KARNEVAL 7

Touya Mikanagi

Translation: Su Mon Han   Lettering: Alexis Eckerman

This book is a work of fiction. Names, characters, places, and incidents are the product of the author's imagination or are used fictitiously. Any resemblance to actual events, locales, or persons, living or dead, is coincidental.

Karneval vols. 13-14 © 2014 by Touya Mikanagi. All rights reserved. First published in Japan in 2014 by ICHIJINSHA. English translation rights arranged with ICHIJINSHA through Tuttle-Mori Agency, Inc., Tokyo.

English translation © 2017 by Yen Press, LLC

Yen Press
1290 Avenue of the Americas
New York, NY 10104

Visit us at yenpress.com • facebook.com/yenpress • twitter.com/yenpress • yenpress.tumblr.com • instagram.com/yenpress

First Yen Press Edition: May 2017

Yen Press is an imprint of Yen Press, LLC.
The Yen Press name and logo are trademarks of Yen Press, LLC.

The publisher is not responsible for websites (or their content) that are not owned by the publisher.

Library of Congress Control Number: 2016936531

ISBNs: 978-0-316-54780-2 (paperback)

10 9 8 7 6 5 4 3 2 1

BVG

Printed in the United States of America

KARNEVAL 7

Touya Mikanagi

STORY

THE VISITOR WHO APPEARS ON THE DOORSTEP OF THE FUGITIVE URO IS NONE OTHER THAN DOCTOR AKARI'S FORMER PROTÉGÉ, AZANA. NOW WORKING WITH KAFKA, AZANA REPORTS BACK ON A CERTAIN RESEARCH PROJECT HE IS CONDUCTING FOR THEM. ABOARD THE 2ND SHIP, KAROKU, HAVING REGAINED HIS MEMORIES, EXPLAINS THAT THE NIJI DESCRIBED IN THE CRYPTIC NOTEBOOK IS INDEED NAI AND INFORMS DOCTOR AKARI THAT NAI'S PRESENCE IS MEANT TO INCREASE THE QUANTITY OF GOOD FORTUNE THAT OCCURS. MEANWHILE, NAI AND COMPANY RECEIVE INVITATIONS TO AN EXCLUSIVE PARTY THROWN BY THEIR FRIEND YANARI, WHOM THEY FIRST MET IN THE CITY OF VANTONAM. AFTER A JOYFUL REUNION, THE BASH RUNS INTO TROUBLE, ALMOST LEADING TO ITS CANCELLATION. HOWEVER, THANKS TO SOME QUICK THINKING FROM GAREKI, THE CRISIS IS AVERTED, AND THE EVENT ENDS AS A GREAT SUCCESS. WITH THEIR BONDS OF FRIENDSHIP FURTHER DEEPENED, THE CREW BIDS YANARI GOOD-BYE AND RETURNS TO THE 2ND SHIP, WHERE GAREKI IS SUMMONED TO A MEETING BY THE SHEEP. WHEN HE ARRIVES AT THE APPOINTED LOCATION, HOWEVER, THE PERSON WAITING FOR HIM IS...

CHARACTERS OF KARNEVAL

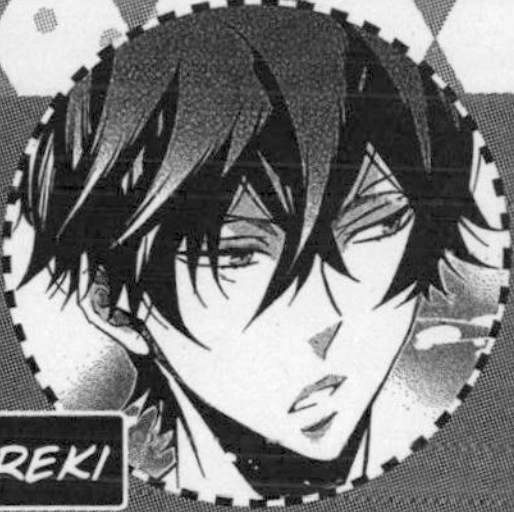

GAREKI

HE MET NAI INSIDE AN EERIE MANSION THAT HE HAD INTENDED TO BURGLARIZE. HE LEFT HIS SCHOOL BEHIND TO HELP NAI AND IS CURRENTLY BACK ABOARD THE 2ND SHIP.

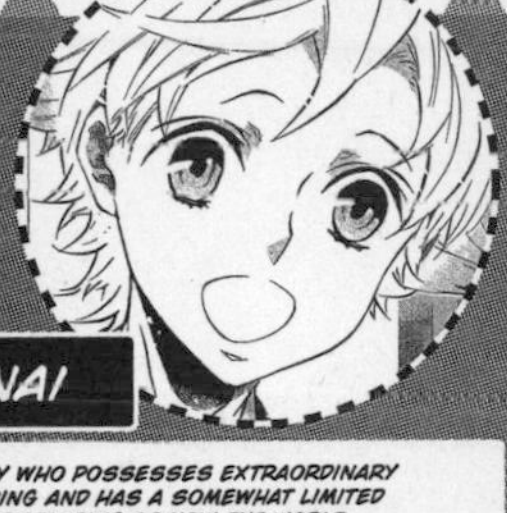

NAI

A BOY WHO POSSESSES EXTRAORDINARY HEARING AND HAS A SOMEWHAT LIMITED UNDERSTANDING OF HOW THE WORLD WORKS. HE IS CURRENTLY LIVING ABOARD CIRCUS'S 2ND SHIP ALONGSIDE KAROKU.

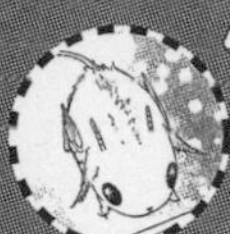

NIJI

THE ANIMAL FROM WHICH NAI WAS CREATED. THEY EXIST ONLY IN THE RAINBOW FOREST, A HIGHLY UNUSUAL ECOSYSTEM THAT ALLOWED THE NIJI TO EVOLVE AS THEY DID.

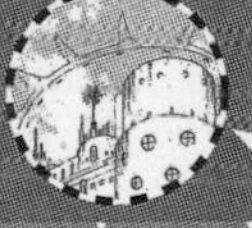

CHRONOMÉ

A VOCATIONAL SCHOOL FOR THOSE HOPING TO WORK FOR THE GOVERNMENT. ITS FOUR PROGRAMS OF STUDY ARE CIRCUS, ENGINEERING, MEDICAL & BIOLOGICAL SCIENCES, AND MANAGEMENT & INTELLIGENCE.

CHILDHOOD FRIENDS

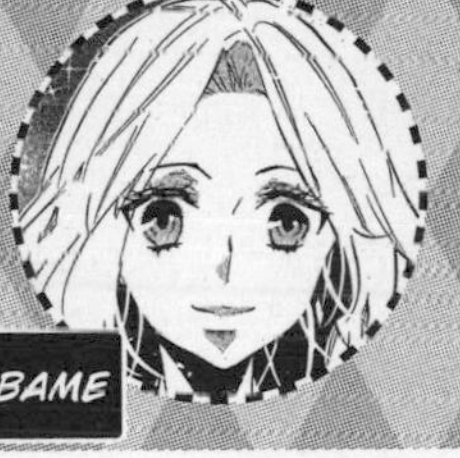

TSUBAME

GAREKI'S CHILDHOOD FRIEND. SHE PREVIOUSLY LIVED IN KARASUNA WITH HER TWIN BROTHER, YOTAKA, WHO WAS KILLED BY KAFKA. SHE CURRENTLY ATTENDS CHRONOMÉ ACADEMY.

NATIONAL SUPREME DEFENSE FORCE "CIRCUS" 2ND SHIP

HIRATO

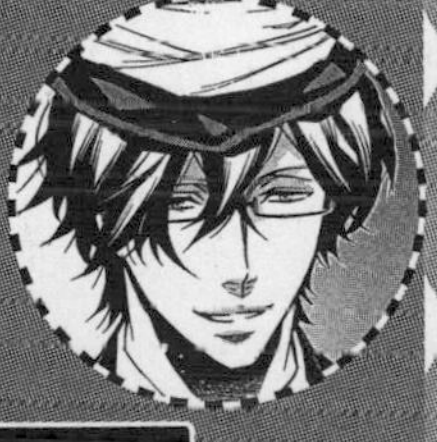

CAPTAIN OF CIRCUS'S 2ND SHIP. NAI (AND GAREKI), WHO BROUGHT HIM A BRACELET BELONGING TO CIRCUS, ARE CURRENTLY UNDER HIS PROTECTION.

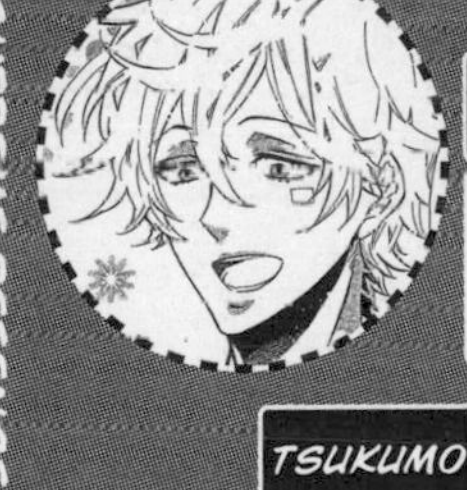

YOGI

CIRCUS'S 2ND SHIP COMBAT SPECIALIST. HE HAS A CHEERFUL, FRIENDLY PERSONALITY. HE WAS BORN THE CROWN PRINCE OF RIMHAKKA, A KINGDOM THAT WAS DESTROYED IN A VARUGA ATTACK.

TSUKUMO

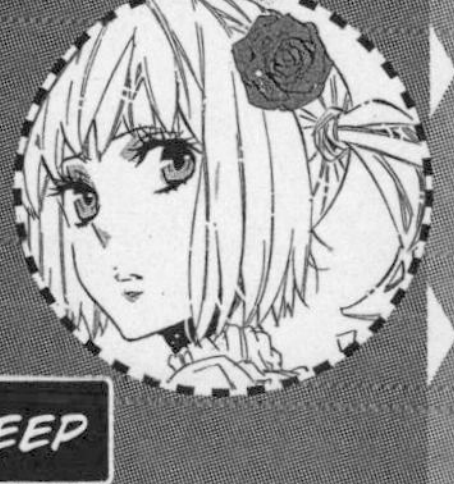

CIRCUS'S 2ND SHIP COMBAT SPECIALIST. A BEAUTIFUL GIRL WITH A COOL, SERIOUS PERSONALITY. RECENTLY, SHE SEEMS TO HAVE TAKEN UP SEWING STUFFED TOYS AS A PASTIME.

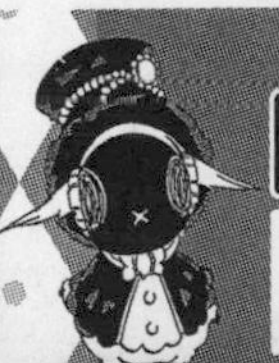

SHEEP

A CIRCUS DEFENSE SYSTEM. DESPITE THEIR CUTE APPEARANCE, THE SHEEP HAVE SOME VERY POWERFUL CAPABILITIES.

Q: WHAT IS CIRCUS?

A: THE EQUIVALENT OF THE REAL-WORLD POLICE. THEY CONDUCT THEIR LARGE-SCALE "OPERATIONS" UTILIZING COORDINATED, POWERFUL ATTACKS AND WITHOUT FOREWARNING TO ENSURE THEIR TARGETS WILL NOT ESCAPE ARREST!! AFTER SUCH AN OPERATION, CIRCUS PERFORMS A "SHOW" FOR THE PEOPLE OF THE CITY AS AN APOLOGY FOR THE FEAR AND INCONVENIENCE THEIR WORK MAY HAVE CAUSED. IN SHORT, "CIRCUS" IS A CHEERFUL(?) AGENCY THAT CARRIES OUT THEIR MISSION DAY AND NIGHT TO APPREHEND EVIL AND PROTECT THE PEACE OF THE LAND.

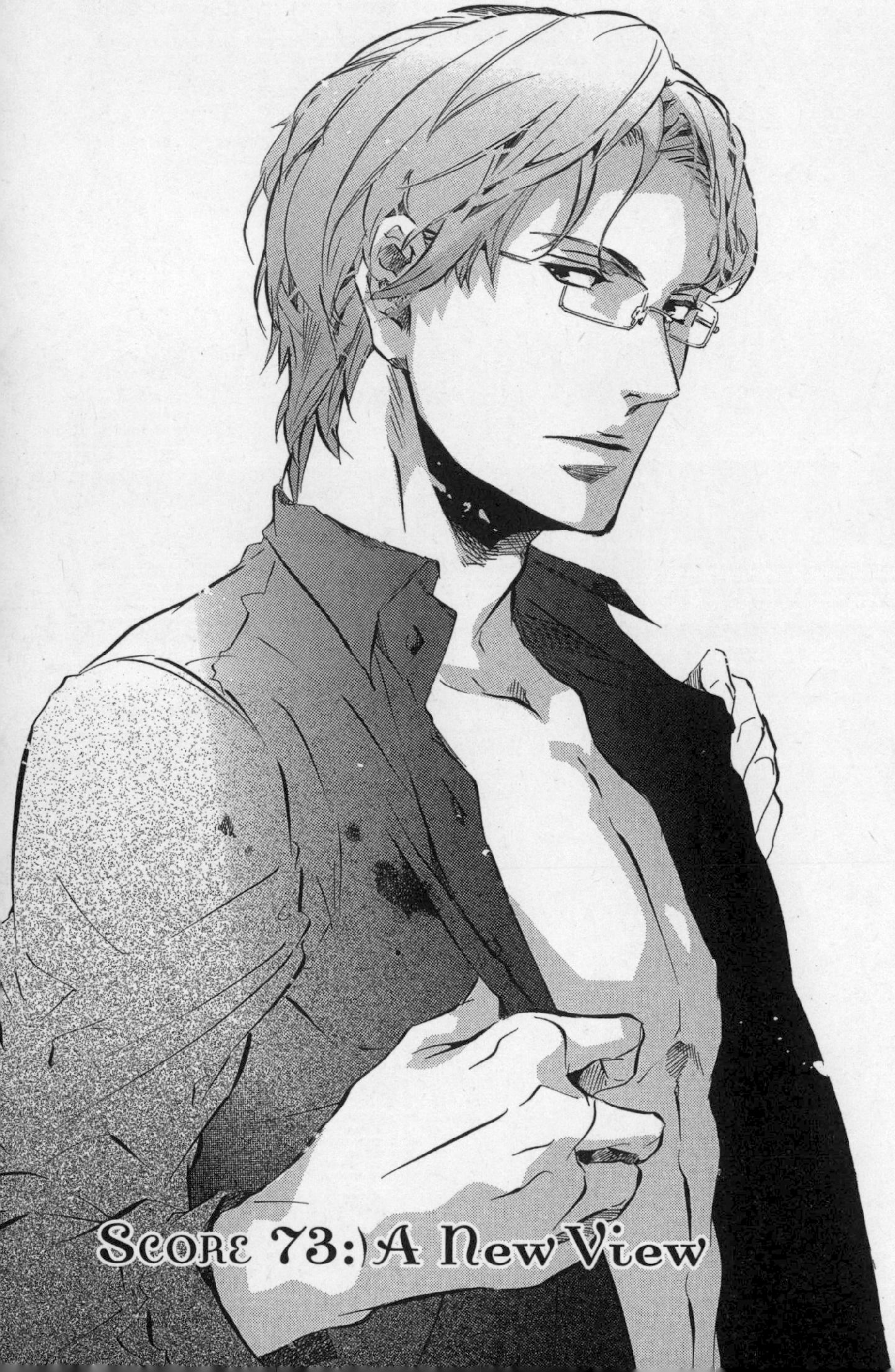
Score 73: A New View

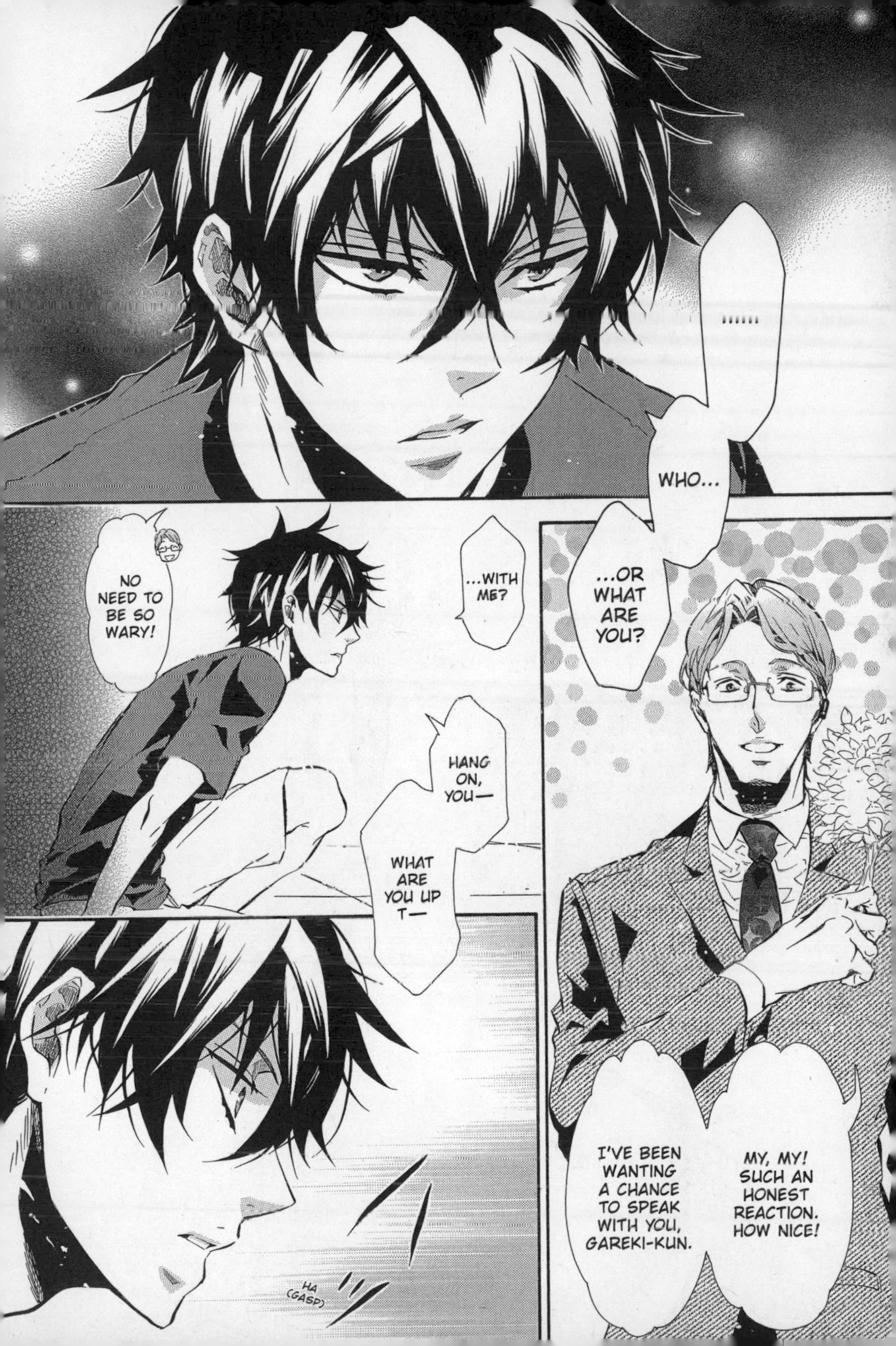
......
WHO...
...OR WHAT ARE YOU?
MY, MY! SUCH AN HONEST REACTION. HOW NICE!
I'VE BEEN WANTING A CHANCE TO SPEAK WITH YOU, GAREKI-KUN.
...WITH ME?
NO NEED TO BE SO WARY!
HANG ON, YOU—
WHAT ARE YOU UP T—
HA (GASP)

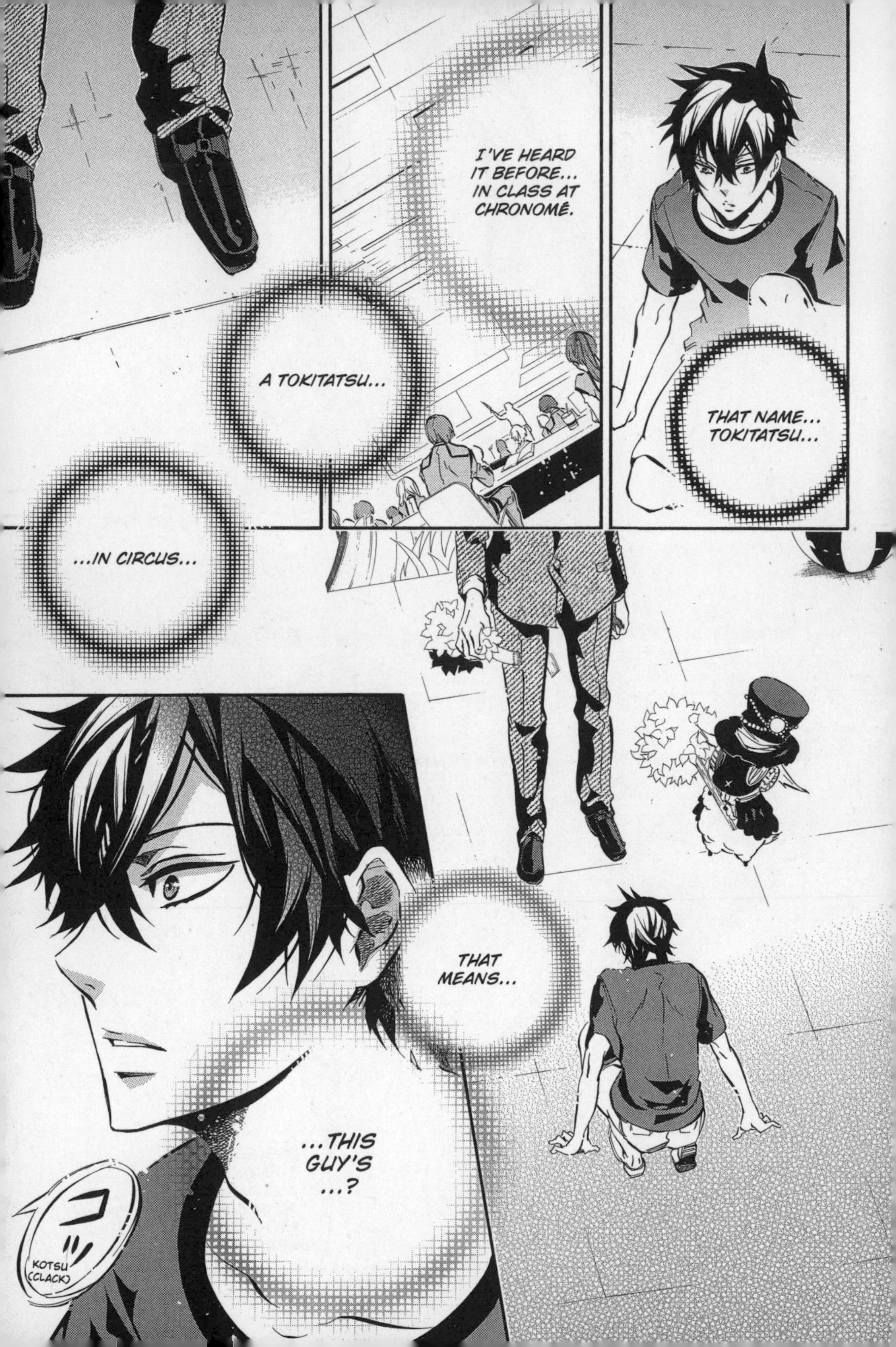
THAT NAME... TOKITATSU...
I'VE HEARD IT BEFORE... IN CLASS AT CHRONOMÉ.
A TOKITATSU...
...IN CIRCUS...
THAT MEANS...
...THIS GUY'S ...?
コツ
KOTSU (CLACK)

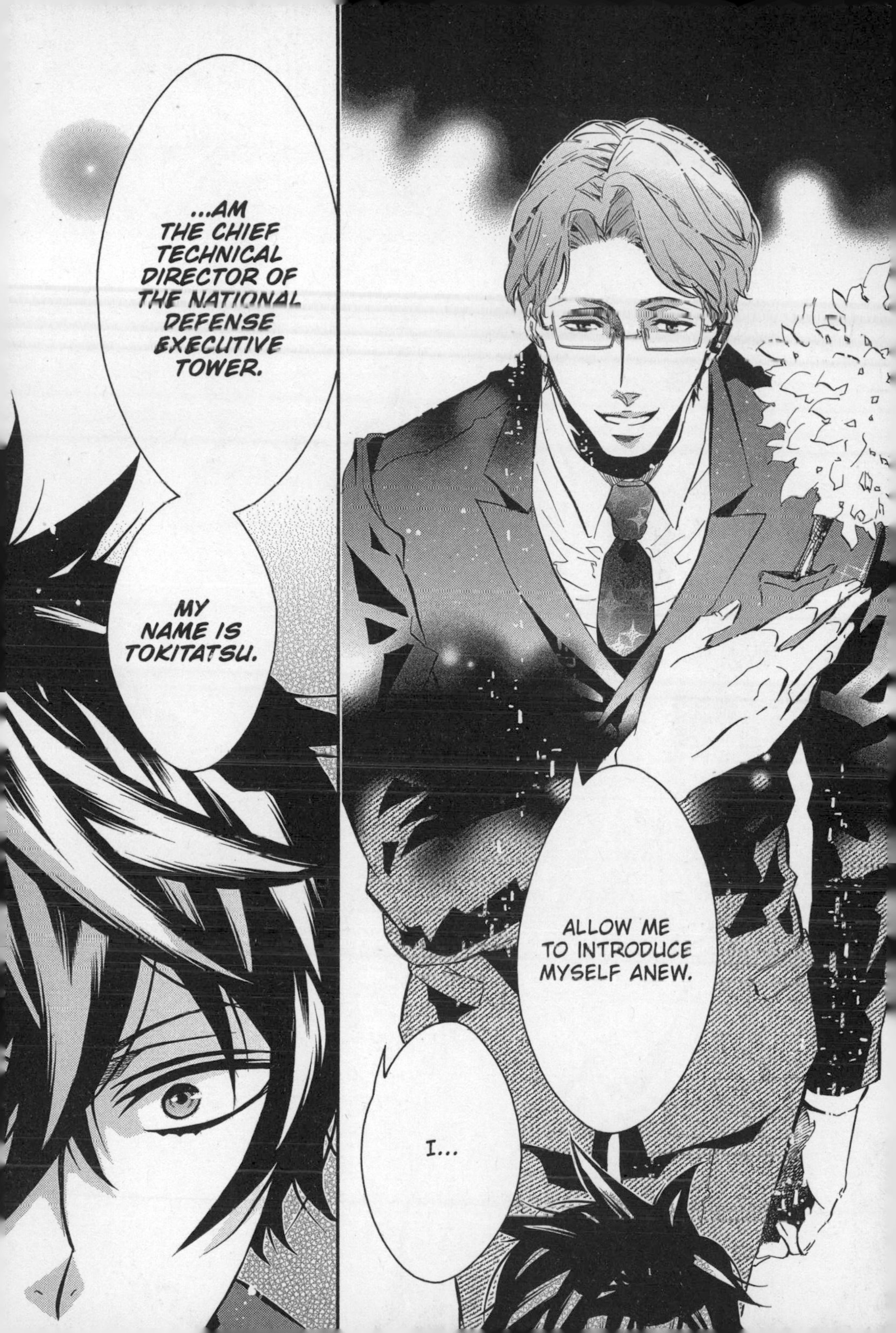
ALLOW ME TO INTRODUCE MYSELF ANEW.
I...
...AM THE CHIEF TECHNICAL DIRECTOR OF THE NATIONAL DEFENSE EXECUTIVE TOWER.
MY NAME IS TOKITATSU.

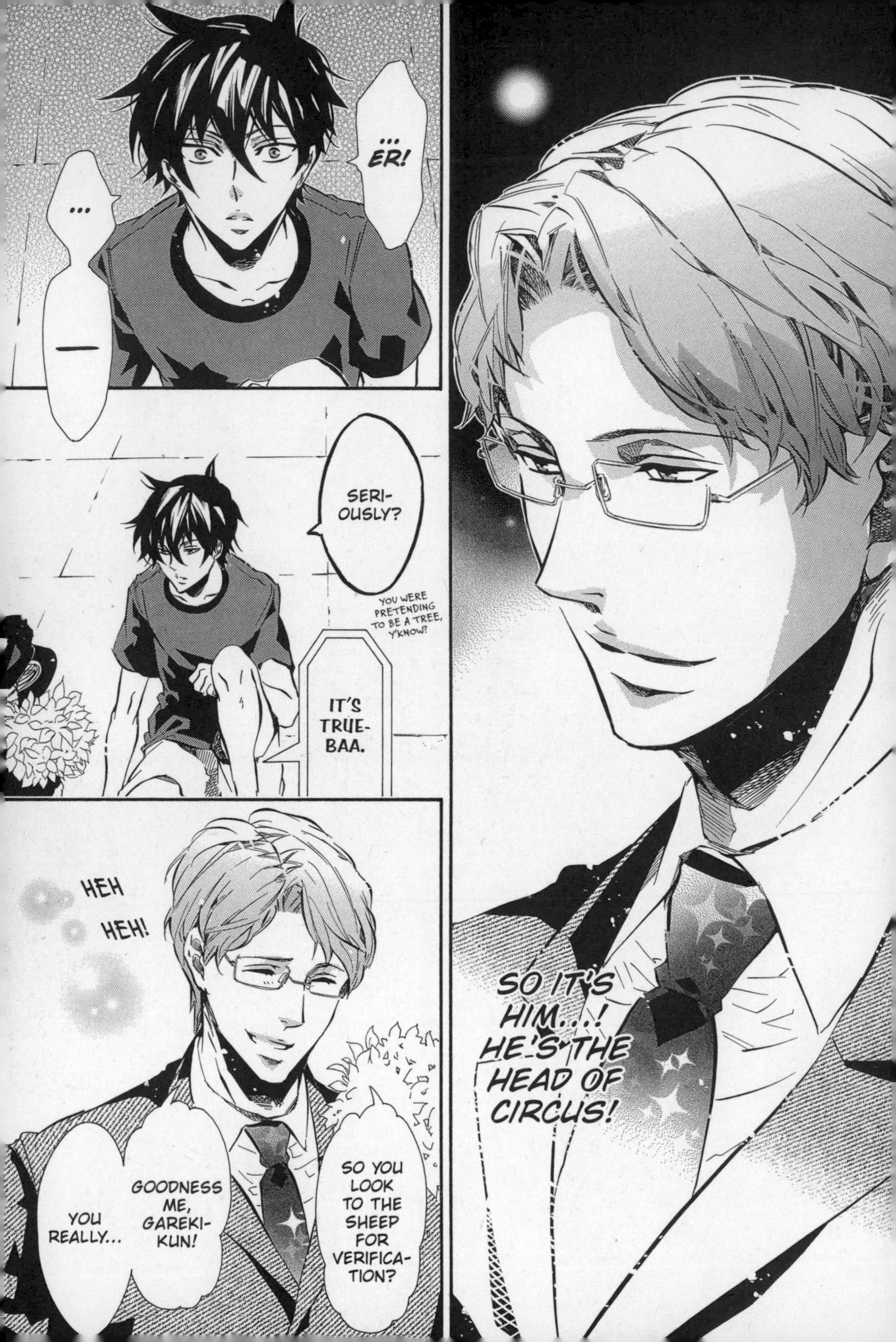
SO IT'S HIM...! HE'S THE HEAD OF CIRCUS!
...ER!
... —
SERI-OUSLY?
YOU WERE PRETENDING TO BE A TREE, Y'KNOW?
IT'S TRUE-BAA.
HEH HEH!
SO YOU LOOK TO THE SHEEP FOR VERIFICA-TION?
GOODNESS ME, GAREKI-KUN!
YOU REALLY...

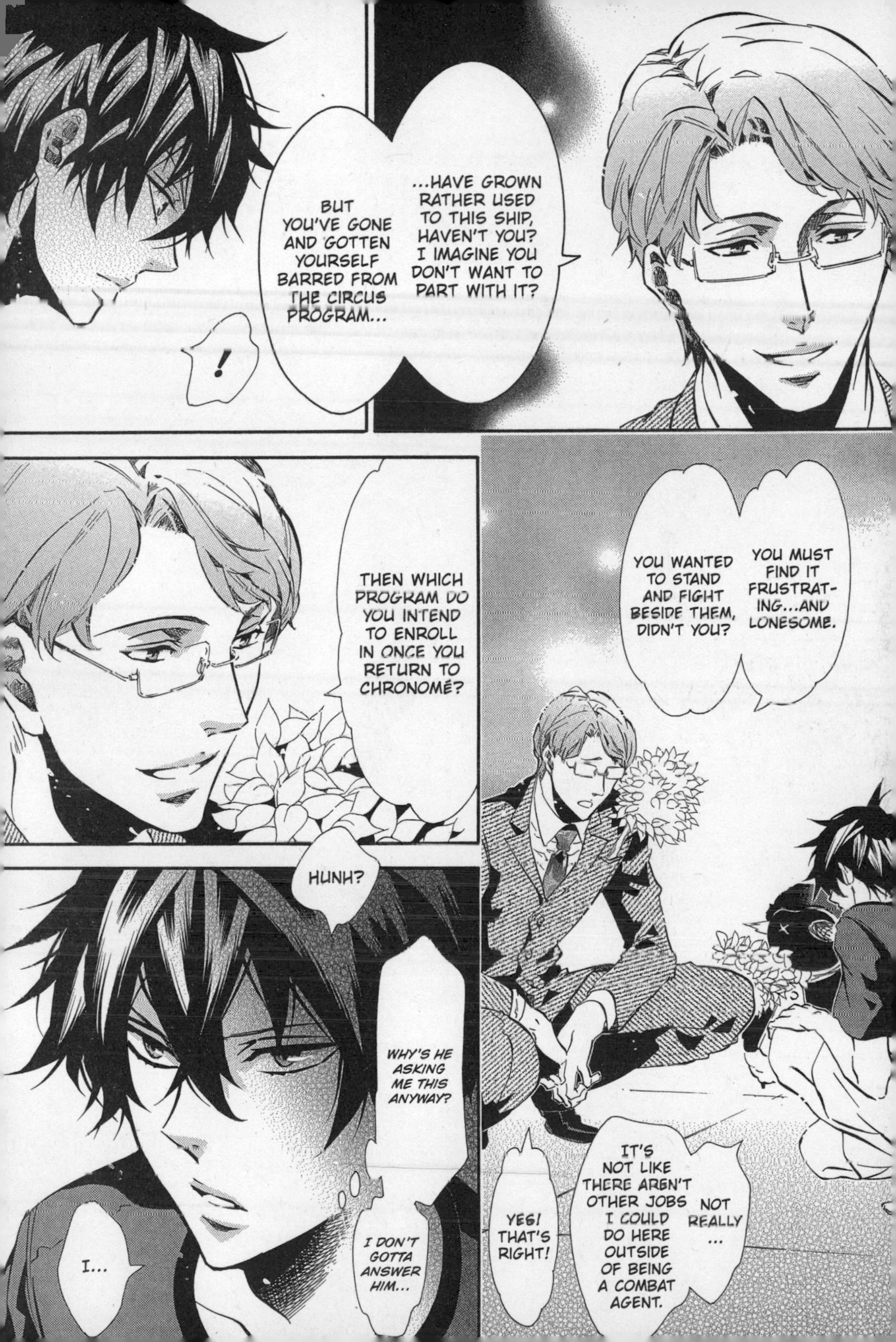
...HAVE GROWN RATHER USED TO THIS SHIP, HAVEN'T YOU? I IMAGINE YOU DON'T WANT TO PART WITH IT?
BUT YOU'VE GONE AND GOTTEN YOURSELF BARRED FROM THE CIRCUS PROGRAM...
!
YOU MUST FIND IT FRUSTRATING...AND LONESOME.
YOU WANTED TO STAND AND FIGHT BESIDE THEM, DIDN'T YOU?
NOT REALLY...
IT'S NOT LIKE THERE AREN'T OTHER JOBS I COULD DO HERE OUTSIDE OF BEING A COMBAT AGENT.
YES! THAT'S RIGHT!
THEN WHICH PROGRAM DO YOU INTEND TO ENROLL IN ONCE YOU RETURN TO CHRONOMÉ?
HUNH?
WHY'S HE ASKING ME THIS ANYWAY?
I DON'T GOTTA ANSWER HIM...
I...

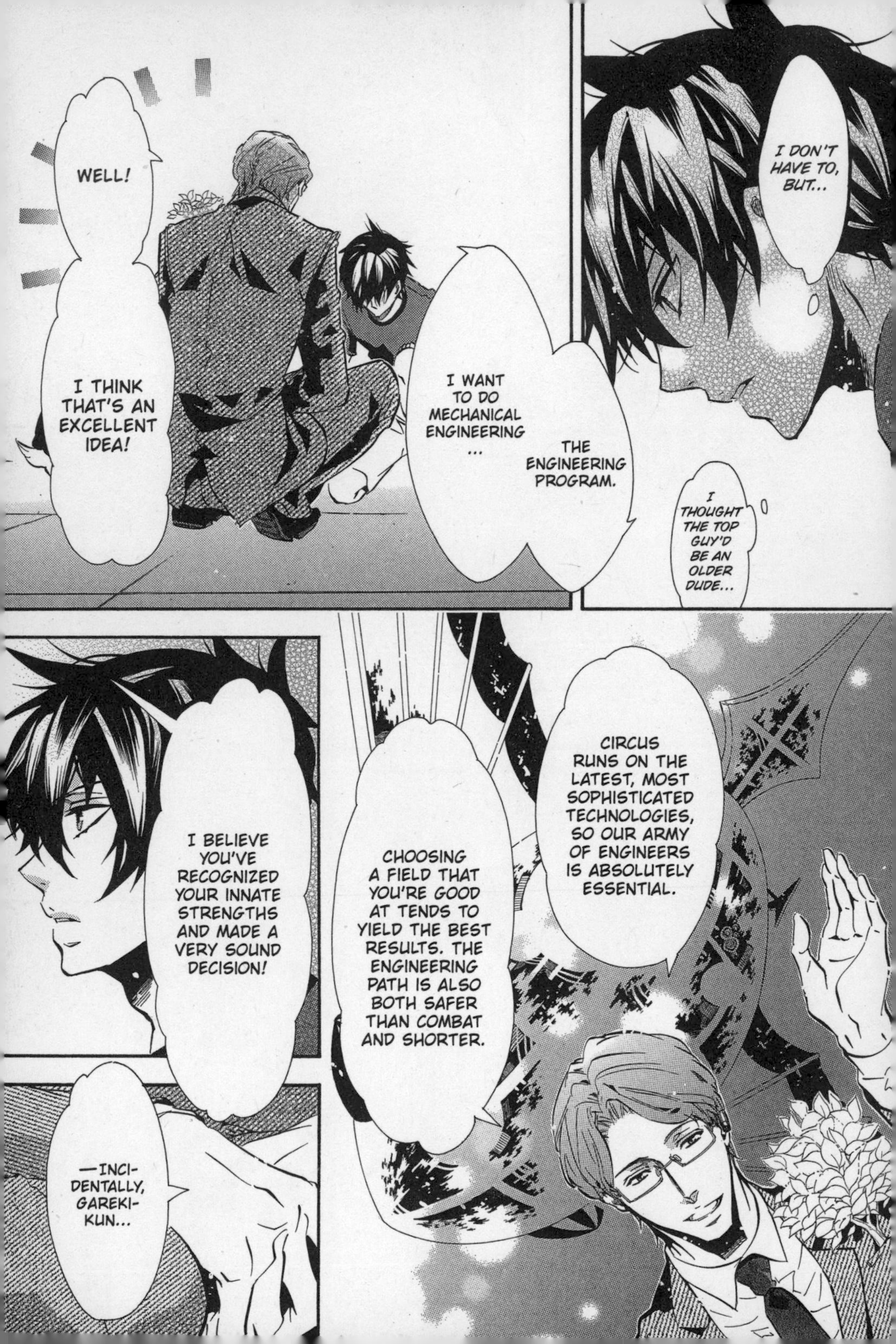
I DON'T HAVE TO, BUT...
I THOUGHT THE TOP GUY'D BE AN OLDER DUDE...
I WANT TO DO MECHANICAL ENGINEERING ...
THE ENGINEERING PROGRAM.
WELL!
I THINK THAT'S AN EXCELLENT IDEA!
CIRCUS RUNS ON THE LATEST, MOST SOPHISTICATED TECHNOLOGIES, SO OUR ARMY OF ENGINEERS IS ABSOLUTELY ESSENTIAL.
CHOOSING A FIELD THAT YOU'RE GOOD AT TENDS TO YIELD THE BEST RESULTS. THE ENGINEERING PATH IS ALSO BOTH SAFER THAN COMBAT AND SHORTER.
I BELIEVE YOU'VE RECOGNIZED YOUR INNATE STRENGTHS AND MADE A VERY SOUND DECISION!
—INCIDENTALLY, GAREKI-KUN...

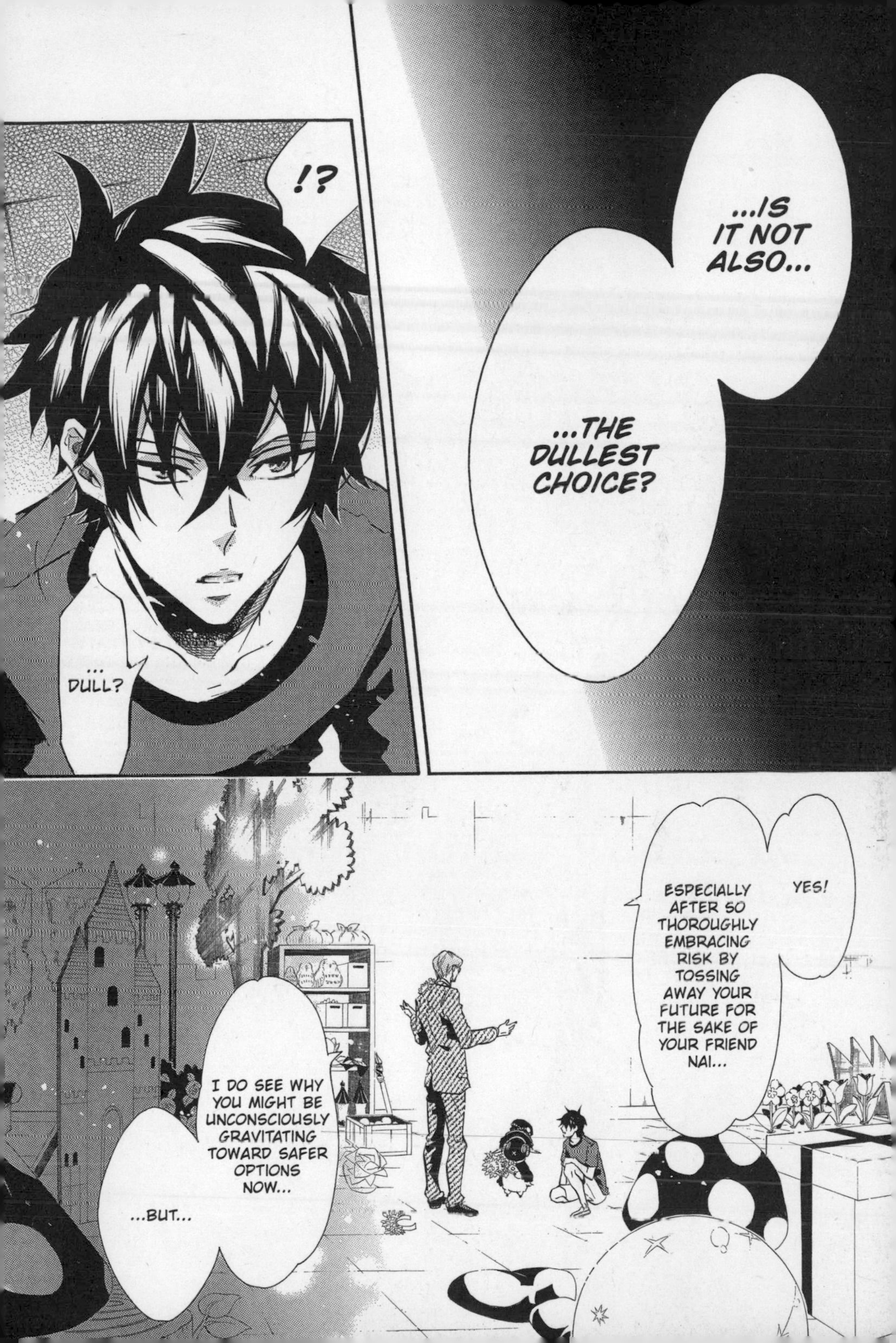
...IS IT NOT ALSO...
...THE DULLEST CHOICE?
!?
... DULL?
YES!
ESPECIALLY AFTER SO THOROUGHLY EMBRACING RISK BY TOSSING AWAY YOUR FUTURE FOR THE SAKE OF YOUR FRIEND NAI...
I DO SEE WHY YOU MIGHT BE UNCONSCIOUSLY GRAVITATING TOWARD SAFER OPTIONS NOW...
...BUT...

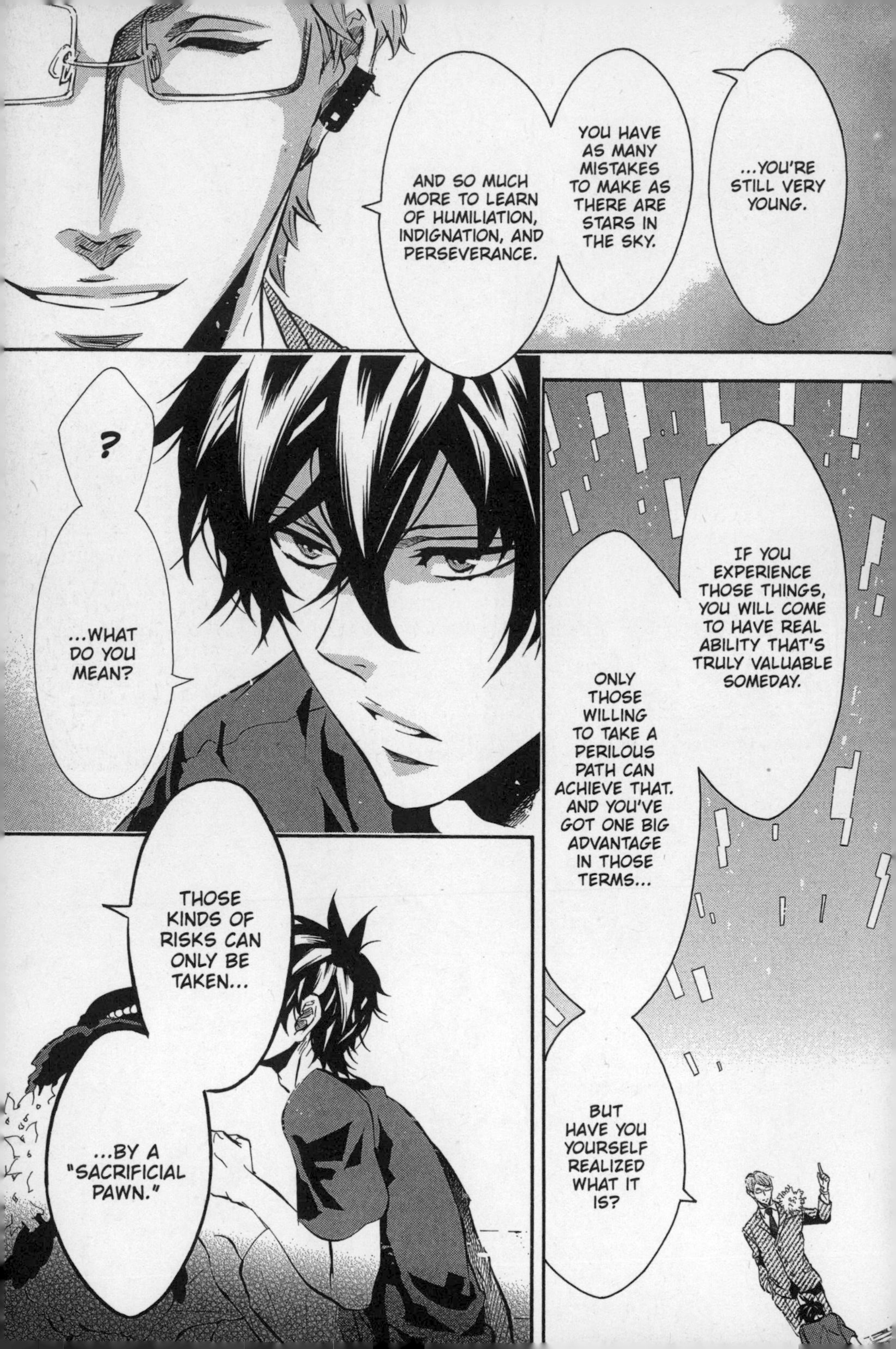
...YOU'RE STILL VERY YOUNG.
YOU HAVE AS MANY MISTAKES TO MAKE AS THERE ARE STARS IN THE SKY.
AND SO MUCH MORE TO LEARN OF HUMILIATION, INDIGNATION, AND PERSEVERANCE.
IF YOU EXPERIENCE THOSE THINGS, YOU WILL COME TO HAVE REAL ABILITY THAT'S TRULY VALUABLE SOMEDAY.
ONLY THOSE WILLING TO TAKE A PERILOUS PATH CAN ACHIEVE THAT. AND YOU'VE GOT ONE BIG ADVANTAGE IN THOSE TERMS...
BUT HAVE YOU YOURSELF REALIZED WHAT IT IS?
?
...WHAT DO YOU MEAN?
THOSE KINDS OF RISKS CAN ONLY BE TAKEN...
...BY A "SACRIFICIAL PAWN."

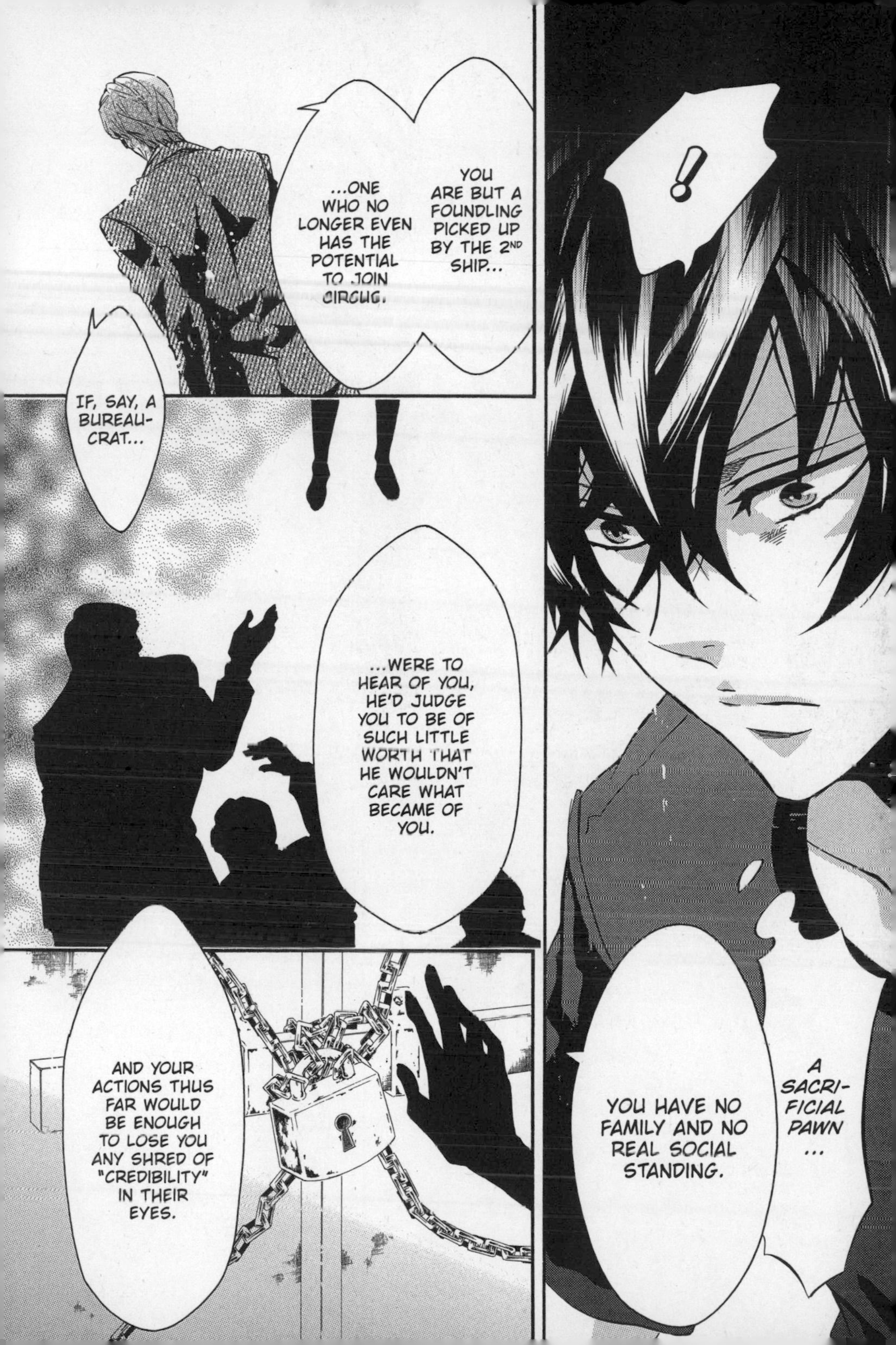
!
A SACRI-FICIAL PAWN ...
YOU HAVE NO FAMILY AND NO REAL SOCIAL STANDING.
YOU ARE BUT A FOUNDLING PICKED UP BY THE 2ND SHIP...
...ONE WHO NO LONGER EVEN HAS THE POTENTIAL TO JOIN CIRCUS.
IF, SAY, A BUREAU-CRAT...
...WERE TO HEAR OF YOU, HE'D JUDGE YOU TO BE OF SUCH LITTLE WORTH THAT HE WOULDN'T CARE WHAT BECAME OF YOU.
AND YOUR ACTIONS THUS FAR WOULD BE ENOUGH TO LOSE YOU ANY SHRED OF "CREDIBILITY" IN THEIR EYES.

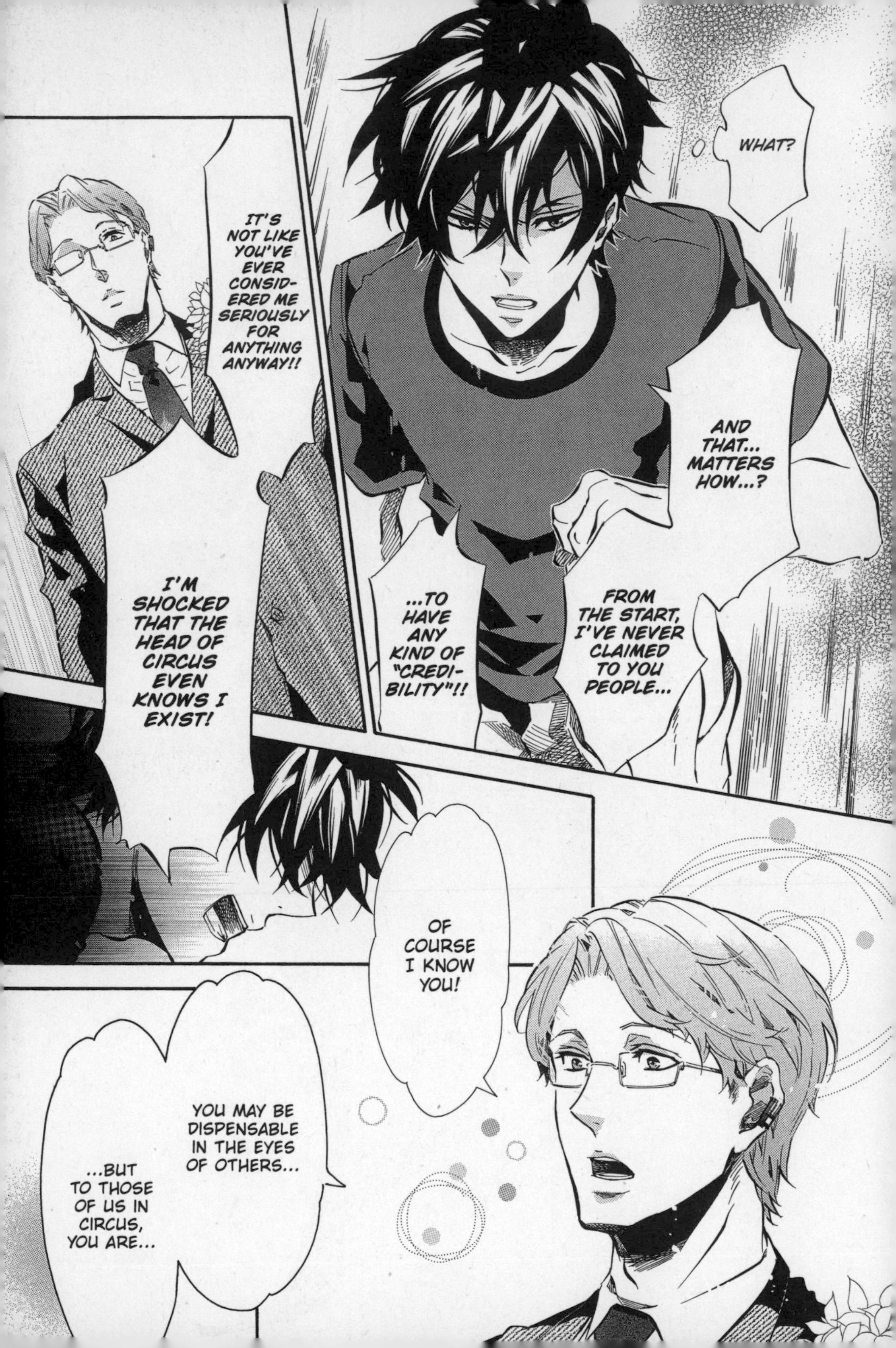

WHAT?
AND THAT... MATTERS HOW...?
FROM THE START, I'VE NEVER CLAIMED TO YOU PEOPLE...
...TO HAVE ANY KIND OF "CREDIBILITY"!!
IT'S NOT LIKE YOU'VE EVER CONSIDERED ME SERIOUSLY FOR ANYTHING ANYWAY!!
I'M SHOCKED THAT THE HEAD OF CIRCUS EVEN KNOWS I EXIST!
OF COURSE I KNOW YOU!
YOU MAY BE DISPENSABLE IN THE EYES OF OTHERS...
...BUT TO THOSE OF US IN CIRCUS, YOU ARE...

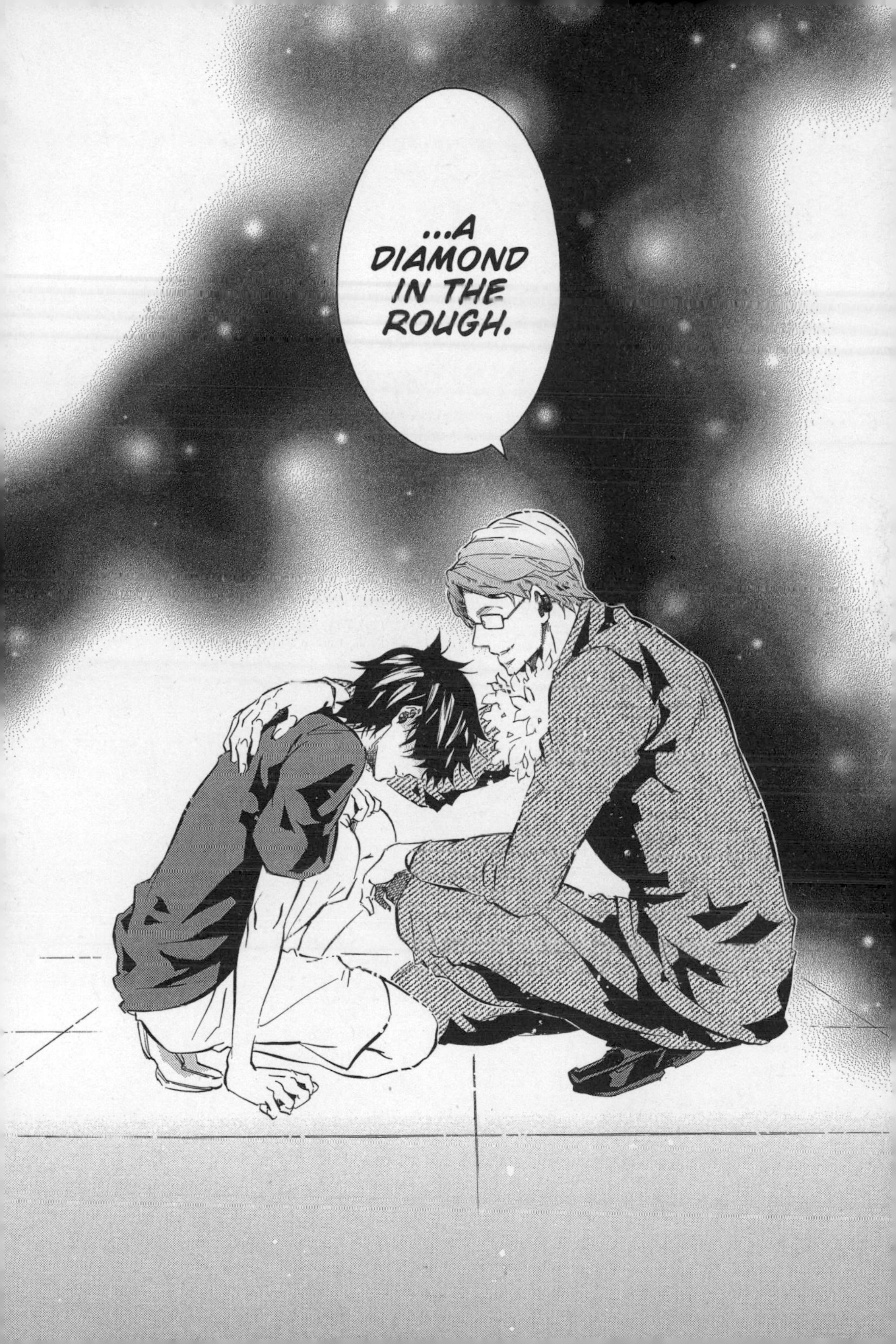
...A DIAMOND IN THE ROUGH.

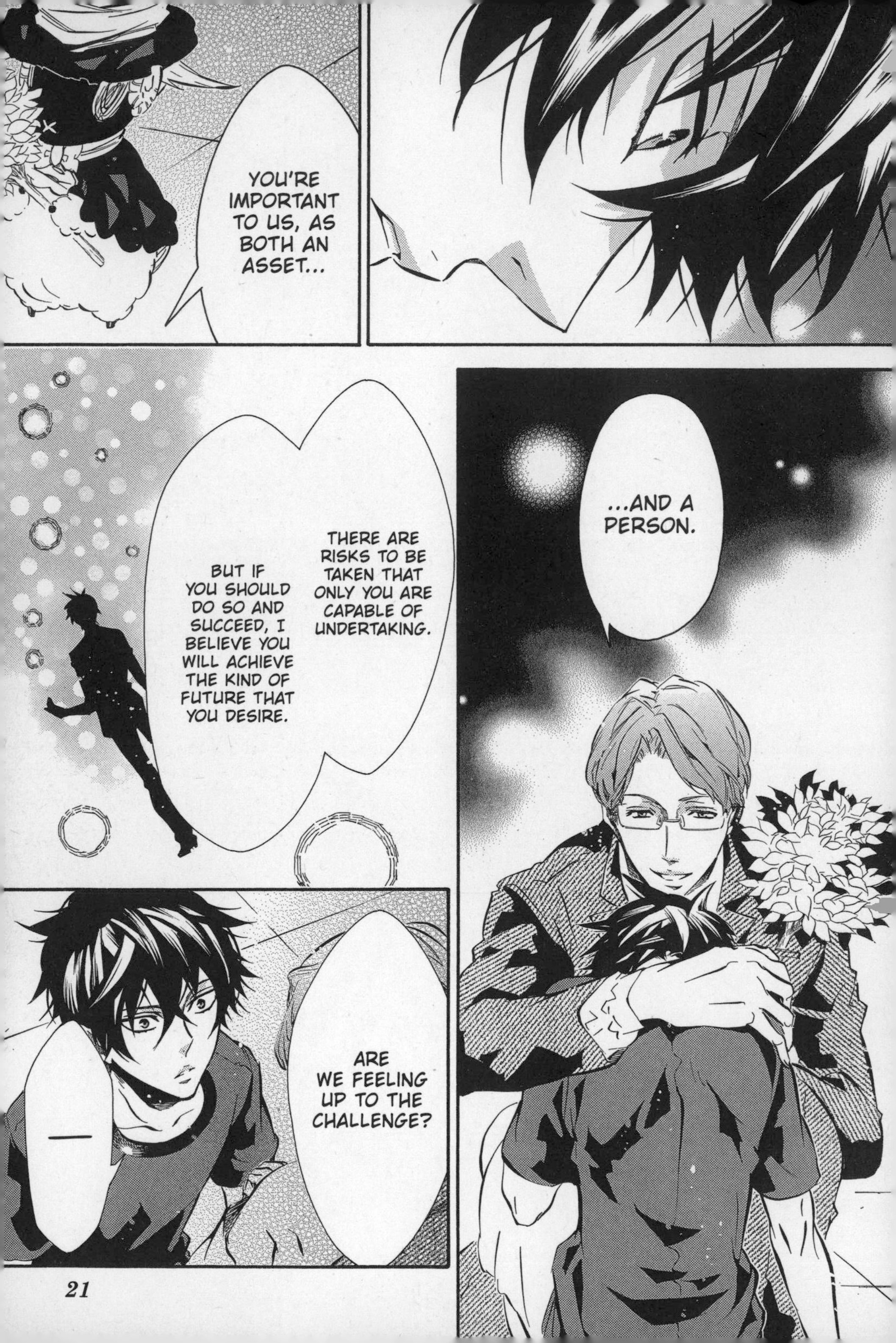
YOU'RE IMPORTANT TO US, AS BOTH AN ASSET...
...AND A PERSON.
THERE ARE RISKS TO BE TAKEN THAT ONLY YOU ARE CAPABLE OF UNDERTAKING.
BUT IF YOU SHOULD DO SO AND SUCCEED, I BELIEVE YOU WILL ACHIEVE THE KIND OF FUTURE THAT YOU DESIRE.
ARE WE FEELING UP TO THE CHALLENGE?
—

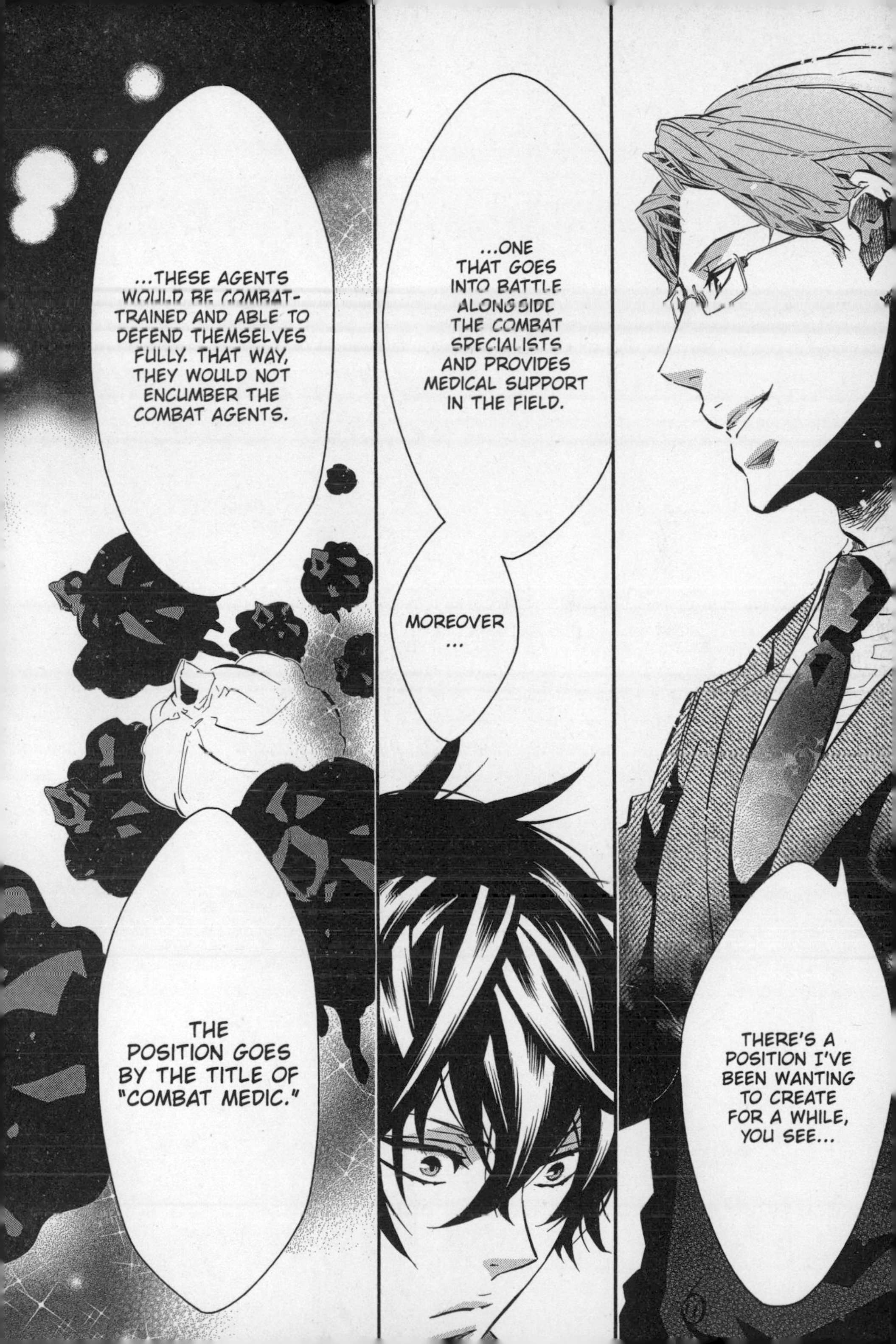
THERE'S A POSITION I'VE BEEN WANTING TO CREATE FOR A WHILE, YOU SEE...
...ONE THAT GOES INTO BATTLE ALONGSIDE THE COMBAT SPECIALISTS AND PROVIDES MEDICAL SUPPORT IN THE FIELD.
MOREOVER...
...THESE AGENTS WOULD BE COMBAT-TRAINED AND ABLE TO DEFEND THEMSELVES FULLY. THAT WAY, THEY WOULD NOT ENCUMBER THE COMBAT AGENTS.
THE POSITION GOES BY THE TITLE OF "COMBAT MEDIC."

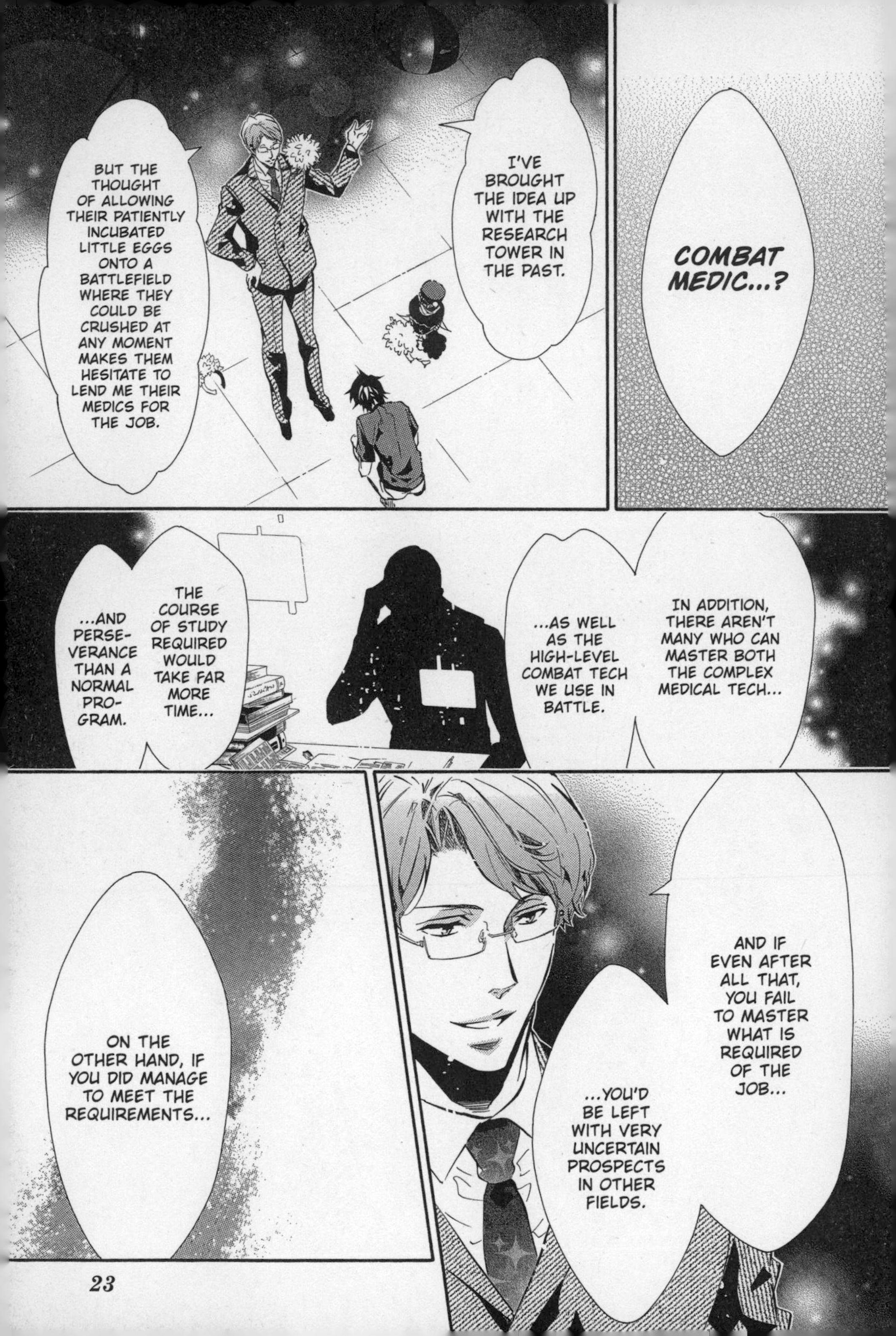
COMBAT MEDIC...?
I'VE BROUGHT THE IDEA UP WITH THE RESEARCH TOWER IN THE PAST.
BUT THE THOUGHT OF ALLOWING THEIR PATIENTLY INCUBATED LITTLE EGGS ONTO A BATTLEFIELD WHERE THEY COULD BE CRUSHED AT ANY MOMENT MAKES THEM HESITATE TO LEND ME THEIR MEDICS FOR THE JOB.
IN ADDITION, THERE AREN'T MANY WHO CAN MASTER BOTH THE COMPLEX MEDICAL TECH...
...AS WELL AS THE HIGH-LEVEL COMBAT TECH WE USE IN BATTLE.
THE COURSE OF STUDY REQUIRED WOULD TAKE FAR MORE TIME...
...AND PERSE-VERANCE THAN A NORMAL PRO-GRAM.
AND IF EVEN AFTER ALL THAT, YOU FAIL TO MASTER WHAT IS REQUIRED OF THE JOB...
...YOU'D BE LEFT WITH VERY UNCERTAIN PROSPECTS IN OTHER FIELDS.
ON THE OTHER HAND, IF YOU DID MANAGE TO MEET THE REQUIREMENTS...

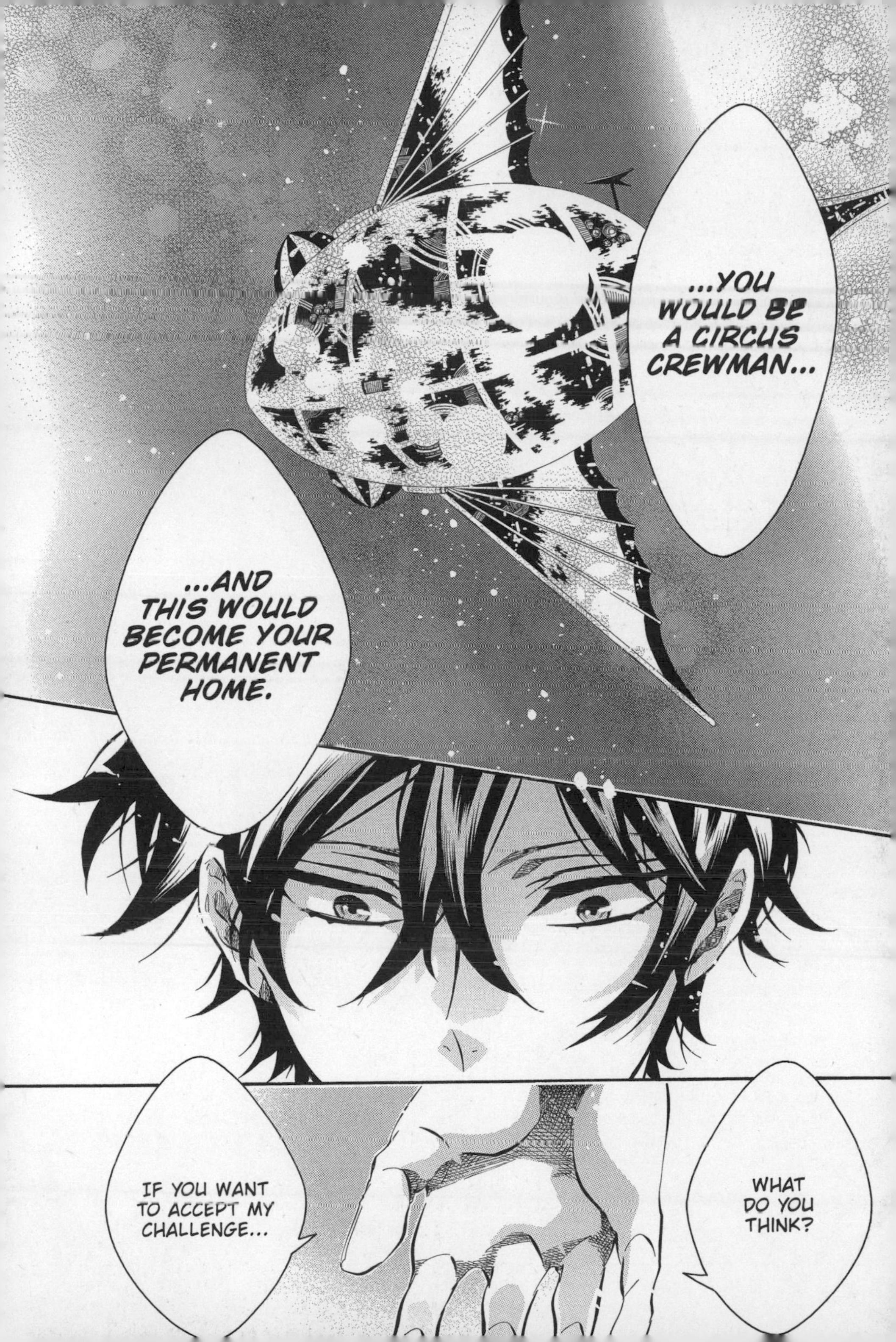
...YOU WOULD BE A CIRCUS CREWMAN...
...AND THIS WOULD BECOME YOUR PERMANENT HOME.
WHAT DO YOU THINK?
IF YOU WANT TO ACCEPT MY CHALLENGE...

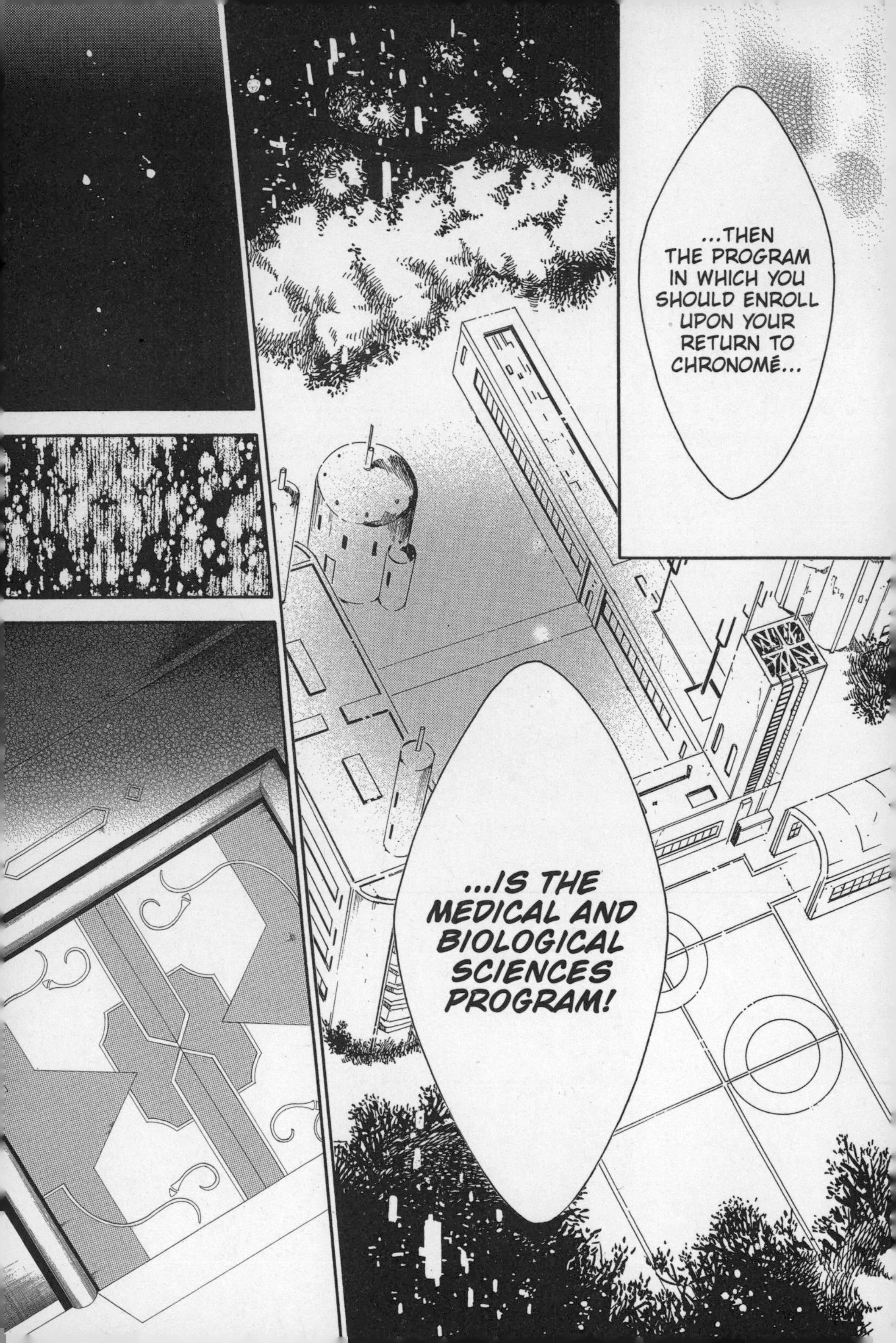
...THEN THE PROGRAM IN WHICH YOU SHOULD ENROLL UPON YOUR RETURN TO CHRONOMÉ...
...IS THE MEDICAL AND BIOLOGICAL SCIENCES PROGRAM!

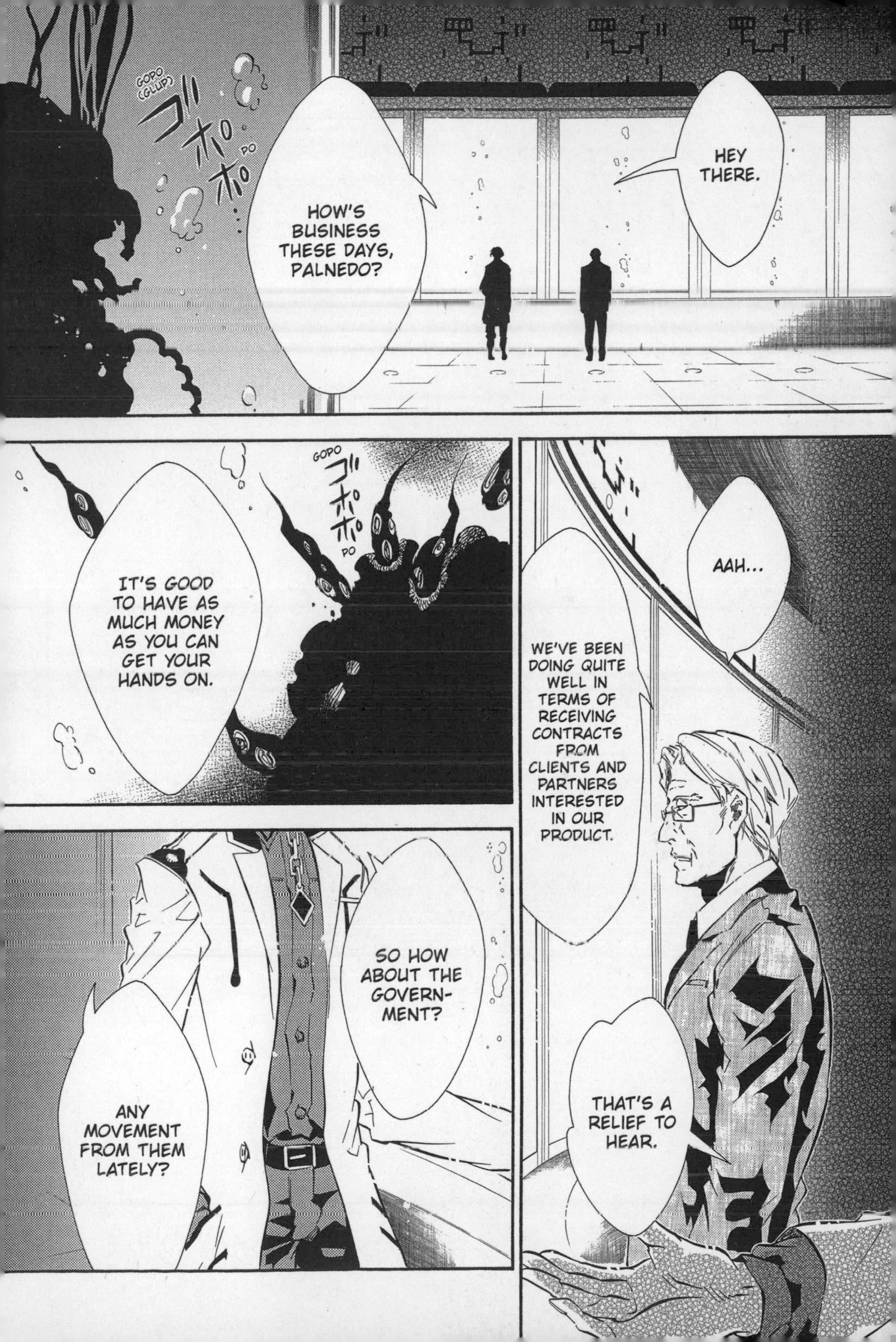
HEY THERE.
HOW'S BUSINESS THESE DAYS, PALNEDO?
GOPO (GLUP)
PO
AAH...
WE'VE BEEN DOING QUITE WELL IN TERMS OF RECEIVING CONTRACTS FROM CLIENTS AND PARTNERS INTERESTED IN OUR PRODUCT.
THAT'S A RELIEF TO HEAR.
GOPO
PO
IT'S GOOD TO HAVE AS MUCH MONEY AS YOU CAN GET YOUR HANDS ON.
SO HOW ABOUT THE GOVERN-MENT?
ANY MOVEMENT FROM THEM LATELY?

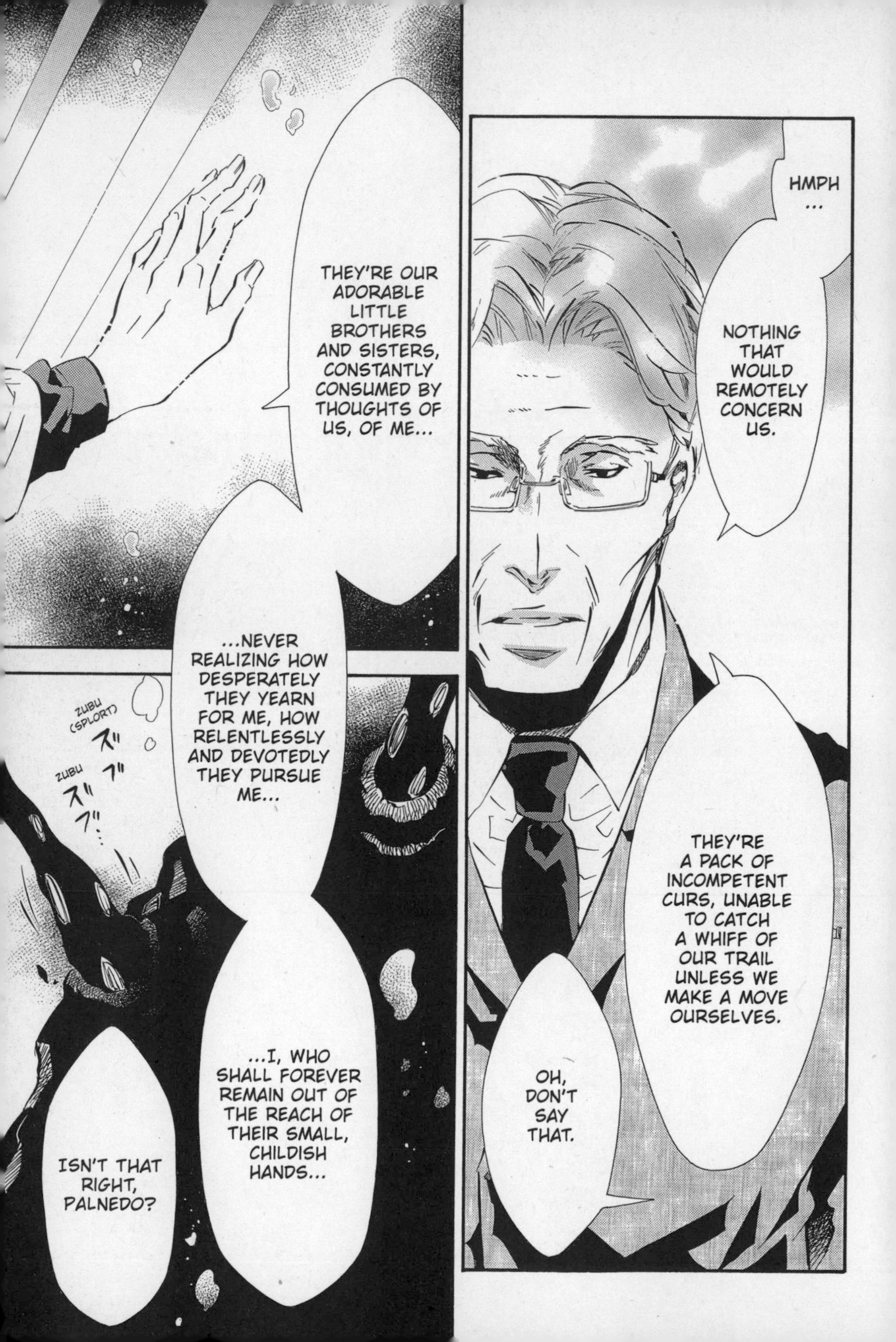
HMPH...
NOTHING THAT WOULD REMOTELY CONCERN US.
THEY'RE A PACK OF INCOMPETENT CURS, UNABLE TO CATCH A WHIFF OF OUR TRAIL UNLESS WE MAKE A MOVE OURSELVES.
OH, DON'T SAY THAT.
THEY'RE OUR ADORABLE LITTLE BROTHERS AND SISTERS, CONSTANTLY CONSUMED BY THOUGHTS OF US, OF ME...
...NEVER REALIZING HOW DESPERATELY THEY YEARN FOR ME, HOW RELENTLESSLY AND DEVOTEDLY THEY PURSUE ME...
ズブ ZUBU (SPLORT)
ズブ... ZUBU
...I, WHO SHALL FOREVER REMAIN OUT OF THE REACH OF THEIR SMALL, CHILDISH HANDS...
ISN'T THAT RIGHT, PALNEDO?

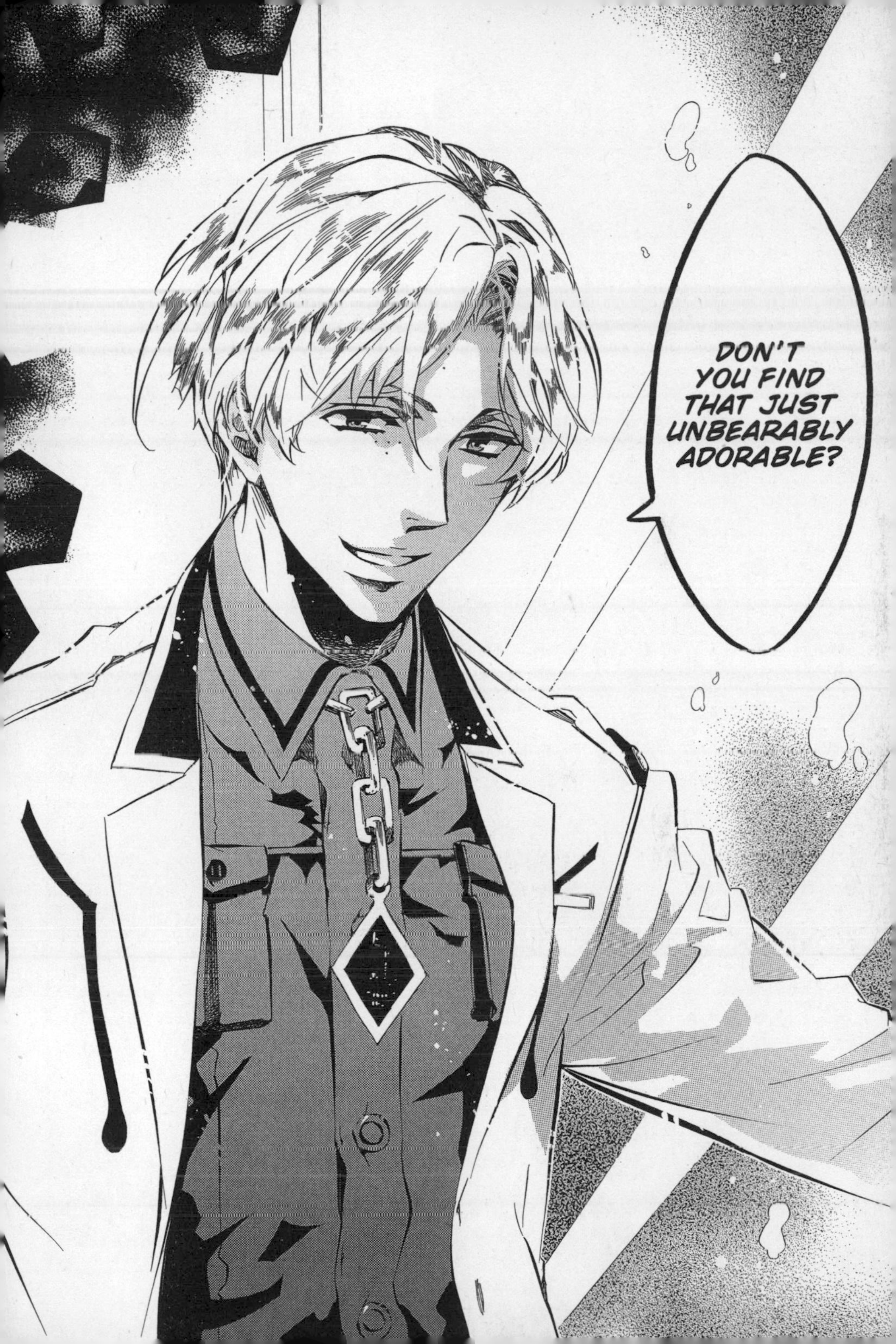
DON'T YOU FIND THAT JUST UNBEARABLY ADORABLE?

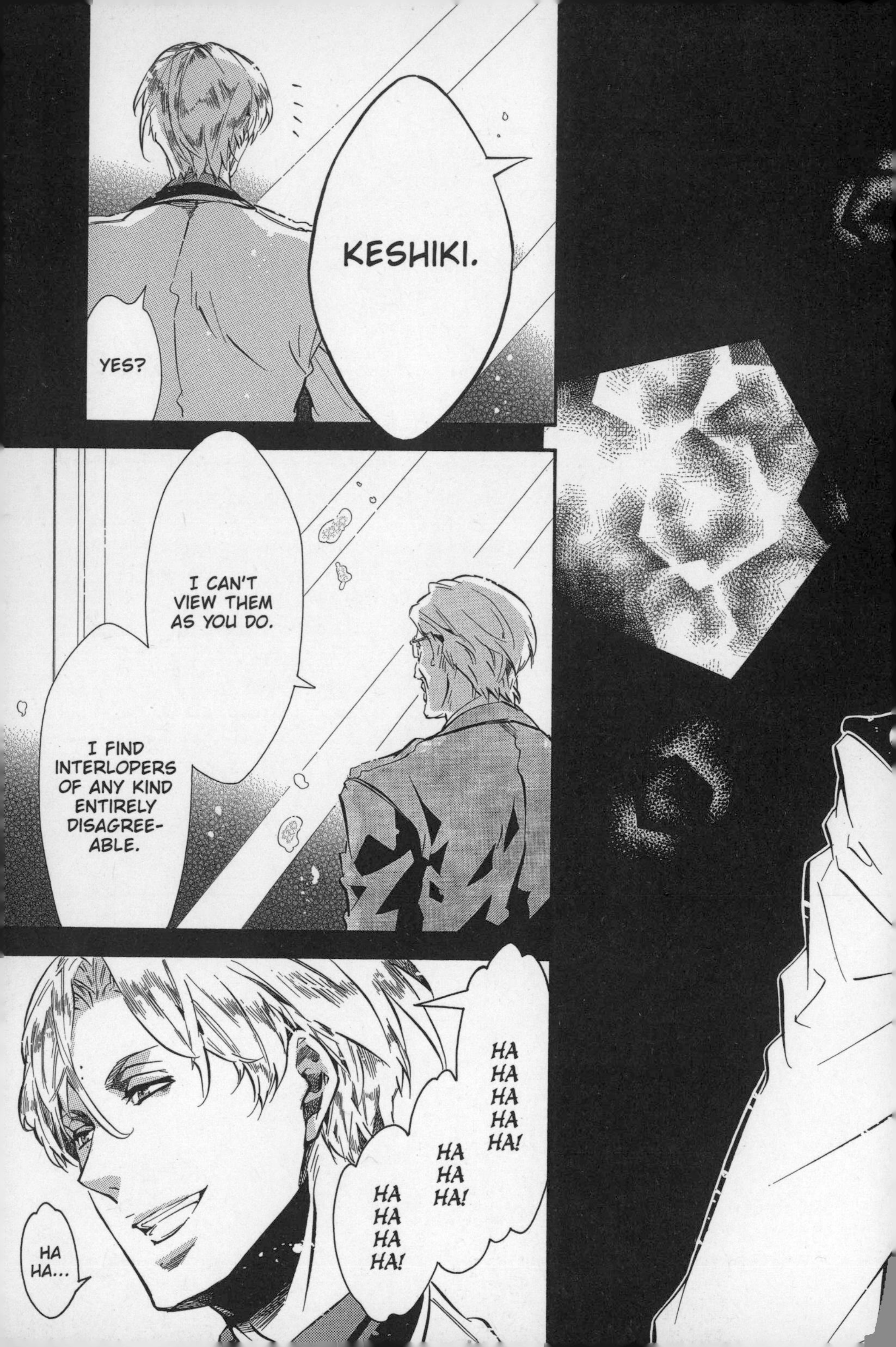
KESHIKI.
YES?
I CAN'T VIEW THEM AS YOU DO.
I FIND INTERLOPERS OF ANY KIND ENTIRELY DISAGREE-ABLE.
HA HA HA HA HA!
HA HA HA!
HA HA HA HA!
HA HA...

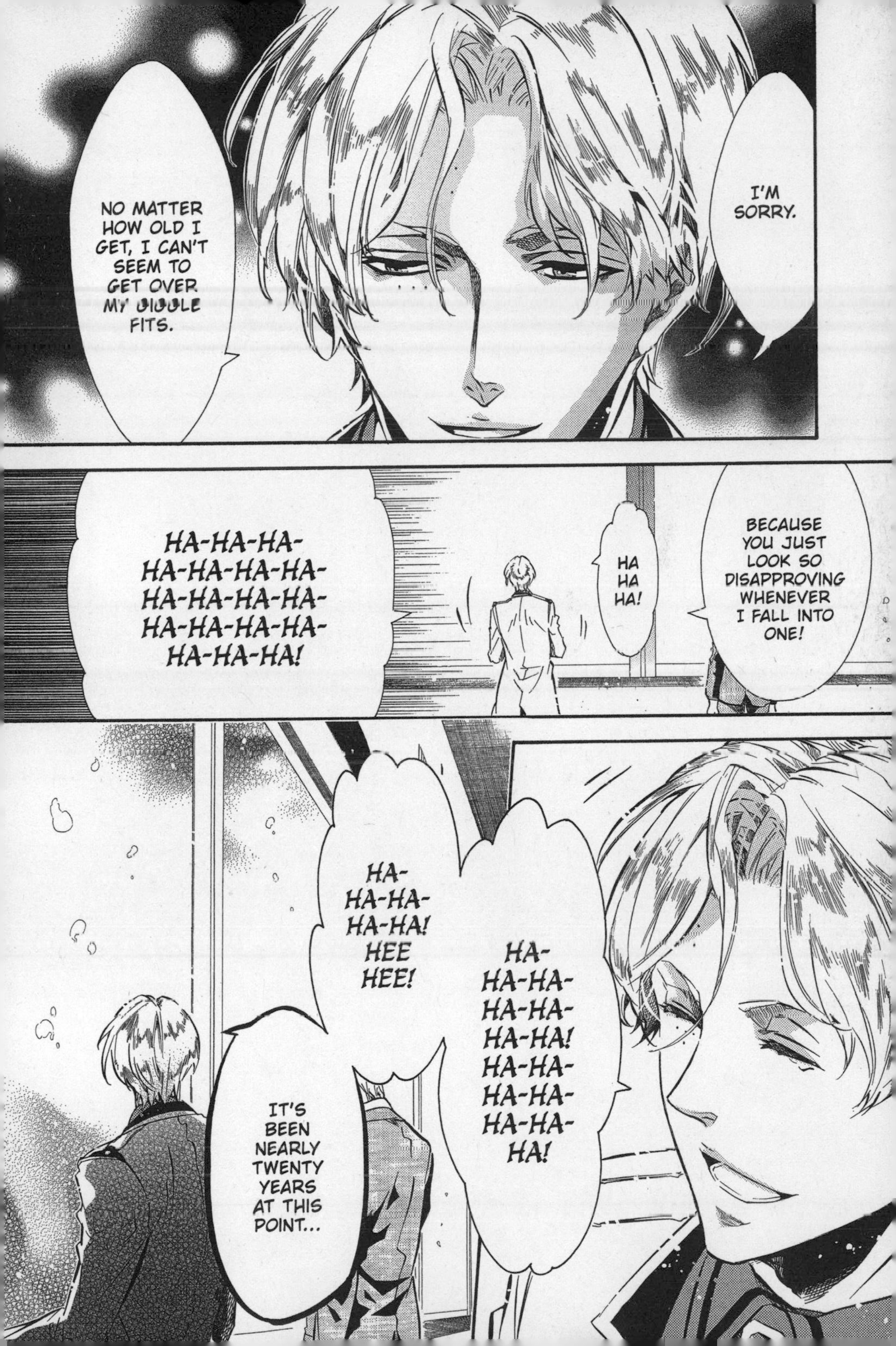
I'M SORRY.
NO MATTER HOW OLD I GET, I CAN'T SEEM TO GET OVER MY GIGGLE FITS.
BECAUSE YOU JUST LOOK SO DISAPPROVING WHENEVER I FALL INTO ONE!
HA HA HA!
HA-HA-HA-HA-HA-HA-HA-HA-HA-HA-HA-HA-HA-HA-HA-HA-HA!
HA-HA-HA-HA-HA-HA-HA! HA-HA-HA-HA-HA-HA-HA!
HA-HA-HA-HA-HA! HEE HEE!
IT'S BEEN NEARLY TWENTY YEARS AT THIS POINT...

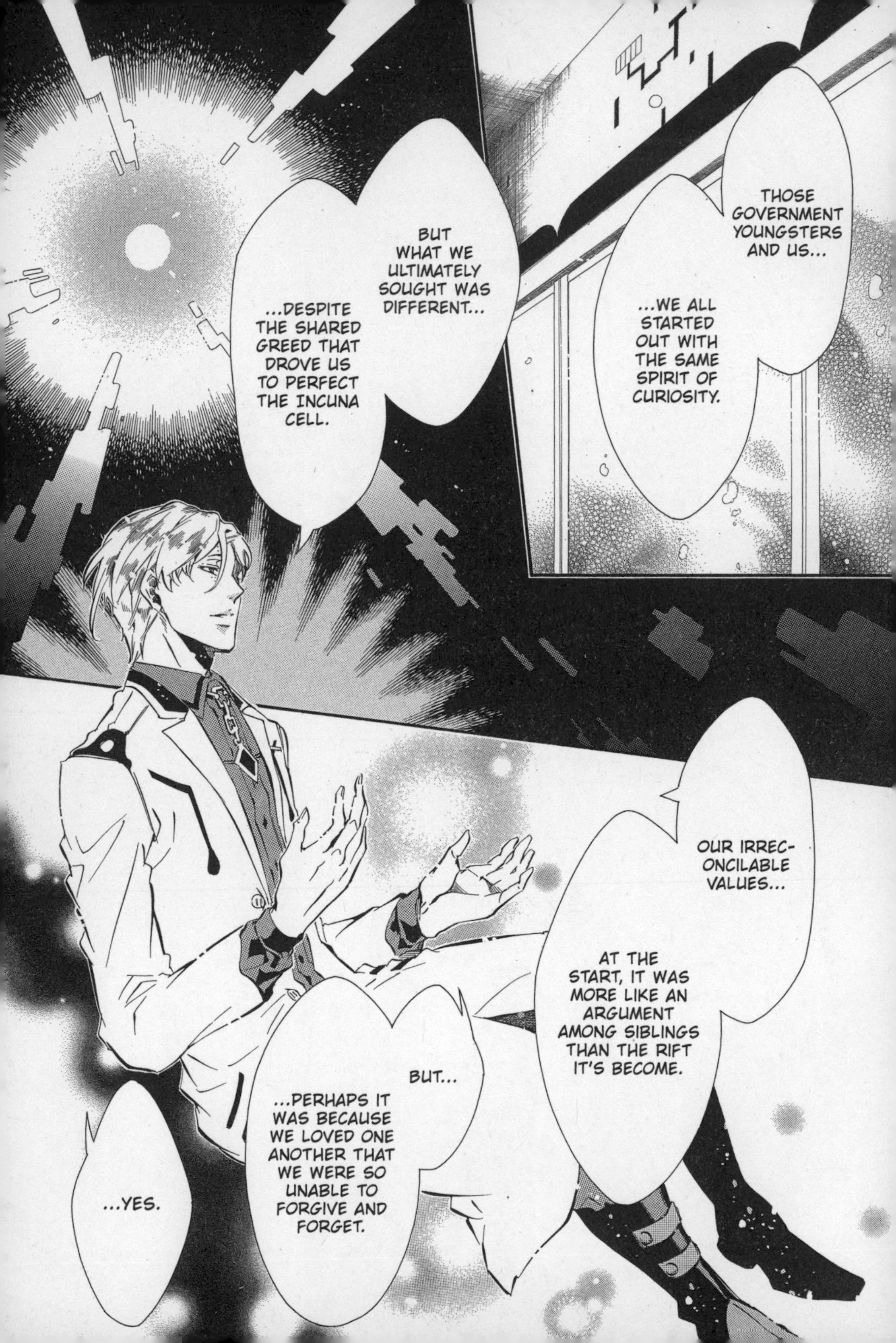
THOSE GOVERNMENT YOUNGSTERS AND US...
...WE ALL STARTED OUT WITH THE SAME SPIRIT OF CURIOSITY.
BUT WHAT WE ULTIMATELY SOUGHT WAS DIFFERENT...
...DESPITE THE SHARED GREED THAT DROVE US TO PERFECT THE INCUNA CELL.
OUR IRREC-ONCILABLE VALUES...
AT THE START, IT WAS MORE LIKE AN ARGUMENT AMONG SIBLINGS THAN THE RIFT IT'S BECOME.
BUT...
...PERHAPS IT WAS BECAUSE WE LOVED ONE ANOTHER THAT WE WERE SO UNABLE TO FORGIVE AND FORGET.
...YES.

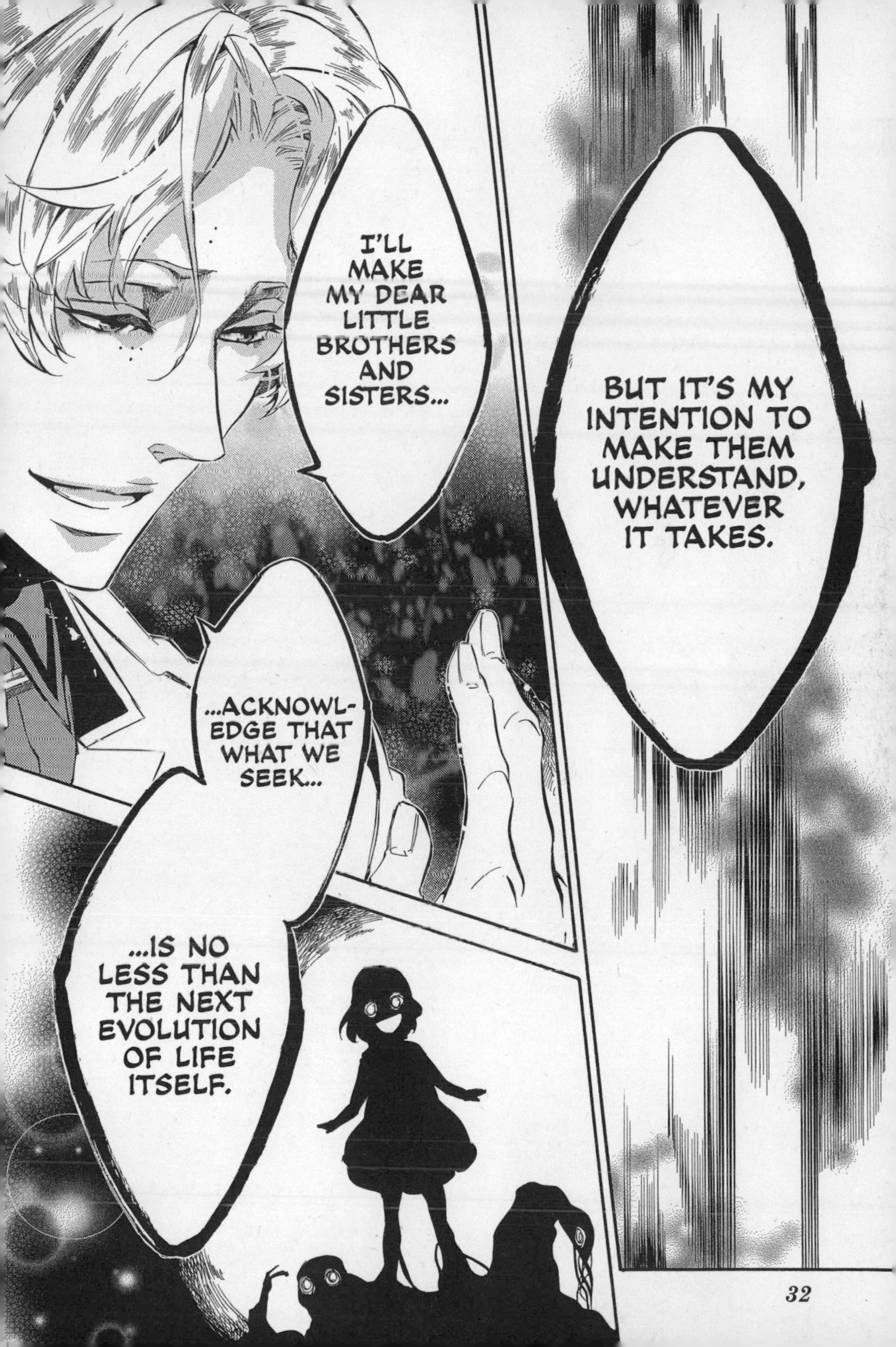
BUT IT'S MY INTENTION TO MAKE THEM UNDERSTAND, WHATEVER IT TAKES.
I'LL MAKE MY DEAR LITTLE BROTHERS AND SISTERS...
...ACKNOWL-EDGE THAT WHAT WE SEEK...
...IS NO LESS THAN THE NEXT EVOLUTION OF LIFE ITSELF.

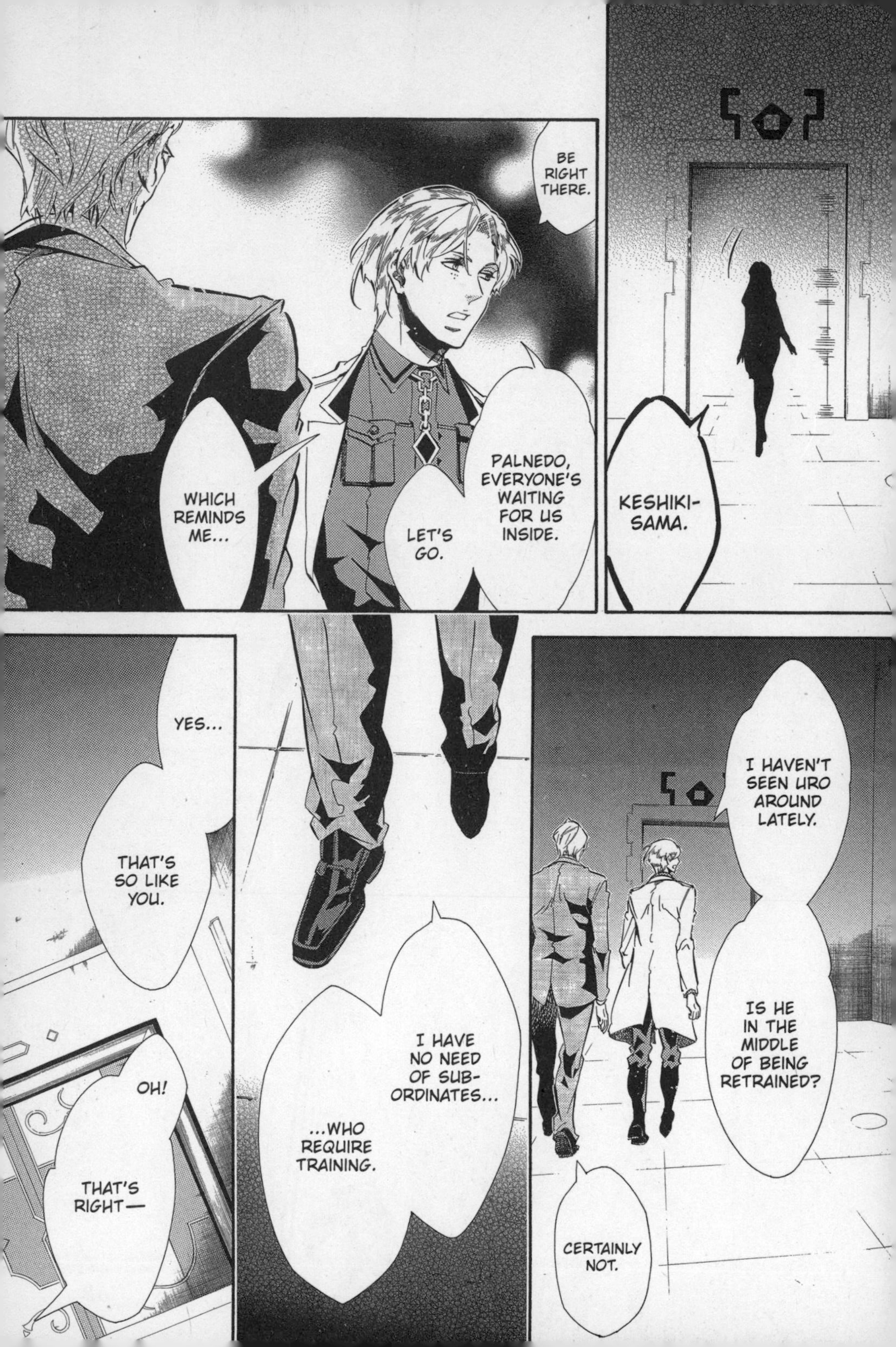
KESHIKI-SAMA.
BE RIGHT THERE.
PALNEDO, EVERYONE'S WAITING FOR US INSIDE.
LET'S GO.
WHICH REMINDS ME...
I HAVEN'T SEEN URO AROUND LATELY.
IS HE IN THE MIDDLE OF BEING RETRAINED?
CERTAINLY NOT.
I HAVE NO NEED OF SUB-ORDINATES...
...WHO REQUIRE TRAINING.
YES...
THAT'S SO LIKE YOU.
OH!
THAT'S RIGHT—

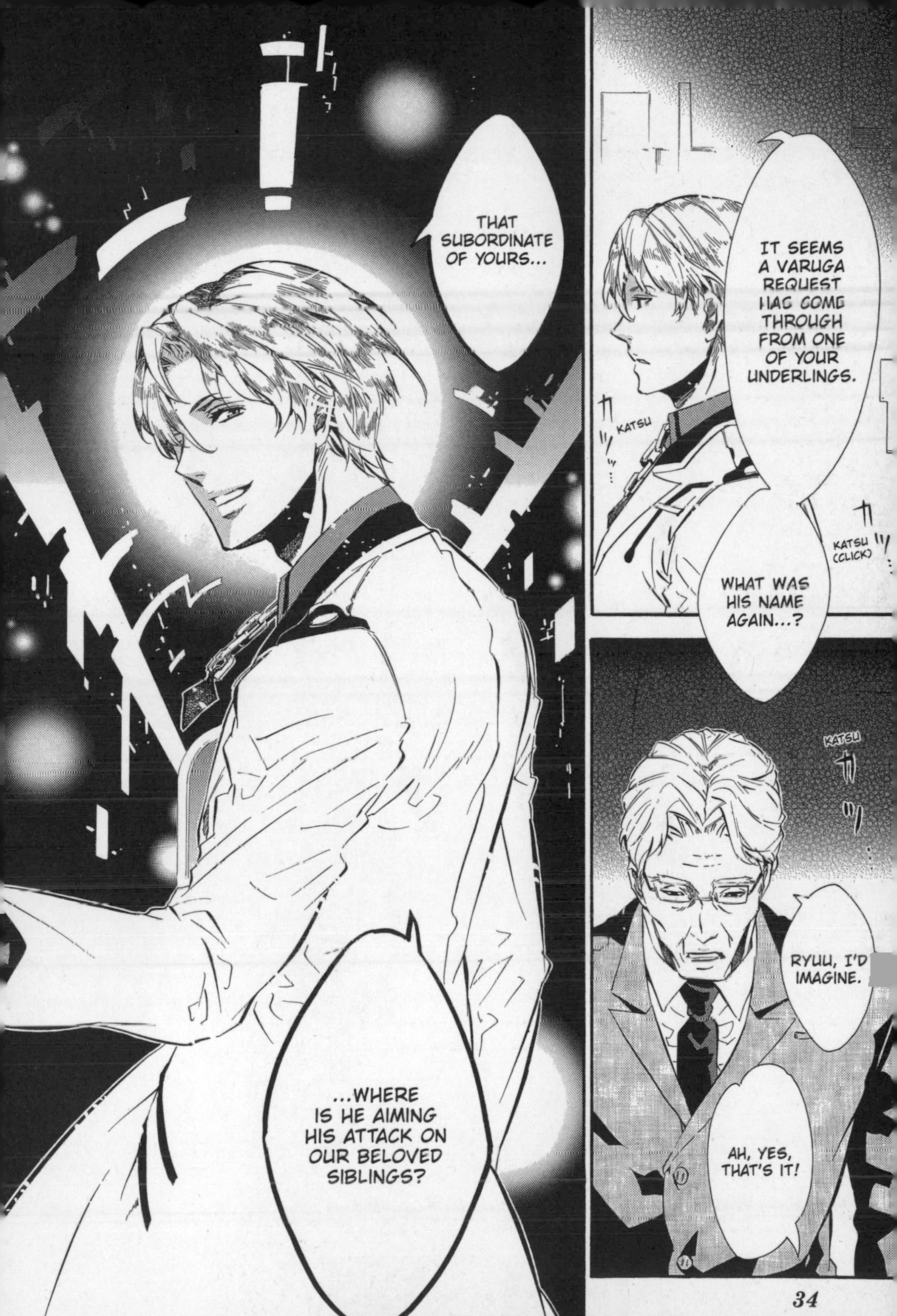
IT SEEMS A VARUGA REQUEST HAS COME THROUGH FROM ONE OF YOUR UNDERLINGS.
KATSU
KATSU (CLICK)
WHAT WAS HIS NAME AGAIN...?
KATSU
RYUU, I'D IMAGINE.
AH, YES, THAT'S IT!
THAT SUBORDINATE OF YOURS...
...WHERE IS HE AIMING HIS ATTACK ON OUR BELOVED SIBLINGS?

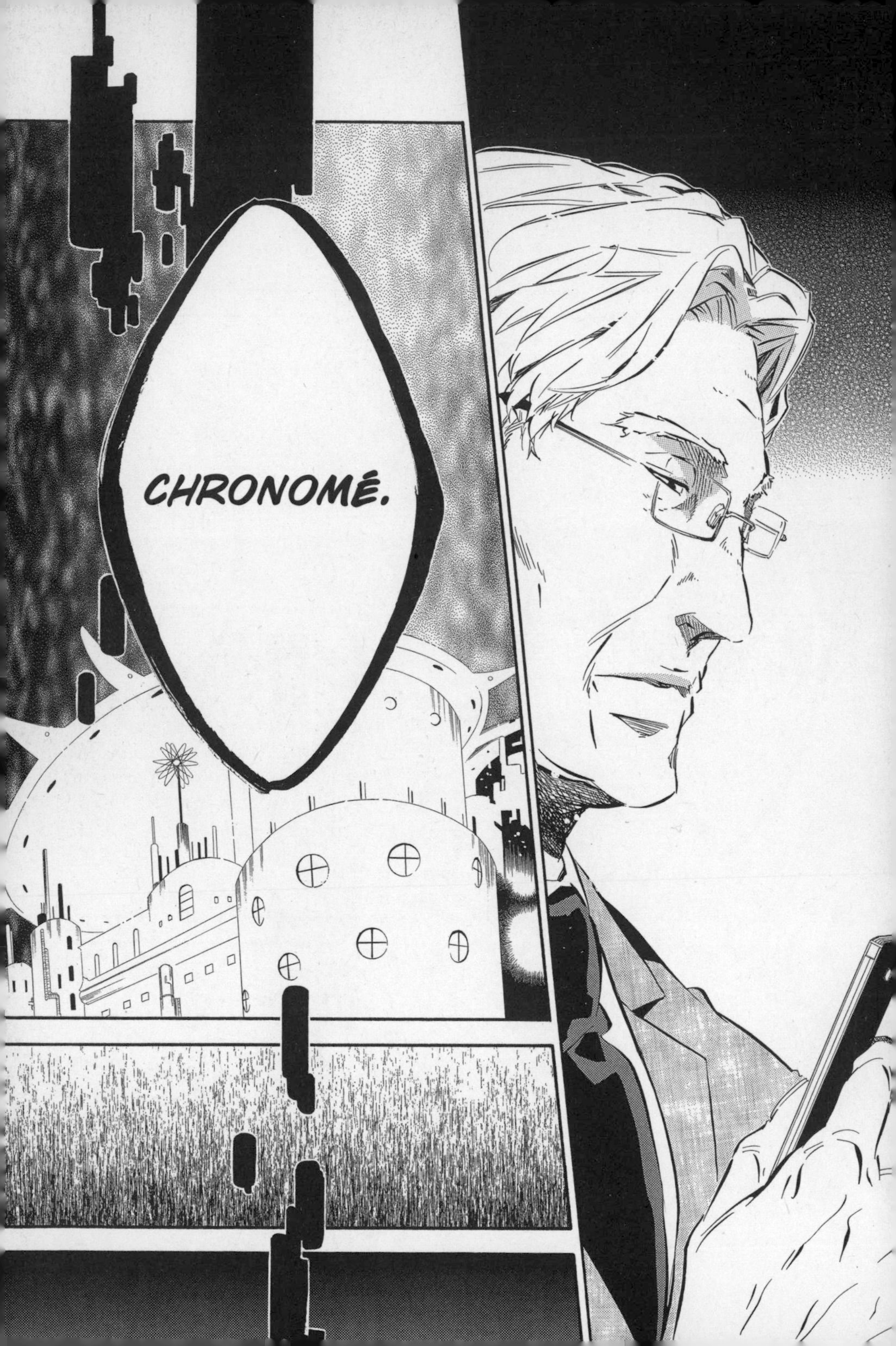
CHRONOMÉ.

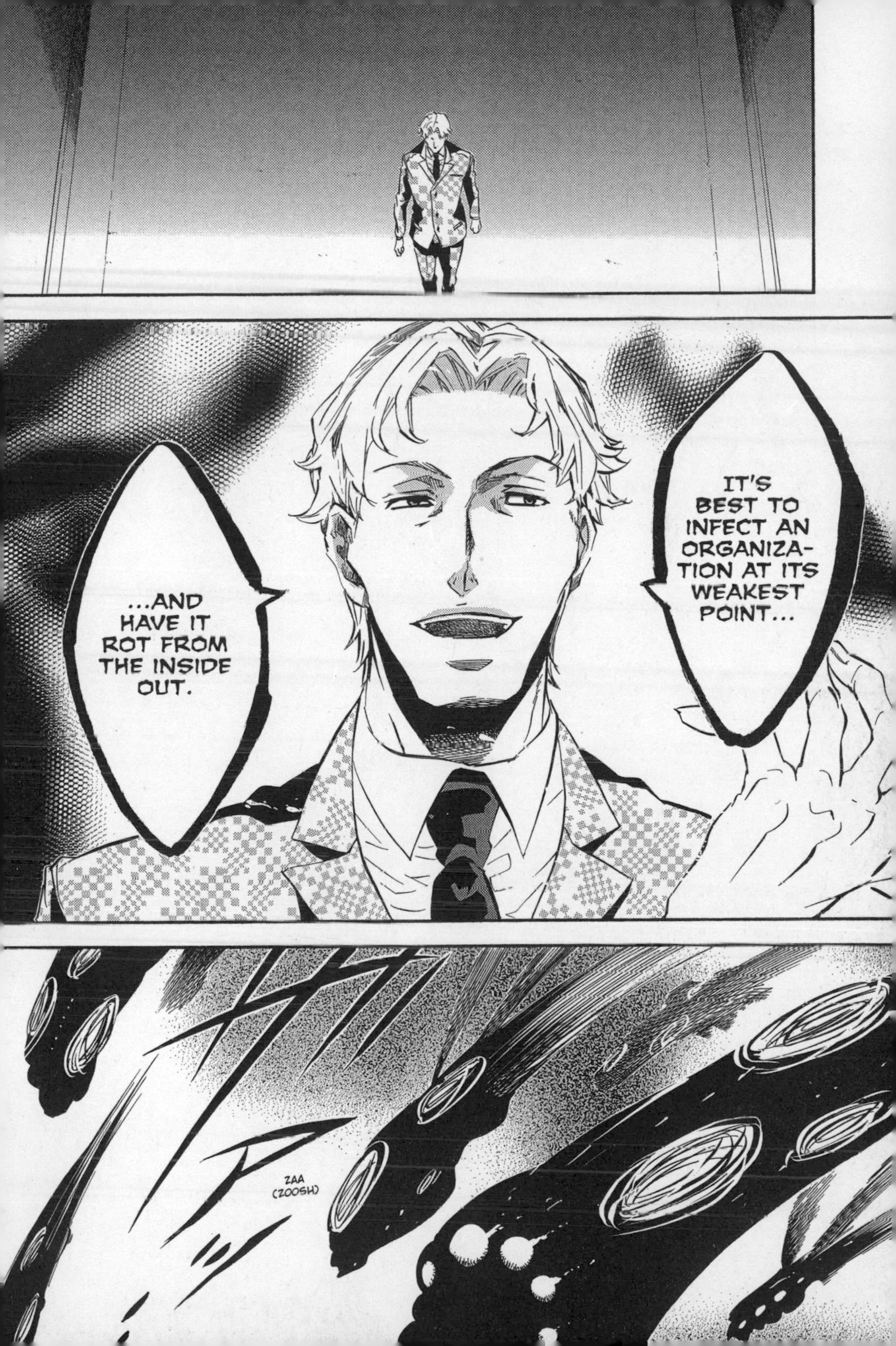
IT'S BEST TO INFECT AN ORGANIZATION AT ITS WEAKEST POINT...
...AND HAVE IT ROT FROM THE INSIDE OUT.
ZAA (ZOOSH)

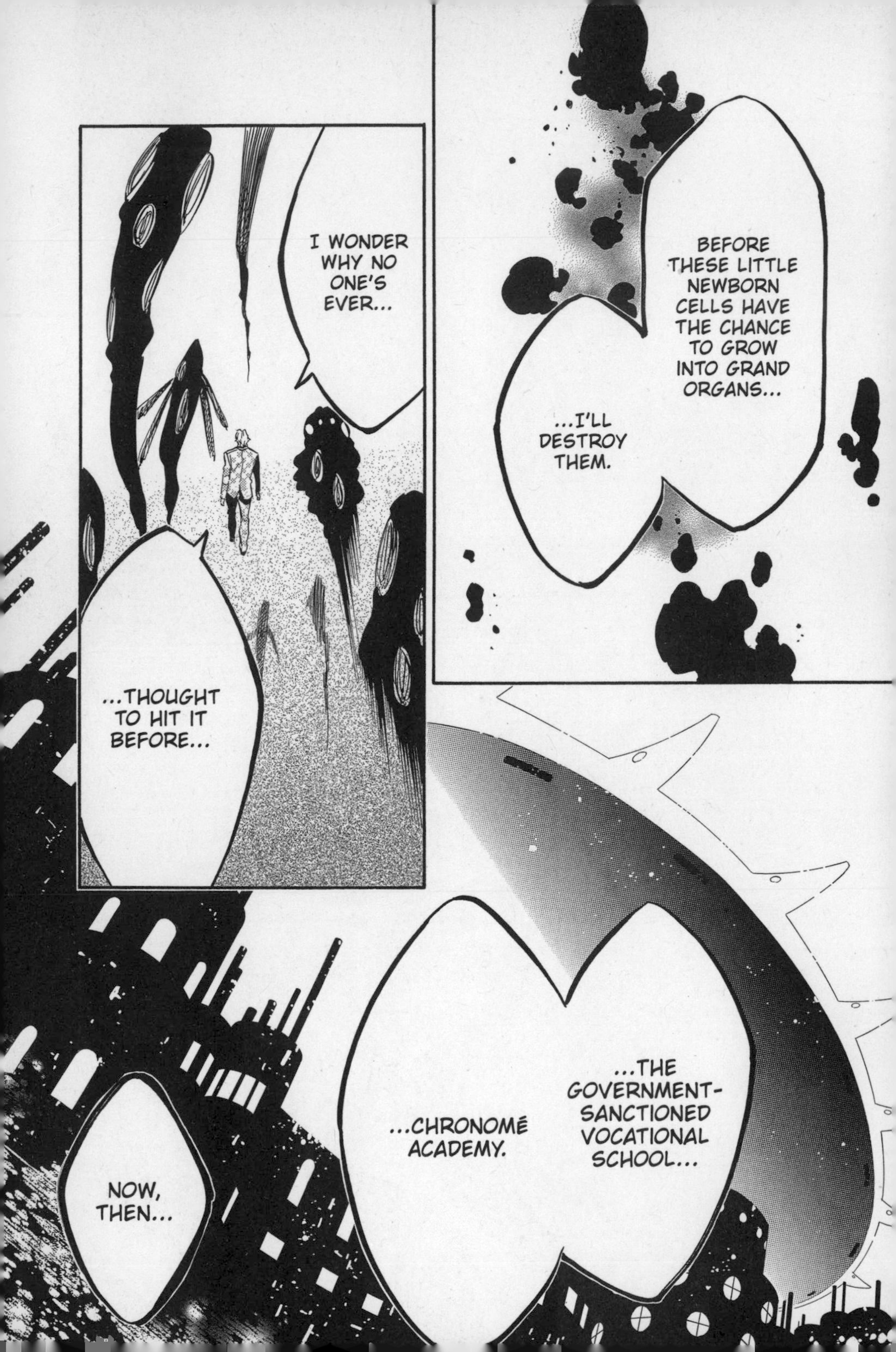
BEFORE THESE LITTLE NEWBORN CELLS HAVE THE CHANCE TO GROW INTO GRAND ORGANS...
...I'LL DESTROY THEM.
I WONDER WHY NO ONE'S EVER...
...THOUGHT TO HIT IT BEFORE...
...THE GOVERNMENT-SANCTIONED VOCATIONAL SCHOOL...
...CHRONOMÉ ACADEMY.
NOW, THEN...

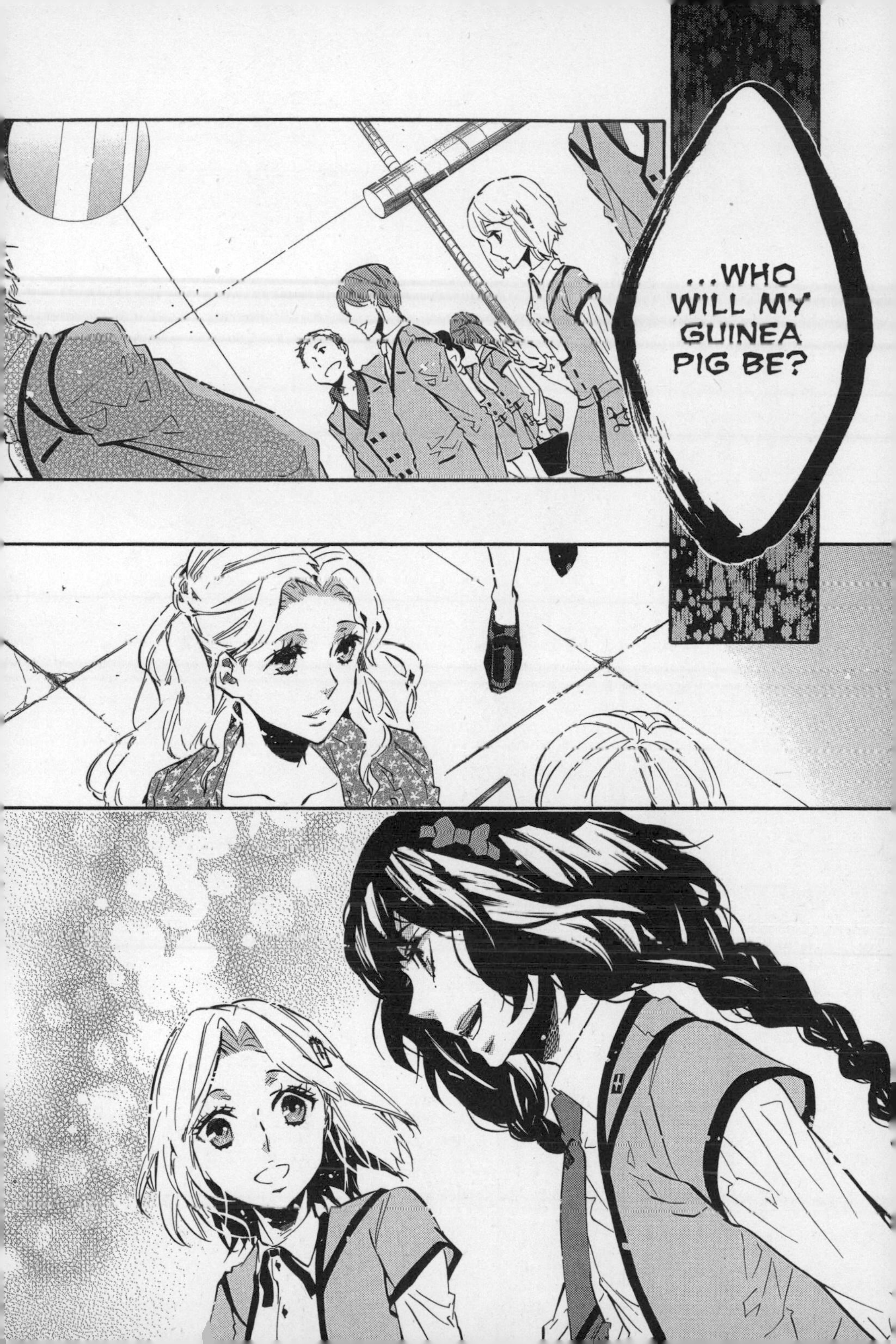
...WHO WILL MY GUINEA PIG BE?

KARNEVAL

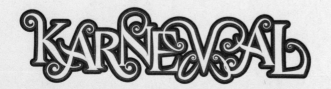

KARNEVAL

Score 74: A Place to Return

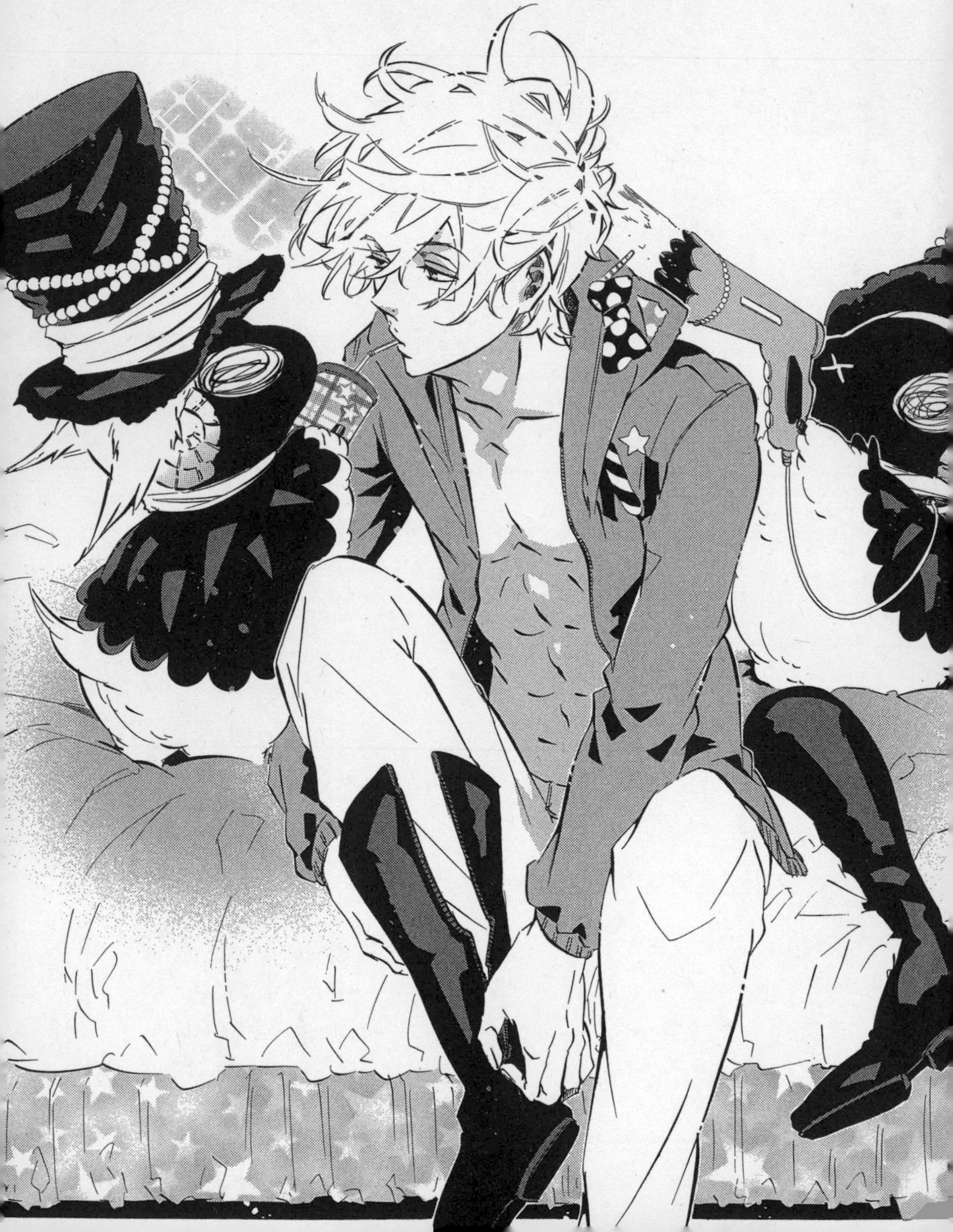

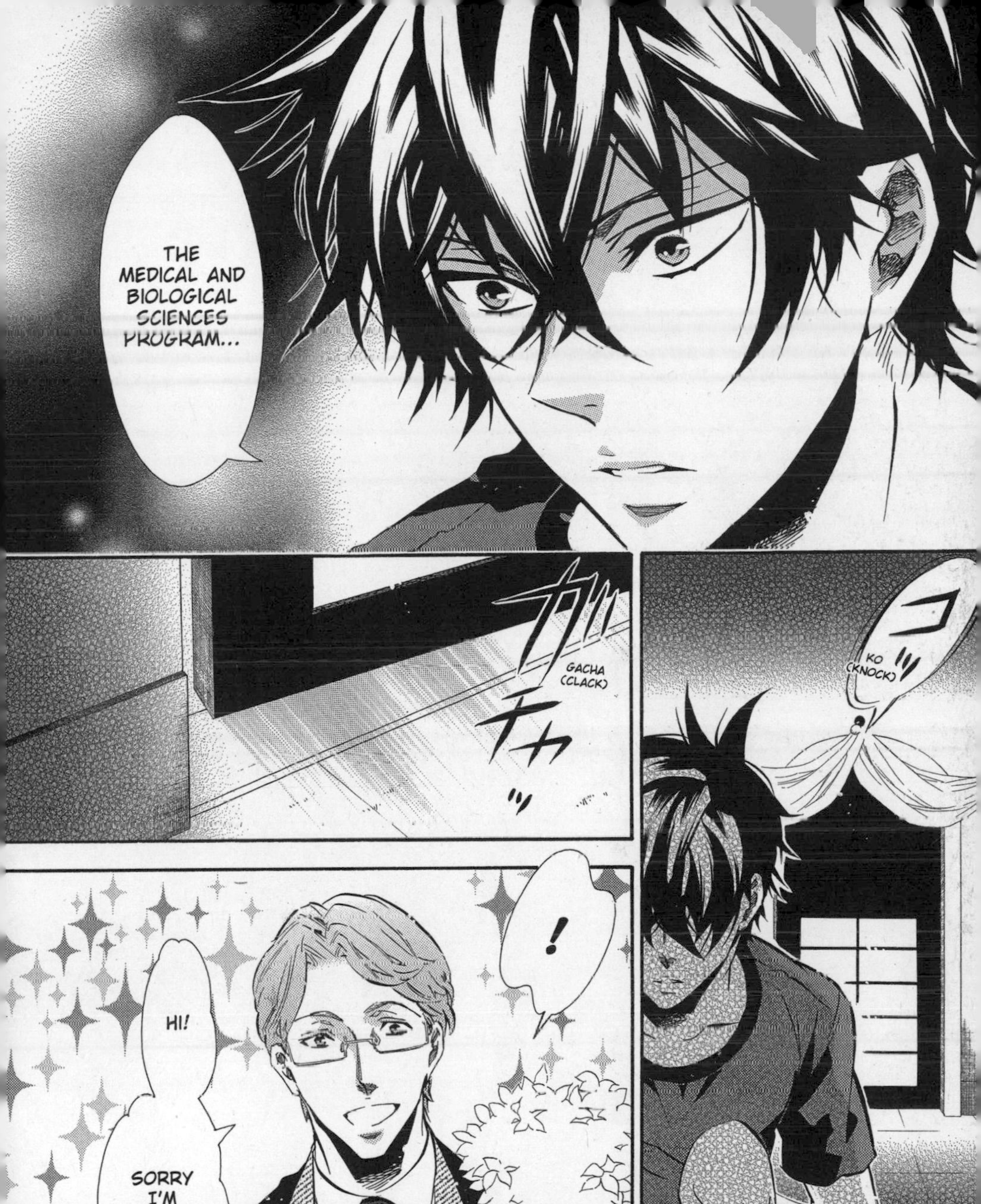
THE MEDICAL AND BIOLOGICAL SCIENCES PROGRAM...
KO (KNOCK)
GACHA (CLACK)
!
HI!
SORRY I'M INTRUDING HERE! ARE YOU COMING OFF-DUTY NOW...

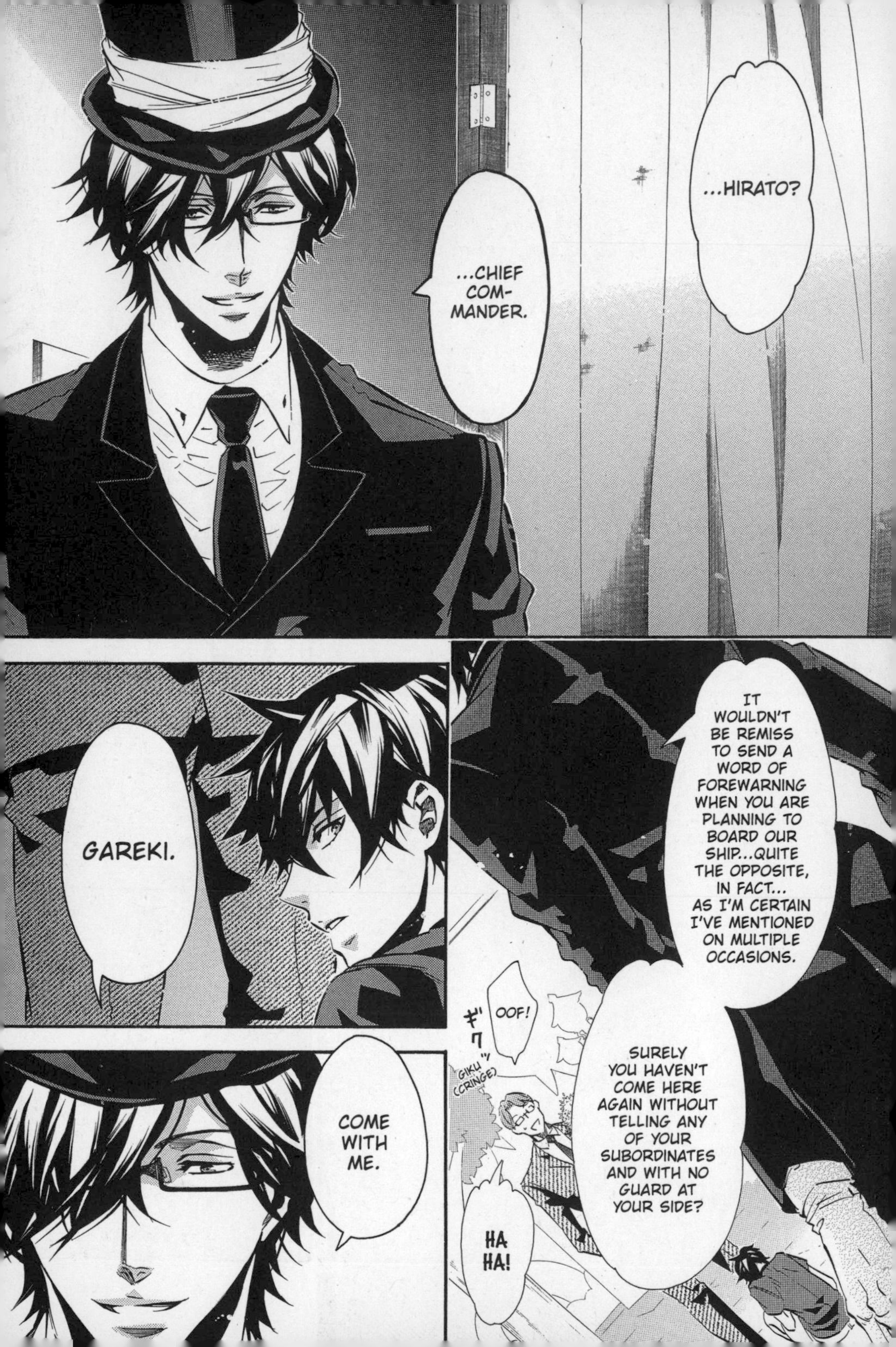
...HIRATO?
...CHIEF COMMANDER.
IT WOULDN'T BE REMISS TO SEND A WORD OF FOREWARNING WHEN YOU ARE PLANNING TO BOARD OUR SHIP...QUITE THE OPPOSITE, IN FACT... AS I'M CERTAIN I'VE MENTIONED ON MULTIPLE OCCASIONS.
OOF!
ギクッ
GIKU (CRINGE)
SURELY YOU HAVEN'T COME HERE AGAIN WITHOUT TELLING ANY OF YOUR SUBORDINATES AND WITH NO GUARD AT YOUR SIDE?
HA HA!
GAREKI.
COME WITH ME.

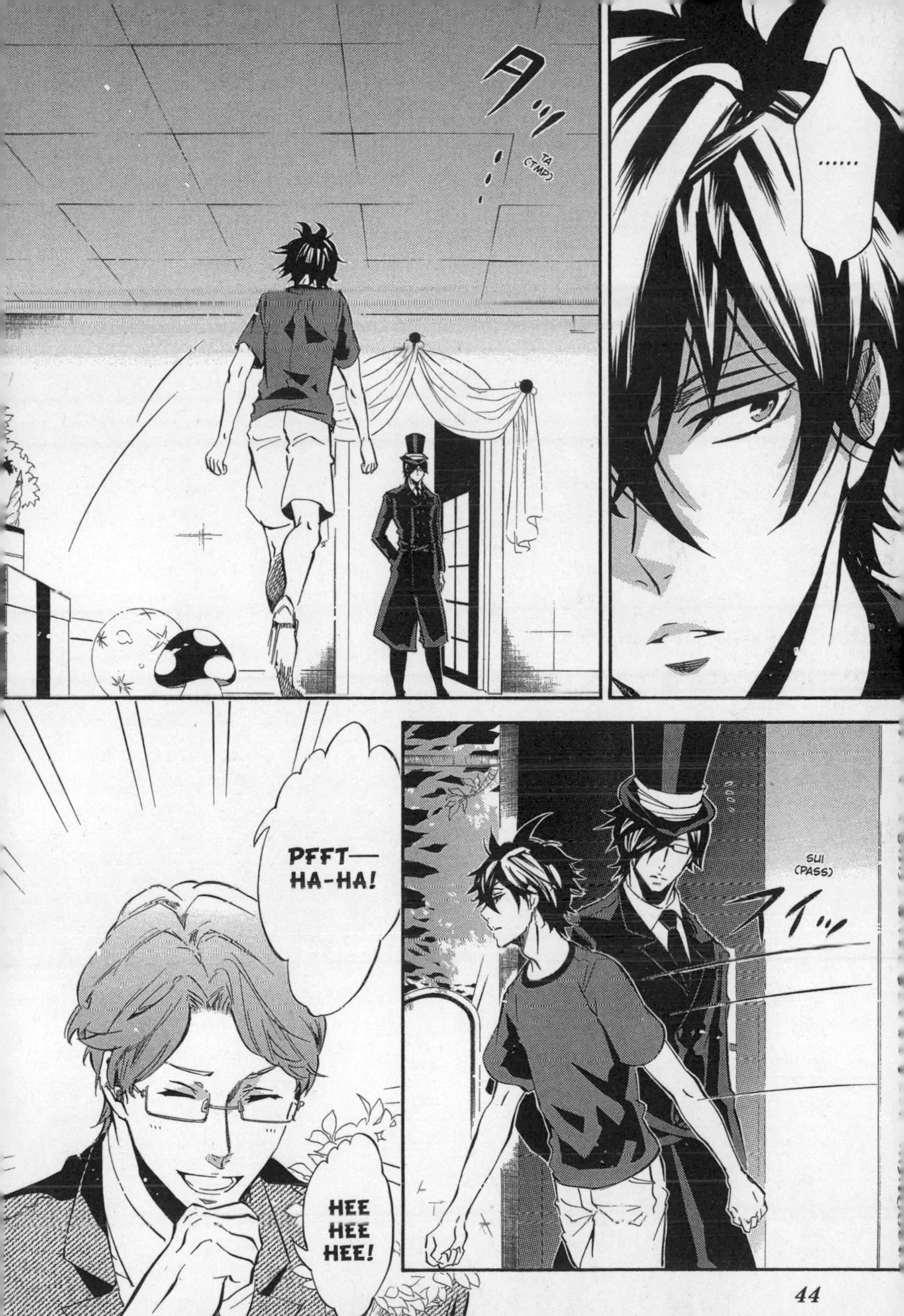
......
TA (TMP)
SUI (PASS)
PFFT— HA-HA!
HEE HEE HEE!

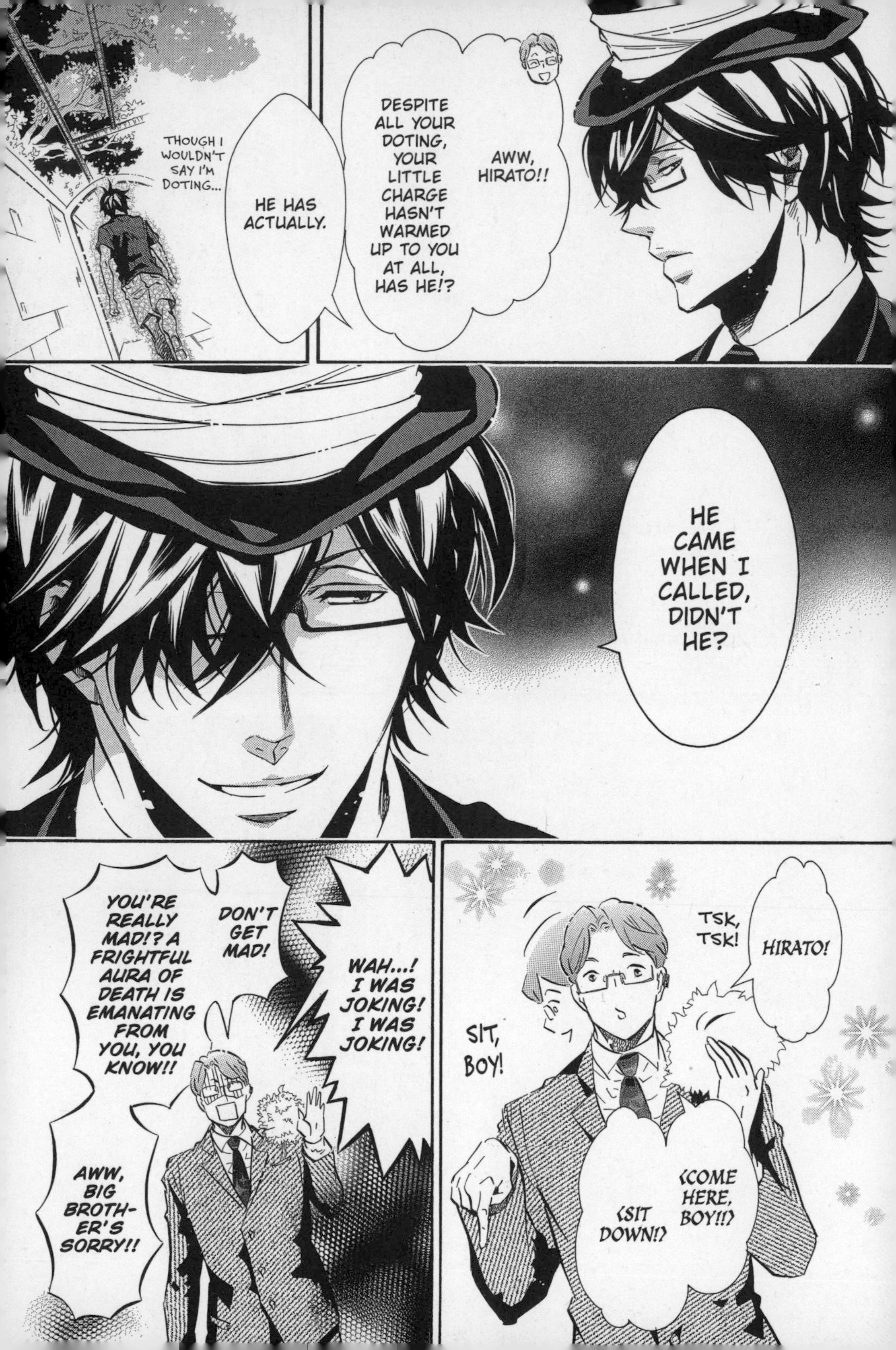
AWW, HIRATO!!
DESPITE ALL YOUR DOTING, YOUR LITTLE CHARGE HASN'T WARMED UP TO YOU AT ALL, HAS HE!?
HE HAS ACTUALLY.
THOUGH I WOULDN'T SAY I'M DOTING...
HE CAME WHEN I CALLED, DIDN'T HE?
HIRATO!
TSK, TSK!
‹COME HERE, BOY!!›
SIT, BOY!
‹SIT DOWN!›
WAH...! I WAS JOKING! I WAS JOKING!
DON'T GET MAD!
YOU'RE REALLY MAD!? A FRIGHTFUL AURA OF DEATH IS EMANATING FROM YOU, YOU KNOW!!
AWW, BIG BROTHER'S SORRY!!

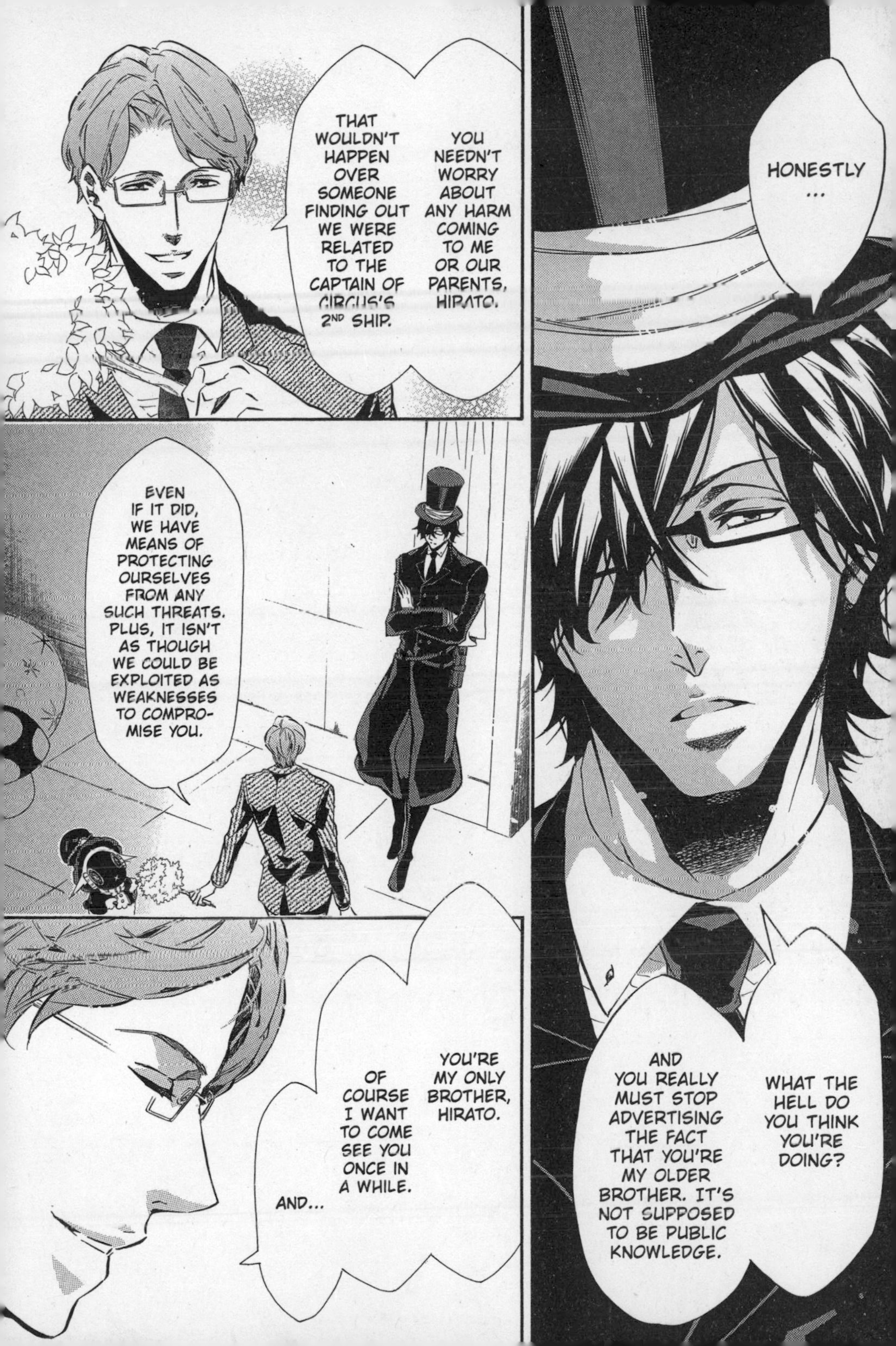
HONESTLY...
WHAT THE HELL DO YOU THINK YOU'RE DOING?
AND YOU REALLY MUST STOP ADVERTISING THE FACT THAT YOU'RE MY OLDER BROTHER. IT'S NOT SUPPOSED TO BE PUBLIC KNOWLEDGE.
YOU NEEDN'T WORRY ABOUT ANY HARM COMING TO ME OR OUR PARENTS, HIRATO.
THAT WOULDN'T HAPPEN OVER SOMEONE FINDING OUT WE WERE RELATED TO THE CAPTAIN OF CIRCUS'S 2ND SHIP.
EVEN IF IT DID, WE HAVE MEANS OF PROTECTING OURSELVES FROM ANY SUCH THREATS. PLUS, IT ISN'T AS THOUGH WE COULD BE EXPLOITED AS WEAKNESSES TO COMPRO-MISE YOU.
YOU'RE MY ONLY BROTHER, HIRATO.
OF COURSE I WANT TO COME SEE YOU ONCE IN A WHILE.
AND...

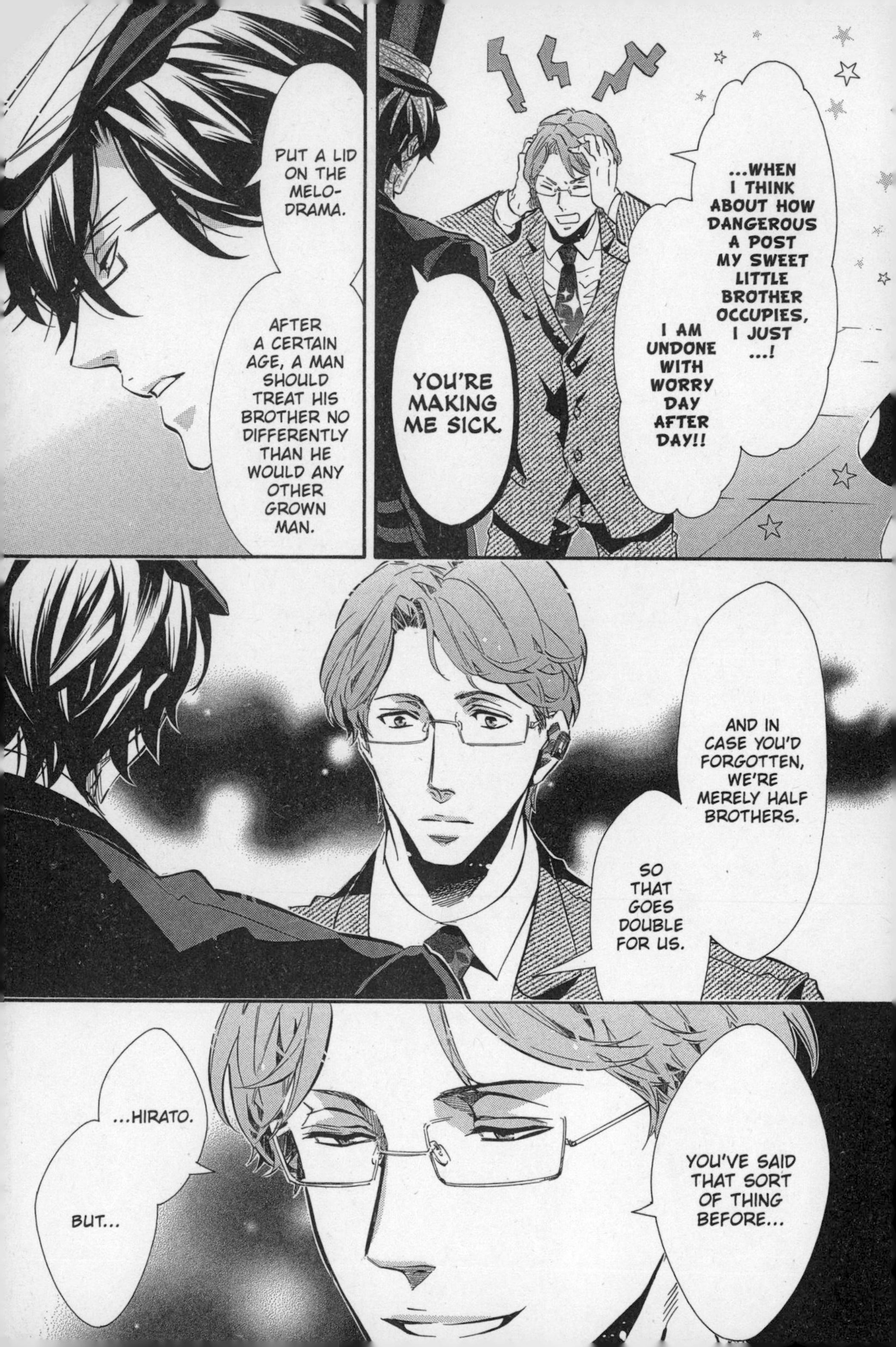
...WHEN I THINK ABOUT HOW DANGEROUS A POST MY SWEET LITTLE BROTHER OCCUPIES, I JUST ...!
I AM UNDONE WITH WORRY DAY AFTER DAY!!
YOU'RE MAKING ME SICK.
PUT A LID ON THE MELO-DRAMA.
AFTER A CERTAIN AGE, A MAN SHOULD TREAT HIS BROTHER NO DIFFERENTLY THAN HE WOULD ANY OTHER GROWN MAN.
AND IN CASE YOU'D FORGOTTEN, WE'RE MERELY HALF BROTHERS.
SO THAT GOES DOUBLE FOR US.
YOU'VE SAID THAT SORT OF THING BEFORE...
...HIRATO.
BUT...

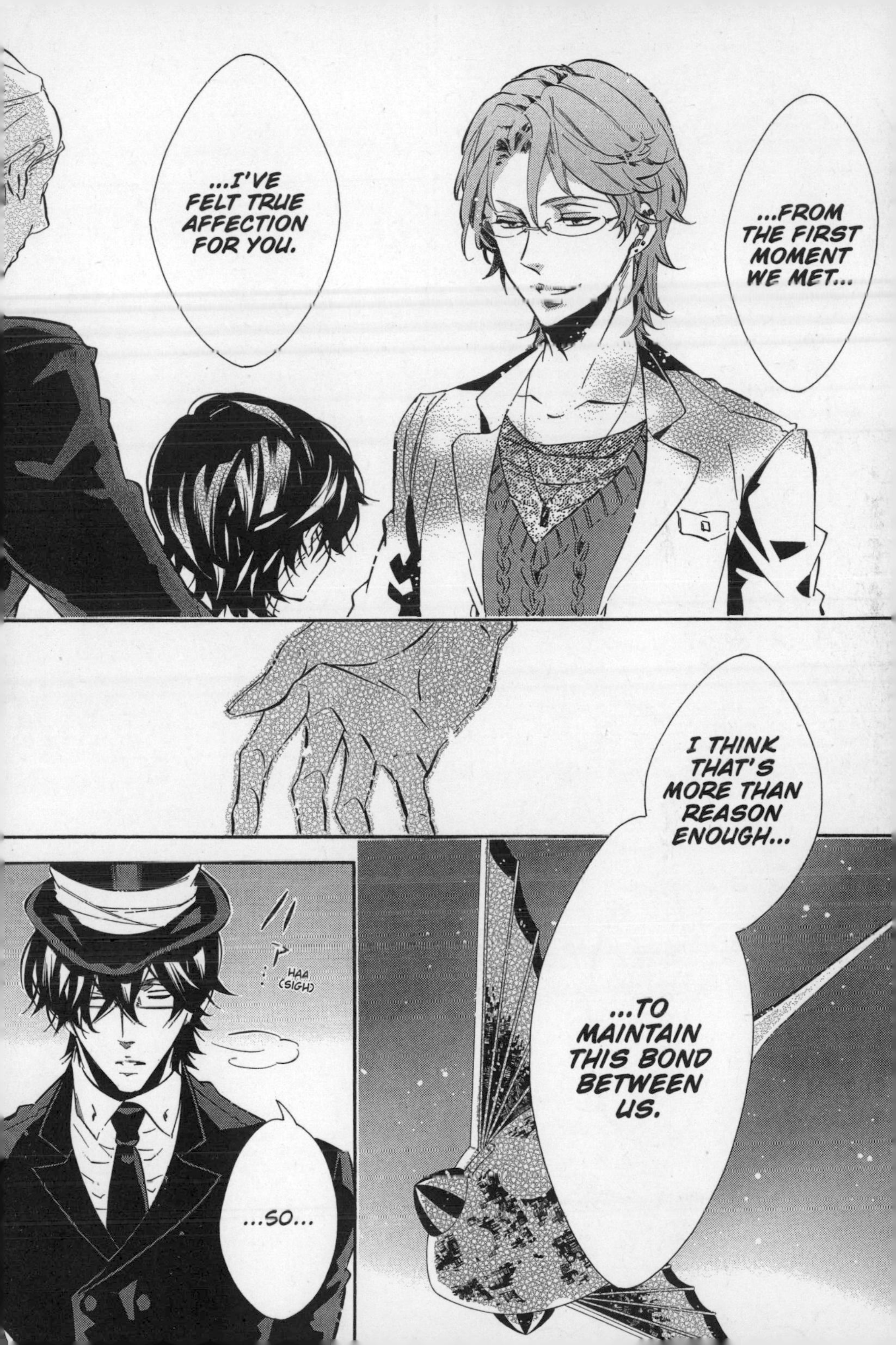
...FROM THE FIRST MOMENT WE MET...
...I'VE FELT TRUE AFFECTION FOR YOU.
I THINK THAT'S MORE THAN REASON ENOUGH...
...TO MAINTAIN THIS BOND BETWEEN US.
HAA (SIGH)
...SO...

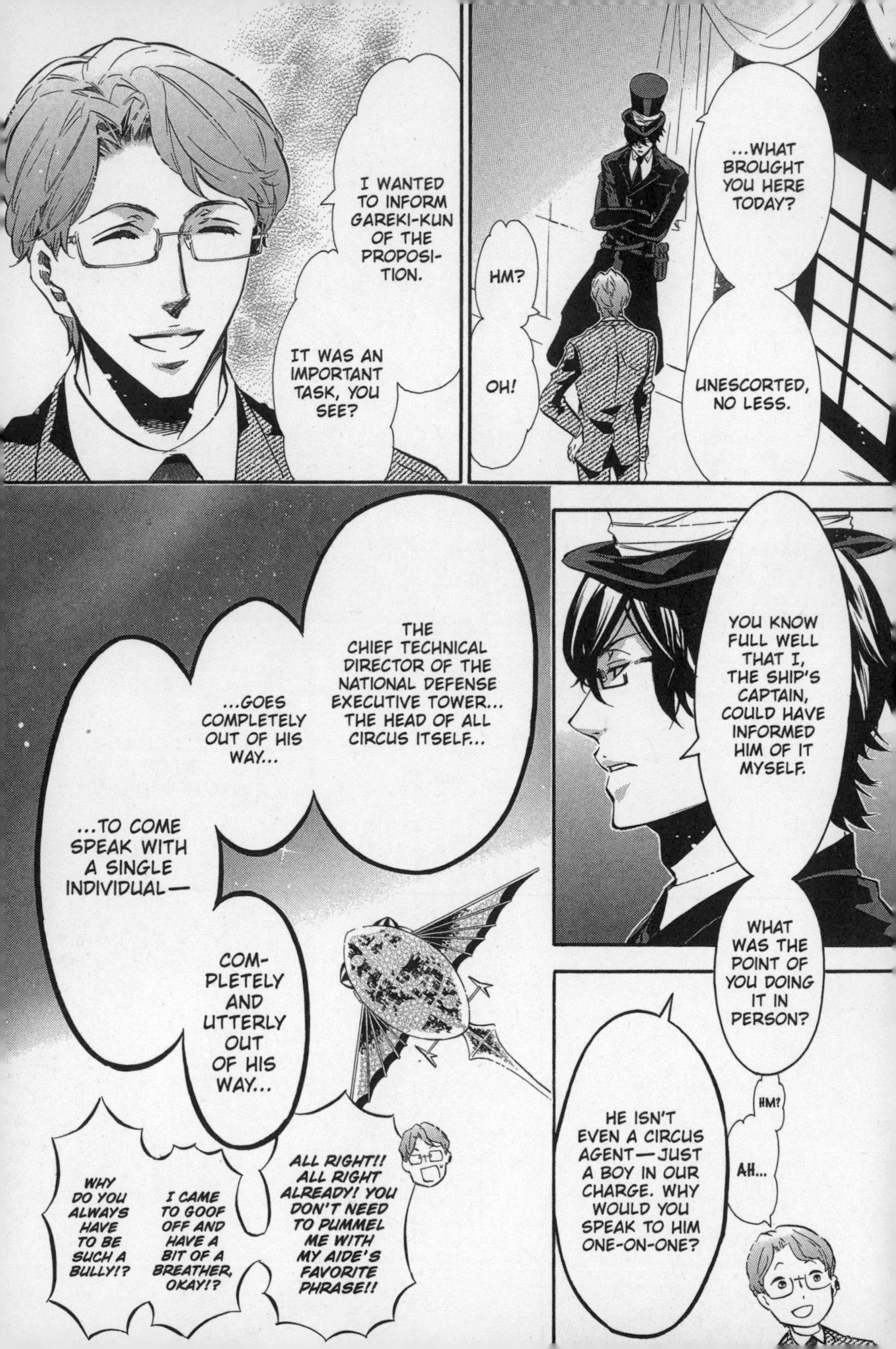
...WHAT BROUGHT YOU HERE TODAY?
UNESCORTED, NO LESS.
HM?
OH!
I WANTED TO INFORM GAREKI-KUN OF THE PROPOSITION.
IT WAS AN IMPORTANT TASK, YOU SEE?
YOU KNOW FULL WELL THAT I, THE SHIP'S CAPTAIN, COULD HAVE INFORMED HIM OF IT MYSELF.
WHAT WAS THE POINT OF YOU DOING IT IN PERSON?
HE ISN'T EVEN A CIRCUS AGENT—JUST A BOY IN OUR CHARGE. WHY WOULD YOU SPEAK TO HIM ONE-ON-ONE?
HM?
AH...
THE CHIEF TECHNICAL DIRECTOR OF THE NATIONAL DEFENSE EXECUTIVE TOWER... THE HEAD OF ALL CIRCUS ITSELF...
...GOES COMPLETELY OUT OF HIS WAY...
...TO COME SPEAK WITH A SINGLE INDIVIDUAL—
COMPLETELY AND UTTERLY OUT OF HIS WAY...
ALL RIGHT!! ALL RIGHT ALREADY! YOU DON'T NEED TO PUMMEL ME WITH MY AIDE'S FAVORITE PHRASE!!
I CAME TO GOOF OFF AND HAVE A BIT OF A BREATHER, OKAY!?
WHY DO YOU ALWAYS HAVE TO BE SUCH A BULLY!?

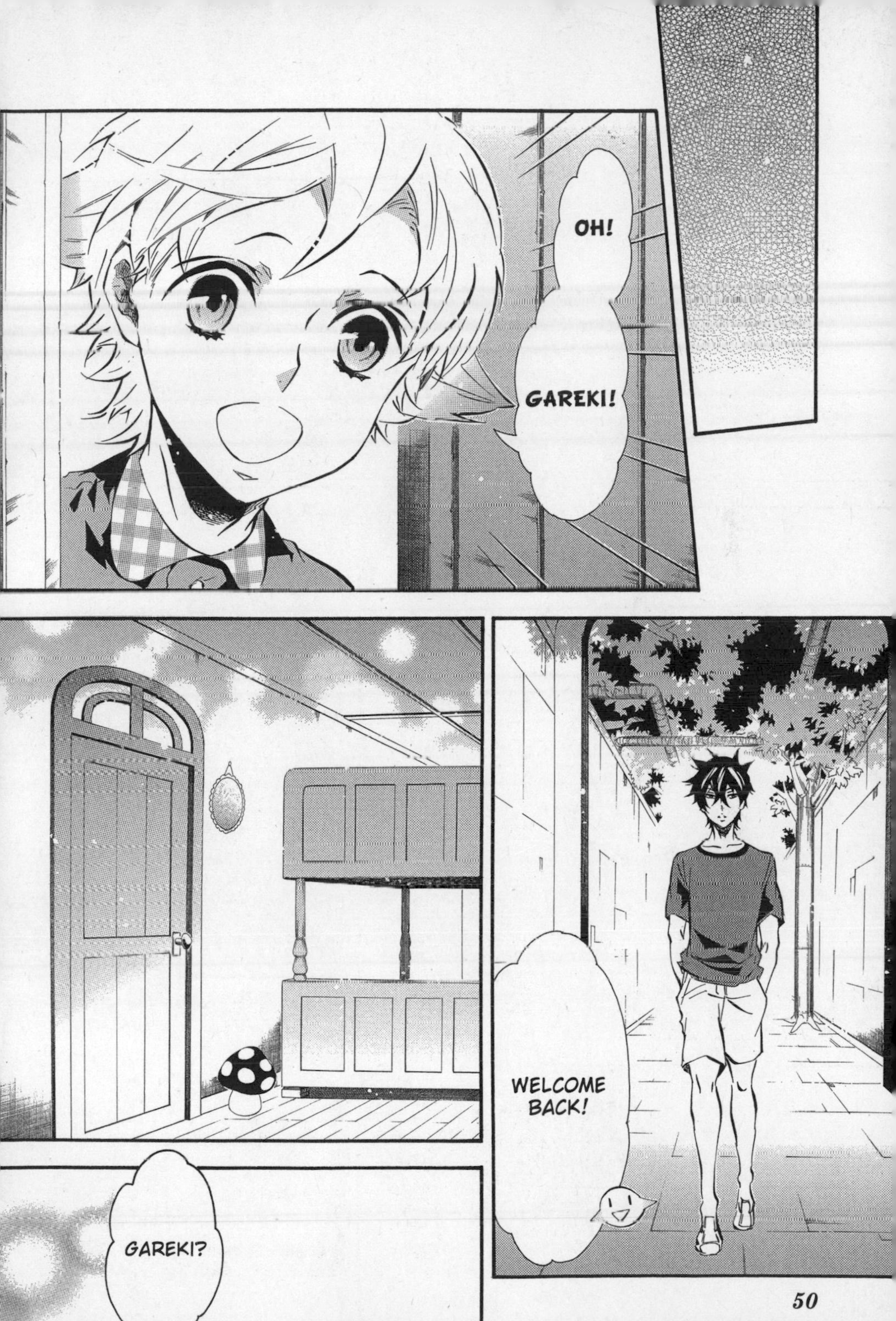
OH!
GAREKI!
WELCOME BACK!
GAREKI?

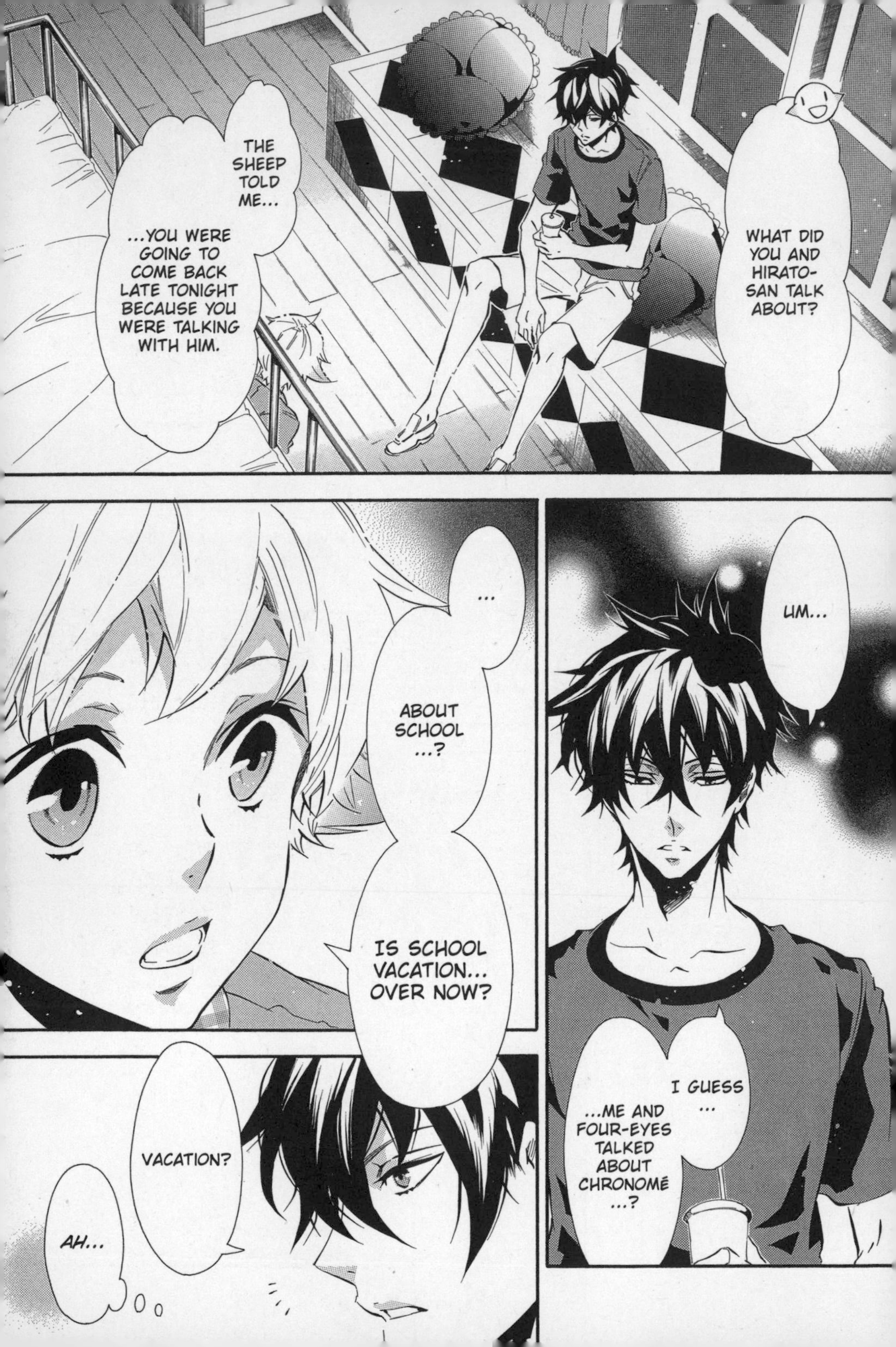
WHAT DID YOU AND HIRATO-SAN TALK ABOUT?
THE SHEEP TOLD ME...
...YOU WERE GOING TO COME BACK LATE TONIGHT BECAUSE YOU WERE TALKING WITH HIM.
UM...
I GUESS ...
...ME AND FOUR-EYES TALKED ABOUT CHRONOMÉ ...?
...
ABOUT SCHOOL ...?
IS SCHOOL VACATION... OVER NOW?
VACATION?
AH...

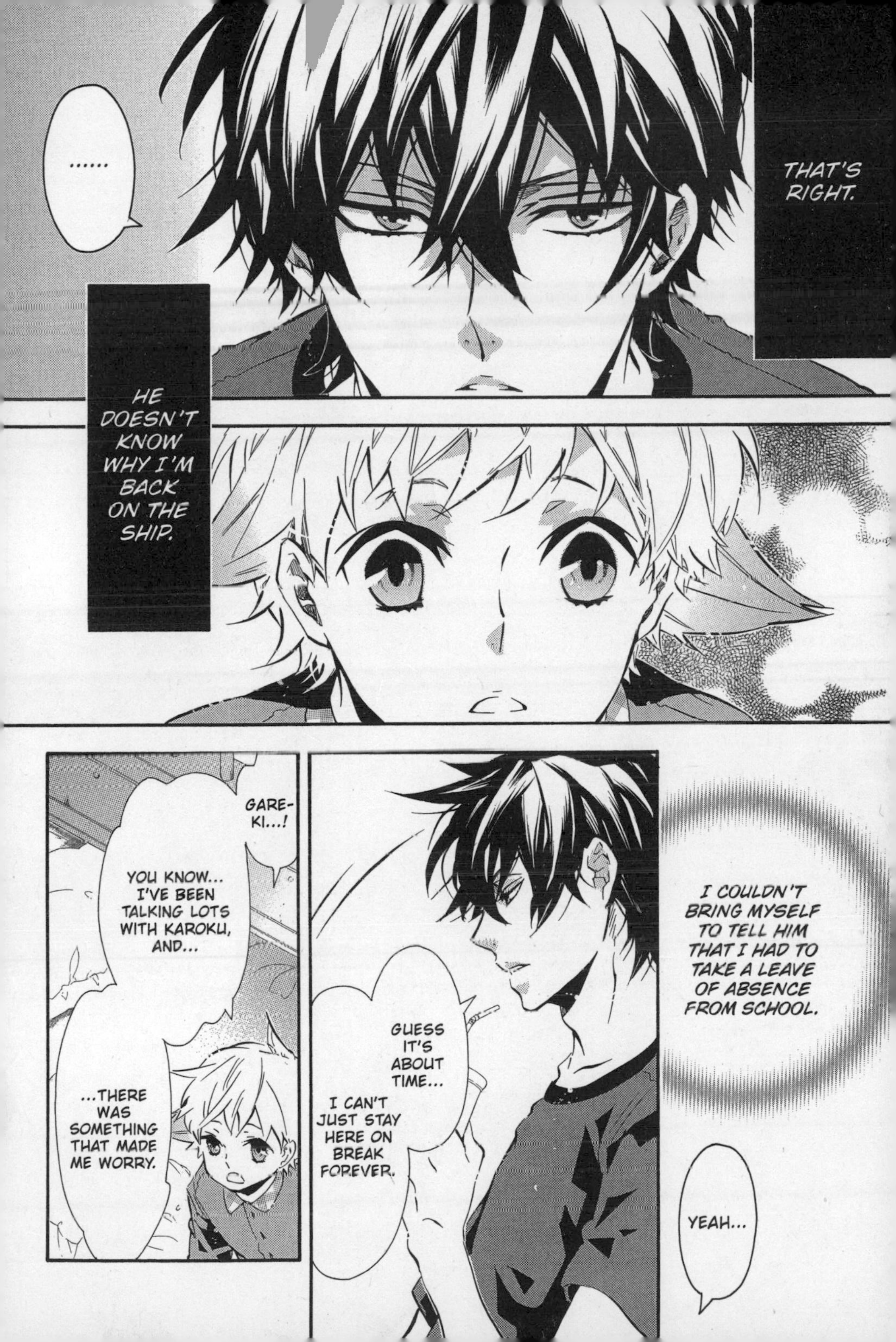
THAT'S RIGHT.
......
HE DOESN'T KNOW WHY I'M BACK ON THE SHIP.
I COULDN'T BRING MYSELF TO TELL HIM THAT I HAD TO TAKE A LEAVE OF ABSENCE FROM SCHOOL.
GUESS IT'S ABOUT TIME... I CAN'T JUST STAY HERE ON BREAK FOREVER.
YEAH...
GARE-KI...!
YOU KNOW... I'VE BEEN TALKING LOTS WITH KAROKU, AND...
...THERE WAS SOMETHING THAT MADE ME WORRY.

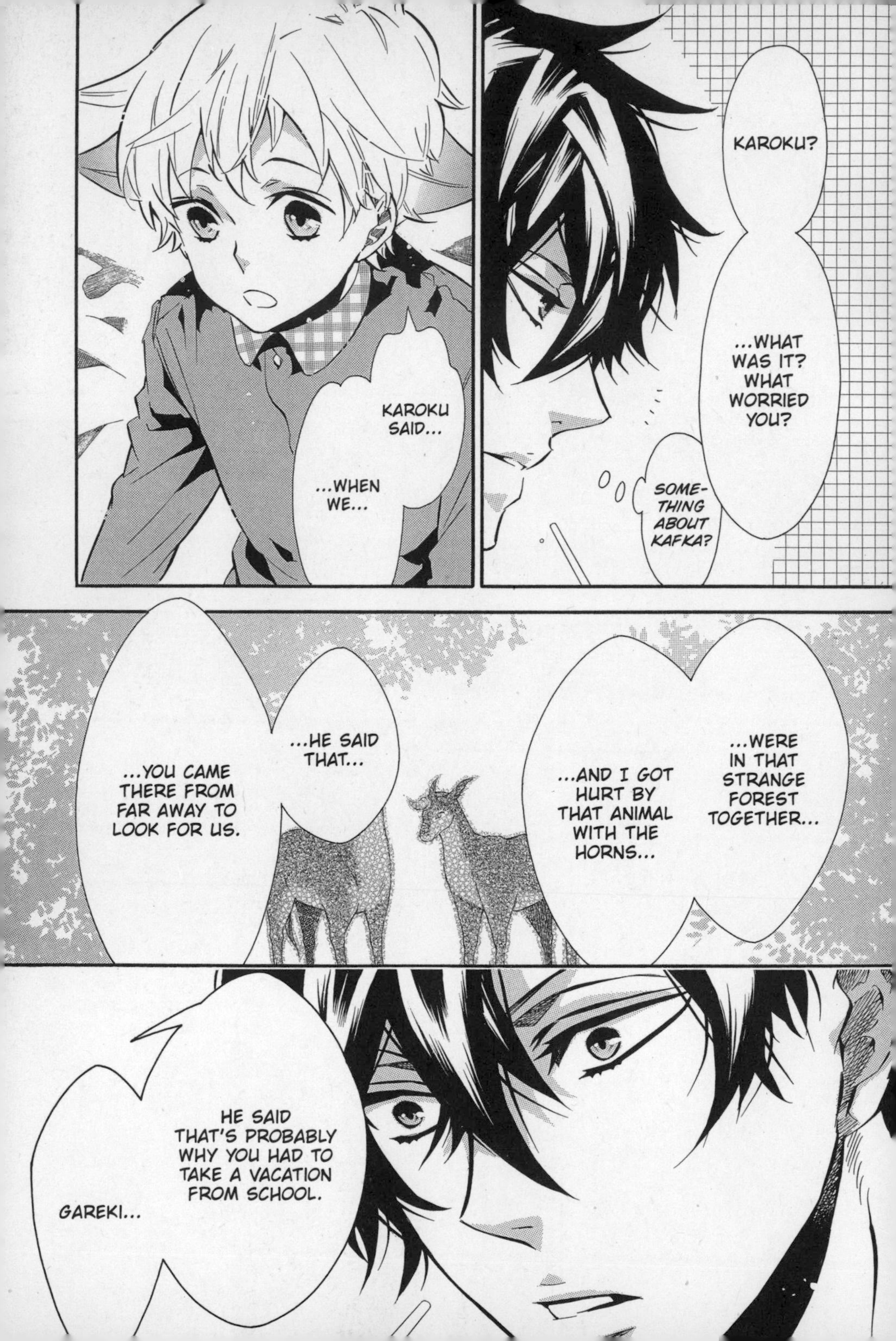
KAROKU?
...WHAT WAS IT? WHAT WORRIED YOU?
SOME-THING ABOUT KAFKA?
KAROKU SAID...
...WHEN WE...
...WERE IN THAT STRANGE FOREST TOGETHER...
...AND I GOT HURT BY THAT ANIMAL WITH THE HORNS...
...HE SAID THAT...
...YOU CAME THERE FROM FAR AWAY TO LOOK FOR US.
HE SAID THAT'S PROBABLY WHY YOU HAD TO TAKE A VACATION FROM SCHOOL.
GAREKI...

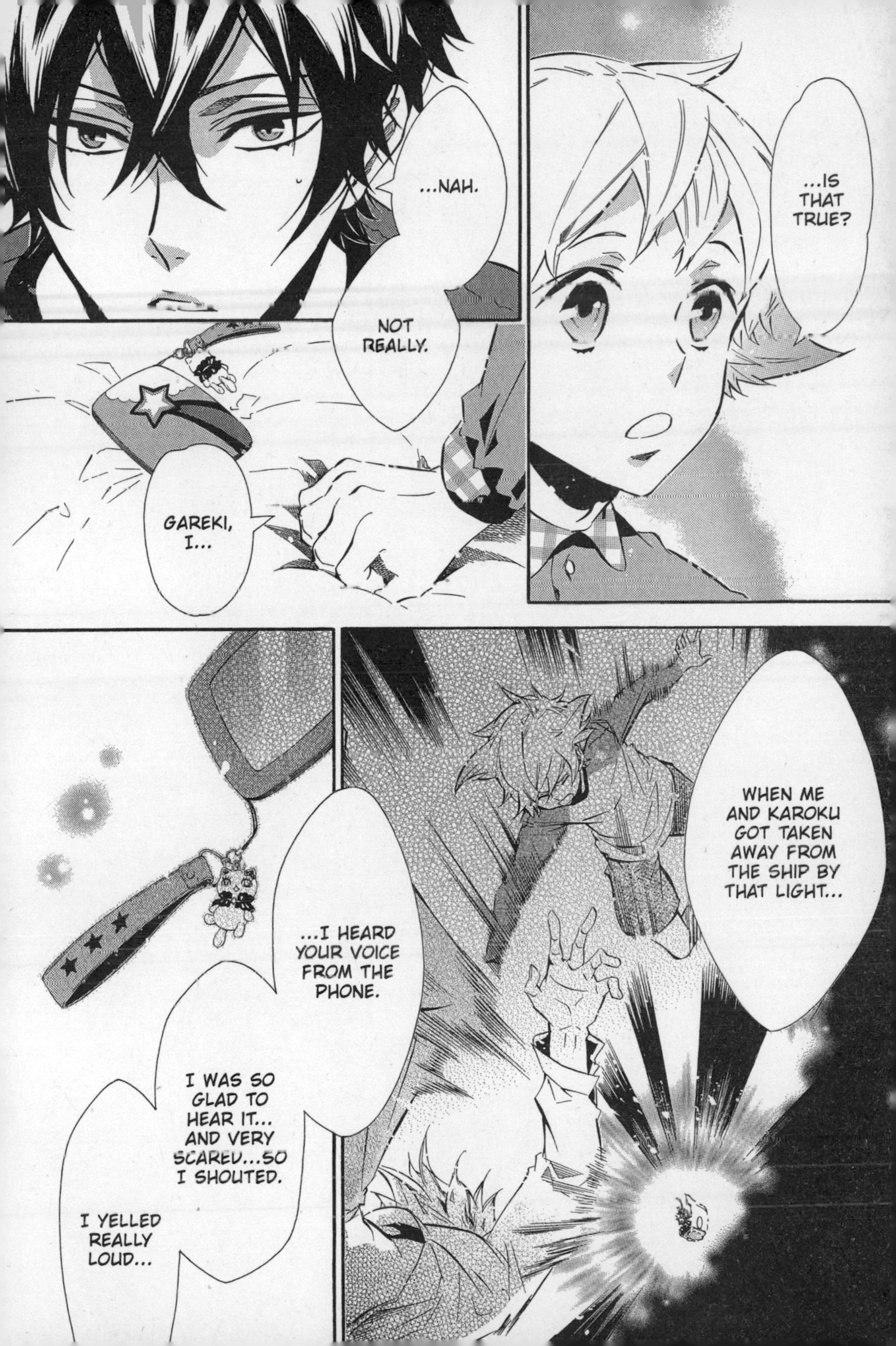
...IS THAT TRUE?
...NAH.
NOT REALLY.
GAREKI, I...
WHEN ME AND KAROKU GOT TAKEN AWAY FROM THE SHIP BY THAT LIGHT...
...I HEARD YOUR VOICE FROM THE PHONE.
I WAS SO GLAD TO HEAR IT... AND VERY SCARED...SO I SHOUTED.
I YELLED REALLY LOUD...

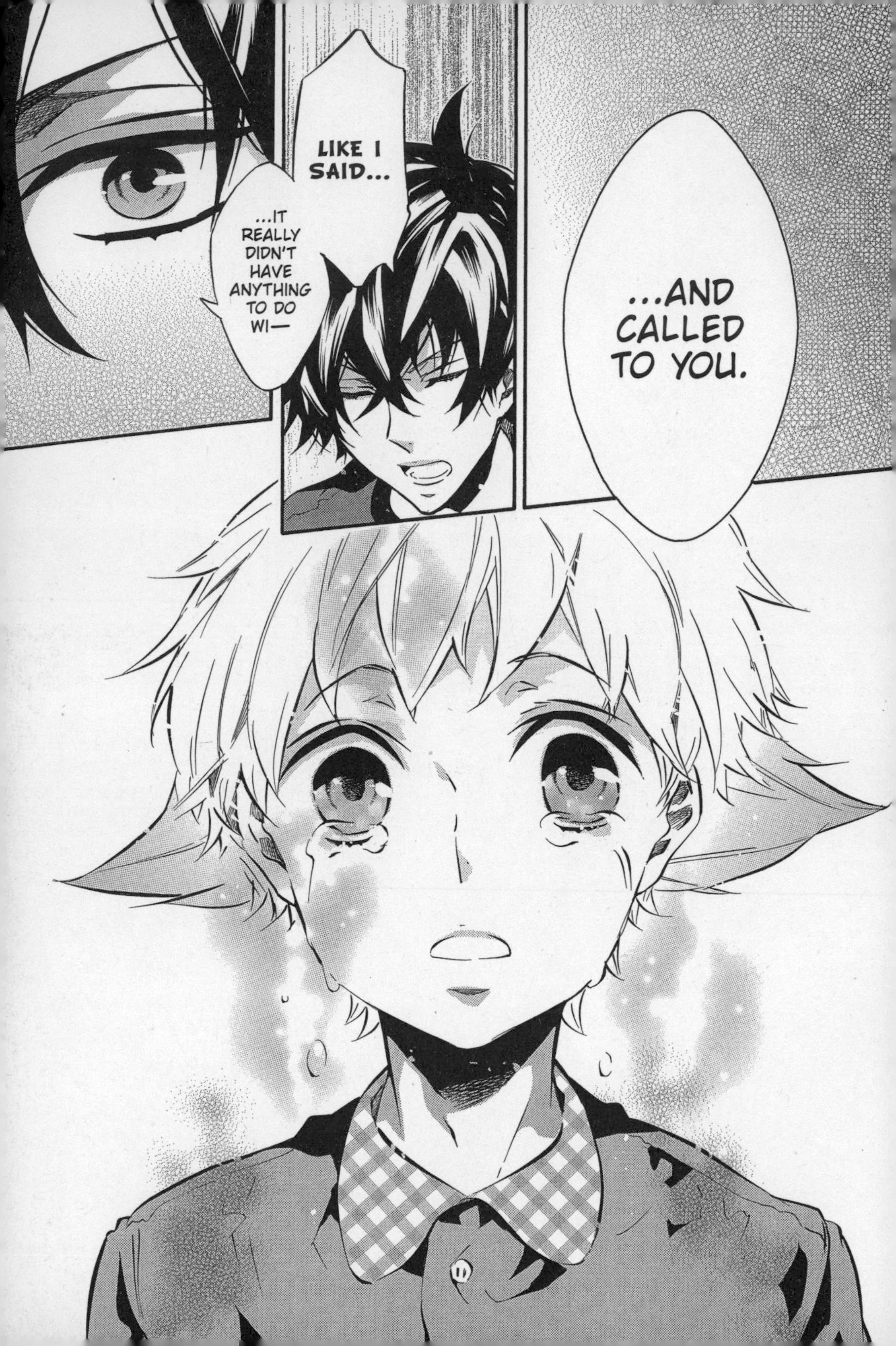
...AND CALLED TO YOU.
LIKE I SAID...
...IT REALLY DIDN'T HAVE ANYTHING TO DO WI—

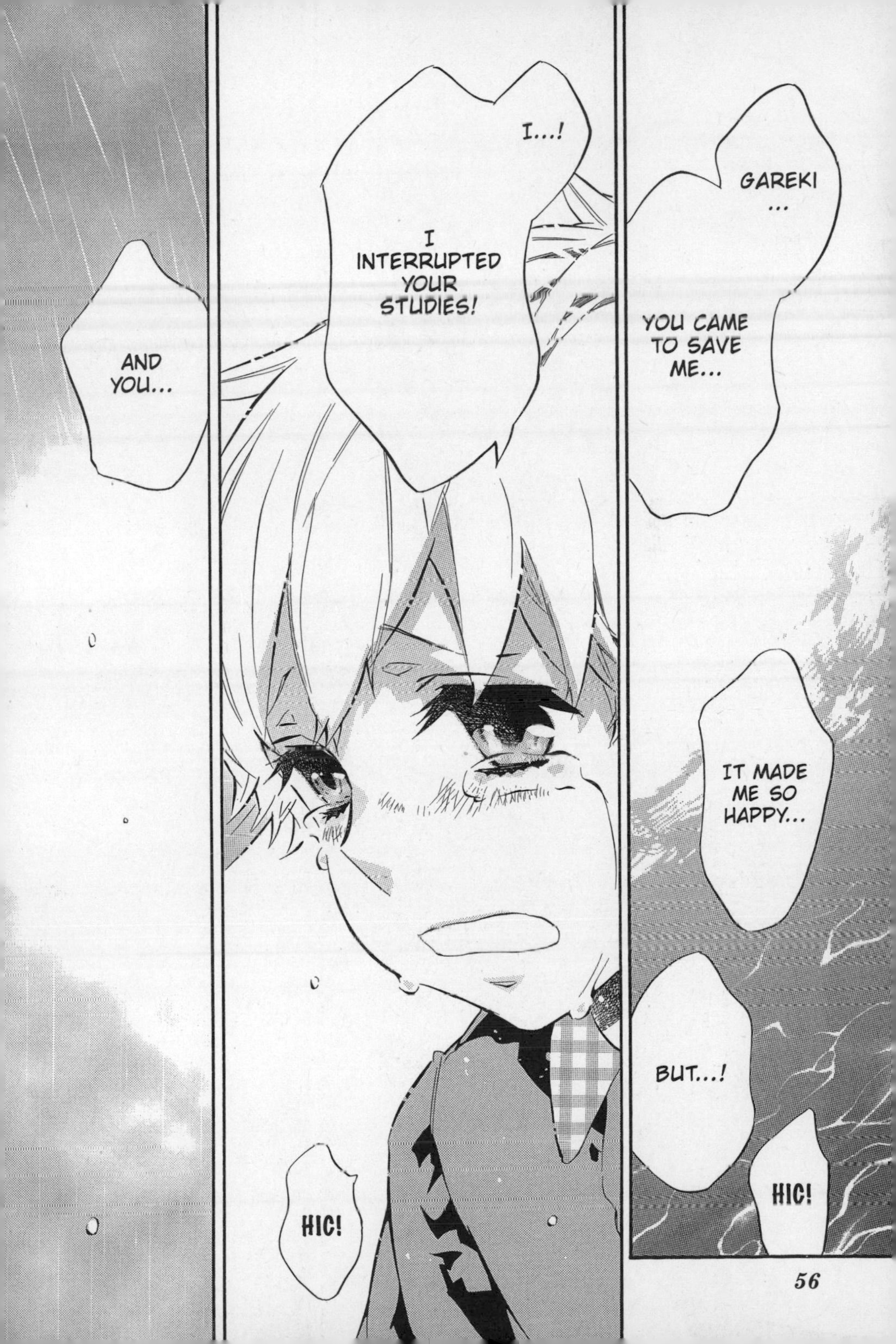
GAREKI ...
YOU CAME TO SAVE ME...
IT MADE ME SO HAPPY...
BUT...!
HIC!
I...!
I INTERRUPTED YOUR STUDIES!
HIC!
AND YOU...

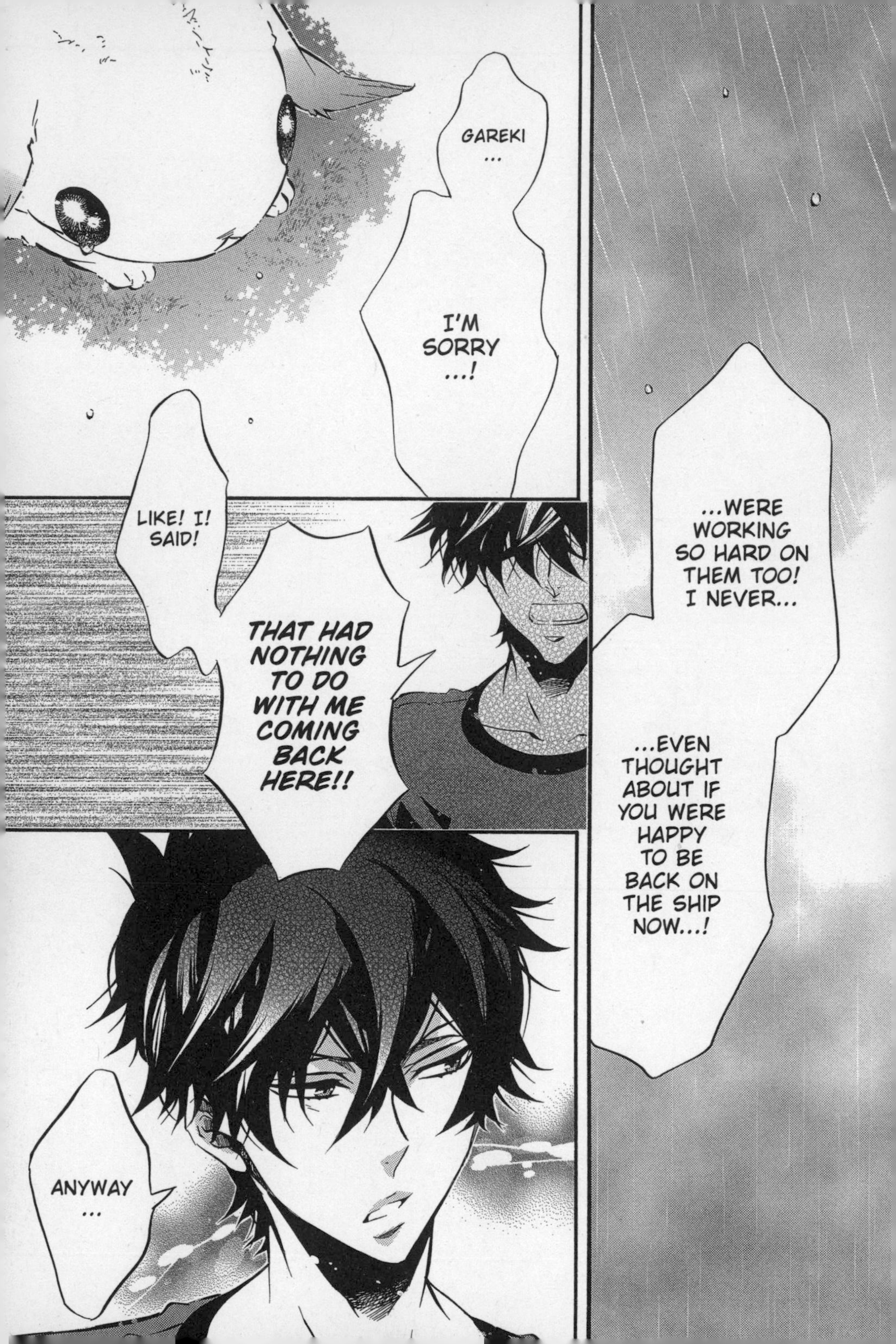
GAREKI...
I'M SORRY...!
...WERE WORKING SO HARD ON THEM TOO! I NEVER...
...EVEN THOUGHT ABOUT IF YOU WERE HAPPY TO BE BACK ON THE SHIP NOW...!
LIKE! I! SAID!
THAT HAD NOTHING TO DO WITH ME COMING BACK HERE!!
ANYWAY...

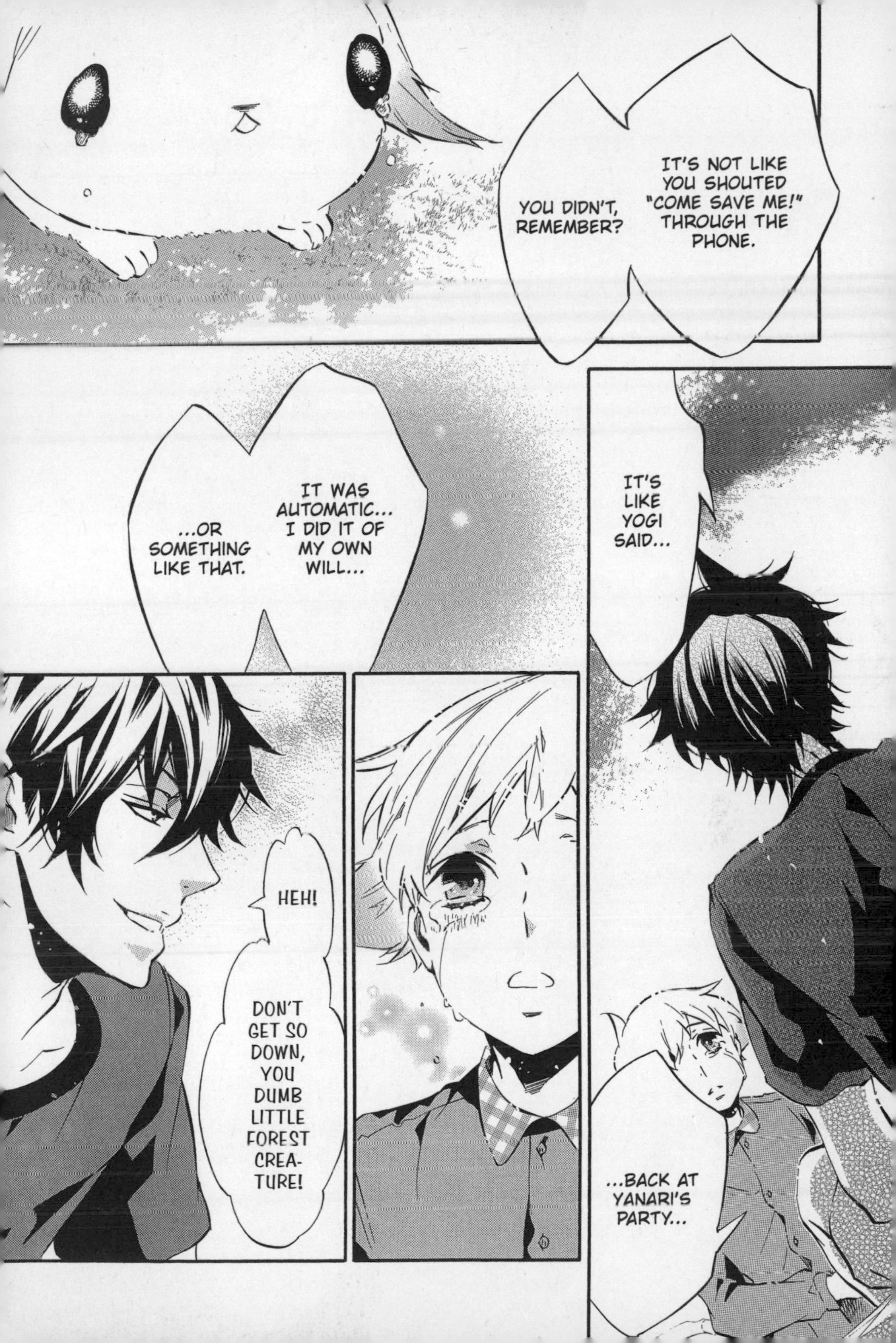
IT'S NOT LIKE YOU SHOUTED "COME SAVE ME!" THROUGH THE PHONE.
YOU DIDN'T, REMEMBER?
IT'S LIKE YOGI SAID...
...BACK AT YANARI'S PARTY...
IT WAS AUTOMATIC... I DID IT OF MY OWN WILL...
...OR SOMETHING LIKE THAT.
HEH!
DON'T GET SO DOWN, YOU DUMB LITTLE FOREST CREA-TURE!

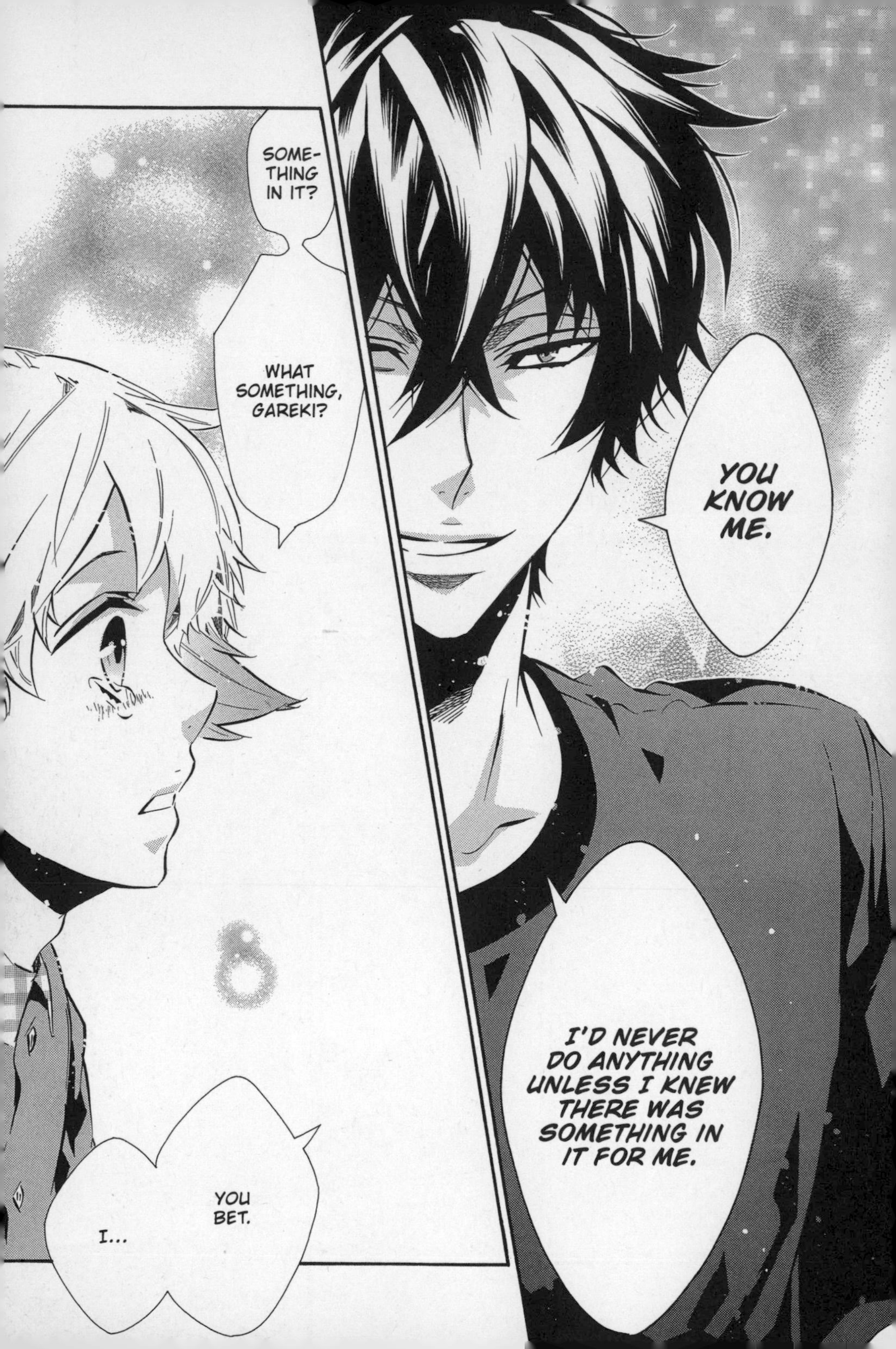
YOU KNOW ME.
I'D NEVER DO ANYTHING UNLESS I KNEW THERE WAS SOMETHING IN IT FOR ME.
SOME-THING IN IT?
WHAT SOMETHING, GAREKI?
YOU BET.
I...

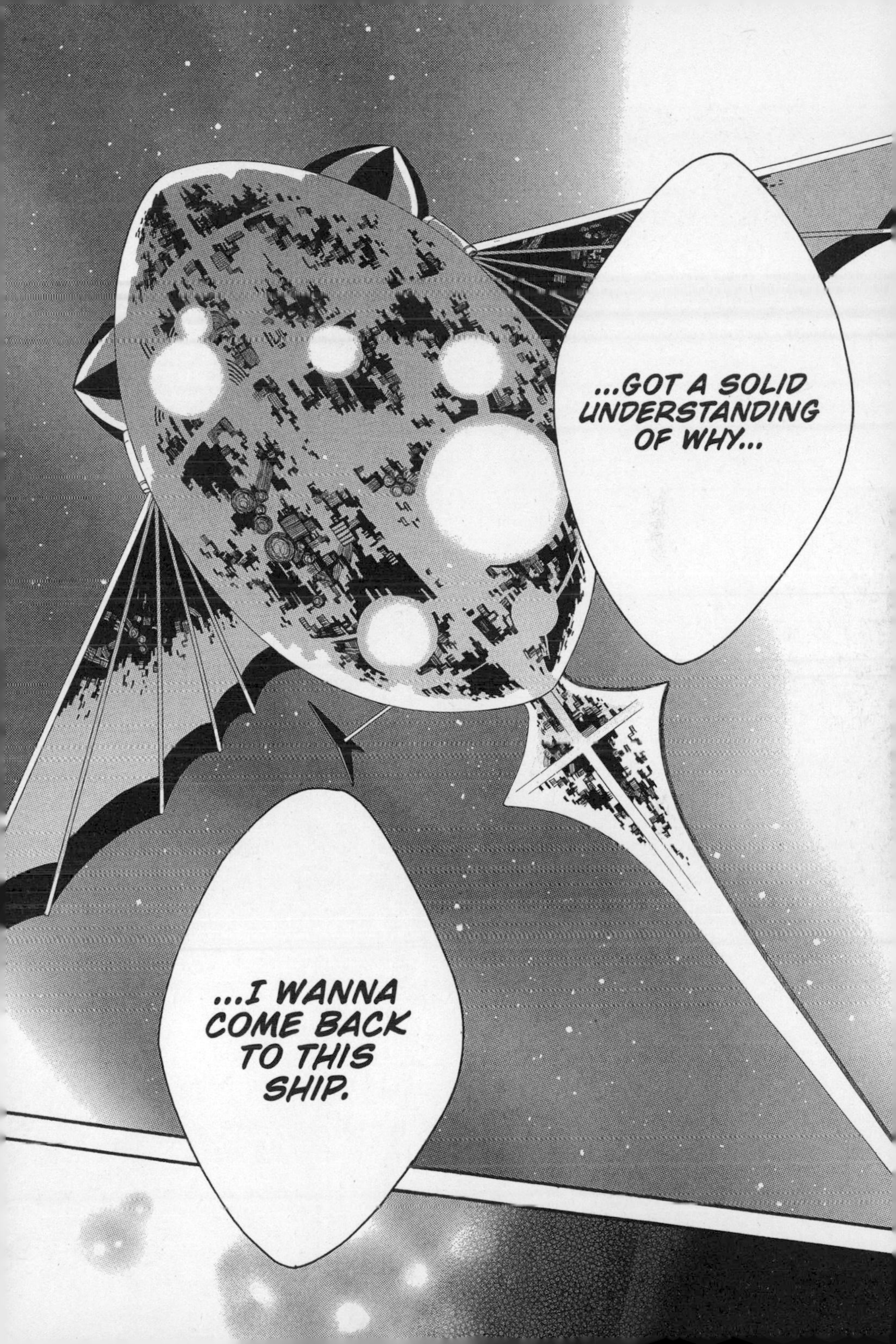
...GOT A SOLID UNDERSTANDING OF WHY...
...I WANNA COME BACK TO THIS SHIP.

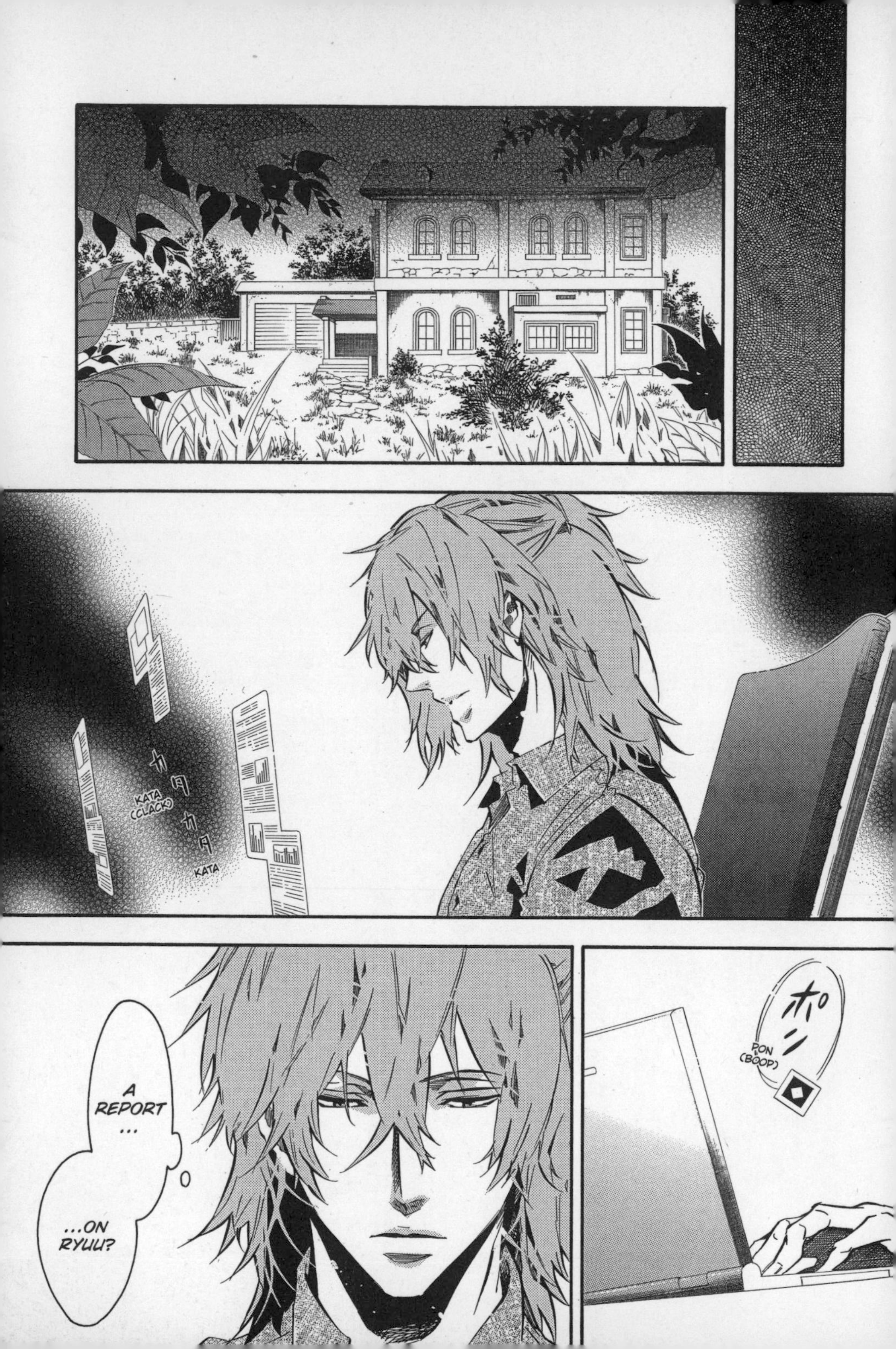
カタ
KATA (CLACK)
カタ
KATA
ポン
PON (BOOP)
A REPORT ...
...ON RYUU?

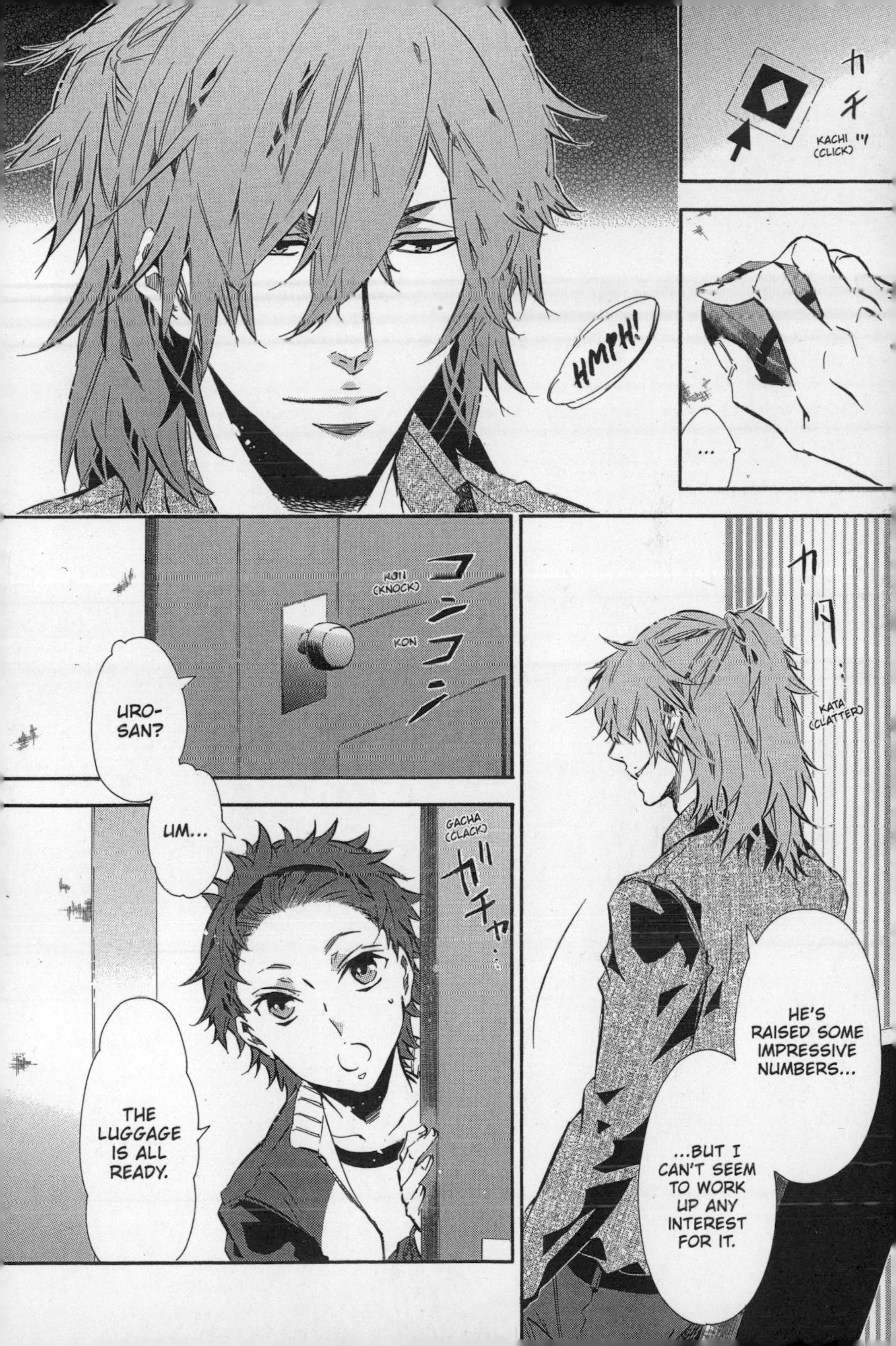
カチ
KACHI (CLICK)
...
HMPH!
カタ
KATA (CLATTER)
HE'S RAISED SOME IMPRESSIVE NUMBERS...
...BUT I CAN'T SEEM TO WORK UP ANY INTEREST FOR IT.
コンコン
KON (KNOCK)
KON
URO-SAN?
UM...
ガチャ...
GACHA (CLACK)
THE LUGGAGE IS ALL READY.

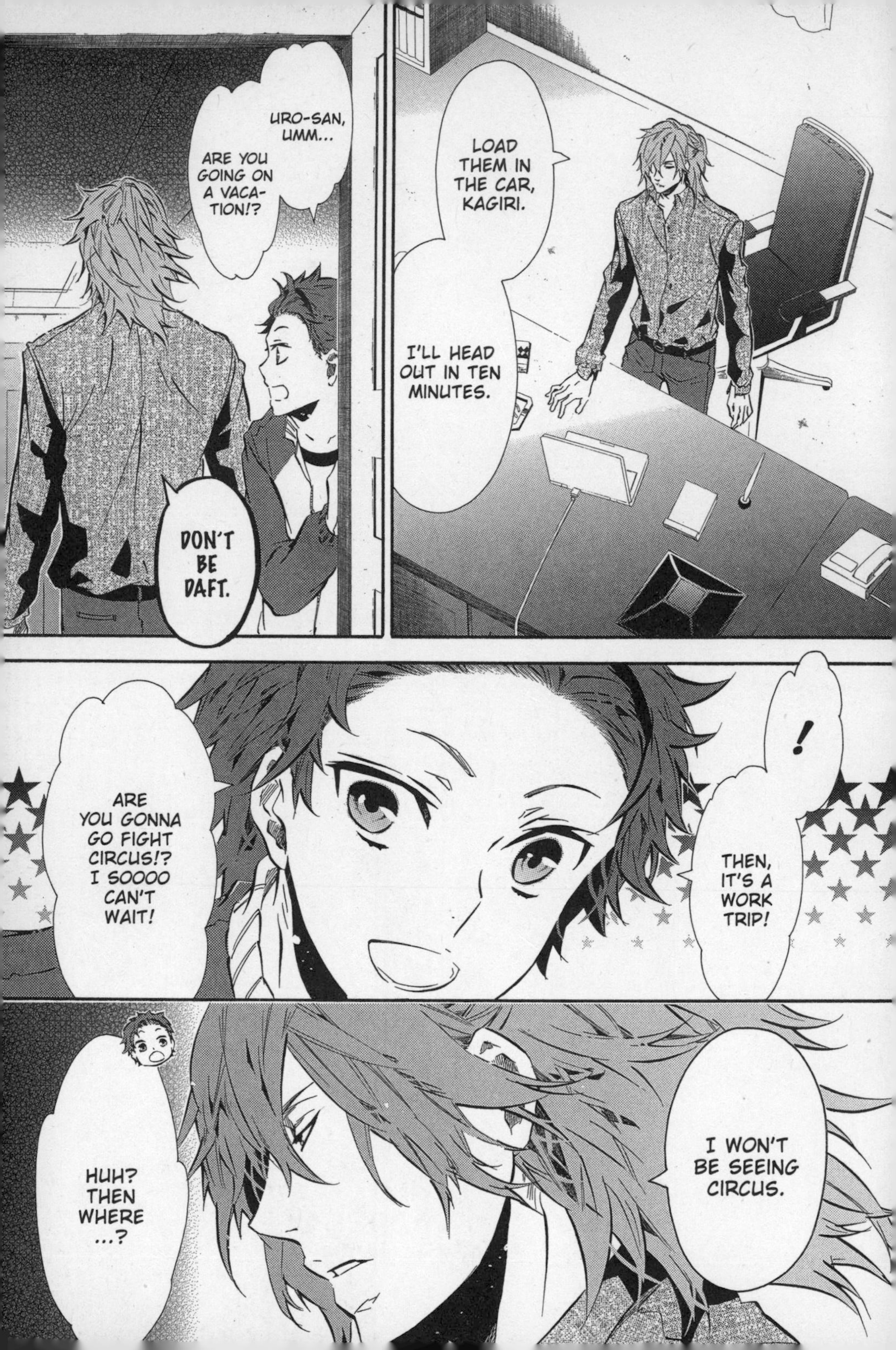
LOAD THEM IN THE CAR, KAGIRI.
I'LL HEAD OUT IN TEN MINUTES.
URO-SAN, UMM...
ARE YOU GOING ON A VACA-TION!?
DON'T BE DAFT.
!
THEN, IT'S A WORK TRIP!
ARE YOU GONNA GO FIGHT CIRCUS!? I SOOOO CAN'T WAIT!
I WON'T BE SEEING CIRCUS.
HUH? THEN WHERE ...?

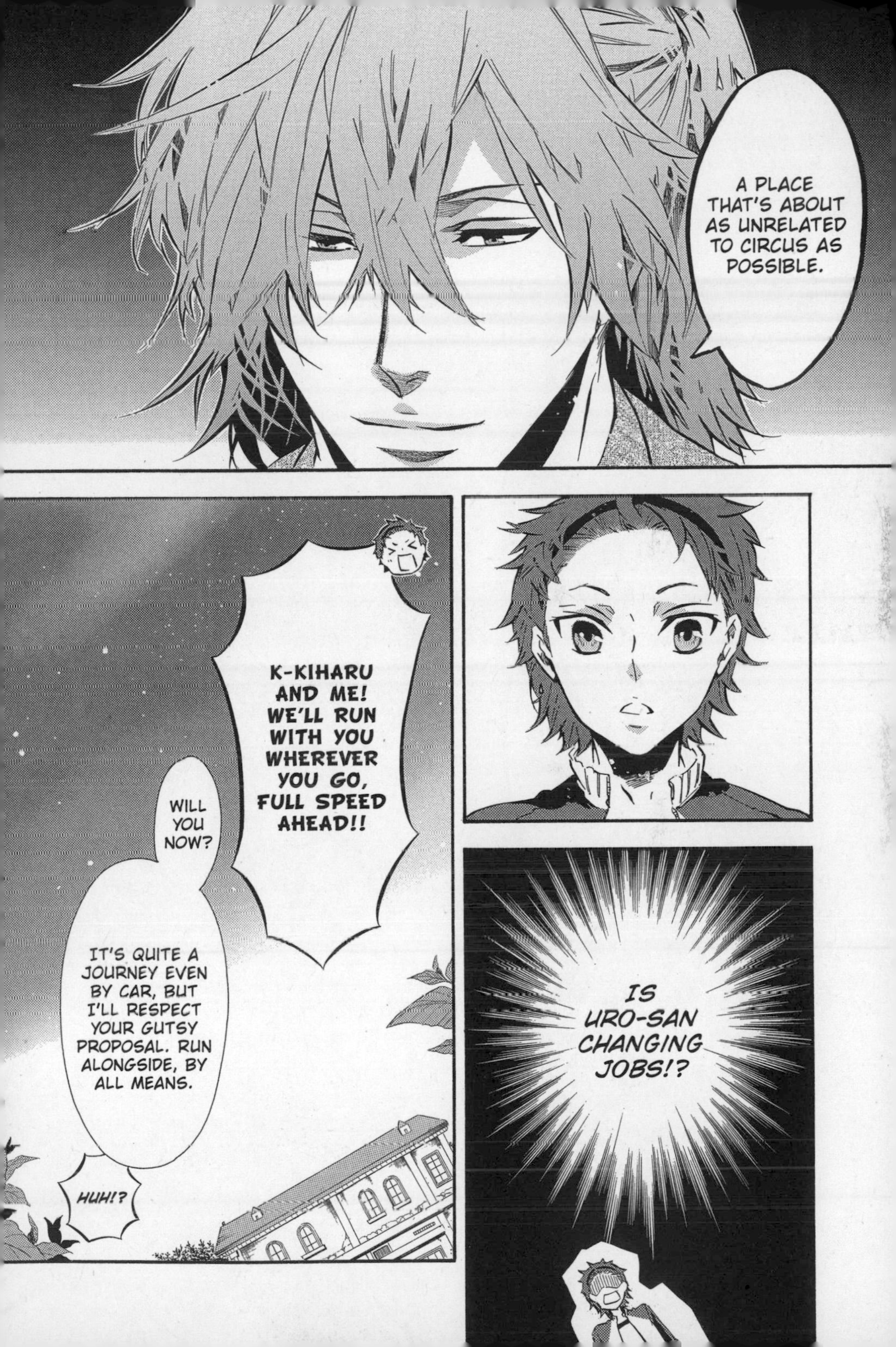
A PLACE THAT'S ABOUT AS UNRELATED TO CIRCUS AS POSSIBLE.
IS URO-SAN CHANGING JOBS!?
K-KIHARU AND ME! WE'LL RUN WITH YOU WHEREVER YOU GO, FULL SPEED AHEAD!!
WILL YOU NOW?
IT'S QUITE A JOURNEY EVEN BY CAR, BUT I'LL RESPECT YOUR GUTSY PROPOSAL. RUN ALONGSIDE, BY ALL MEANS.
HUH!?

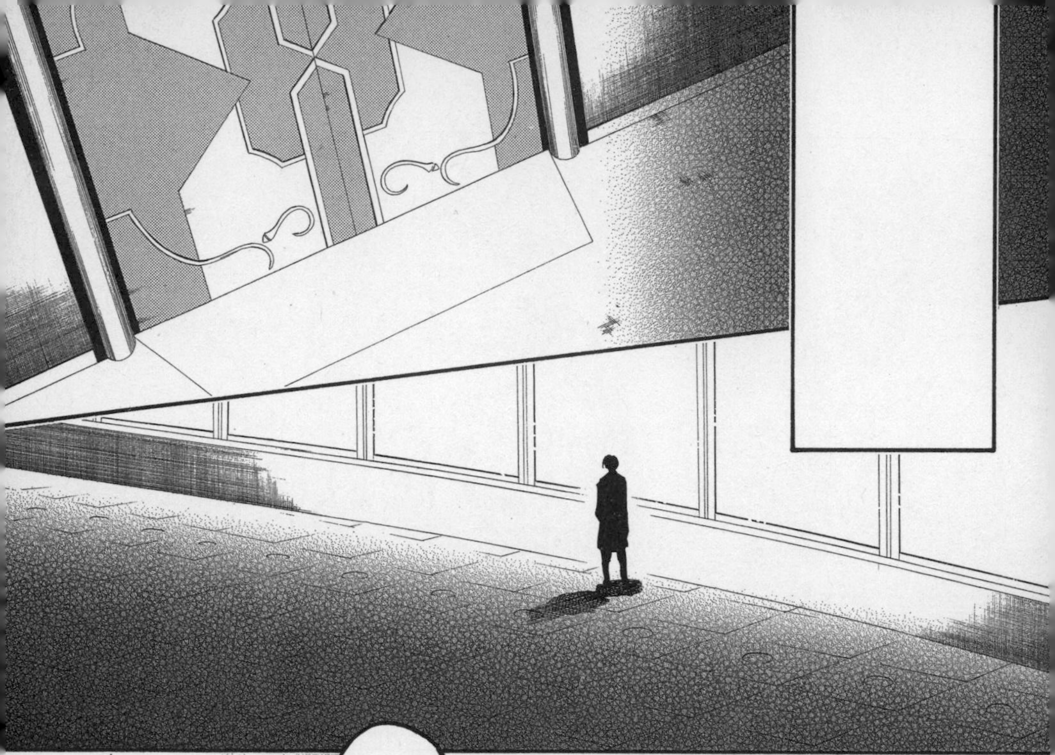

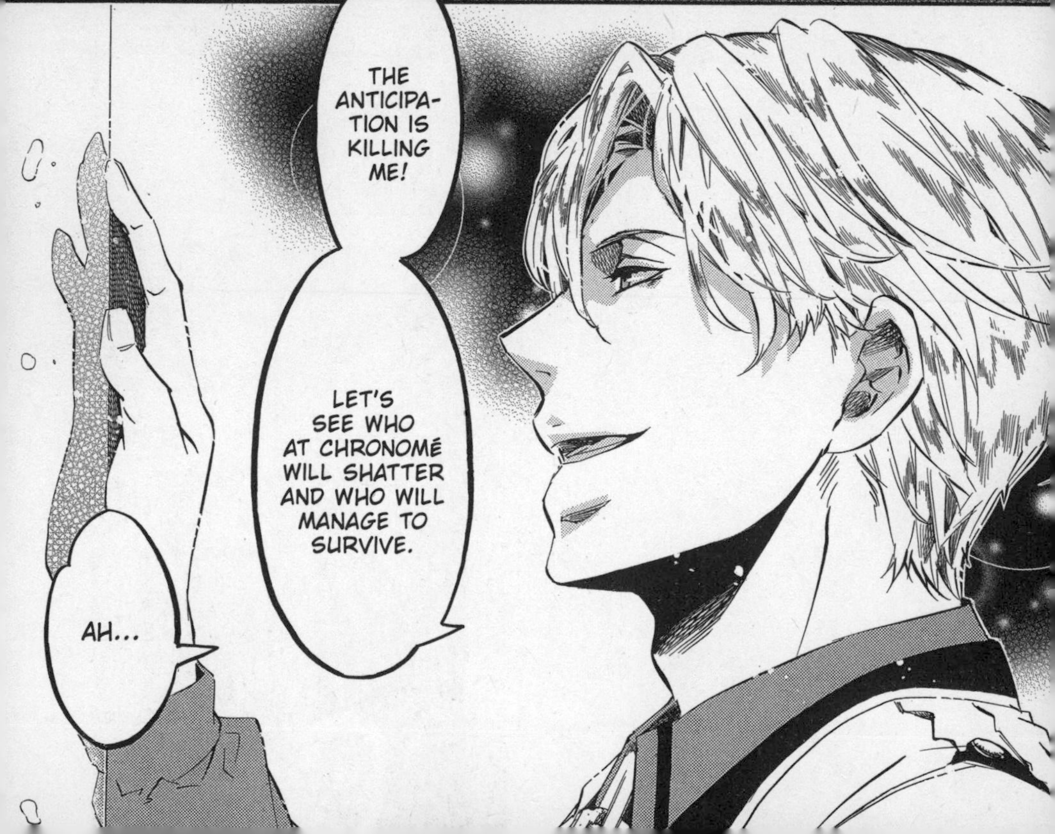
THE ANTICIPATION IS KILLING ME!
LET'S SEE WHO AT CHRONOMÉ WILL SHATTER AND WHO WILL MANAGE TO SURVIVE.
AH...

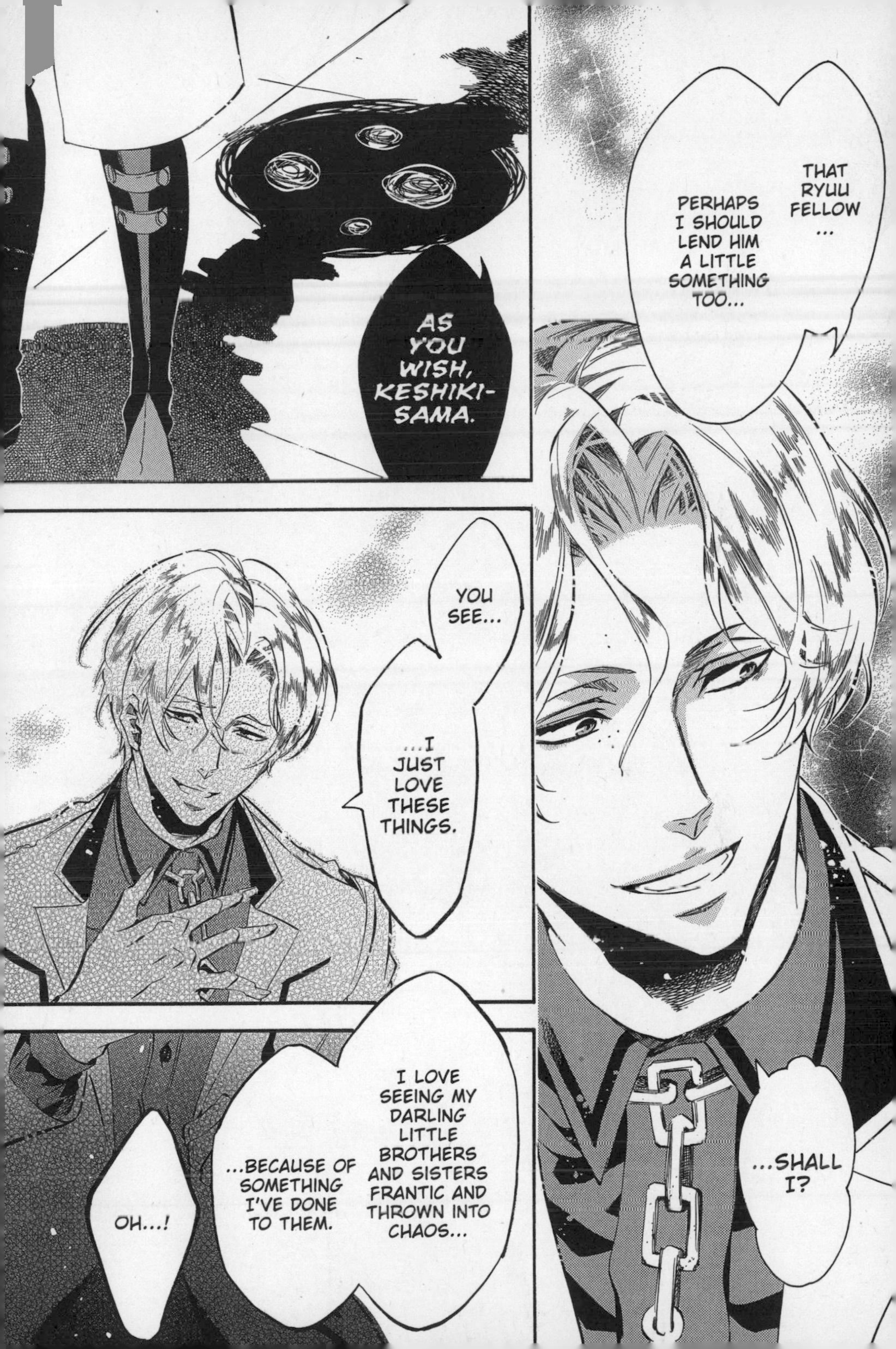
THAT RYUU FELLOW...
PERHAPS I SHOULD LEND HIM A LITTLE SOMETHING TOO...
...SHALL I?
AS YOU WISH, KESHIKI-SAMA.
YOU SEE...
...I JUST LOVE THESE THINGS.
I LOVE SEEING MY DARLING LITTLE BROTHERS AND SISTERS FRANTIC AND THROWN INTO CHAOS...
...BECAUSE OF SOMETHING I'VE DONE TO THEM.
OH...!

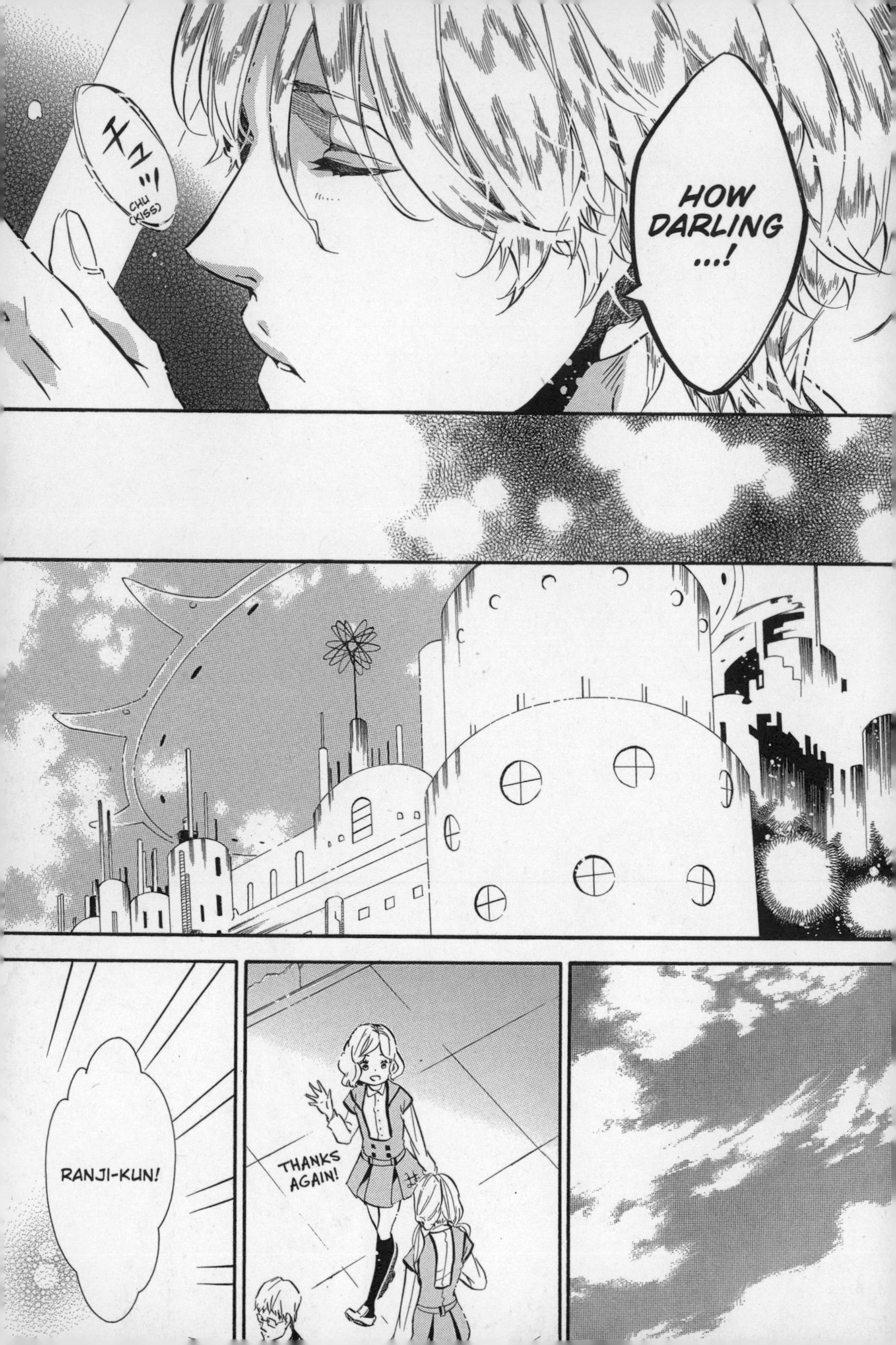
HOW DARLING ...!
チュッ
CHU (KISS)
THANKS AGAIN!
RANJI-KUN!

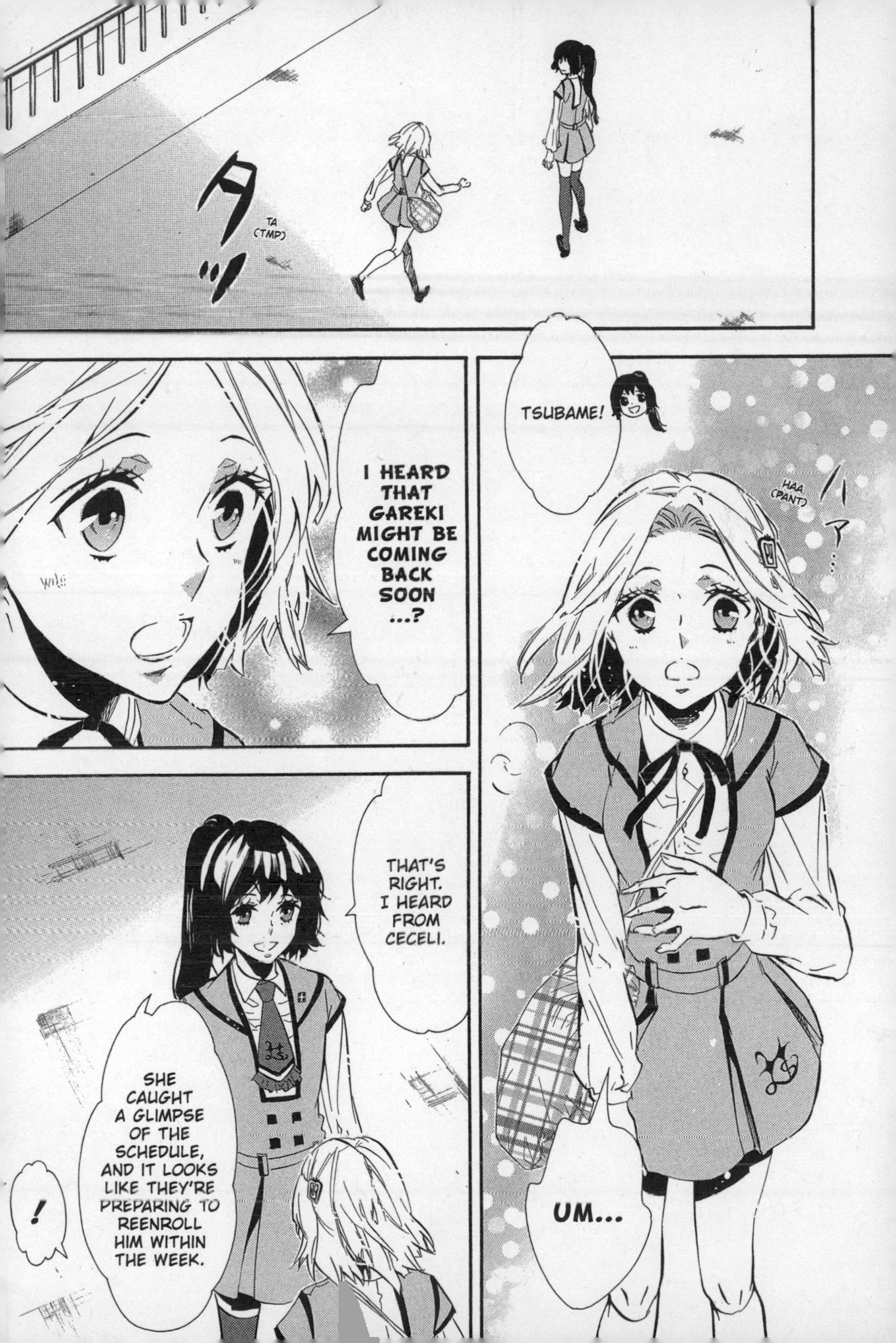
タッ
TA (TMP)
TSUBAME!
ハァ…
HAA (PANT)
UM...
I HEARD THAT GAREKI MIGHT BE COMING BACK SOON ...?
THAT'S RIGHT. I HEARD FROM CECELI.
SHE CAUGHT A GLIMPSE OF THE SCHEDULE, AND IT LOOKS LIKE THEY'RE PREPARING TO REENROLL HIM WITHIN THE WEEK.
!

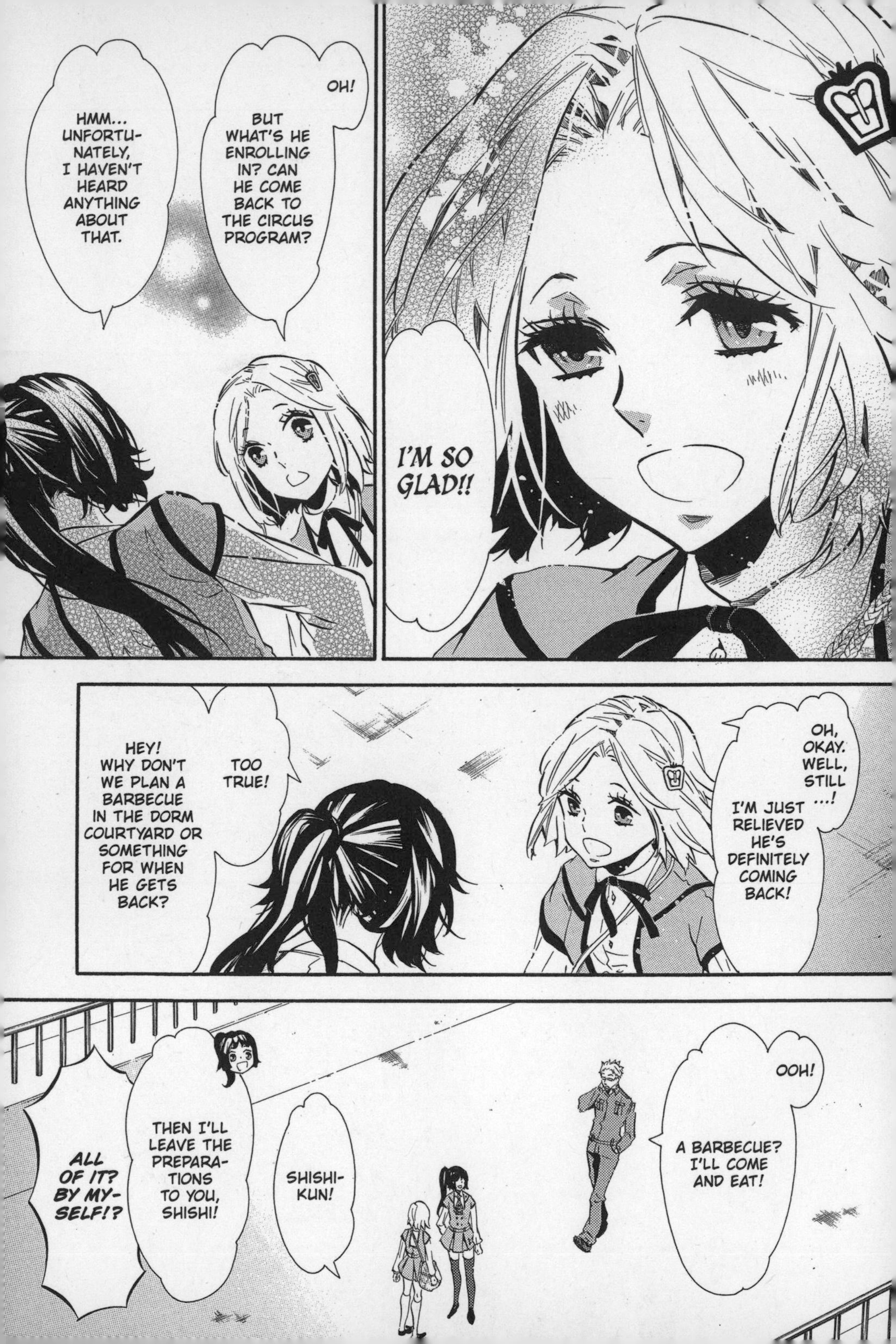
I'M SO GLAD!!
OH!
BUT WHAT'S HE ENROLLING IN? CAN HE COME BACK TO THE CIRCUS PROGRAM?
HMM... UNFORTUNATELY, I HAVEN'T HEARD ANYTHING ABOUT THAT.
OH, OKAY. WELL, STILL...!
I'M JUST RELIEVED HE'S DEFINITELY COMING BACK!
TOO TRUE!
HEY! WHY DON'T WE PLAN A BARBECUE IN THE DORM COURTYARD OR SOMETHING FOR WHEN HE GETS BACK?
OOH!
A BARBECUE? I'LL COME AND EAT!
SHISHI-KUN!
THEN I'LL LEAVE THE PREPARATIONS TO YOU, SHISHI!
ALL OF IT? BY MYSELF!?

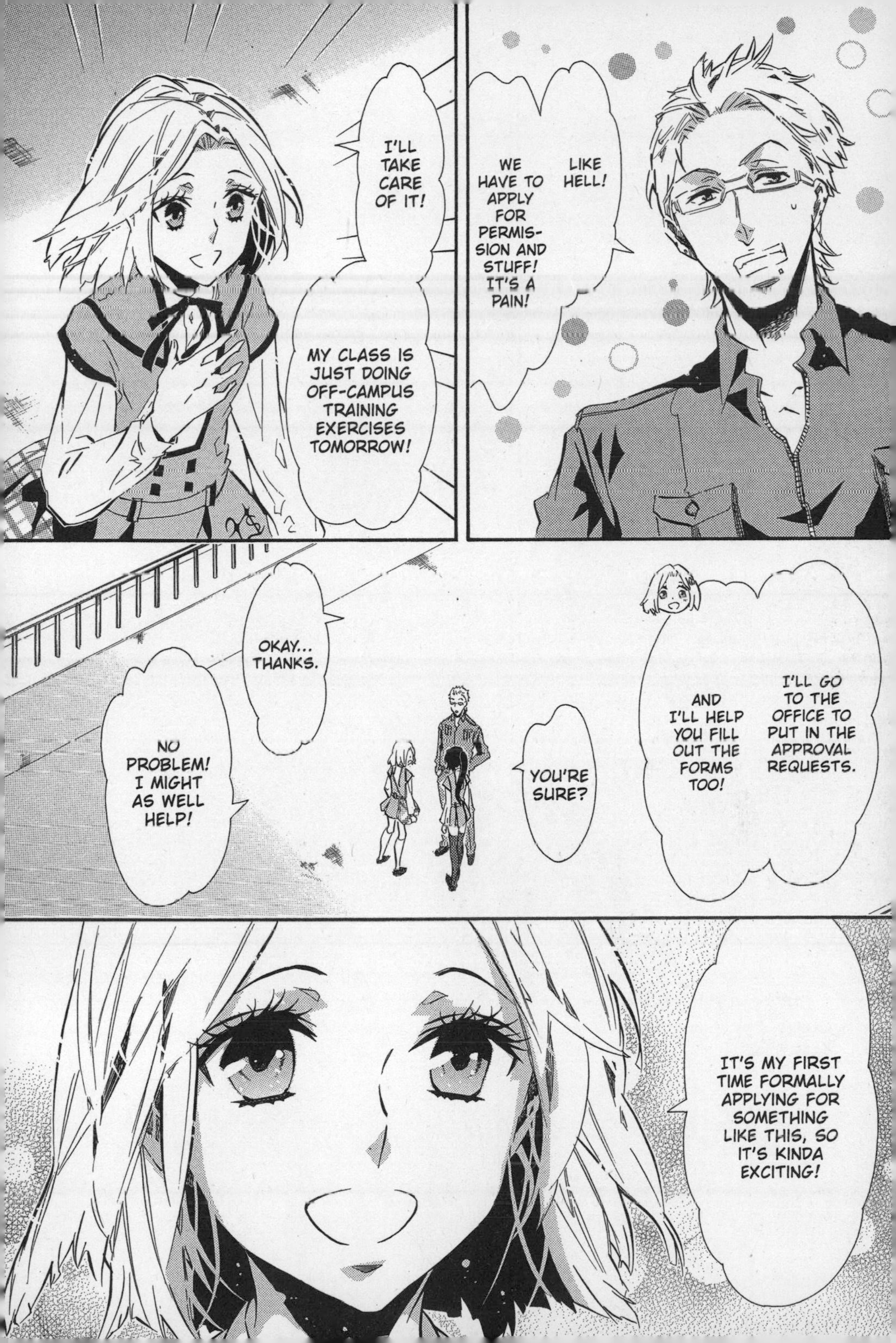
LIKE HELL!
WE HAVE TO APPLY FOR PERMISSION AND STUFF! IT'S A PAIN!
I'LL TAKE CARE OF IT!
MY CLASS IS JUST DOING OFF-CAMPUS TRAINING EXERCISES TOMORROW!
I'LL GO TO THE OFFICE TO PUT IN THE APPROVAL REQUESTS.
AND I'LL HELP YOU FILL OUT THE FORMS TOO!
YOU'RE SURE?
OKAY... THANKS.
NO PROBLEM! I MIGHT AS WELL HELP!
IT'S MY FIRST TIME FORMALLY APPLYING FOR SOMETHING LIKE THIS, SO IT'S KINDA EXCITING!

HEY!

YOUR HEART IS SO SPLENDIDLY PURE! SO UTTERLY THE OPPOSITE OF SHISHI'S!

HUH!? THAT STUFF AGAIN...?

OH, BUT I APOLOGIZE IN ADVANCE IF I SCREW SOMETHING UP...

...ON THE FORMS...

NO WORRIES!

WE'LL BE JOINTLY RESPONSIBLE... ACTUALLY...

...SHISHI WILL BE JOINTLY RESPONSIBLE, SO...

RANJI, YOU JERK!!

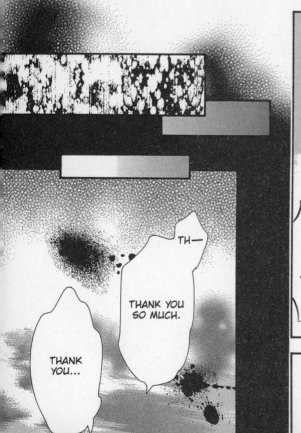

TH—

THANK YOU SO MUCH.

THANK YOU...

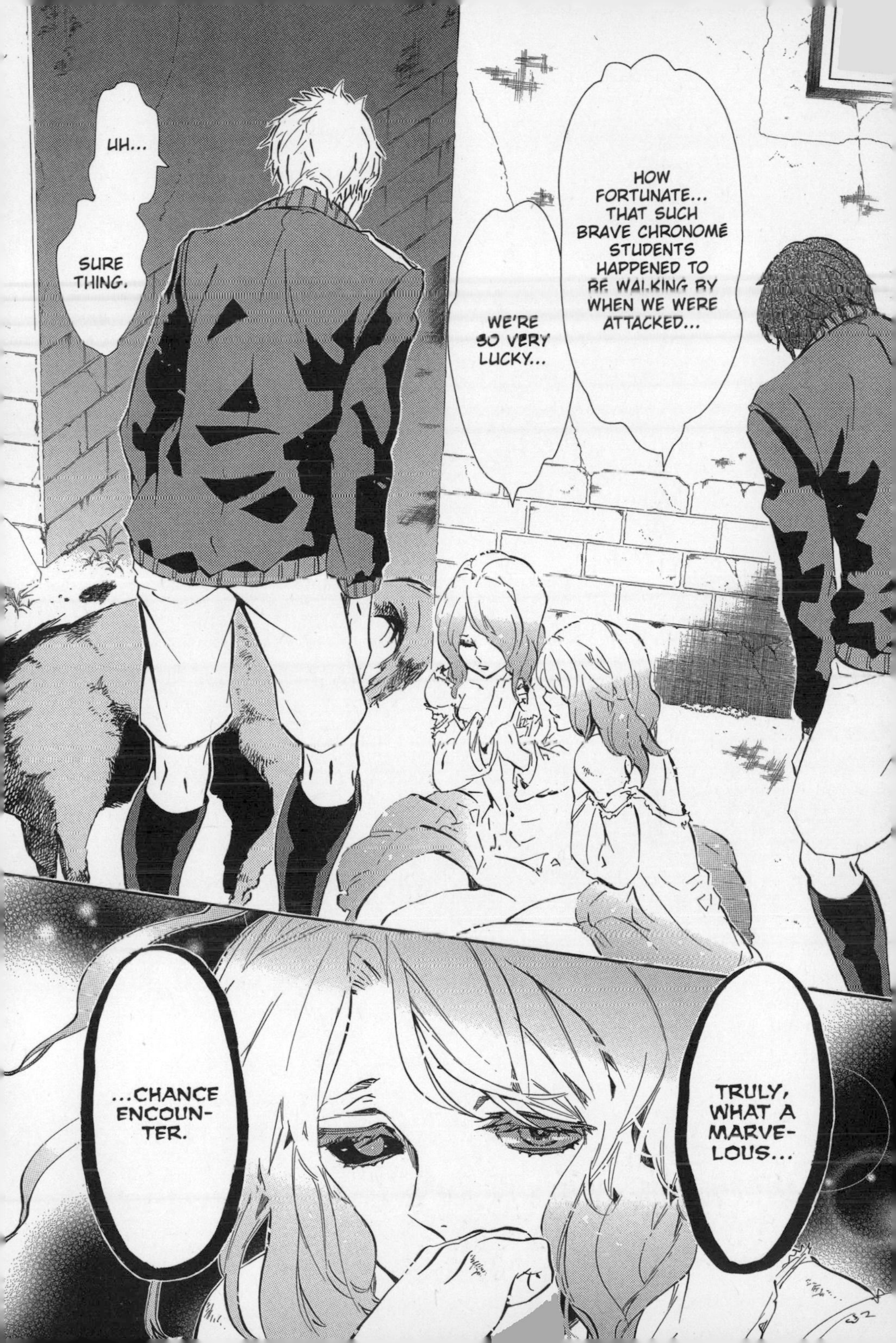
HOW FORTUNATE... THAT SUCH BRAVE CHRONOME STUDENTS HAPPENED TO BE WALKING BY WHEN WE WERE ATTACKED...
WE'RE SO VERY LUCKY...
UH...
SURE THING.
TRULY, WHAT A MARVE-LOUS...
...CHANCE ENCOUN-TER.

KARNEVAL

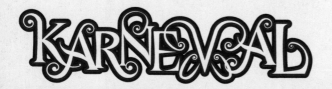

KARNEVAL

Score 75:
The Pinpoint of Infiltration

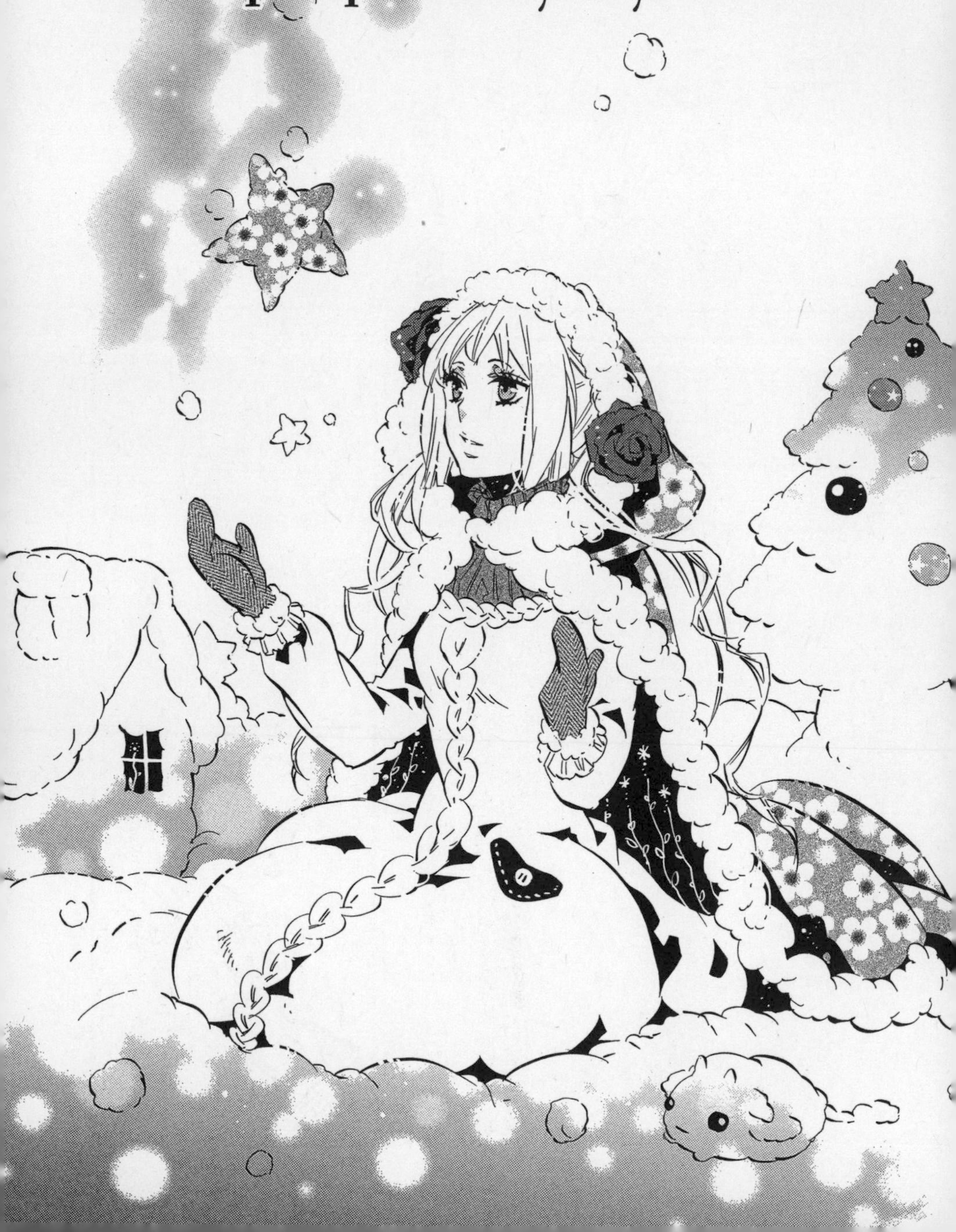

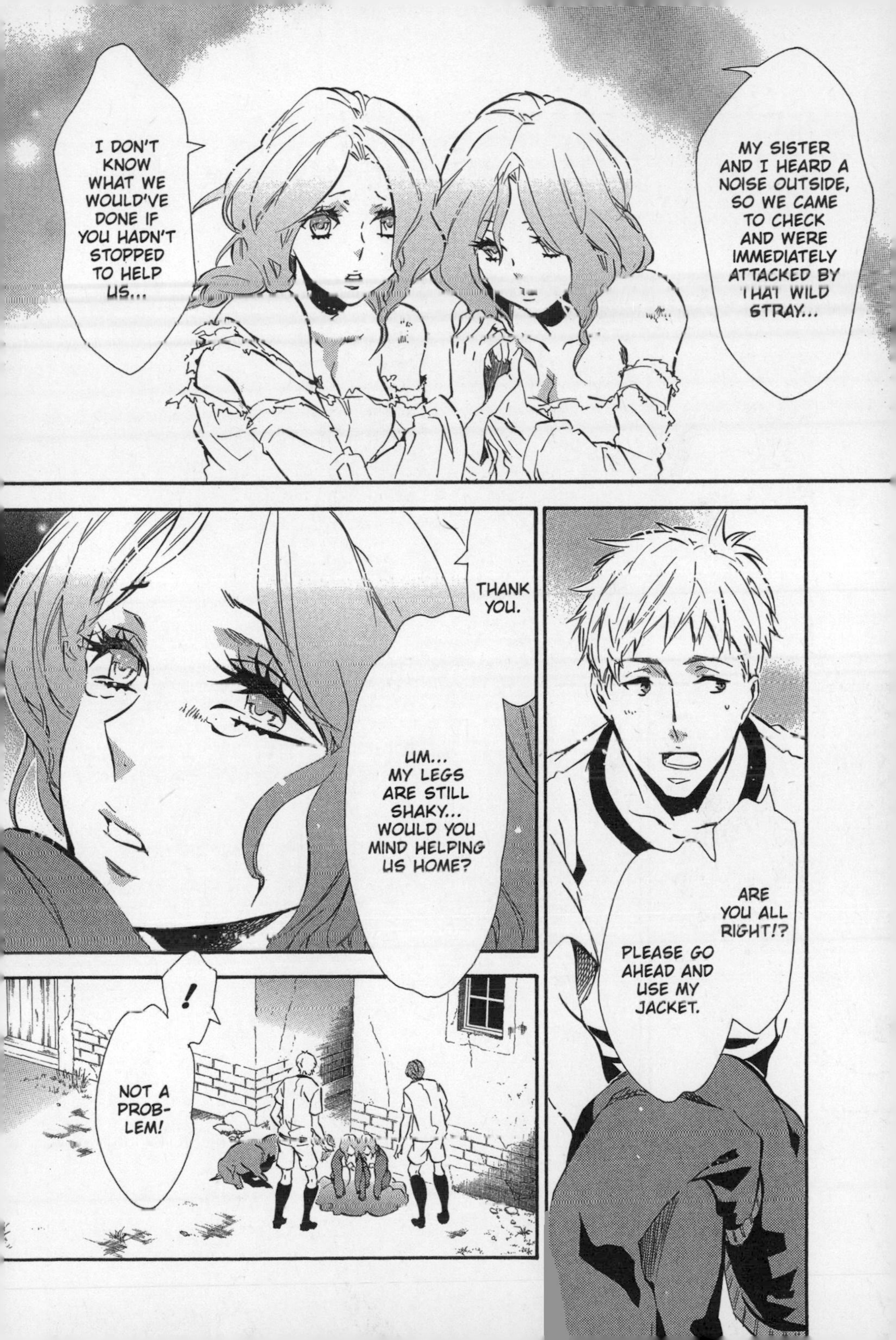
MY SISTER AND I HEARD A NOISE OUTSIDE, SO WE CAME TO CHECK AND WERE IMMEDIATELY ATTACKED BY THAT WILD STRAY...
I DON'T KNOW WHAT WE WOULD'VE DONE IF YOU HADN'T STOPPED TO HELP US...
ARE YOU ALL RIGHT!?
PLEASE GO AHEAD AND USE MY JACKET.
THANK YOU.
UM... MY LEGS ARE STILL SHAKY... WOULD YOU MIND HELPING US HOME?
!
NOT A PROB-LEM!

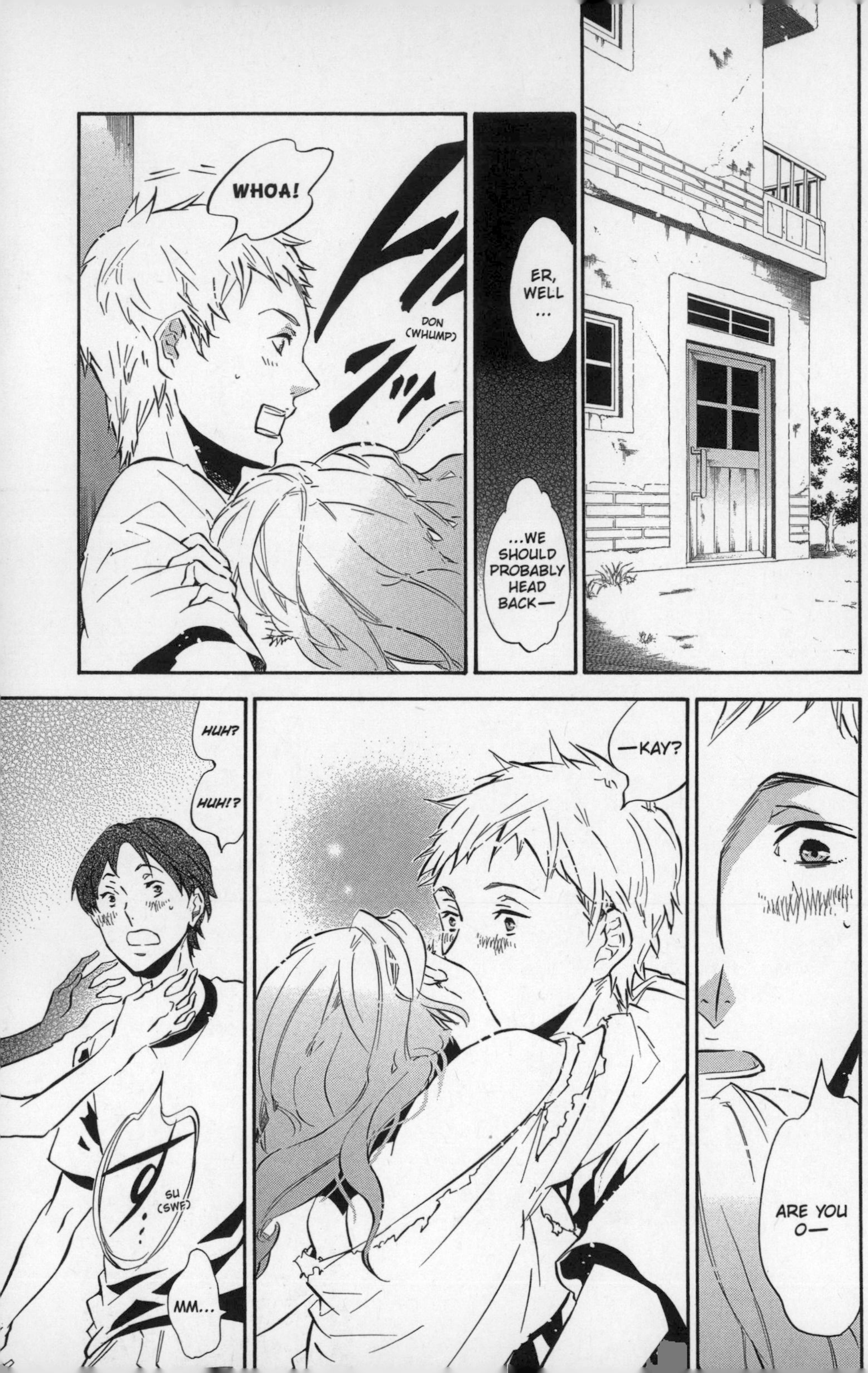
ER, WELL ...
...WE SHOULD PROBABLY HEAD BACK—
WHOA!
DON (WHUMP)
ARE YOU O—
—KAY?
HUH?
HUH!?
SU (SWF)
MM...

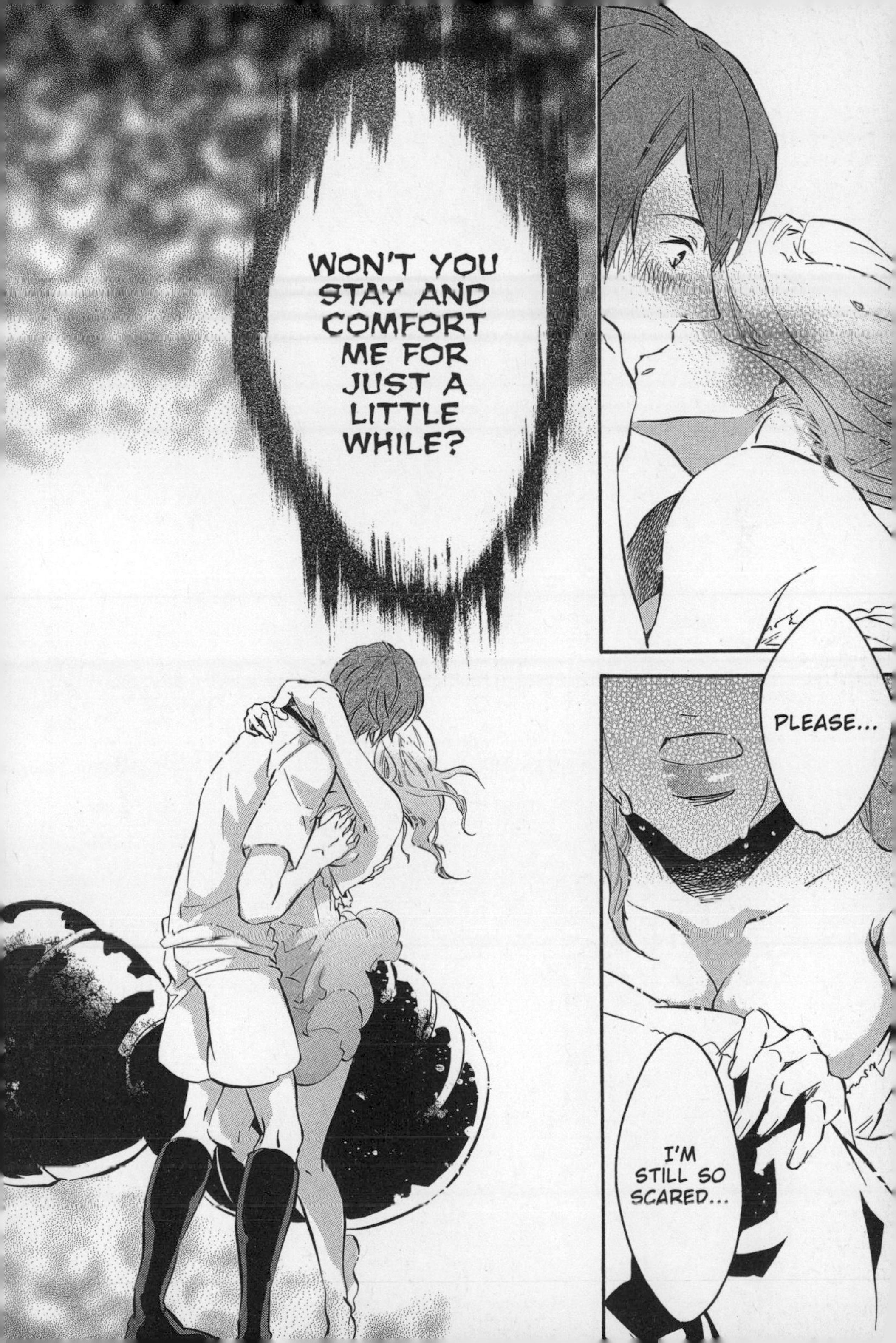
PLEASE...
I'M STILL SO SCARED...
WON'T YOU STAY AND COMFORT ME FOR JUST A LITTLE WHILE?

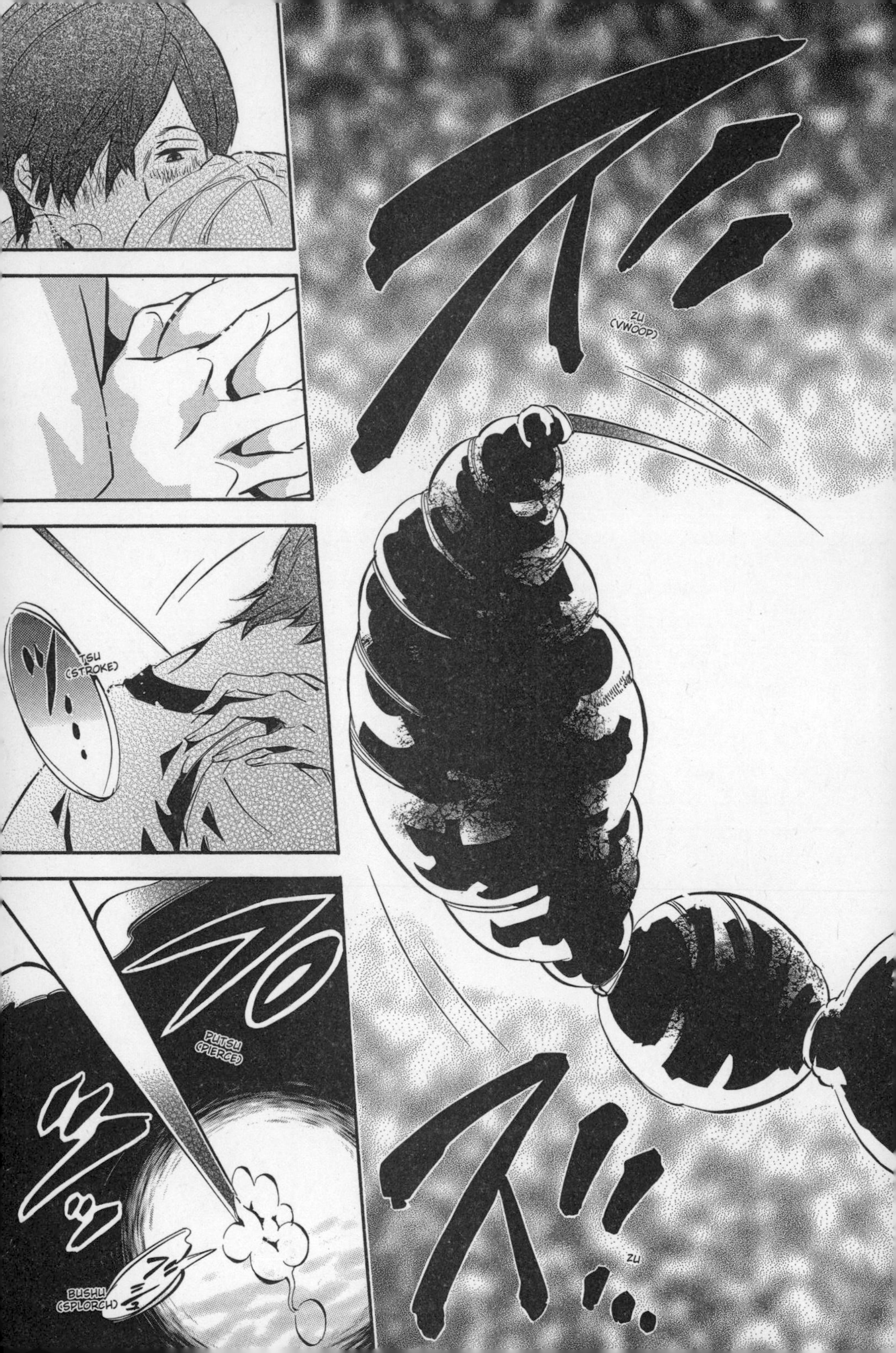
ZU
(VWOOP)
ZU
TSU
(STROKE)
PUTSU
(PIERCE)
BUSHU
(SPLORCH)

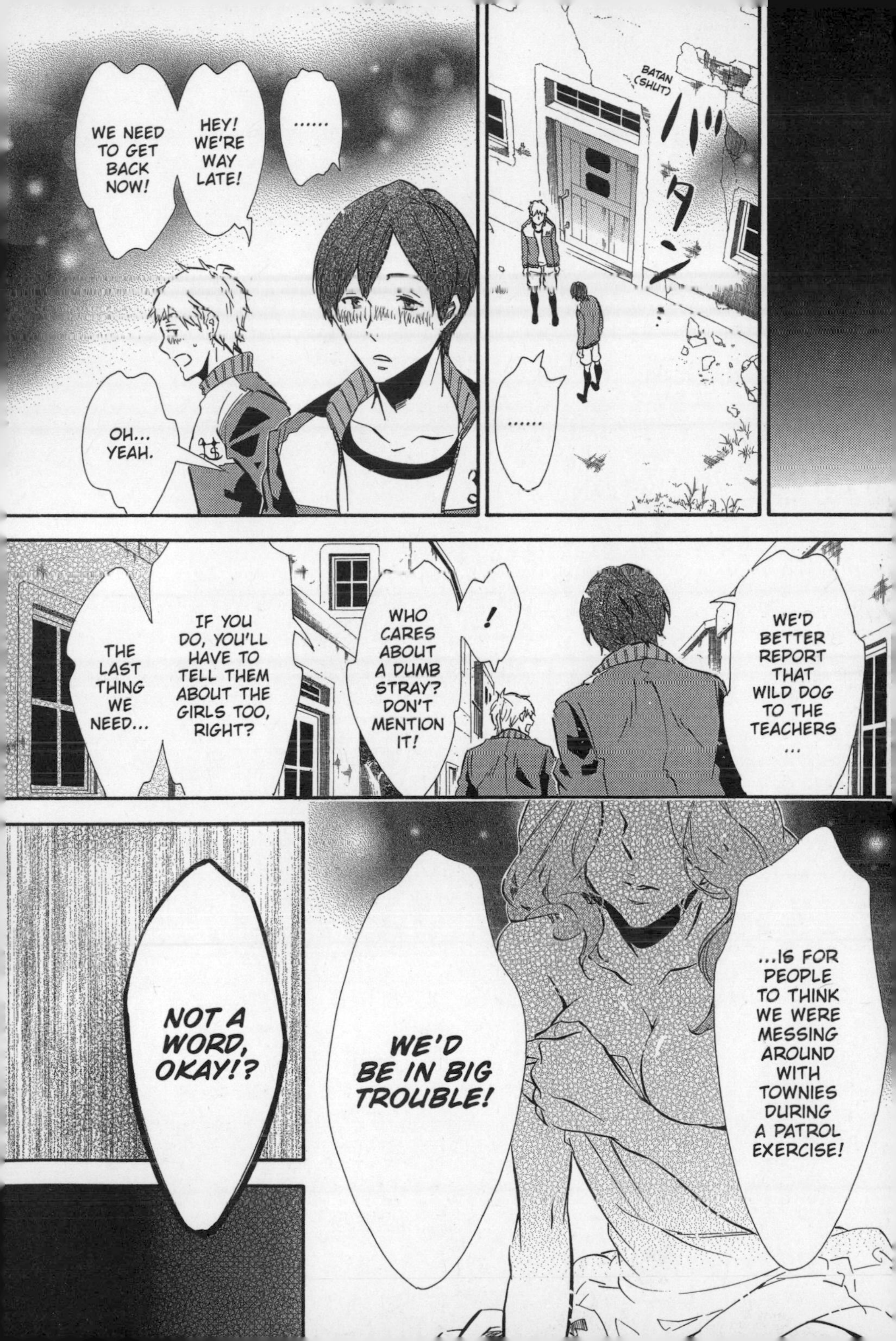
BATAN (SHUT)
......
......
HEY! WE'RE WAY LATE!
WE NEED TO GET BACK NOW!
OH... YEAH.
WE'D BETTER REPORT THAT WILD DOG TO THE TEACHERS ...
!
WHO CARES ABOUT A DUMB STRAY? DON'T MENTION IT!
IF YOU DO, YOU'LL HAVE TO TELL THEM ABOUT THE GIRLS TOO, RIGHT?
THE LAST THING WE NEED...
...IS FOR PEOPLE TO THINK WE WERE MESSING AROUND WITH TOWNIES DURING A PATROL EXERCISE!
WE'D BE IN BIG TROUBLE!
NOT A WORD, OKAY!?

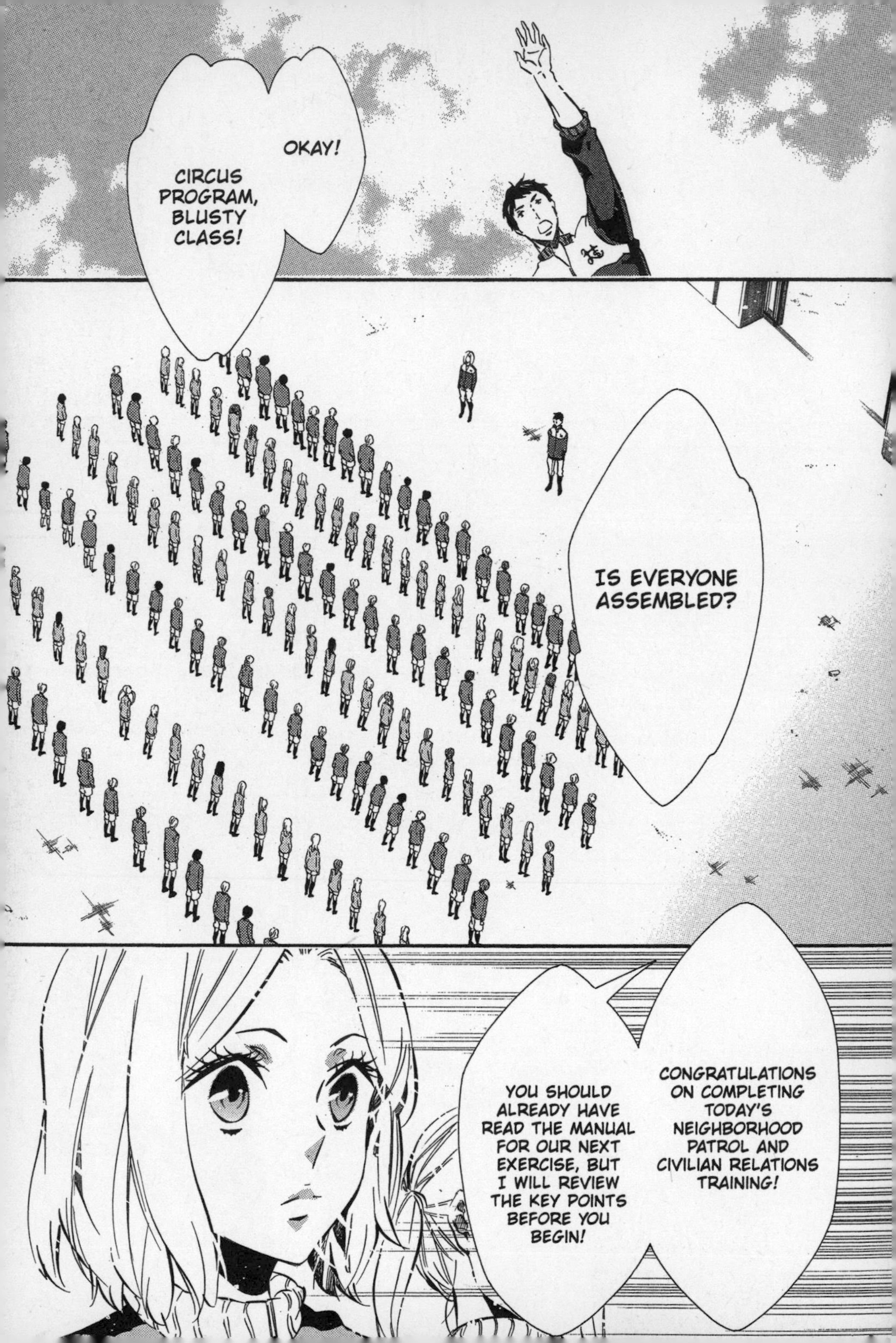
OKAY!
CIRCUS PROGRAM, BLUSTY CLASS!
IS EVERYONE ASSEMBLED?
CONGRATULATIONS ON COMPLETING TODAY'S NEIGHBORHOOD PATROL AND CIVILIAN RELATIONS TRAINING!
YOU SHOULD ALREADY HAVE READ THE MANUAL FOR OUR NEXT EXERCISE, BUT I WILL REVIEW THE KEY POINTS BEFORE YOU BEGIN!

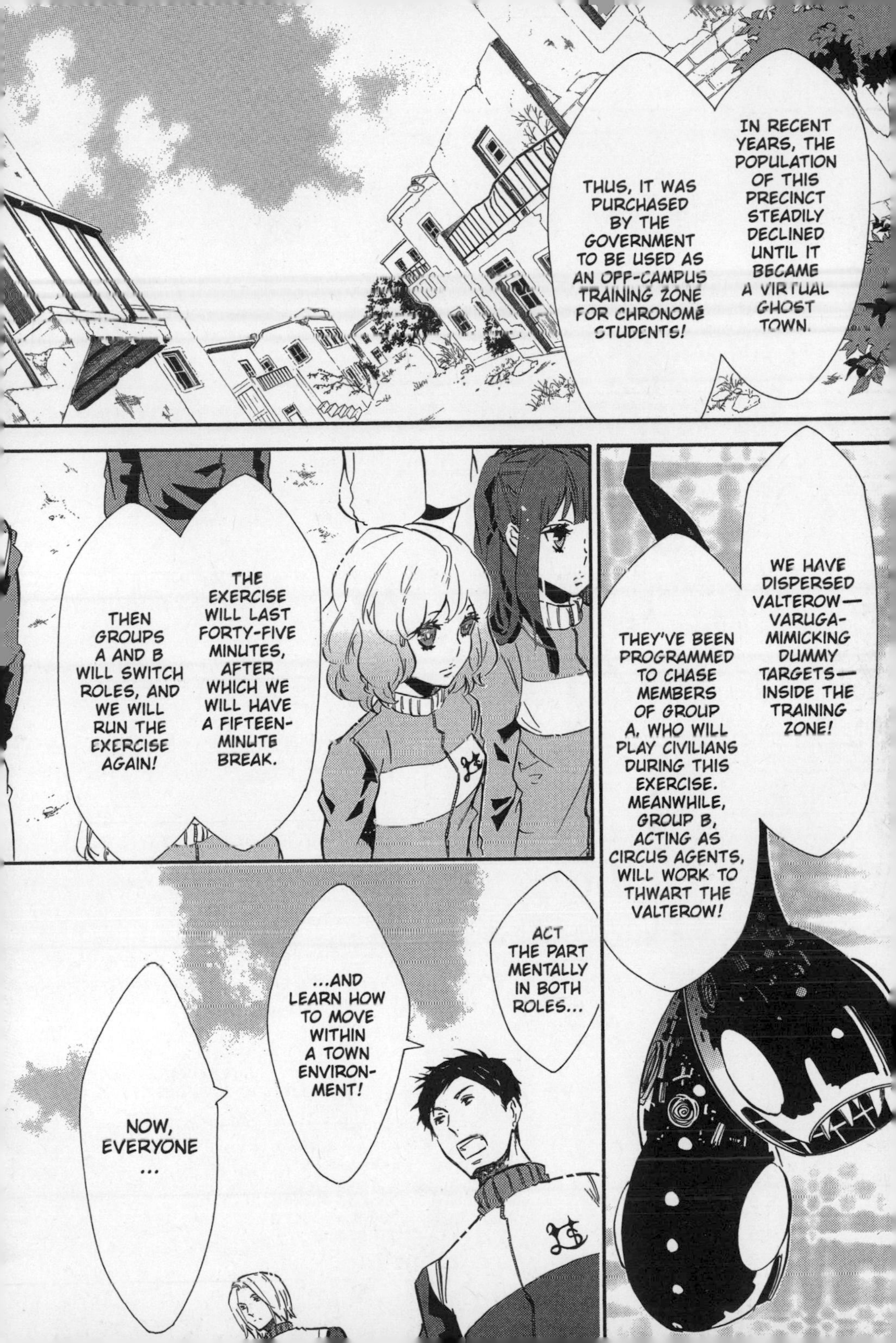
IN RECENT YEARS, THE POPULATION OF THIS PRECINCT STEADILY DECLINED UNTIL IT BECAME A VIRTUAL GHOST TOWN.
THUS, IT WAS PURCHASED BY THE GOVERNMENT TO BE USED AS AN OFF-CAMPUS TRAINING ZONE FOR CHRONOMÉ STUDENTS!
WE HAVE DISPERSED VALTEROW—VARUGA-MIMICKING DUMMY TARGETS—INSIDE THE TRAINING ZONE!
THEY'VE BEEN PROGRAMMED TO CHASE MEMBERS OF GROUP A, WHO WILL PLAY CIVILIANS DURING THIS EXERCISE. MEANWHILE, GROUP B, ACTING AS CIRCUS AGENTS, WILL WORK TO THWART THE VALTEROW!
THE EXERCISE WILL LAST FORTY-FIVE MINUTES, AFTER WHICH WE WILL HAVE A FIFTEEN-MINUTE BREAK.
THEN GROUPS A AND B WILL SWITCH ROLES, AND WE WILL RUN THE EXERCISE AGAIN!
ACT THE PART MENTALLY IN BOTH ROLES...
...AND LEARN HOW TO MOVE WITHIN A TOWN ENVIRON-MENT!
NOW, EVERYONE ...

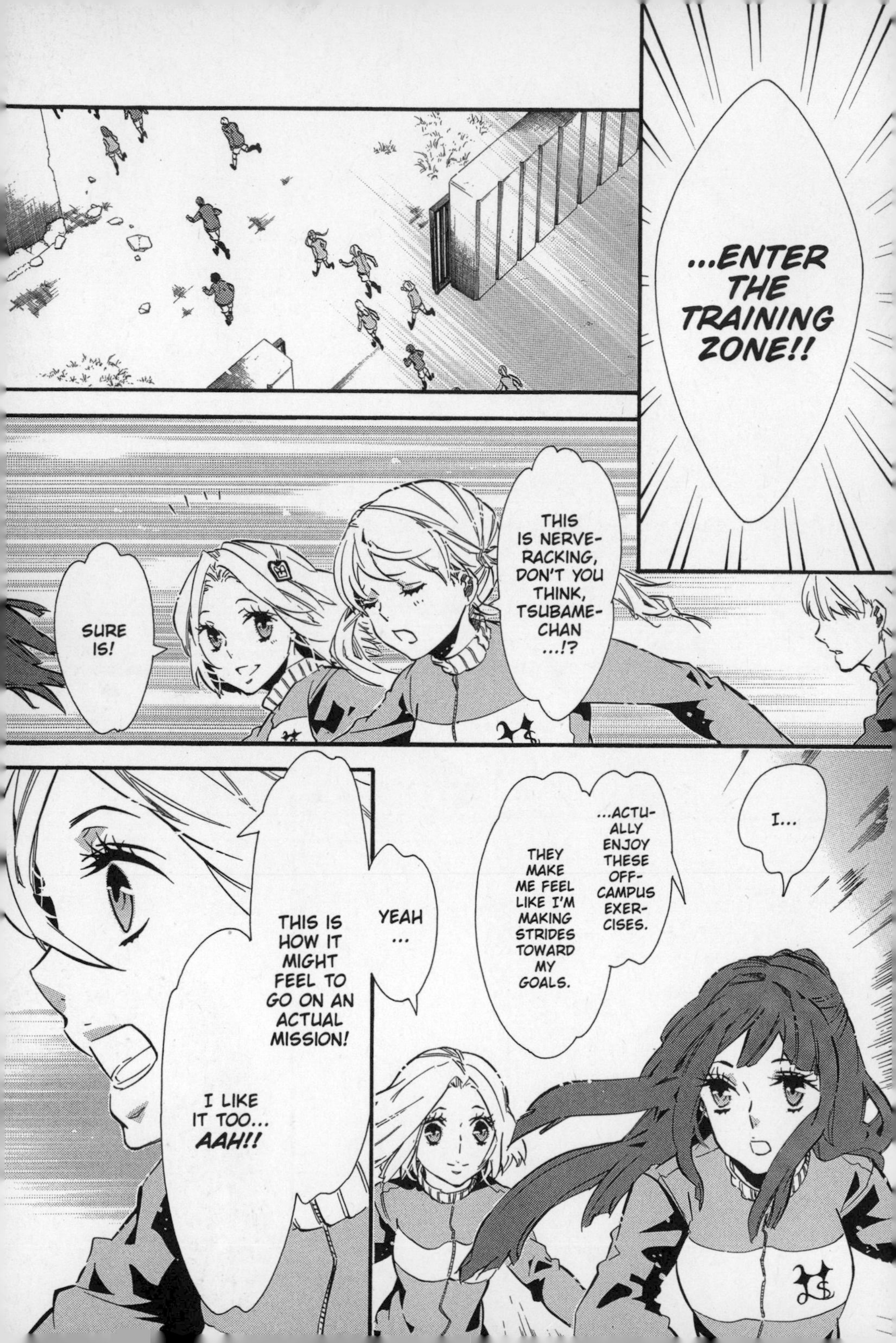

...ENTER THE TRAINING ZONE!!
THIS IS NERVE-RACKING, DON'T YOU THINK, TSUBAME-CHAN ...!?
SURE IS!
I...
...ACTU-ALLY ENJOY THESE OFF-CAMPUS EXER-CISES.
THEY MAKE ME FEEL LIKE I'M MAKING STRIDES TOWARD MY GOALS.
YEAH ...
THIS IS HOW IT MIGHT FEEL TO GO ON AN ACTUAL MISSION!
I LIKE IT TOO... *AAH!!*

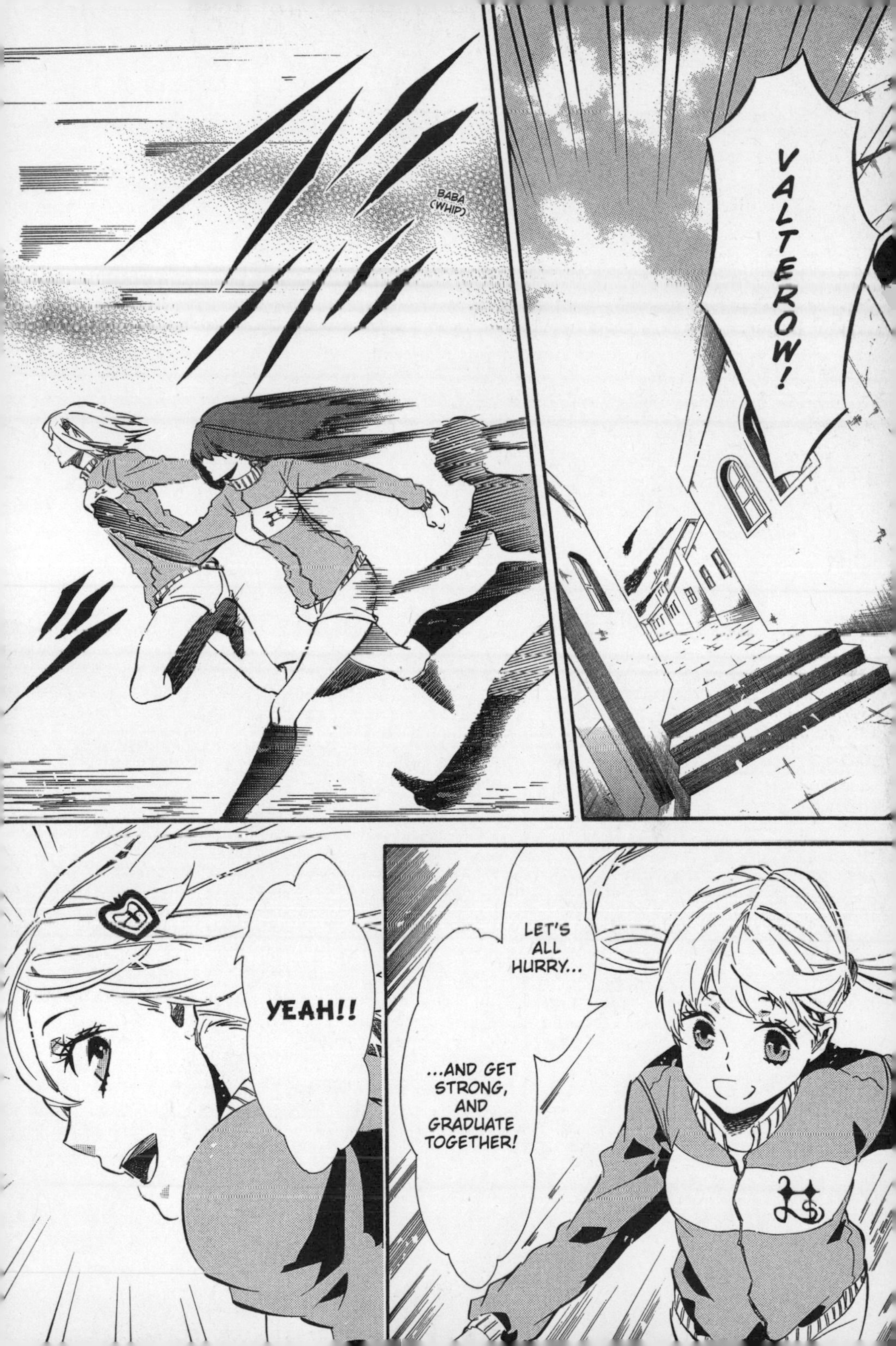
VALTEROW!
BABA (WHIP)
LET'S ALL HURRY...
...AND GET STRONG, AND GRADUATE TOGETHER!
YEAH!!

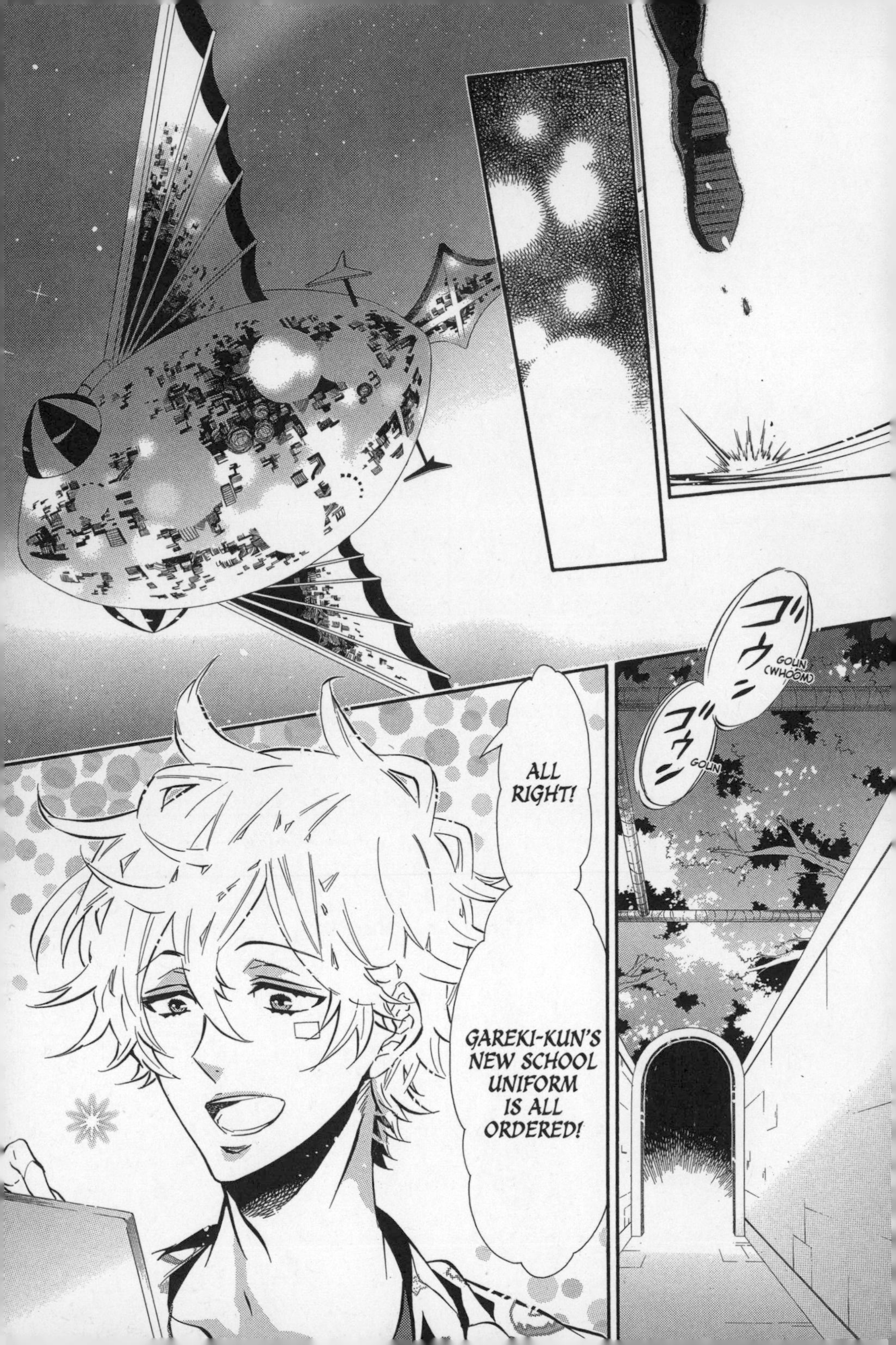
ゴウン
GOUN (WHOOM)
ゴウン
GOUN
ALL RIGHT!
GAREKI-KUN'S NEW SCHOOL UNIFORM IS ALL ORDERED!

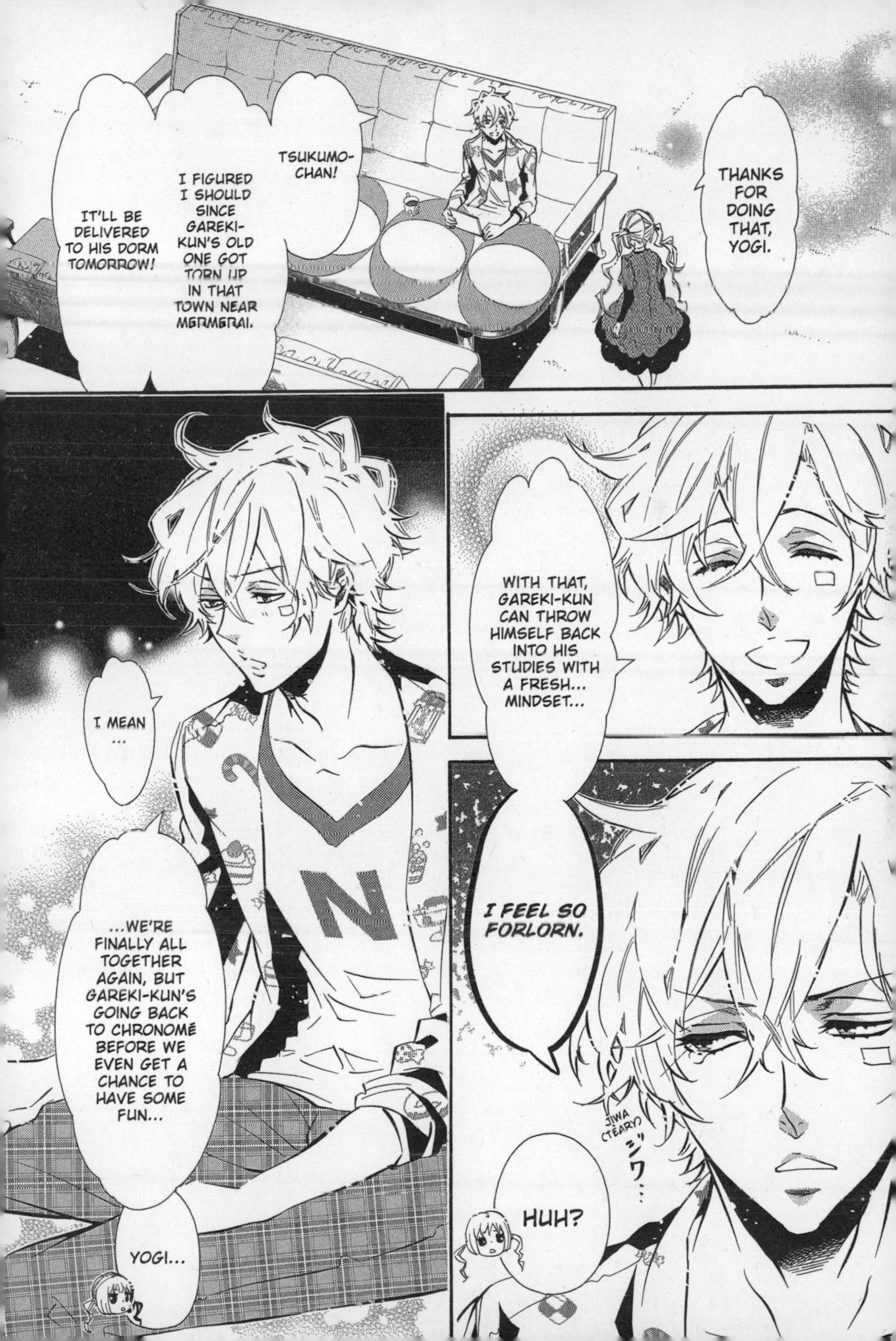
THANKS FOR DOING THAT, YOGI.
TSUKUMO-CHAN!
I FIGURED I SHOULD SINCE GAREKI-KUN'S OLD ONE GOT TORN UP IN THAT TOWN NEAR MERMERAI.
IT'LL BE DELIVERED TO HIS DORM TOMORROW!
WITH THAT, GAREKI-KUN CAN THROW HIMSELF BACK INTO HIS STUDIES WITH A FRESH... MINDSET...
I FEEL SO FORLORN.
JIWA (TEARY)
ジワ…
HUH?
I MEAN ...
...WE'RE FINALLY ALL TOGETHER AGAIN, BUT GAREKI-KUN'S GOING BACK TO CHRONOMÉ BEFORE WE EVEN GET A CHANCE TO HAVE SOME FUN...
YOGI...

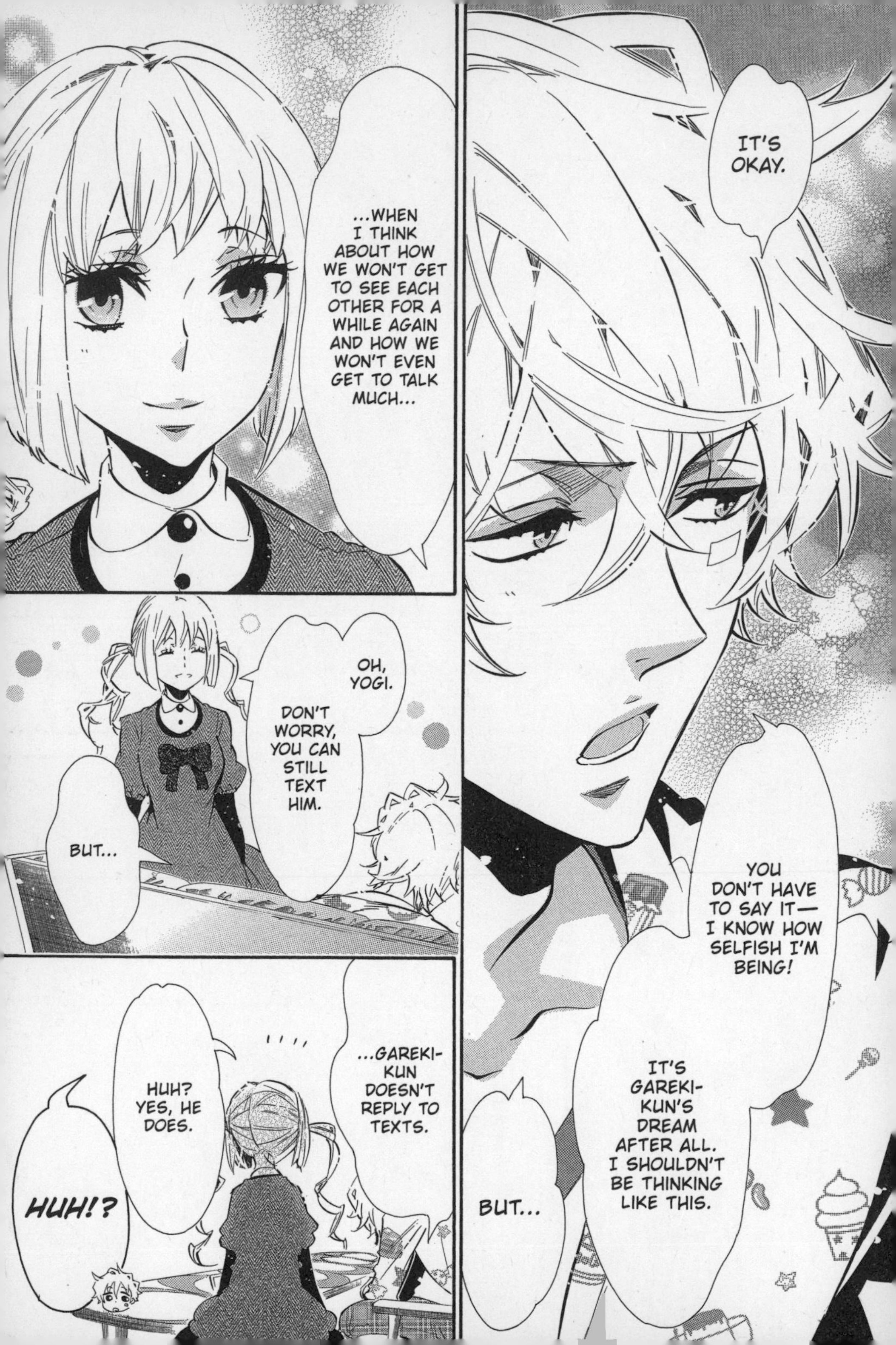
IT'S OKAY.
YOU DON'T HAVE TO SAY IT— I KNOW HOW SELFISH I'M BEING!
IT'S GAREKI-KUN'S DREAM AFTER ALL. I SHOULDN'T BE THINKING LIKE THIS.
BUT...
...WHEN I THINK ABOUT HOW WE WON'T GET TO SEE EACH OTHER FOR A WHILE AGAIN AND HOW WE WON'T EVEN GET TO TALK MUCH...
OH, YOGI.
DON'T WORRY, YOU CAN STILL TEXT HIM.
BUT...
...GAREKI-KUN DOESN'T REPLY TO TEXTS.
HUH? YES, HE DOES.
HUH!?

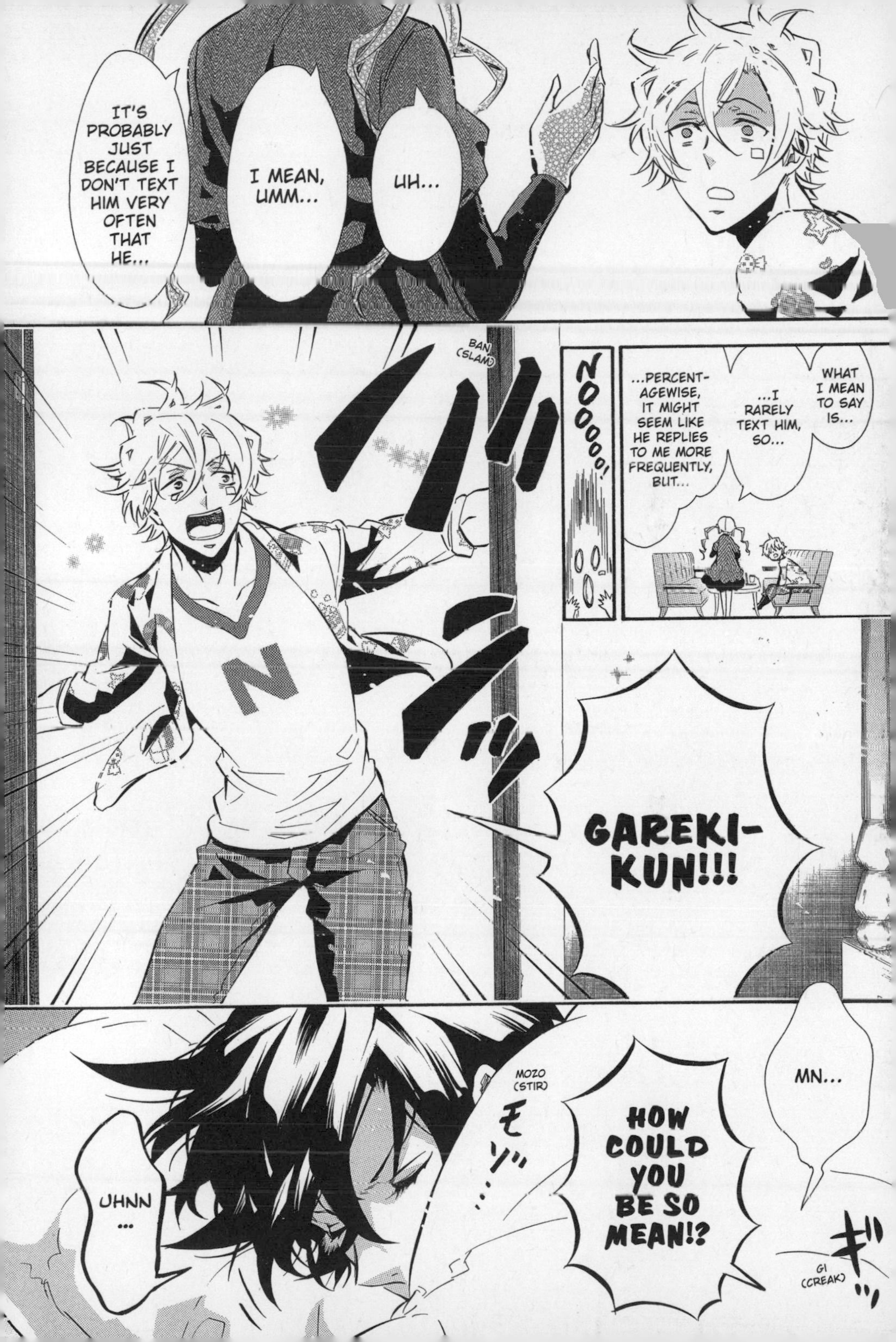
UH...
I MEAN, UMM...
IT'S PROBABLY JUST BECAUSE I DON'T TEXT HIM VERY OFTEN THAT HE...
WHAT I MEAN TO SAY IS...
...I RARELY TEXT HIM, SO...
...PERCENT-AGEWISE, IT MIGHT SEEM LIKE HE REPLIES TO ME MORE FREQUENTLY, BUT...
NOOOOO!
GAREKI-KUN!!!
BAN (SLAM)
MN...
GI (CREAK)
HOW COULD YOU BE SO MEAN!?
MOZO (STIR)
UHNN...

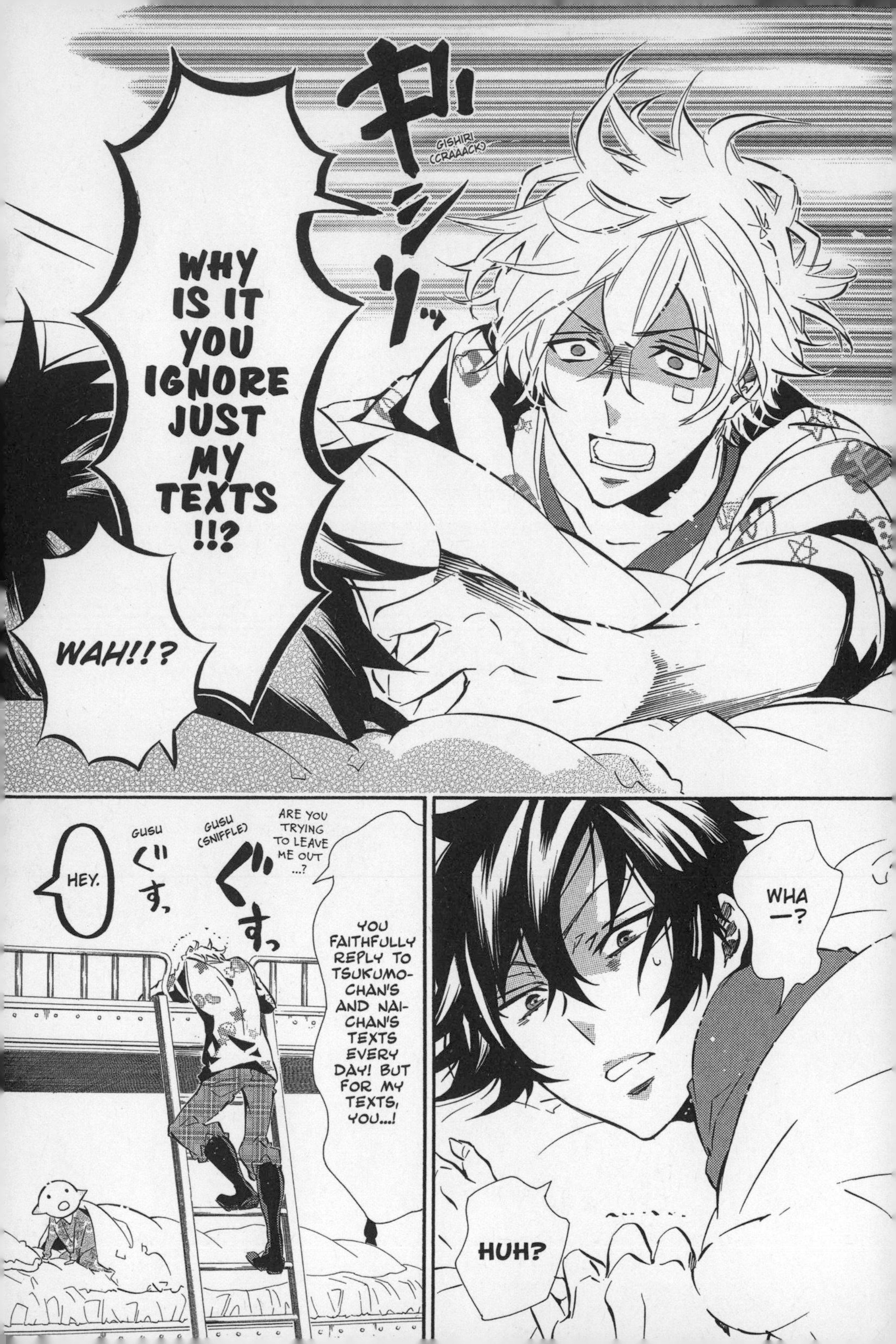
ギシッ
GISHIRI (CRAAACK)
WHY IS IT YOU IGNORE JUST MY TEXTS!!?
WAH!!?
WHA—?
YOU FAITHFULLY REPLY TO TSUKUMO-CHAN'S AND NAI-CHAN'S TEXTS EVERY DAY! BUT FOR MY TEXTS, YOU...!
......
HUH?
ARE YOU TRYING TO LEAVE ME OUT ...?
GUSU (SNIFFLE)
ぐすっ
GUSU
ぐすっ
HEY.

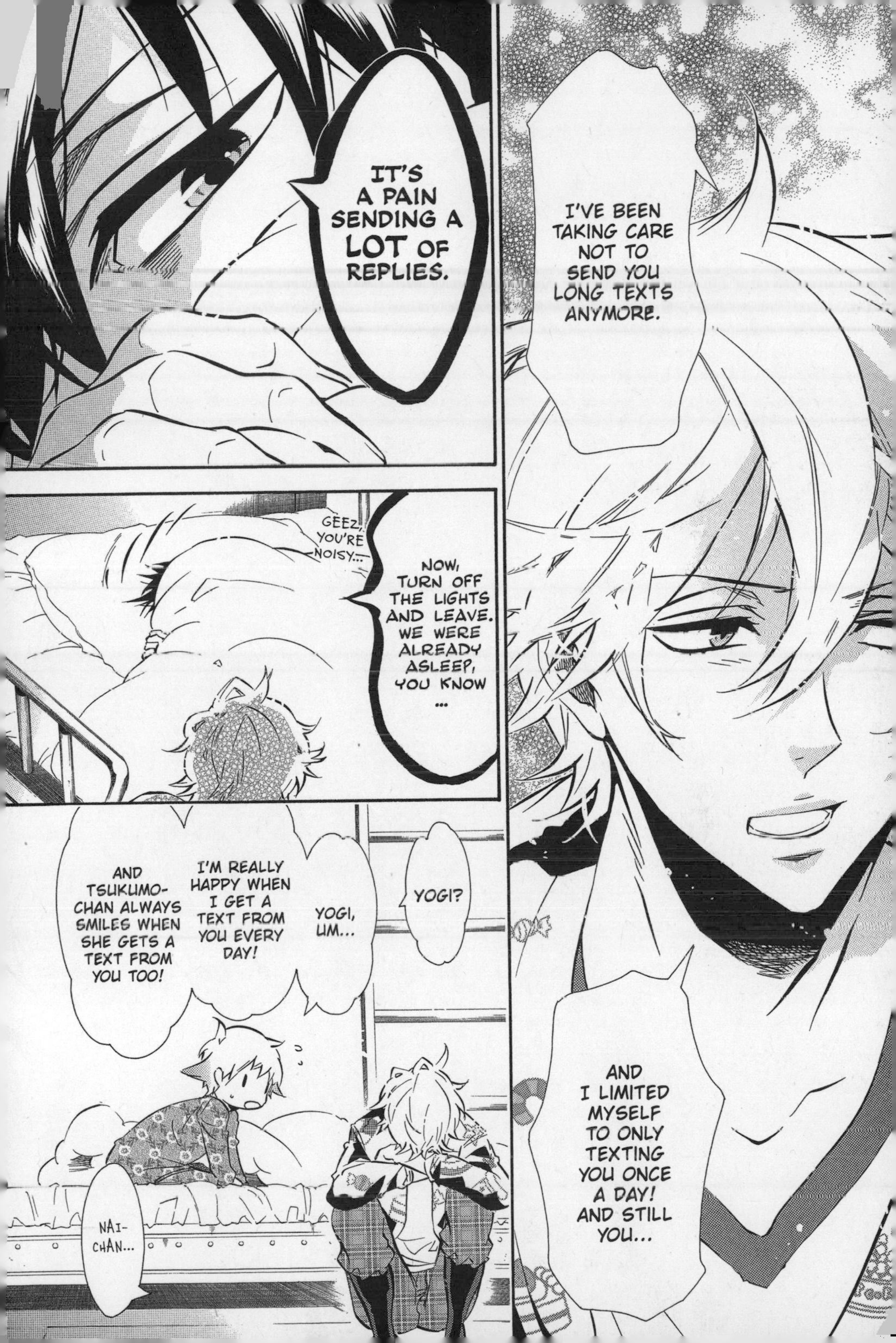

I'VE BEEN TAKING CARE NOT TO SEND YOU LONG TEXTS ANYMORE.
AND I LIMITED MYSELF TO ONLY TEXTING YOU ONCE A DAY! AND STILL YOU...
IT'S A PAIN SENDING A LOT OF REPLIES.
GEEZ, YOU'RE NOISY...
NOW, TURN OFF THE LIGHTS AND LEAVE. WE WERE ALREADY ASLEEP, YOU KNOW ...
YOGI?
YOGI, UM...
I'M REALLY HAPPY WHEN I GET A TEXT FROM YOU EVERY DAY!
AND TSUKUMO-CHAN ALWAYS SMILES WHEN SHE GETS A TEXT FROM YOU TOO!
NAI-CHAN...

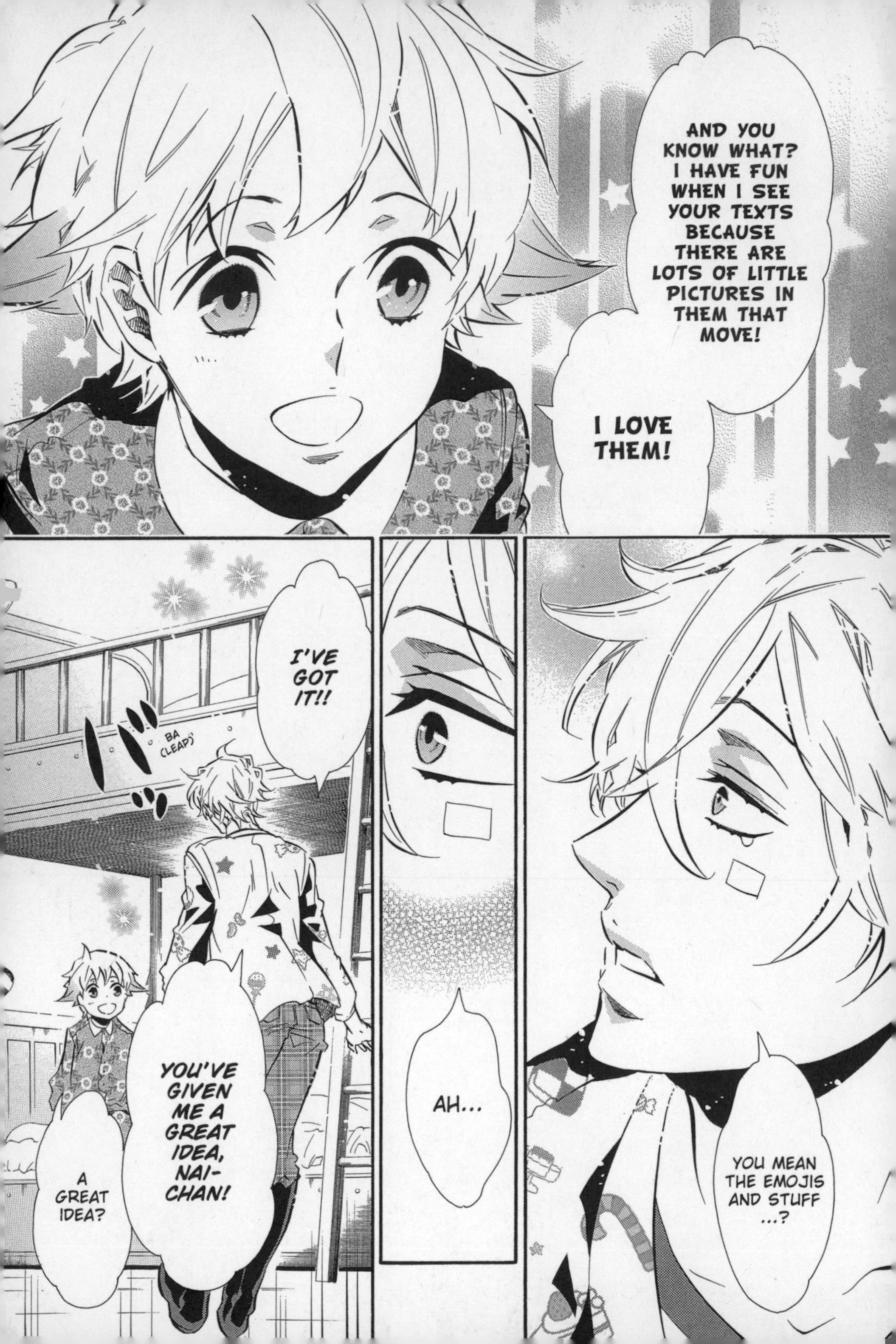
AND YOU KNOW WHAT? I HAVE FUN WHEN I SEE YOUR TEXTS BECAUSE THERE ARE LOTS OF LITTLE PICTURES IN THEM THAT MOVE!
I LOVE THEM!
YOU MEAN THE EMOJIS AND STUFF ...?
AH...
I'VE GOT IT!!
BA (LEAP)
YOU'VE GIVEN ME A GREAT IDEA, NAI-CHAN!
A GREAT IDEA?

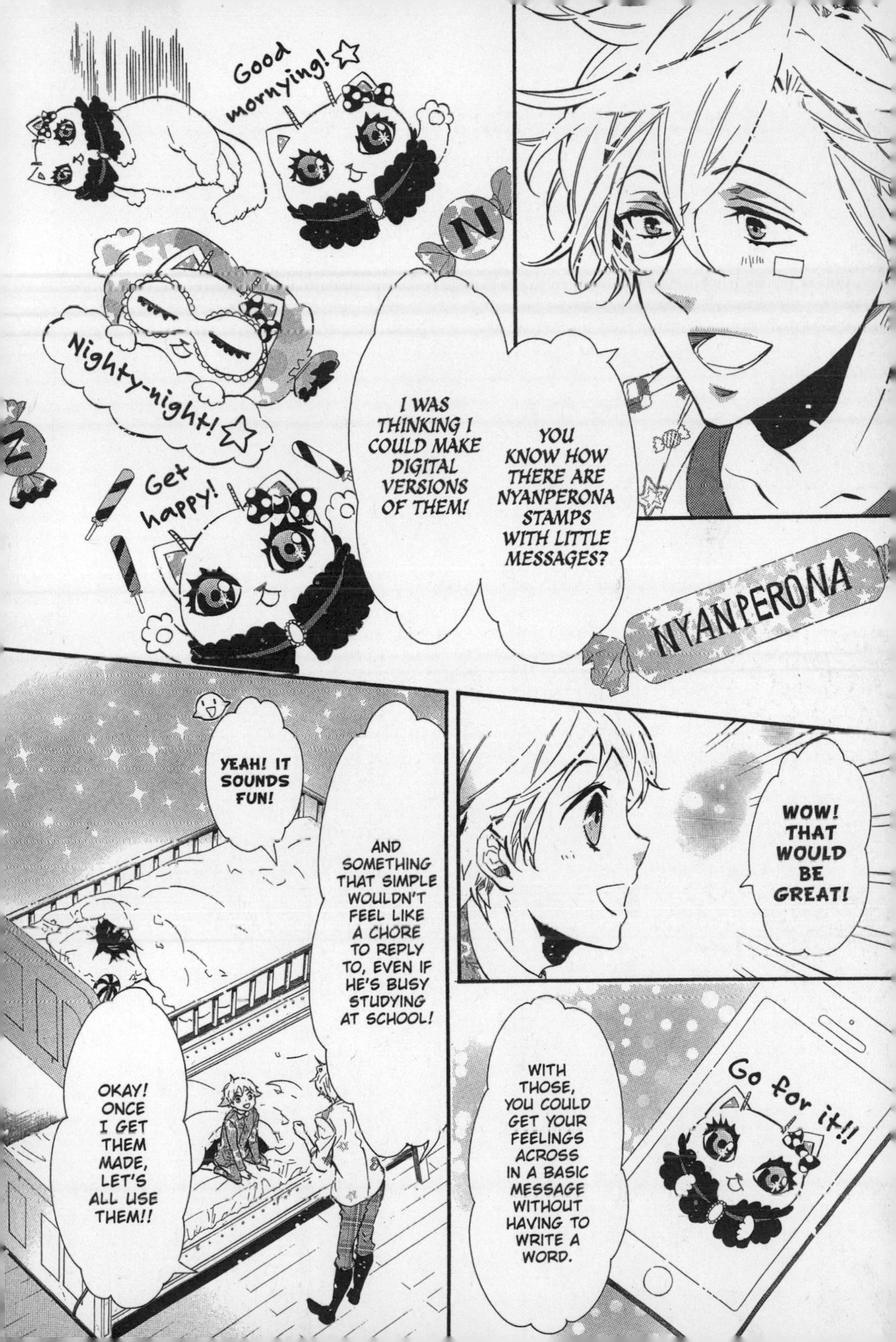
YOU KNOW HOW THERE ARE NYANPERONA STAMPS WITH LITTLE MESSAGES?
NYANPERONA
I WAS THINKING I COULD MAKE DIGITAL VERSIONS OF THEM!
Good mornying! ☆
Nighty-night! ☆
Get happy!
WOW! THAT WOULD BE GREAT!
WITH THOSE, YOU COULD GET YOUR FEELINGS ACROSS IN A BASIC MESSAGE WITHOUT HAVING TO WRITE A WORD.
Go for it!!
AND SOMETHING THAT SIMPLE WOULDN'T FEEL LIKE A CHORE TO REPLY TO, EVEN IF HE'S BUSY STUDYING AT SCHOOL!
YEAH! IT SOUNDS FUN!
OKAY! ONCE I GET THEM MADE, LET'S ALL USE THEM!!

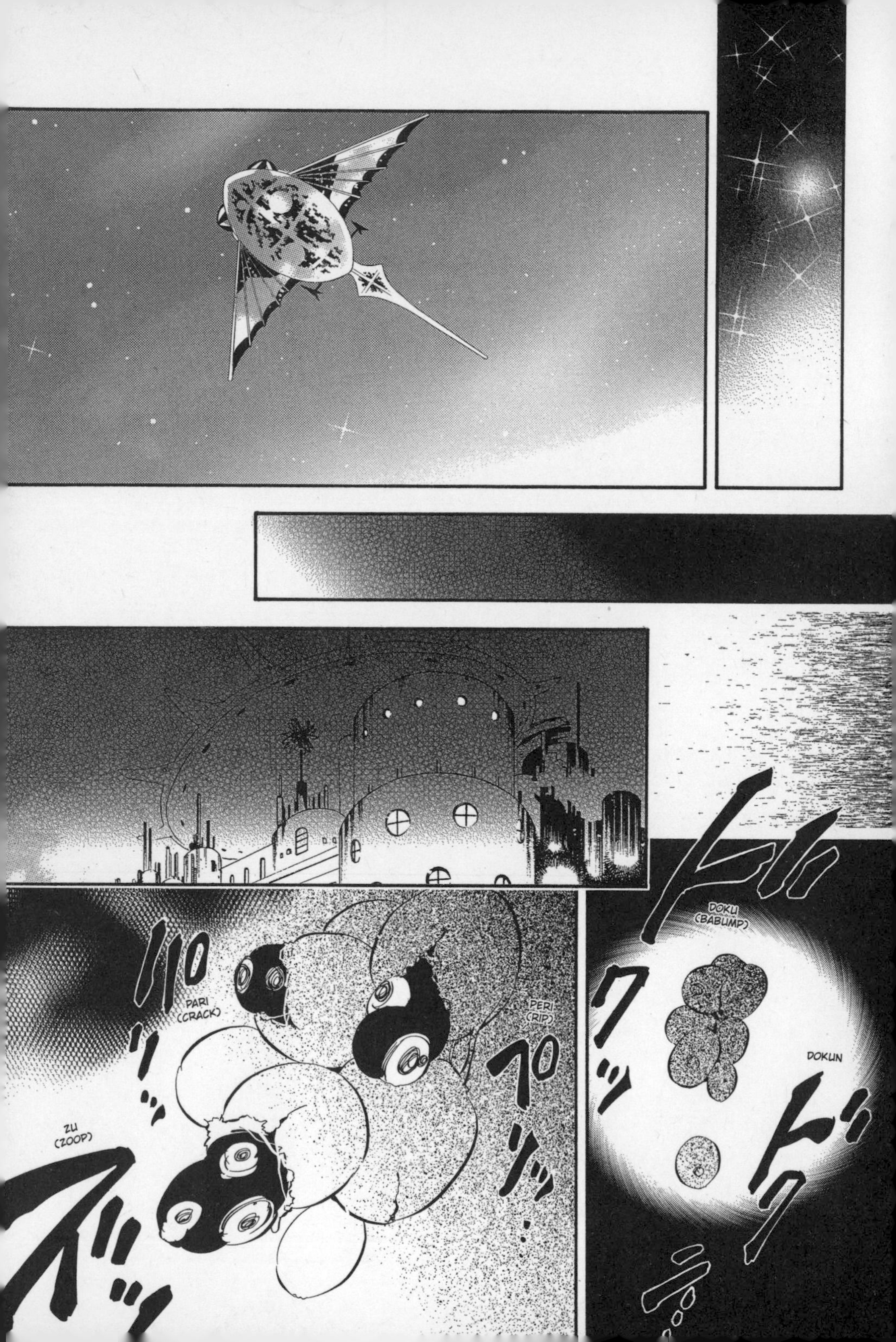
DOKU
(BABUMP)
DOKUN
PERI
(RIP)
PARI
(CRACK)
ZU
(ZOOP)

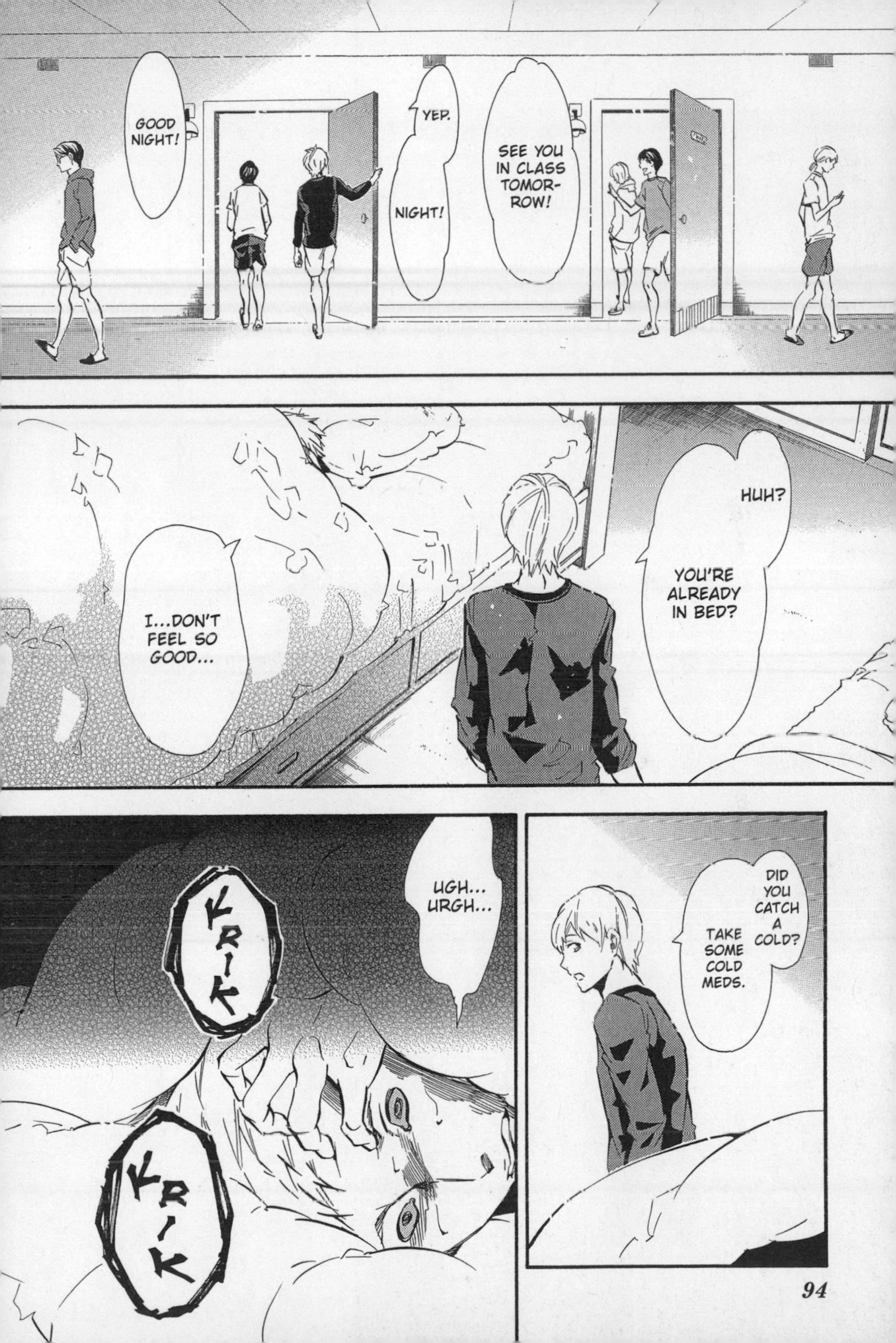

SEE YOU IN CLASS TOMORROW!
YEP.
NIGHT!
GOOD NIGHT!
HUH?
YOU'RE ALREADY IN BED?
I...DON'T FEEL SO GOOD...
DID YOU CATCH A COLD?
TAKE SOME COLD MEDS.
UGH... URGH...
KRIK
KRIK

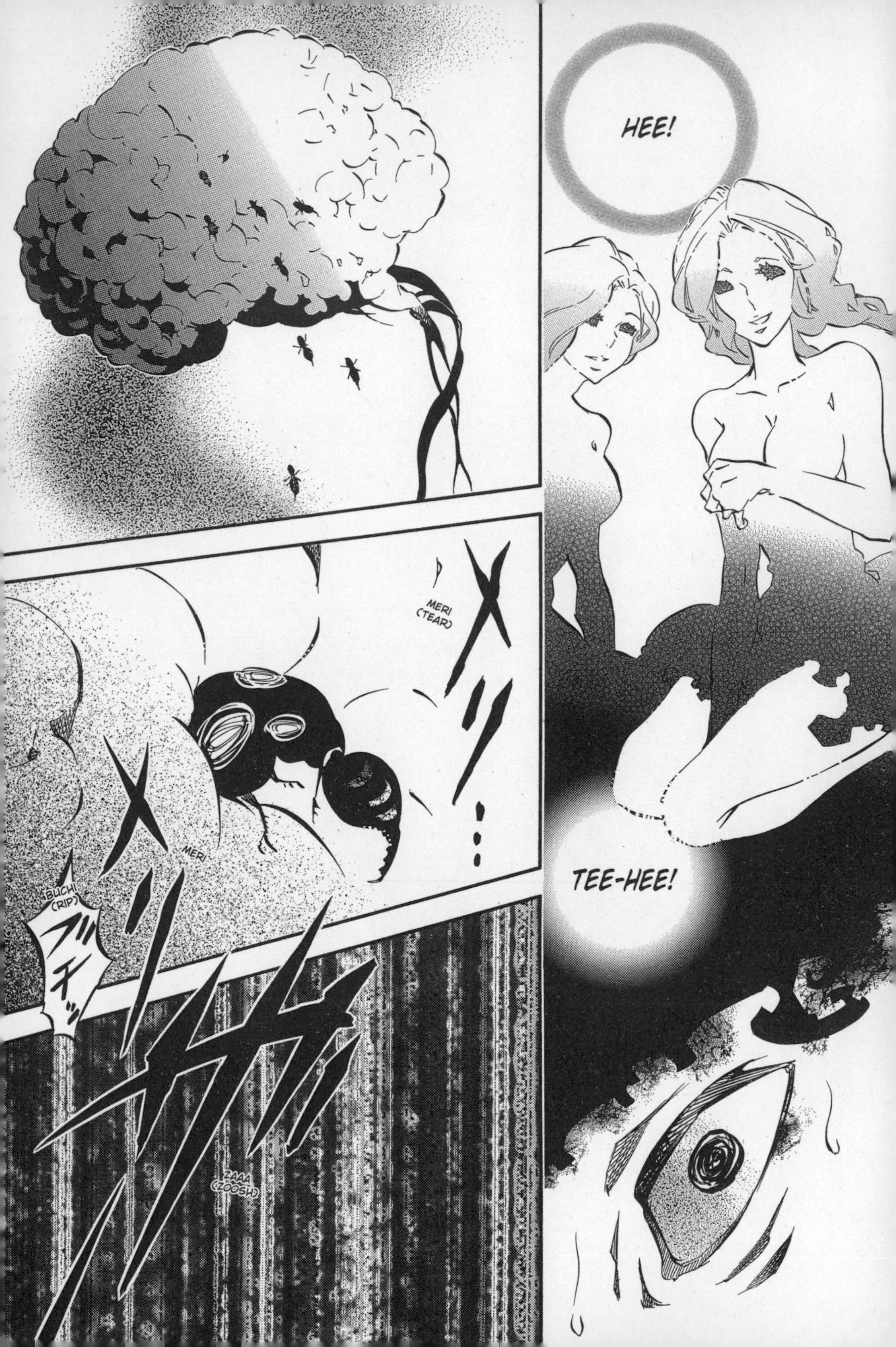
HEE!
TEE-HEE!
MERI (TEAR)
MERI
BUCHI (RIP)
ZAAA (ZOOSH)

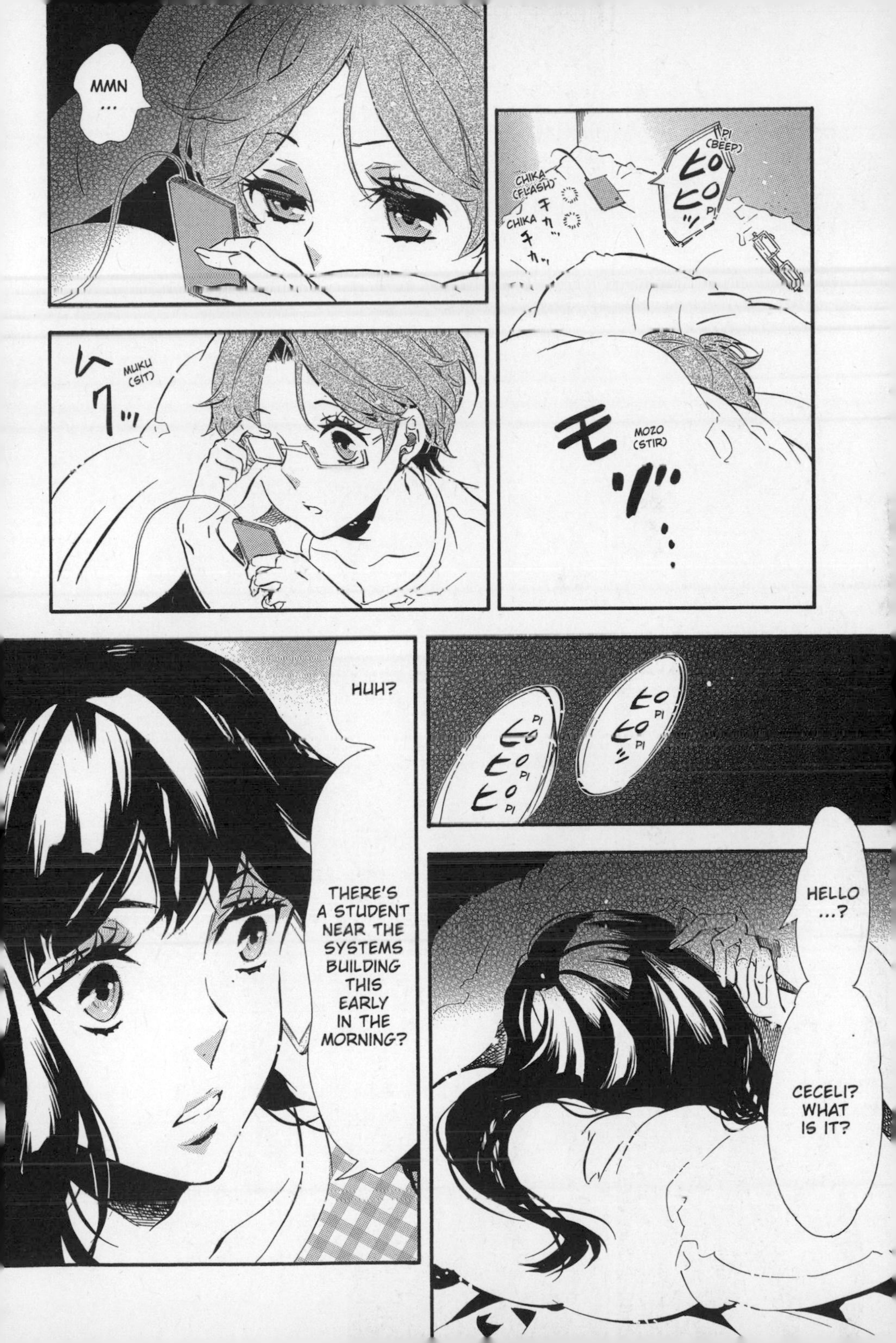
PI (BEEP) PI
CHIKA (FLASH) CHIKA
MOZO (STIR)
MMN ...
MUKU (SIT)
PI PI
PI PI PI
HELLO ...?
CECELI? WHAT IS IT?
HUH?
THERE'S A STUDENT NEAR THE SYSTEMS BUILDING THIS EARLY IN THE MORNING?

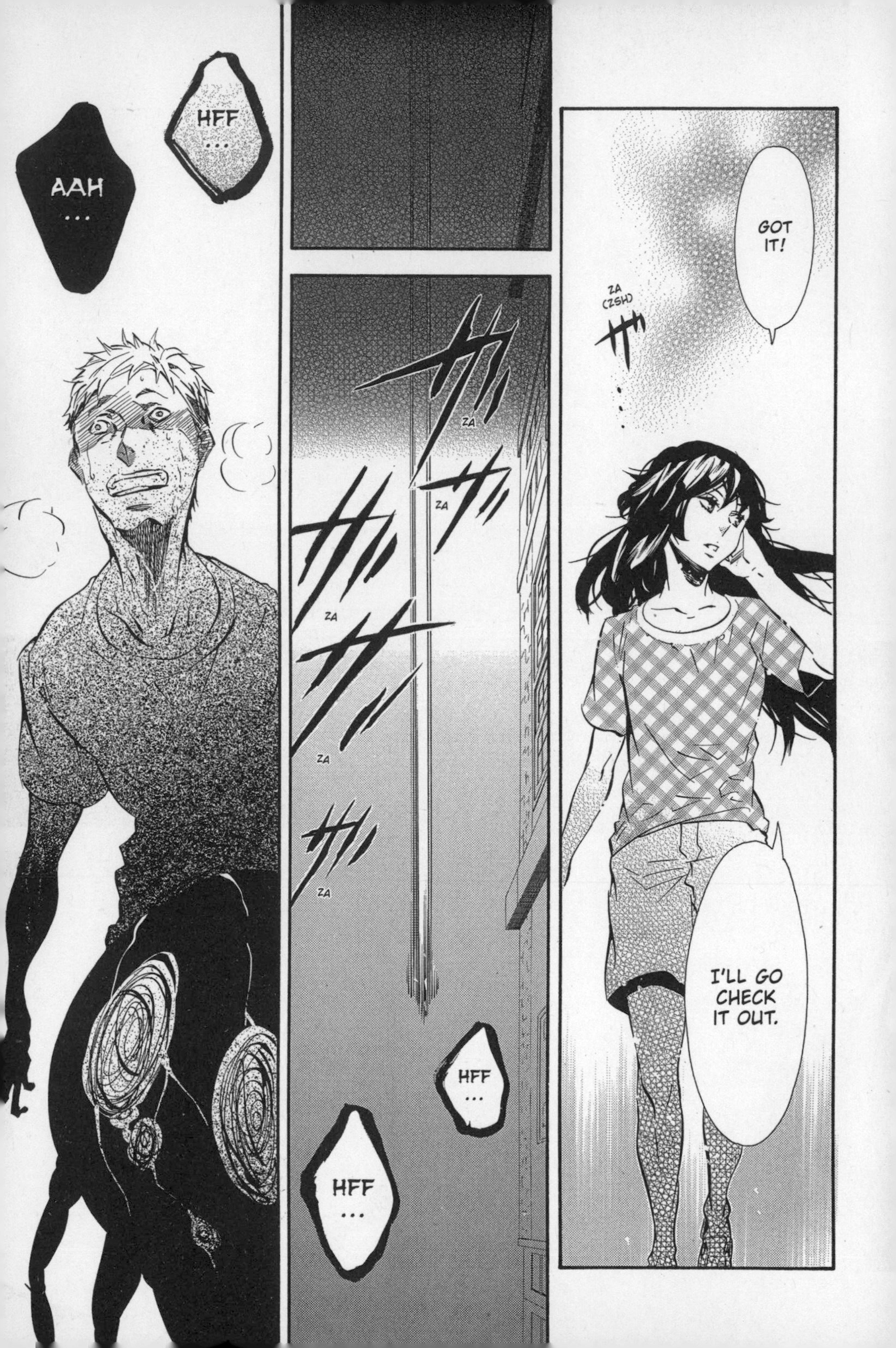
GOT IT!
ZA (ZSH)
I'LL GO CHECK IT OUT.
ZA
ZA
ZA
ZA
ZA
HFF …
HFF …
HFF …
AAH …

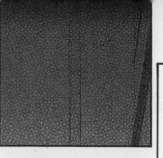

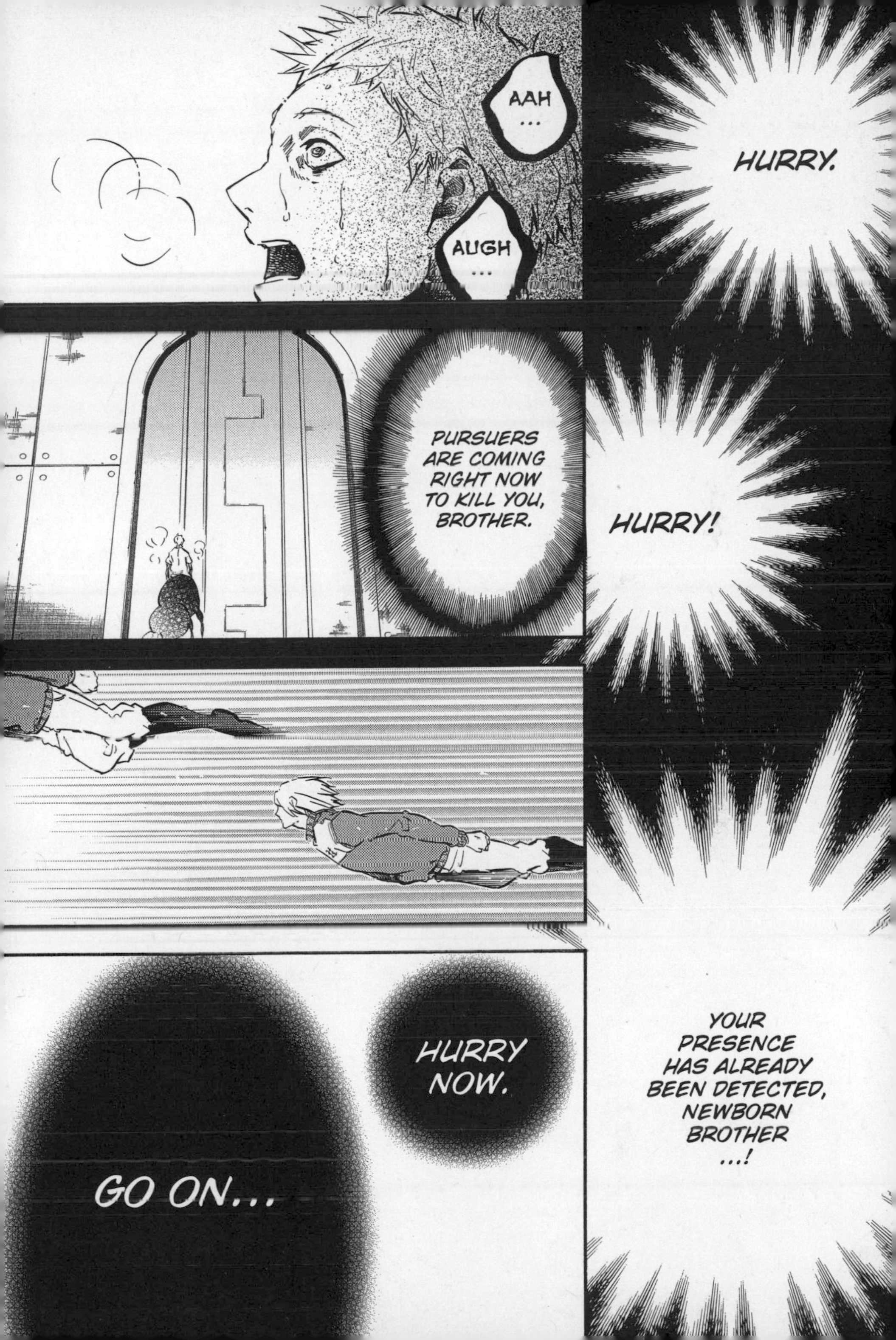
HURRY.
HURRY!
AAH ...
AUGH ...
PURSUERS ARE COMING RIGHT NOW TO KILL YOU, BROTHER.
YOUR PRESENCE HAS ALREADY BEEN DETECTED, NEWBORN BROTHER ...!
HURRY NOW.
GO ON...

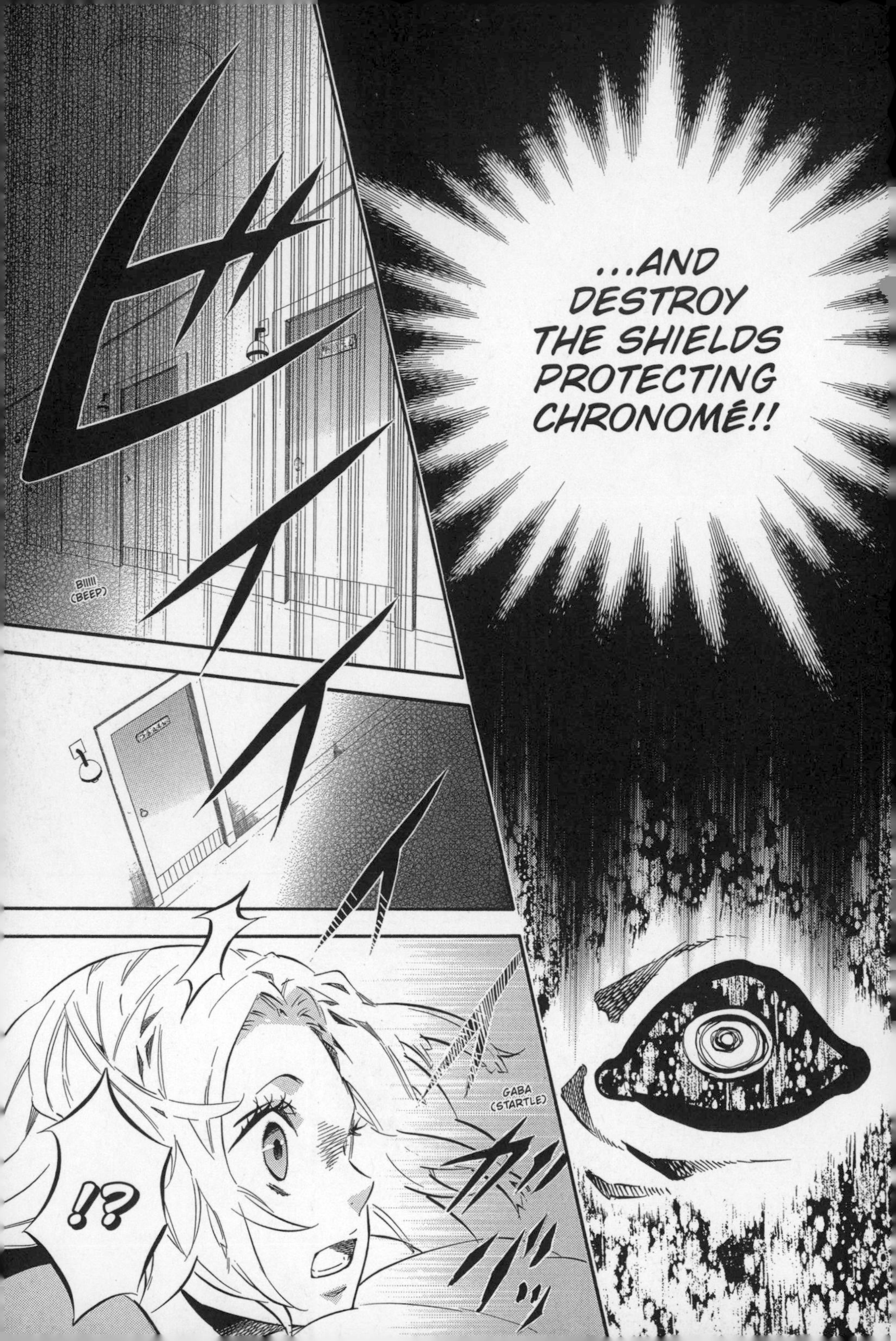

...AND DESTROY THE SHIELDS PROTECTING CHRONOMÉ!!
BIIII (BEEP)
GABA (STARTLE)
!?

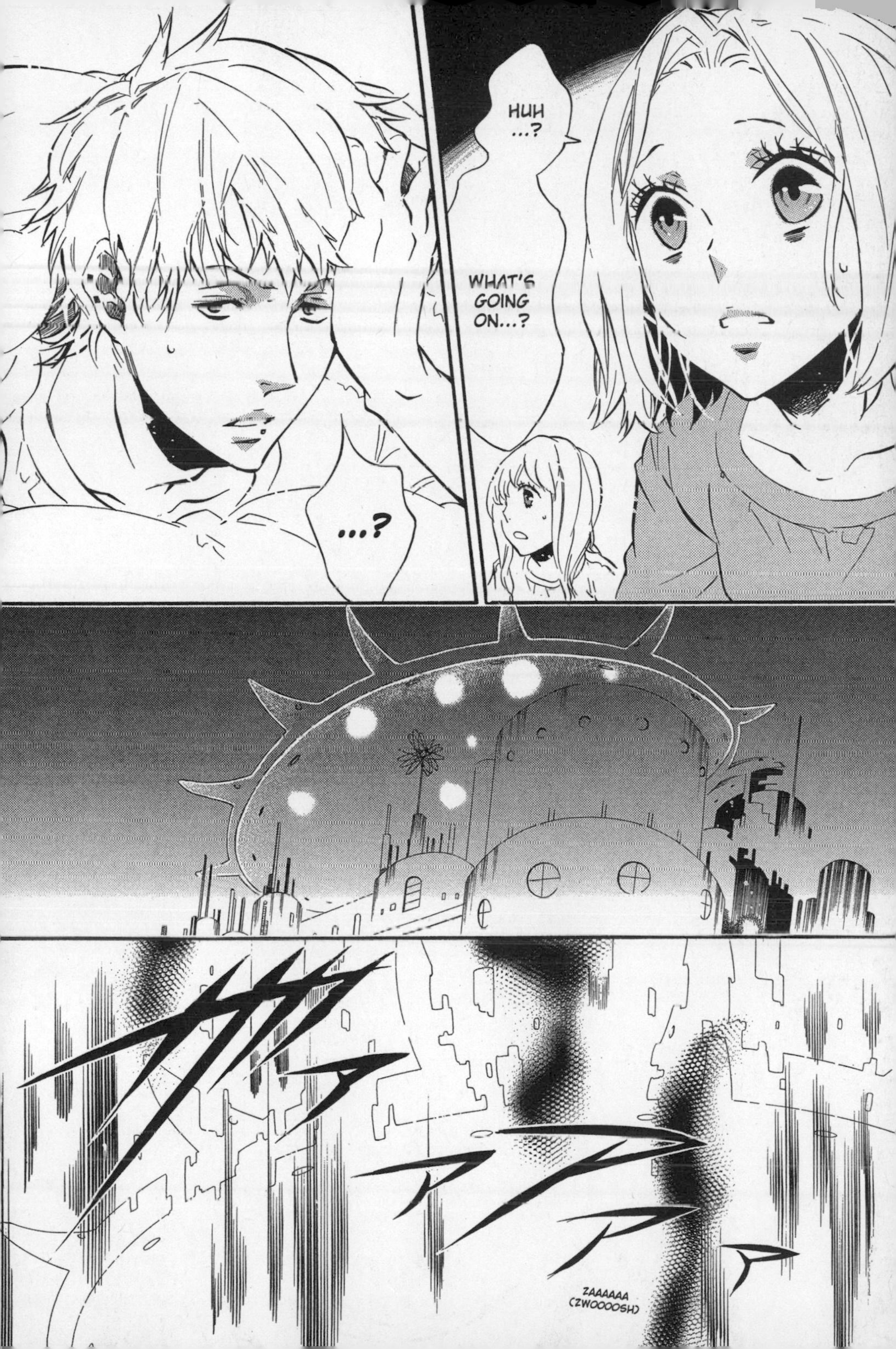
HUH ...?
WHAT'S GOING ON...?
...?
ZAAAAAA (ZWOOOOSH)

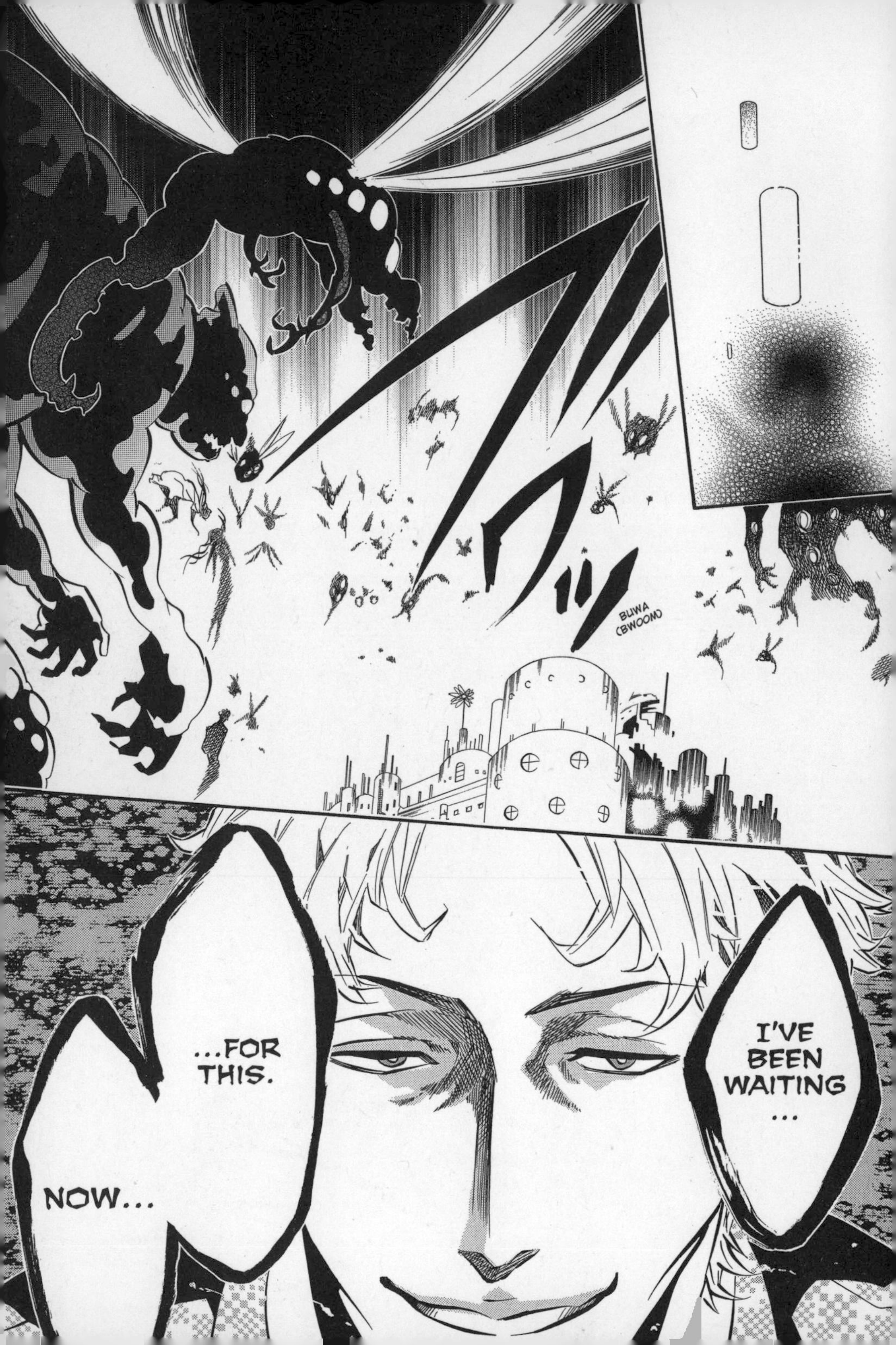
BUWA (BWOOM)
I'VE BEEN WAITING ...
...FOR THIS.
NOW...

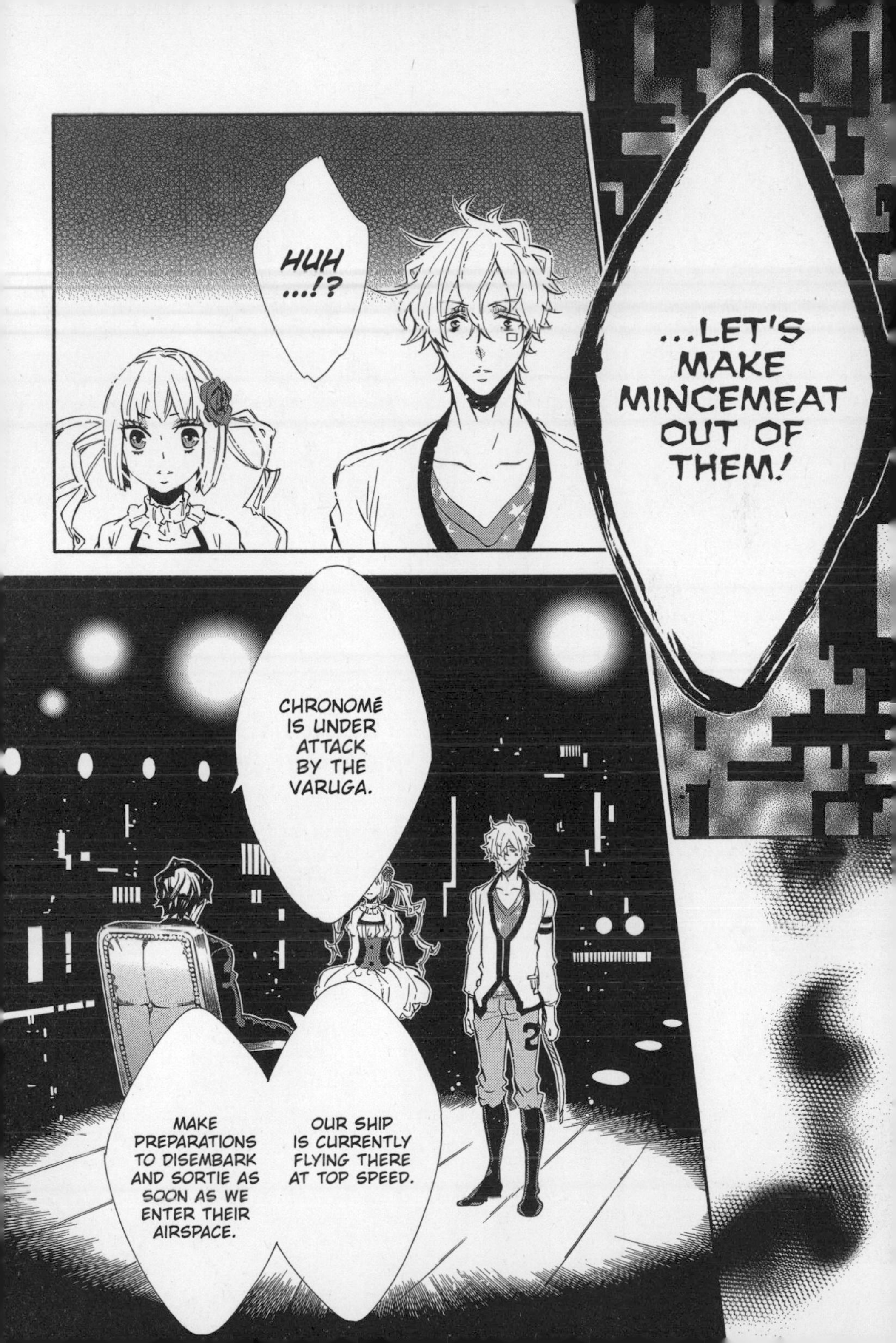
...LET'S MAKE MINCEMEAT OUT OF THEM!
HUH ...!?
CHRONOMÉ IS UNDER ATTACK BY THE VARUGA.
OUR SHIP IS CURRENTLY FLYING THERE AT TOP SPEED.
MAKE PREPARATIONS TO DISEMBARK AND SORTIE AS SOON AS WE ENTER THEIR AIRSPACE.

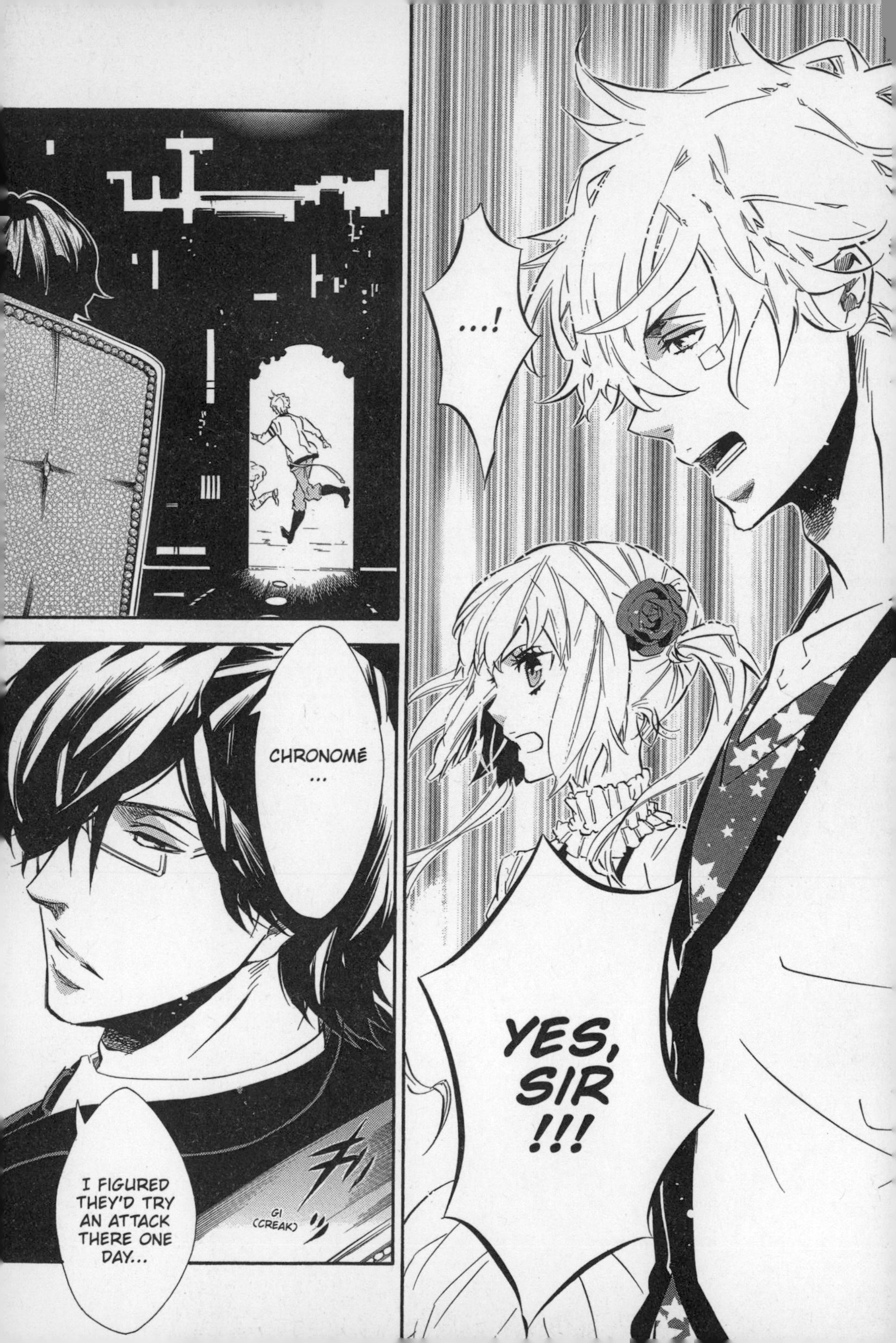
...!
YES, SIR!!!
CHRONOME ...
I FIGURED THEY'D TRY AN ATTACK THERE ONE DAY...
GI (CREAK)

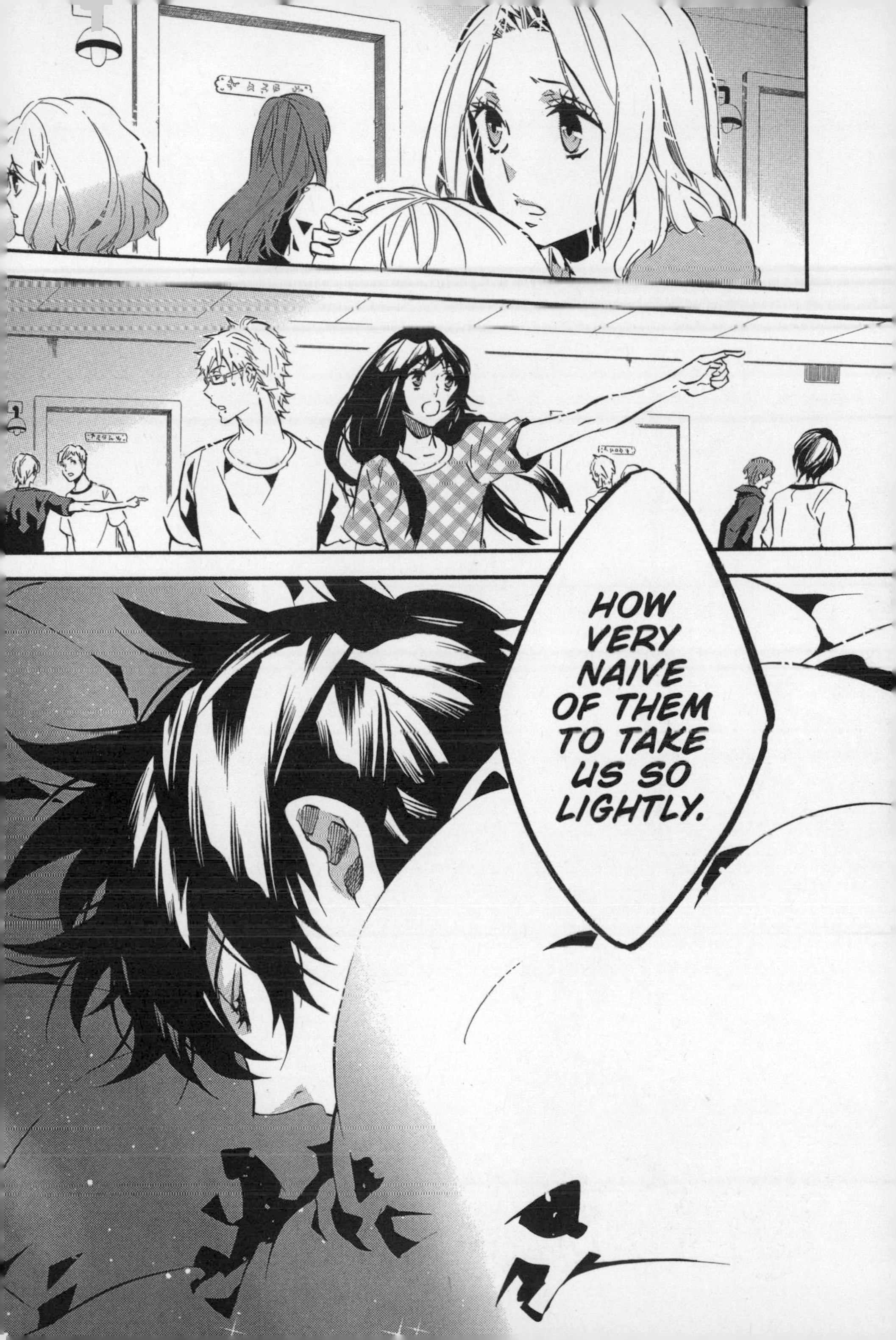
HOW VERY NAIVE OF THEM TO TAKE US SO LIGHTLY.

KARNEVAL

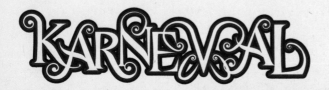

Good mornying! ☆

Nighty-night! ☆

Get happy!

KARNEVAL

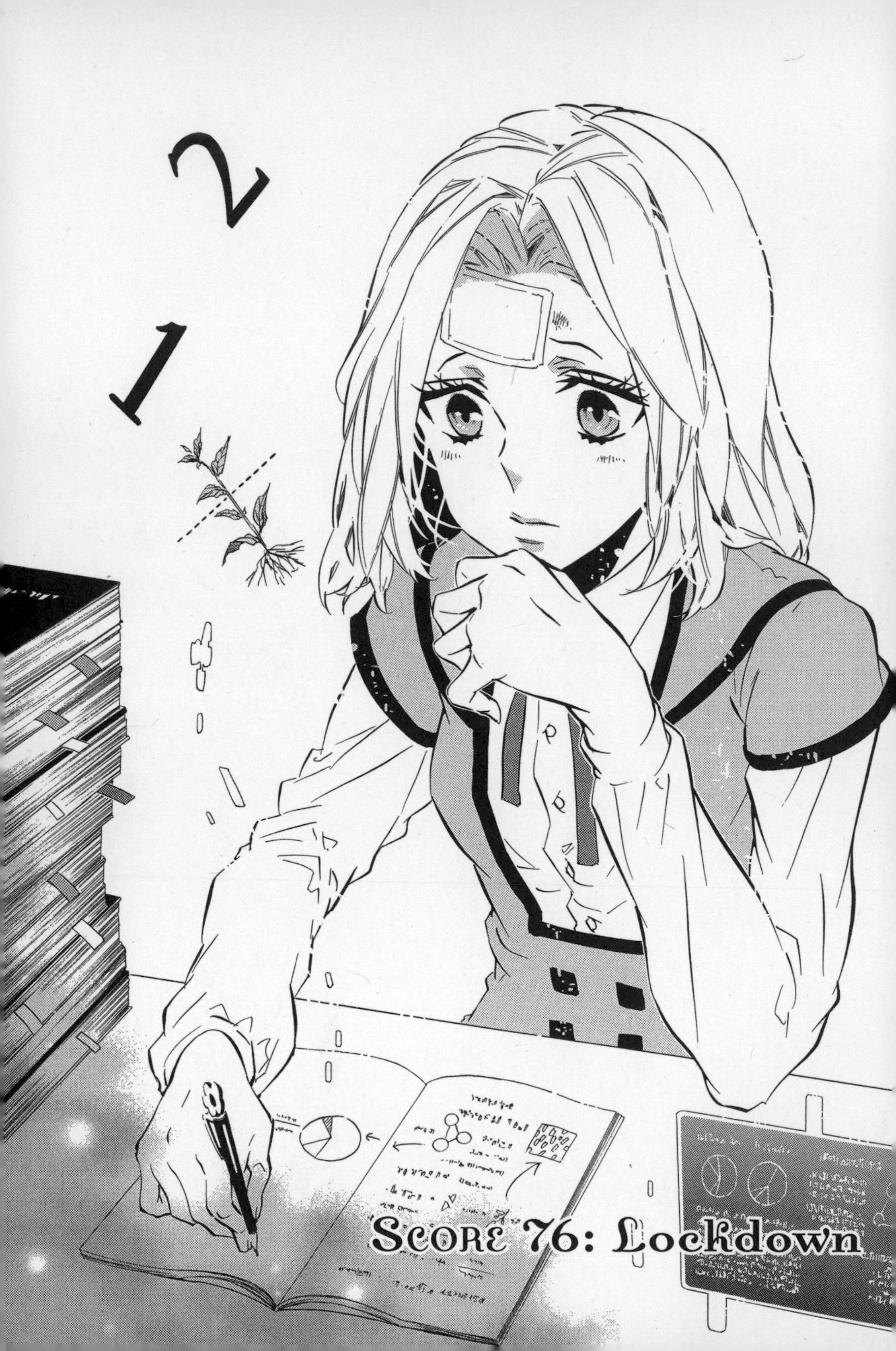
1
2
Score 76: Lockdown

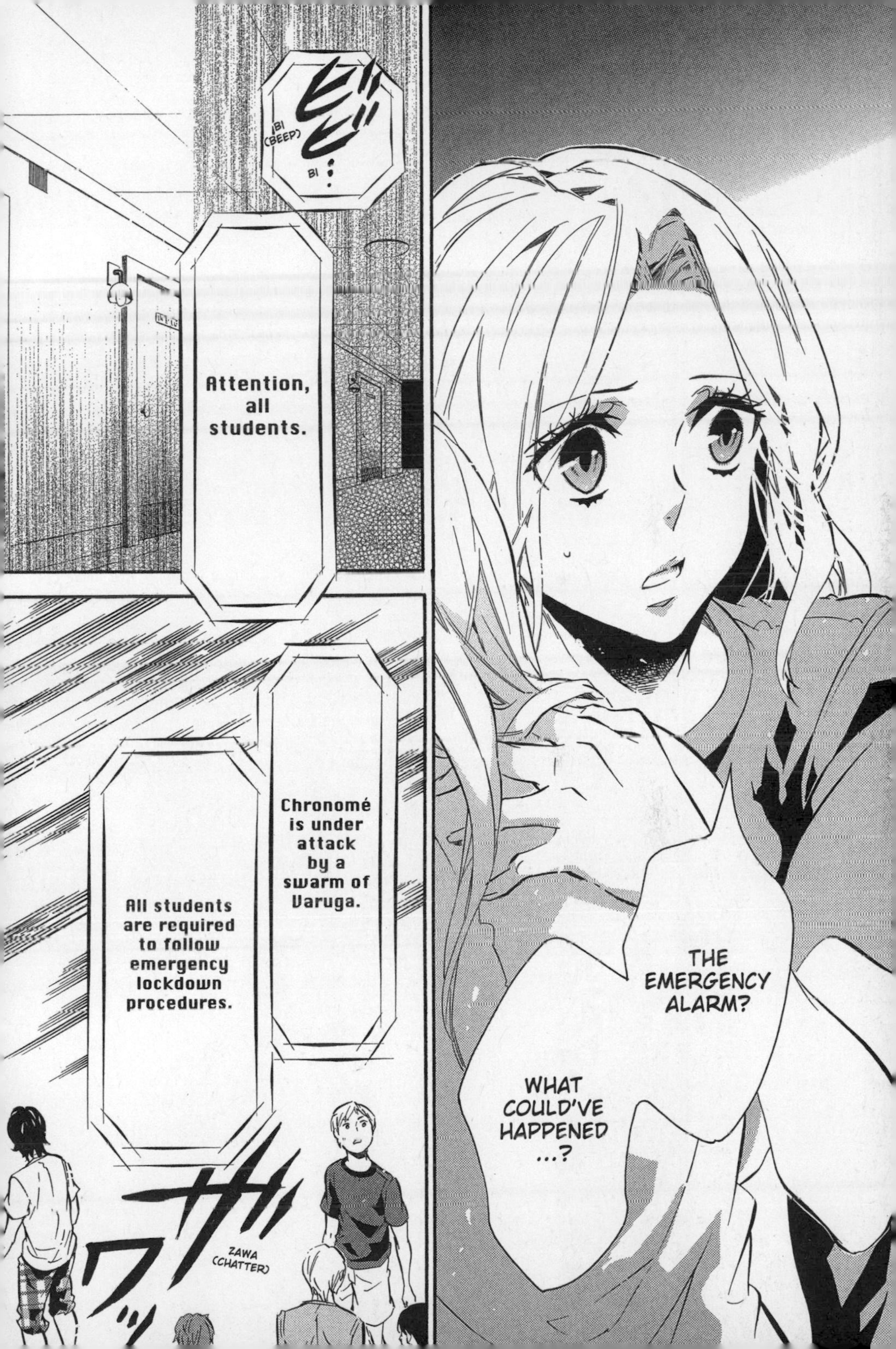
THE EMERGENCY ALARM?
WHAT COULD'VE HAPPENED ...?
BI (BEEP) BI
Attention, all students.
Chronomé is under attack by a swarm of Varuga.
All students are required to follow emergency lockdown procedures.
ZAWA (CHATTER)

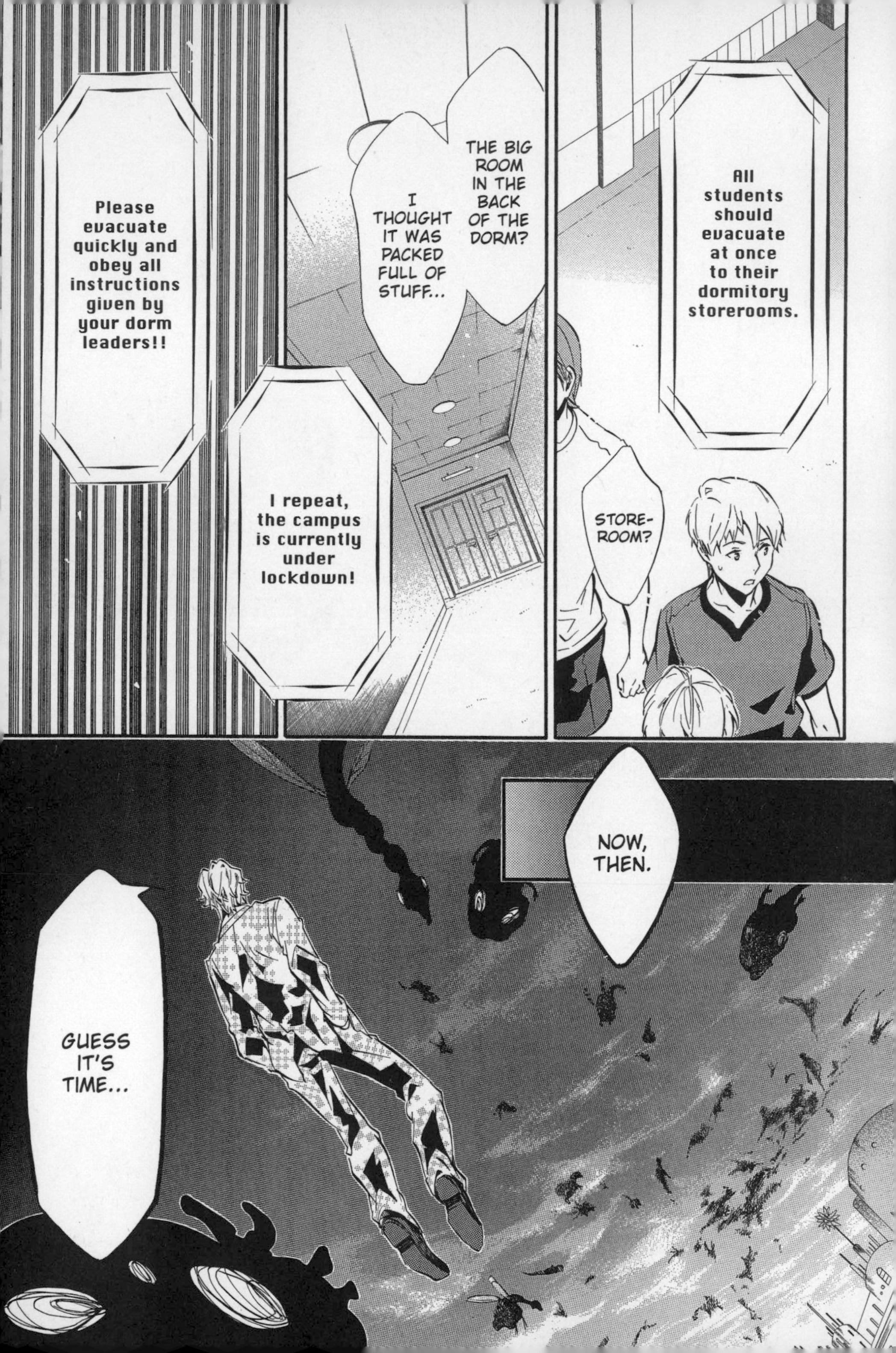
All students should evacuate at once to their dormitory storerooms.
STORE-ROOM?
THE BIG ROOM IN THE BACK OF THE DORM?
I THOUGHT IT WAS PACKED FULL OF STUFF...
I repeat, the campus is currently under lockdown!
Please evacuate quickly and obey all instructions given by your dorm leaders!!
NOW, THEN.
GUESS IT'S TIME...

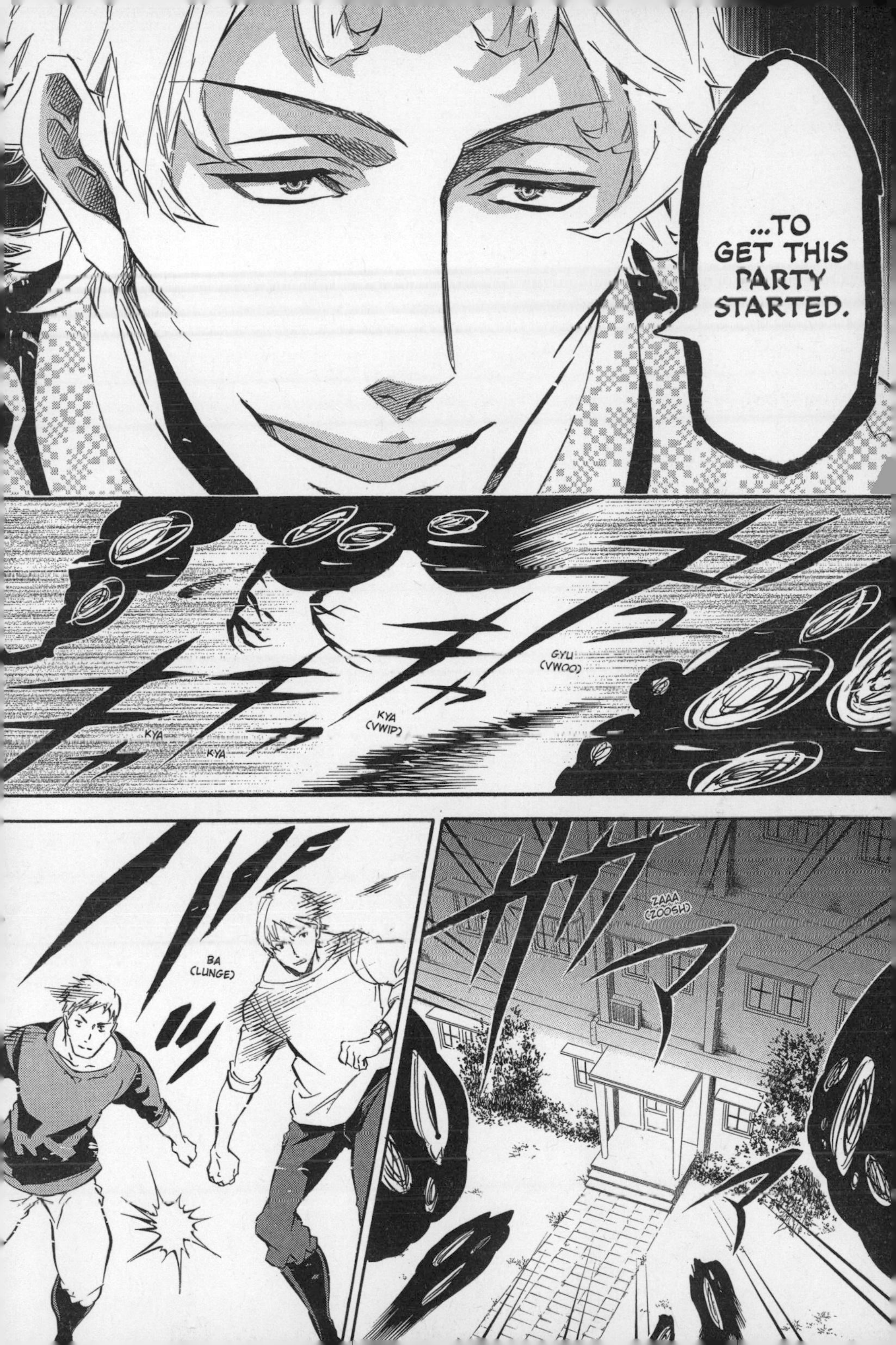
...TO GET THIS PARTY STARTED.
GYU (VWOO)
KYA (VWIP)
KYA
KYA
ZAAA (ZOOSH)
BA (LUNGE)

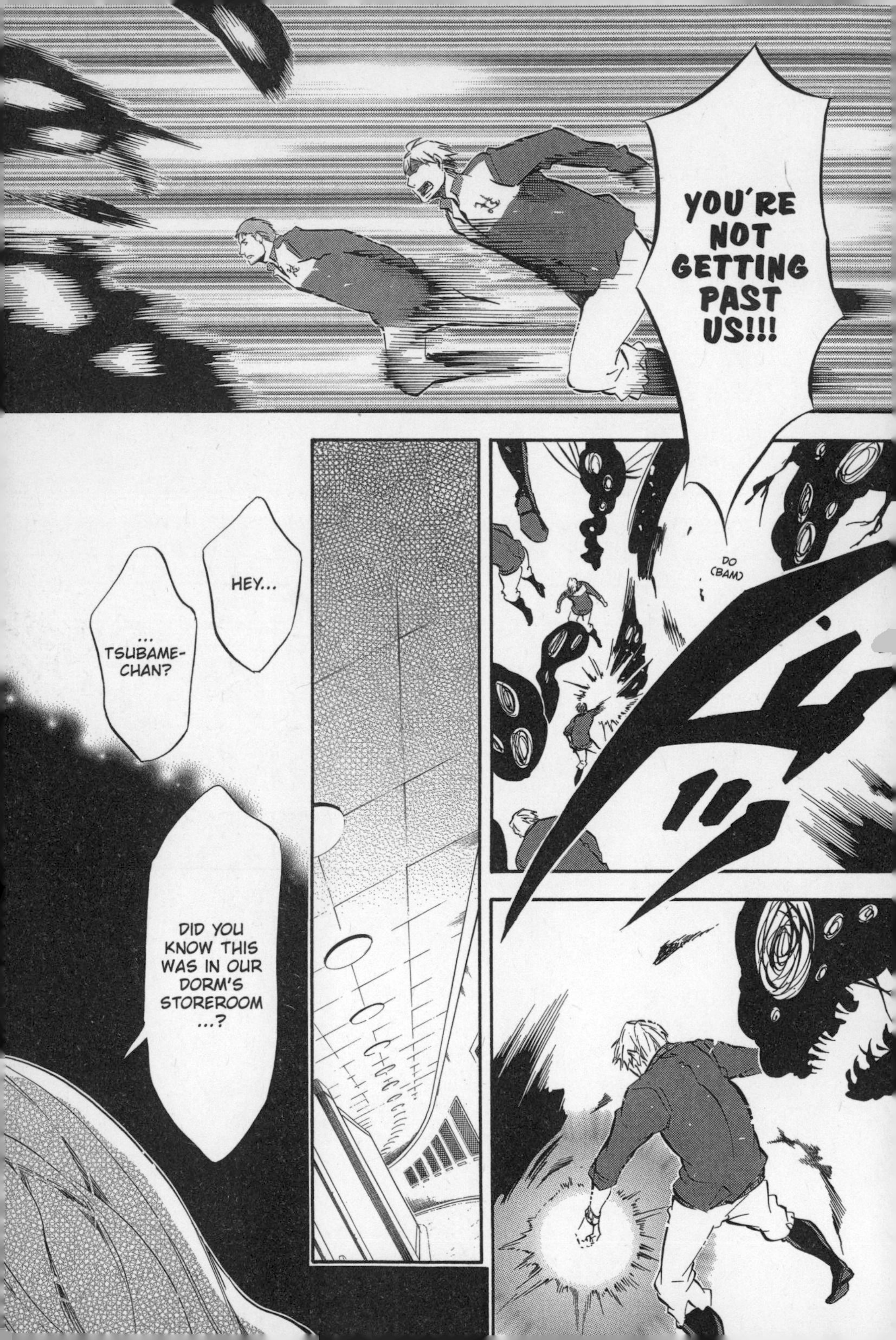

YOU'RE NOT GETTING PAST US!!!
DO (BAM)
HEY...
...TSUBAME-CHAN?
DID YOU KNOW THIS WAS IN OUR DORM'S STOREROOM ...?

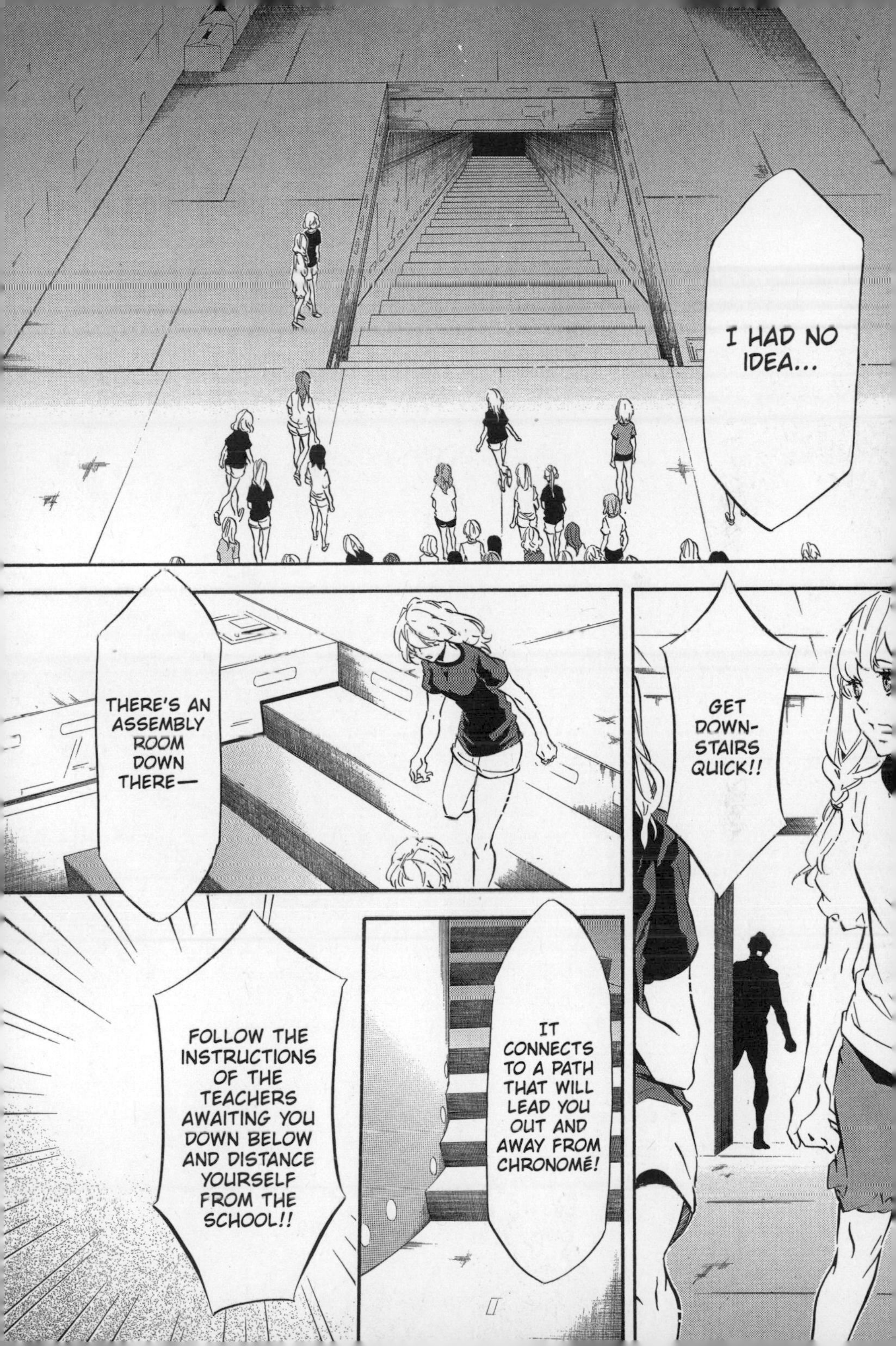
I HAD NO IDEA...
GET DOWN-STAIRS QUICK!!
THERE'S AN ASSEMBLY ROOM DOWN THERE—
IT CONNECTS TO A PATH THAT WILL LEAD YOU OUT AND AWAY FROM CHRONOMÉ!
FOLLOW THE INSTRUCTIONS OF THE TEACHERS AWAITING YOU DOWN BELOW AND DISTANCE YOURSELF FROM THE SCHOOL!!

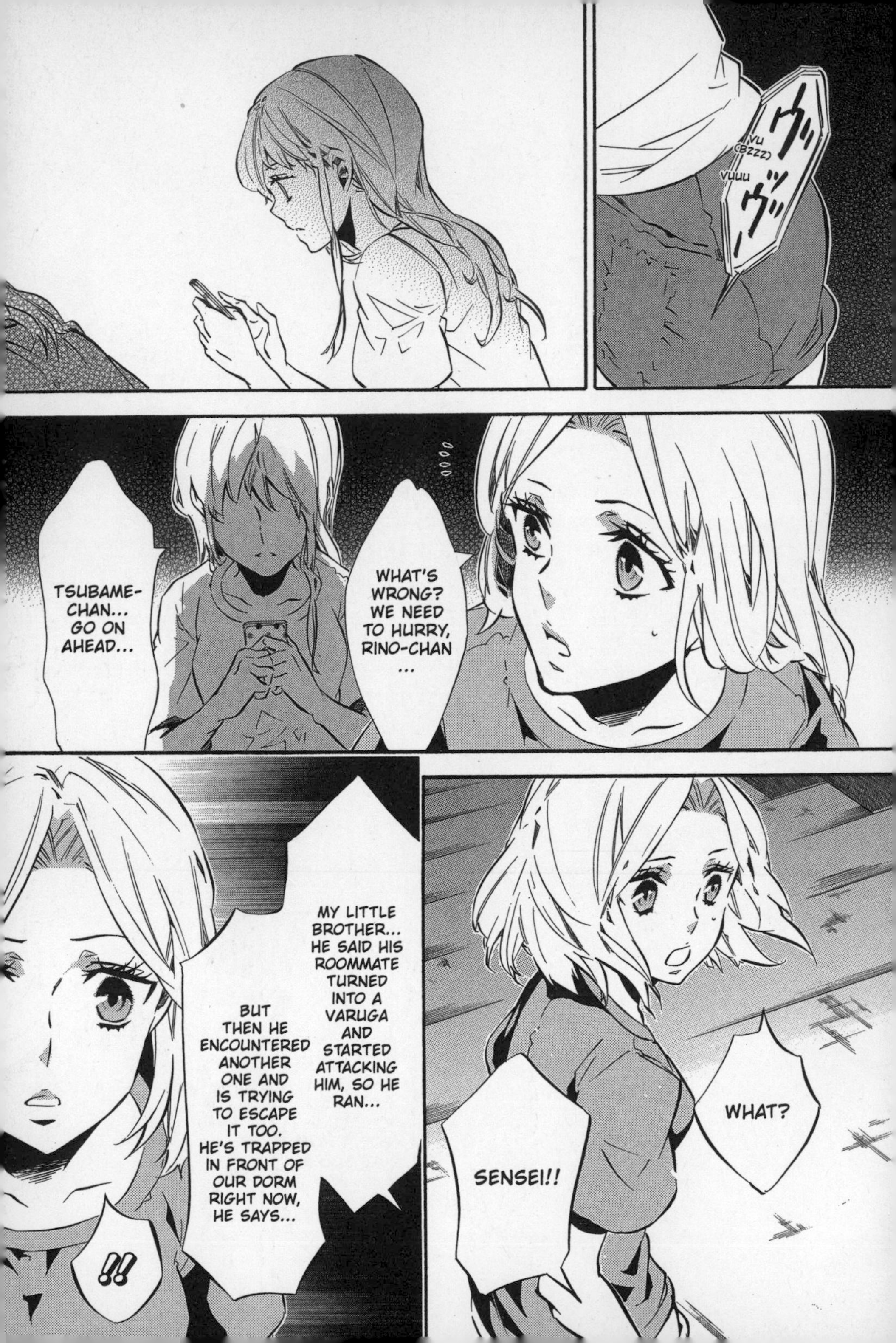
VU (BZZZ) VUUU
WHAT'S WRONG? WE NEED TO HURRY, RINO-CHAN...
TSUBAME-CHAN... GO ON AHEAD...
WHAT?
SENSEI!!
MY LITTLE BROTHER... HE SAID HIS ROOMMATE TURNED INTO A VARUGA AND STARTED ATTACKING HIM, SO HE RAN...
BUT THEN HE ENCOUNTERED ANOTHER ONE AND IS TRYING TO ESCAPE IT TOO. HE'S TRAPPED IN FRONT OF OUR DORM RIGHT NOW, HE SAYS...
!!

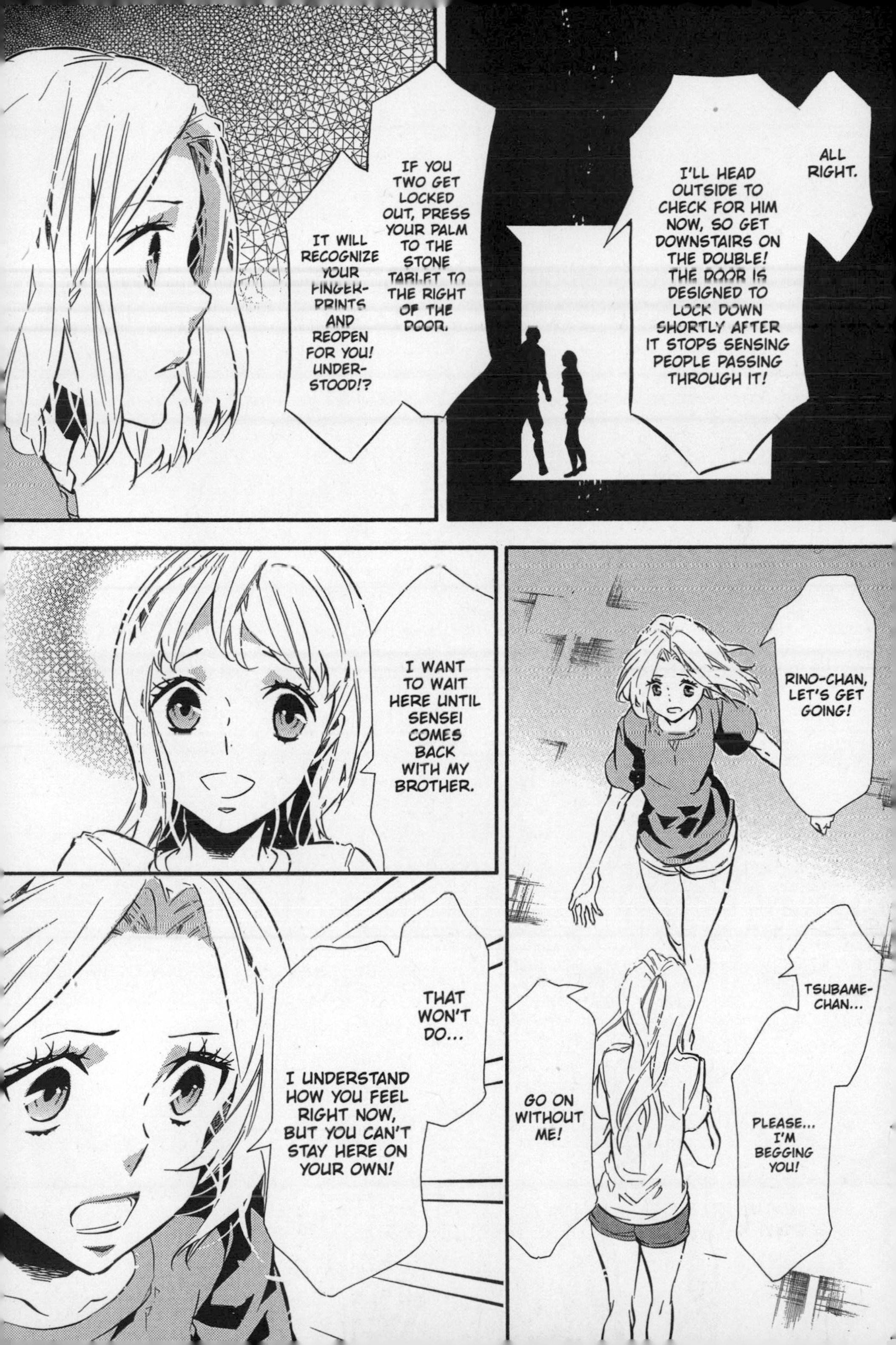
ALL RIGHT.
I'LL HEAD OUTSIDE TO CHECK FOR HIM NOW, SO GET DOWNSTAIRS ON THE DOUBLE! THE DOOR IS DESIGNED TO LOCK DOWN SHORTLY AFTER IT STOPS SENSING PEOPLE PASSING THROUGH IT!
IF YOU TWO GET LOCKED OUT, PRESS YOUR PALM TO THE STONE TABLET TO THE RIGHT OF THE DOOR.
IT WILL RECOGNIZE YOUR FINGER-PRINTS AND REOPEN FOR YOU! UNDER-STOOD!?
RINO-CHAN, LET'S GET GOING!
TSUBAME-CHAN...
PLEASE... I'M BEGGING YOU!
GO ON WITHOUT ME!
I WANT TO WAIT HERE UNTIL SENSEI COMES BACK WITH MY BROTHER.
THAT WON'T DO...
I UNDERSTAND HOW YOU FEEL RIGHT NOW, BUT YOU CAN'T STAY HERE ON YOUR OWN!

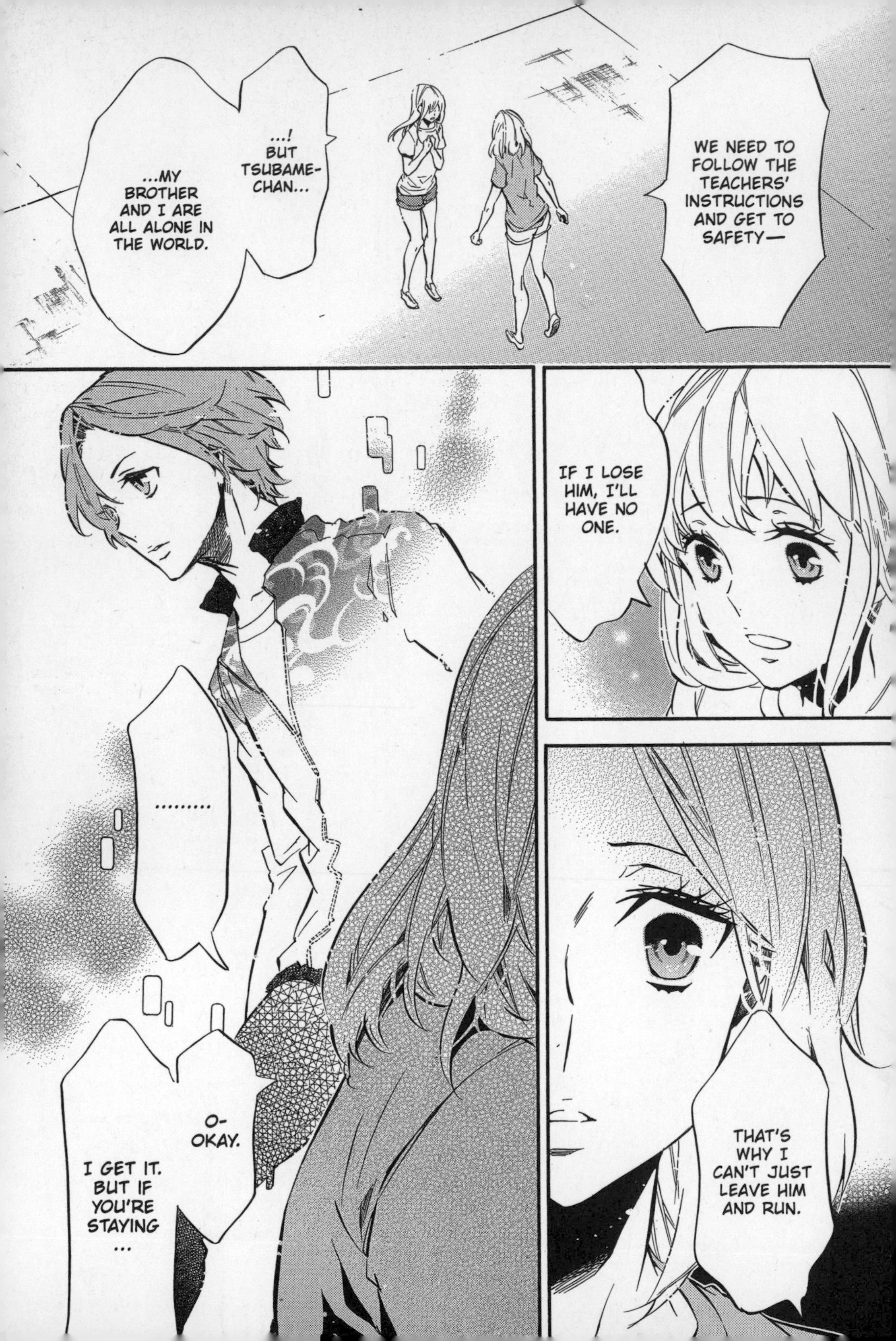
WE NEED TO FOLLOW THE TEACHERS' INSTRUCTIONS AND GET TO SAFETY—
...! BUT TSUBAME-CHAN...
...MY BROTHER AND I ARE ALL ALONE IN THE WORLD.
IF I LOSE HIM, I'LL HAVE NO ONE.
THAT'S WHY I CAN'T JUST LEAVE HIM AND RUN.
....
O-OKAY.
I GET IT. BUT IF YOU'RE STAYING ...

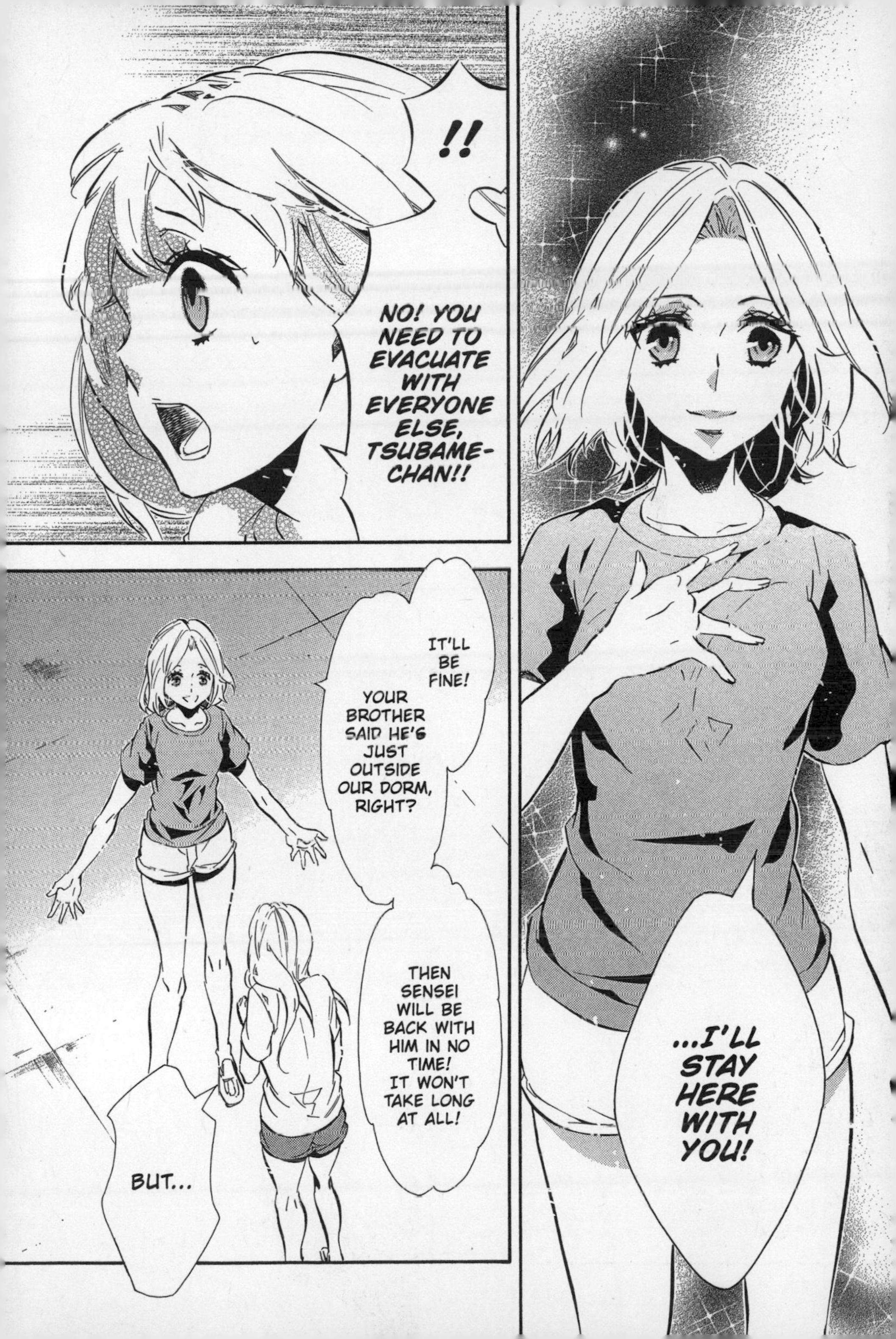
...I'LL STAY HERE WITH YOU!
!!
NO! YOU NEED TO EVACUATE WITH EVERYONE ELSE, TSUBAME-CHAN!!
IT'LL BE FINE!
YOUR BROTHER SAID HE'S JUST OUTSIDE OUR DORM, RIGHT?
THEN SENSEI WILL BE BACK WITH HIM IN NO TIME! IT WON'T TAKE LONG AT ALL!
BUT...

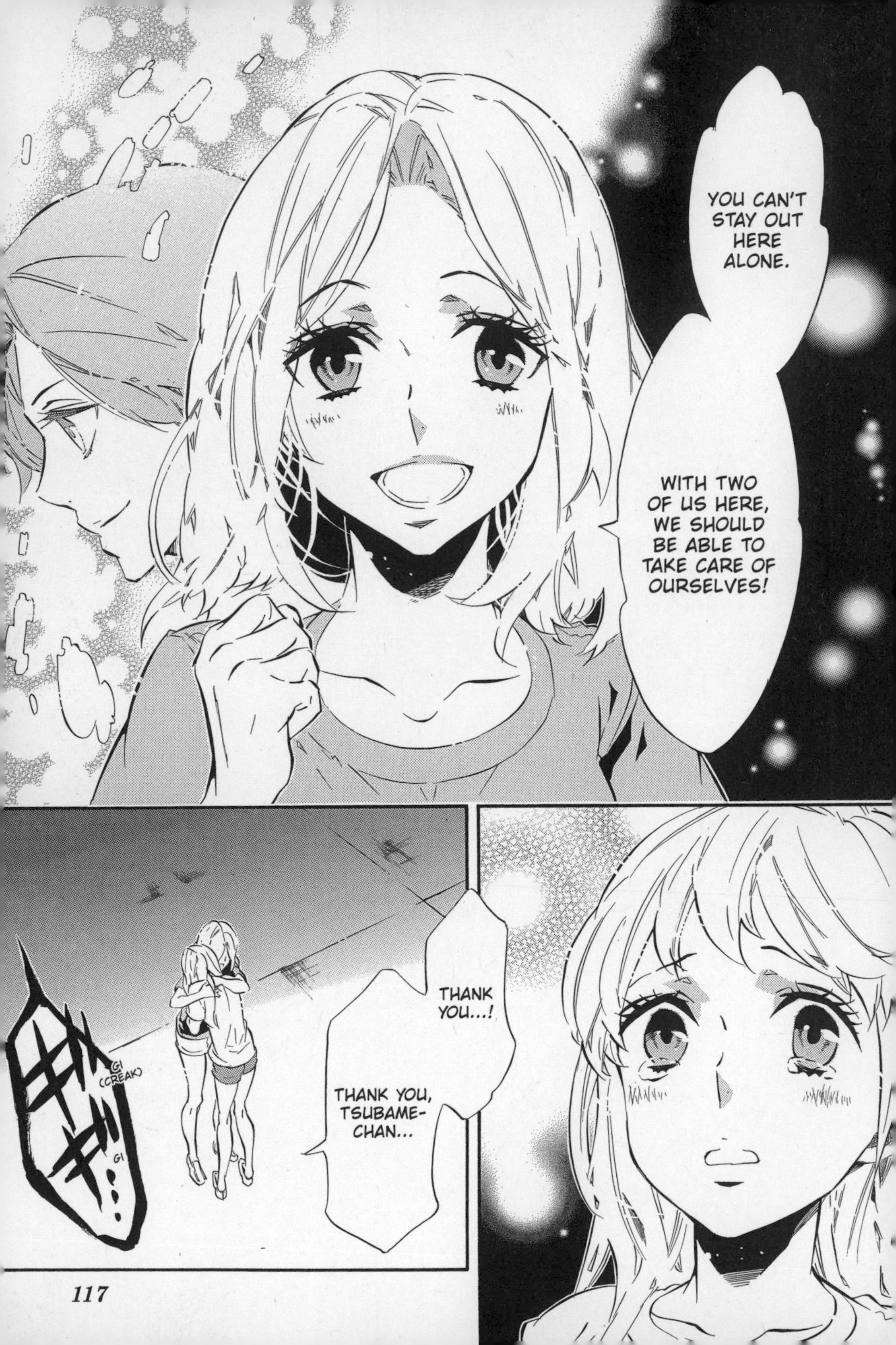
YOU CAN'T STAY OUT HERE ALONE.
WITH TWO OF US HERE, WE SHOULD BE ABLE TO TAKE CARE OF OURSELVES!
THANK YOU...!
THANK YOU, TSUBAME-CHAN...
GI (CREAK)
GI

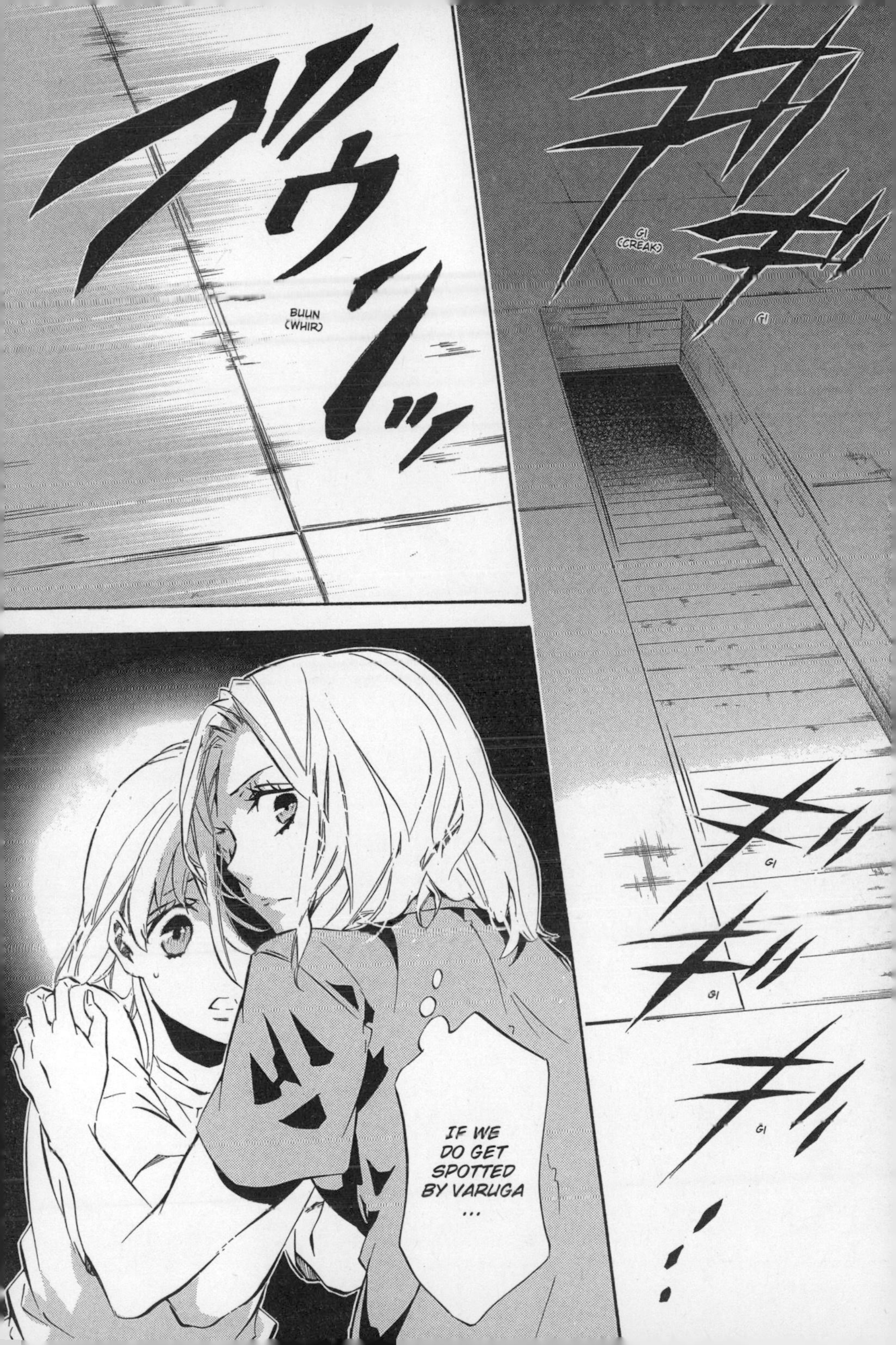
GI (CREAK)
GI
GI
GI
GI
BUUN (WHIR)
IF WE DO GET SPOTTED BY VARUGA...

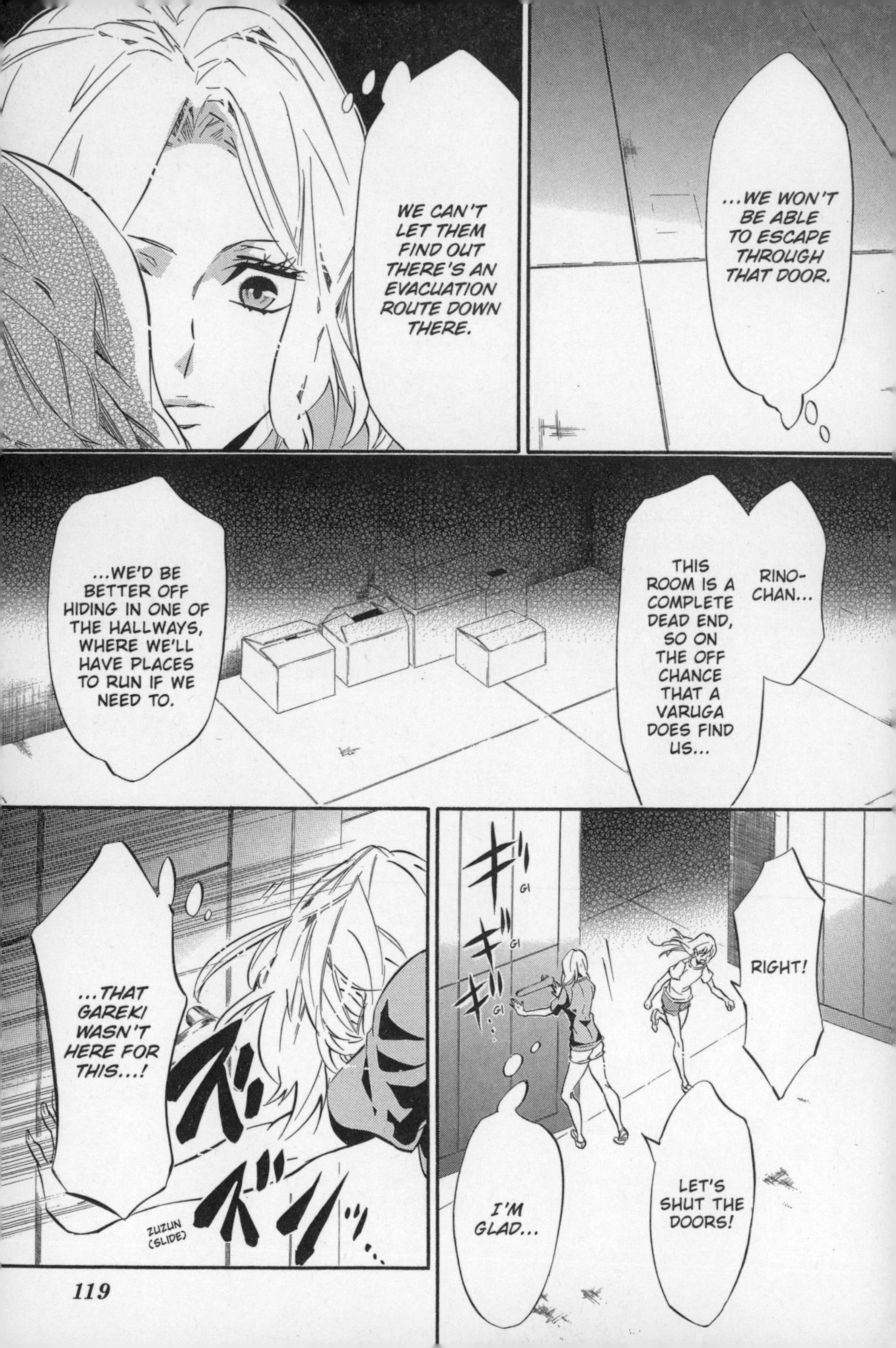
...WE WON'T BE ABLE TO ESCAPE THROUGH THAT DOOR.
WE CAN'T LET THEM FIND OUT THERE'S AN EVACUATION ROUTE DOWN THERE.
RINO-CHAN...
THIS ROOM IS A COMPLETE DEAD END, SO ON THE OFF CHANCE THAT A VARUGA DOES FIND US...
...WE'D BE BETTER OFF HIDING IN ONE OF THE HALLWAYS, WHERE WE'LL HAVE PLACES TO RUN IF WE NEED TO.
RIGHT!
GI
GI
GI
LET'S SHUT THE DOORS!
I'M GLAD...
...THAT GAREKI WASN'T HERE FOR THIS...!
ZUZUN (SLIDE)

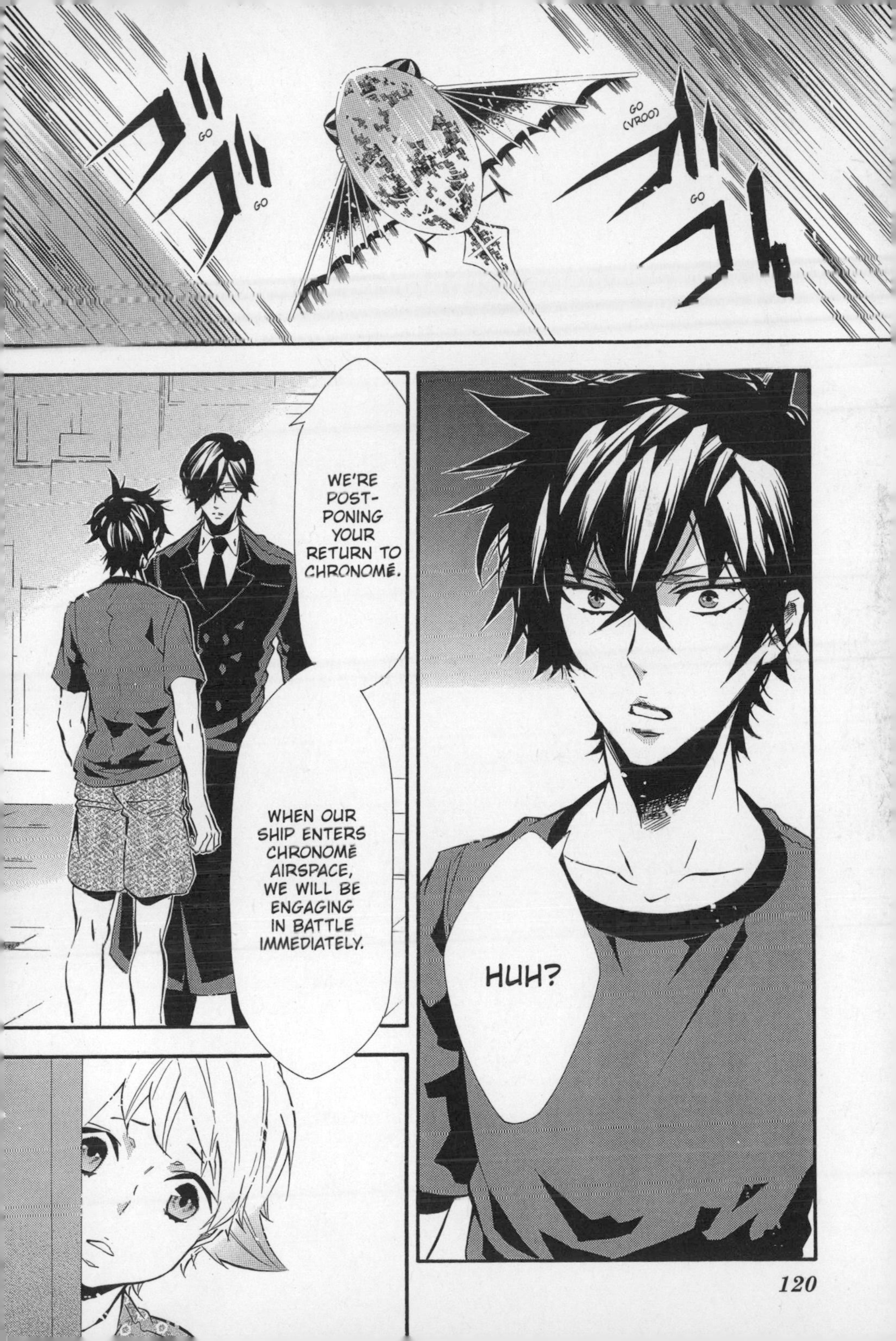
GO
(VROO)
GO
GO
GO
HUH?
WE'RE POST-PONING YOUR RETURN TO CHRONOMÉ.
WHEN OUR SHIP ENTERS CHRONOMÉ AIRSPACE, WE WILL BE ENGAGING IN BATTLE IMMEDIATELY.

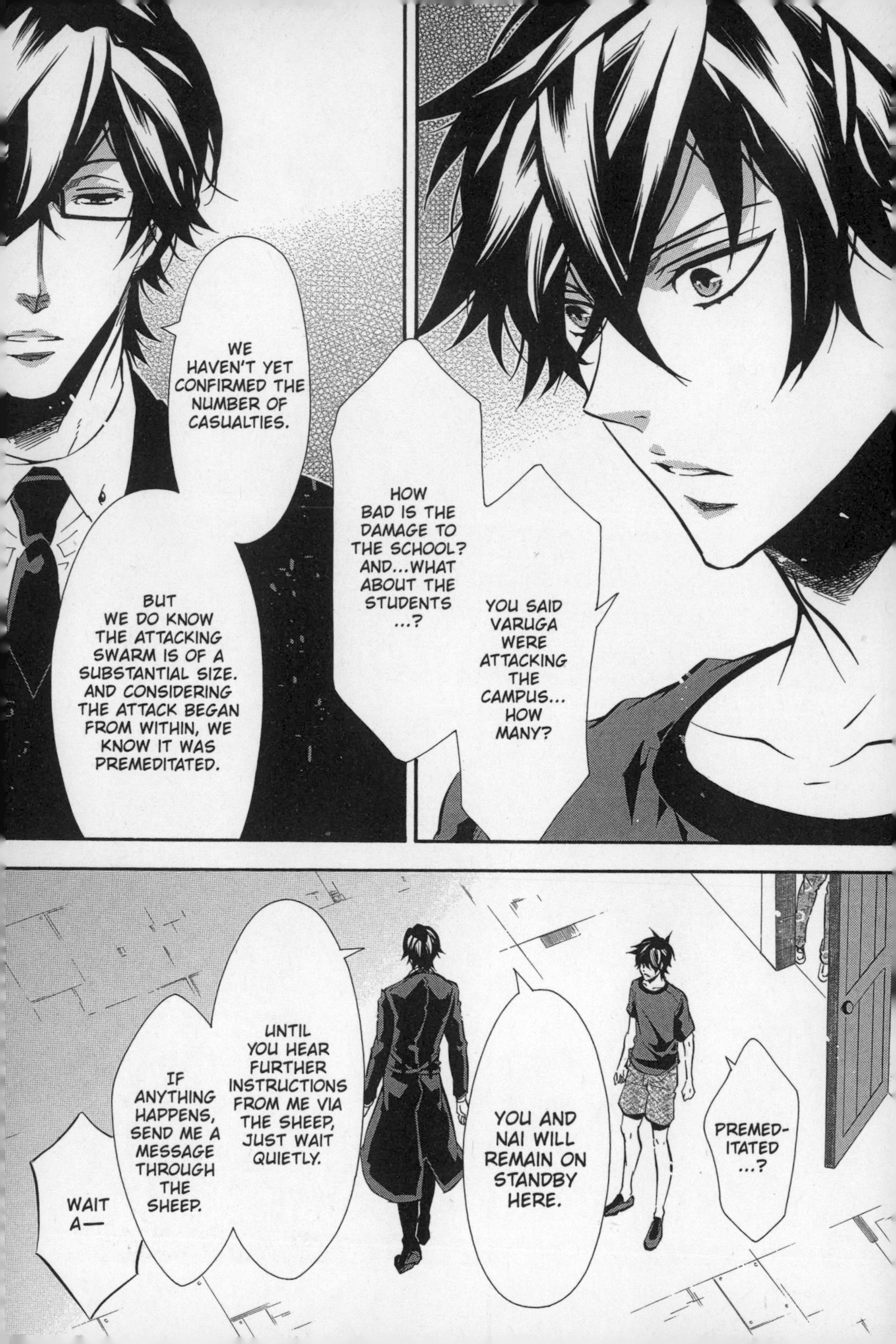
YOU SAID VARUGA WERE ATTACKING THE CAMPUS... HOW MANY?
HOW BAD IS THE DAMAGE TO THE SCHOOL? AND...WHAT ABOUT THE STUDENTS ...?
WE HAVEN'T YET CONFIRMED THE NUMBER OF CASUALTIES.
BUT WE DO KNOW THE ATTACKING SWARM IS OF A SUBSTANTIAL SIZE. AND CONSIDERING THE ATTACK BEGAN FROM WITHIN, WE KNOW IT WAS PREMEDITATED.
PREMED-ITATED ...?
YOU AND NAI WILL REMAIN ON STANDBY HERE.
UNTIL YOU HEAR FURTHER INSTRUCTIONS FROM ME VIA THE SHEEP, JUST WAIT QUIETLY.
IF ANYTHING HAPPENS, SEND ME A MESSAGE THROUGH THE SHEEP.
WAIT A—

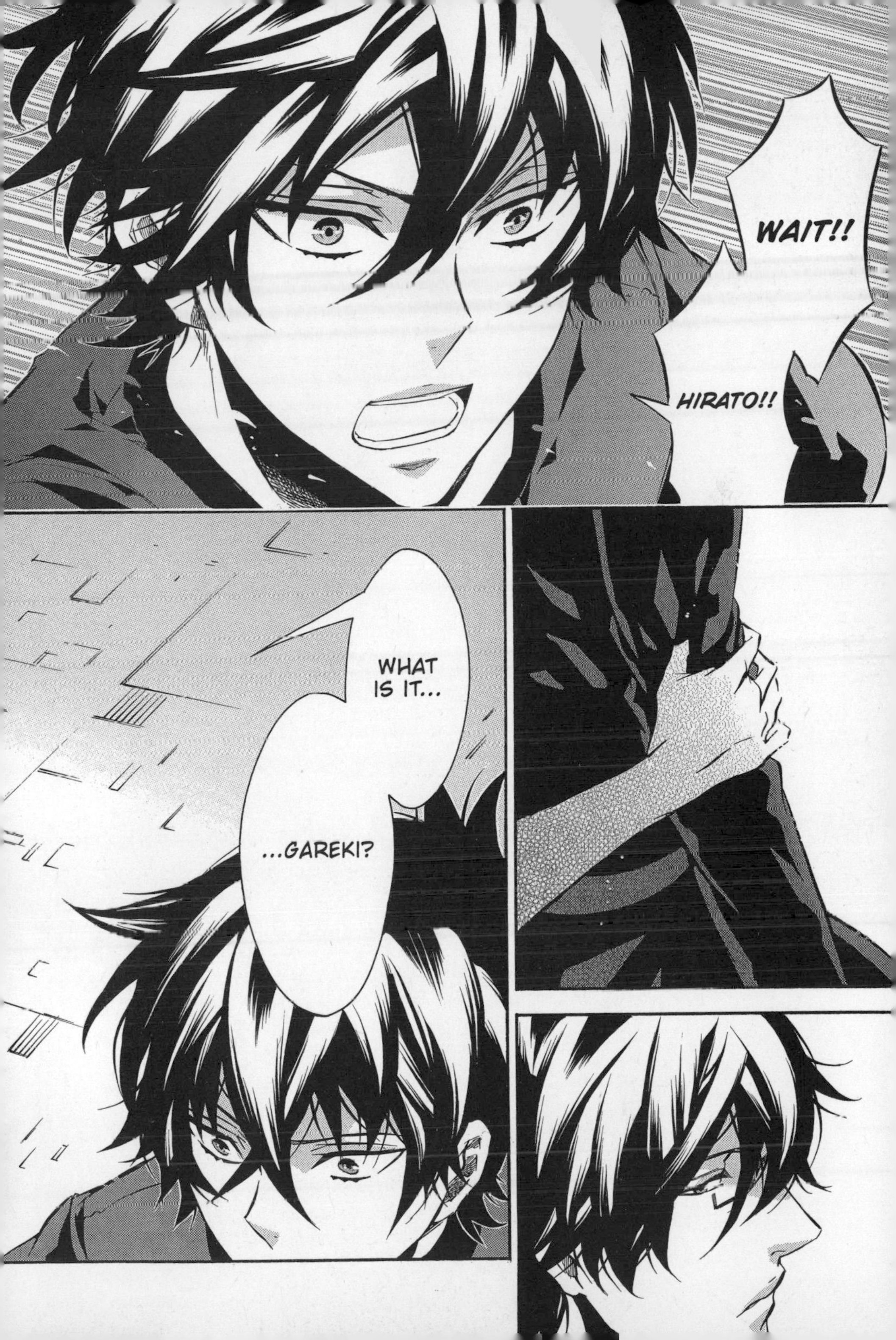
WAIT!!
HIRATO!!
WHAT IS IT...
...GAREKI?

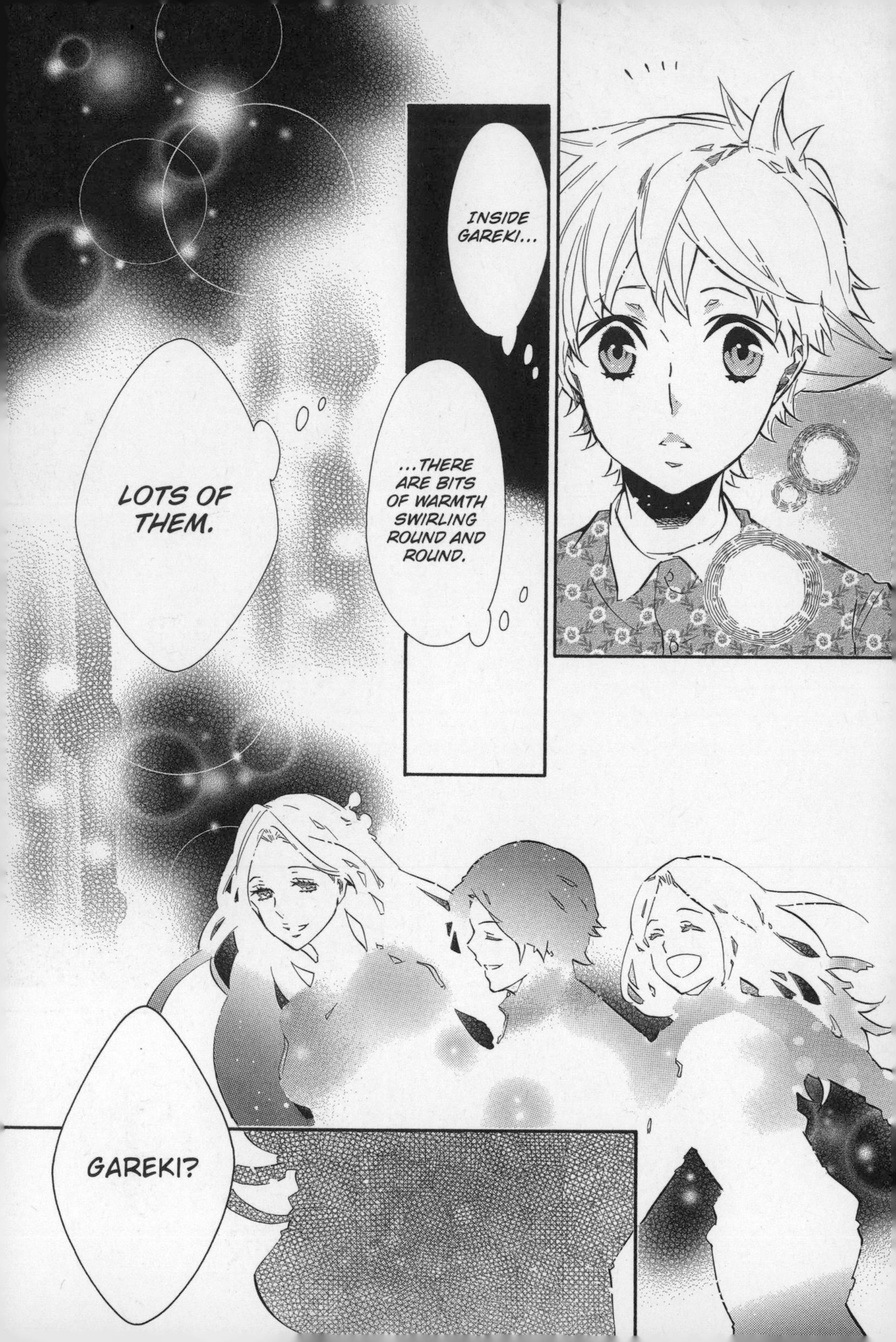
INSIDE GAREKI...
...THERE ARE BITS OF WARMTH SWIRLING ROUND AND ROUND.
LOTS OF THEM.
GAREKI?

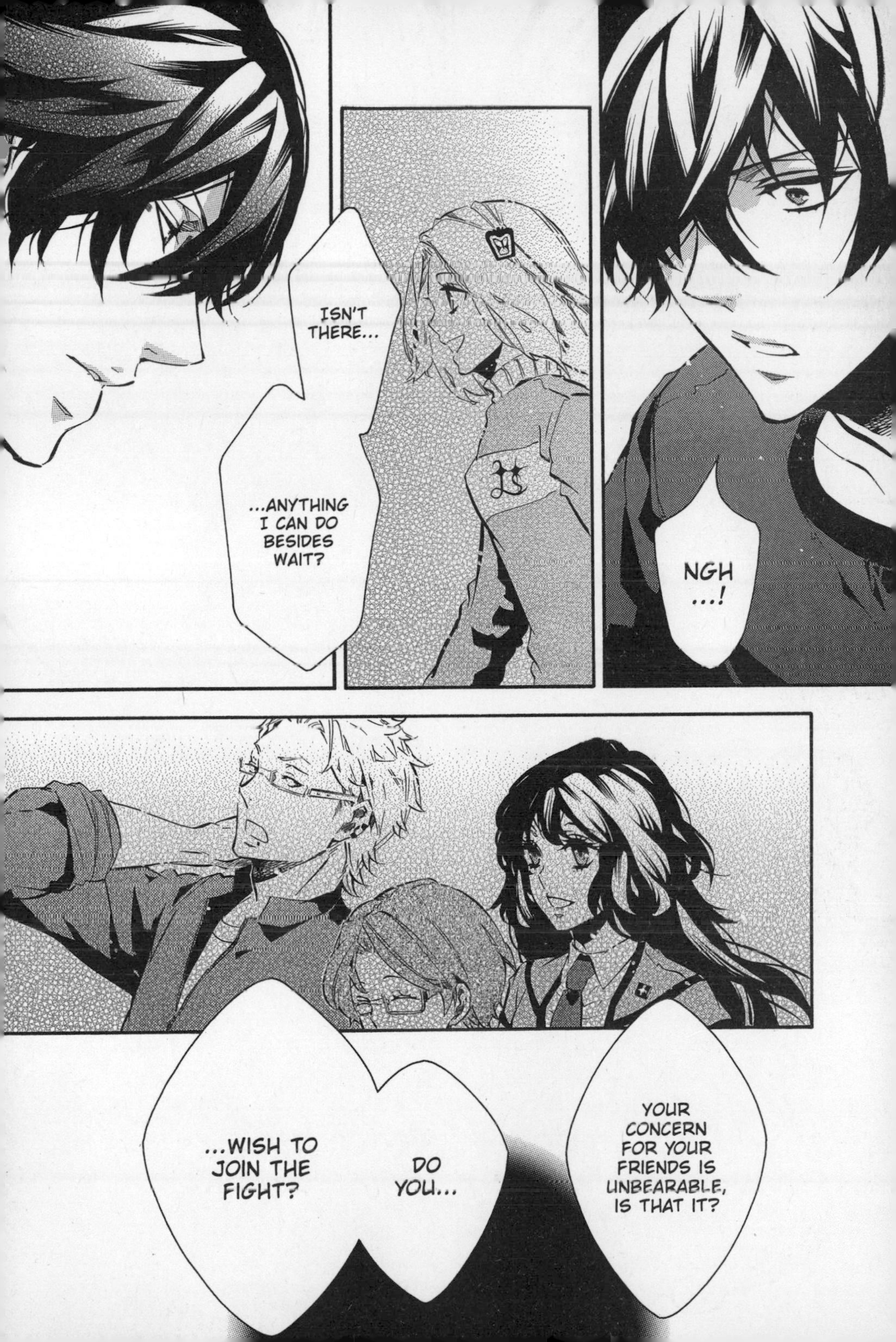
NGH ...!
ISN'T THERE...
...ANYTHING I CAN DO BESIDES WAIT?
YOUR CONCERN FOR YOUR FRIENDS IS UNBEARABLE, IS THAT IT?
DO YOU...
...WISH TO JOIN THE FIGHT?

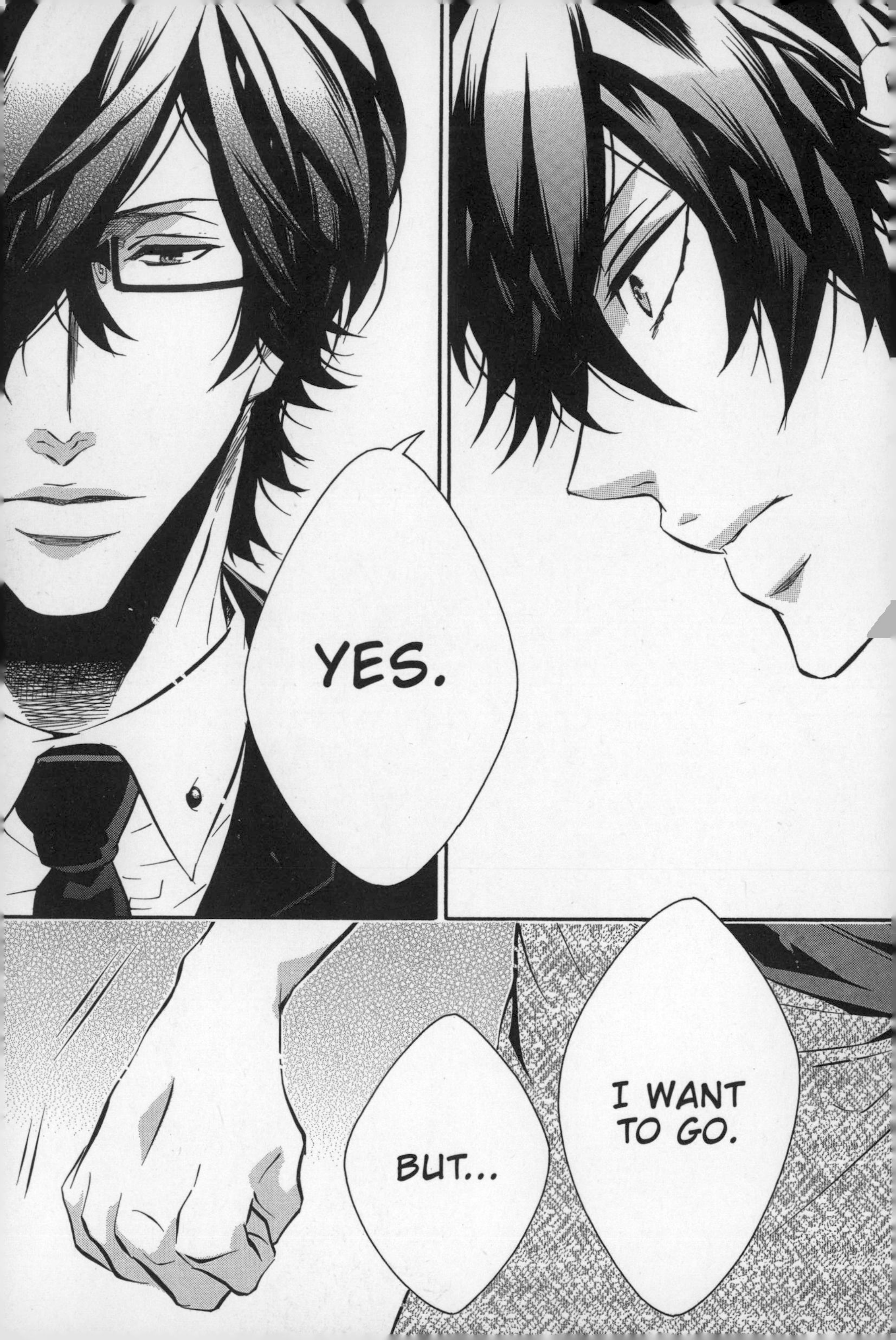
YES.
I WANT TO GO.
BUT...

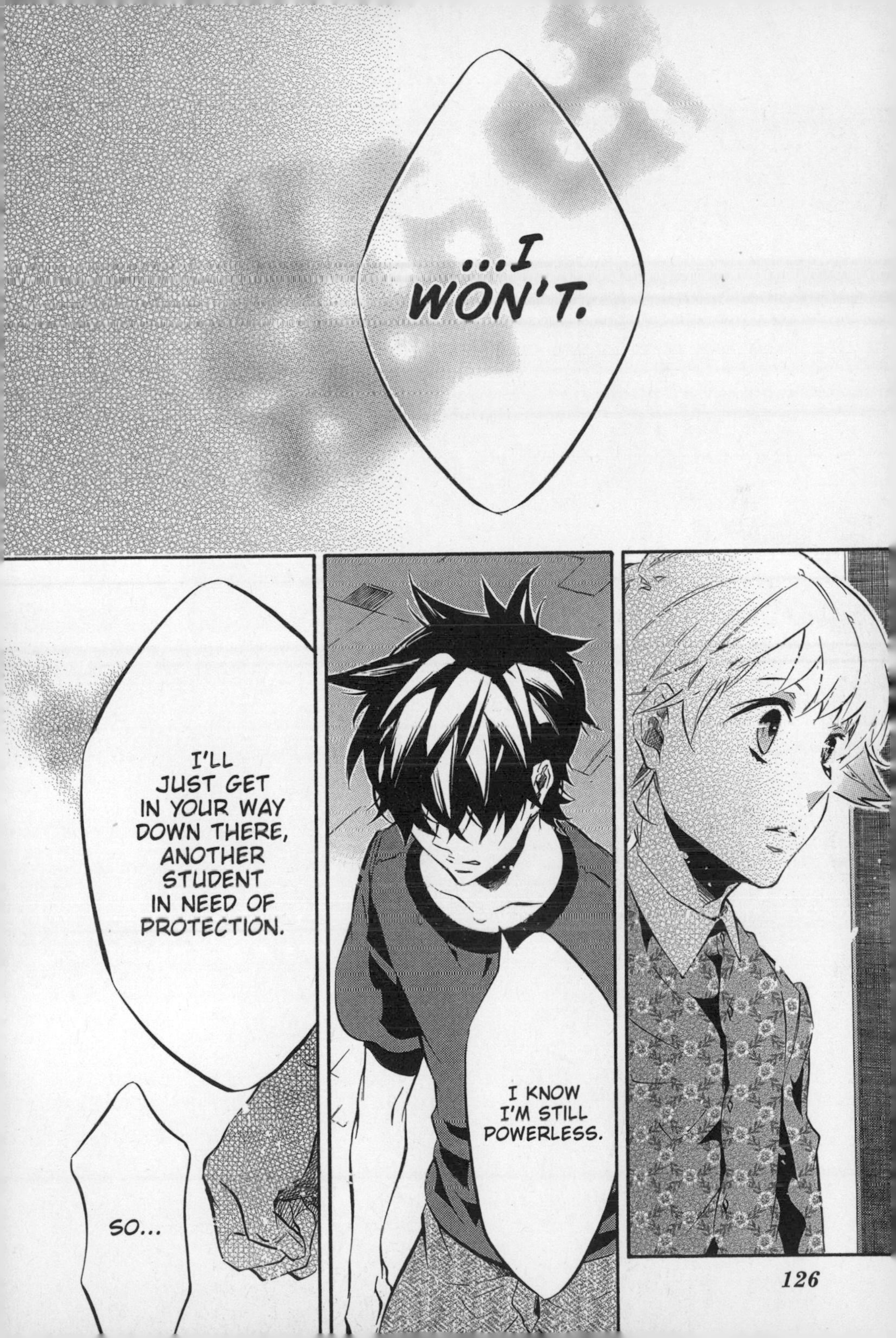
...I WON'T.
I KNOW I'M STILL POWERLESS.
I'LL JUST GET IN YOUR WAY DOWN THERE, ANOTHER STUDENT IN NEED OF PROTECTION.
SO...

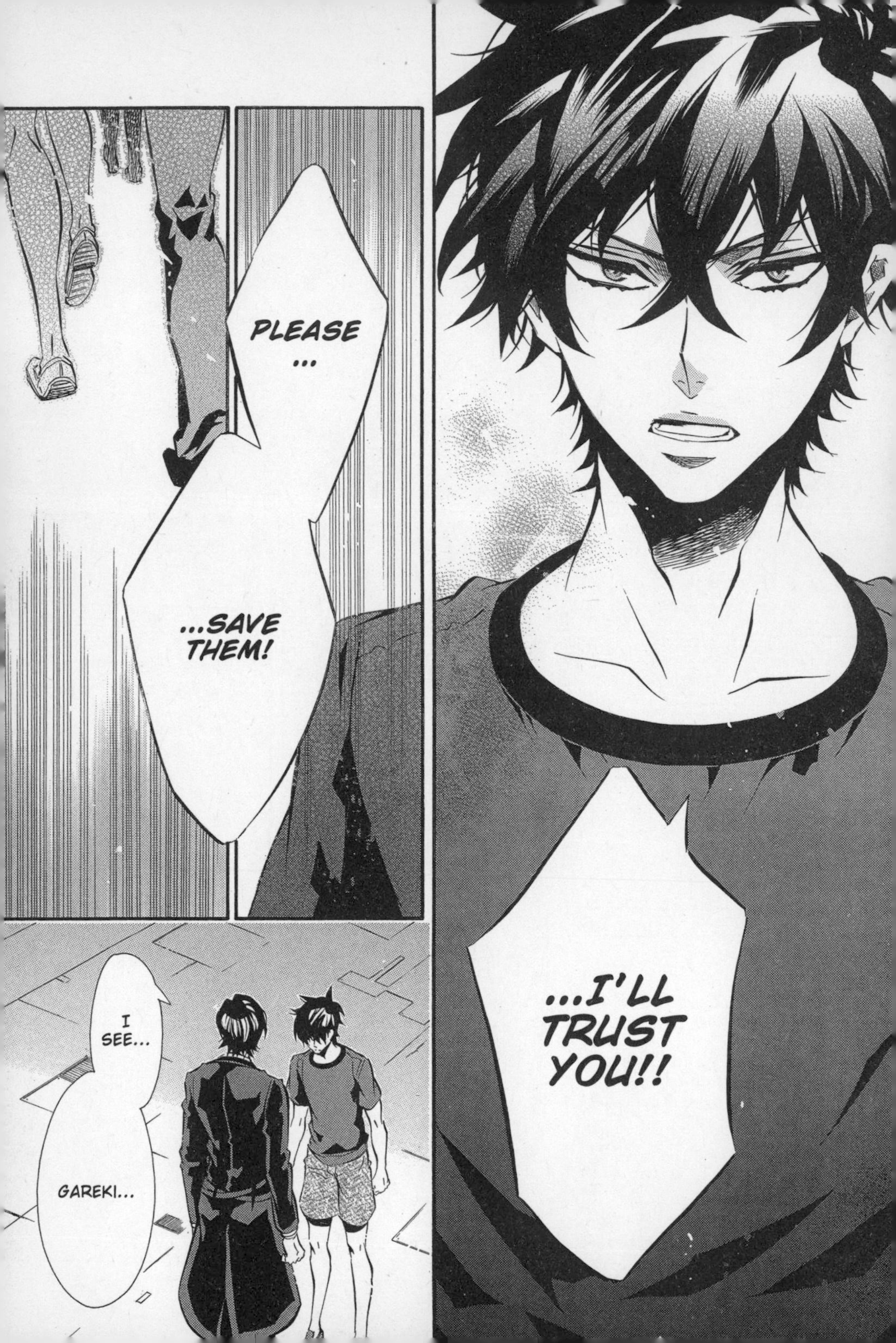
...I'LL TRUST YOU!!
PLEASE ...
...SAVE THEM!
I SEE...
GAREKI...

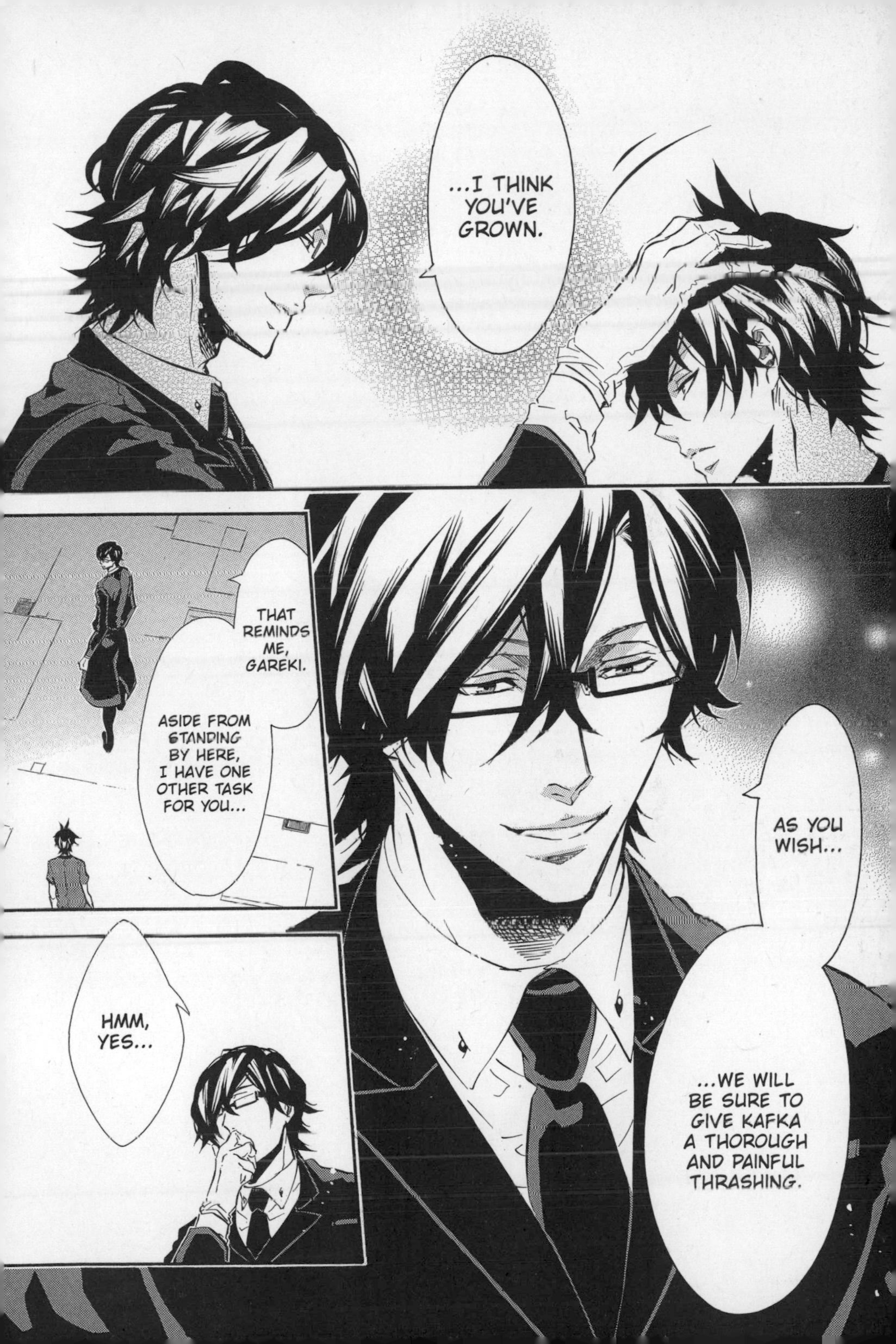
...I THINK YOU'VE GROWN.
AS YOU WISH...
...WE WILL BE SURE TO GIVE KAFKA A THOROUGH AND PAINFUL THRASHING.
THAT REMINDS ME, GAREKI.
ASIDE FROM STANDING BY HERE, I HAVE ONE OTHER TASK FOR YOU...
HMM, YES...

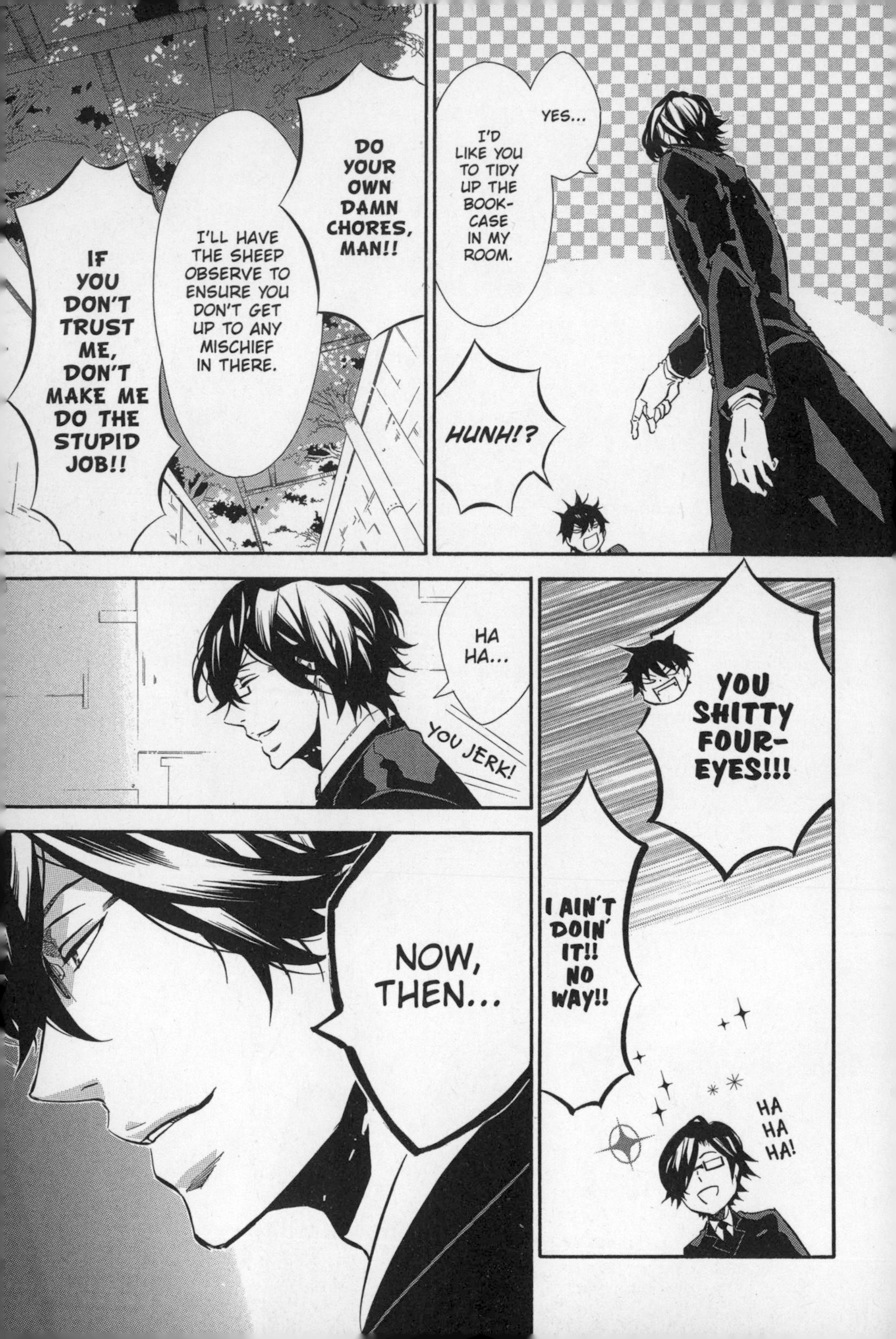
YES...
I'D LIKE YOU TO TIDY UP THE BOOK-CASE IN MY ROOM.
HUNH!?
DO YOUR OWN DAMN CHORES, MAN!!
I'LL HAVE THE SHEEP OBSERVE TO ENSURE YOU DON'T GET UP TO ANY MISCHIEF IN THERE.
IF YOU DON'T TRUST ME, DON'T MAKE ME DO THE STUPID JOB!!
YOU SHITTY FOUR-EYES!!!
I AIN'T DOIN' IT!! NO WAY!!
HA HA HA!
HA HA...
YOU JERK!
NOW, THEN...

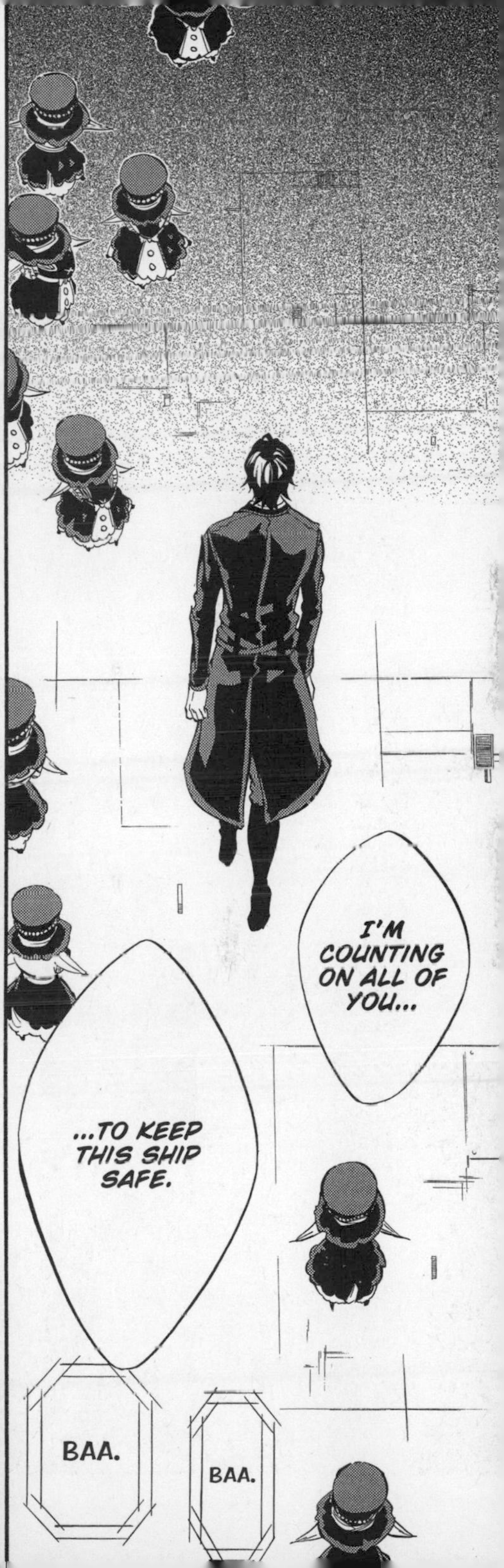
I'M COUNTING ON ALL OF YOU...
...TO KEEP THIS SHIP SAFE.
BAA.
BAA.
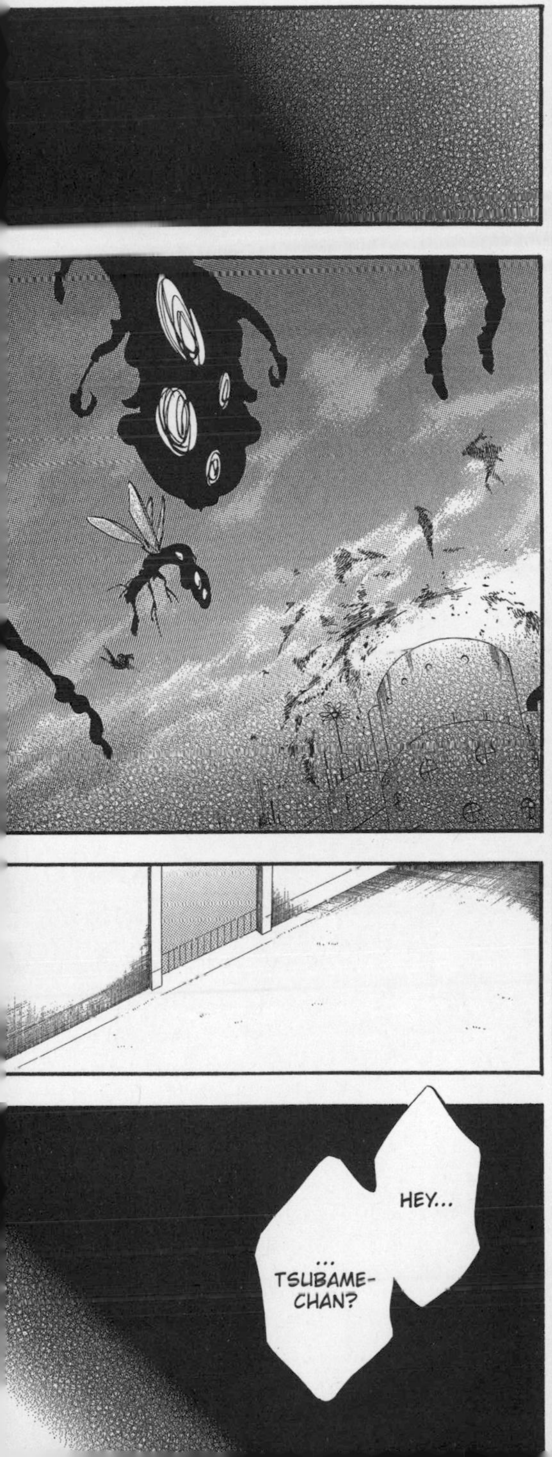
HEY...
...TSUBAME-CHAN?

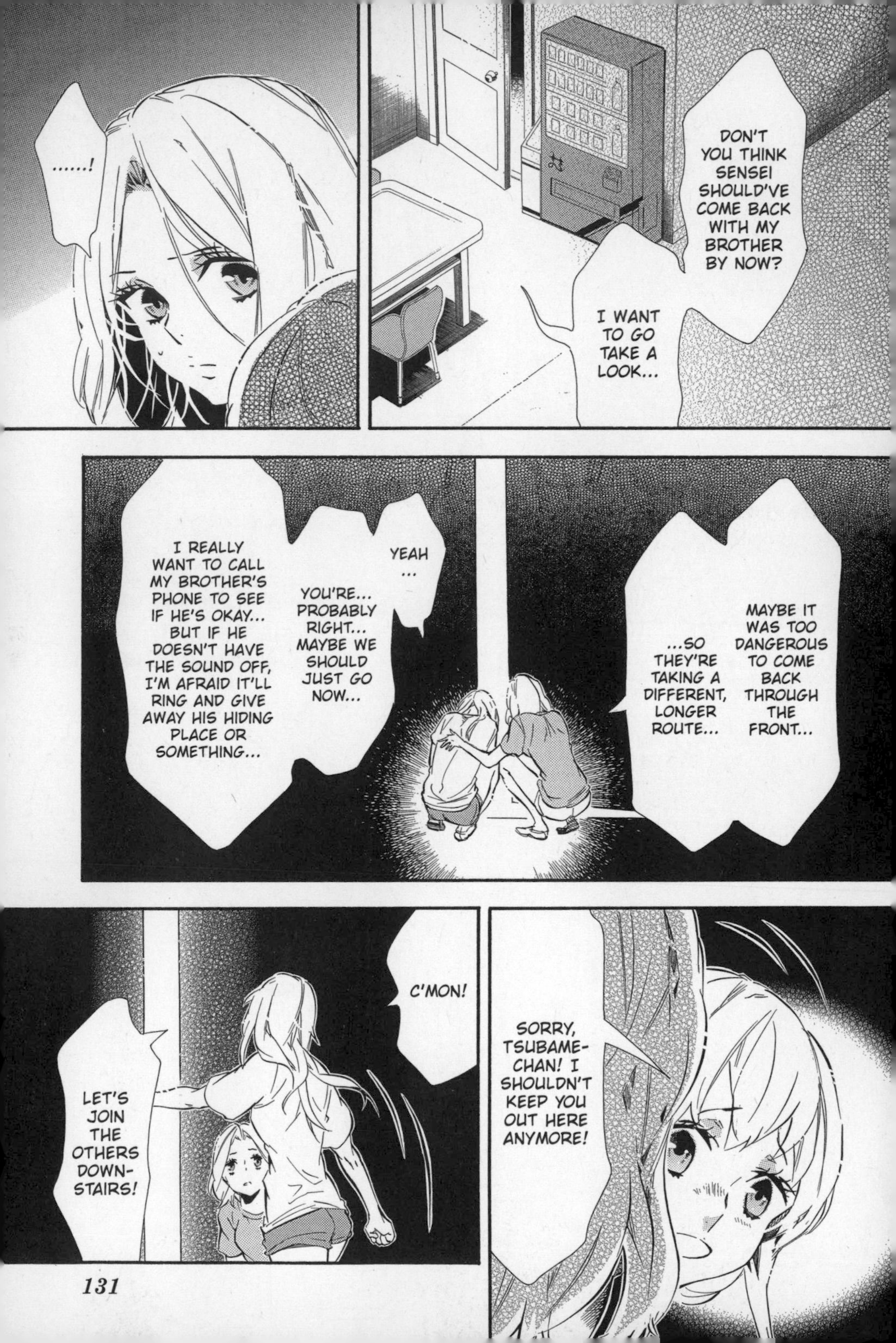
DON'T YOU THINK SENSEI SHOULD'VE COME BACK WITH MY BROTHER BY NOW?
I WANT TO GO TAKE A LOOK...
......!
MAYBE IT WAS TOO DANGEROUS TO COME BACK THROUGH THE FRONT...
...SO THEY'RE TAKING A DIFFERENT, LONGER ROUTE...
YEAH...
YOU'RE... PROBABLY RIGHT... MAYBE WE SHOULD JUST GO NOW...
I REALLY WANT TO CALL MY BROTHER'S PHONE TO SEE IF HE'S OKAY... BUT IF HE DOESN'T HAVE THE SOUND OFF, I'M AFRAID IT'LL RING AND GIVE AWAY HIS HIDING PLACE OR SOMETHING...
SORRY, TSUBAME-CHAN! I SHOULDN'T KEEP YOU OUT HERE ANYMORE!
C'MON!
LET'S JOIN THE OTHERS DOWN-STAIRS!

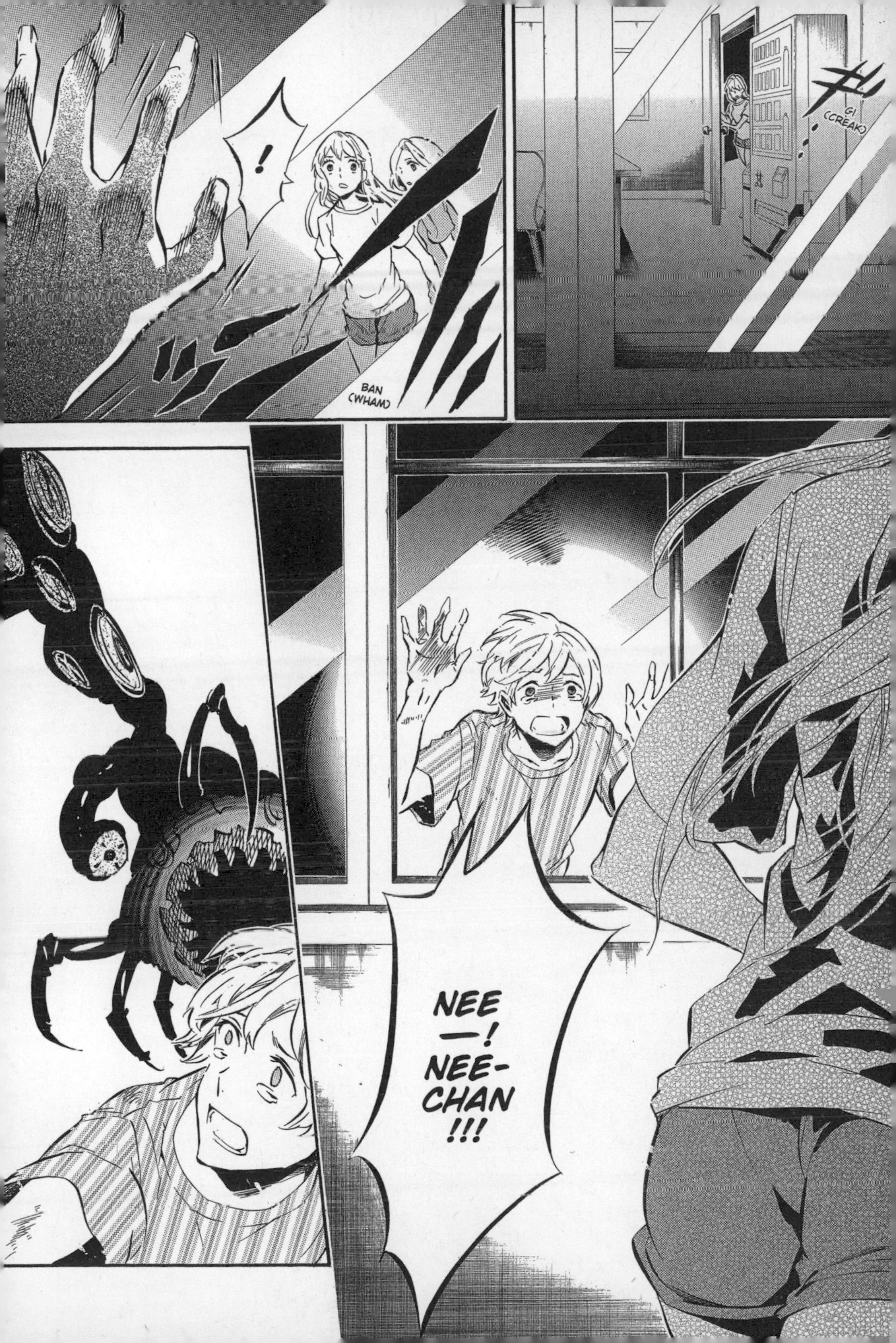
GI
(CREAK)
!
BAN
(WHAM)
NEE—! NEE-CHAN!!!

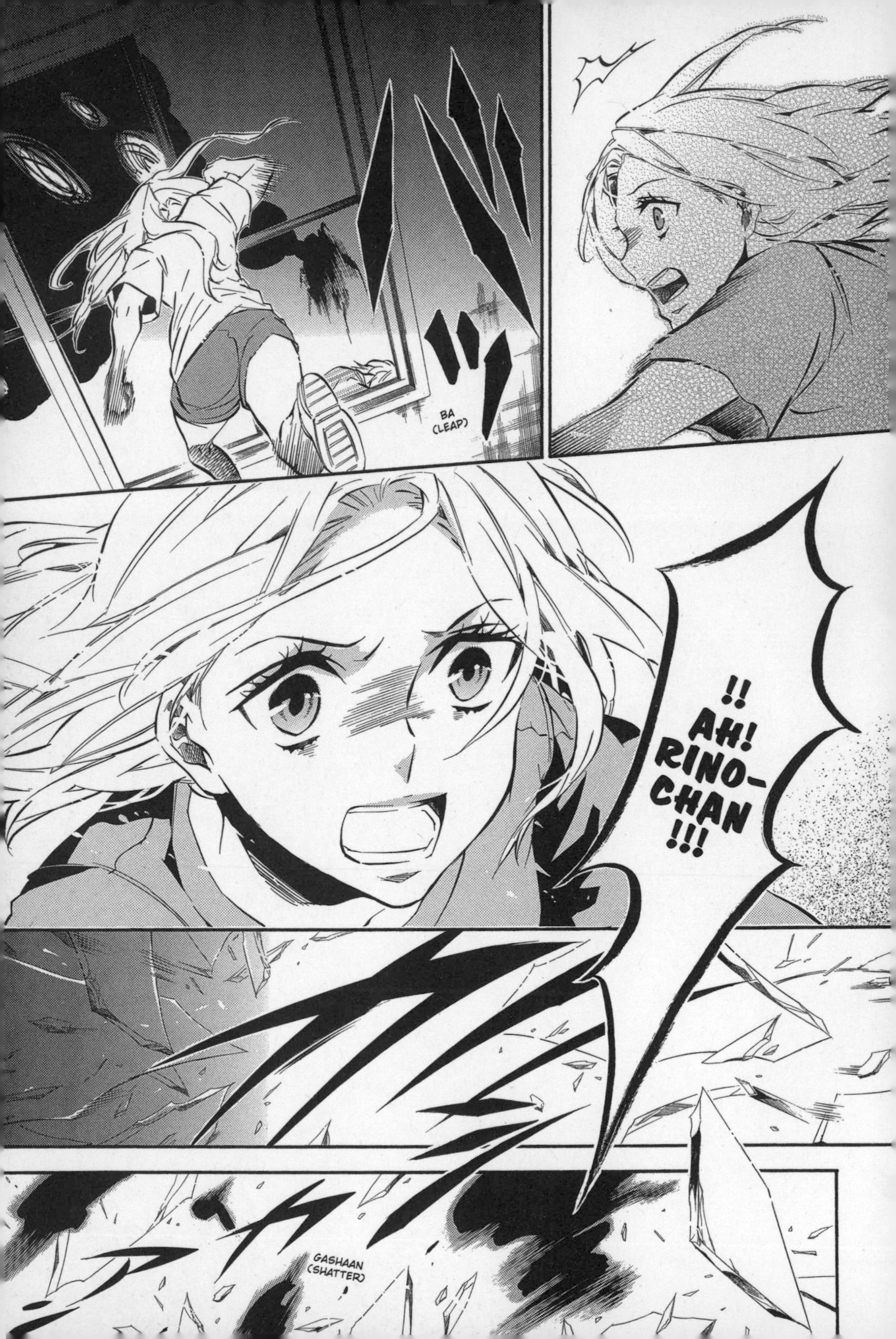
BA
(LEAP)
!! AH! RINO-CHAN!!!
GASHAAN
(SHATTER)

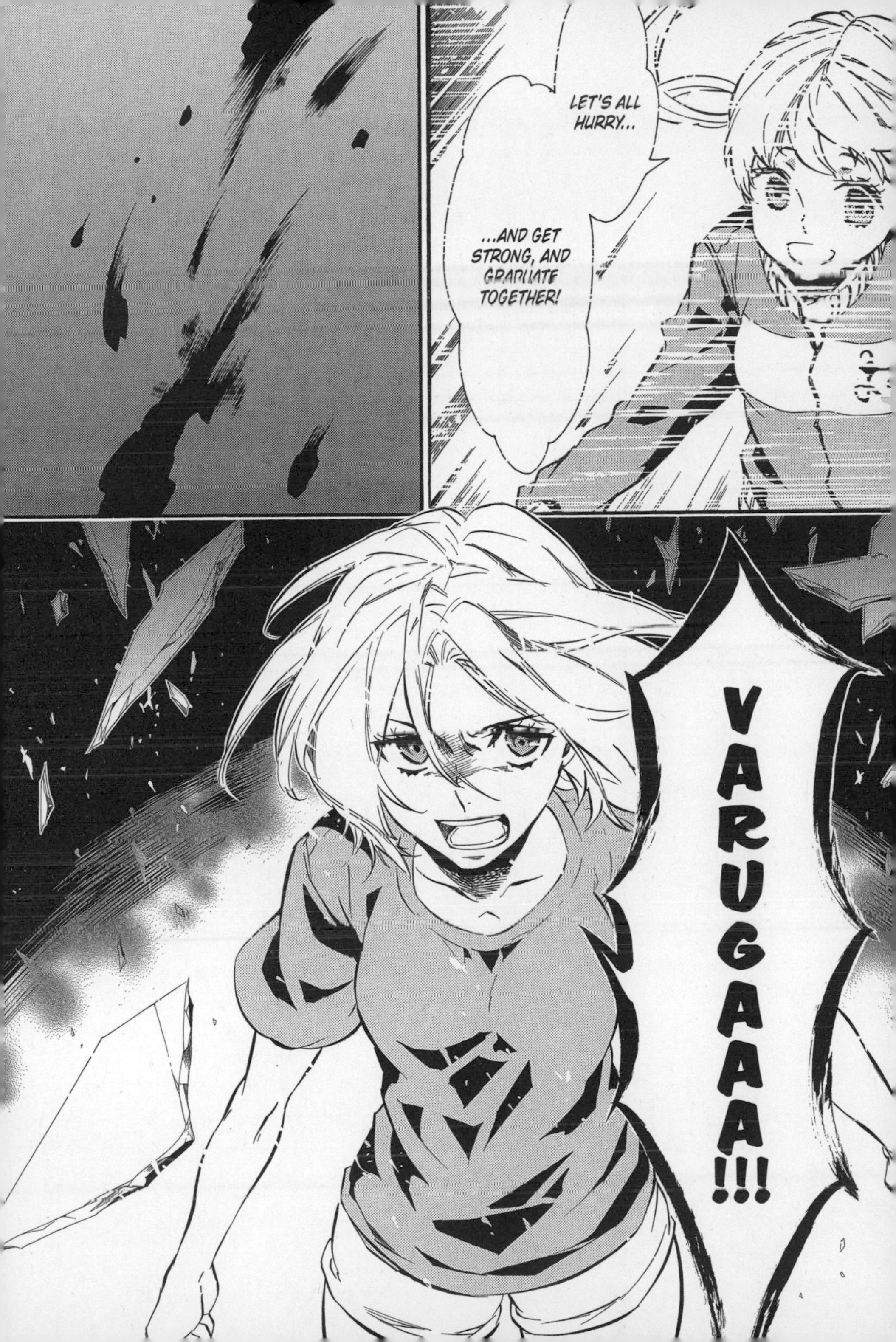
LET'S ALL HURRY...
...AND GET STRONG, AND GRADUATE TOGETHER!
VARUGAAA!!!

KARNEVAL

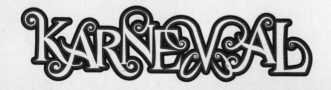

HA HA HA!

KARNEVAL

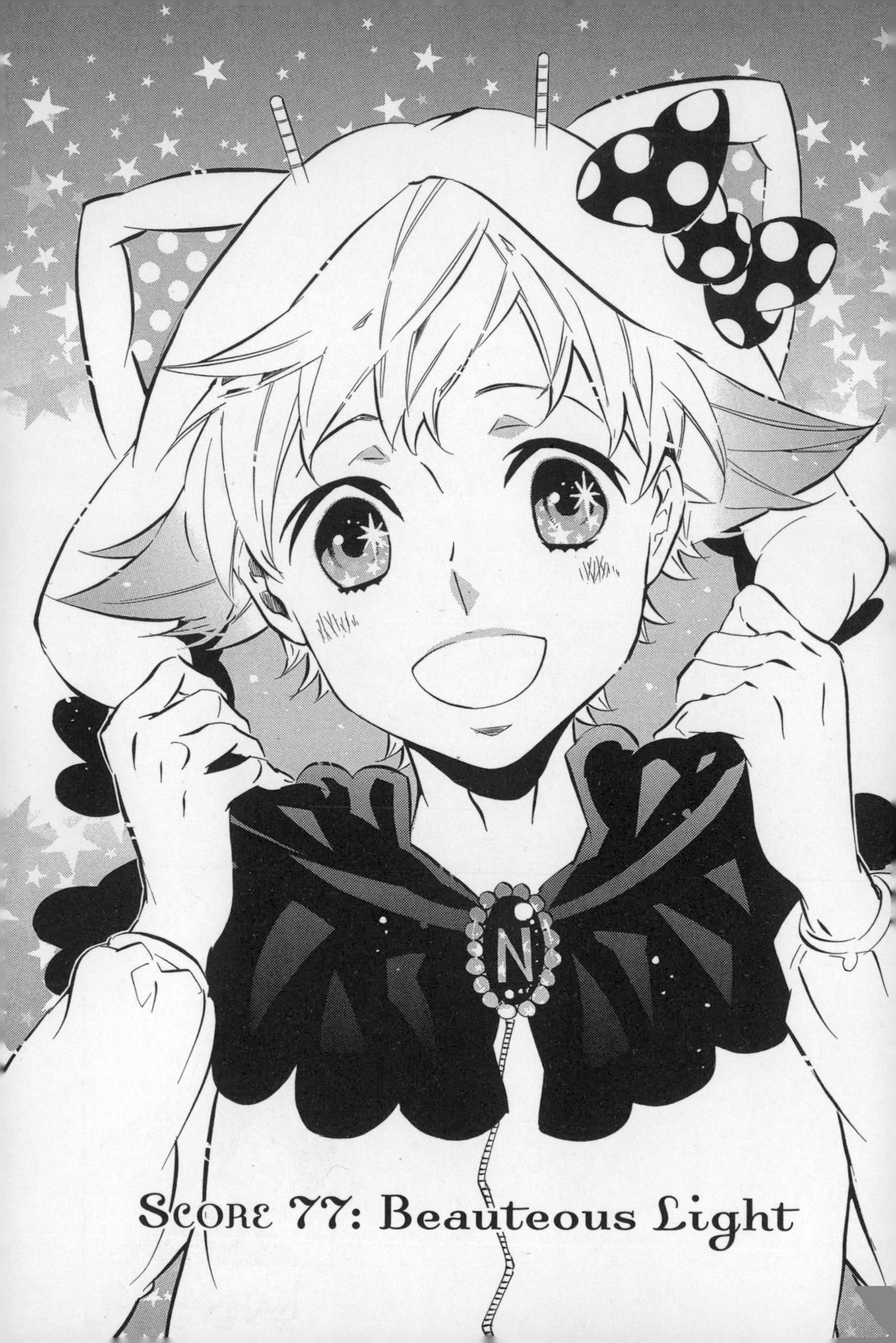
N
SCORE 77: Beauteous Light

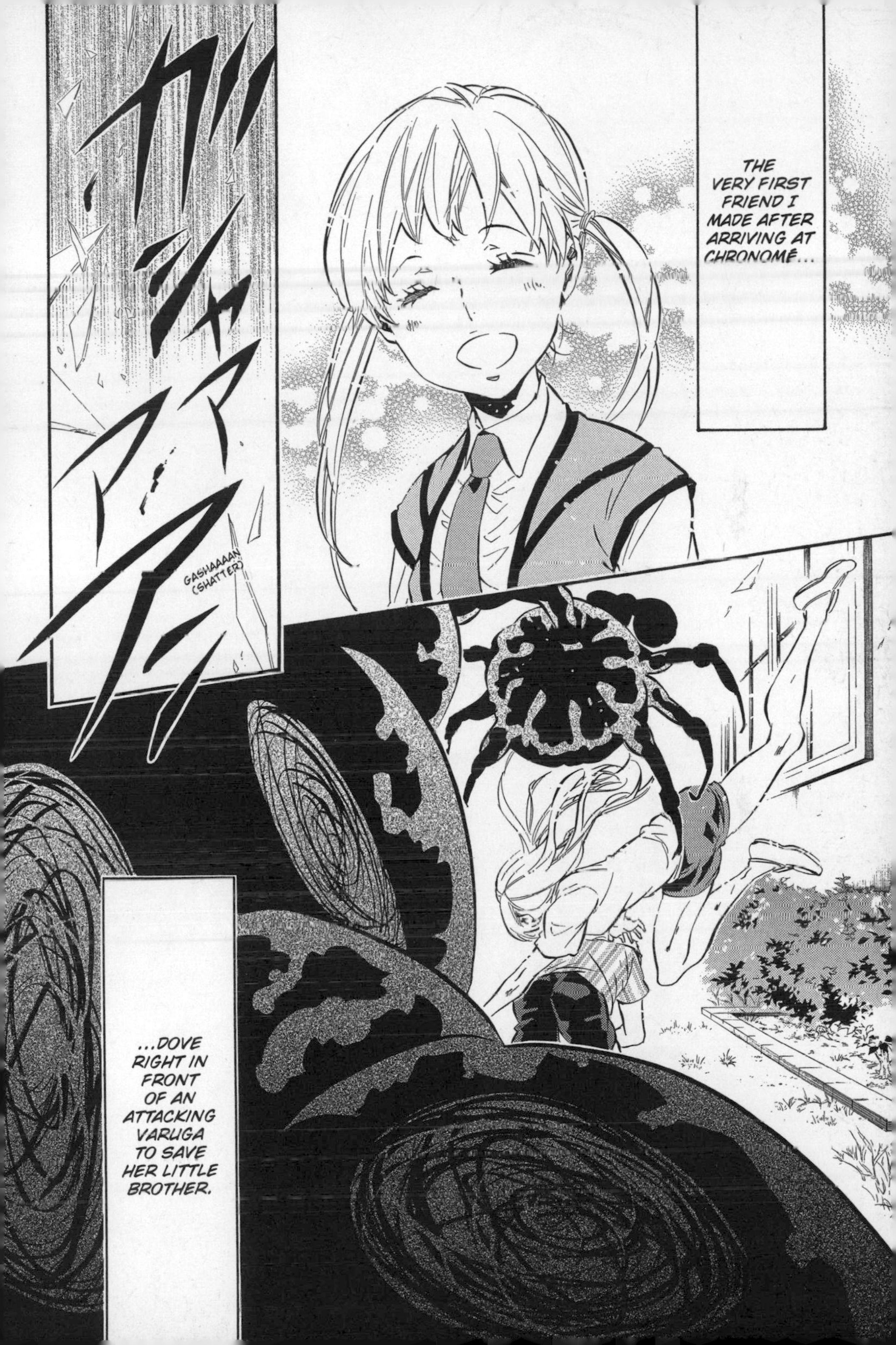
THE VERY FIRST FRIEND I MADE AFTER ARRIVING AT CHRONOMÉ...
GASHAAAAN (SHATTER)
...DOVE RIGHT IN FRONT OF AN ATTACKING VARUGA TO SAVE HER LITTLE BROTHER.

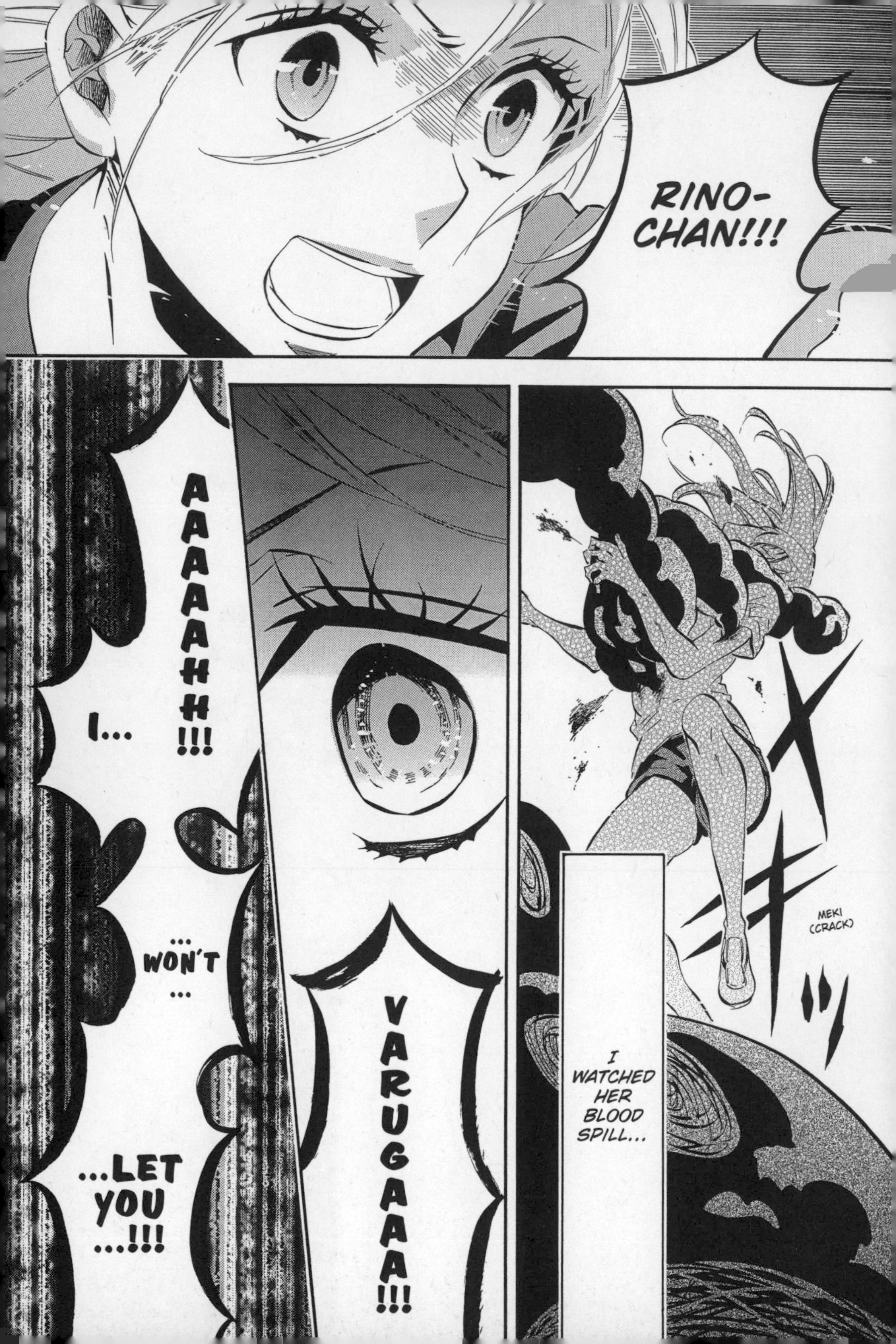
RINO-CHAN!!!
MEKI (CRACK)
I WATCHED HER BLOOD SPILL...
VARUGAAA!!!
AAAAAHH!!!
I...
...WON'T...
...LET YOU ...!!!

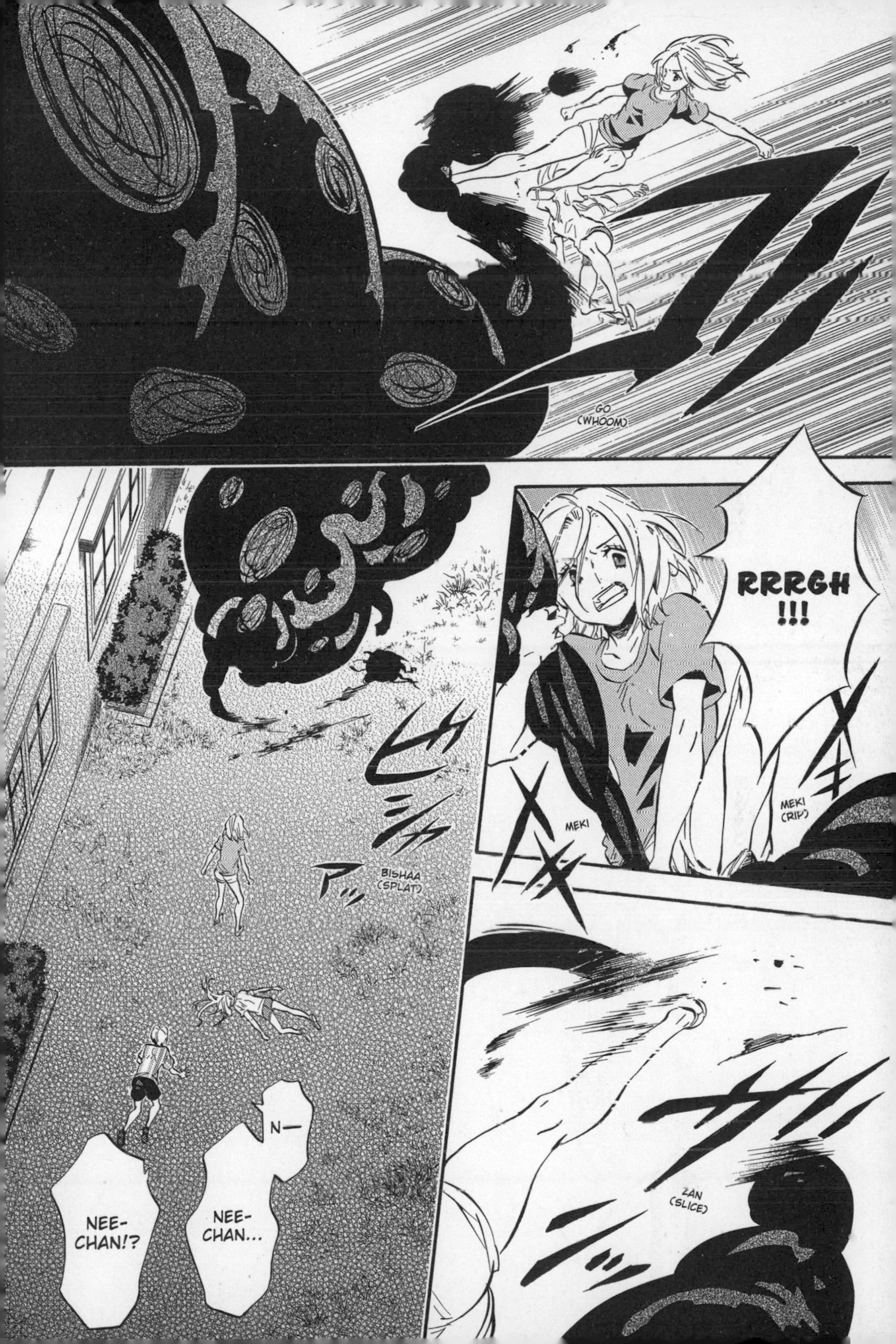
GO
(WHOOM)
RRRGH
!!!
MEKI
(RIP)
MEKI
ZAN
(SLICE)
BISHAA
(SPLAT)
N—
NEE-
CHAN...
NEE-
CHAN!?

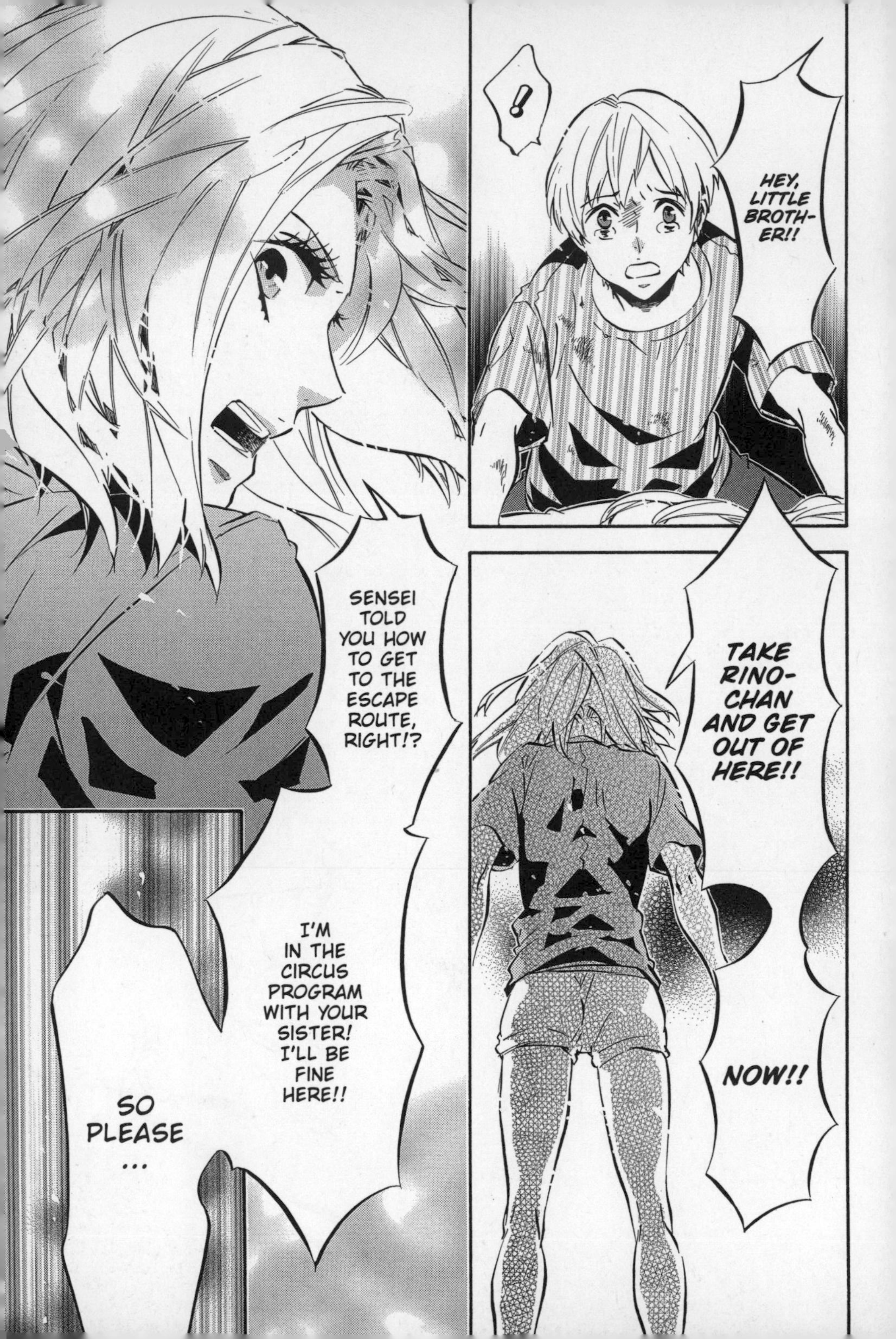
!
HEY, LITTLE BROTHER!!
TAKE RINO-CHAN AND GET OUT OF HERE!!
NOW!!
SENSEI TOLD YOU HOW TO GET TO THE ESCAPE ROUTE, RIGHT!?
I'M IN THE CIRCUS PROGRAM WITH YOUR SISTER! I'LL BE FINE HERE!!
SO PLEASE ...

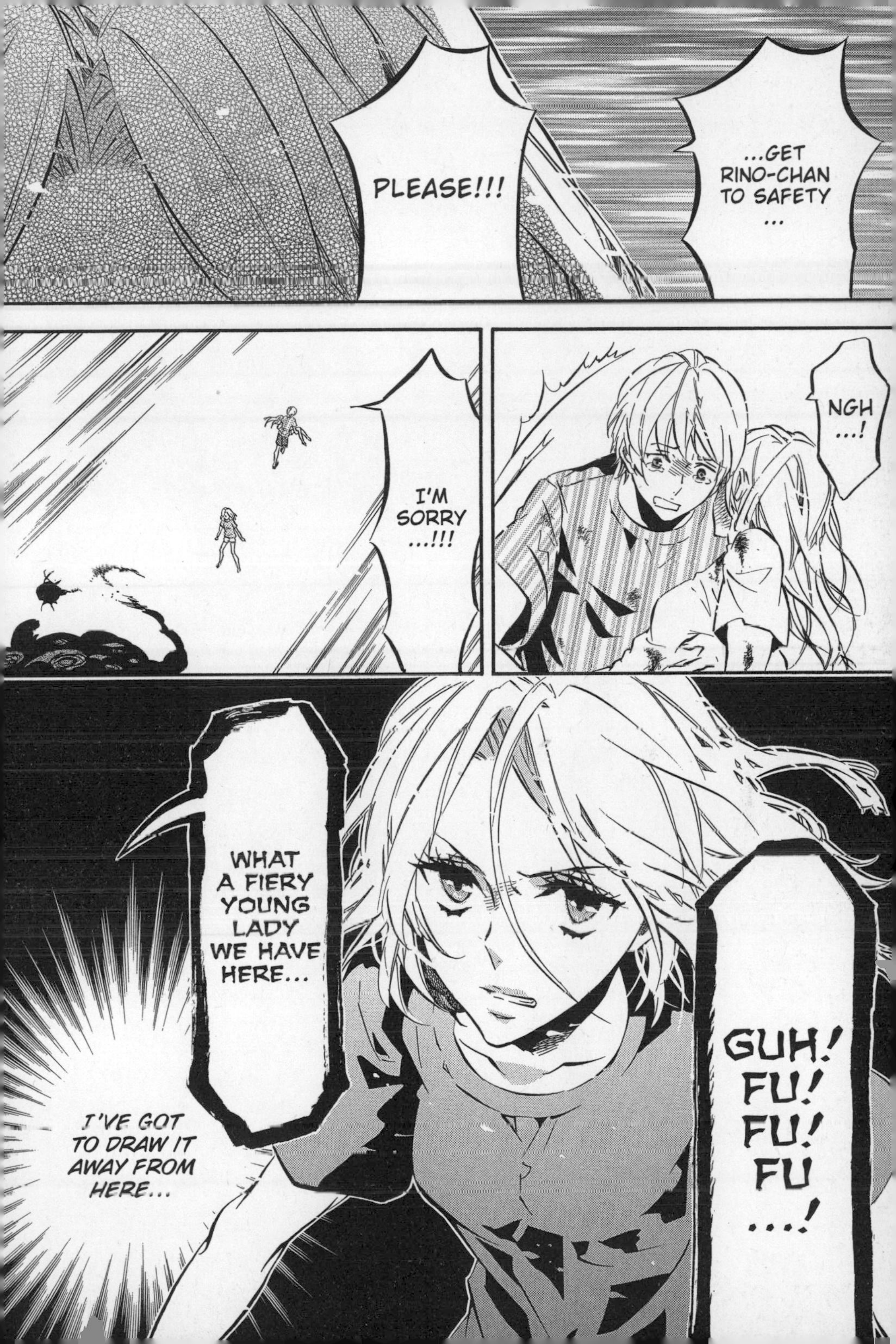
...GET RINO-CHAN TO SAFETY ...
PLEASE!!!
NGH ...!
I'M SORRY ...!!!
GUH! FU! FU! FU ...!
WHAT A FIERY YOUNG LADY WE HAVE HERE...
I'VE GOT TO DRAW IT AWAY FROM HERE...

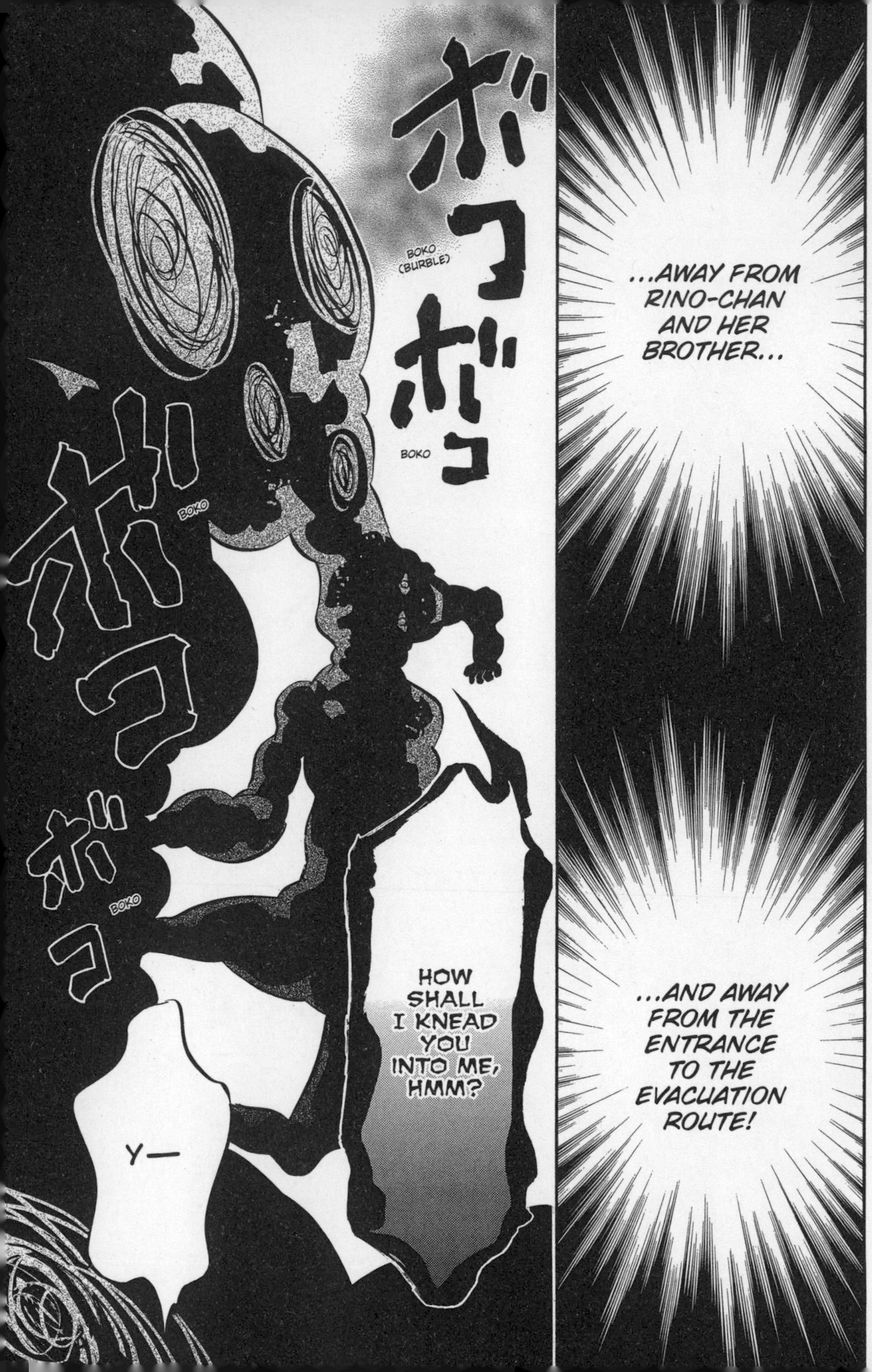
...AWAY FROM RINO-CHAN AND HER BROTHER...
...AND AWAY FROM THE ENTRANCE TO THE EVACUATION ROUTE!
ボコボコ
BOKO (BURBLE)
BOKO
ボコボコっ
BOKO
BOKO
HOW SHALL I KNEAD YOU INTO ME, HMM?
Y—

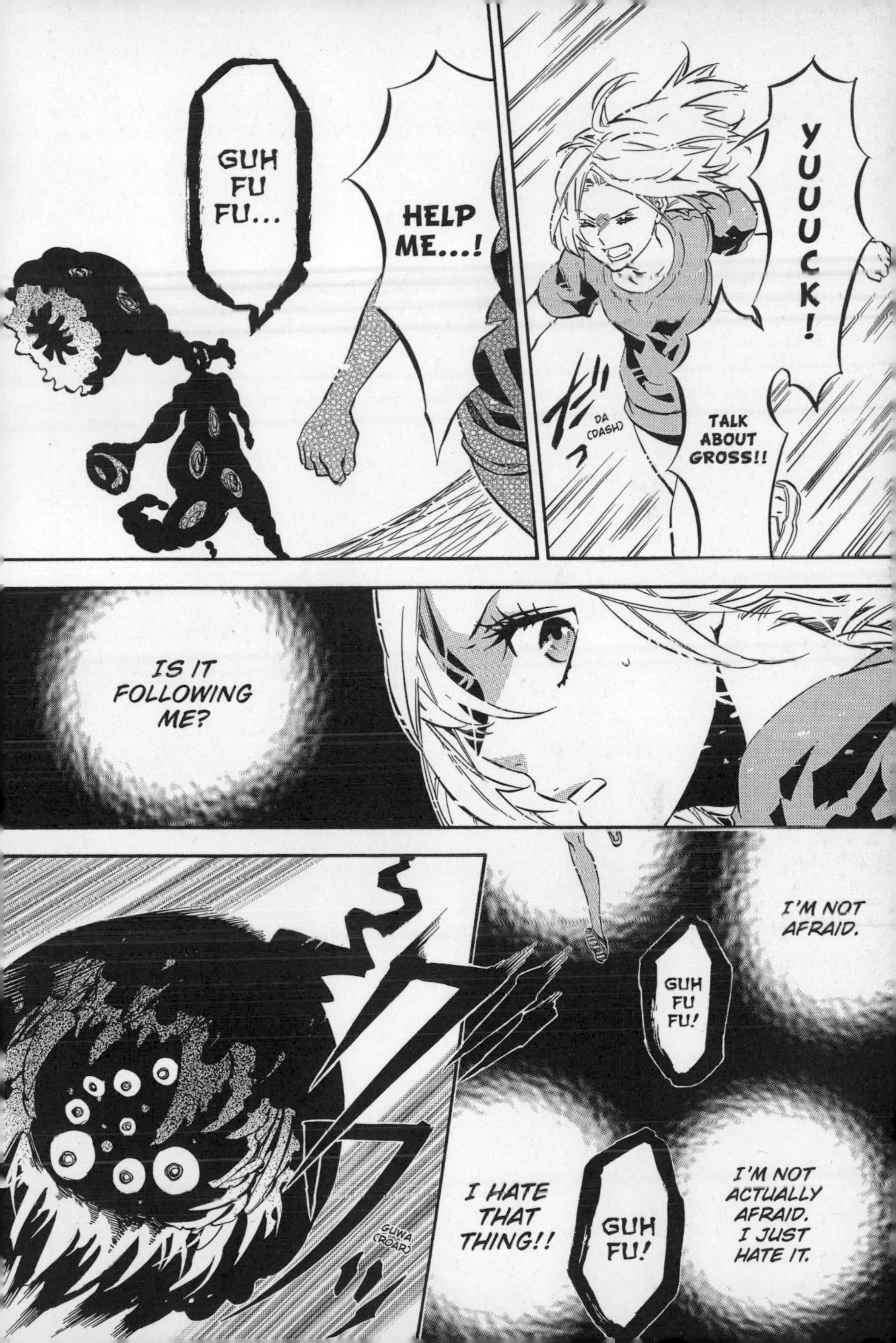
YUUUCK!
DA (DASH)
TALK ABOUT GROSS!!
HELP ME...!
GUH FU FU...
IS IT FOLLOWING ME?
I'M NOT AFRAID.
GUH FU FU!
I'M NOT ACTUALLY AFRAID. I JUST HATE IT.
GUH FU!
I HATE THAT THING!!
GUWA (ROAR)

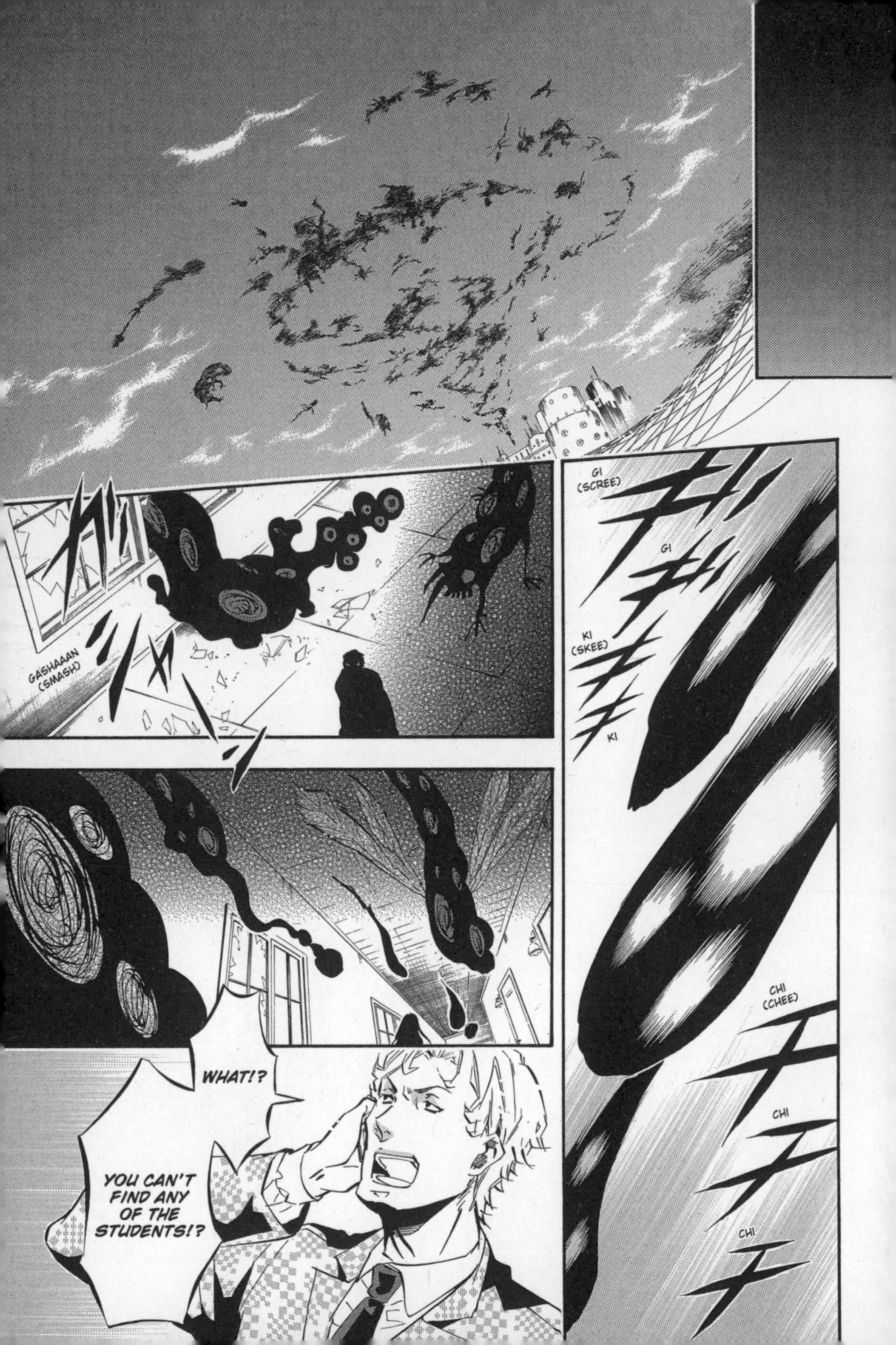
GI (SCREE)
GI
KI (SKEE)
KI
CHI (CHEE)
CHI
CHI
GASHAAAN (SMASH)
WHAT!?
YOU CAN'T FIND ANY OF THE STUDENTS!?

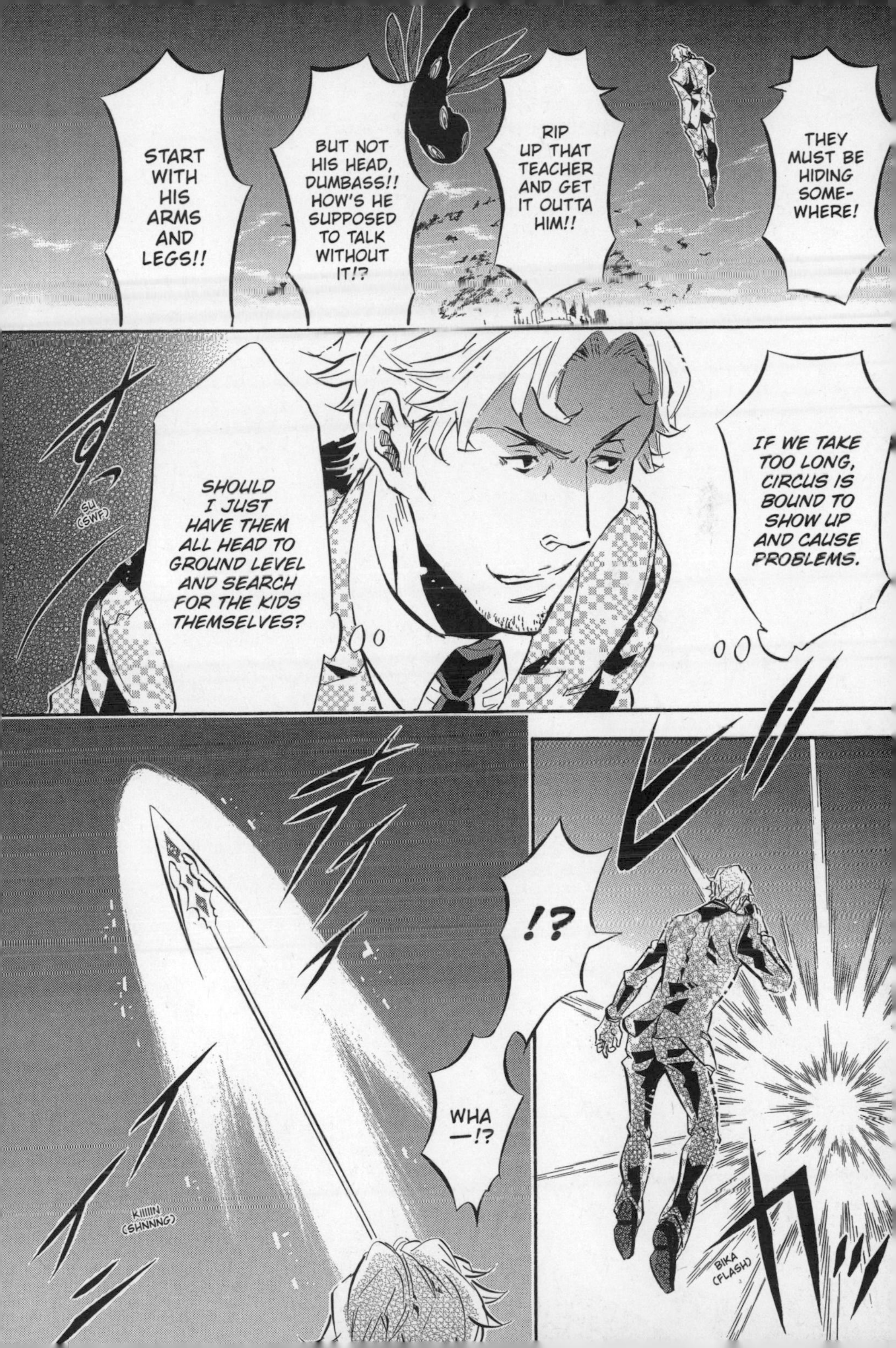
THEY MUST BE HIDING SOME-WHERE!
RIP UP THAT TEACHER AND GET IT OUTTA HIM!!
BUT NOT HIS HEAD, DUMBASS!! HOW'S HE SUPPOSED TO TALK WITHOUT IT!?
START WITH HIS ARMS AND LEGS!!
IF WE TAKE TOO LONG, CIRCUS IS BOUND TO SHOW UP AND CAUSE PROBLEMS.
SHOULD I JUST HAVE THEM ALL HEAD TO GROUND LEVEL AND SEARCH FOR THE KIDS THEMSELVES?
SU (SWF)
!?
WHA—!?
BIKA (FLASH)
KIIIIN (SHNNNG)

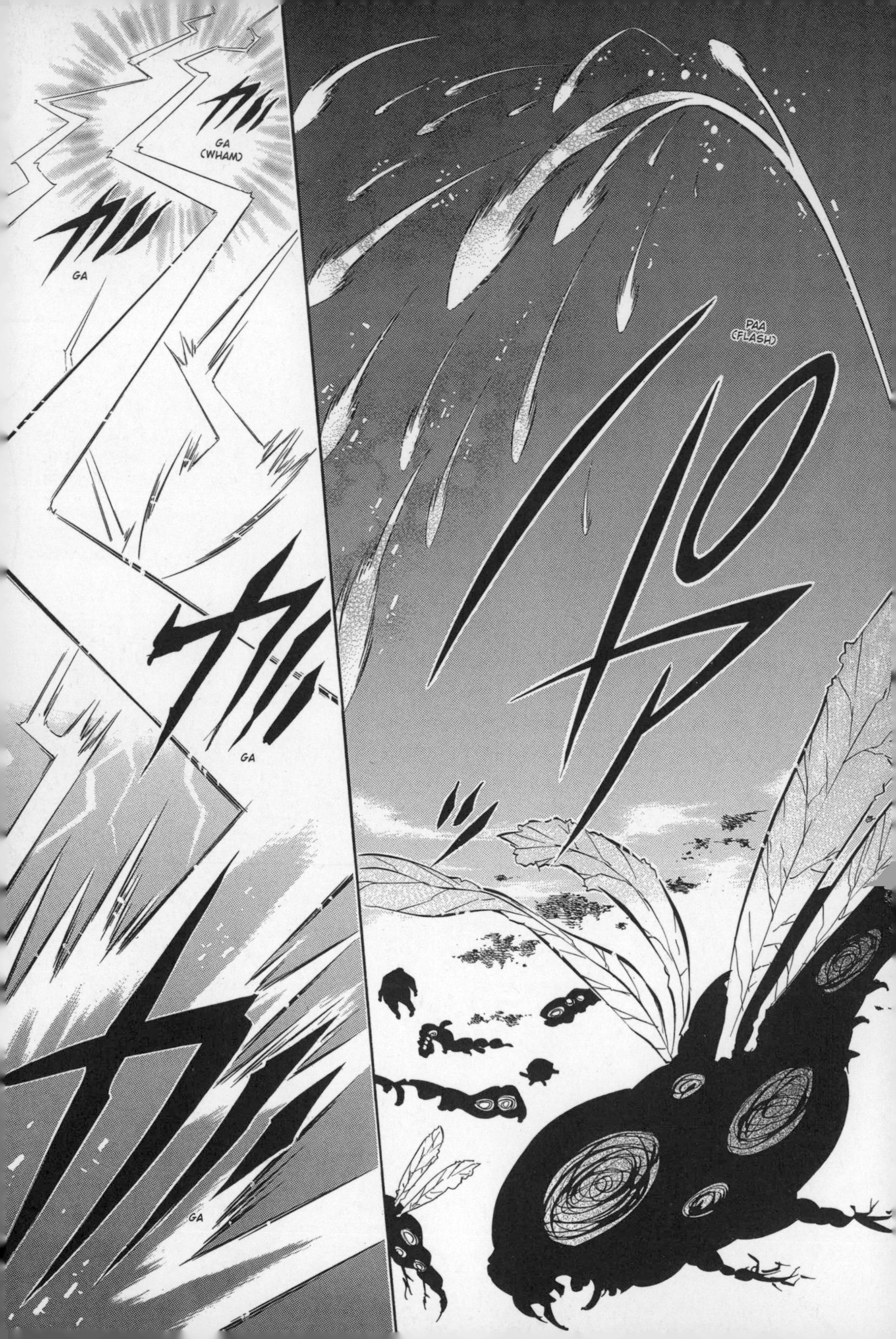
PAA (FLASH)
GA (WHAM)
GA
GA
GA

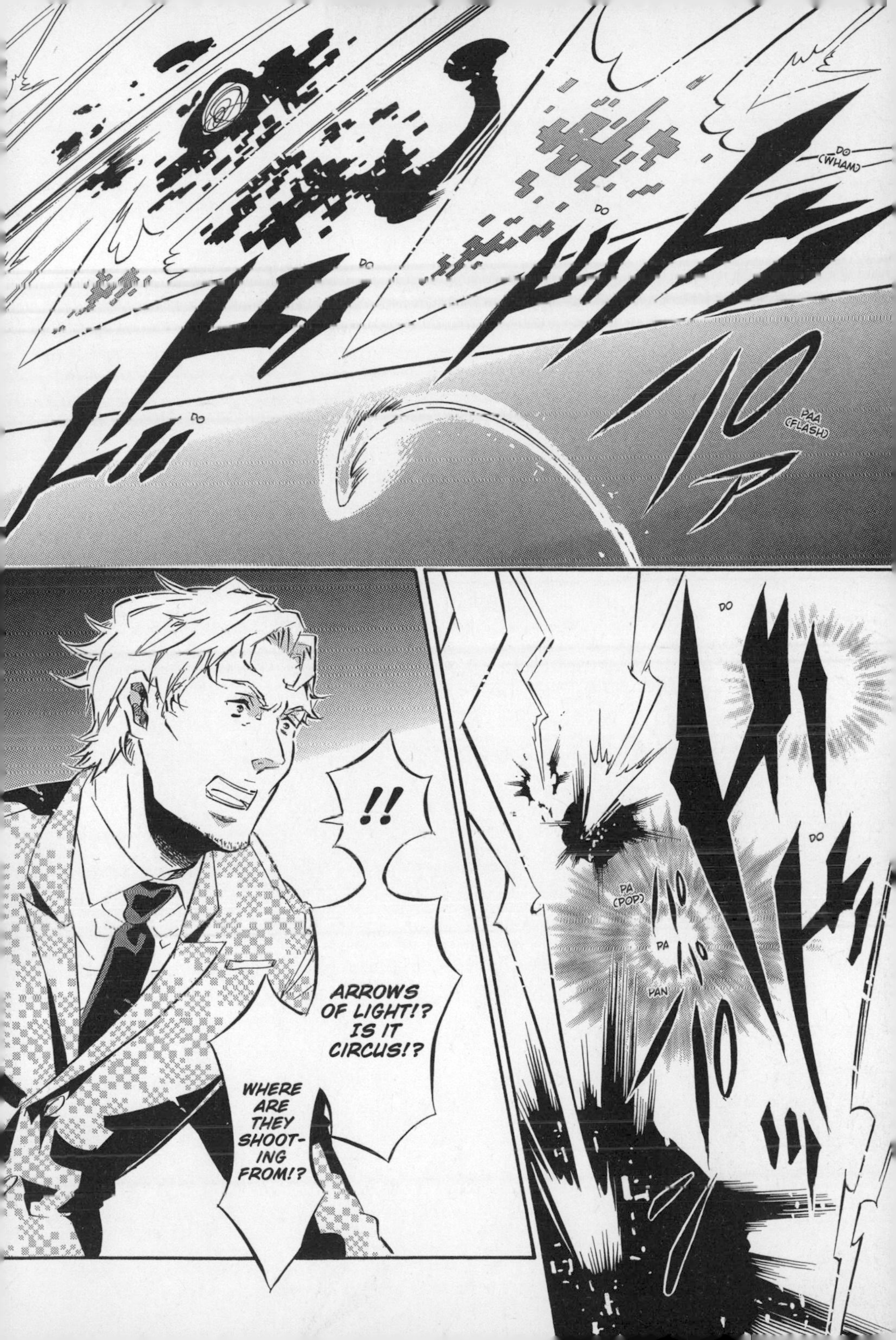
DO (WHAM)
DO
DO
PAA (FLASH)
DO
DO
DO
PA (POP)
PA
PAN
!!
ARROWS OF LIGHT!? IS IT CIRCUS!?
WHERE ARE THEY SHOOTING FROM!?

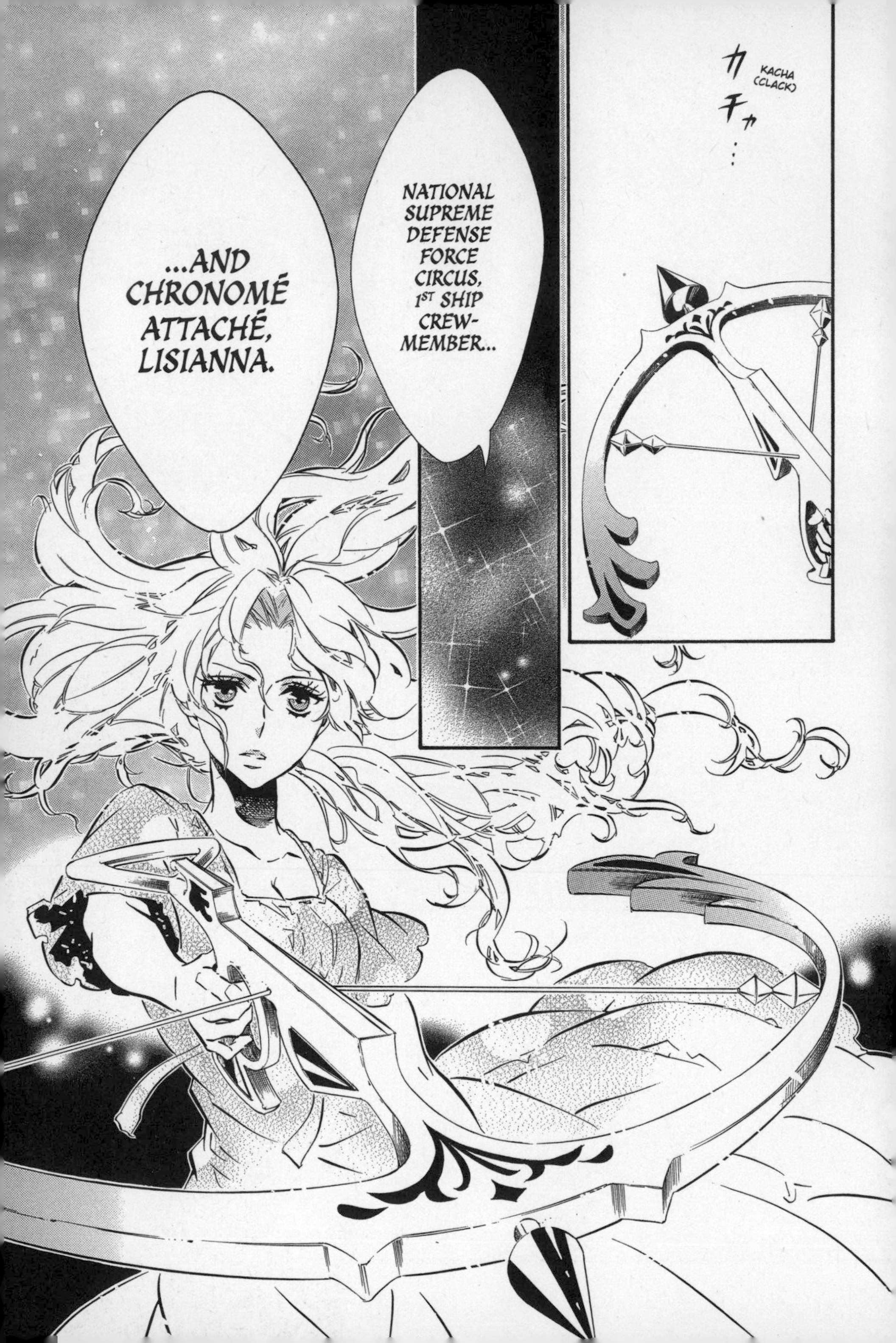
カチャ…
KACHA (CLACK)
NATIONAL SUPREME DEFENSE FORCE CIRCUS, 1ST SHIP CREW-MEMBER...
...AND CHRONOMÉ ATTACHÉ, LISIANNA.

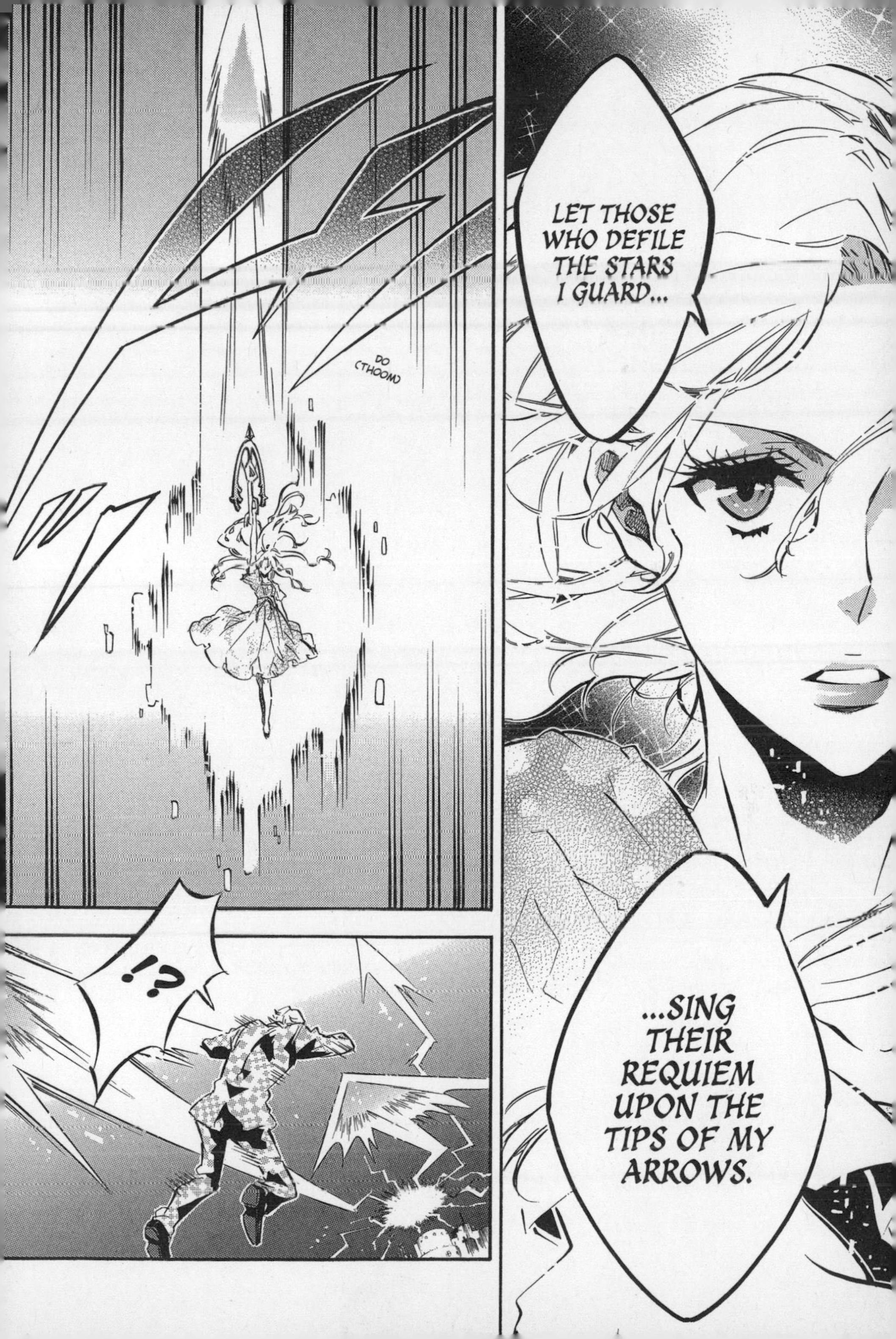
LET THOSE WHO DEFILE THE STARS I GUARD...
DO (THOOM)
...SING THEIR REQUIEM UPON THE TIPS OF MY ARROWS.
!?

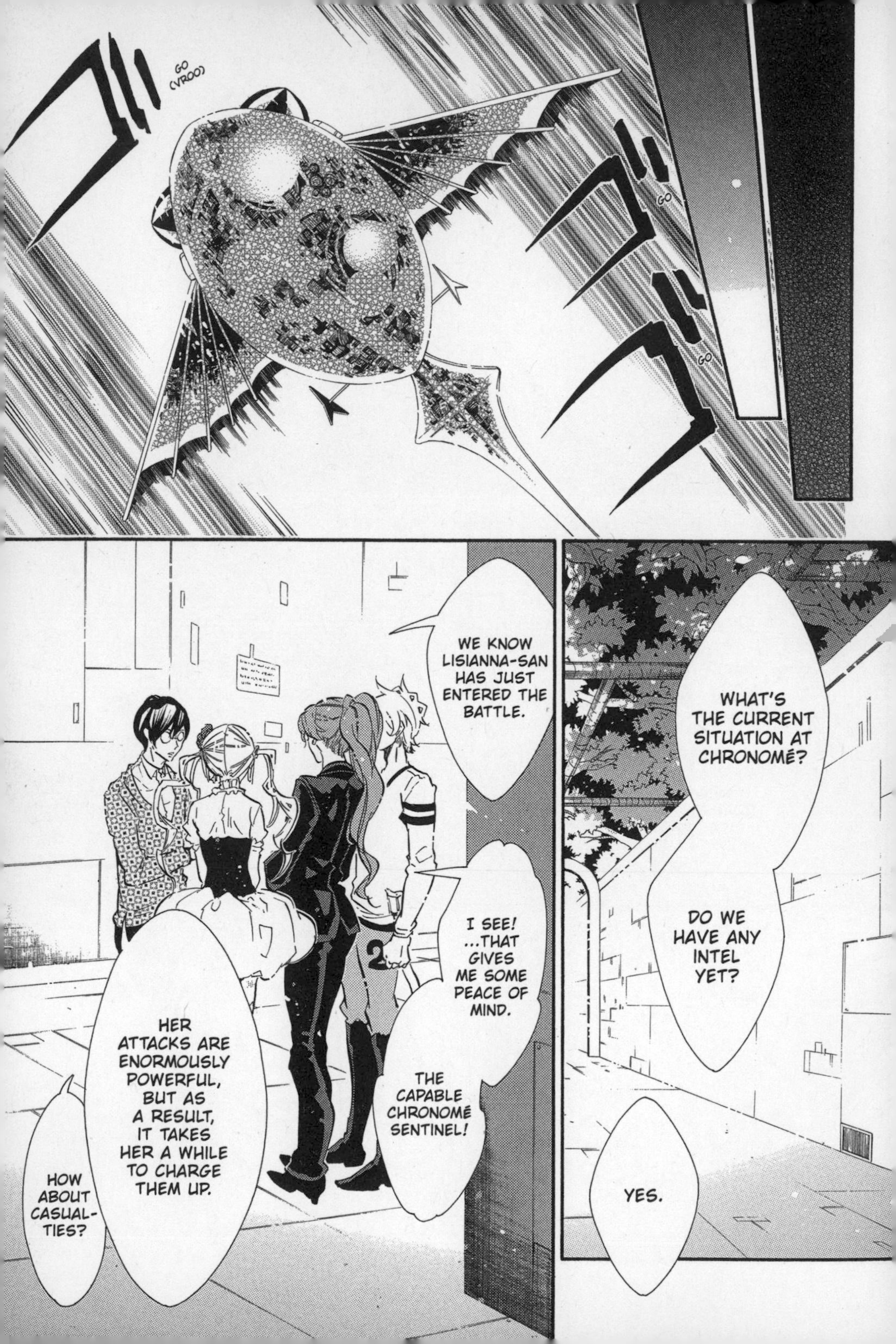
GO
GO
GO (VROO)
WHAT'S THE CURRENT SITUATION AT CHRONOMÉ?
DO WE HAVE ANY INTEL YET?
YES.
WE KNOW LISIANNA-SAN HAS JUST ENTERED THE BATTLE.
I SEE! ...THAT GIVES ME SOME PEACE OF MIND.
THE CAPABLE CHRONOMÉ SENTINEL!
HER ATTACKS ARE ENORMOUSLY POWERFUL, BUT AS A RESULT, IT TAKES HER A WHILE TO CHARGE THEM UP.
HOW ABOUT CASUALTIES?

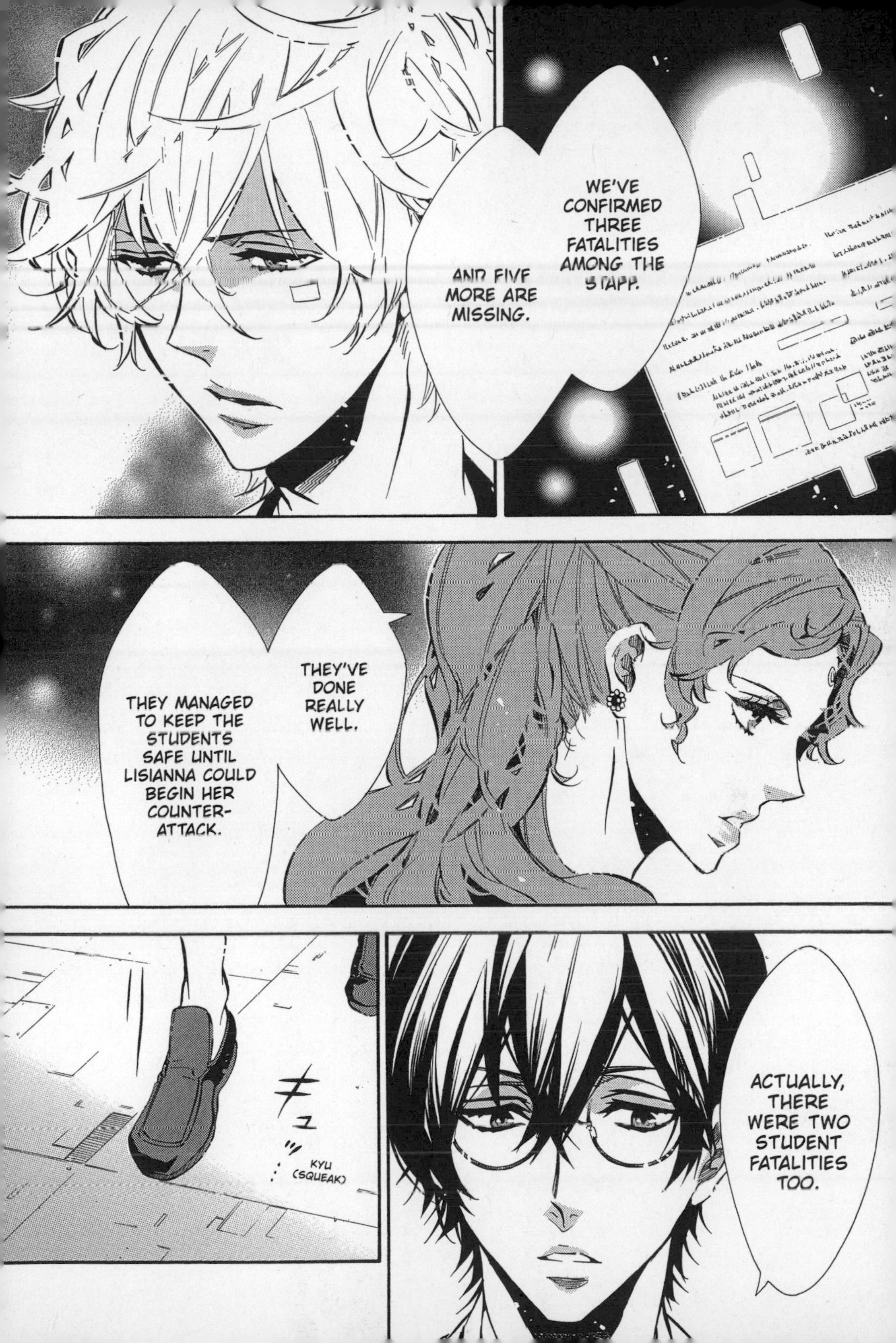
WE'VE CONFIRMED THREE FATALITIES AMONG THE STAFF.
AND FIVE MORE ARE MISSING.
THEY'VE DONE REALLY WELL.
THEY MANAGED TO KEEP THE STUDENTS SAFE UNTIL LISIANNA COULD BEGIN HER COUNTER-ATTACK.
ACTUALLY, THERE WERE TWO STUDENT FATALITIES TOO.
KYU (SQUEAK)

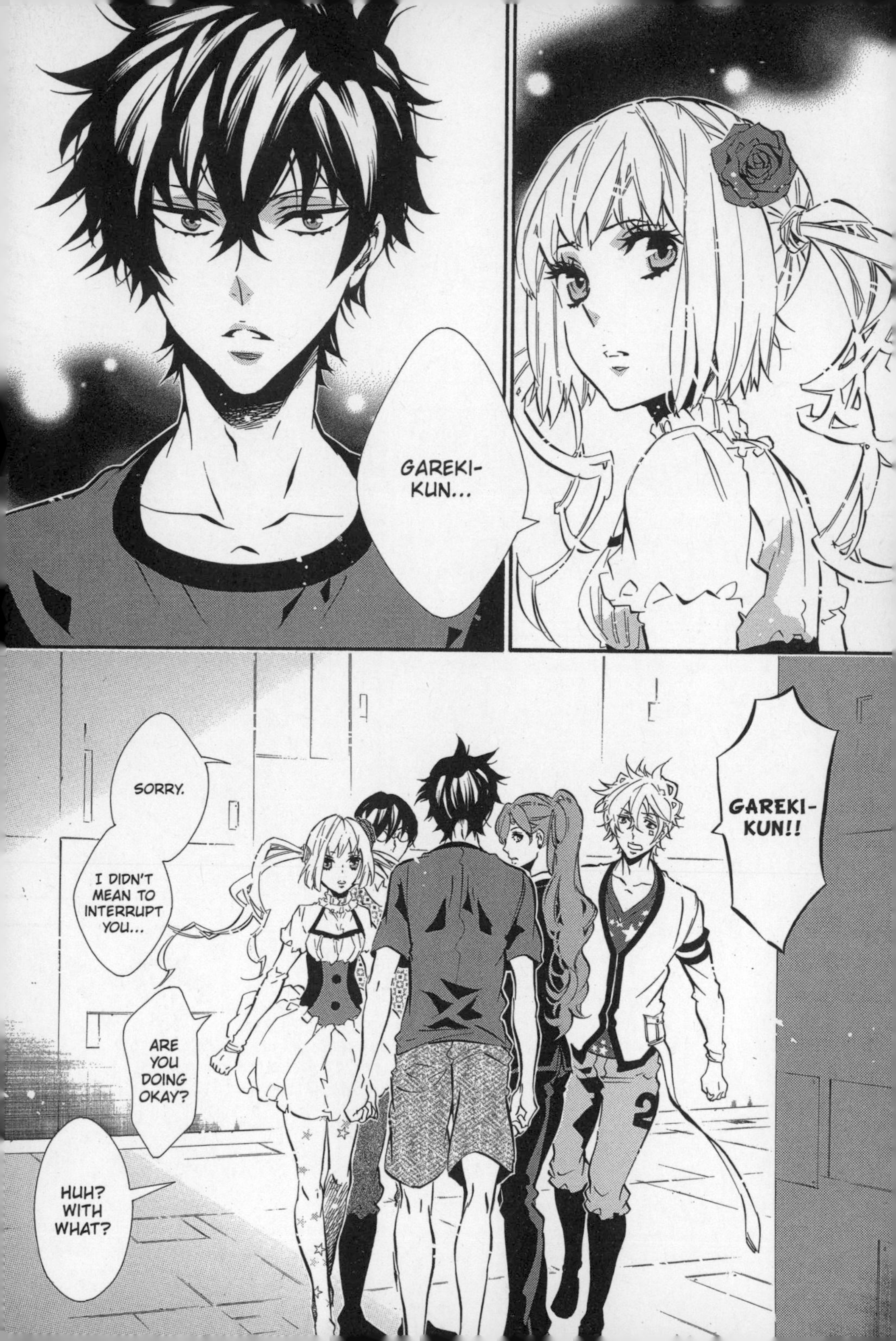
GAREKI-KUN...
GAREKI-KUN!!
SORRY.
I DIDN'T MEAN TO INTERRUPT YOU...
ARE YOU DOING OKAY?
HUH? WITH WHAT?

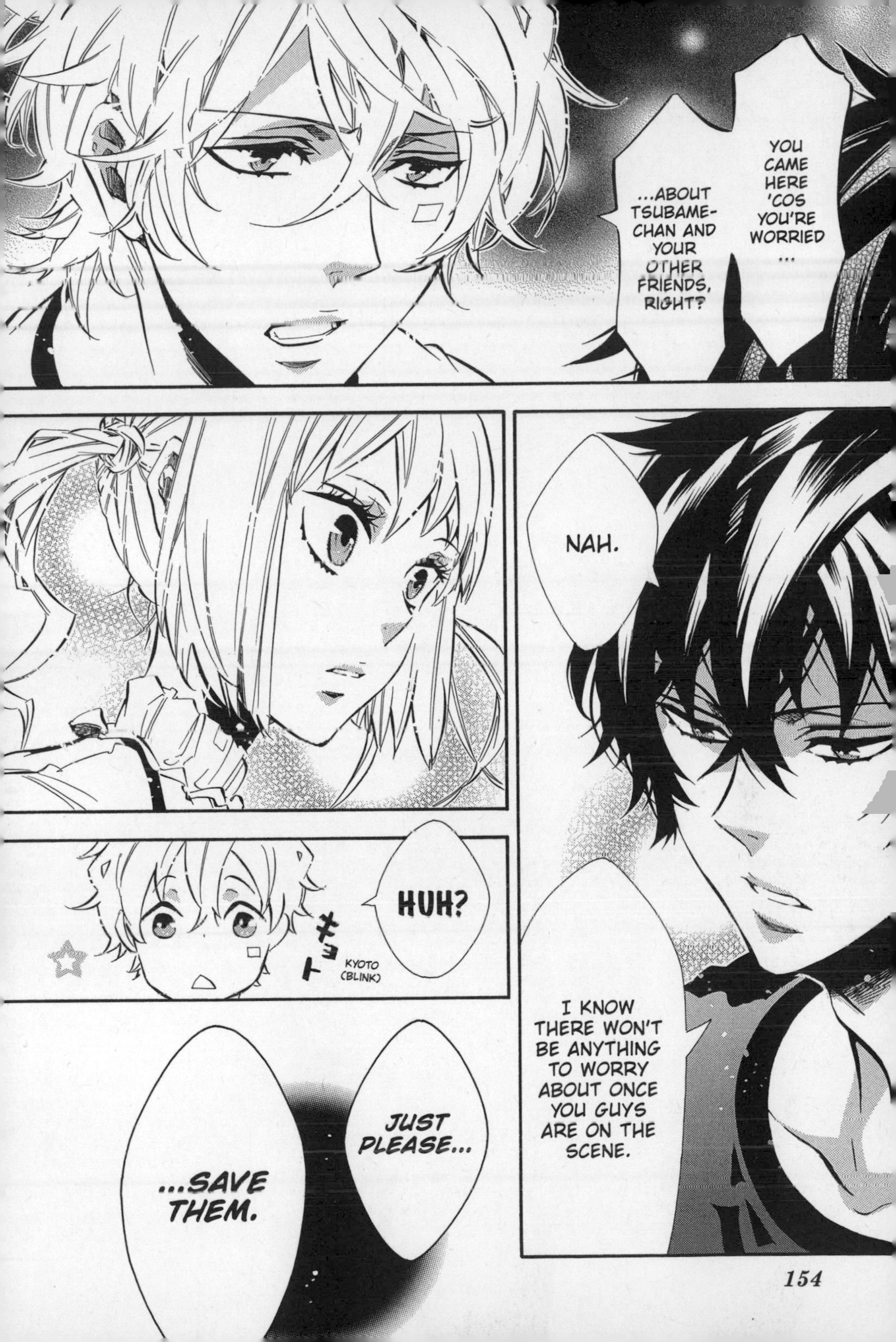

YOU CAME HERE 'COS YOU'RE WORRIED...
...ABOUT TSUBAME-CHAN AND YOUR OTHER FRIENDS, RIGHT?
NAH.
I KNOW THERE WON'T BE ANYTHING TO WORRY ABOUT ONCE YOU GUYS ARE ON THE SCENE.
HUH?
キョト
KYOTO (BLINK)
JUST PLEASE...
...SAVE THEM.

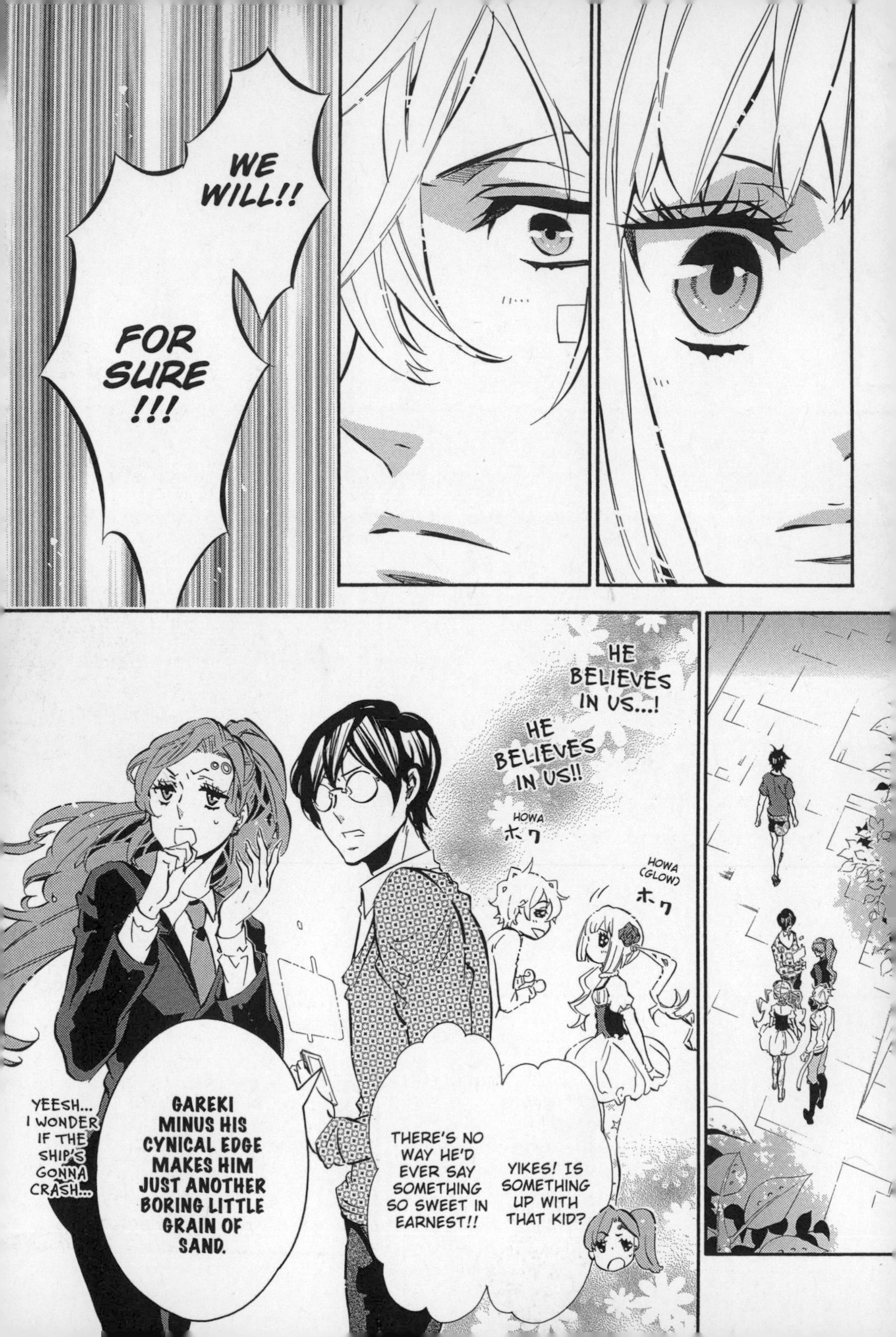
WE WILL!!
FOR SURE!!!
HE BELIEVES IN US...!
HE BELIEVES IN US!!
HOWA (GLOW)
ホワ
HOWA
ホワ
YIKES! IS SOMETHING UP WITH THAT KID?
THERE'S NO WAY HE'D EVER SAY SOMETHING SO SWEET IN EARNEST!!
GAREKI MINUS HIS CYNICAL EDGE MAKES HIM JUST ANOTHER BORING LITTLE GRAIN OF SAND.
YEESH... I WONDER IF THE SHIP'S GONNA CRASH...

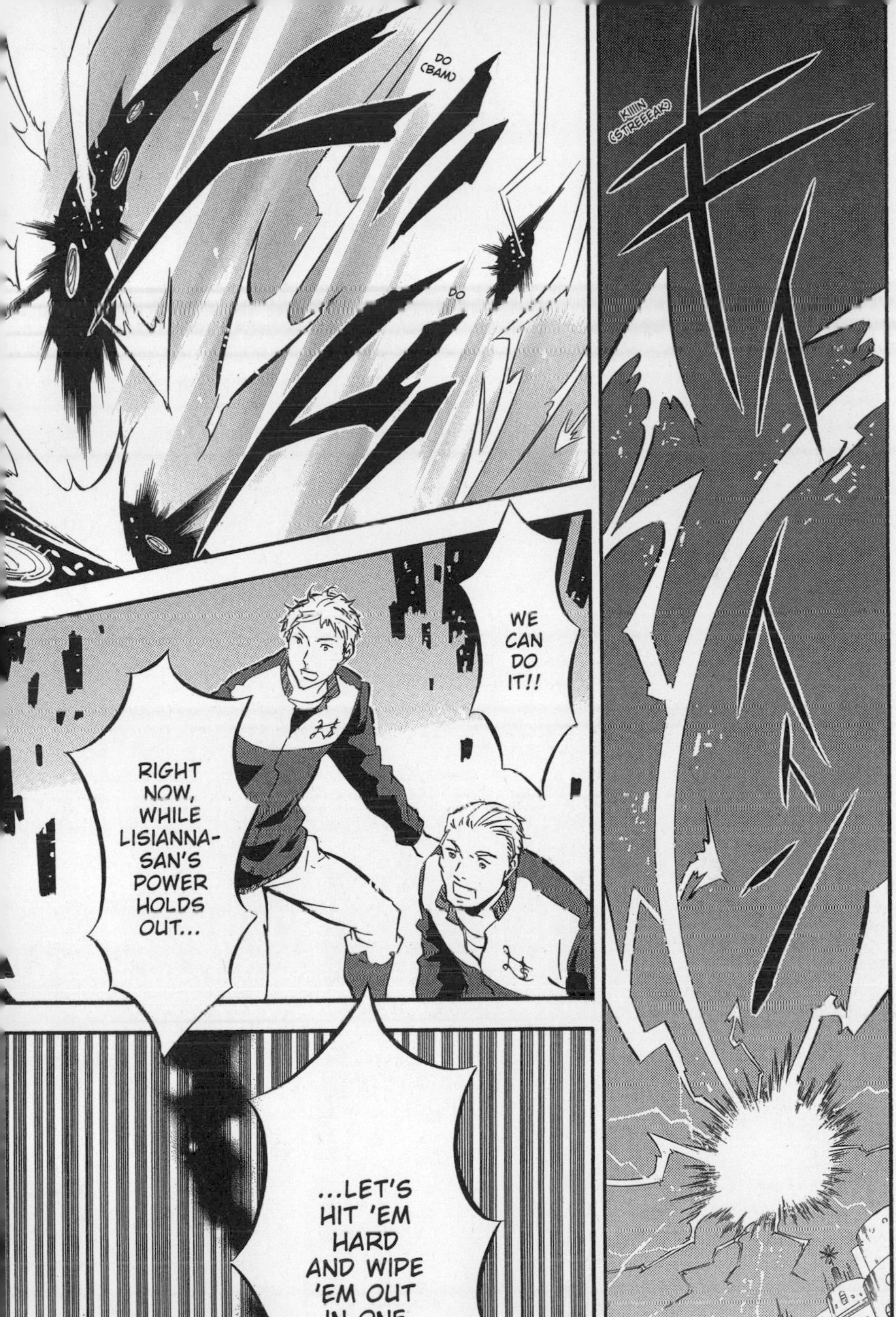
KIIIN (STREEEAK)
DO (BAM)
DO
WE CAN DO IT!!
RIGHT NOW, WHILE LISIANNA-SAN'S POWER HOLDS OUT...
...LET'S HIT 'EM HARD AND WIPE 'EM OUT IN ONE GO!!

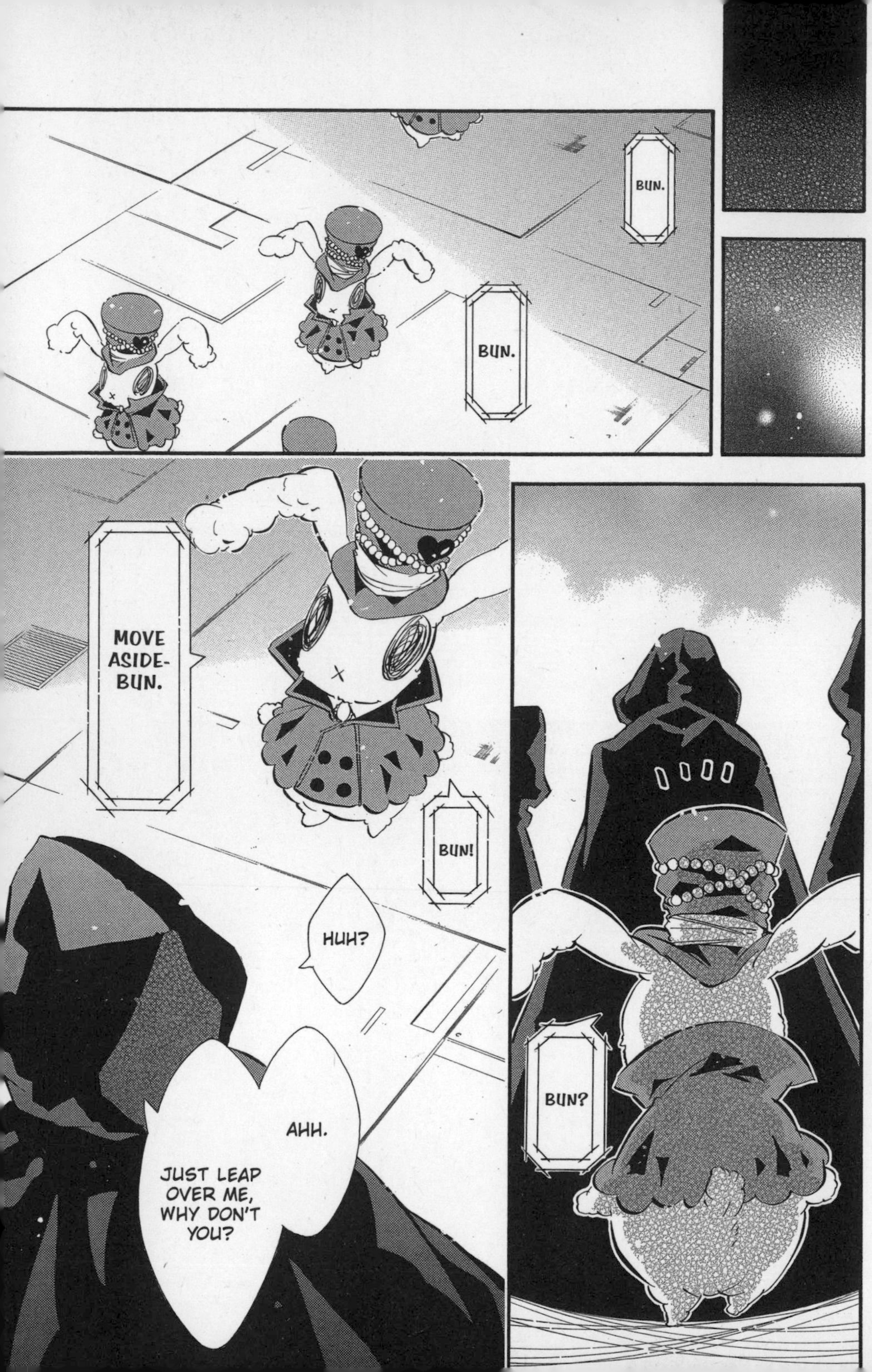
BUN.
BUN.
BUN?
MOVE ASIDE-BUN.
BUN!
HUH?
AHH.
JUST LEAP OVER ME, WHY DON'T YOU?

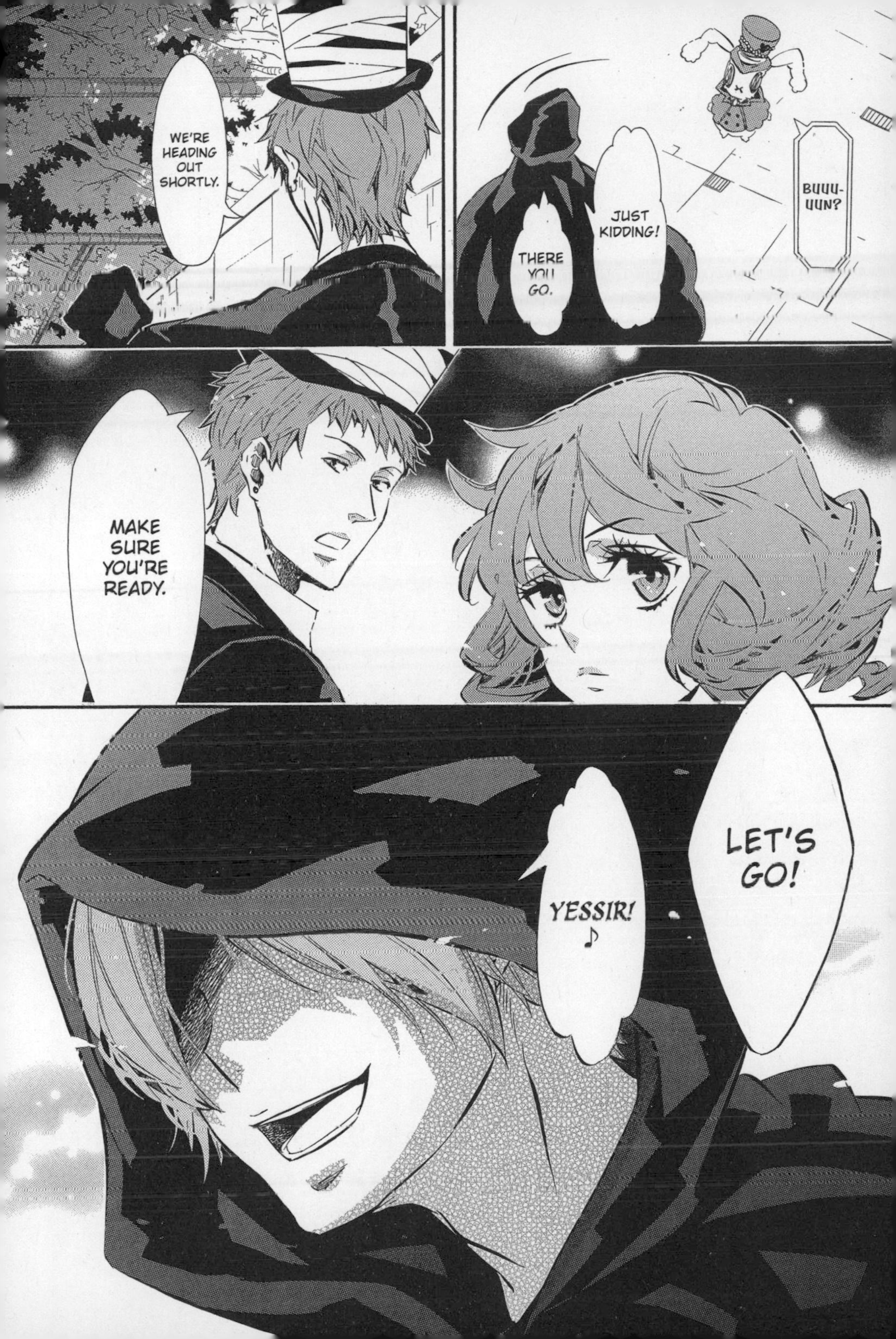
BUUU-UUN?
JUST KIDDING!
THERE YOU GO.
WE'RE HEADING OUT SHORTLY.
MAKE SURE YOU'RE READY.
LET'S GO!
YESSIR! ♪

KARNEVAL

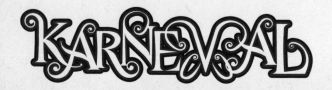

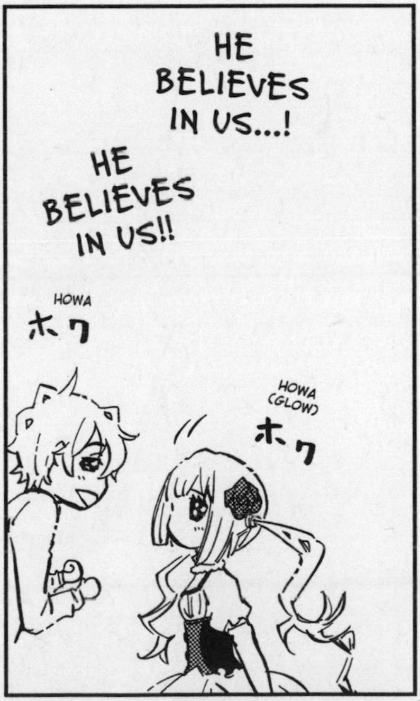
HE BELIEVES IN US...!
HE BELIEVES IN US!!
HOWA (GLOW)
ホワ
HOWA
ホワ

KARNEVAL

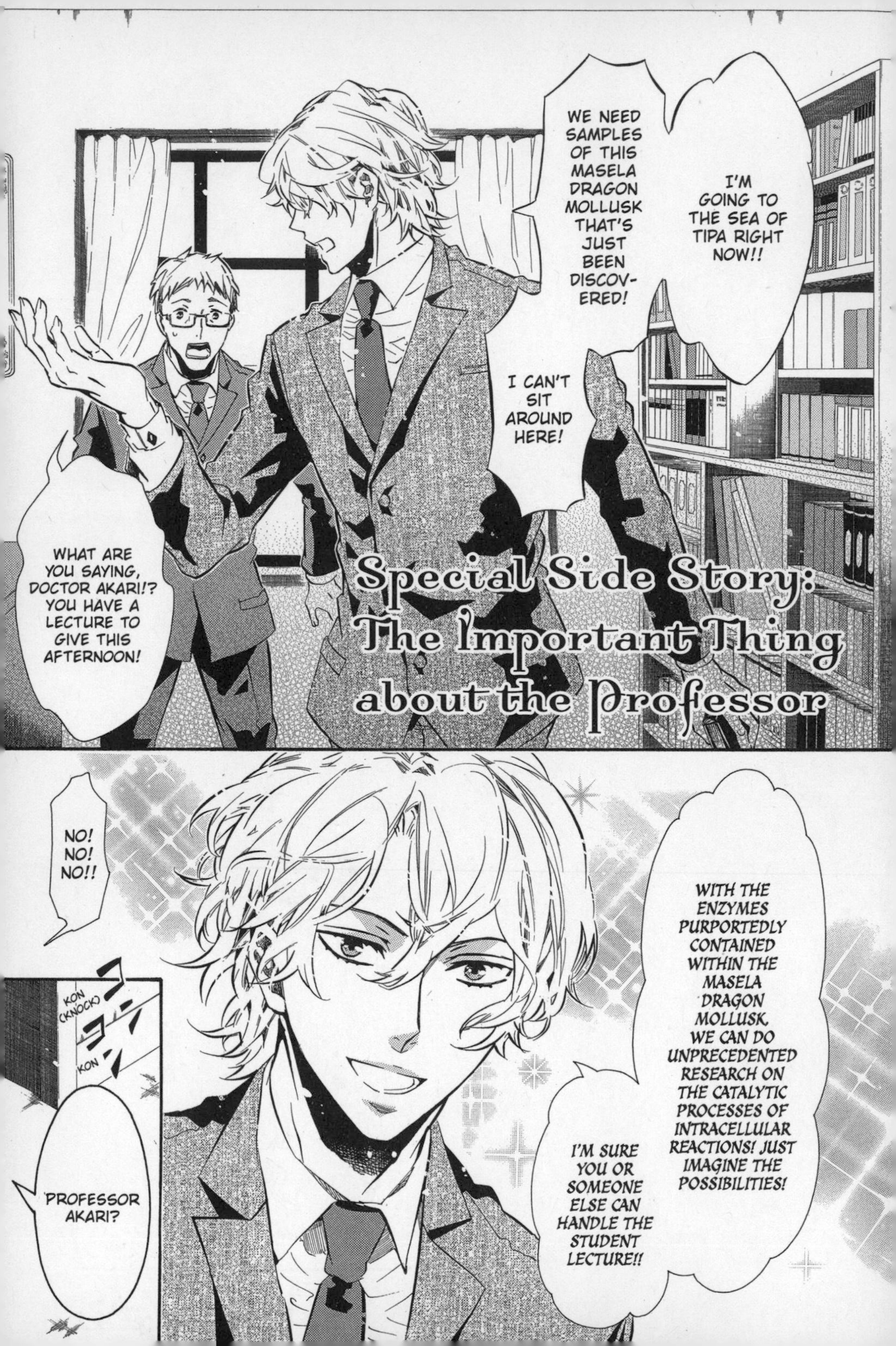
WE NEED SAMPLES OF THIS MASELA DRAGON MOLLUSK THAT'S JUST BEEN DISCOV-ERED!
I'M GOING TO THE SEA OF TIPA RIGHT NOW!!
I CAN'T SIT AROUND HERE!
WHAT ARE YOU SAYING, DOCTOR AKARI!? YOU HAVE A LECTURE TO GIVE THIS AFTERNOON!
Special Side Story: The Important Thing about the Professor
WITH THE ENZYMES PURPORTEDLY CONTAINED WITHIN THE MASELA DRAGON MOLLUSK, WE CAN DO UNPRECEDENTED RESEARCH ON THE CATALYTIC PROCESSES OF INTRACELLULAR REACTIONS! JUST IMAGINE THE POSSIBILITIES!
I'M SURE YOU OR SOMEONE ELSE CAN HANDLE THE STUDENT LECTURE!!
NO! NO! NO!!
KON (KNOCK)
KON
PROFESSOR AKARI?

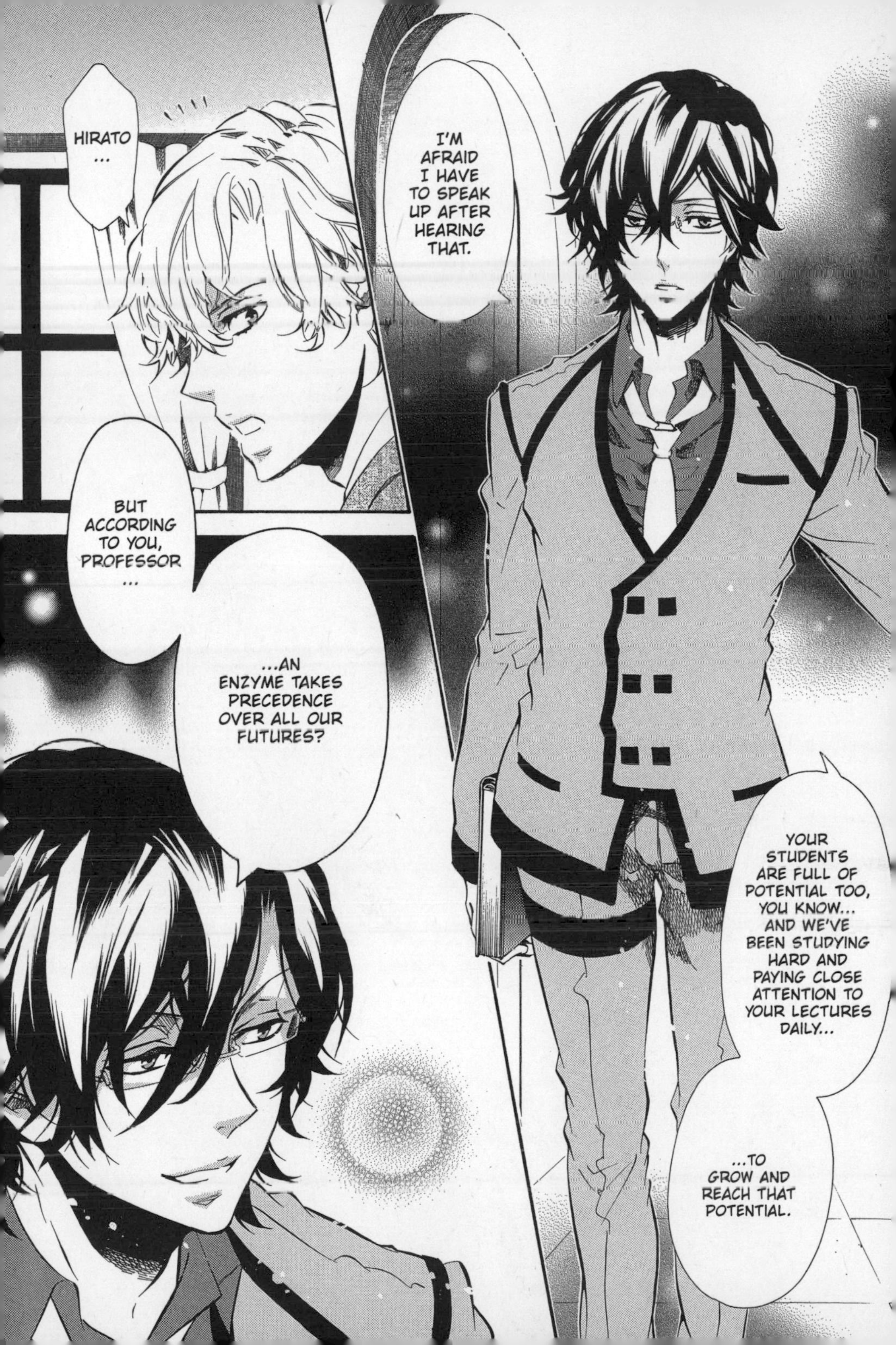
I'M AFRAID I HAVE TO SPEAK UP AFTER HEARING THAT.
HIRATO...
BUT ACCORDING TO YOU, PROFESSOR...
...AN ENZYME TAKES PRECEDENCE OVER ALL OUR FUTURES?
YOUR STUDENTS ARE FULL OF POTENTIAL TOO, YOU KNOW... AND WE'VE BEEN STUDYING HARD AND PAYING CLOSE ATTENTION TO YOUR LECTURES DAILY...
...TO GROW AND REACH THAT POTENTIAL.

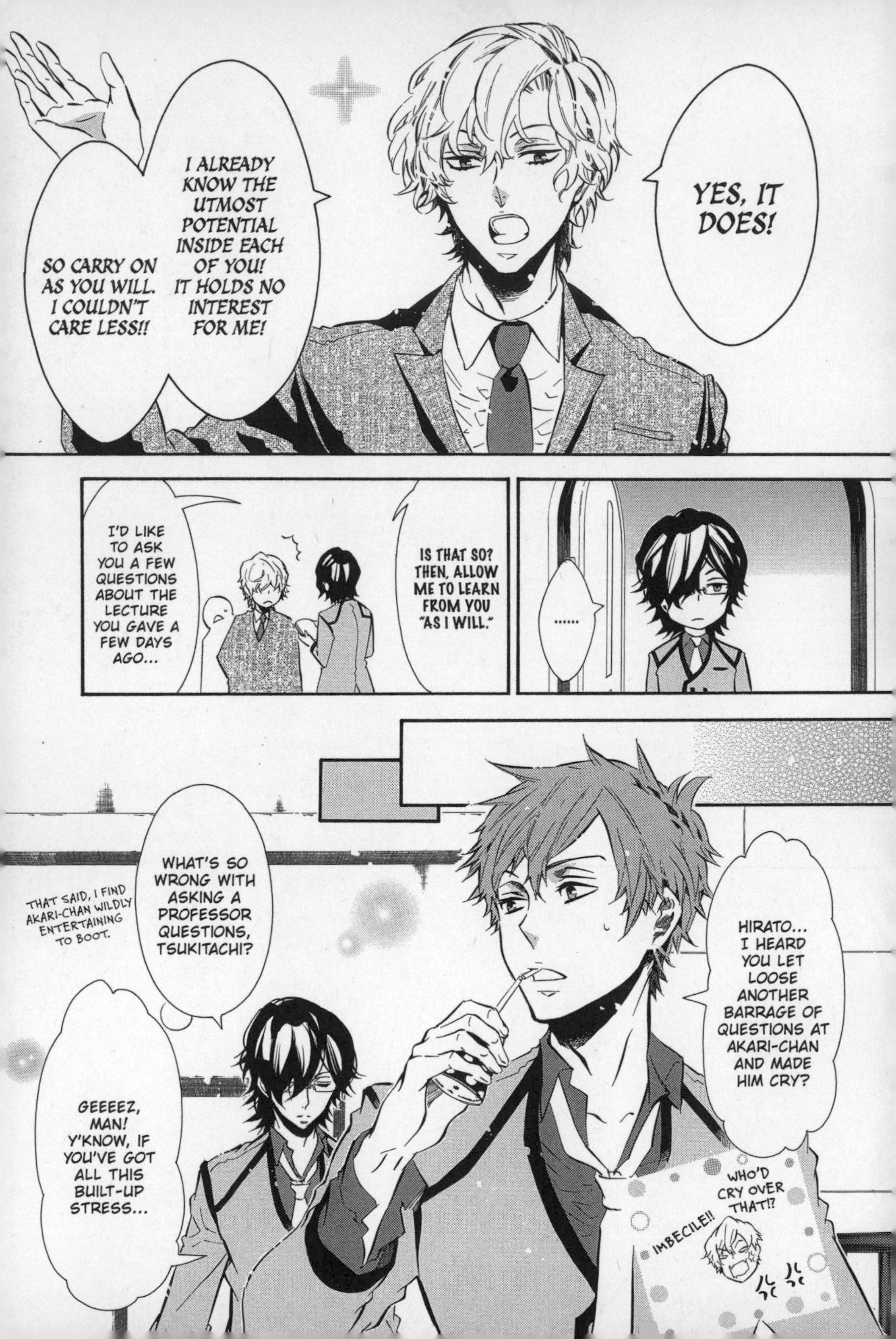

YES, IT DOES!
I ALREADY KNOW THE UTMOST POTENTIAL INSIDE EACH OF YOU! IT HOLDS NO INTEREST FOR ME!
SO CARRY ON AS YOU WILL. I COULDN'T CARE LESS!!
......
IS THAT SO? THEN, ALLOW ME TO LEARN FROM YOU "AS I WILL."
I'D LIKE TO ASK YOU A FEW QUESTIONS ABOUT THE LECTURE YOU GAVE A FEW DAYS AGO...
HIRATO... I HEARD YOU LET LOOSE ANOTHER BARRAGE OF QUESTIONS AT AKARI-CHAN AND MADE HIM CRY?
WHAT'S SO WRONG WITH ASKING A PROFESSOR QUESTIONS, TSUKITACHI?
THAT SAID, I FIND AKARI-CHAN WILDLY ENTERTAINING TO BOOT.
WHO'D CRY OVER THAT!?
IMBECILE!!
GEEEEZ, MAN! Y'KNOW, IF YOU'VE GOT ALL THIS BUILT-UP STRESS...

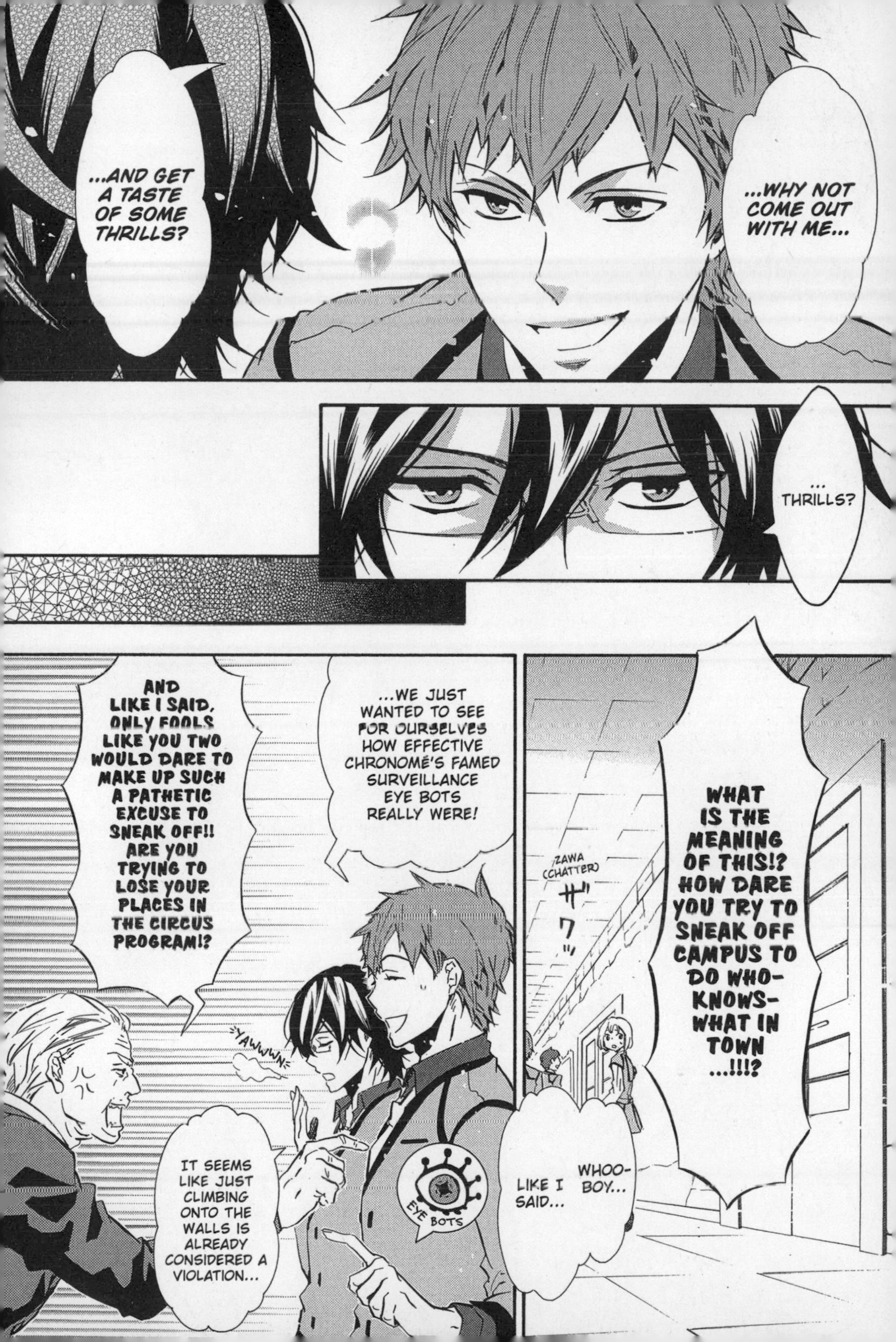
...WHY NOT COME OUT WITH ME...
...AND GET A TASTE OF SOME THRILLS?
... THRILLS?
WHAT IS THE MEANING OF THIS!? HOW DARE YOU TRY TO SNEAK OFF CAMPUS TO DO WHO-KNOWS-WHAT IN TOWN ...!!!?
ZAWA (CHATTER)
ザワッ
WHOO-BOY...
LIKE I SAID...
...WE JUST WANTED TO SEE FOR OURSELVES HOW EFFECTIVE CHRONOMÉ'S FAMED SURVEILLANCE EYE BOTS REALLY WERE!
AND LIKE I SAID, ONLY FOOLS LIKE YOU TWO WOULD DARE TO MAKE UP SUCH A PATHETIC EXCUSE TO SNEAK OFF!! ARE YOU TRYING TO LOSE YOUR PLACES IN THE CIRCUS PROGRAM!?
YAWWWN
IT SEEMS LIKE JUST CLIMBING ONTO THE WALLS IS ALREADY CONSIDERED A VIOLATION...
EYE BOTS

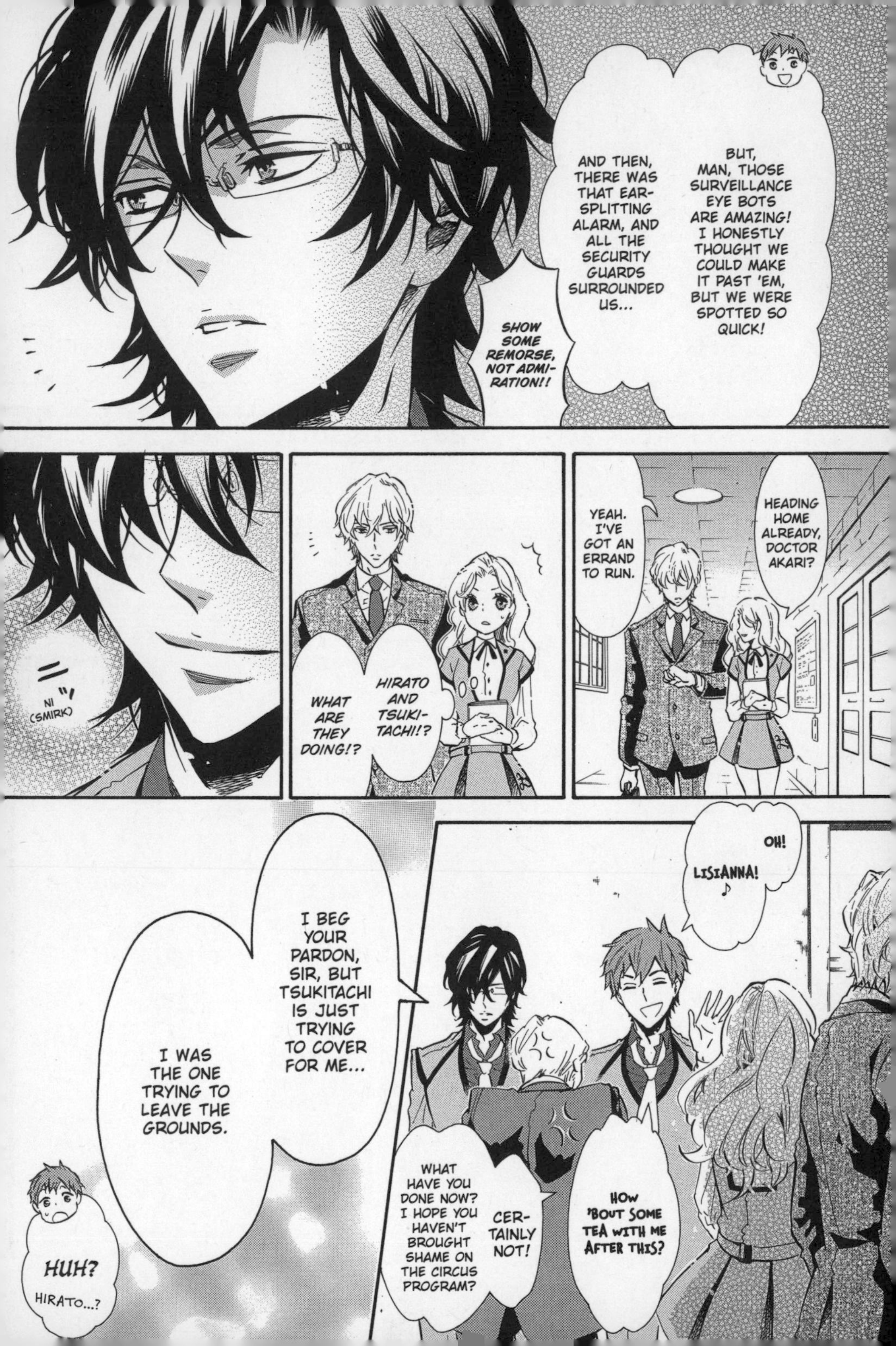
BUT, MAN, THOSE SURVEILLANCE EYE BOTS ARE AMAZING! I HONESTLY THOUGHT WE COULD MAKE IT PAST 'EM, BUT WE WERE SPOTTED SO QUICK!
AND THEN, THERE WAS THAT EAR-SPLITTING ALARM, AND ALL THE SECURITY GUARDS SURROUNDED US...
SHOW SOME REMORSE, NOT ADMIRATION!!
HEADING HOME ALREADY, DOCTOR AKARI?
YEAH. I'VE GOT AN ERRAND TO RUN.
HIRATO AND TSUKITACHI!?
WHAT ARE THEY DOING!?
NI (SMIRK)
OH!
LISIANNA! ♪
HOW 'BOUT SOME TEA WITH ME AFTER THIS?
CERTAINLY NOT!
WHAT HAVE YOU DONE NOW? I HOPE YOU HAVEN'T BROUGHT SHAME ON THE CIRCUS PROGRAM?
I BEG YOUR PARDON, SIR, BUT TSUKITACHI IS JUST TRYING TO COVER FOR ME...
I WAS THE ONE TRYING TO LEAVE THE GROUNDS.
HUH?
HIRATO...?

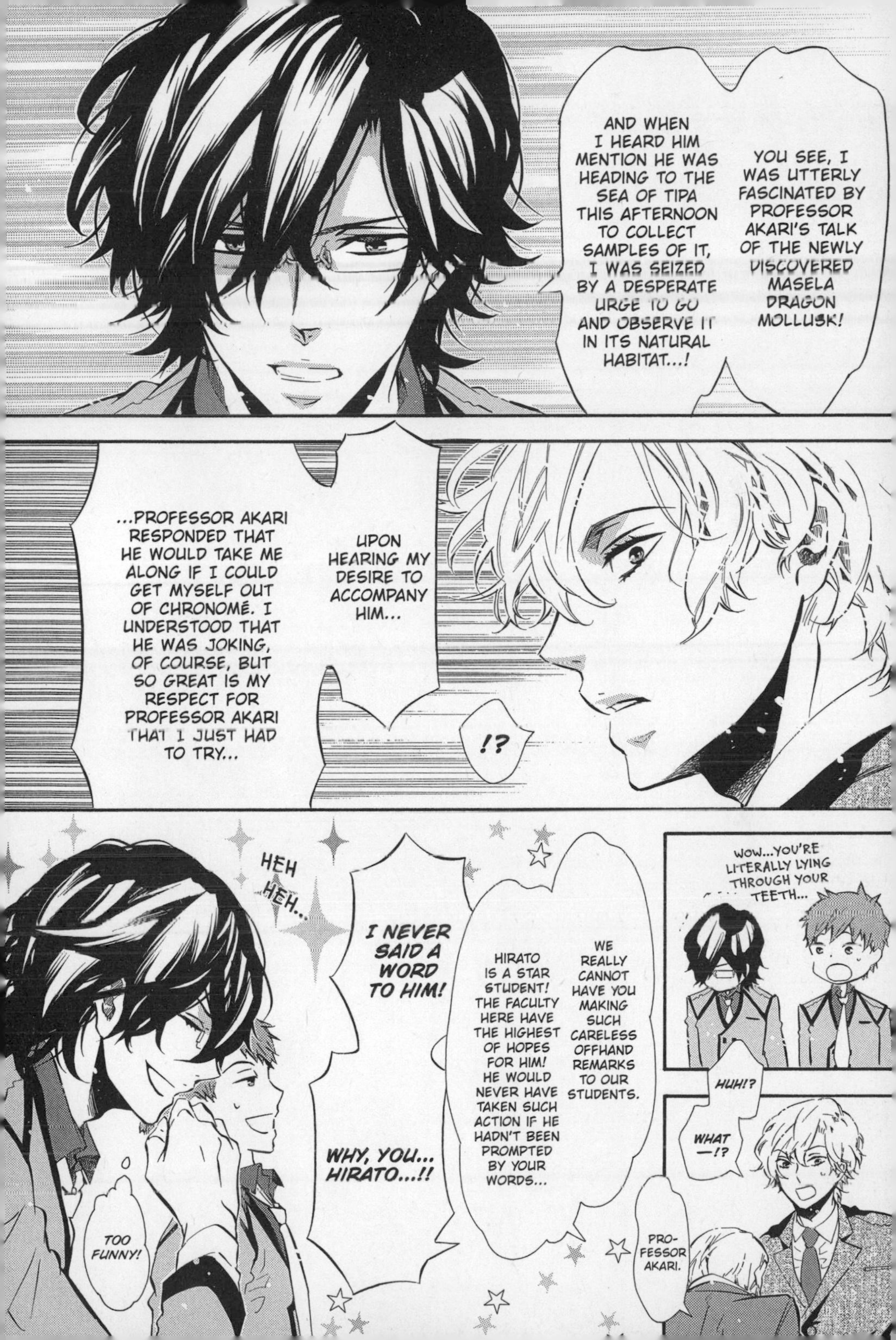
YOU SEE, I WAS UTTERLY FASCINATED BY PROFESSOR AKARI'S TALK OF THE NEWLY DISCOVERED MASELA DRAGON MOLLUSK!
AND WHEN I HEARD HIM MENTION HE WAS HEADING TO THE SEA OF TIPA THIS AFTERNOON TO COLLECT SAMPLES OF IT, I WAS SEIZED BY A DESPERATE URGE TO GO AND OBSERVE IT IN ITS NATURAL HABITAT...!
UPON HEARING MY DESIRE TO ACCOMPANY HIM...
...PROFESSOR AKARI RESPONDED THAT HE WOULD TAKE ME ALONG IF I COULD GET MYSELF OUT OF CHRONOMÉ. I UNDERSTOOD THAT HE WAS JOKING, OF COURSE, BUT SO GREAT IS MY RESPECT FOR PROFESSOR AKARI THAT I JUST HAD TO TRY...
!?
WOW...YOU'RE LITERALLY LYING THROUGH YOUR TEETH...
HUH!?
WHAT—!?
PRO-FESSOR AKARI.
WE REALLY CANNOT HAVE YOU MAKING SUCH CARELESS OFFHAND REMARKS TO OUR STUDENTS.
HIRATO IS A STAR STUDENT! THE FACULTY HERE HAVE THE HIGHEST OF HOPES FOR HIM! HE WOULD NEVER HAVE TAKEN SUCH ACTION IF HE HADN'T BEEN PROMPTED BY YOUR WORDS...
I NEVER SAID A WORD TO HIM!
HEH HEH...
WHY, YOU... HIRATO...!!
TOO FUNNY!

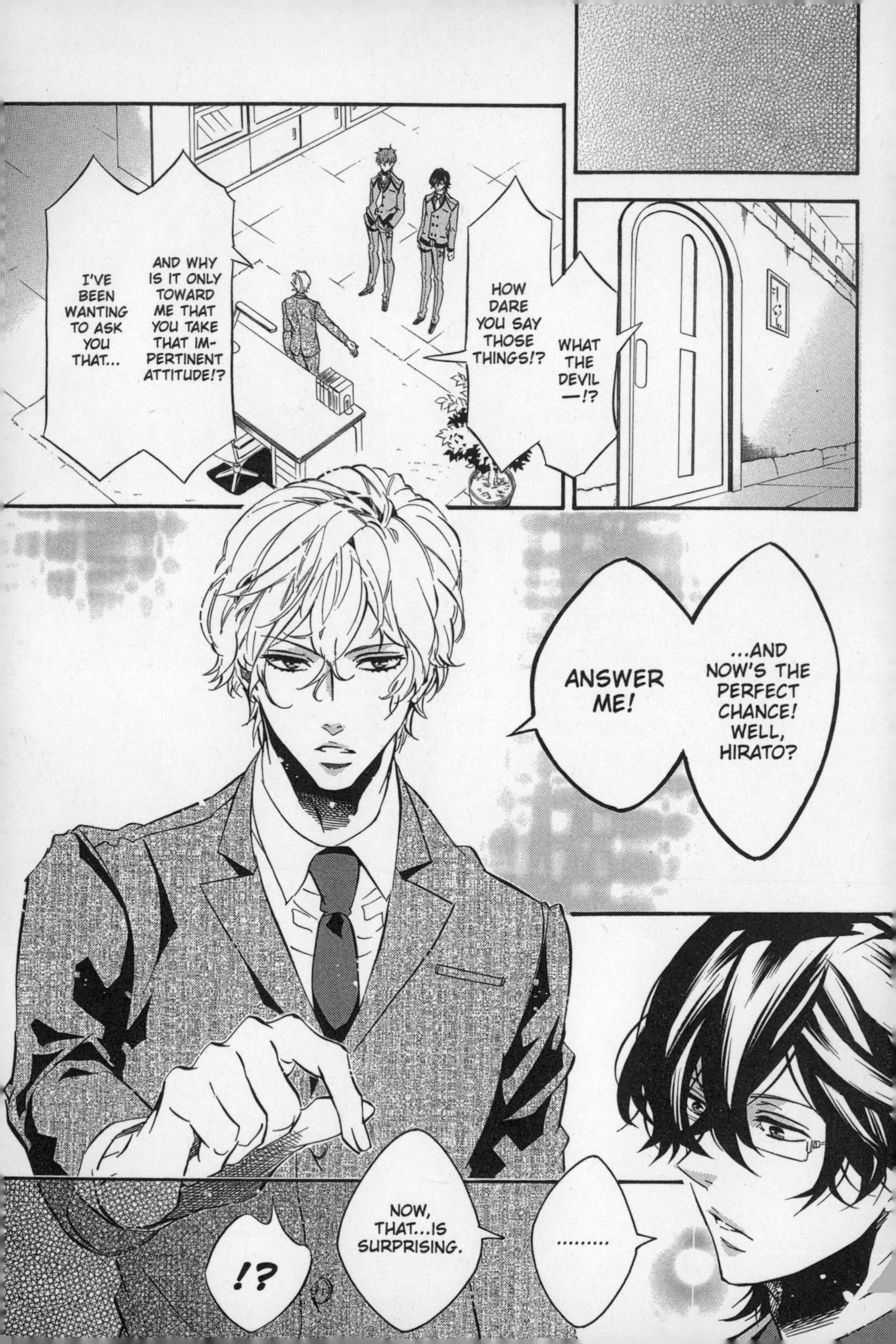
WHAT THE DEVIL—!?
HOW DARE YOU SAY THOSE THINGS!?
AND WHY IS IT ONLY TOWARD ME THAT YOU TAKE THAT IM-PERTINENT ATTITUDE!?
I'VE BEEN WANTING TO ASK YOU THAT...
...AND NOW'S THE PERFECT CHANCE! WELL, HIRATO?
ANSWER ME!
....
NOW, THAT...IS SURPRISING.
!?

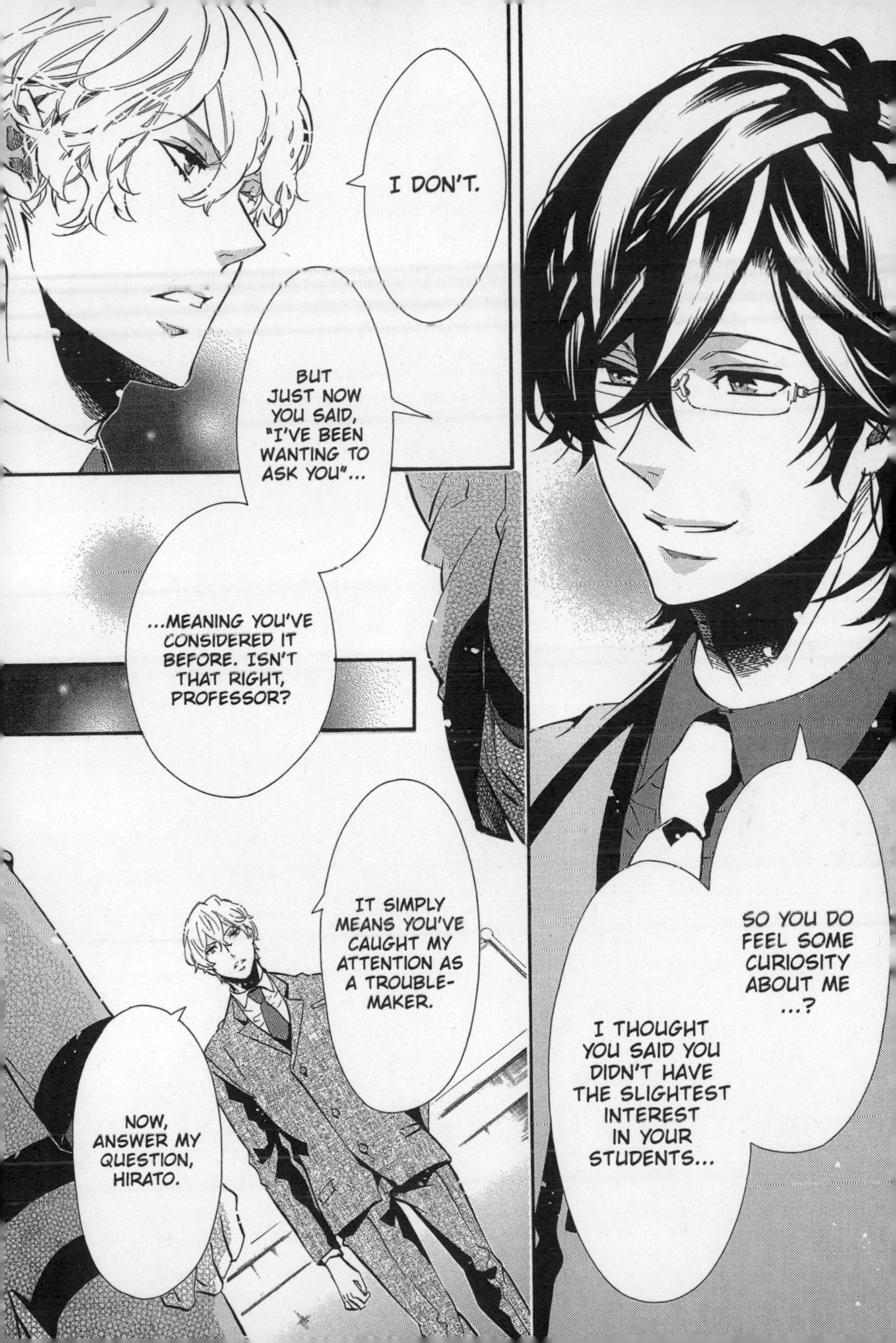
SO YOU DO FEEL SOME CURIOSITY ABOUT ME ...?
I THOUGHT YOU SAID YOU DIDN'T HAVE THE SLIGHTEST INTEREST IN YOUR STUDENTS...
I DON'T.
BUT JUST NOW YOU SAID, "I'VE BEEN WANTING TO ASK YOU"...
...MEANING YOU'VE CONSIDERED IT BEFORE. ISN'T THAT RIGHT, PROFESSOR?
IT SIMPLY MEANS YOU'VE CAUGHT MY ATTENTION AS A TROUBLE-MAKER.
NOW, ANSWER MY QUESTION, HIRATO.

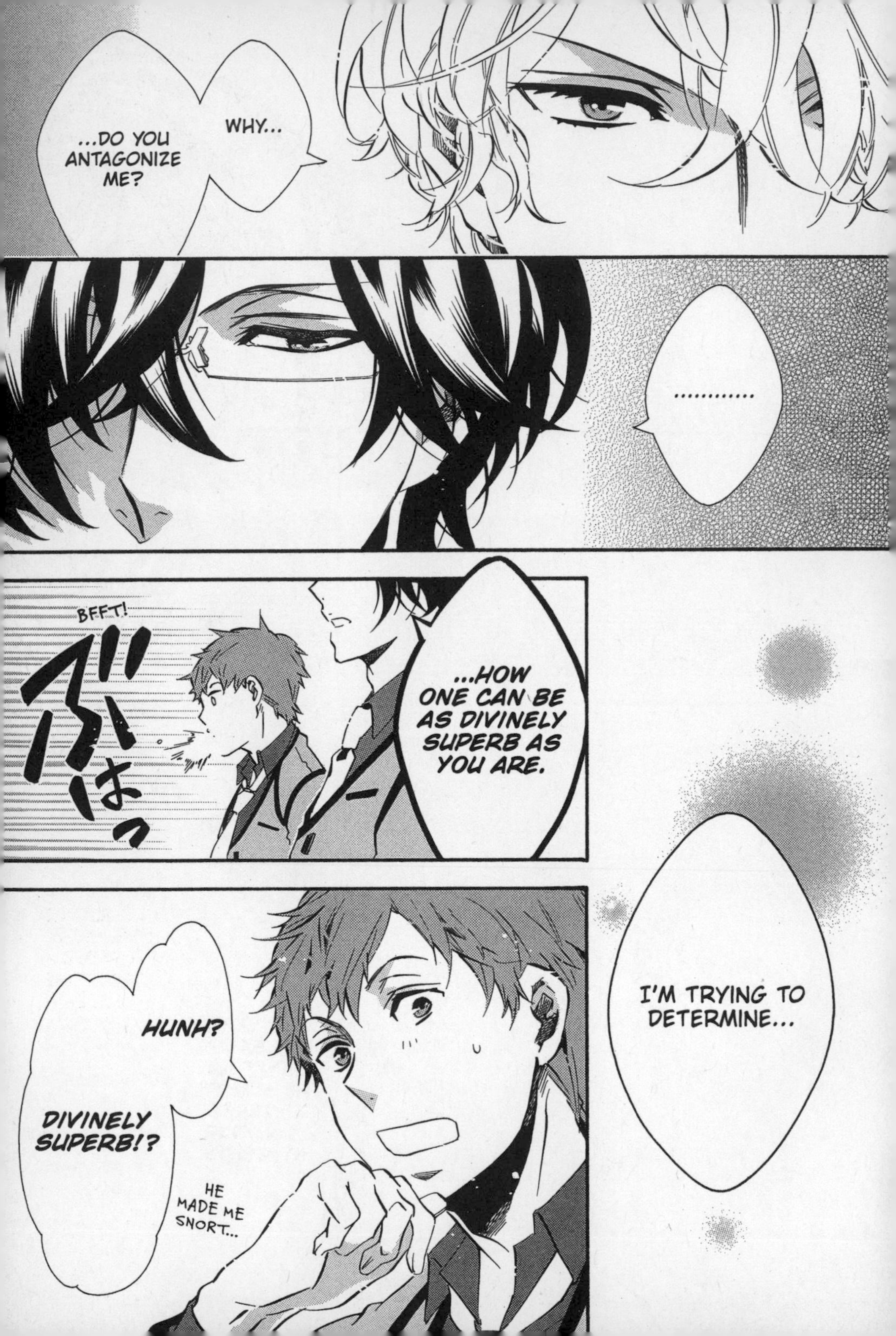
WHY...
...DO YOU ANTAGONIZE ME?
....
I'M TRYING TO DETERMINE...
...HOW ONE CAN BE AS DIVINELY SUPERB AS YOU ARE.
BFFT!
ぶはっ
HUNH?
DIVINELY SUPERB!?
HE MADE ME SNORT...

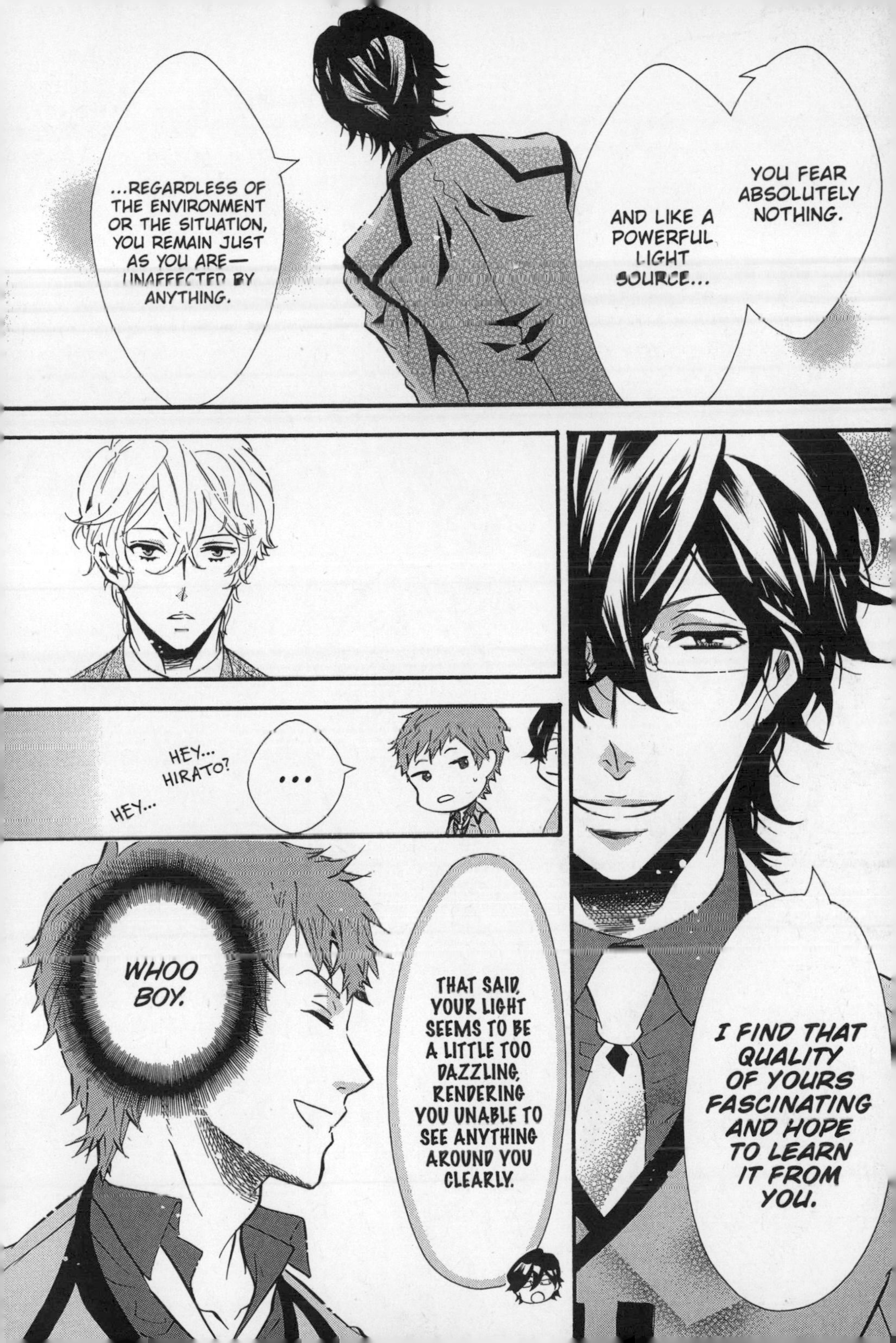
YOU FEAR ABSOLUTELY NOTHING.
AND LIKE A POWERFUL LIGHT SOURCE...
...REGARDLESS OF THE ENVIRONMENT OR THE SITUATION, YOU REMAIN JUST AS YOU ARE—UNAFFECTED BY ANYTHING.
I FIND THAT QUALITY OF YOURS FASCINATING AND HOPE TO LEARN IT FROM YOU.
THAT SAID, YOUR LIGHT SEEMS TO BE A LITTLE TOO DAZZLING, RENDERING YOU UNABLE TO SEE ANYTHING AROUND YOU CLEARLY.
...
HEY... HIRATO?
HEY...
WHOO BOY.

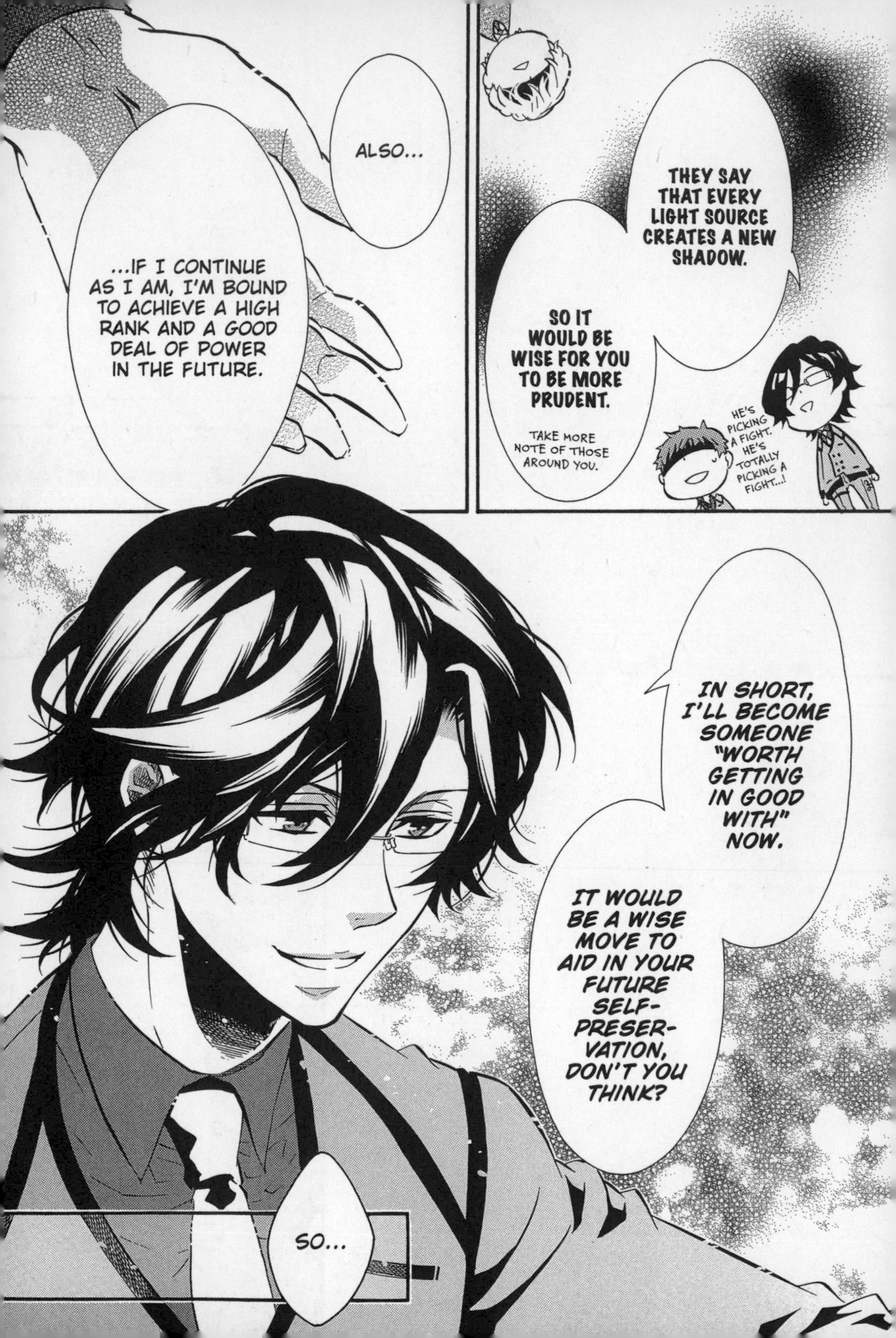
THEY SAY THAT EVERY LIGHT SOURCE CREATES A NEW SHADOW.
SO IT WOULD BE WISE FOR YOU TO BE MORE PRUDENT.
TAKE MORE NOTE OF THOSE AROUND YOU.
HE'S PICKING A FIGHT. HE'S TOTALLY PICKING A FIGHT...!
ALSO...
...IF I CONTINUE AS I AM, I'M BOUND TO ACHIEVE A HIGH RANK AND A GOOD DEAL OF POWER IN THE FUTURE.
IN SHORT, I'LL BECOME SOMEONE "WORTH GETTING IN GOOD WITH" NOW.
IT WOULD BE A WISE MOVE TO AID IN YOUR FUTURE SELF-PRESERVATION, DON'T YOU THINK?
SO...

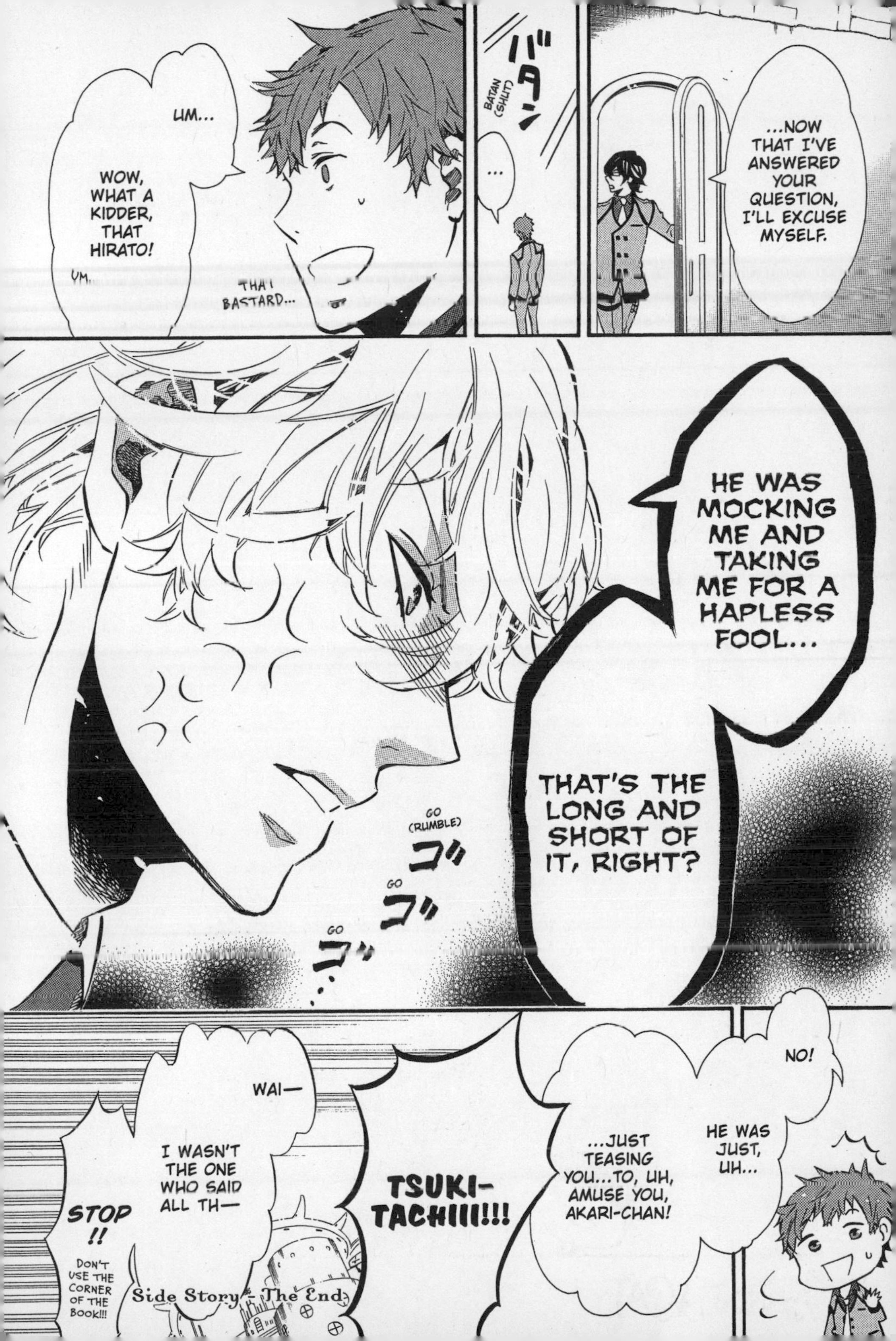
...NOW THAT I'VE ANSWERED YOUR QUESTION, I'LL EXCUSE MYSELF.
バタン
BATAN (SHUT)
...
UM...
WOW, WHAT A KIDDER, THAT HIRATO!
UM.
THAT BASTARD...
HE WAS MOCKING ME AND TAKING ME FOR A HAPLESS FOOL...
THAT'S THE LONG AND SHORT OF IT, RIGHT?
GO (RUMBLE)
ゴ
GO
ゴ
GO
ゴ
NO!
HE WAS JUST, UH...
...JUST TEASING YOU...TO, UH, AMUSE YOU, AKARI-CHAN!
TSUKI-TACHIIII!!!
WAI—
I WASN'T THE ONE WHO SAID ALL TH—
STOP !!
DON'T USE THE CORNER OF THE BOOK!!!
Side Story - The End

HE'S PICKING A FIGHT. HE'S TOTALLY PICKING A FIGHT...!

KARNEVAL

KARNEVAL

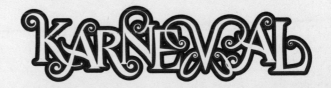

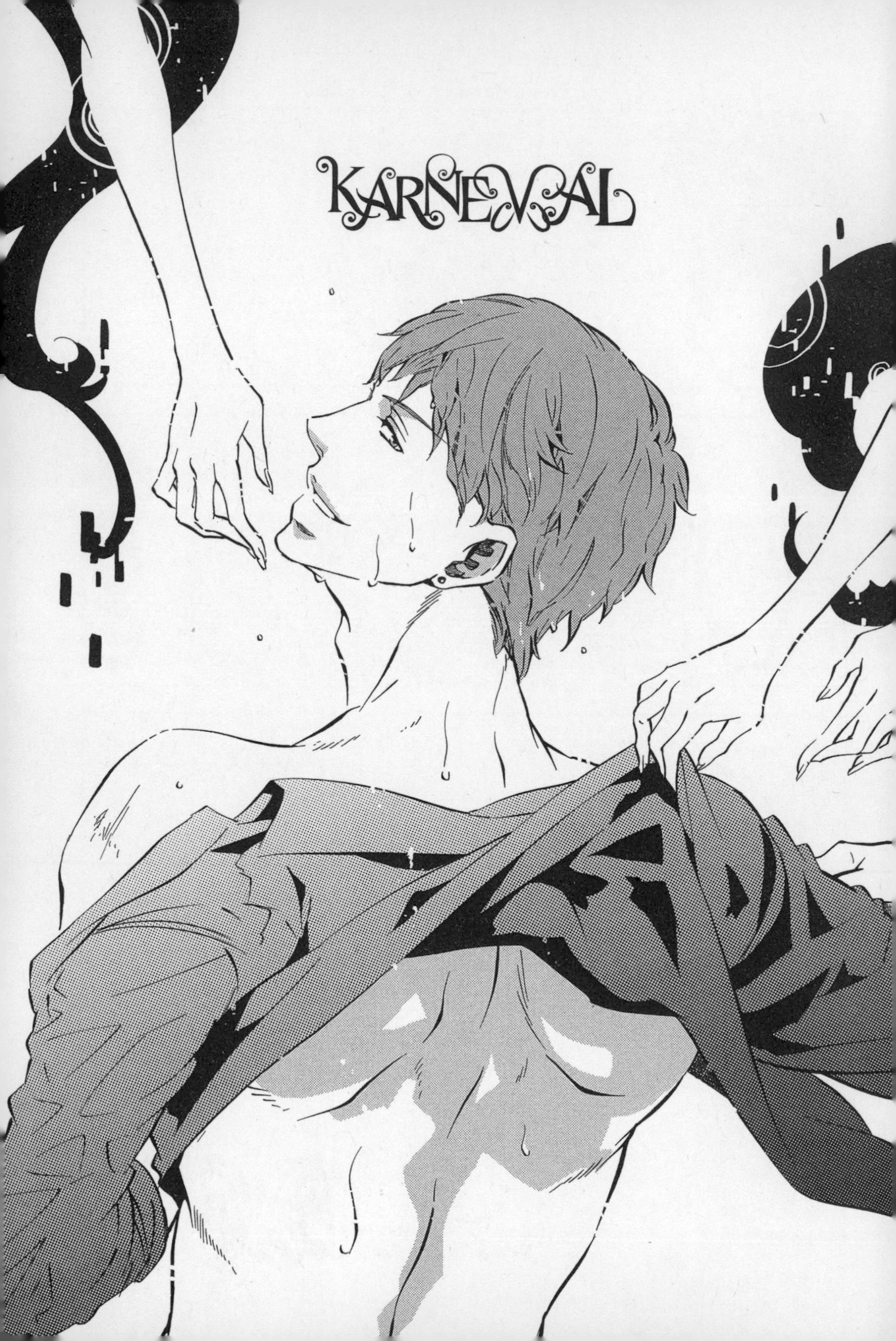
KARNEVAL

Bonus Comic 1 - I Think You Were Being Silly...

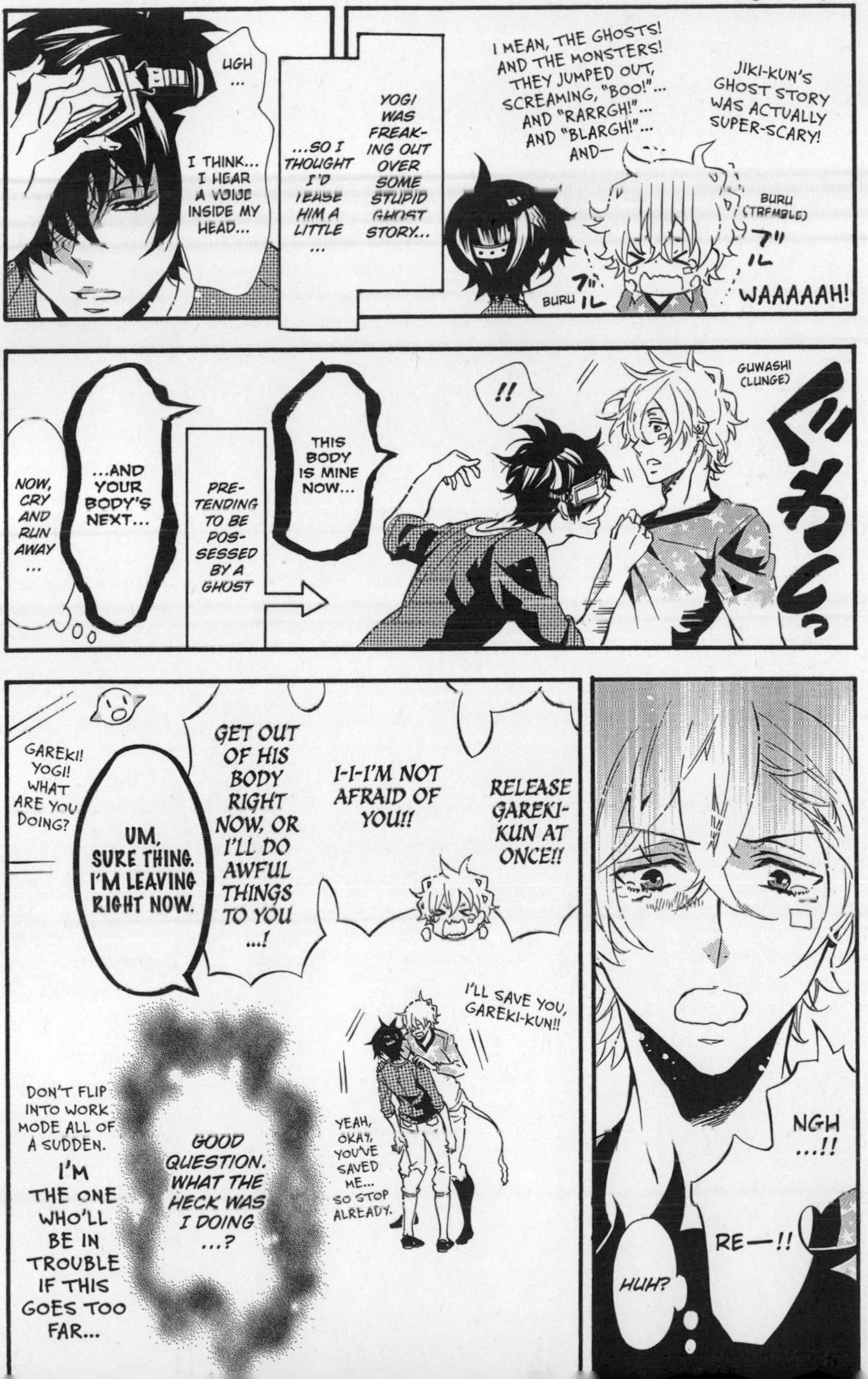
JIKI-KUN'S GHOST STORY WAS ACTUALLY SUPER-SCARY!
I MEAN, THE GHOSTS! AND THE MONSTERS! THEY JUMPED OUT, SCREAMING, "BOO!"... AND "RARRGH!"... AND "BLARGH!"... AND—
BURU (TREMBLE)
WAAAAAH!
BURU
YOGI WAS FREAKING OUT OVER SOME STUPID GHOST STORY...
...SO I THOUGHT I'D TEASE HIM A LITTLE...
UGH...
I THINK... I HEAR A VOICE INSIDE MY HEAD...
GUWASHI (LUNGE)
!!
THIS BODY IS MINE NOW...
PRETENDING TO BE POSSESSED BY A GHOST
...AND YOUR BODY'S NEXT...
NOW, CRY AND RUN AWAY...
NGH ...!!
RE—!!
HUH?
RELEASE GAREKI-KUN AT ONCE!!
I-I-I'M NOT AFRAID OF YOU!!
GET OUT OF HIS BODY RIGHT NOW, OR I'LL DO AWFUL THINGS TO YOU ...!
UM, SURE THING. I'M LEAVING RIGHT NOW.
GAREKI! YOGI! WHAT ARE YOU DOING?
I'LL SAVE YOU, GAREKI-KUN!!
YEAH, OKAY, YOU'VE SAVED ME... SO STOP ALREADY.
GOOD QUESTION. WHAT THE HECK WAS I DOING ...?
DON'T FLIP INTO WORK MODE ALL OF A SUDDEN. I'M THE ONE WHO'LL BE IN TROUBLE IF THIS GOES TOO FAR...

Bonus Comic 2 - I Was Watching

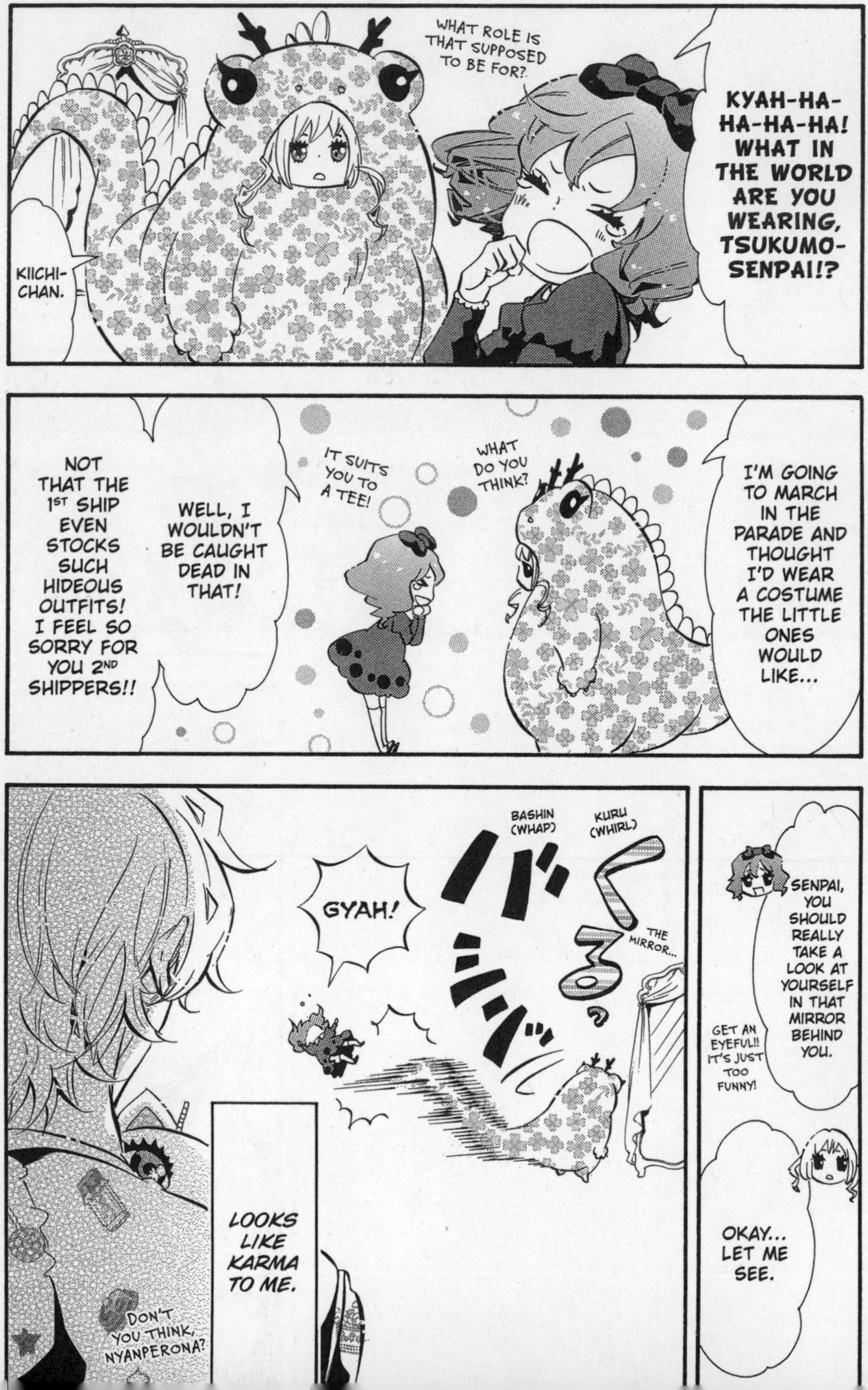
KYAH-HA-HA-HA-HA! WHAT IN THE WORLD ARE YOU WEARING, TSUKUMO-SENPAI!?
WHAT ROLE IS THAT SUPPOSED TO BE FOR?
KIICHI-CHAN.
I'M GOING TO MARCH IN THE PARADE AND THOUGHT I'D WEAR A COSTUME THE LITTLE ONES WOULD LIKE...
WHAT DO YOU THINK?
IT SUITS YOU TO A TEE!
WELL, I WOULDN'T BE CAUGHT DEAD IN THAT!
NOT THAT THE 1st SHIP EVEN STOCKS SUCH HIDEOUS OUTFITS! I FEEL SO SORRY FOR YOU 2nd SHIPPERS!!
SENPAI, YOU SHOULD REALLY TAKE A LOOK AT YOURSELF IN THAT MIRROR BEHIND YOU.
GET AN EYEFUL!! IT'S JUST TOO FUNNY!
OKAY... LET ME SEE.
KURU (WHIRL)
BASHIN (WHAP)
THE MIRROR...
GYAH!
LOOKS LIKE KARMA TO ME.
DON'T YOU THINK, NYANPERONA?

Bonus Comic 3 - Research Tower Daily Log

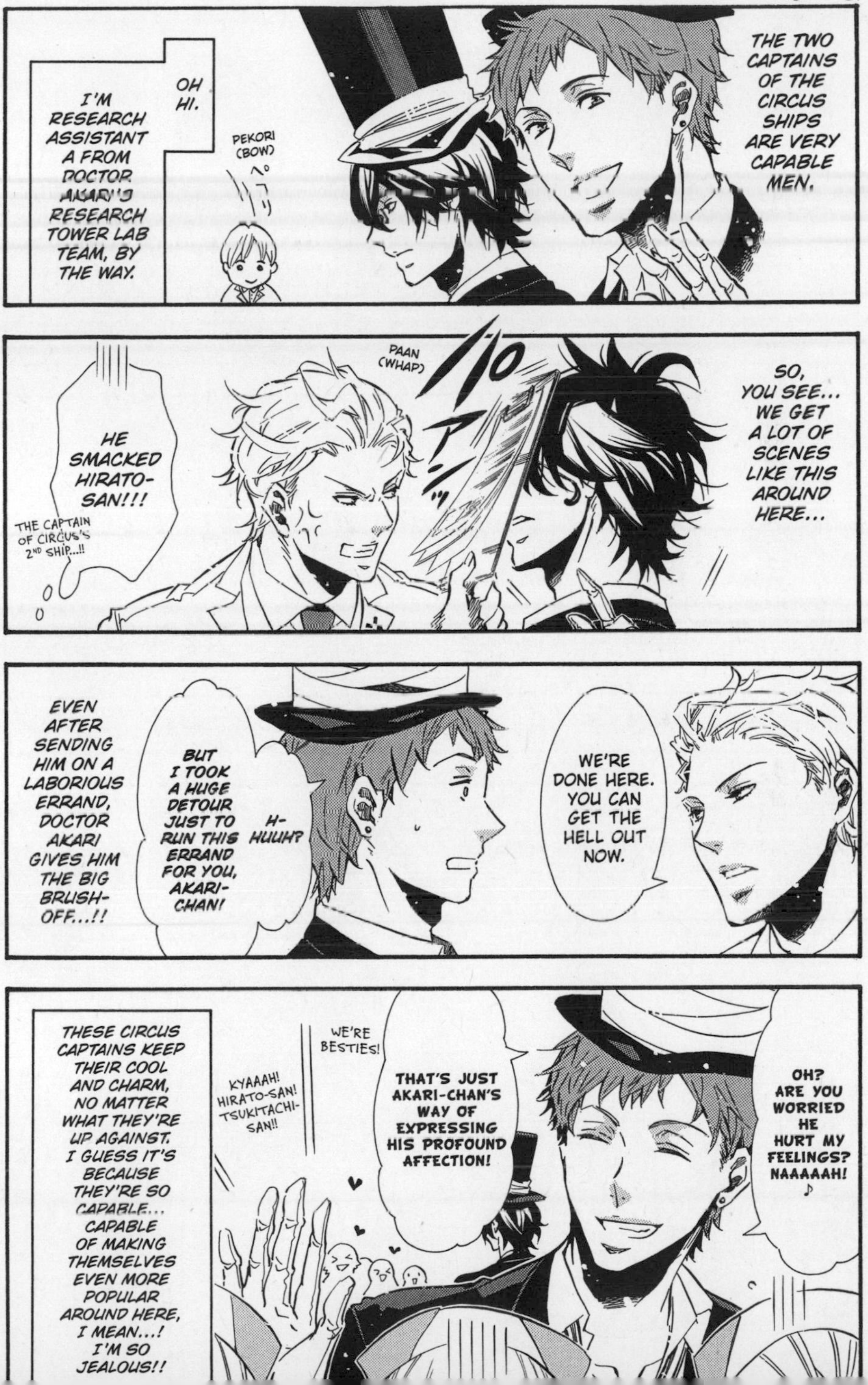
THE TWO CAPTAINS OF THE CIRCUS SHIPS ARE VERY CAPABLE MEN.
OH HI.
PEKORI (BOW)
I'M RESEARCH ASSISTANT A FROM DOCTOR AKARI'S RESEARCH TOWER LAB TEAM, BY THE WAY.
SO, YOU SEE... WE GET A LOT OF SCENES LIKE THIS AROUND HERE...
PAAN (WHAP)
HE SMACKED HIRATO-SAN!!!
THE CAPTAIN OF CIRCUS'S 2ND SHIP...!!
WE'RE DONE HERE. YOU CAN GET THE HELL OUT NOW.
H-HUUH?
BUT I TOOK A HUGE DETOUR JUST TO RUN THIS ERRAND FOR YOU, AKARI-CHAN!
EVEN AFTER SENDING HIM ON A LABORIOUS ERRAND, DOCTOR AKARI GIVES HIM THE BIG BRUSH-OFF...!!
OH? ARE YOU WORRIED HE HURT MY FEELINGS? NAAAAAH! ♪
THAT'S JUST AKARI-CHAN'S WAY OF EXPRESSING HIS PROFOUND AFFECTION!
WE'RE BESTIES!
KYAAAH! HIRATO-SAN! TSUKITACHI-SAN!!
THESE CIRCUS CAPTAINS KEEP THEIR COOL AND CHARM, NO MATTER WHAT THEY'RE UP AGAINST. I GUESS IT'S BECAUSE THEY'RE SO CAPABLE... CAPABLE OF MAKING THEMSELVES EVEN MORE POPULAR AROUND HERE, I MEAN...! I'M SO JEALOUS!!

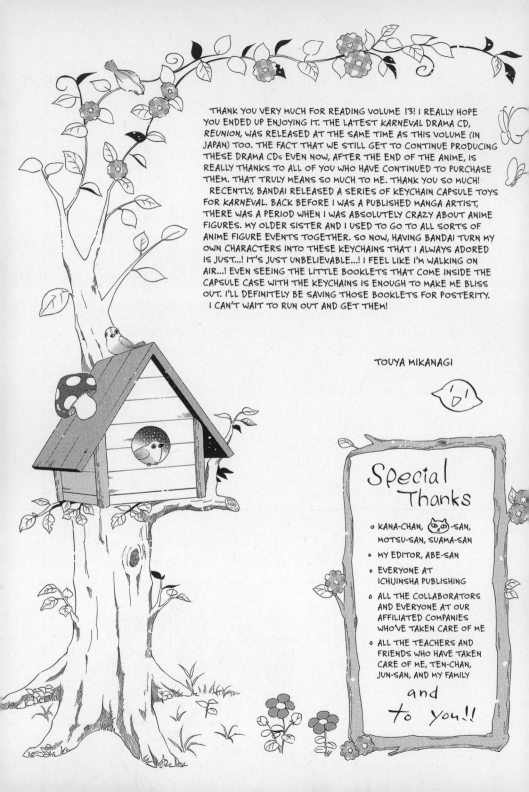

THANK YOU VERY MUCH FOR READING VOLUME 13! I REALLY HOPE YOU ENDED UP ENJOYING IT. THE LATEST *KARNEVAL* DRAMA CD, *REUNION*, WAS RELEASED AT THE SAME TIME AS THIS VOLUME (IN JAPAN) TOO. THE FACT THAT WE STILL GET TO CONTINUE PRODUCING THESE DRAMA CDs EVEN NOW, AFTER THE END OF THE ANIME, IS REALLY THANKS TO ALL OF YOU WHO HAVE CONTINUED TO PURCHASE THEM. THAT TRULY MEANS SO MUCH TO ME. THANK YOU SO MUCH!

RECENTLY, BANDAI RELEASED A SERIES OF KEYCHAIN CAPSULE TOYS FOR KARNEVAL. BACK BEFORE I WAS A PUBLISHED MANGA ARTIST, THERE WAS A PERIOD WHEN I WAS ABSOLUTELY CRAZY ABOUT ANIME FIGURES. MY OLDER SISTER AND I USED TO GO TO ALL SORTS OF ANIME FIGURE EVENTS TOGETHER. SO NOW, HAVING BANDAI TURN MY OWN CHARACTERS INTO THESE KEYCHAINS THAT I ALWAYS ADORED IS JUST...! IT'S JUST UNBELIEVABLE...! I FEEL LIKE I'M WALKING ON AIR...! EVEN SEEING THE LITTLE BOOKLETS THAT COME INSIDE THE CAPSULE CASE WITH THE KEYCHAINS IS ENOUGH TO MAKE ME BLISS OUT. I'LL DEFINITELY BE SAVING THOSE BOOKLETS FOR POSTERITY. I CAN'T WAIT TO RUN OUT AND GET THEM!

TOUYA MIKANAGI

Special Thanks

- KANA-CHAN, 🐱-SAN, MOTSU-SAN, SUAMA-SAN
- MY EDITOR, ABE-SAN
- EVERYONE AT ICHIJINSHA PUBLISHING
- ALL THE COLLABORATORS AND EVERYONE AT OUR AFFILIATED COMPANIES WHO'VE TAKEN CARE OF ME
- ALL THE TEACHERS AND FRIENDS WHO HAVE TAKEN CARE OF ME, TEN-CHAN, JUN-SAN, AND MY FAMILY

and

to you!!

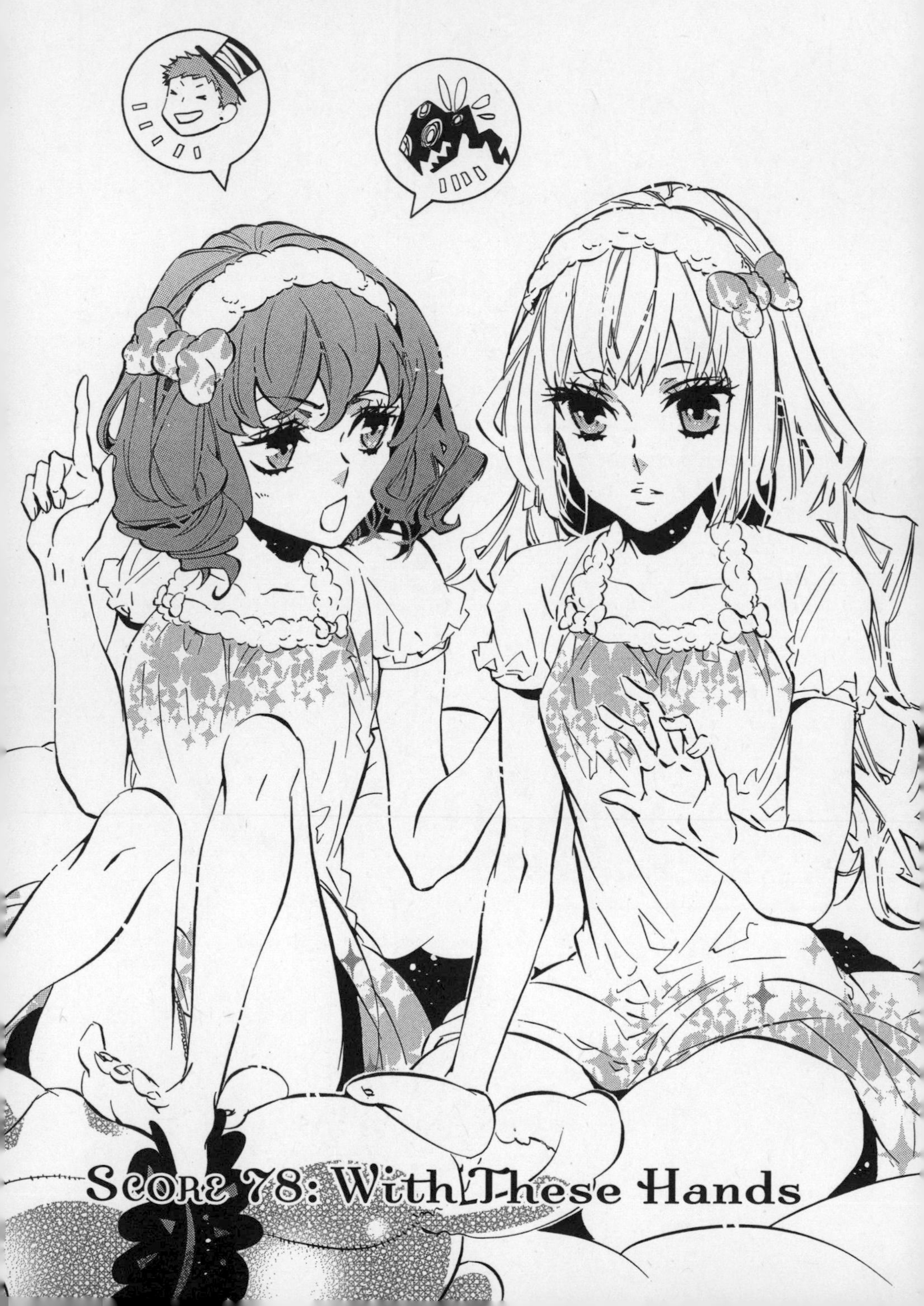
Score 78: With These Hands

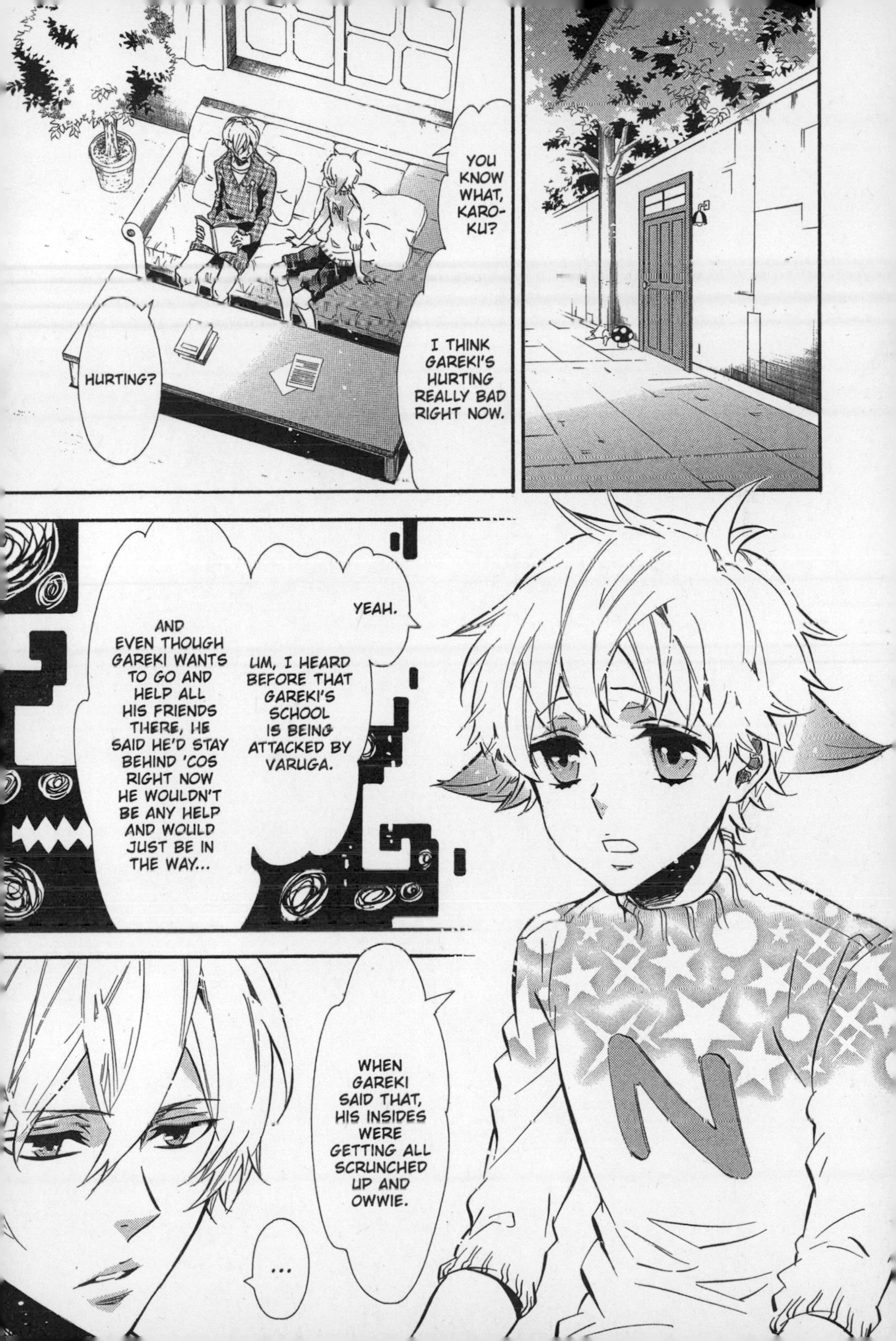
YOU KNOW WHAT, KARO-KU?
I THINK GAREKI'S HURTING REALLY BAD RIGHT NOW.
HURTING?
YEAH.
UM, I HEARD BEFORE THAT GAREKI'S SCHOOL IS BEING ATTACKED BY VARUGA.
AND EVEN THOUGH GAREKI WANTS TO GO AND HELP ALL HIS FRIENDS THERE, HE SAID HE'D STAY BEHIND 'COS RIGHT NOW HE WOULDN'T BE ANY HELP AND WOULD JUST BE IN THE WAY...
WHEN GAREKI SAID THAT, HIS INSIDES WERE GETTING ALL SCRUNCHED UP AND OWWIE.
...

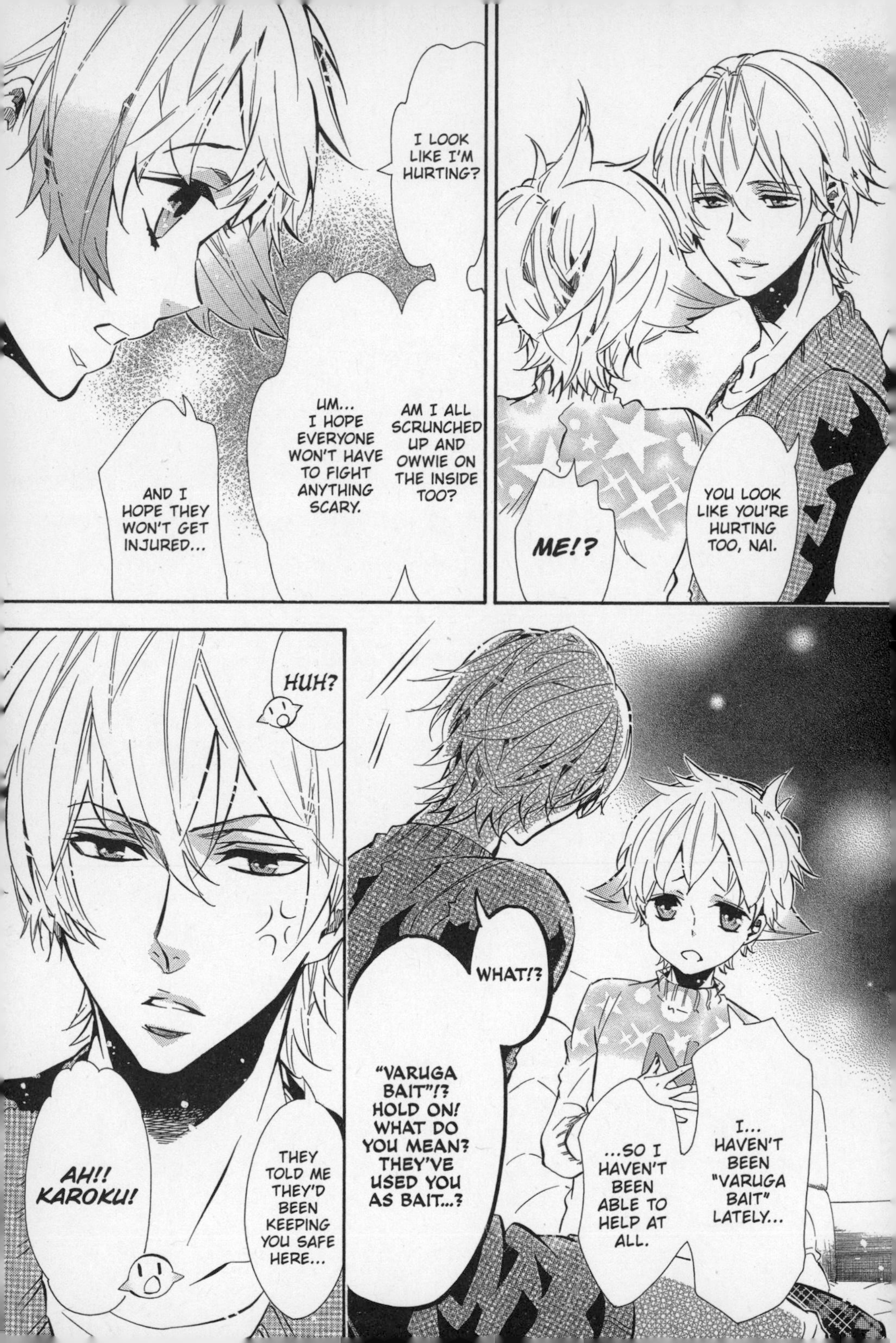
YOU LOOK LIKE YOU'RE HURTING TOO, NAI.
ME!?
I LOOK LIKE I'M HURTING?
AM I ALL SCRUNCHED UP AND OWWIE ON THE INSIDE TOO?
UM... I HOPE EVERYONE WON'T HAVE TO FIGHT ANYTHING SCARY.
AND I HOPE THEY WON'T GET INJURED...
I... HAVEN'T BEEN "VARUGA BAIT" LATELY...
...SO I HAVEN'T BEEN ABLE TO HELP AT ALL.
WHAT!?
"VARUGA BAIT"!? HOLD ON! WHAT DO YOU MEAN? THEY'VE USED YOU AS BAIT...?
HUH?
THEY TOLD ME THEY'D BEEN KEEPING YOU SAFE HERE...
AH!! KAROKU!

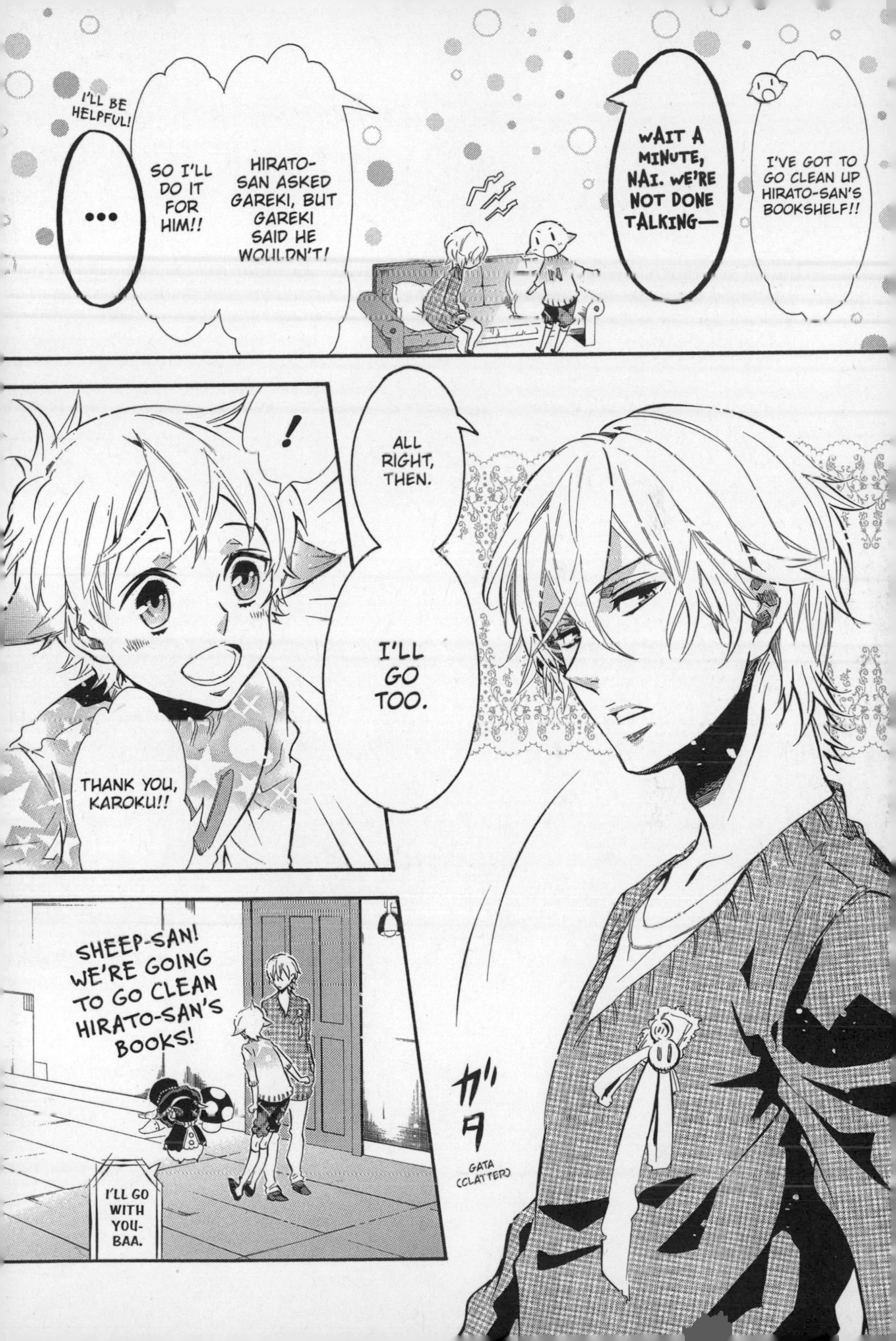
I'VE GOT TO GO CLEAN UP HIRATO-SAN'S BOOKSHELF!!
WAIT A MINUTE, NAI. WE'RE NOT DONE TALKING—
HIRATO-SAN ASKED GAREKI, BUT GAREKI SAID HE WOULDN'T!
SO I'LL DO IT FOR HIM!!
I'LL BE HELPFUL!
...
ALL RIGHT, THEN.
I'LL GO TOO.
ガタ
GATA (CLATTER)
!
THANK YOU, KAROKU!!
SHEEP-SAN! WE'RE GOING TO GO CLEAN HIRATO-SAN'S BOOKS!
I'LL GO WITH YOU-BAA.

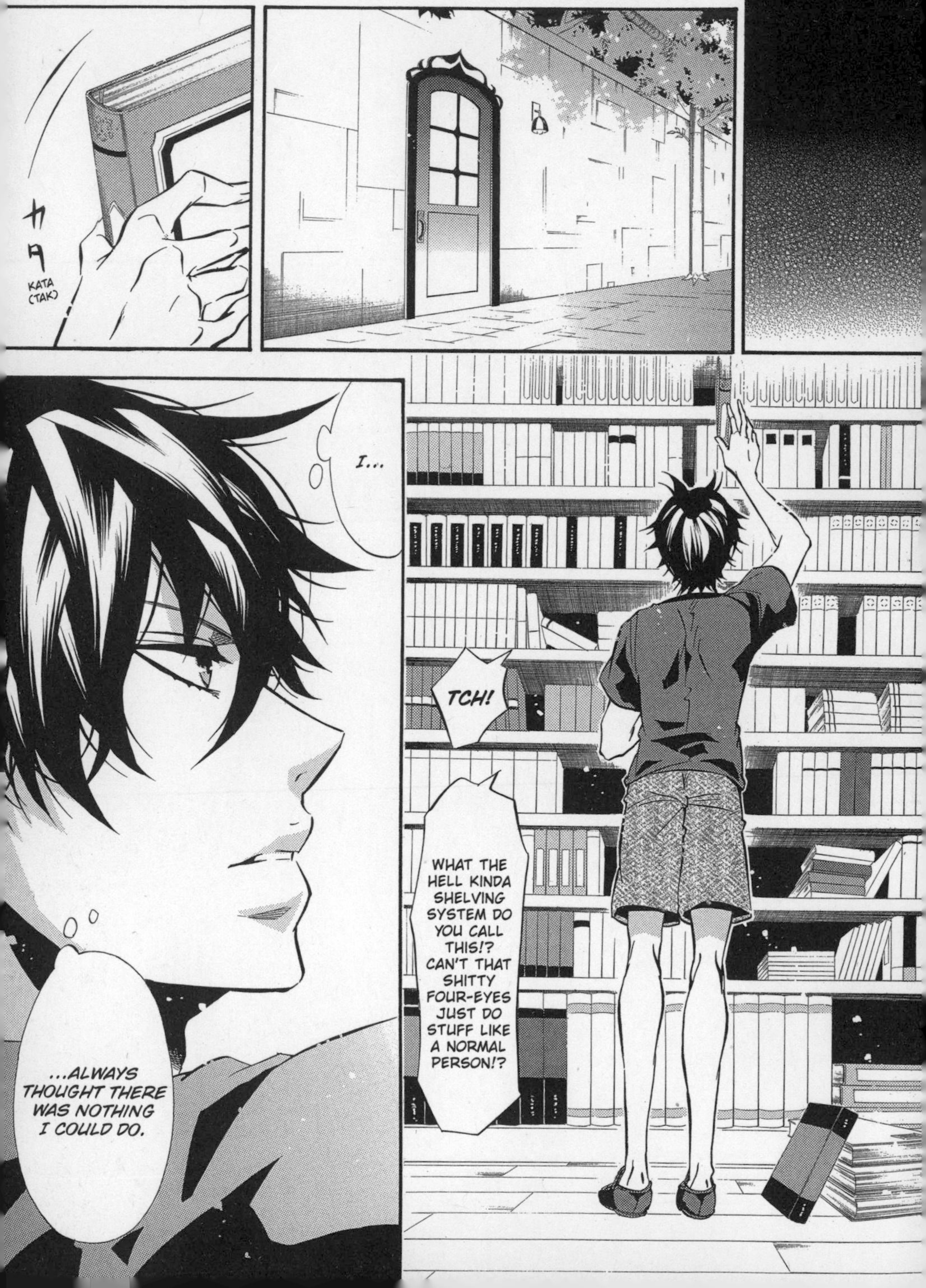
カタ
KATA (TAK)
TCH!
WHAT THE HELL KINDA SHELVING SYSTEM DO YOU CALL THIS!? CAN'T THAT SHITTY FOUR-EYES JUST DO STUFF LIKE A NORMAL PERSON!?
I...
...ALWAYS THOUGHT THERE WAS NOTHING I COULD DO.

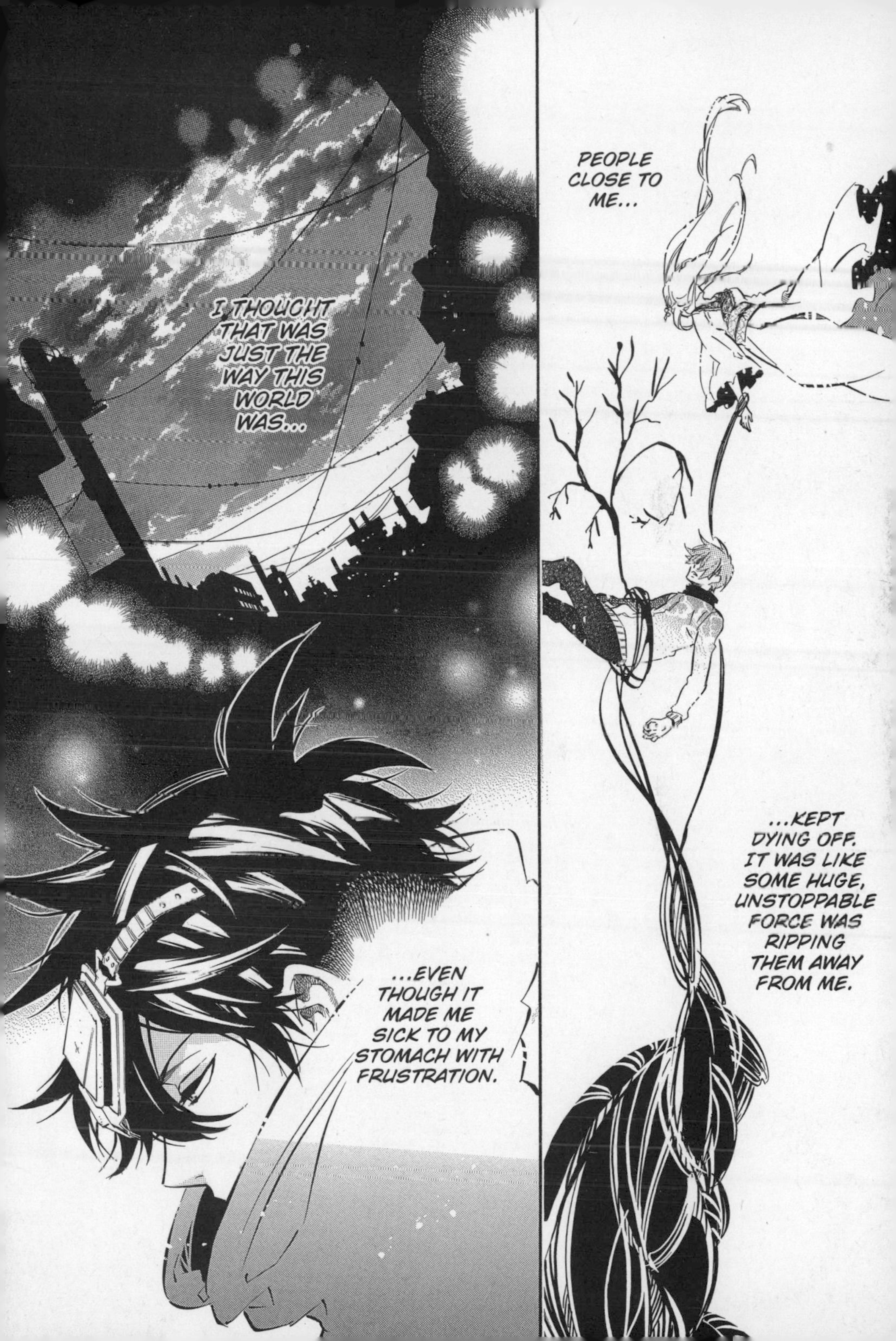
PEOPLE CLOSE TO ME...
...KEPT DYING OFF. IT WAS LIKE SOME HUGE, UNSTOPPABLE FORCE WAS RIPPING THEM AWAY FROM ME.
I THOUGHT THAT WAS JUST THE WAY THIS WORLD WAS...
...EVEN THOUGH IT MADE ME SICK TO MY STOMACH WITH FRUSTRATION.

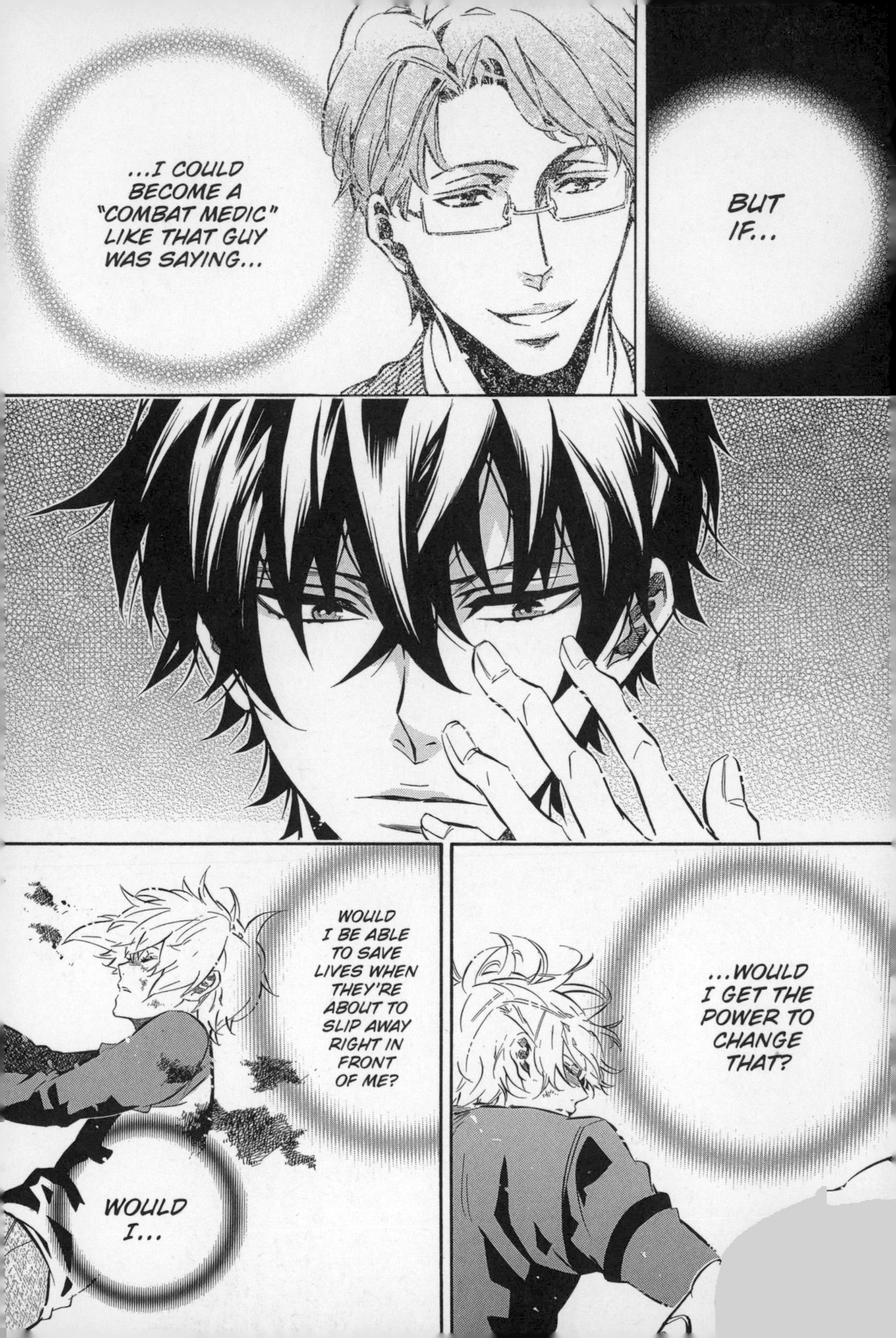
BUT IF...
...I COULD BECOME A "COMBAT MEDIC" LIKE THAT GUY WAS SAYING...
...WOULD I GET THE POWER TO CHANGE THAT?
WOULD I BE ABLE TO SAVE LIVES WHEN THEY'RE ABOUT TO SLIP AWAY RIGHT IN FRONT OF ME?
WOULD I...

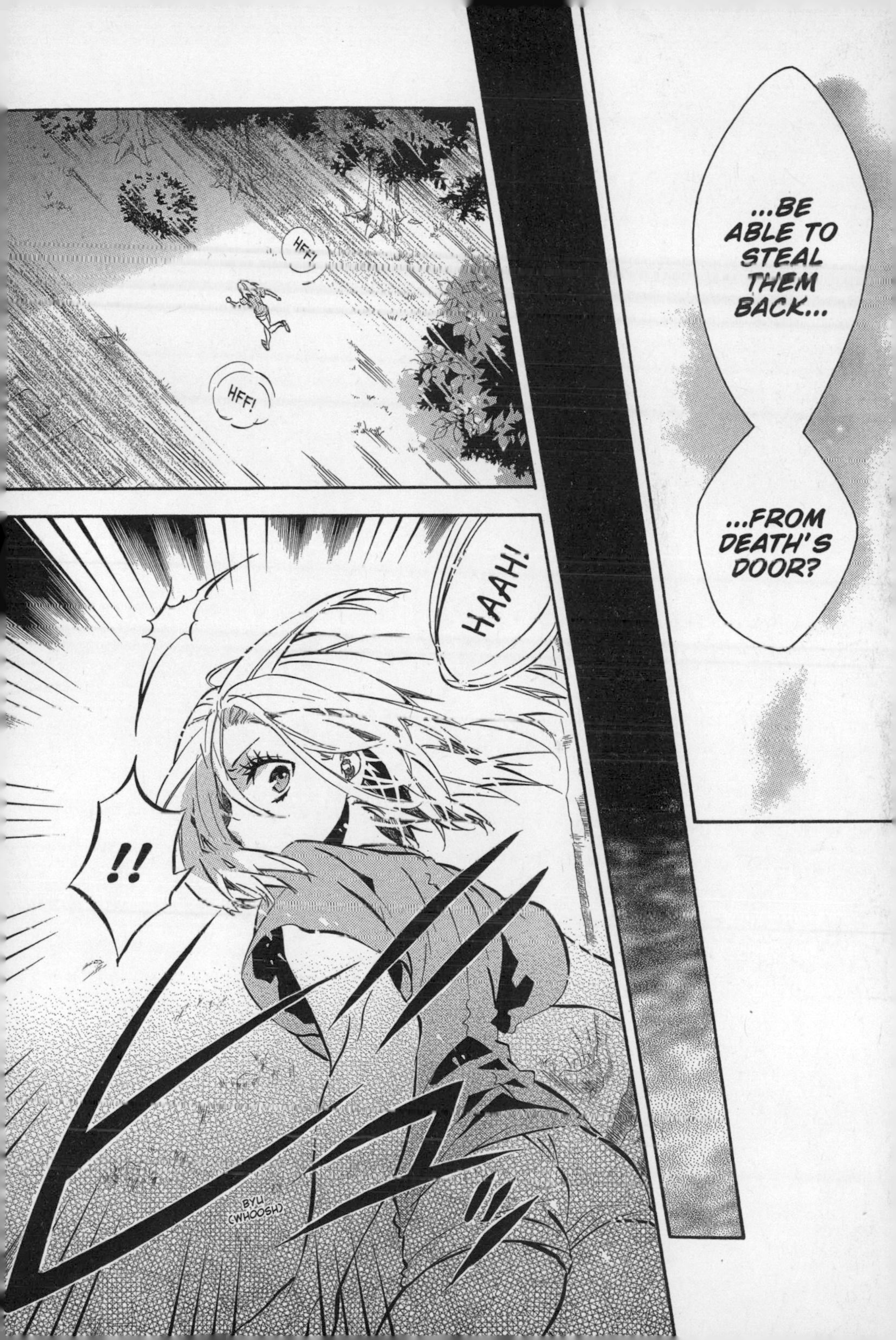
...BE ABLE TO STEAL THEM BACK...
...FROM DEATH'S DOOR?
HFF!
HFF!
HAAH!
!!
BYU (WHOOSH)

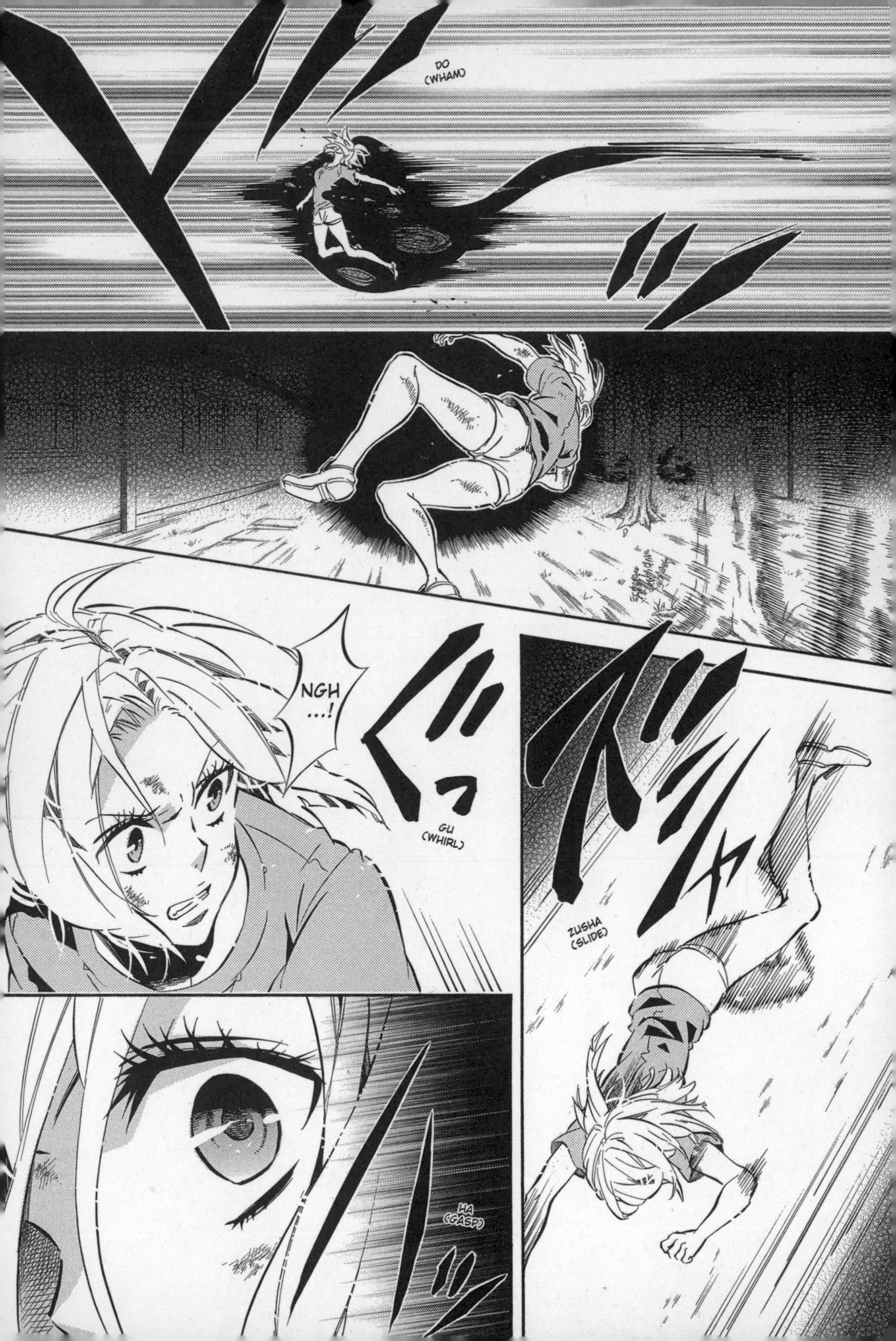
DO
(WHAM)
ZUSHA
(SLIDE)
NGH
...!
GU
(WHIRL)
HA
(GASP)

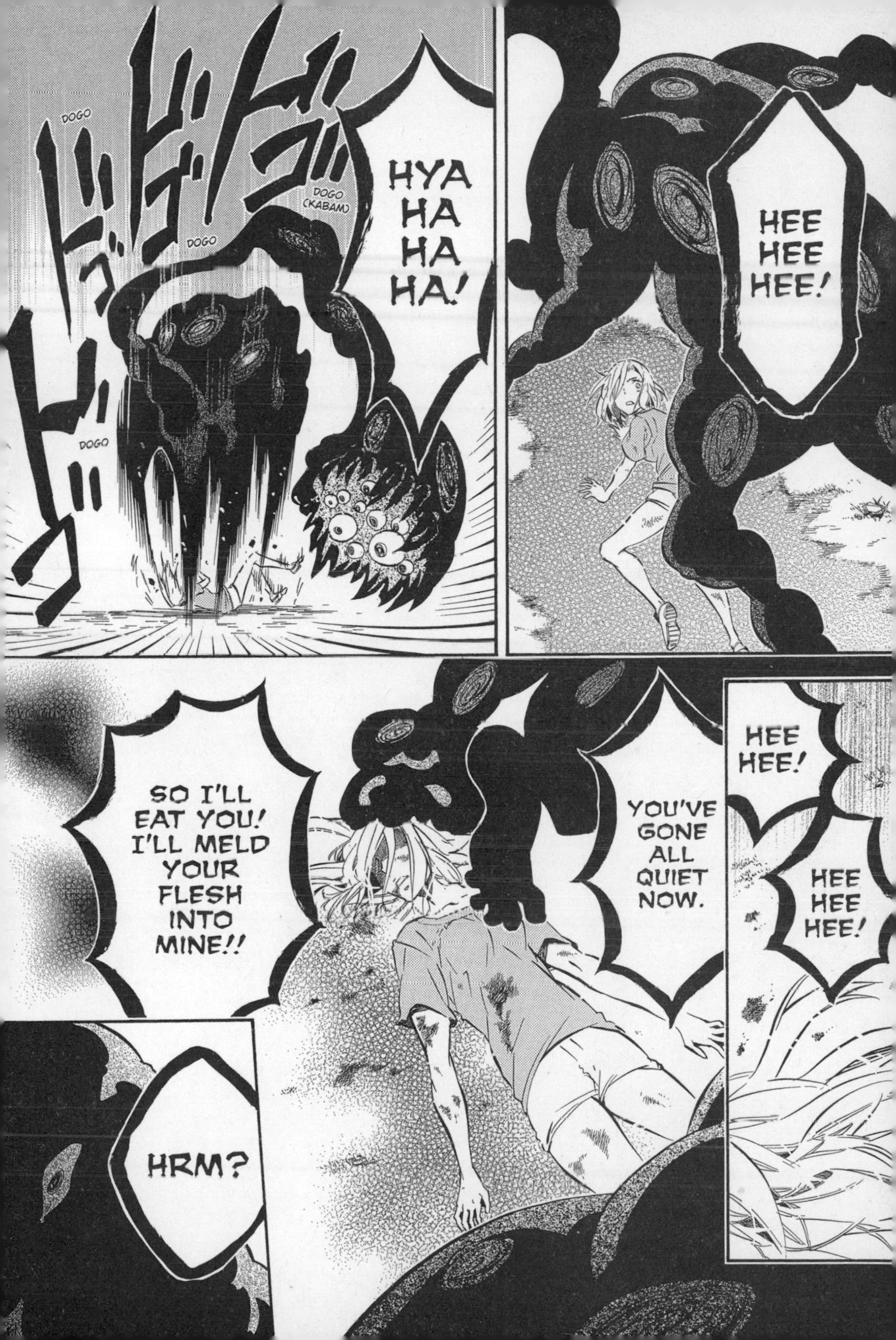
HEE HEE HEE!
HYA HA HA HA!
DOGO (KABAM)
DOGO
DOGO
DOGO
HEE HEE!
HEE HEE HEE!
YOU'VE GONE ALL QUIET NOW.
SO I'LL EAT YOU! I'LL MELD YOUR FLESH INTO MINE!!
HRM?

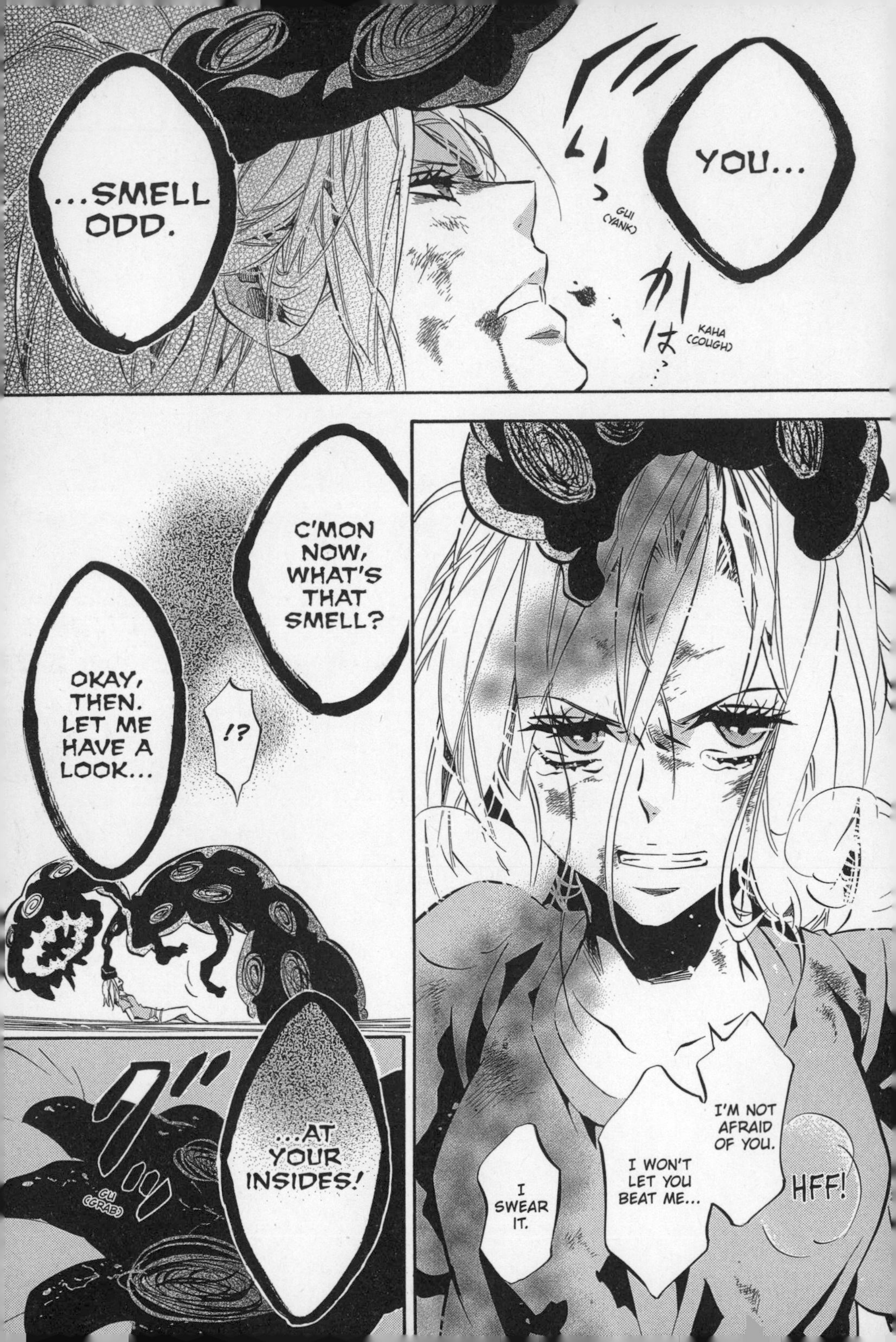
YOU...
GUI (YANK)
KAHA (COUGH)
...SMELL ODD.
HFF!
I'M NOT AFRAID OF YOU.
I WON'T LET YOU BEAT ME...
I SWEAR IT.
C'MON NOW, WHAT'S THAT SMELL?
!?
OKAY, THEN. LET ME HAVE A LOOK...
...AT YOUR INSIDES!
GU (GRAB)

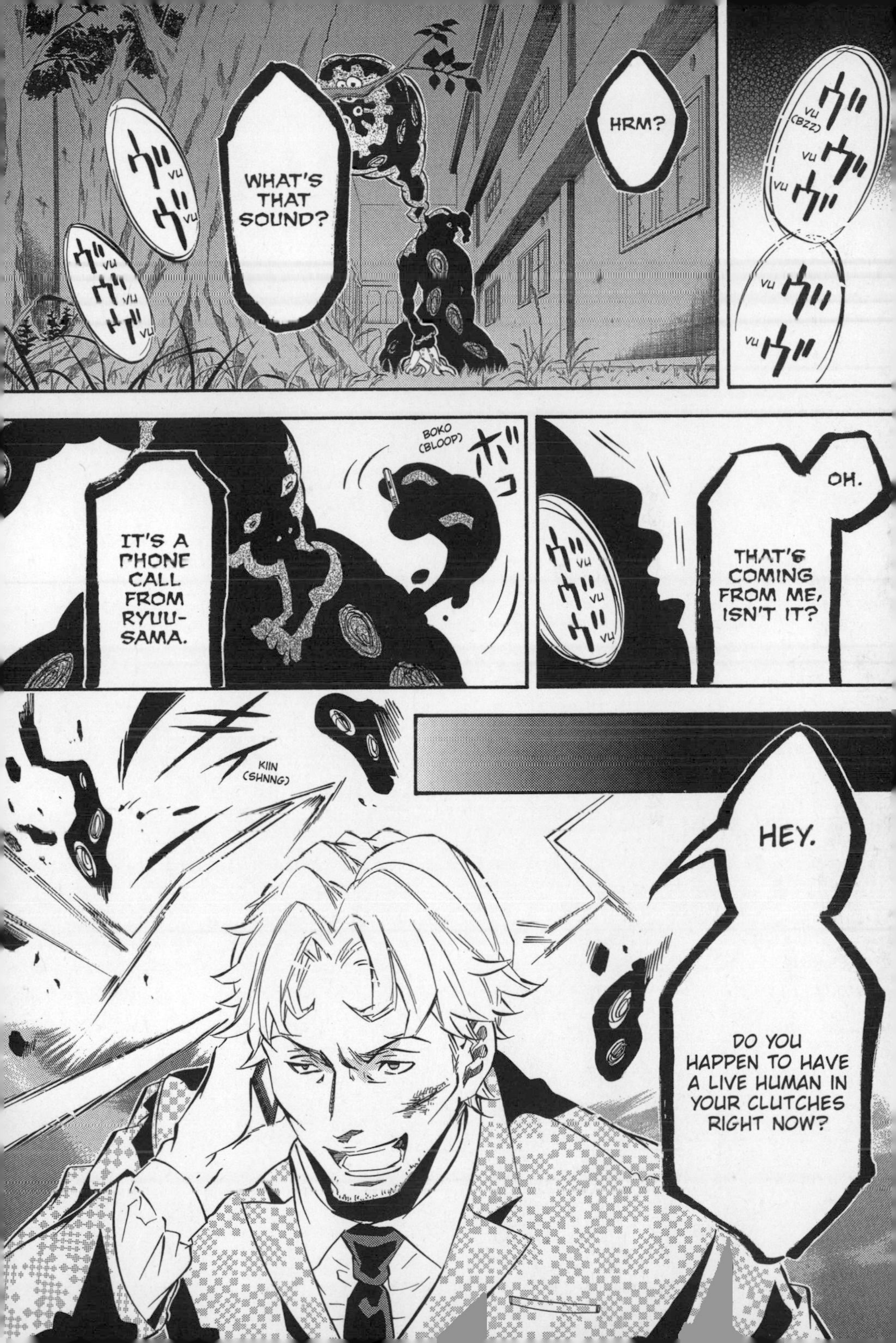
VU (BZZ) VU VU
VU VU
HRM?
WHAT'S THAT SOUND?
VU VU
VU VU VU
OH.
THAT'S COMING FROM ME, ISN'T IT?
VU VU VU
BOKO (BLOOP)
IT'S A PHONE CALL FROM RYUU-SAMA.
HEY.
DO YOU HAPPEN TO HAVE A LIVE HUMAN IN YOUR CLUTCHES RIGHT NOW?
KIIN (SHNNG)

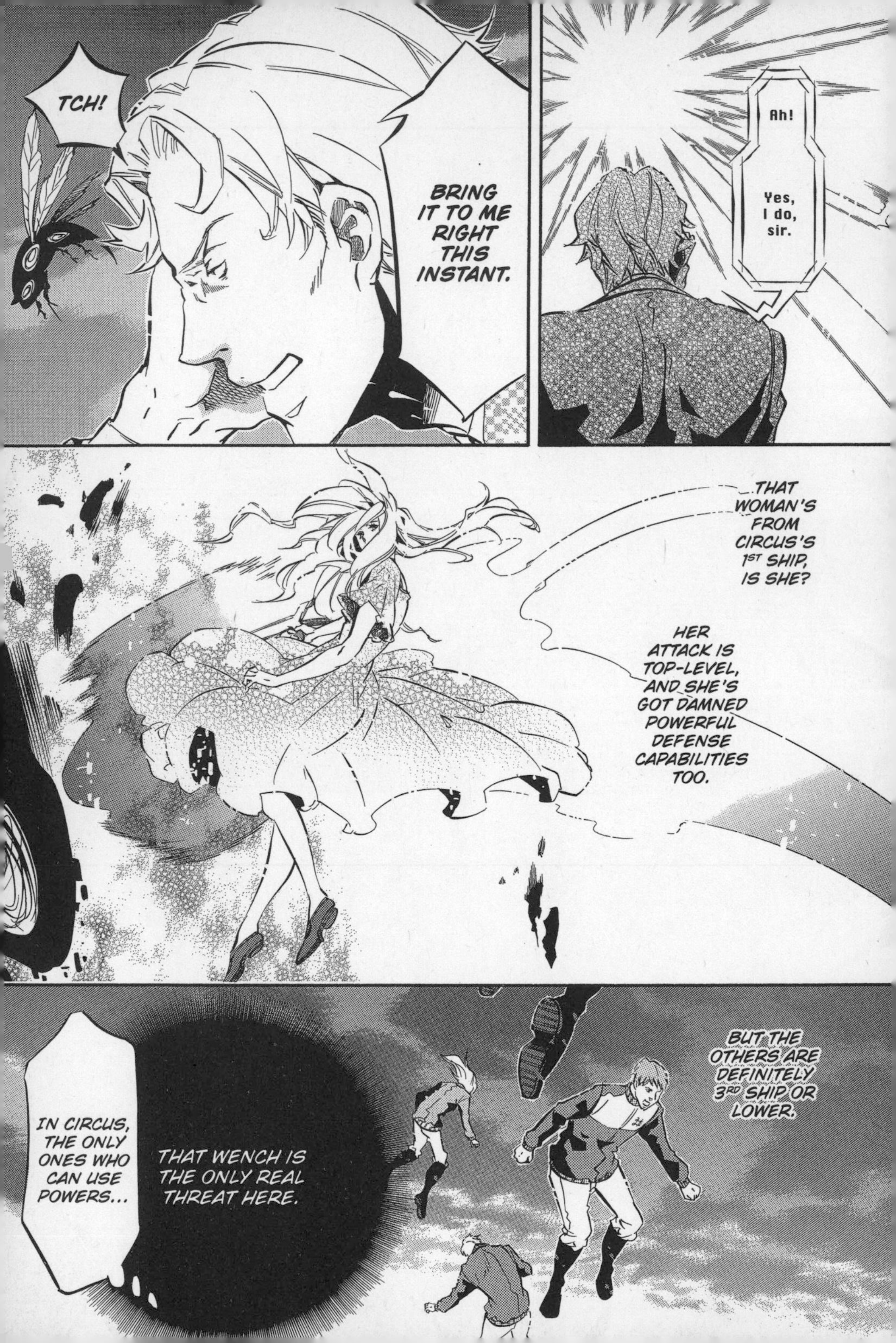
Ah!
Yes, I do, sir.
TCH!
BRING IT TO ME RIGHT THIS INSTANT.
THAT WOMAN'S FROM CIRCUS'S 1ST SHIP, IS SHE?
HER ATTACK IS TOP-LEVEL, AND SHE'S GOT DAMNED POWERFUL DEFENSE CAPABILITIES TOO.
BUT THE OTHERS ARE DEFINITELY 3RD SHIP OR LOWER.
THAT WENCH IS THE ONLY REAL THREAT HERE.
IN CIRCUS, THE ONLY ONES WHO CAN USE POWERS...

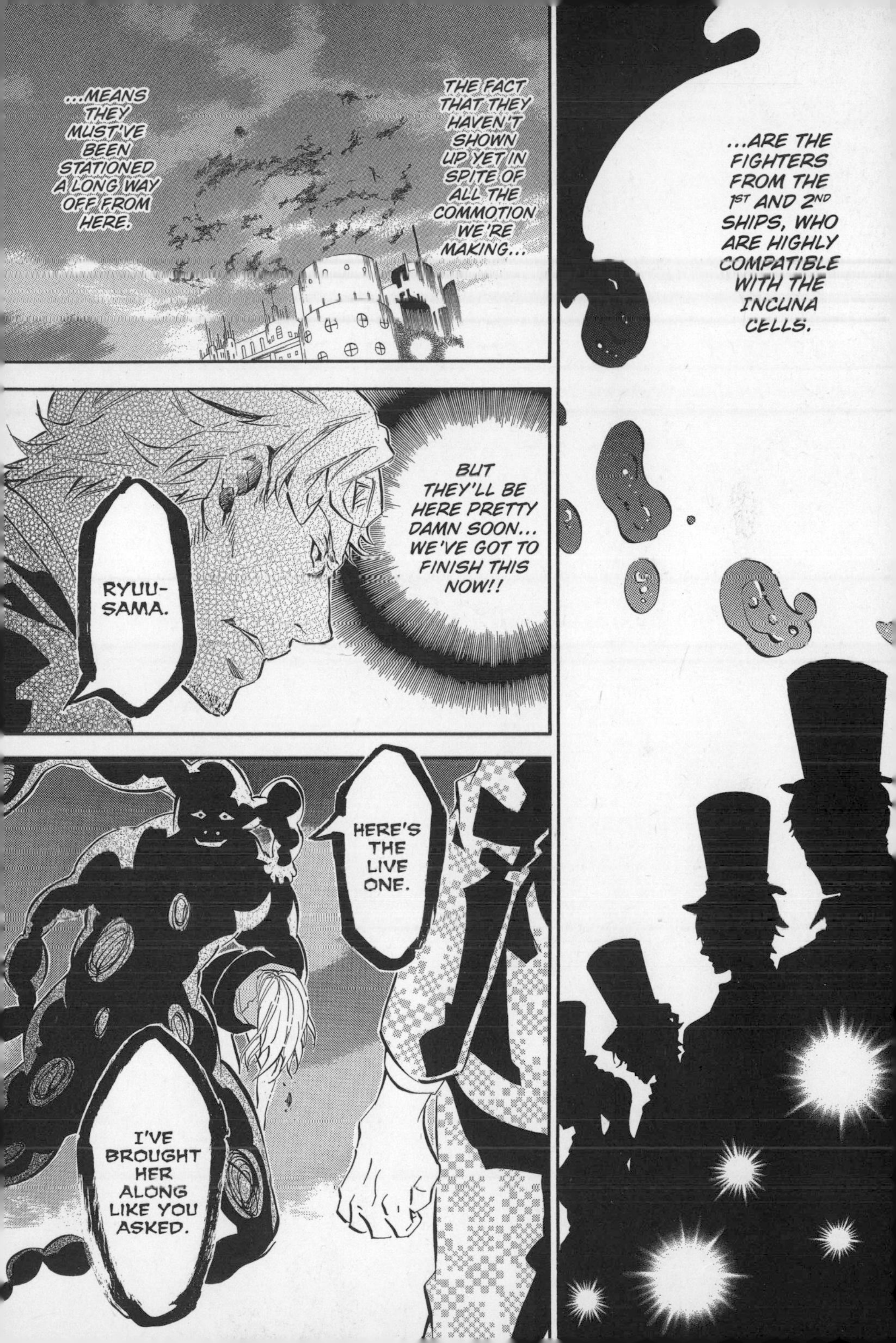
...ARE THE FIGHTERS FROM THE 1ST AND 2ND SHIPS, WHO ARE HIGHLY COMPATIBLE WITH THE INCUNA CELLS.
THE FACT THAT THEY HAVEN'T SHOWN UP YET IN SPITE OF ALL THE COMMOTION WE'RE MAKING...
...MEANS THEY MUST'VE BEEN STATIONED A LONG WAY OFF FROM HERE.
BUT THEY'LL BE HERE PRETTY DAMN SOON... WE'VE GOT TO FINISH THIS NOW!!
RYUU-SAMA.
HERE'S THE LIVE ONE.
I'VE BROUGHT HER ALONG LIKE YOU ASKED.

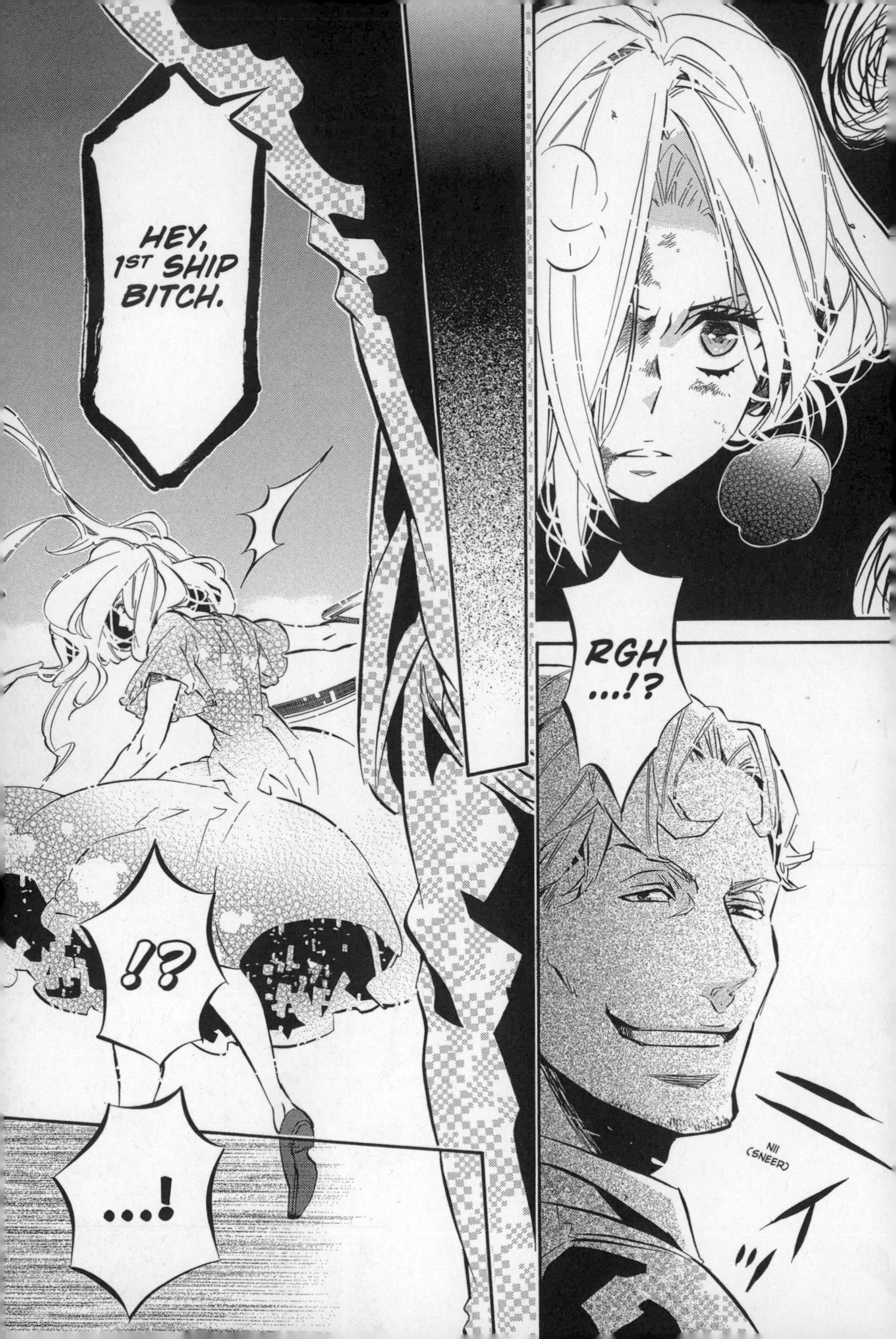
RGH...!?
NII (SNEER)
HEY, 1st SHIP BITCH.
!?
...!

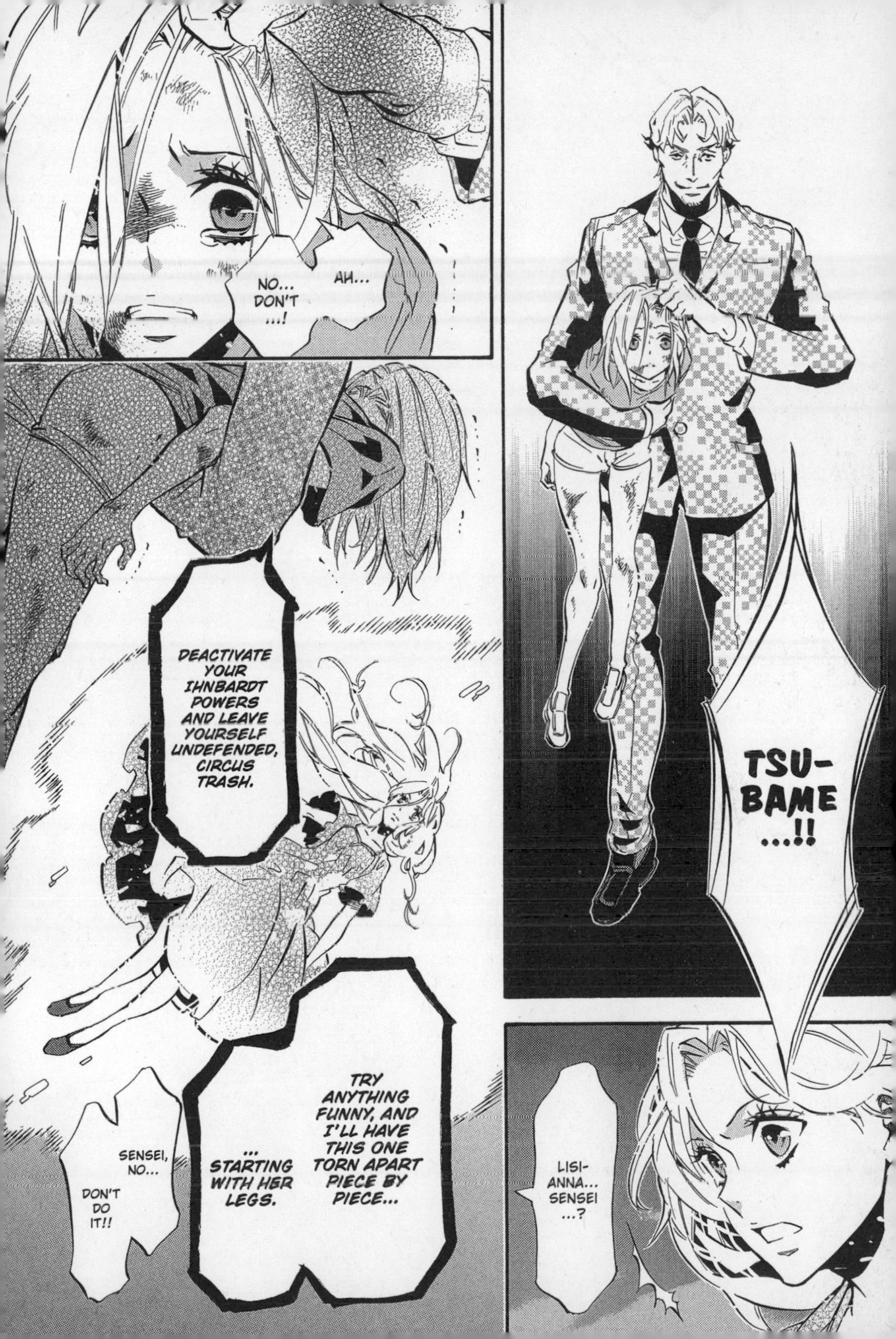
TSU-BAME ...!!
LISI-ANNA... SENSEI ...?
AH...
NO... DON'T ...!
DEACTIVATE YOUR IHNBARDT POWERS AND LEAVE YOURSELF UNDEFENDED, CIRCUS TRASH.
TRY ANYTHING FUNNY, AND I'LL HAVE THIS ONE TORN APART PIECE BY PIECE...
... STARTING WITH HER LEGS.
SENSEI, NO...
DON'T DO IT!!

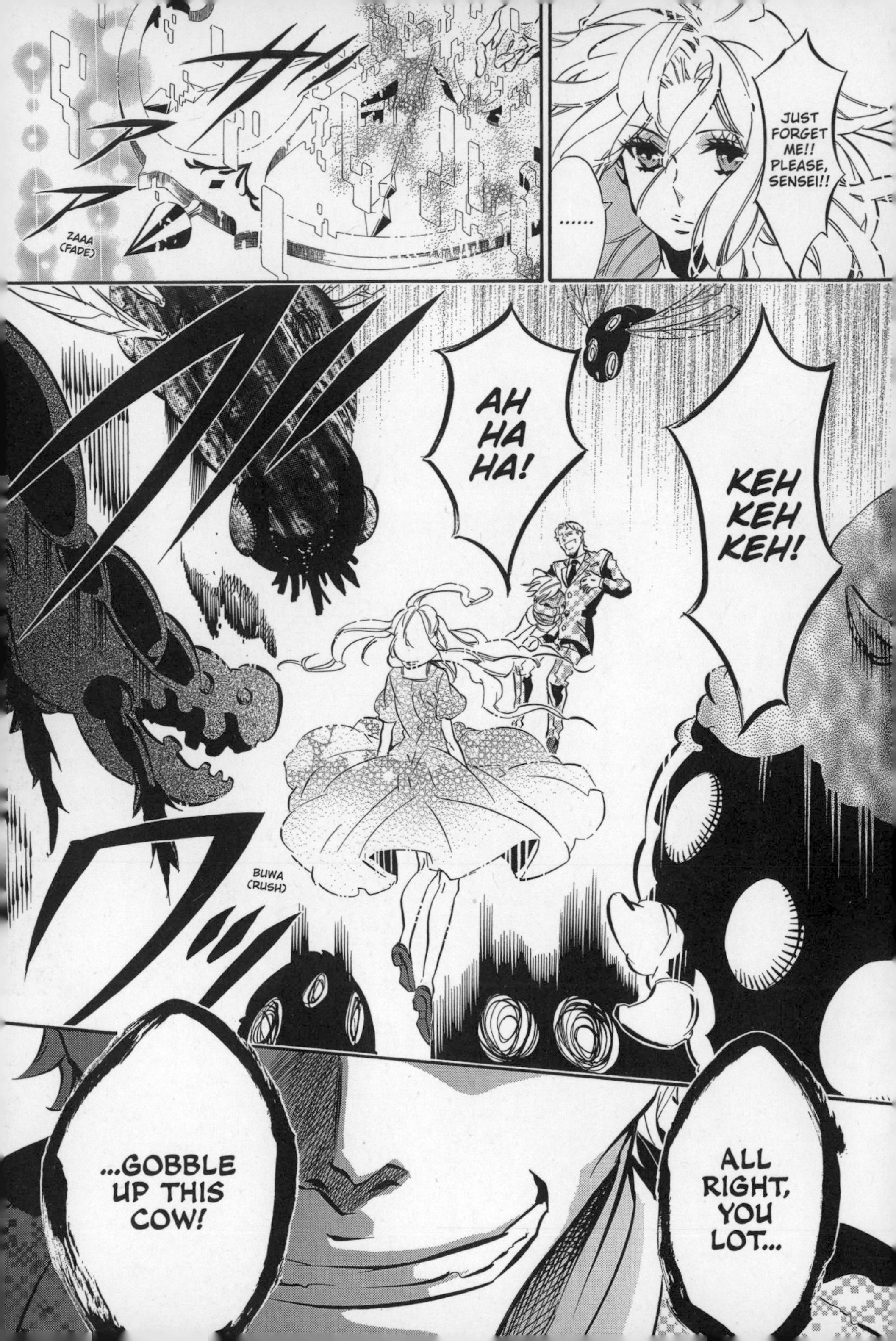
JUST FORGET ME!! PLEASE, SENSEI!!
......
ZAAA (FADE)
KEH KEH KEH!
AH HA HA!
BUWA (RUSH)
ALL RIGHT, YOU LOT...
...GOBBLE UP THIS COW!

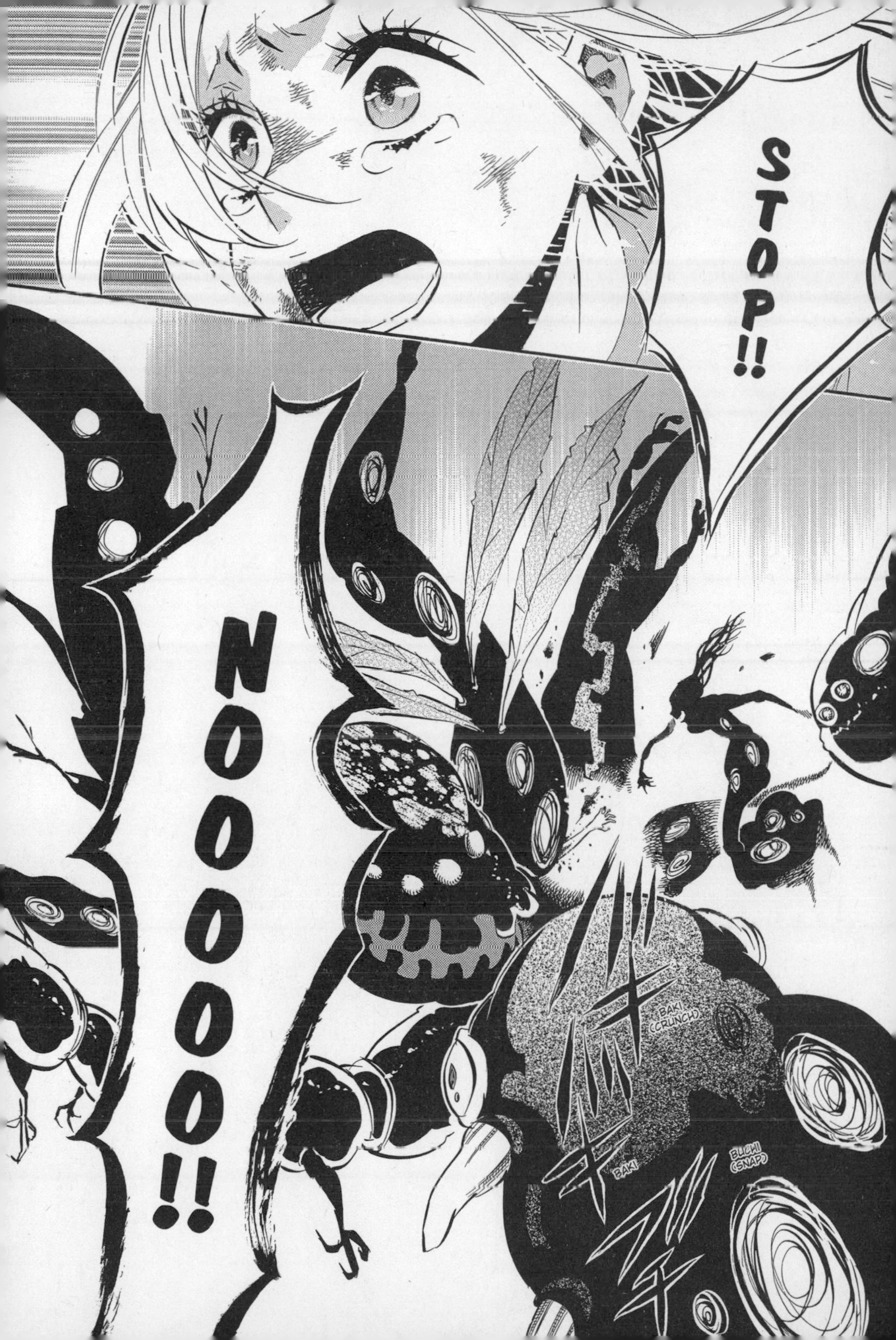
STOP!!
NOOOOOO!!
BAKI (CRUNCH)
BUCHI (SNAP)
BAKI

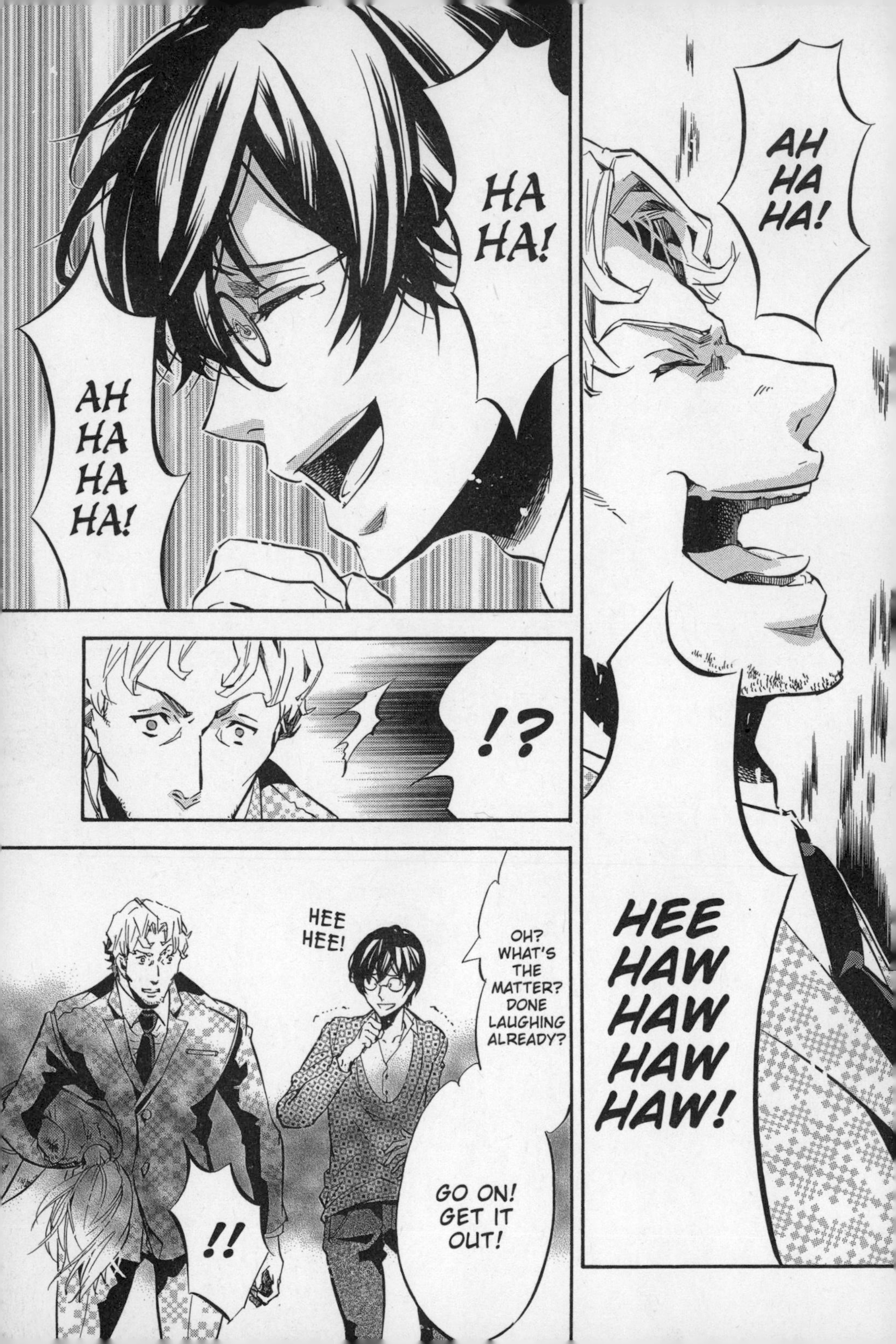
AH HA HA!
HEE HAW HAW HAW HAW!
HA HA!
AH HA HA HA HA!
!?
OH? WHAT'S THE MATTER? DONE LAUGHING ALREADY?
HEE HEE!
GO ON! GET IT OUT!
!!

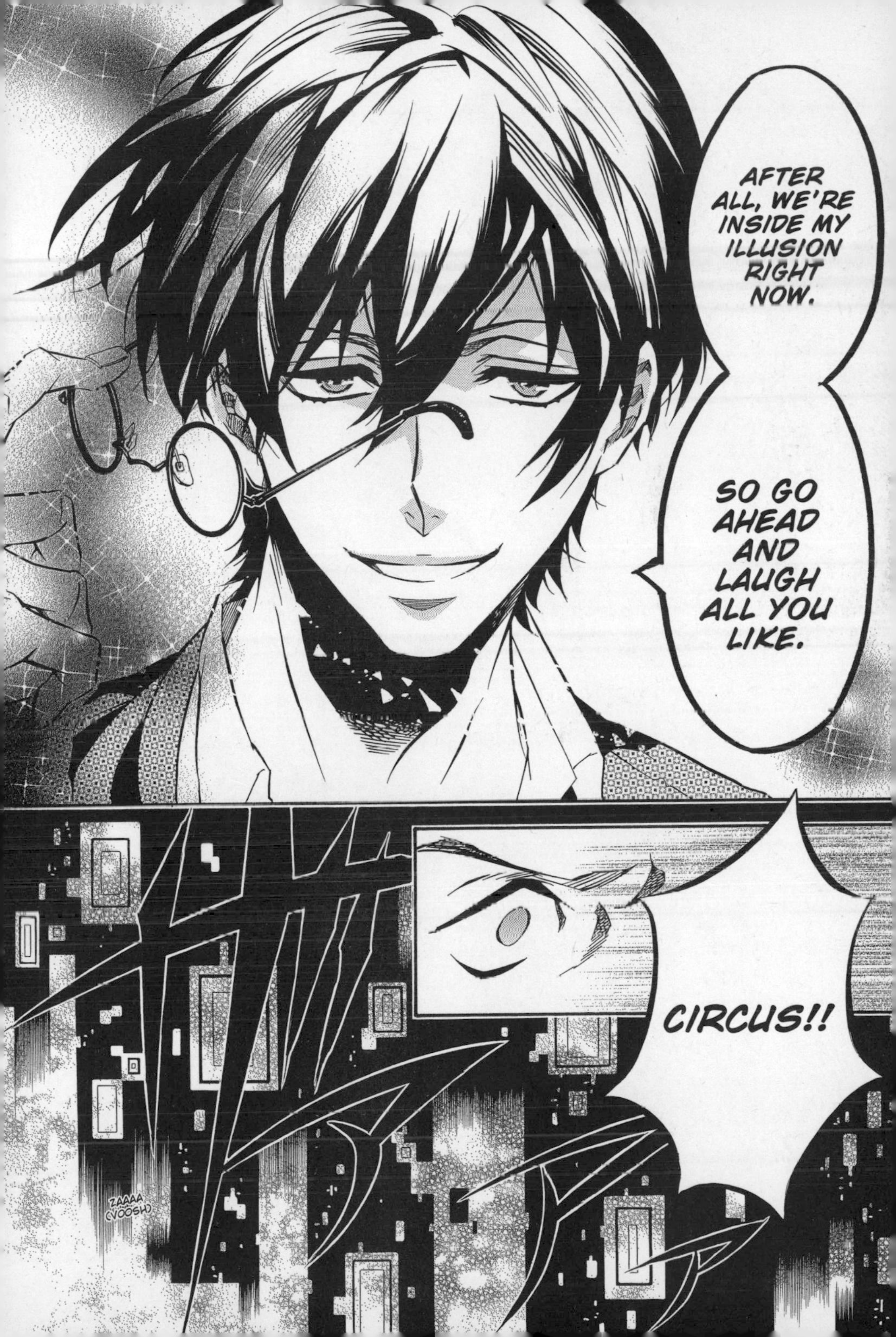
AFTER ALL, WE'RE INSIDE MY ILLUSION RIGHT NOW.
SO GO AHEAD AND LAUGH ALL YOU LIKE.
CIRCUS!!
ZAAAA (VOOSH)

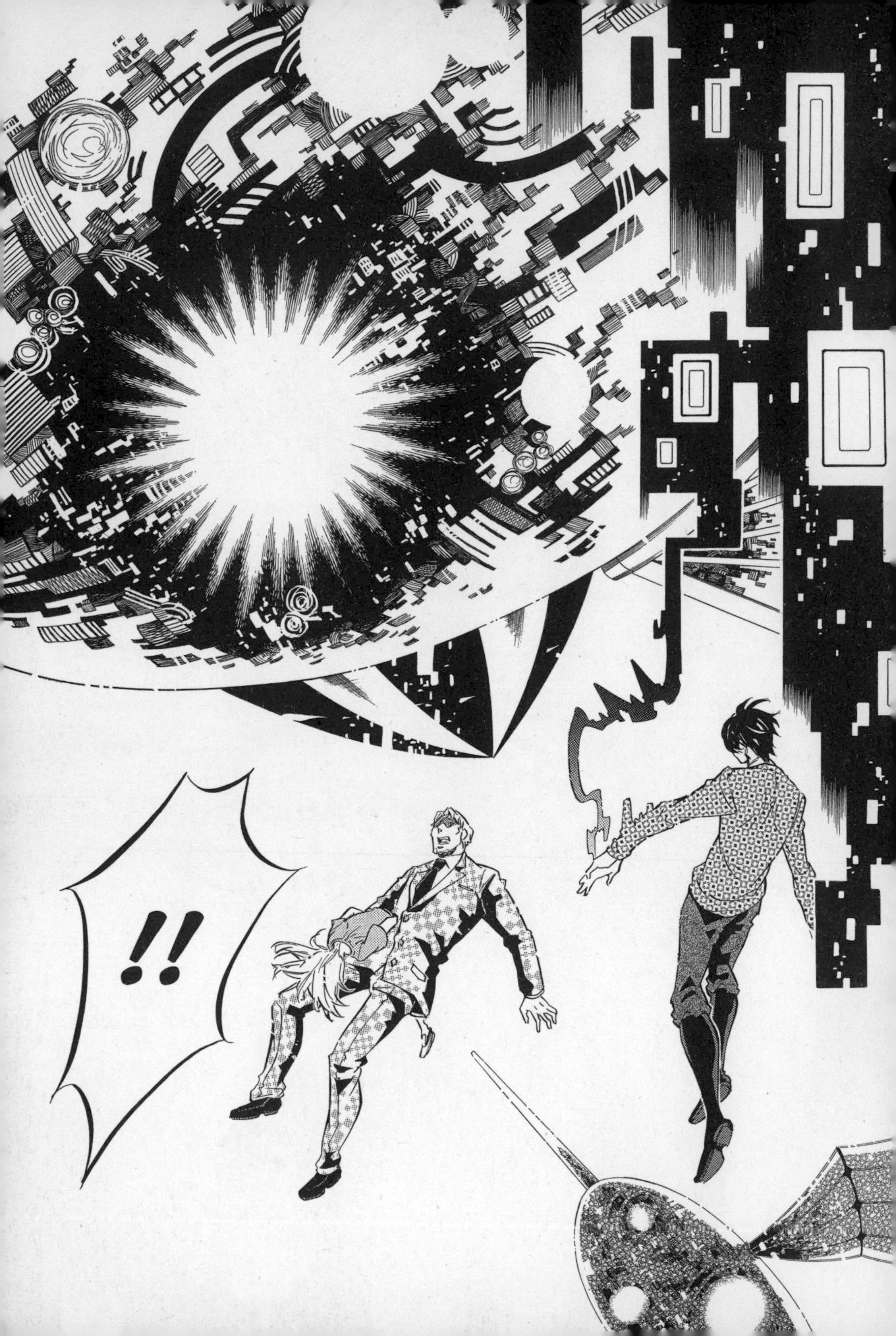
!!

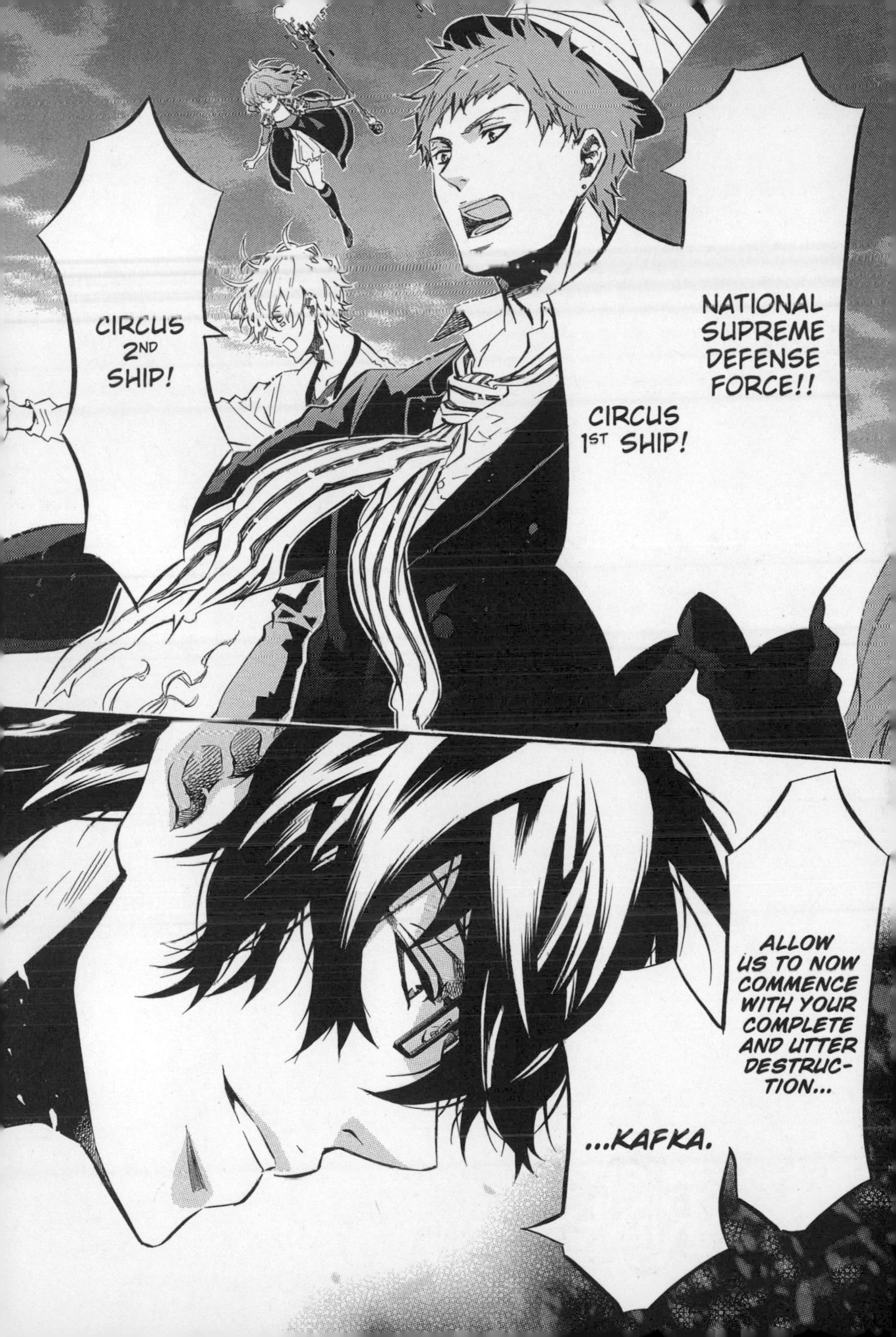
NATIONAL SUPREME DEFENSE FORCE!!
CIRCUS 1ST SHIP!
CIRCUS 2ND SHIP!
ALLOW US TO NOW COMMENCE WITH YOUR COMPLETE AND UTTER DESTRUCTION...
...KAFKA.

KARNEVAL

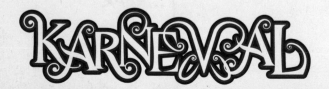

KARNEVAL

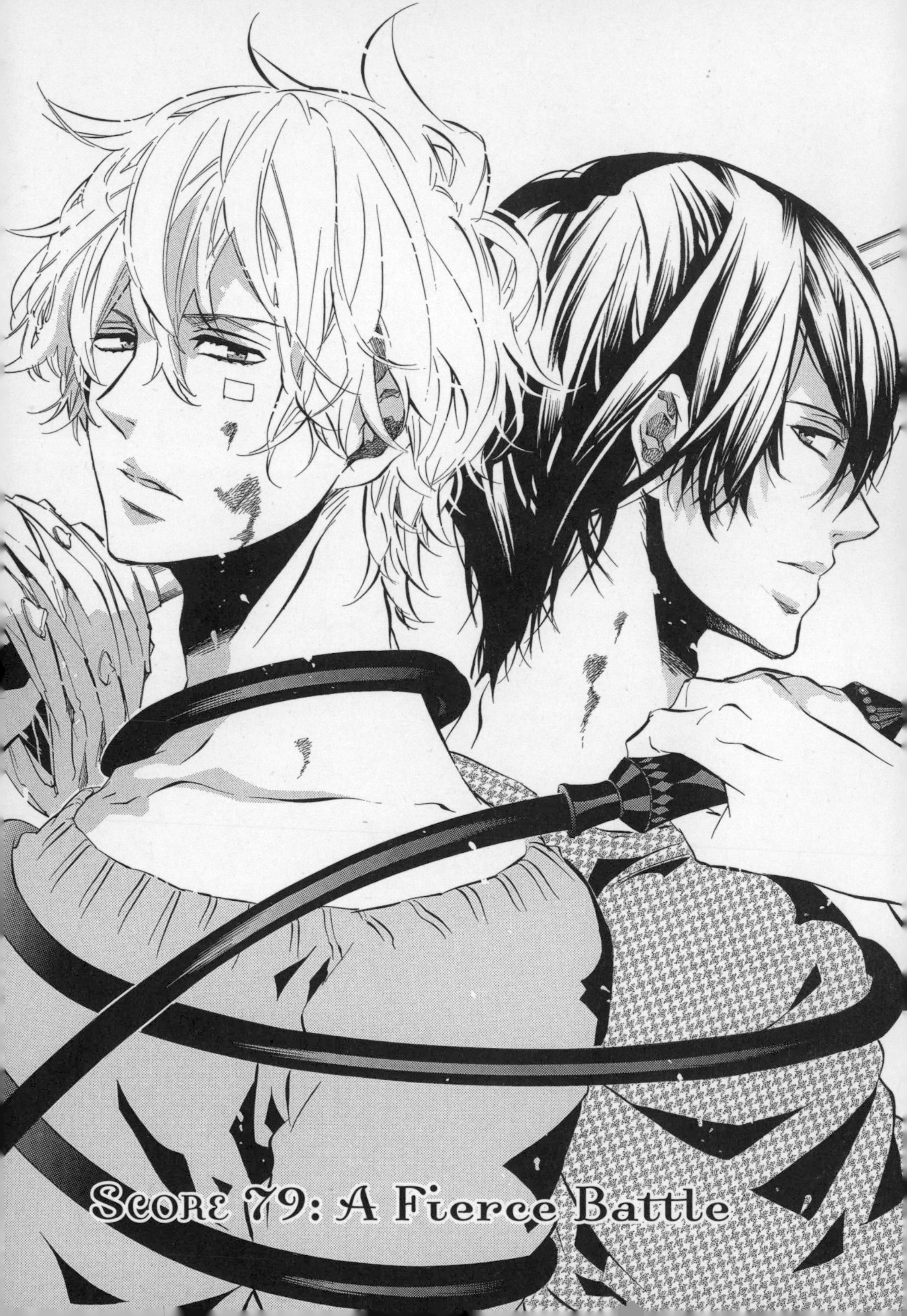

Score 79: A Fierce Battle

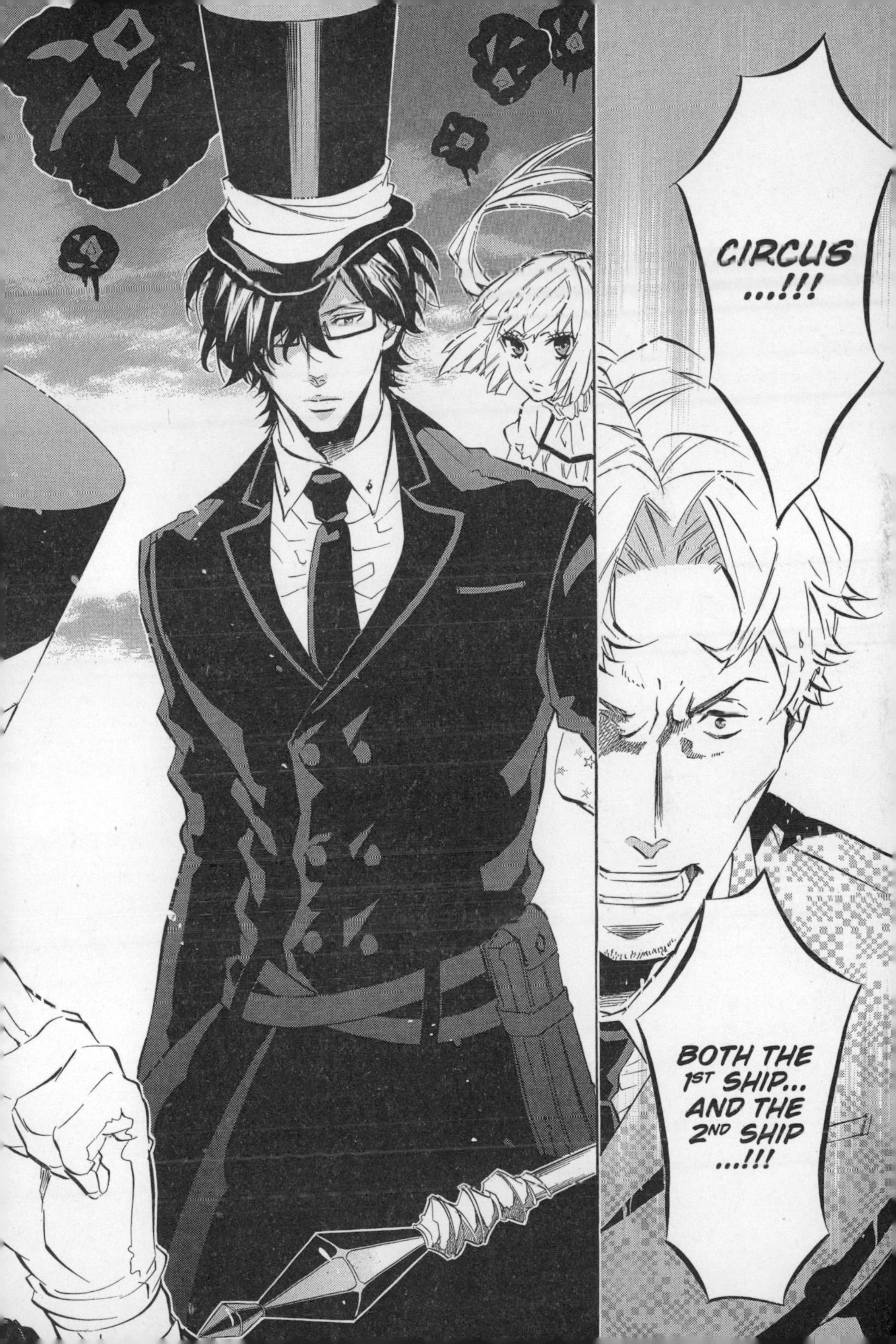
CIRCUS ...!!!
BOTH THE 1ST SHIP... AND THE 2ND SHIP ...!!!

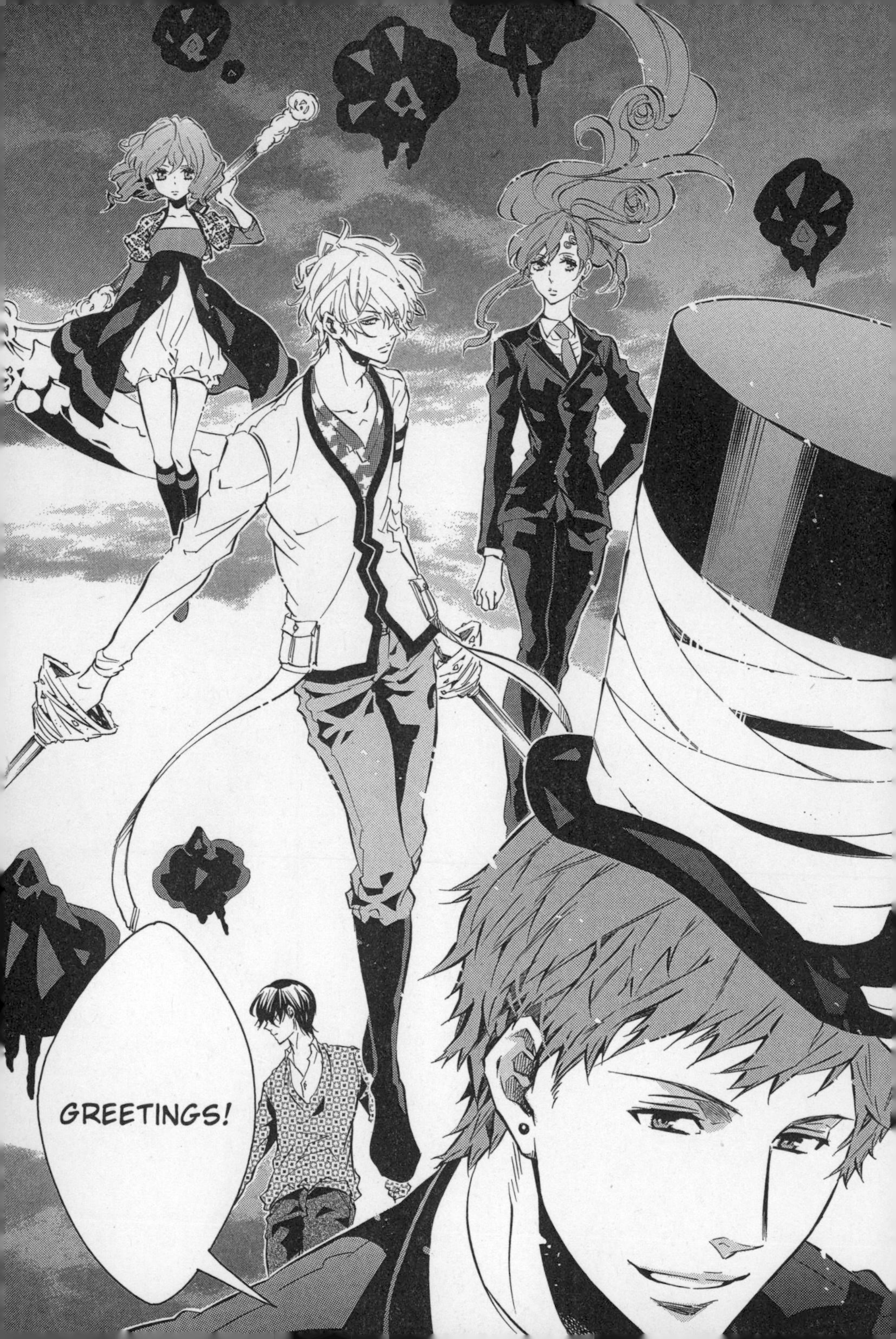
GREETINGS!

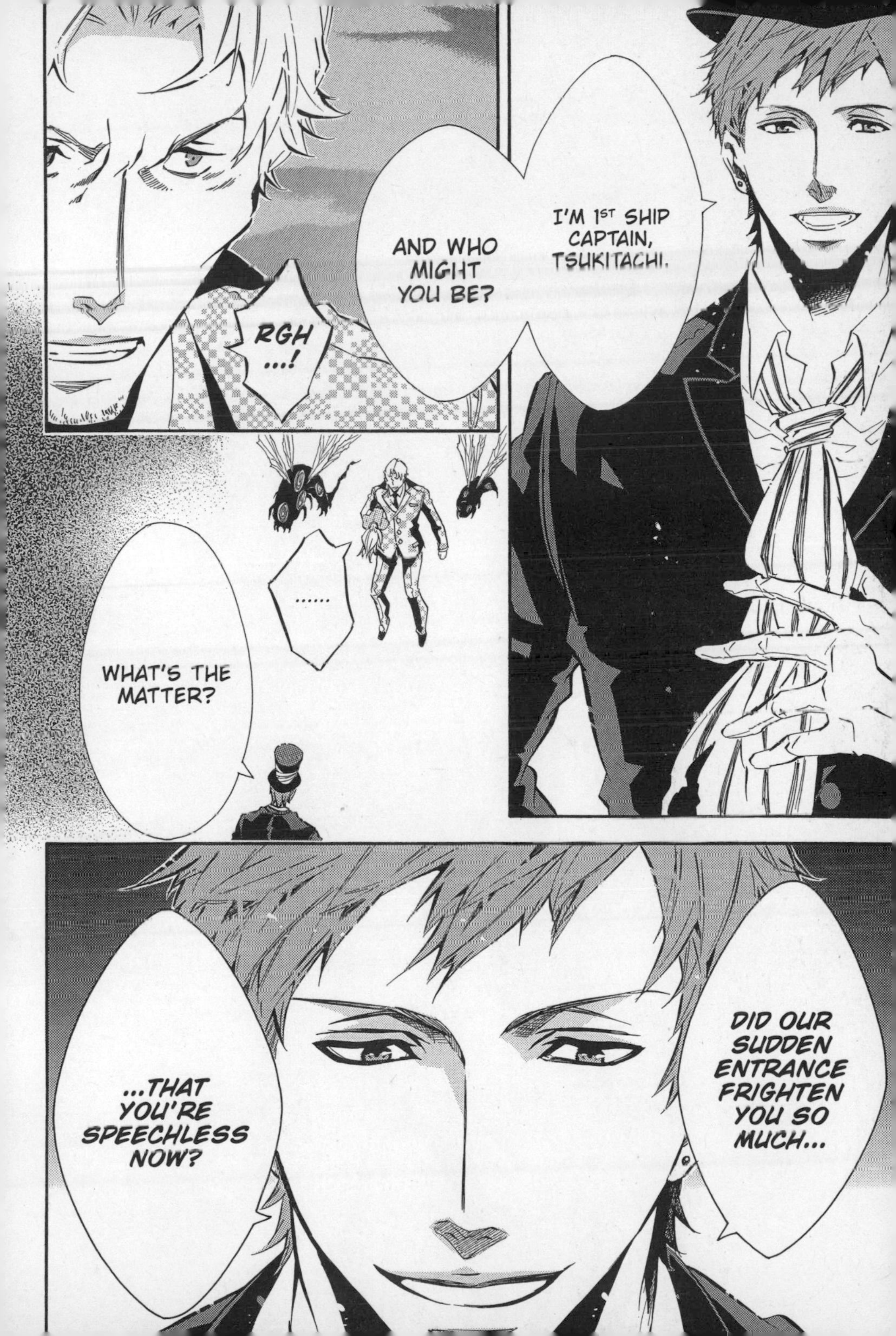
I'M 1st SHIP CAPTAIN, TSUKITACHI.
AND WHO MIGHT YOU BE?
RGH ...!
......
WHAT'S THE MATTER?
DID OUR SUDDEN ENTRANCE FRIGHTEN YOU SO MUCH...
...THAT YOU'RE SPEECHLESS NOW?

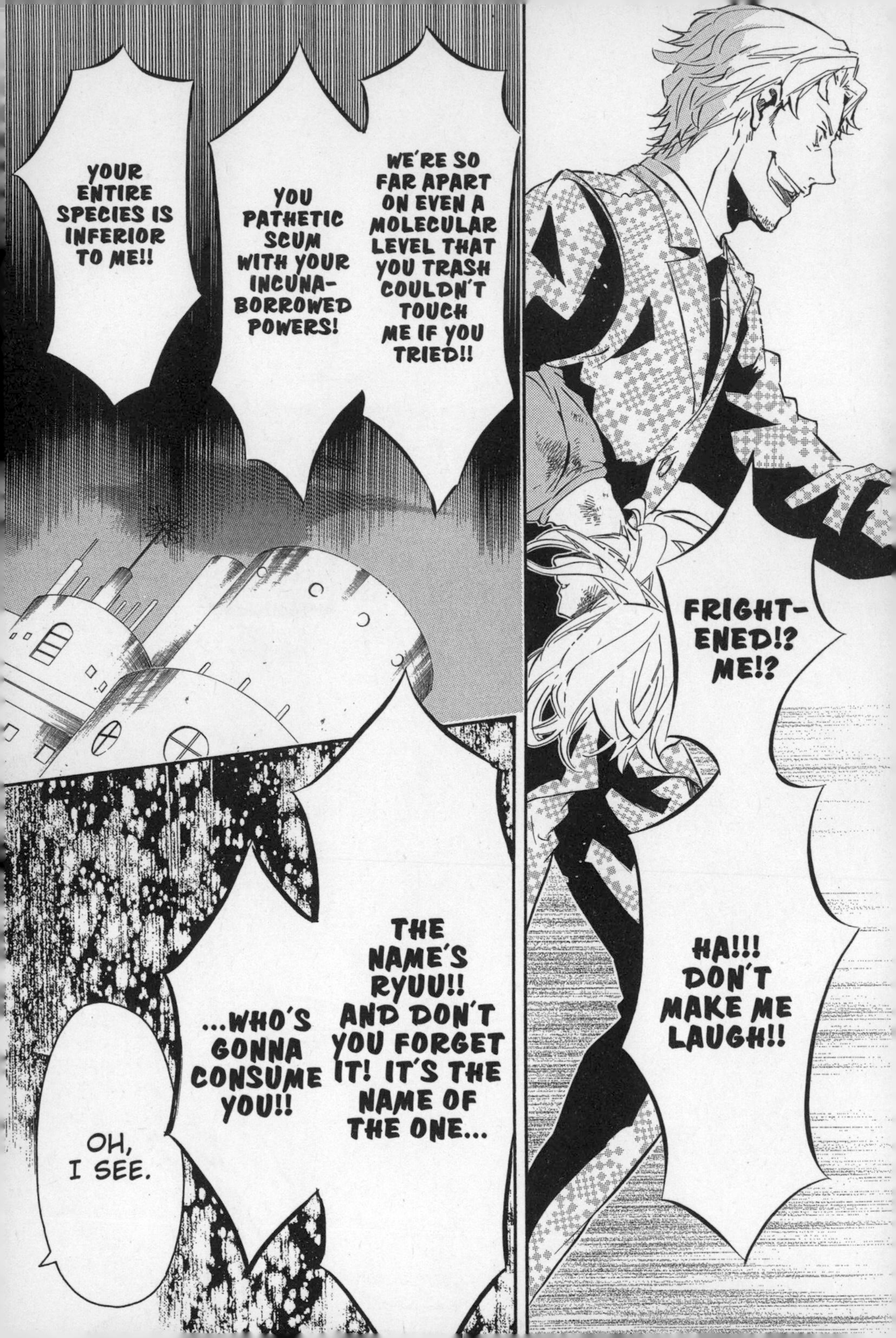
FRIGHT-ENED!? ME!?
HA!!! DON'T MAKE ME LAUGH!!
WE'RE SO FAR APART ON EVEN A MOLECULAR LEVEL THAT YOU TRASH COULDN'T TOUCH ME IF YOU TRIED!!
YOU PATHETIC SCUM WITH YOUR INCUNA-BORROWED POWERS!
YOUR ENTIRE SPECIES IS INFERIOR TO ME!!
THE NAME'S RYUU!! AND DON'T YOU FORGET IT! IT'S THE NAME OF THE ONE...
...WHO'S GONNA CONSUME YOU!!
OH, I SEE.

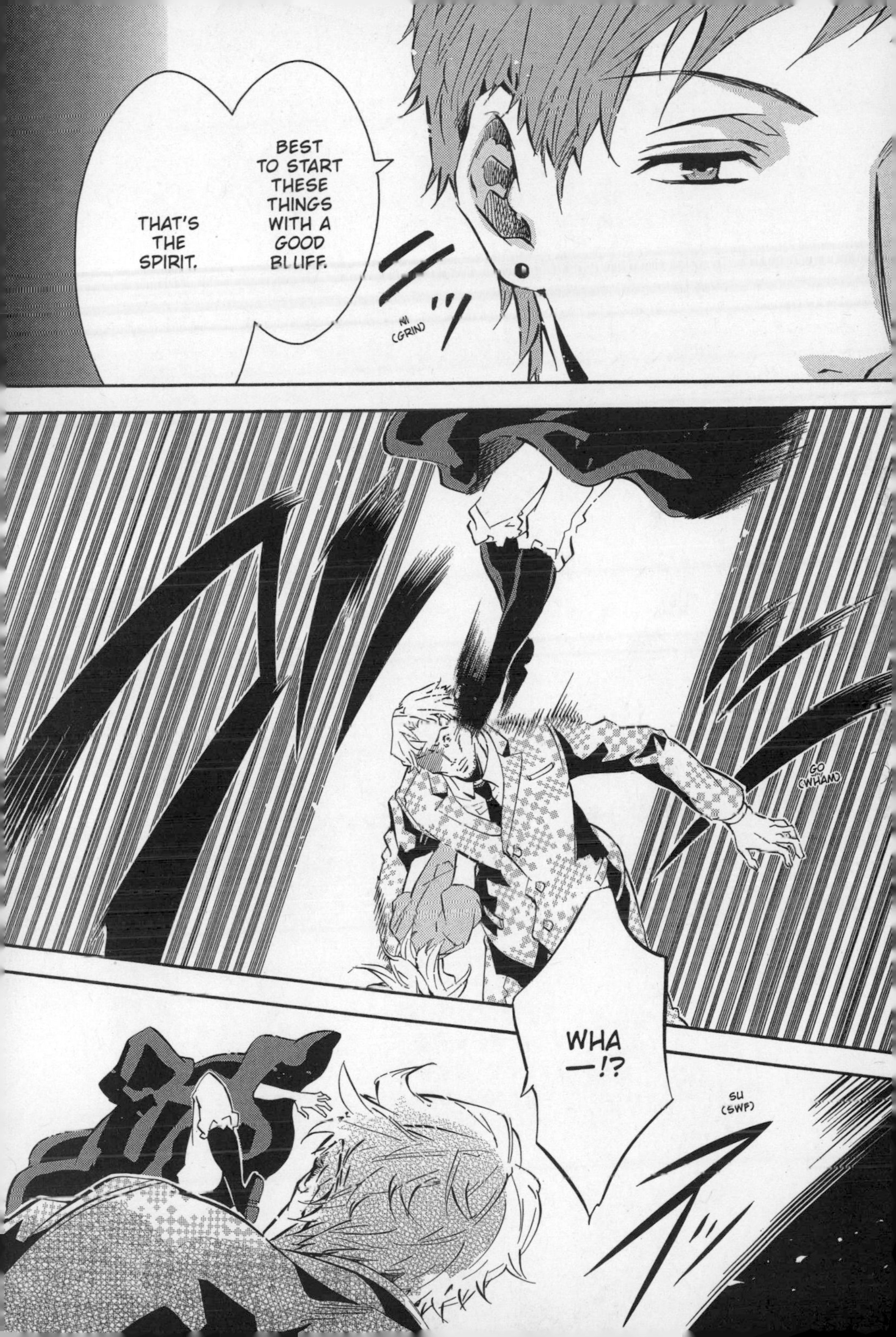
THAT'S THE SPIRIT.
BEST TO START THESE THINGS WITH A GOOD BLUFF.
NI (GRIN)
GO (WHAM)
WHA—!?
SU (SWF)

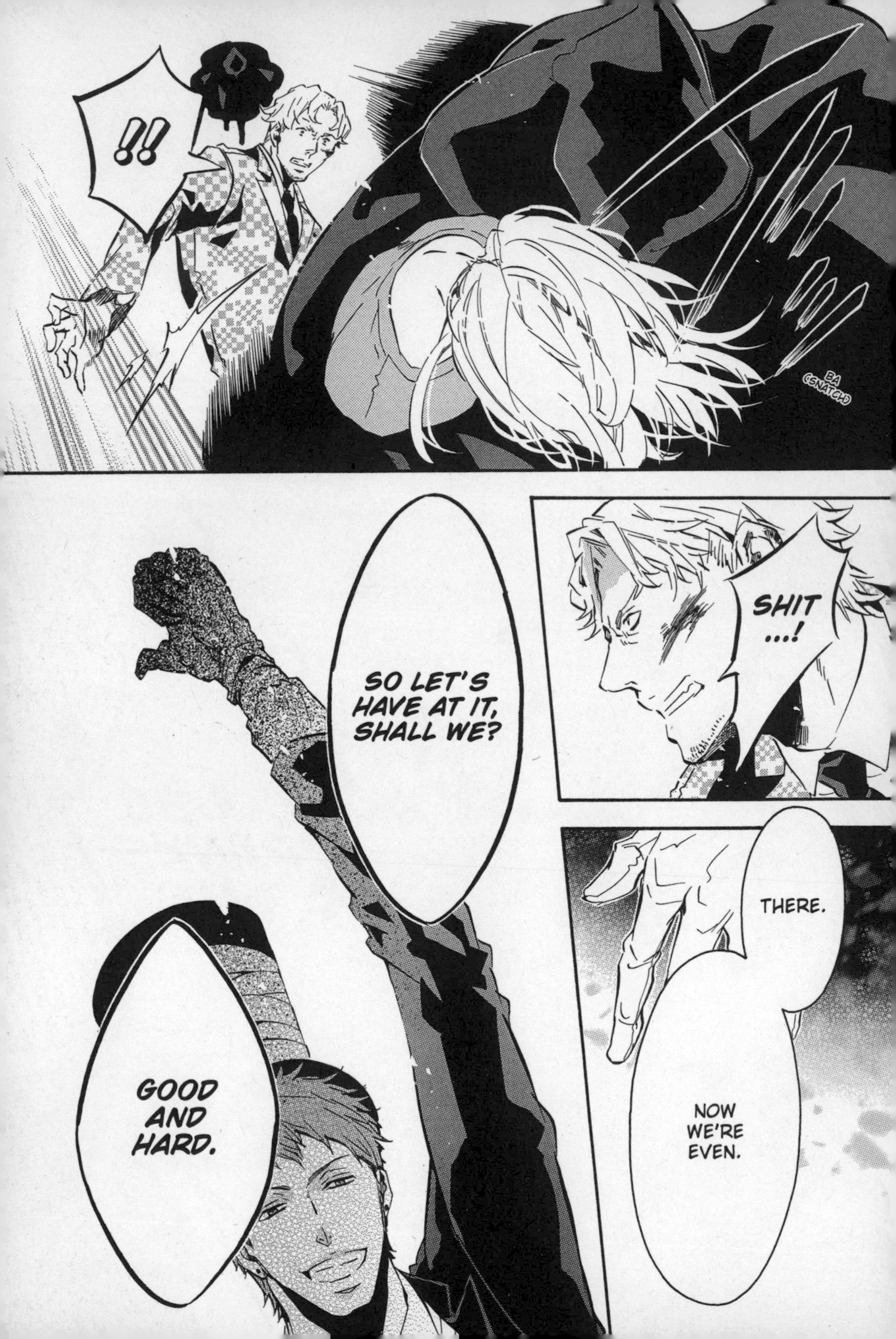
BA (SNATCH)
!!
SHIT ...!
THERE.
NOW WE'RE EVEN.
SO LET'S HAVE AT IT, SHALL WE?
GOOD AND HARD.

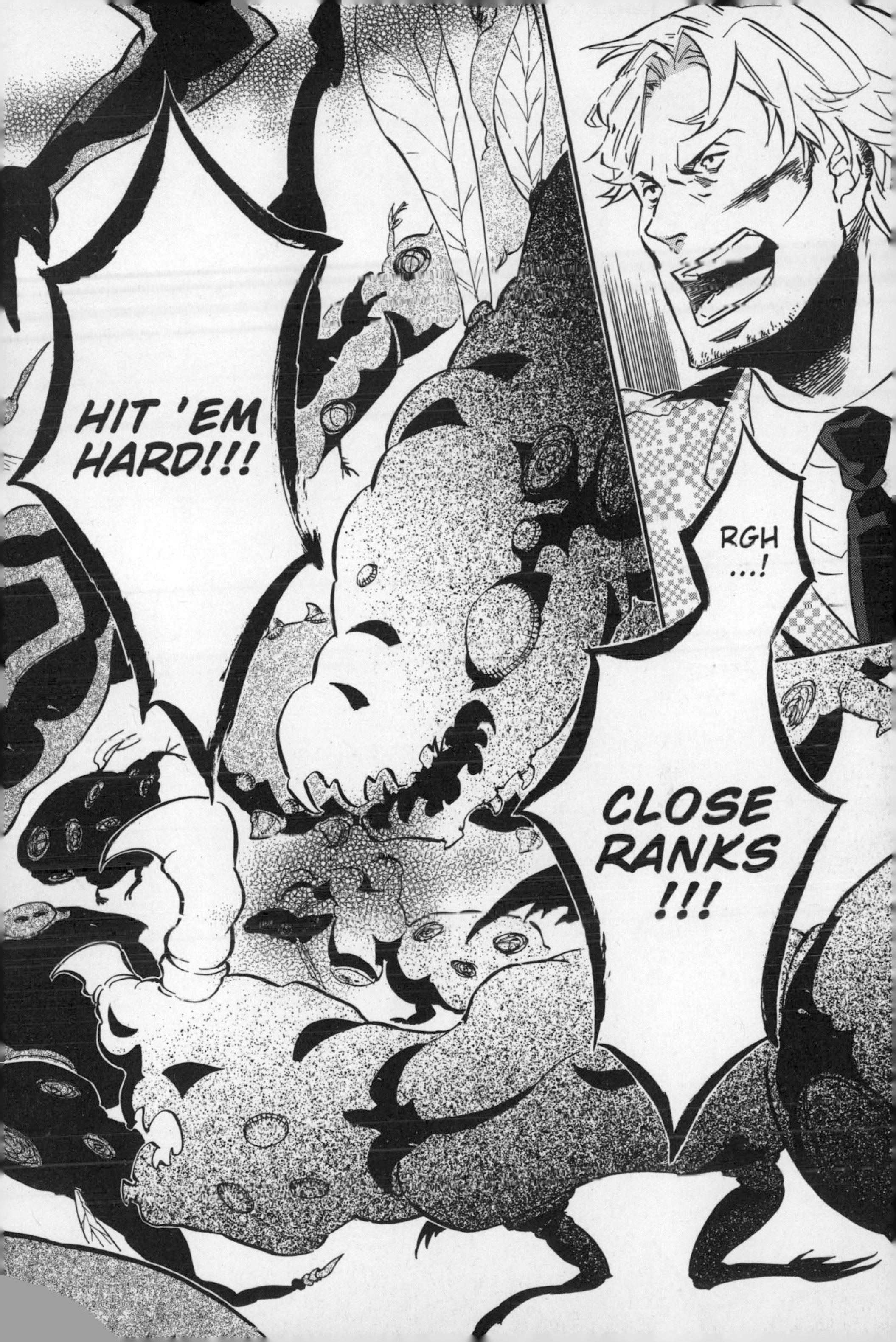
RGH ...!
CLOSE RANKS !!!
HIT 'EM HARD!!!

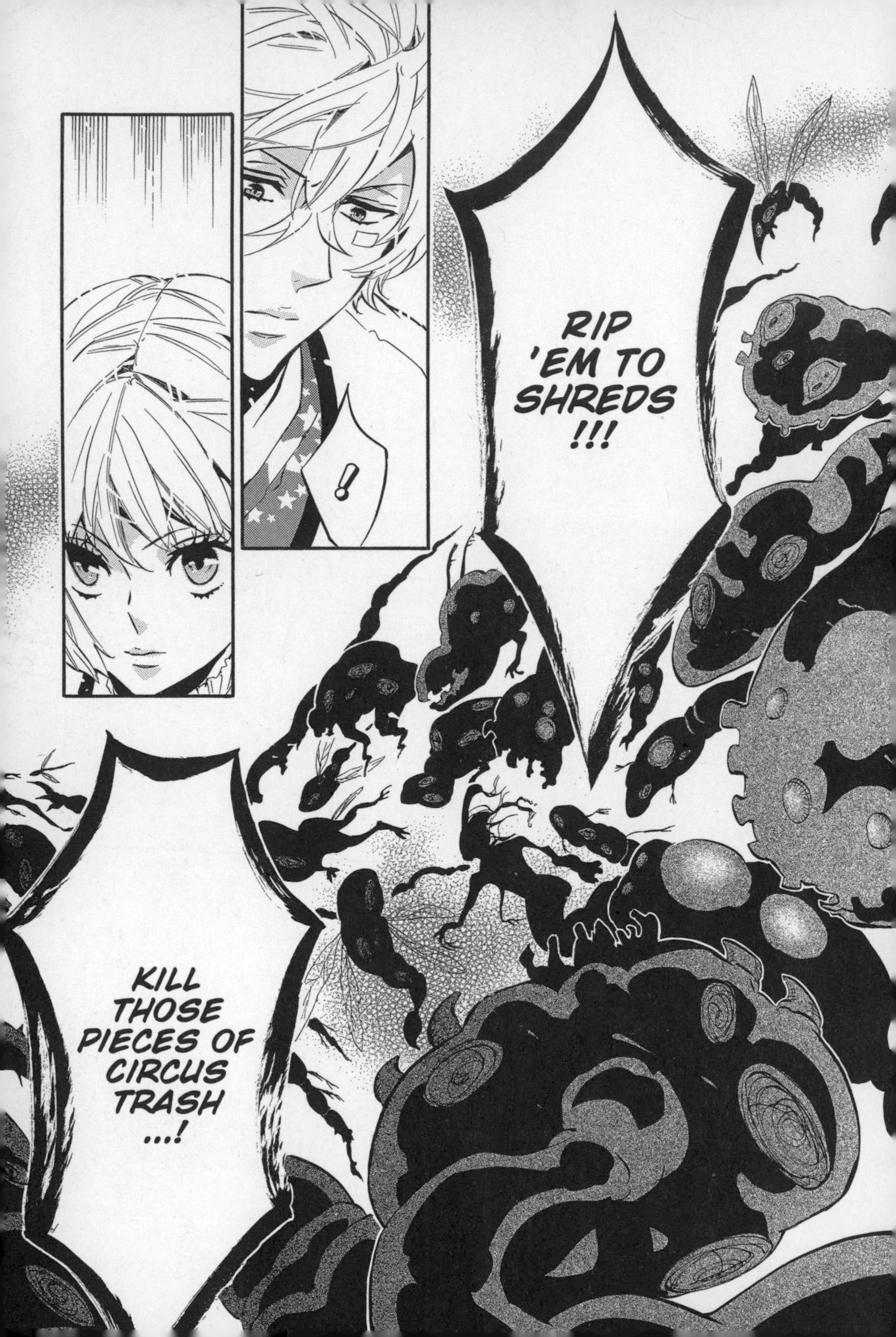
!
RIP 'EM TO SHREDS !!!
KILL THOSE PIECES OF CIRCUS TRASH ...!

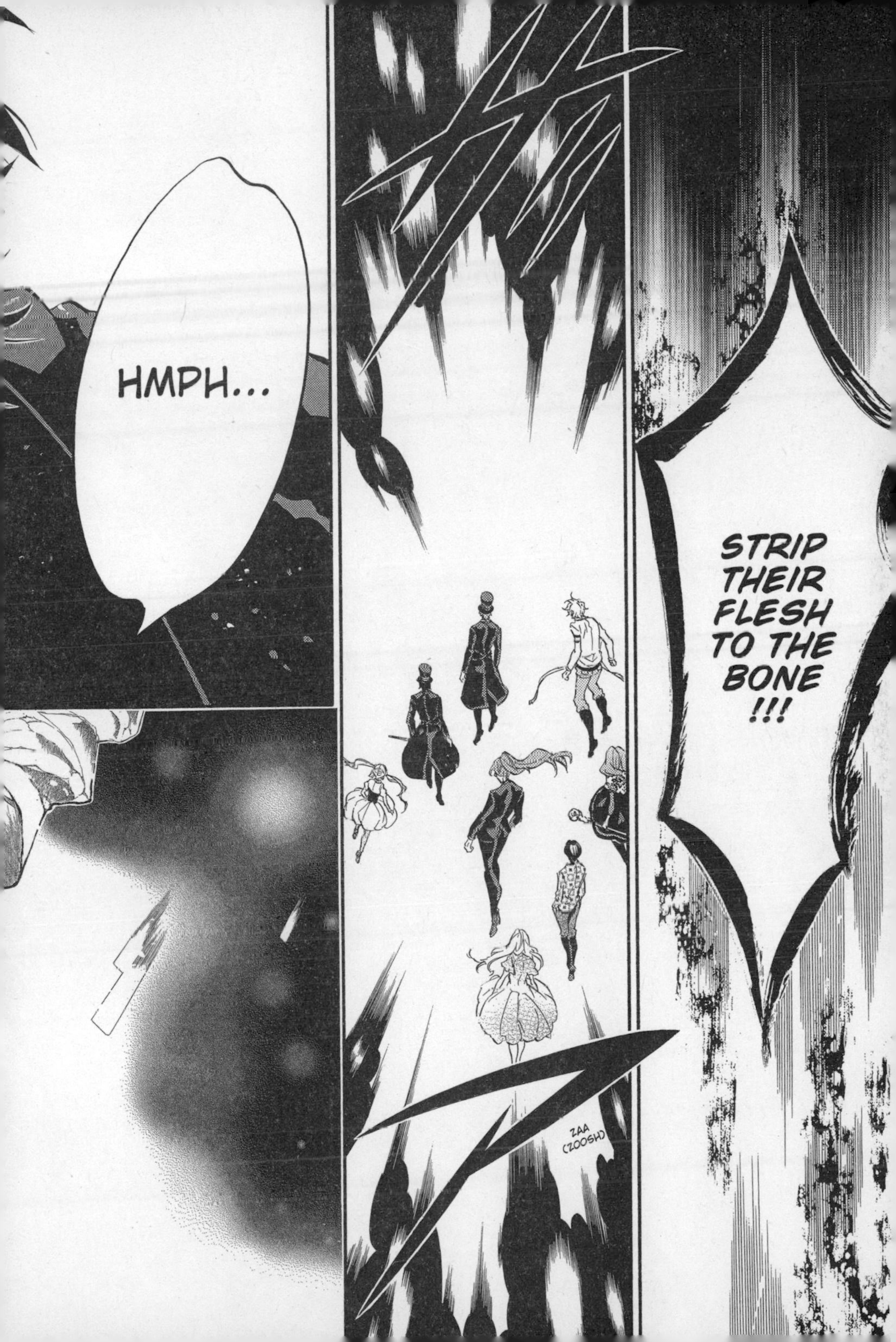
STRIP THEIR FLESH TO THE BONE!!!
ZAA (ZOOSH)
HMPH...

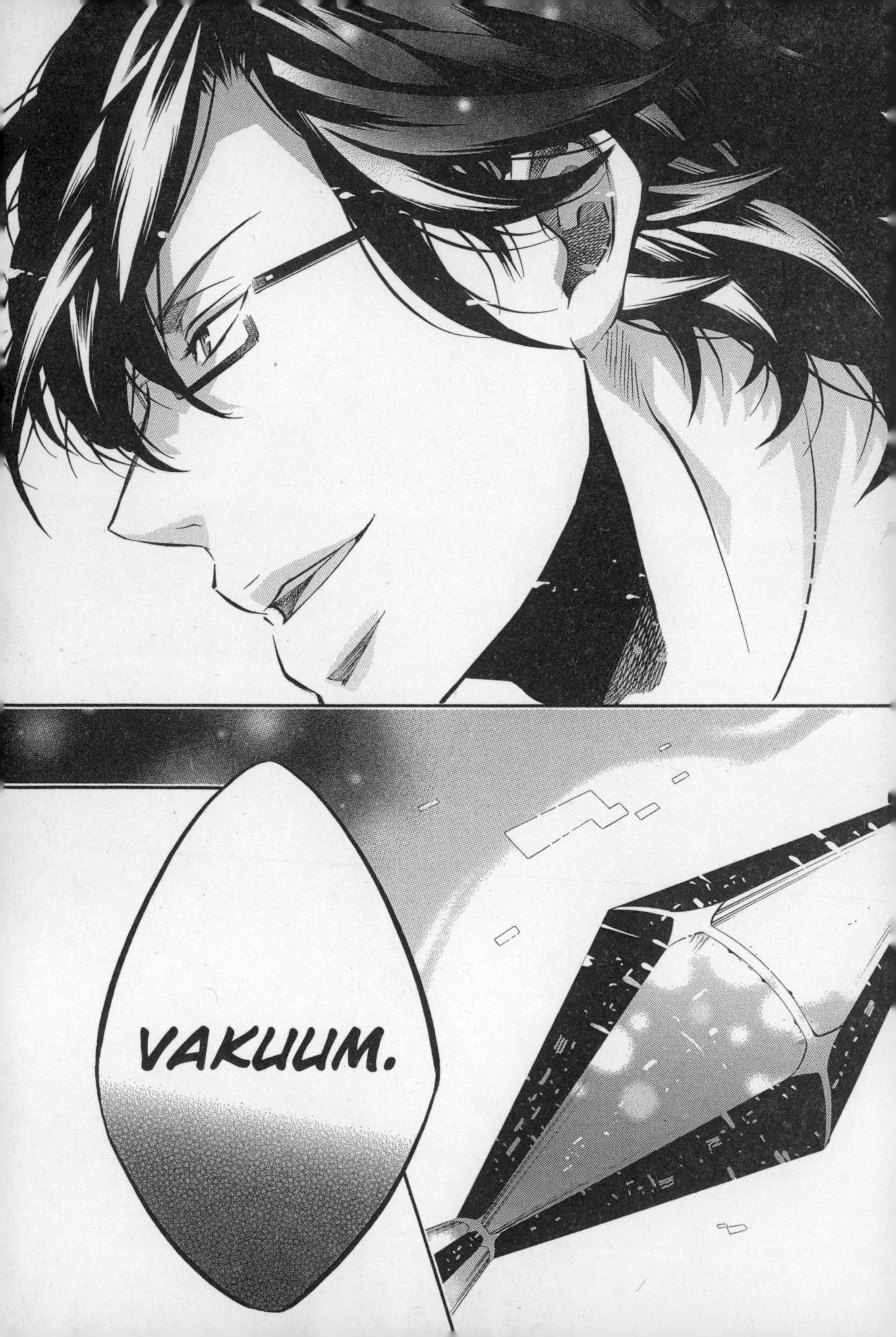
VAKUUM.

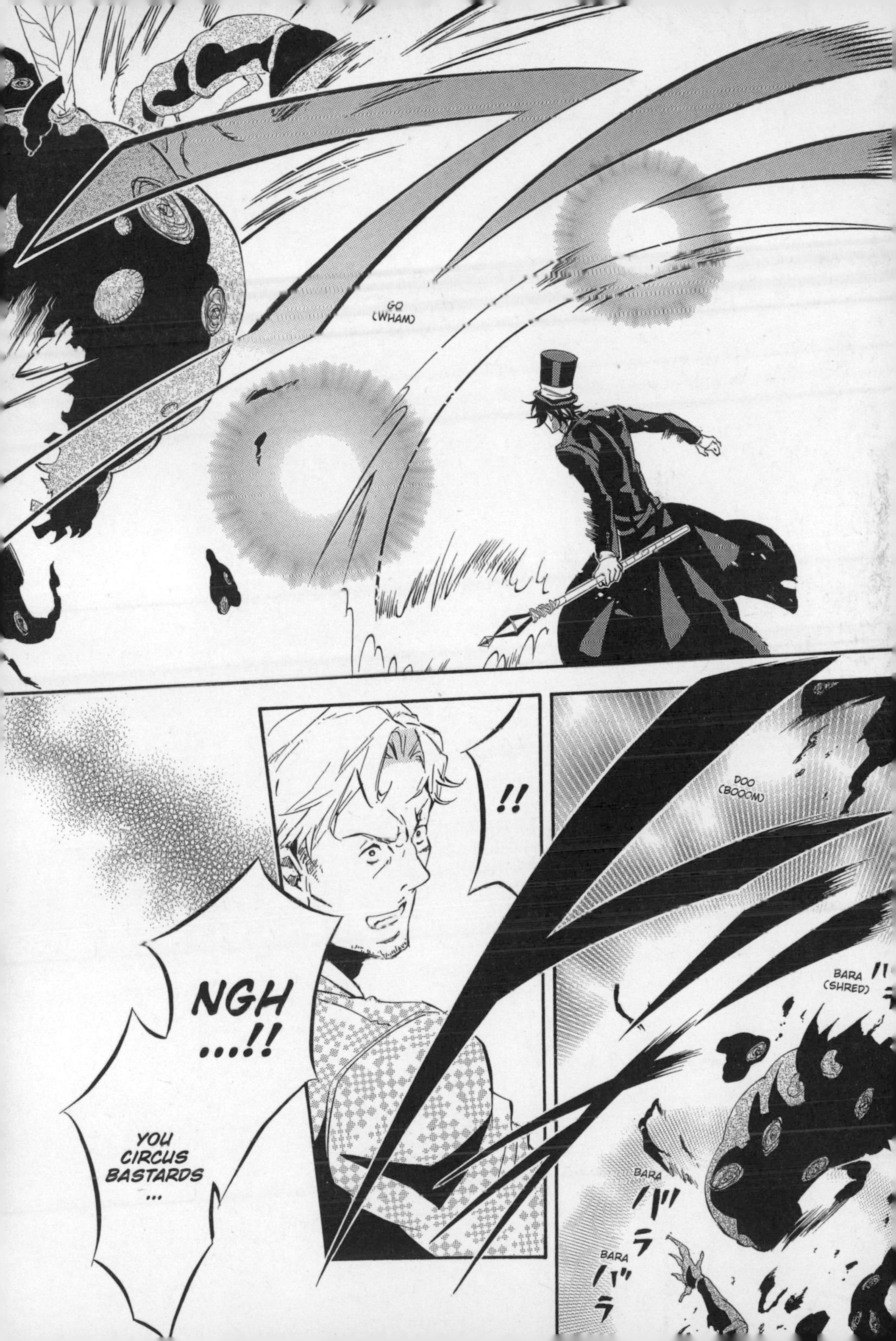
GO
(WHAM)
DOO
(BOOOM)
BARA
(SHRED)
BARA
BARA
!!
NGH
...!!
YOU CIRCUS BASTARDS...

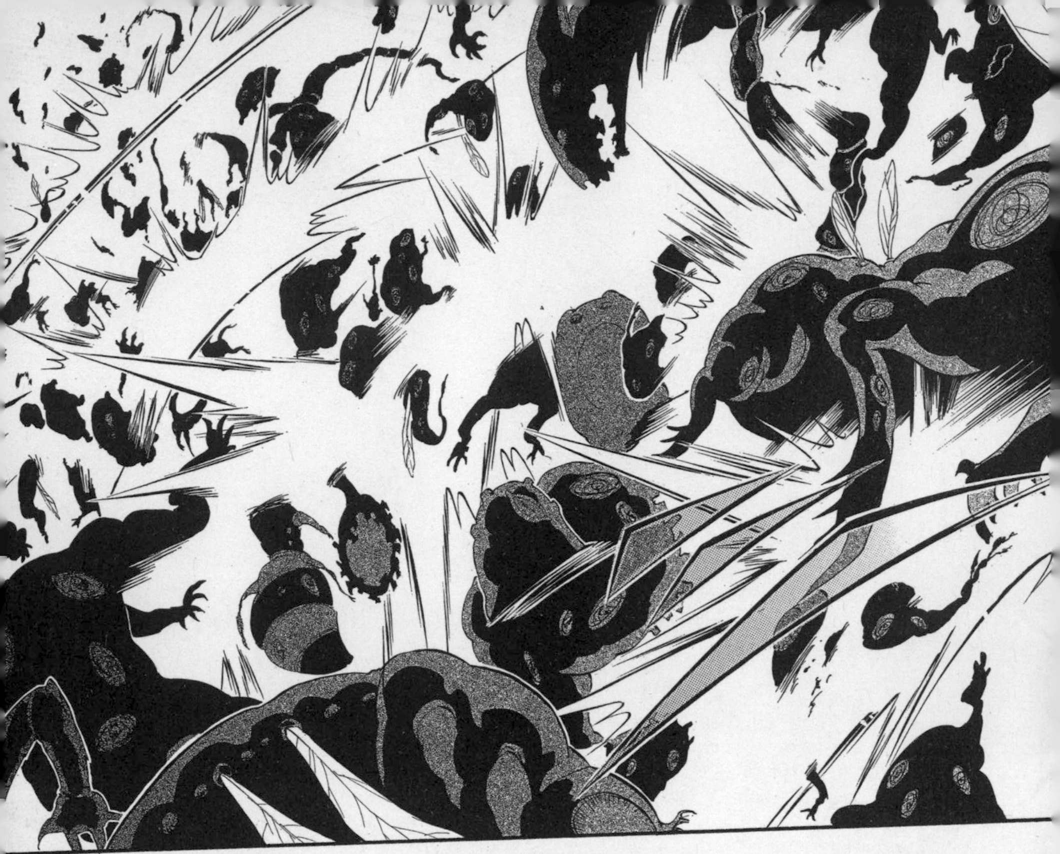

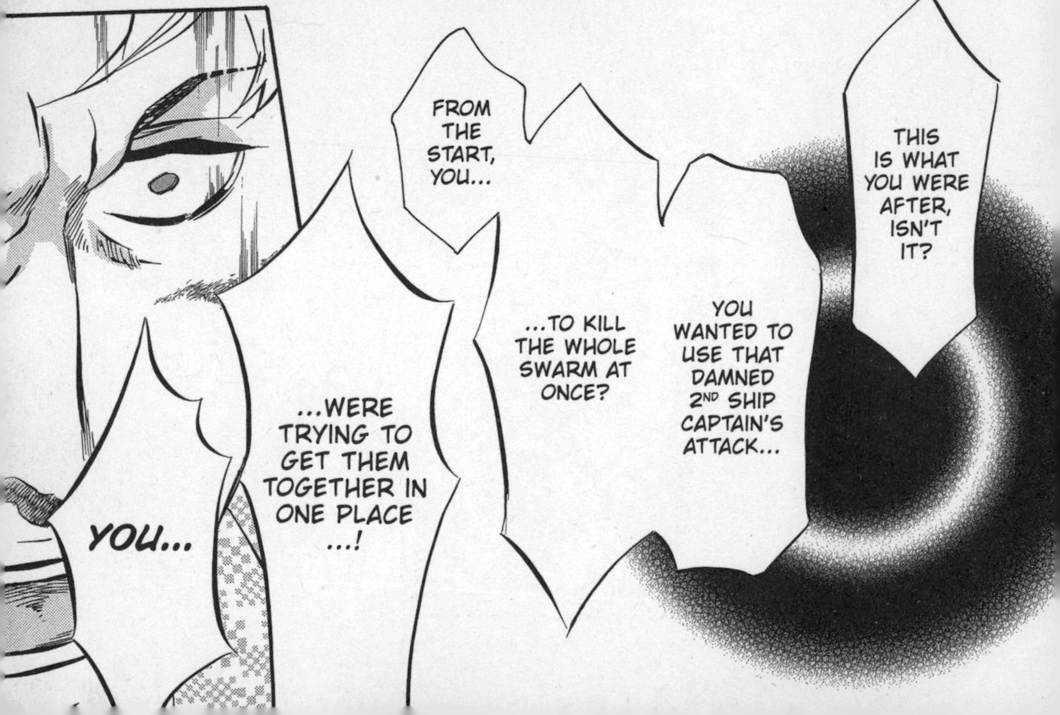
THIS IS WHAT YOU WERE AFTER, ISN'T IT?
FROM THE START, YOU...
YOU WANTED TO USE THAT DAMNED 2ND SHIP CAPTAIN'S ATTACK...
...TO KILL THE WHOLE SWARM AT ONCE?
...WERE TRYING TO GET THEM TOGETHER IN ONE PLACE ...!
YOU...

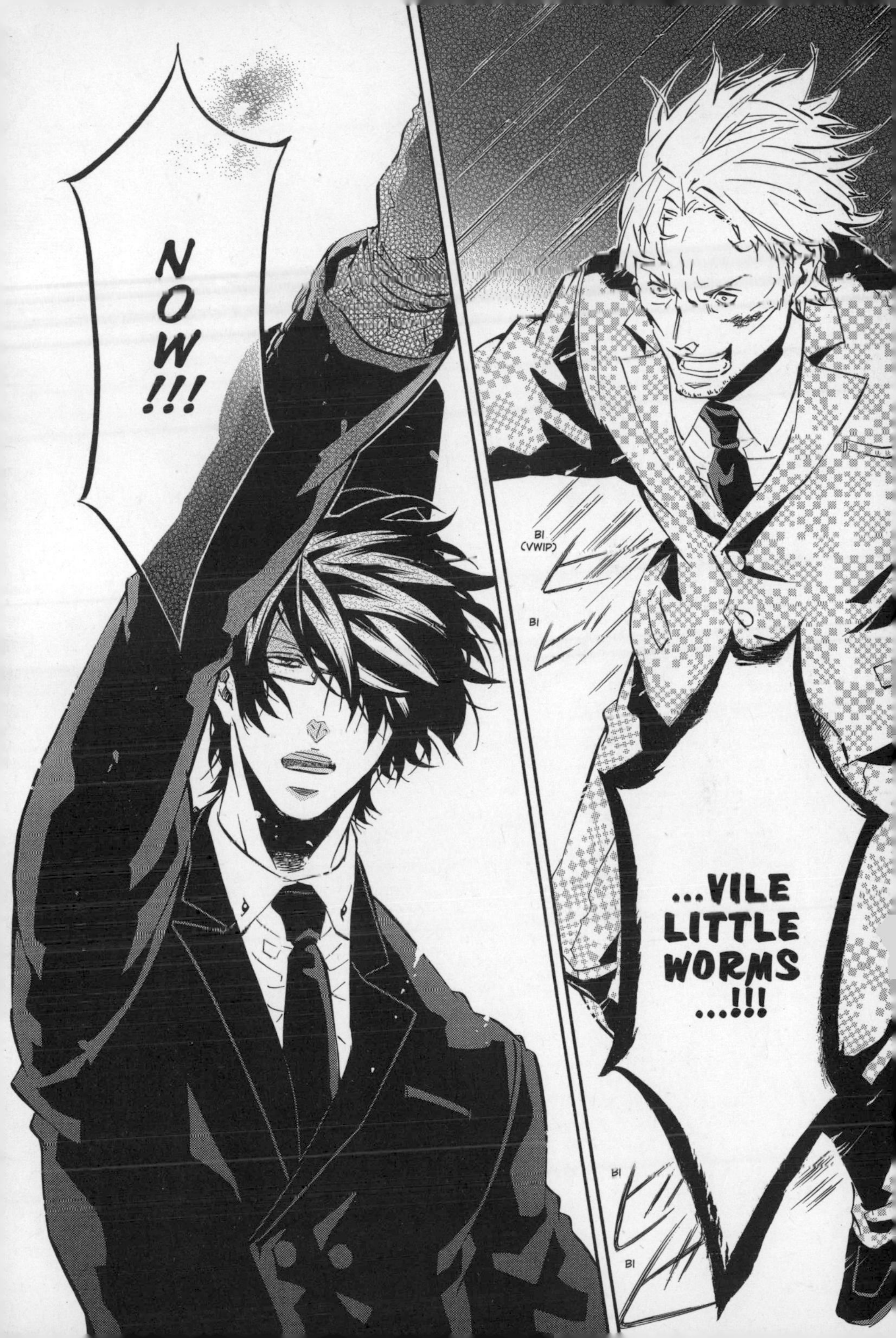
BI (VWIP)
BI
...VILE LITTLE WORMS ...!!!
BI
BI
NOW!!!

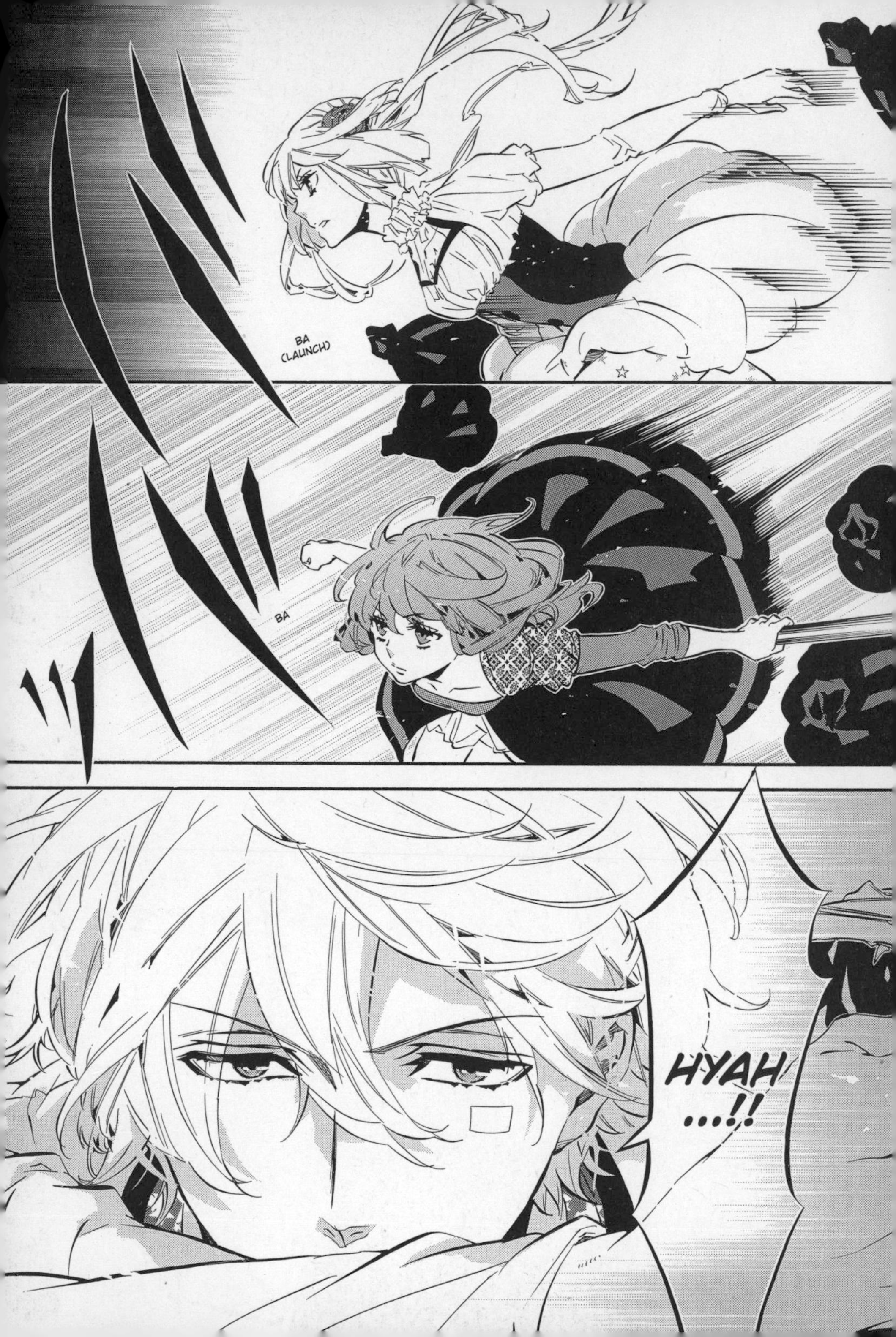
BA
(LAUNCH)
BA
HYAH
...!!

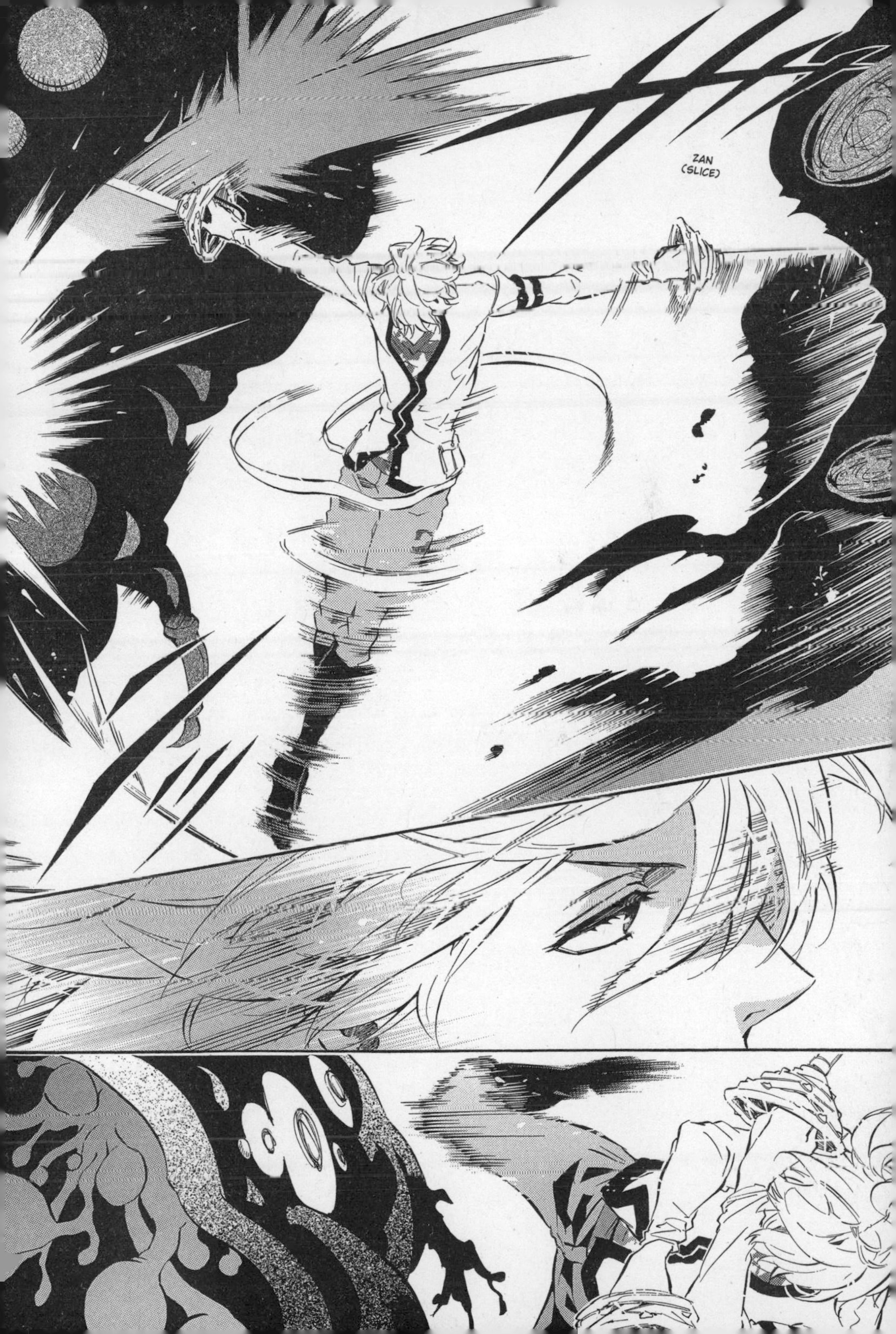
ZAN
(SLICE)

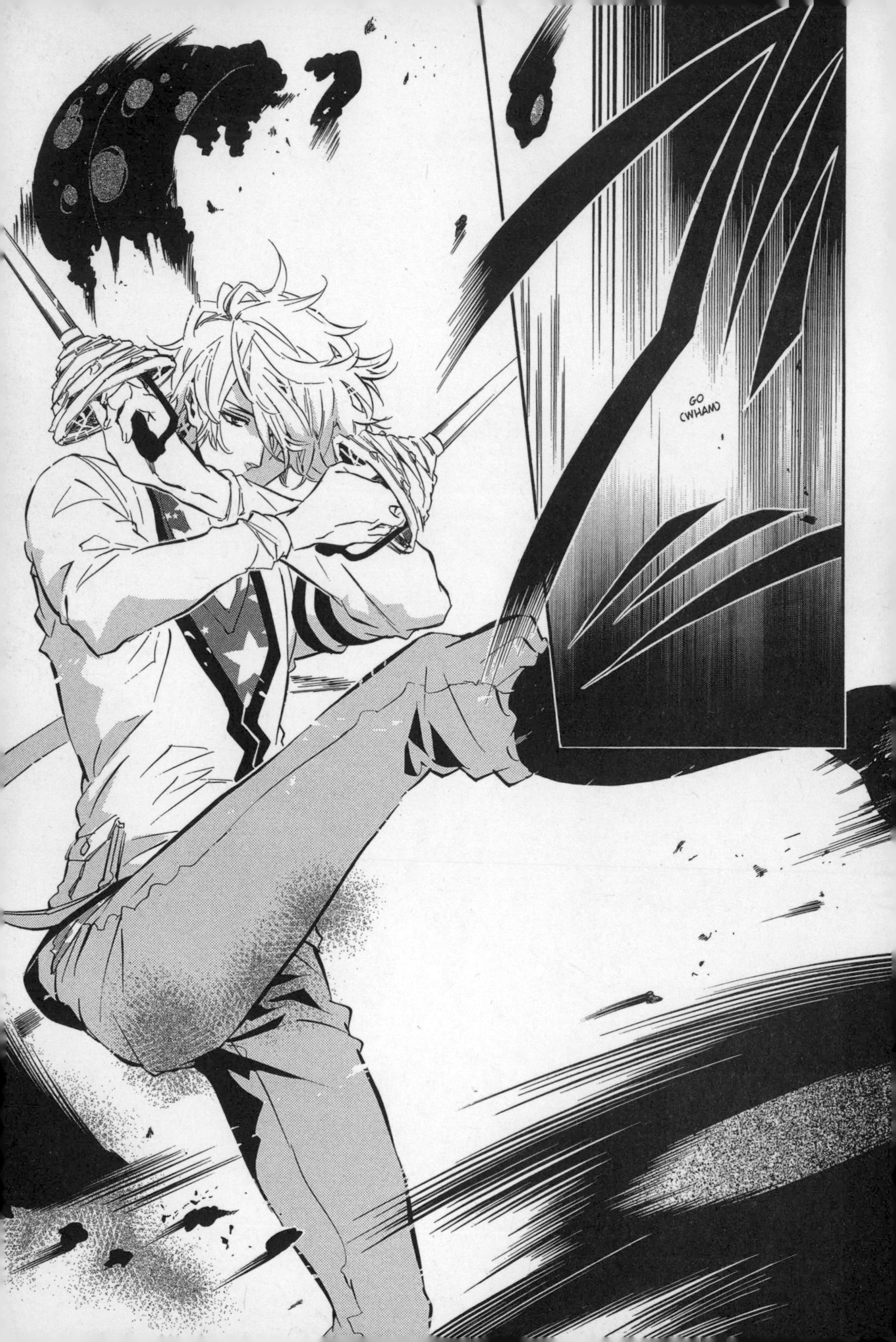
GO
(WHAM)

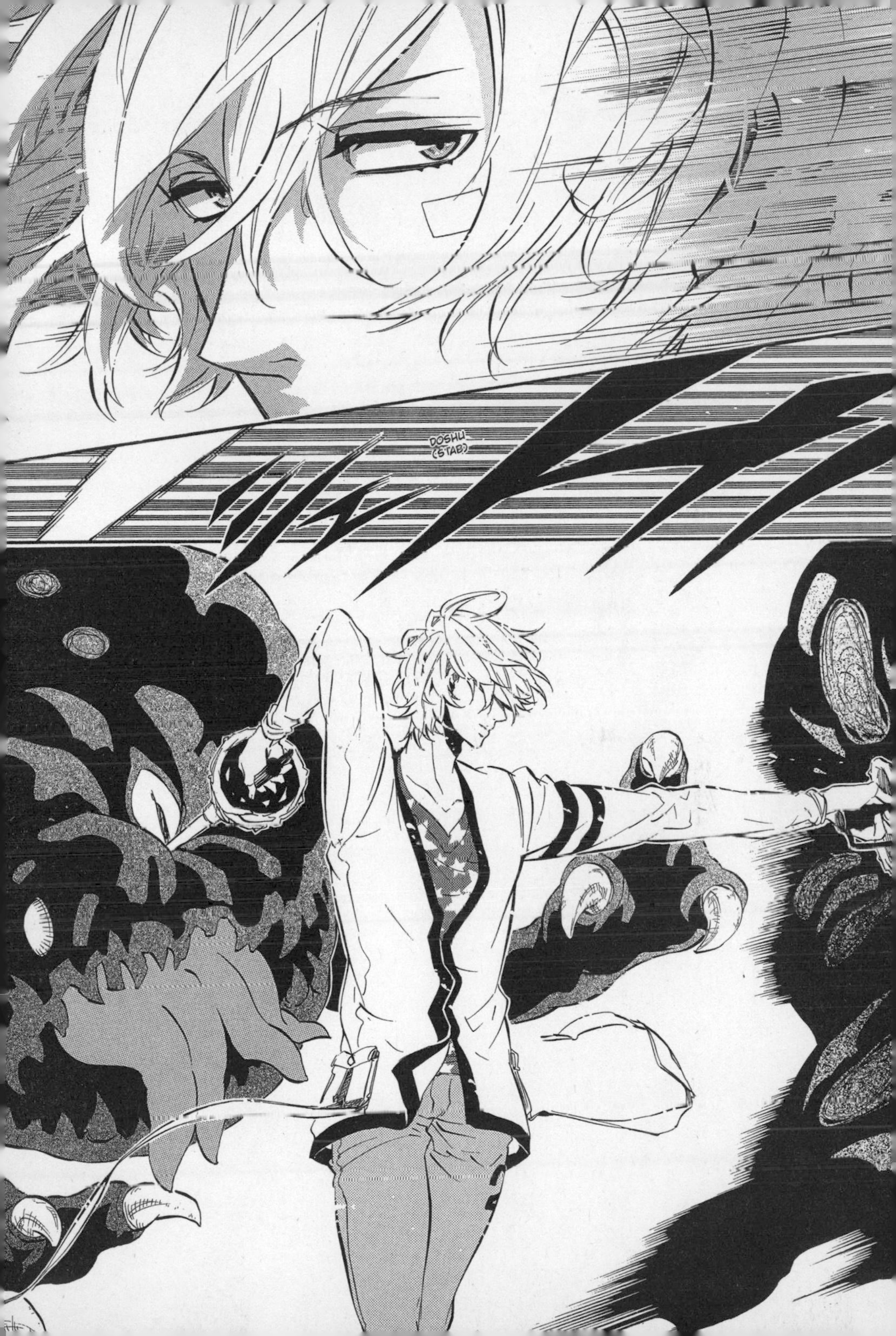
DOSHU
(STAB)

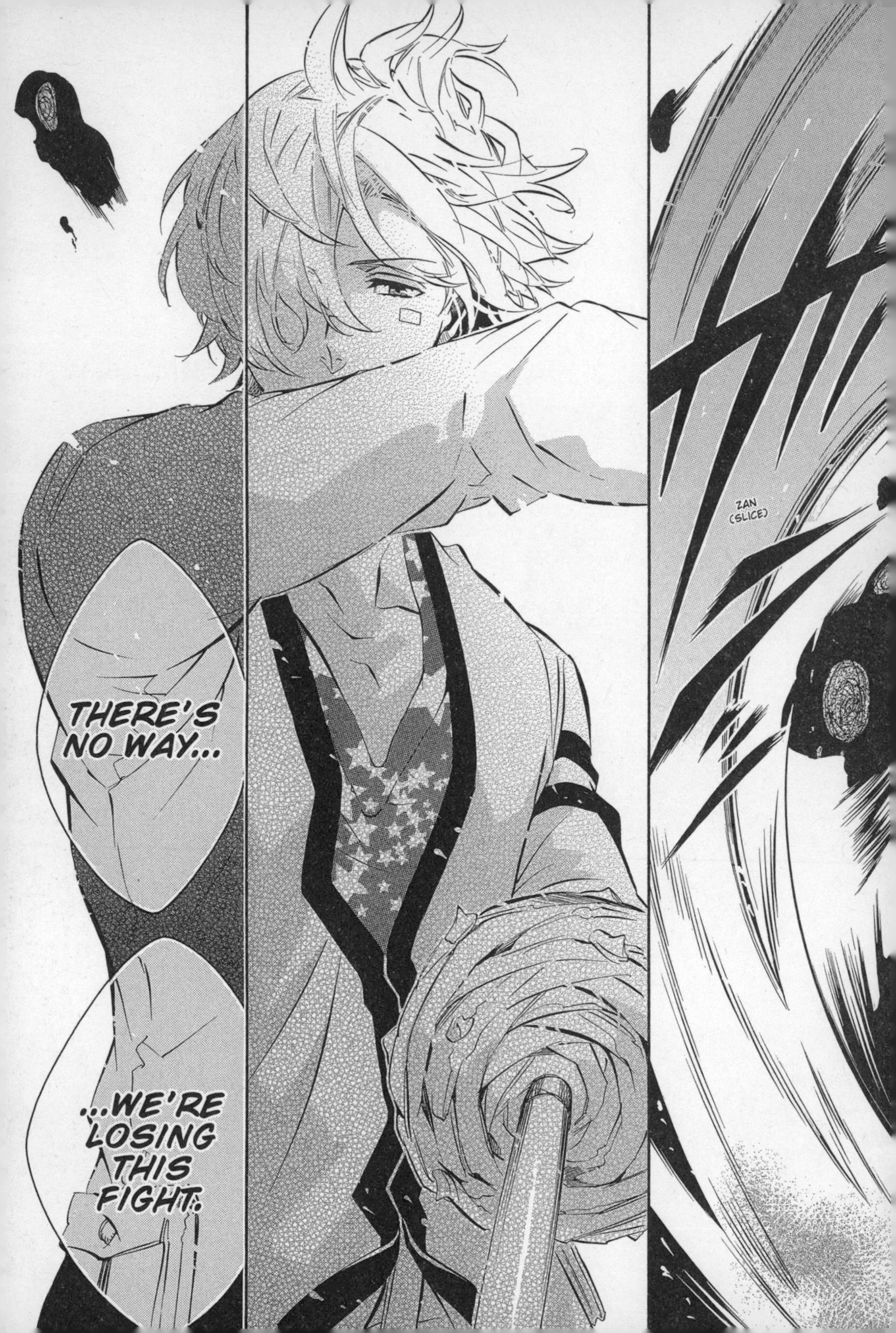
ZAN (SLICE)
THERE'S NO WAY...
...WE'RE LOSING THIS FIGHT.

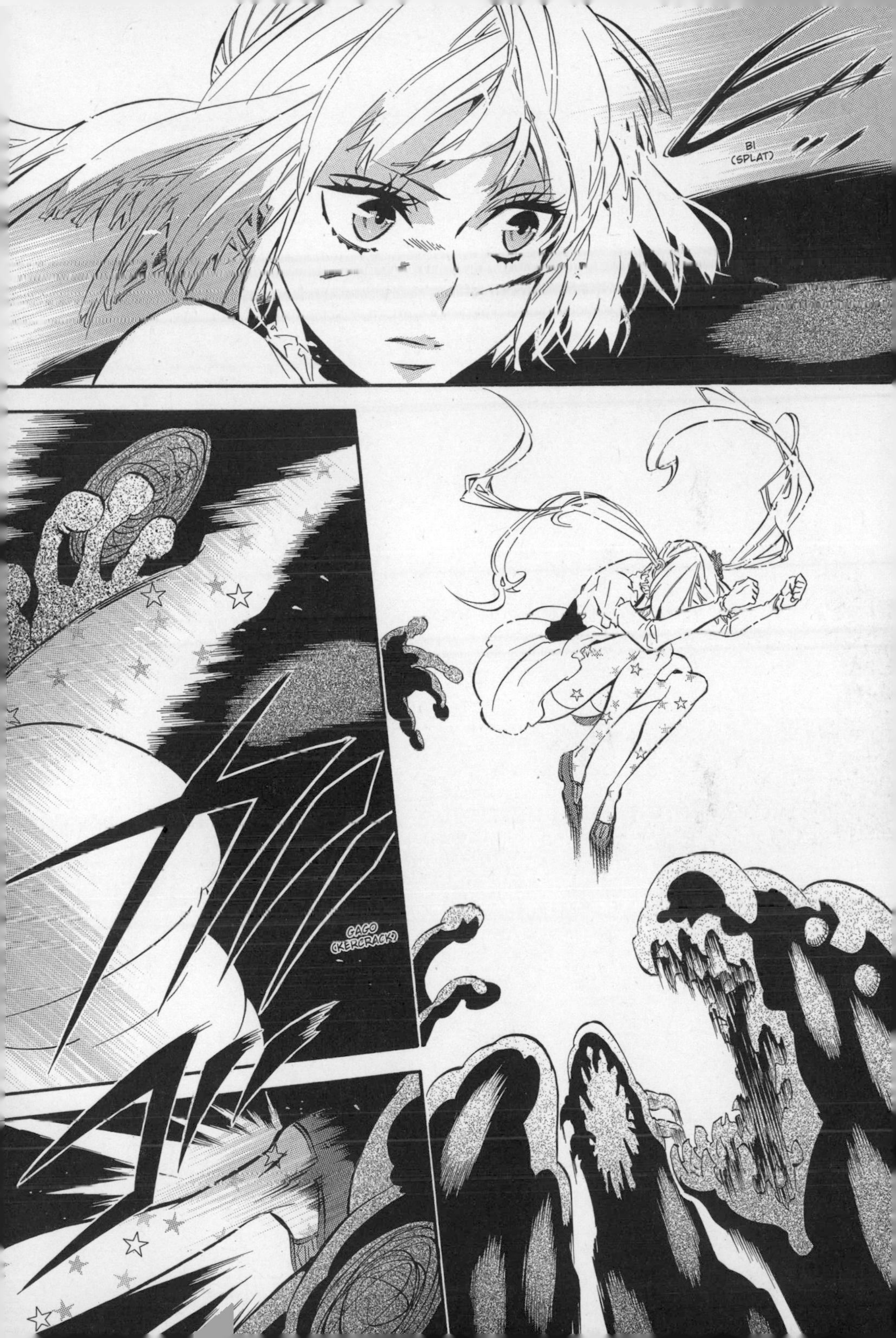
BI
(SPLAT)
GAGO
(KERCRACK)

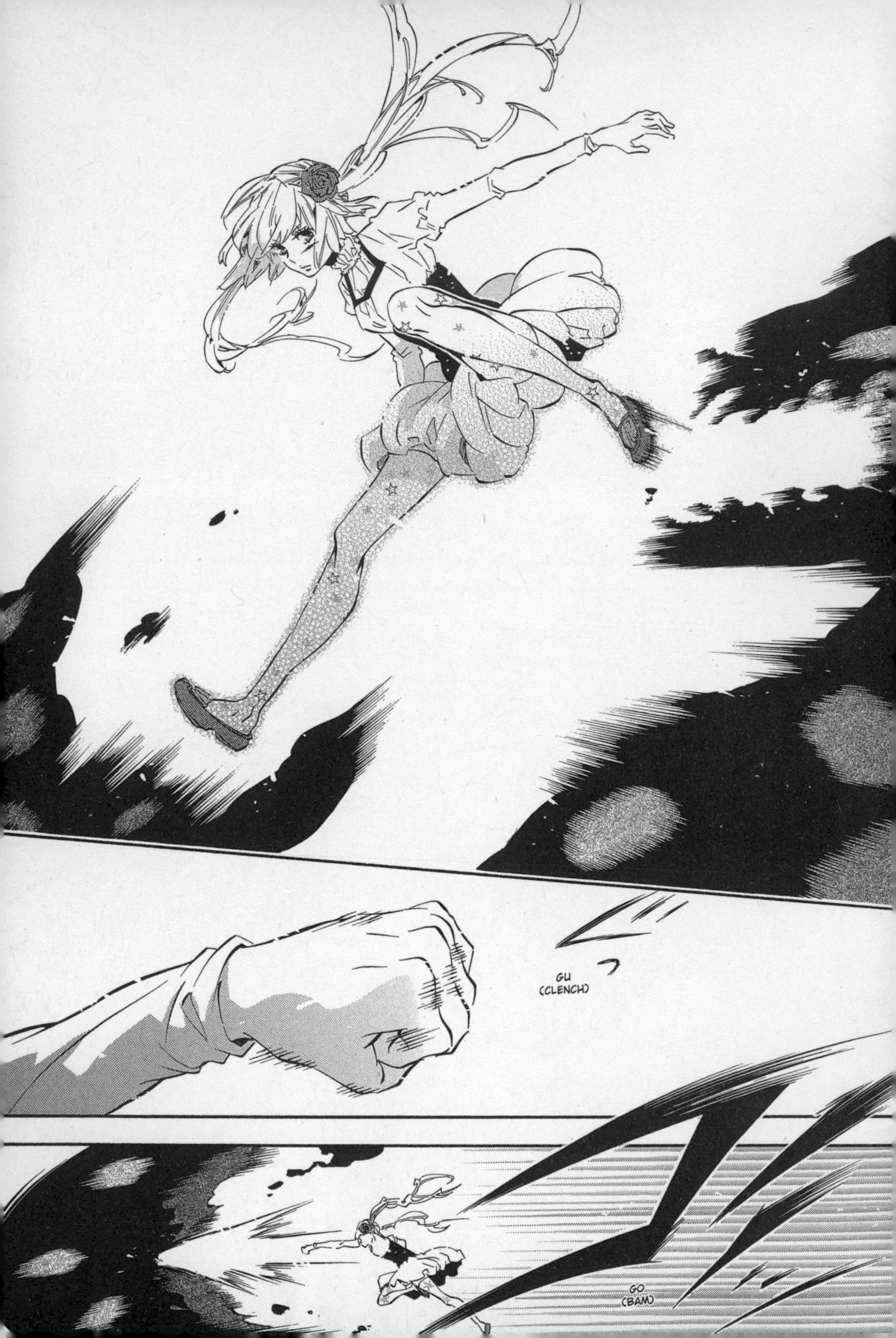
GU
(CLENCH)
GO
(BAM)

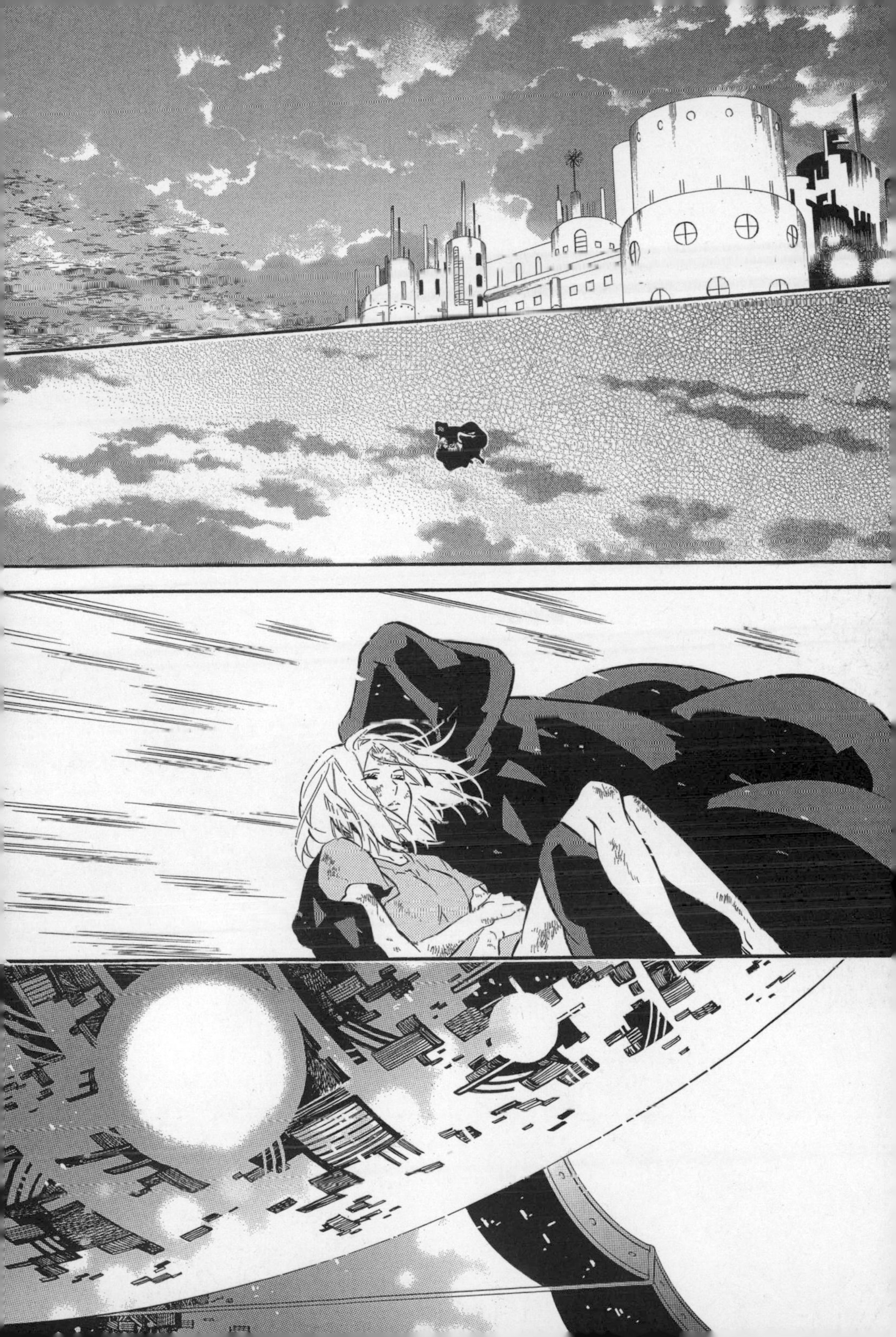

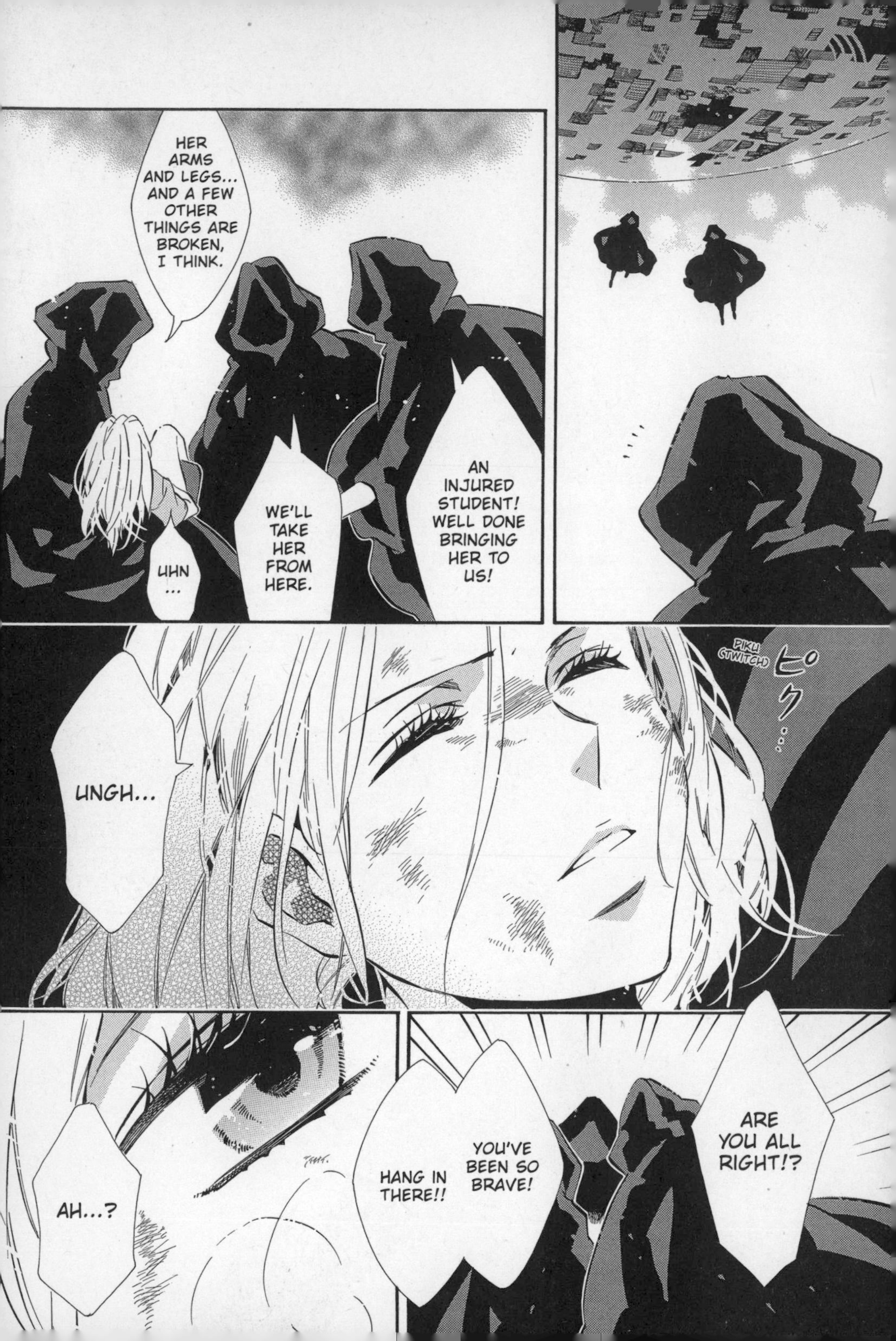
HER ARMS AND LEGS... AND A FEW OTHER THINGS ARE BROKEN, I THINK.
AN INJURED STUDENT! WELL DONE BRINGING HER TO US!
WE'LL TAKE HER FROM HERE.
UHN ...
PIKU (TWITCH)
ピク…
UNGH...
ARE YOU ALL RIGHT!?
YOU'VE BEEN SO BRAVE!
HANG IN THERE!!
AH...?

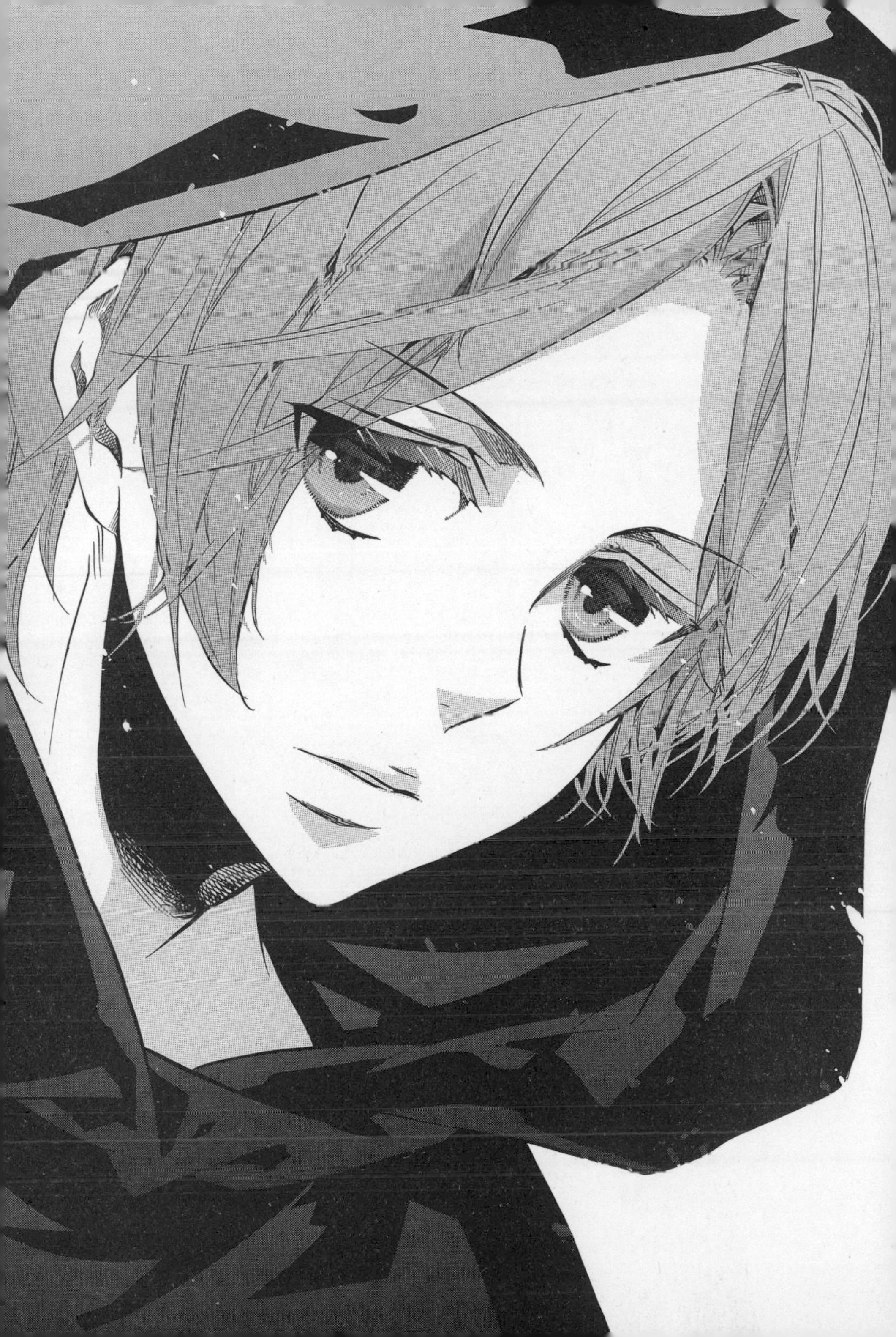

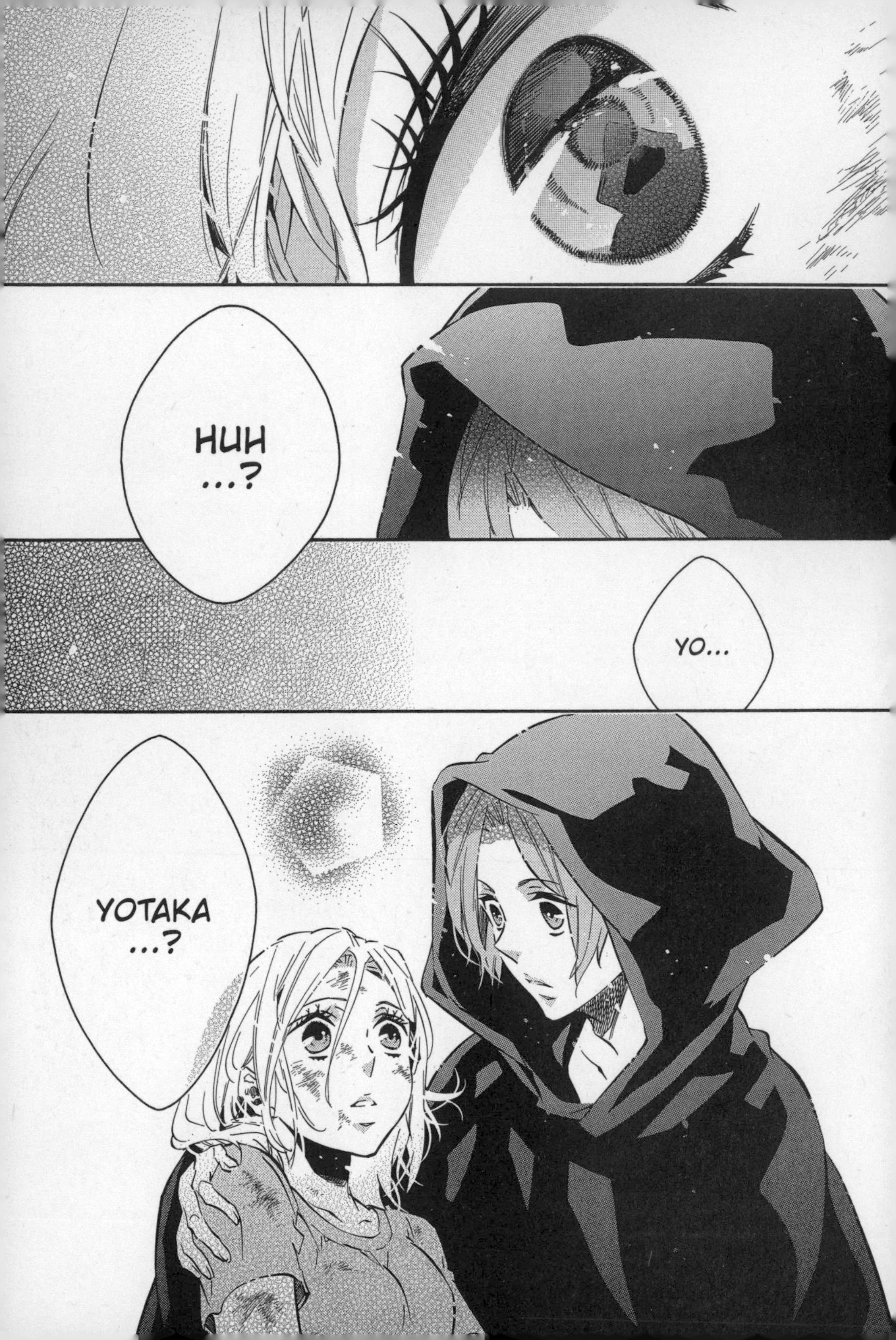
HUH ...?
YO...
YOTAKA ...?

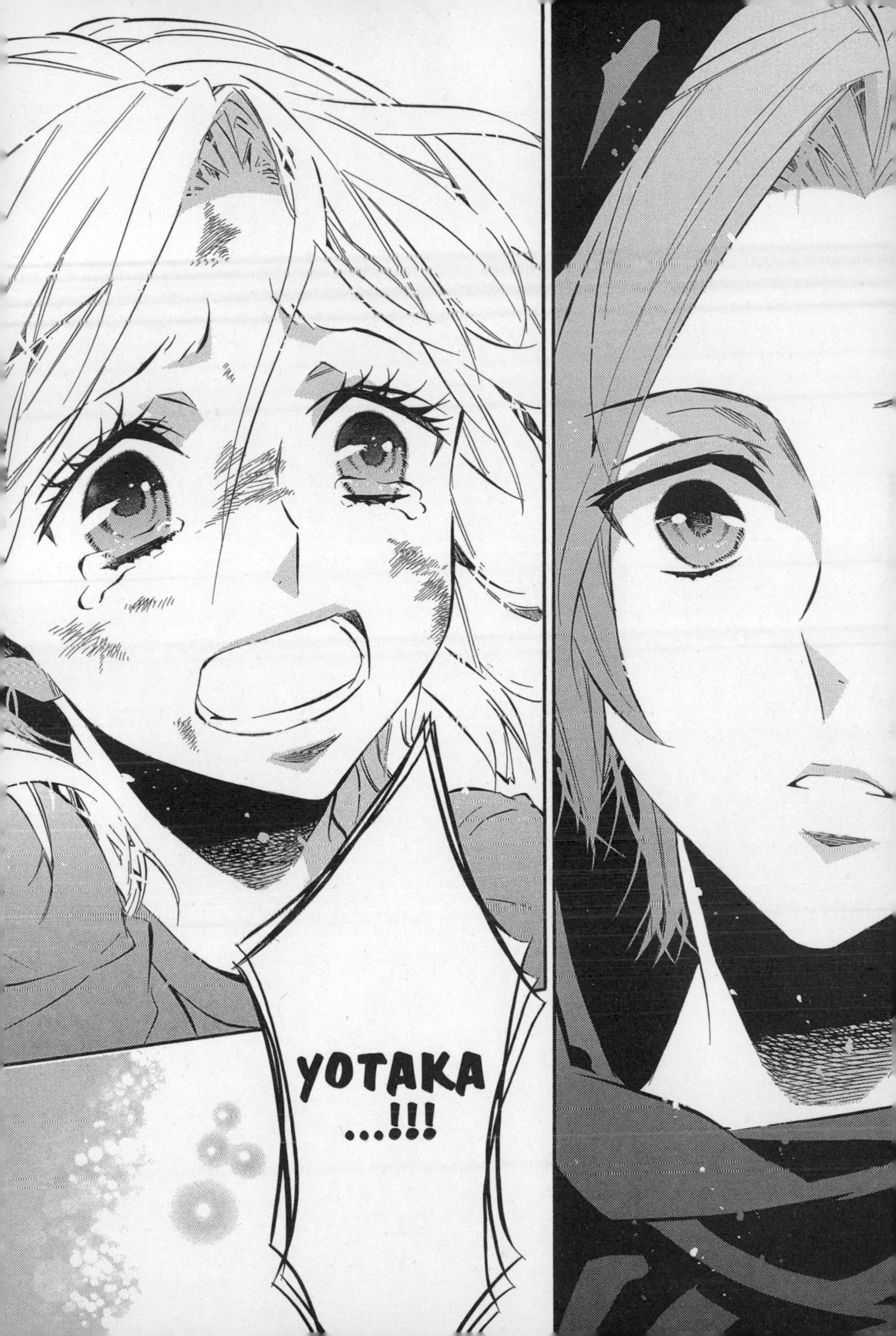
YOTAKA
...!!!

KARNEVAL

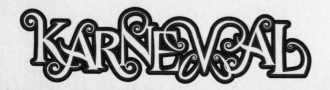

KARNEVAL

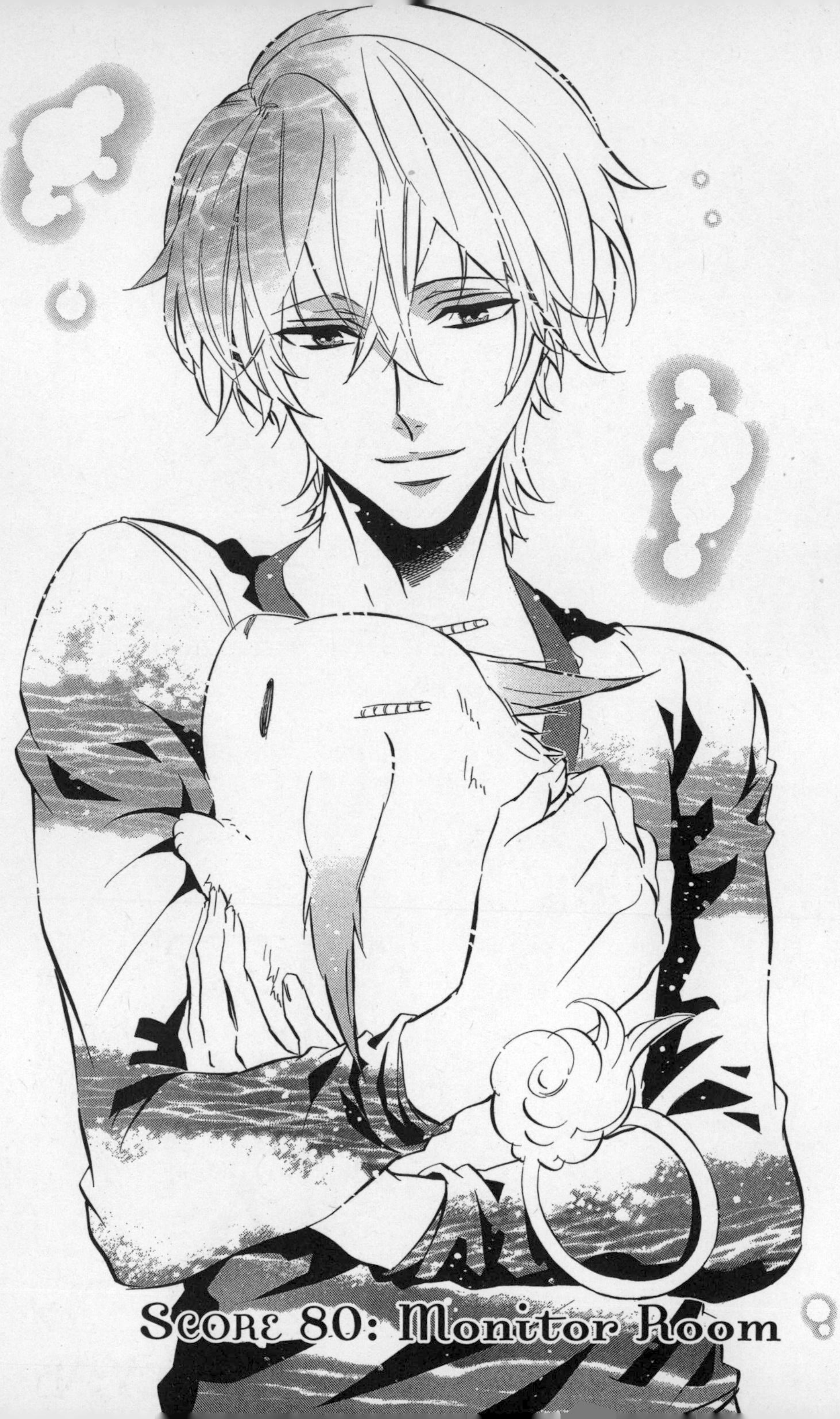

Score 80: Monitor Room

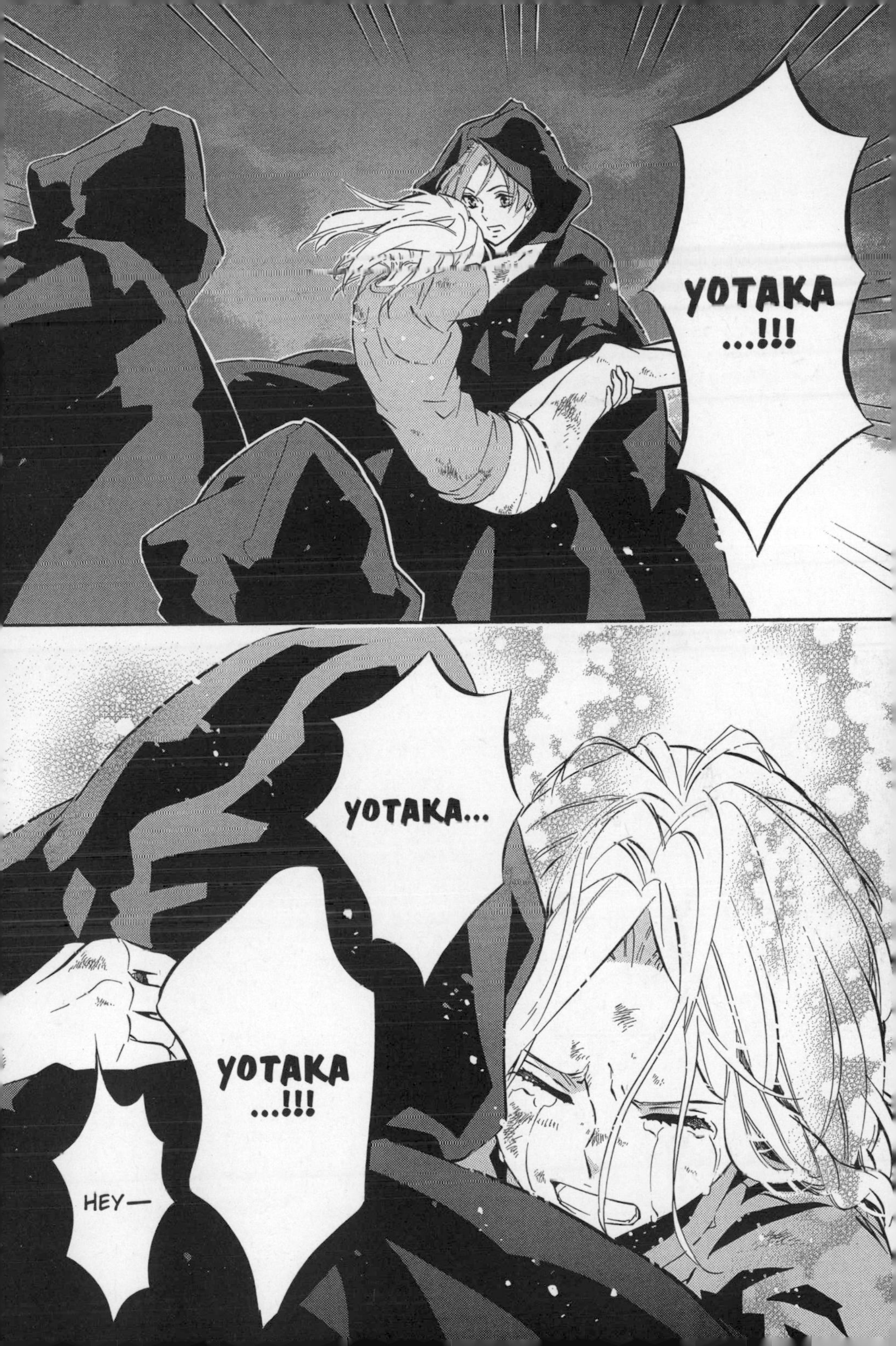
YOTAKA ...!!!
YOTAKA...
YOTAKA ...!!!
HEY—

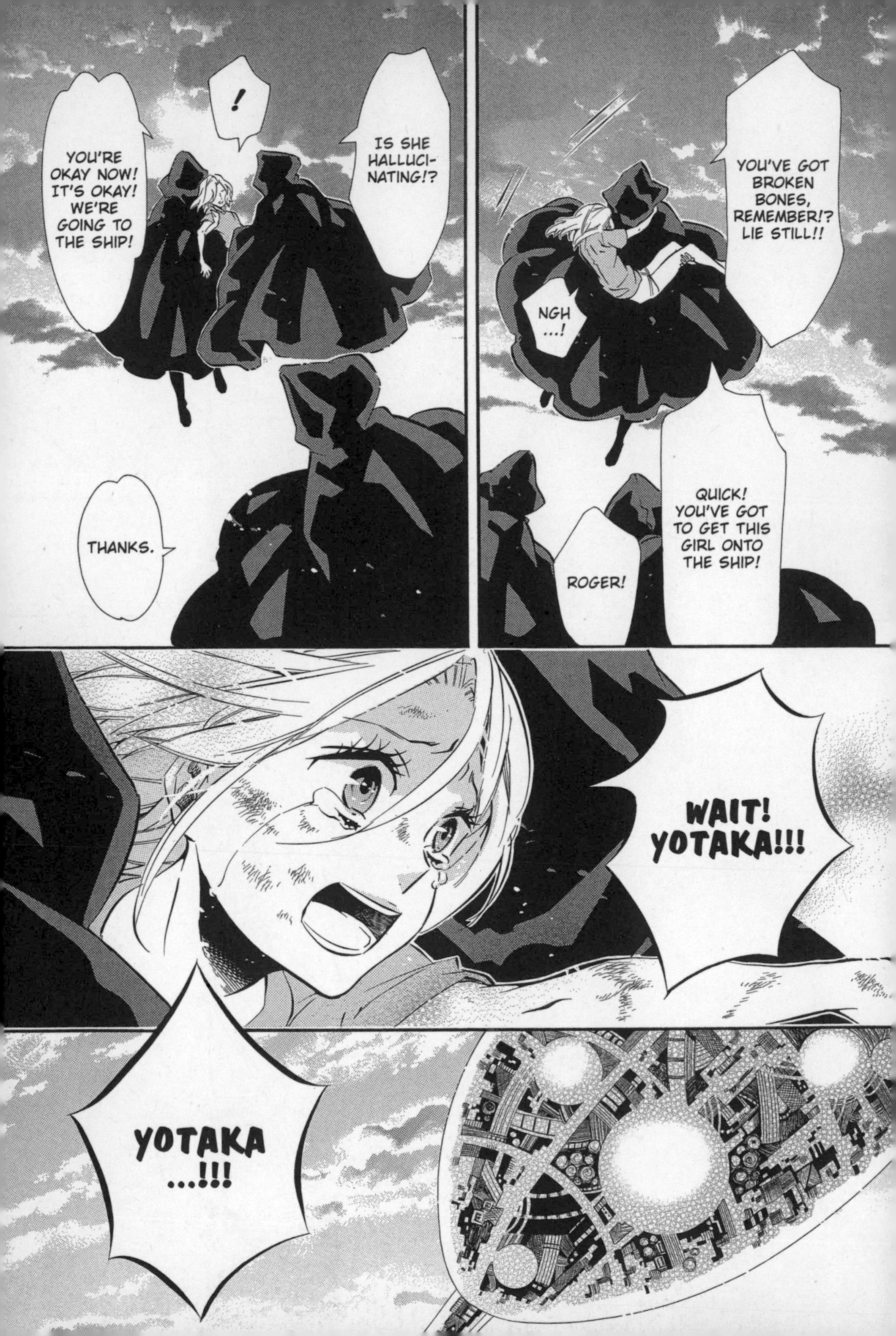
YOU'VE GOT BROKEN BONES, REMEMBER!? LIE STILL!!
NGH ...!
QUICK! YOU'VE GOT TO GET THIS GIRL ONTO THE SHIP!
ROGER!
IS SHE HALLUCI-NATING!?
!
YOU'RE OKAY NOW! IT'S OKAY! WE'RE GOING TO THE SHIP!
THANKS.
WAIT! YOTAKA!!!
YOTAKA ...!!!

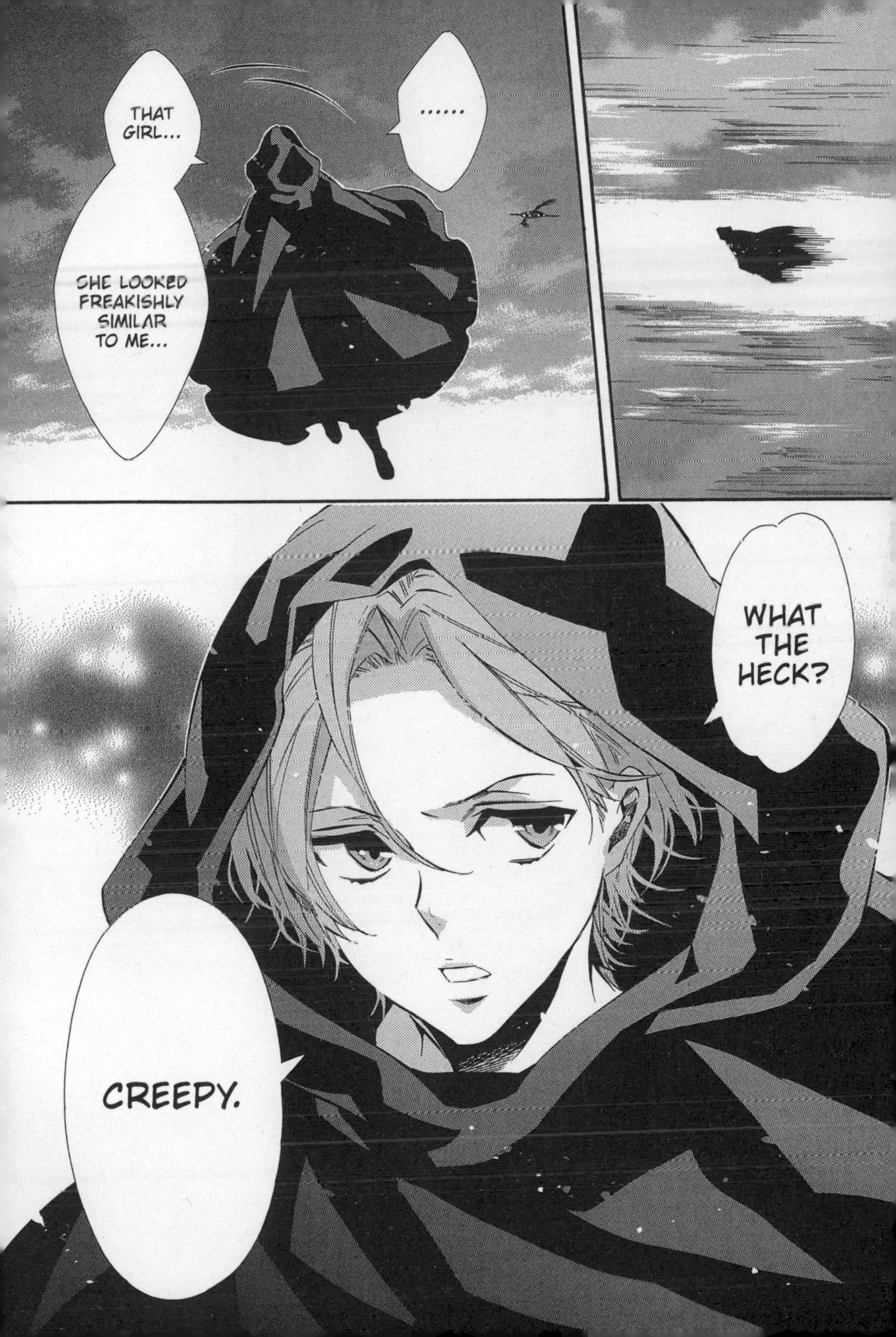
......
THAT GIRL...
SHE LOOKED FREAKISHLY SIMILAR TO ME...
WHAT THE HECK?
CREEPY.

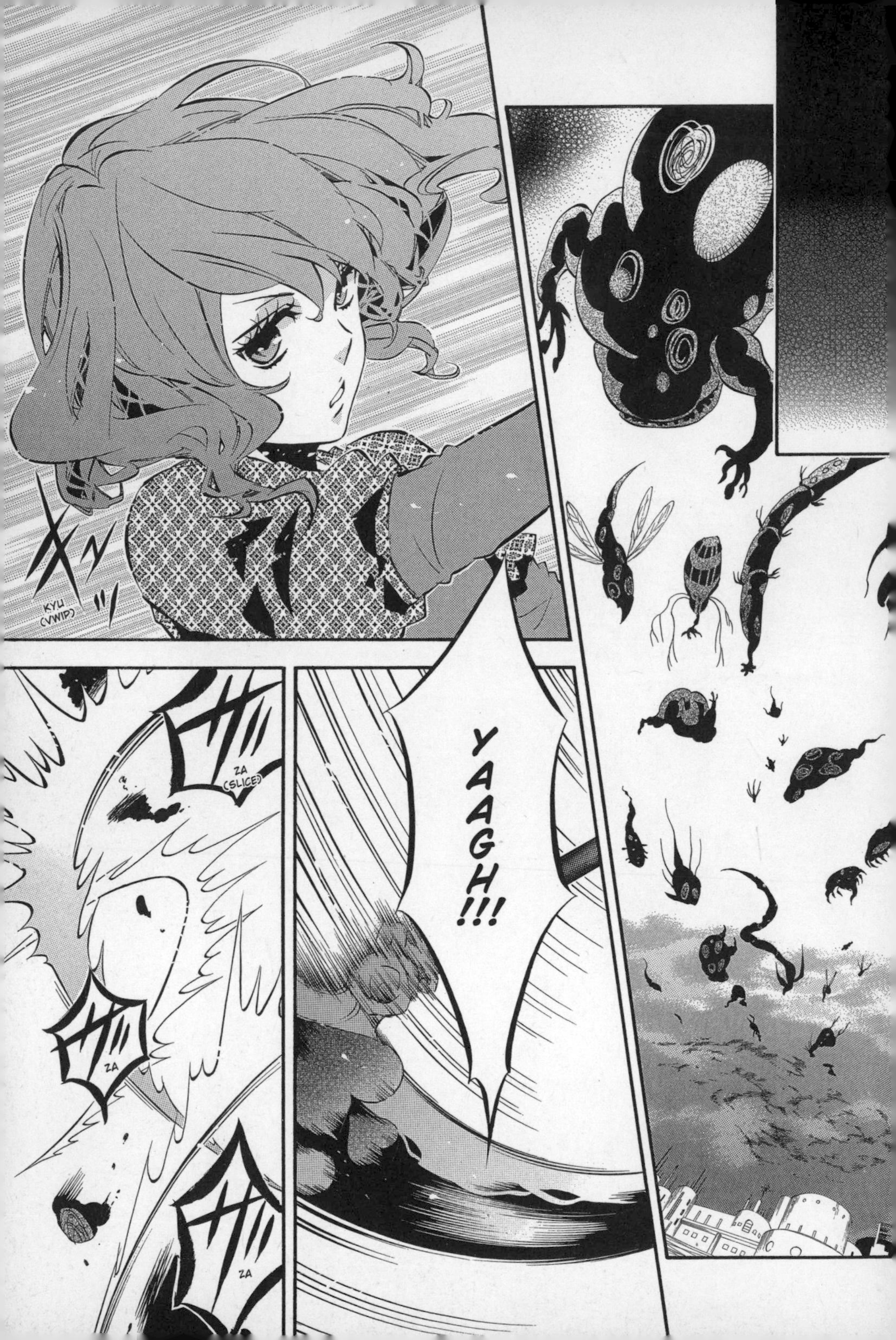
KYU (VWIP)
YAAGH!!!
ZA (SLICE)
ZA
ZA

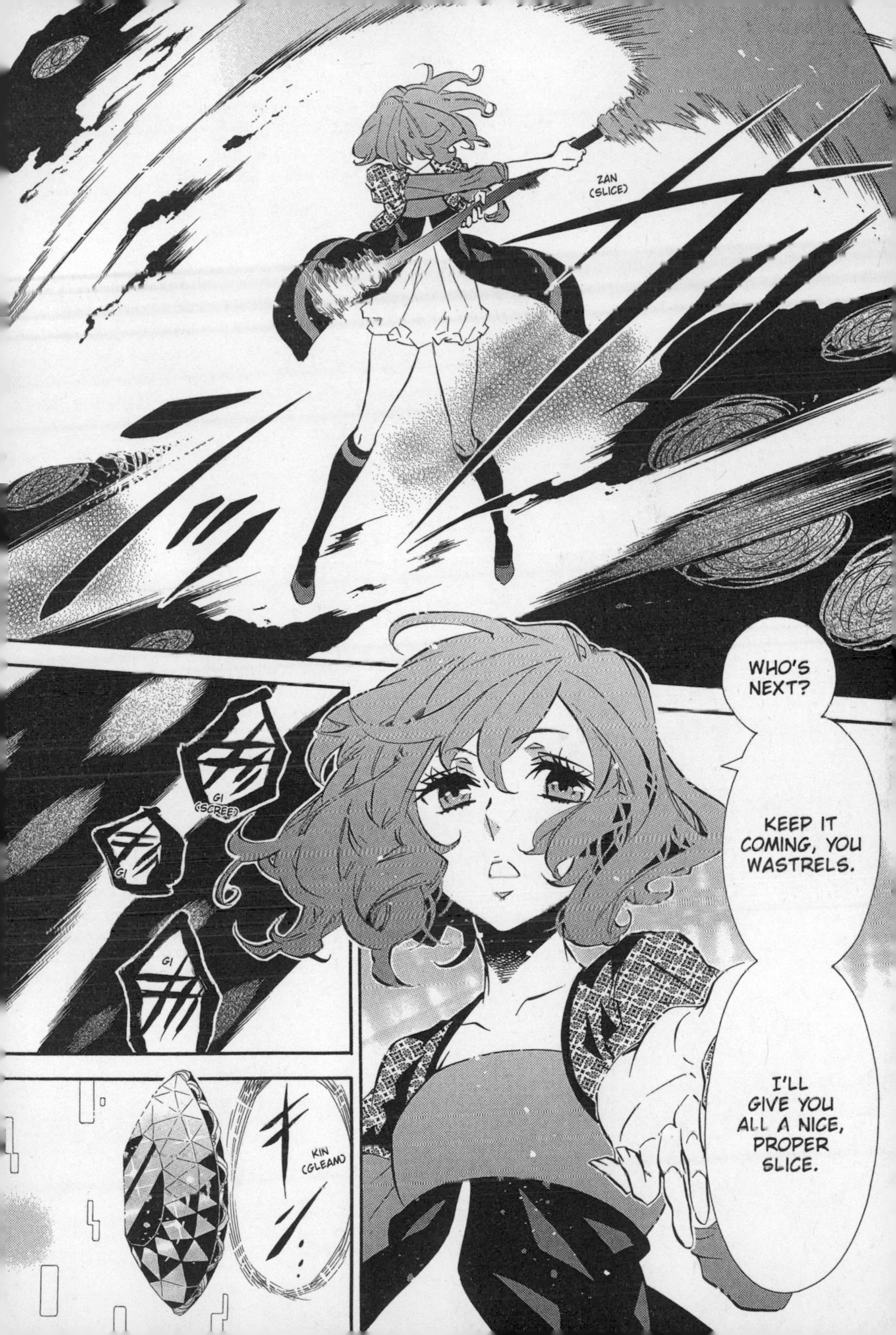
ZAN (SLICE)
WHO'S NEXT?
KEEP IT COMING, YOU WASTRELS.
I'LL GIVE YOU ALL A NICE, PROPER SLICE.
GI (SCREE)
GI
GI
KIN (GLEAM)

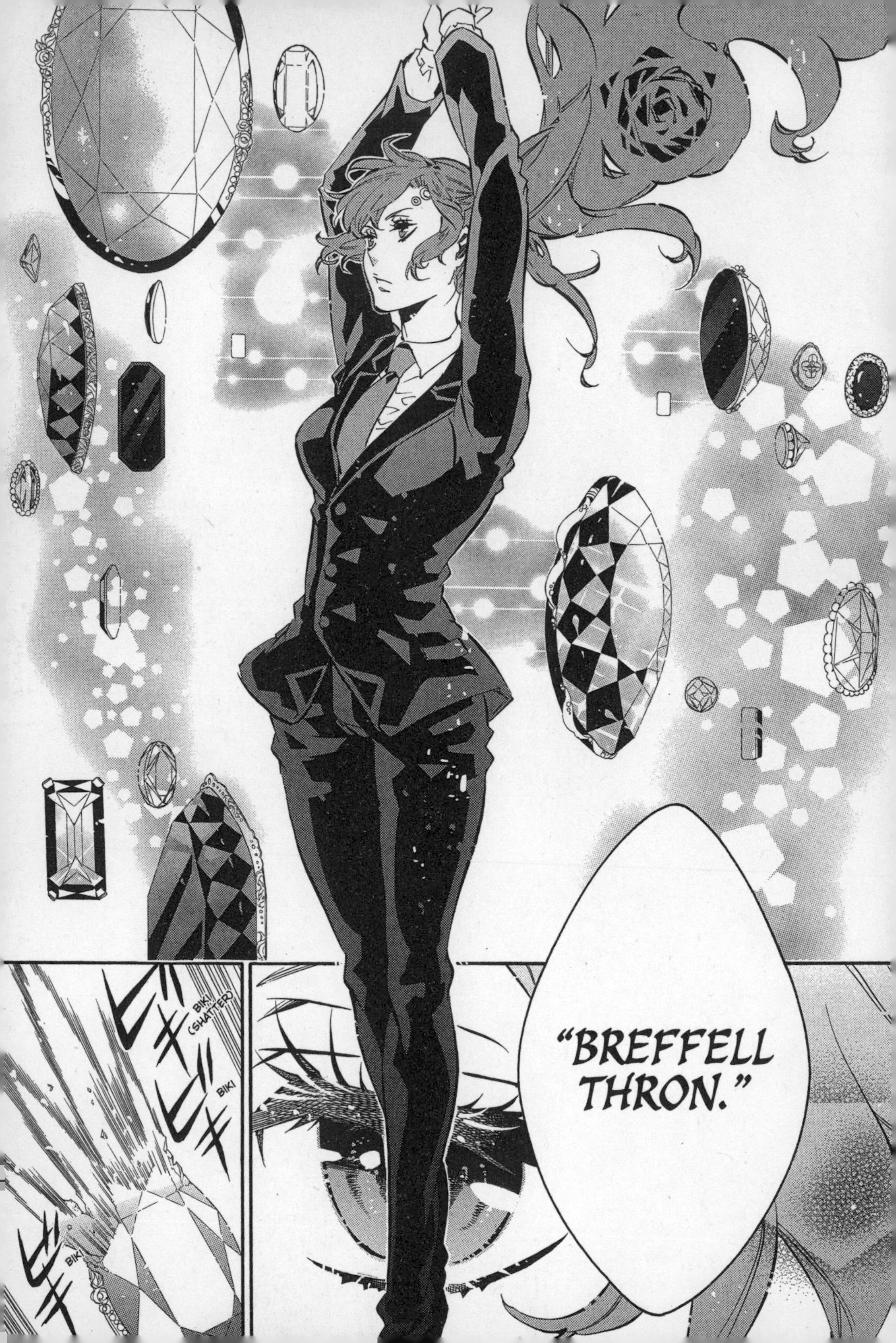
"BREFFELL THRON."
BIKI (SHATTER)
BIKI
BIKI

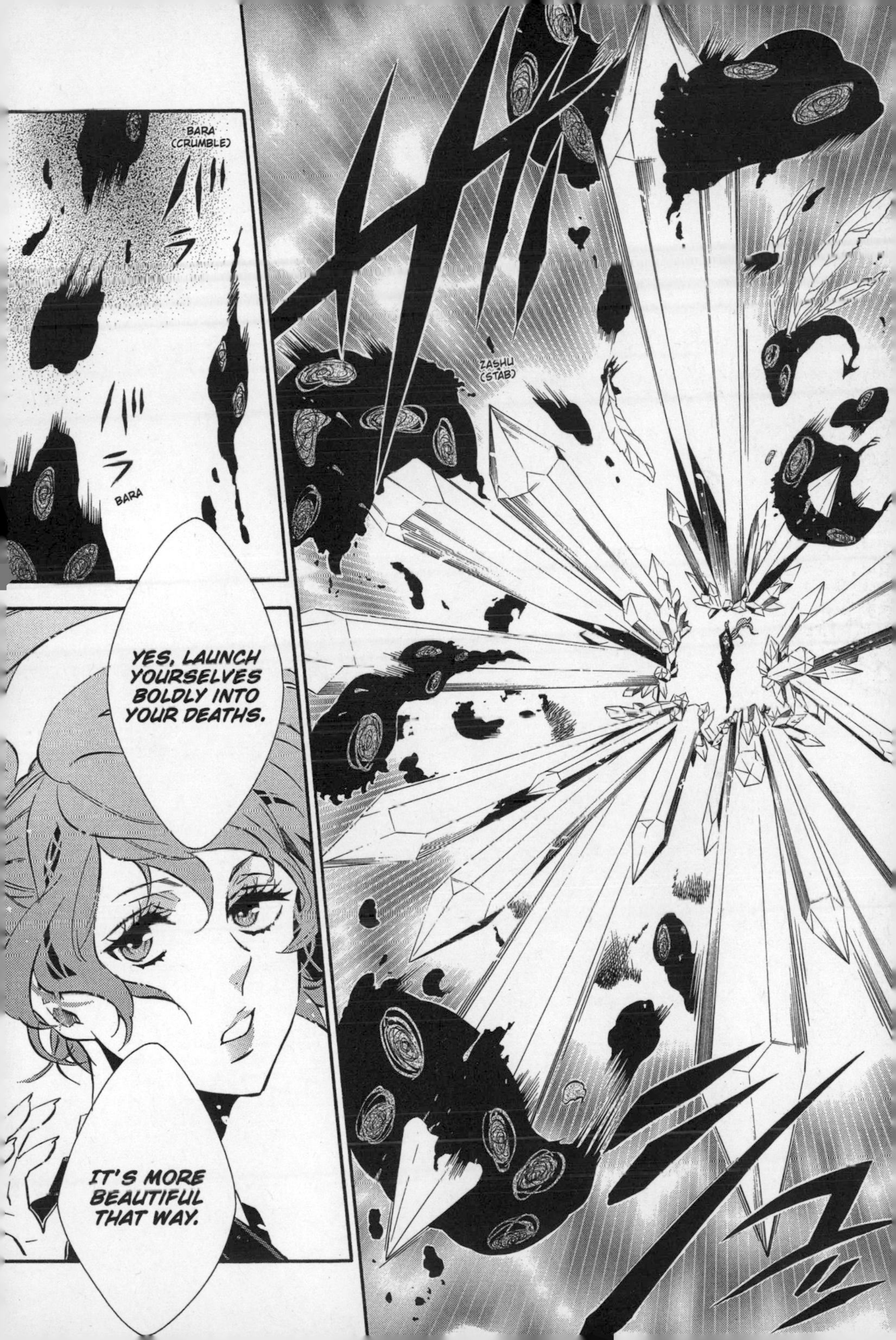
ZASHU
(STAB)
BARA
(CRUMBLE)
BARA
YES, LAUNCH YOURSELVES BOLDLY INTO YOUR DEATHS.
IT'S MORE BEAUTIFUL THAT WAY.

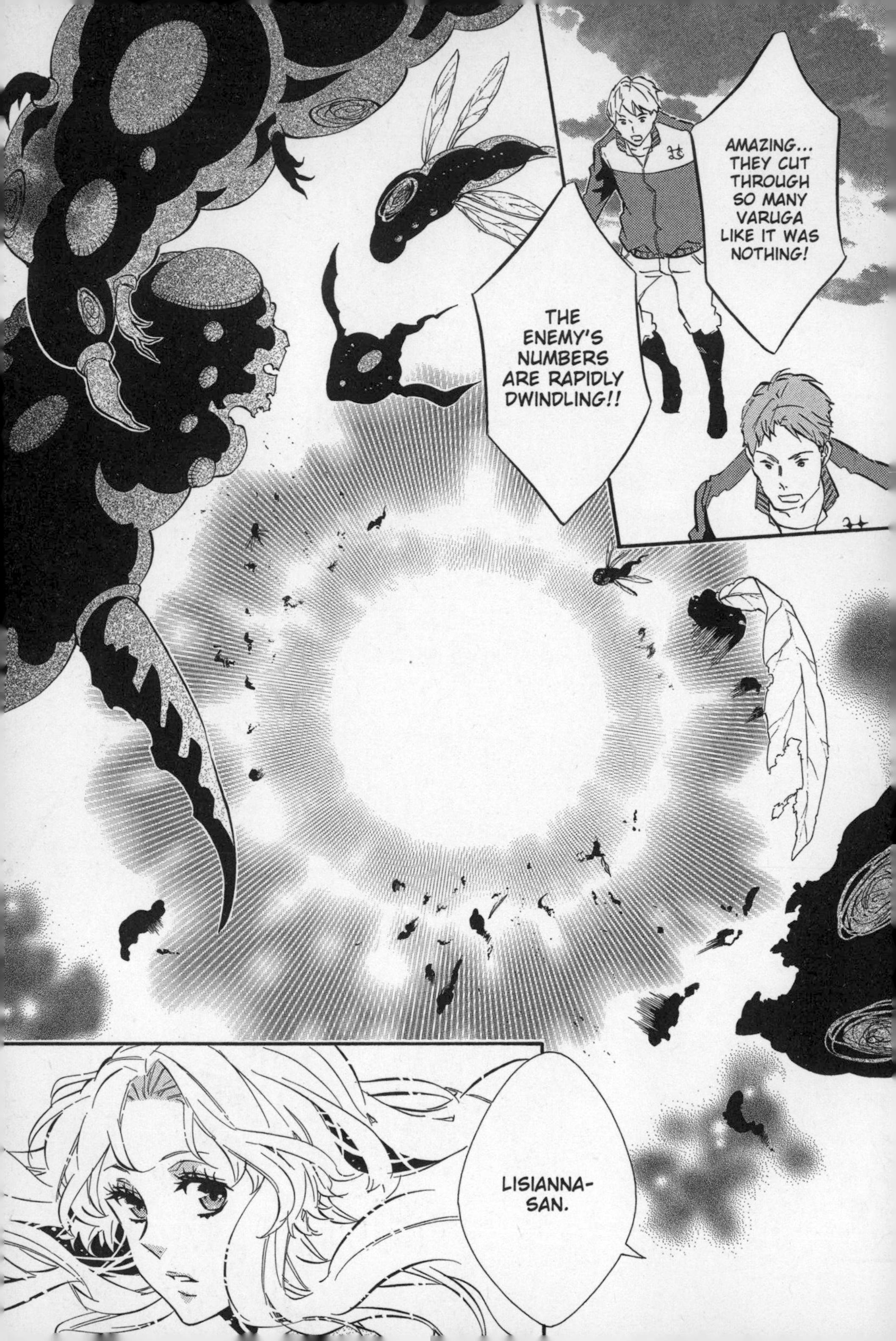
AMAZING... THEY CUT THROUGH SO MANY VARUGA LIKE IT WAS NOTHING!
THE ENEMY'S NUMBERS ARE RAPIDLY DWINDLING!!
LISIANNA-SAN.

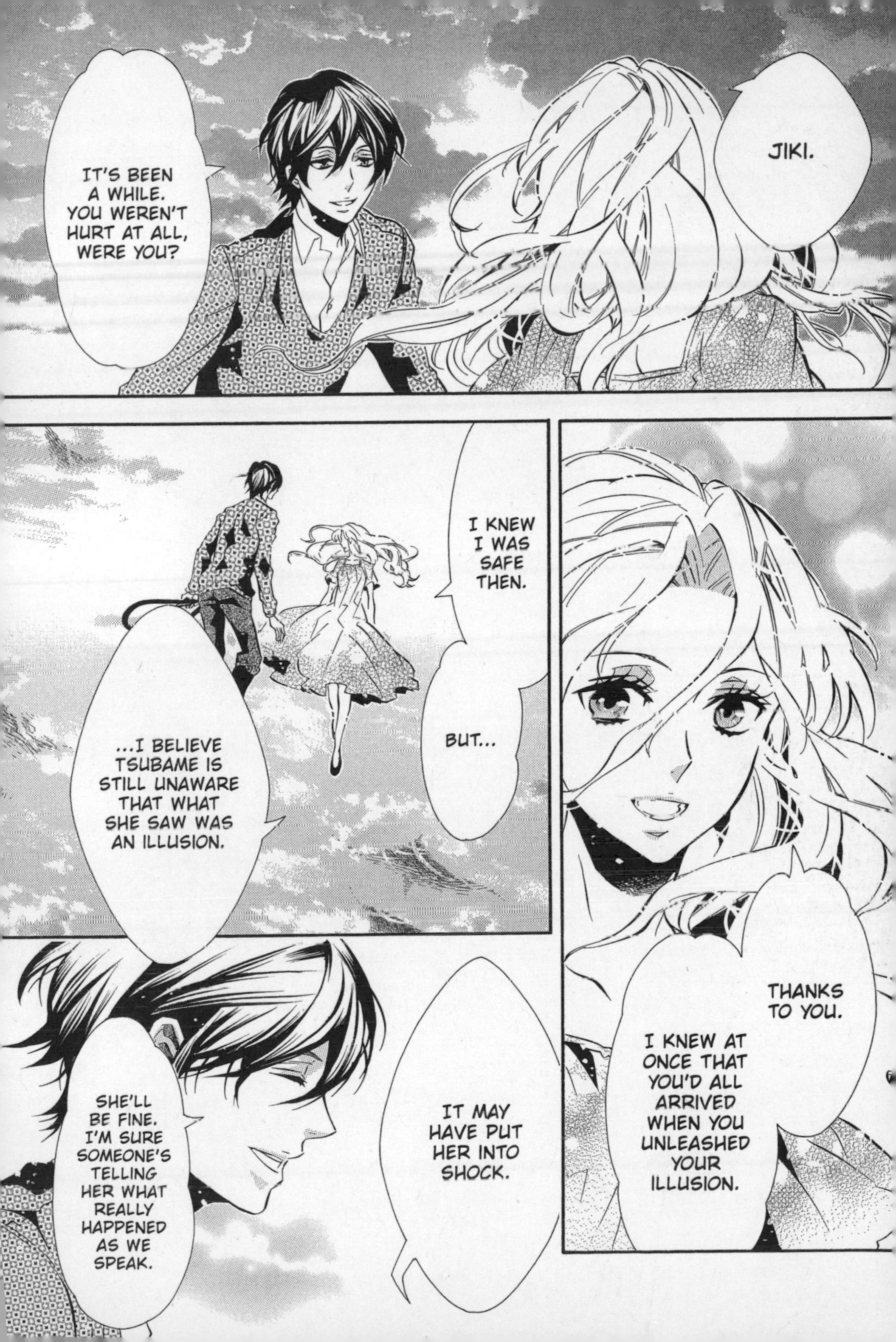
JIKI.
IT'S BEEN A WHILE. YOU WEREN'T HURT AT ALL, WERE YOU?
THANKS TO YOU.
I KNEW AT ONCE THAT YOU'D ALL ARRIVED WHEN YOU UNLEASHED YOUR ILLUSION.
I KNEW I WAS SAFE THEN.
BUT...
...I BELIEVE TSUBAME IS STILL UNAWARE THAT WHAT SHE SAW WAS AN ILLUSION.
IT MAY HAVE PUT HER INTO SHOCK.
SHE'LL BE FINE. I'M SURE SOMEONE'S TELLING HER WHAT REALLY HAPPENED AS WE SPEAK.

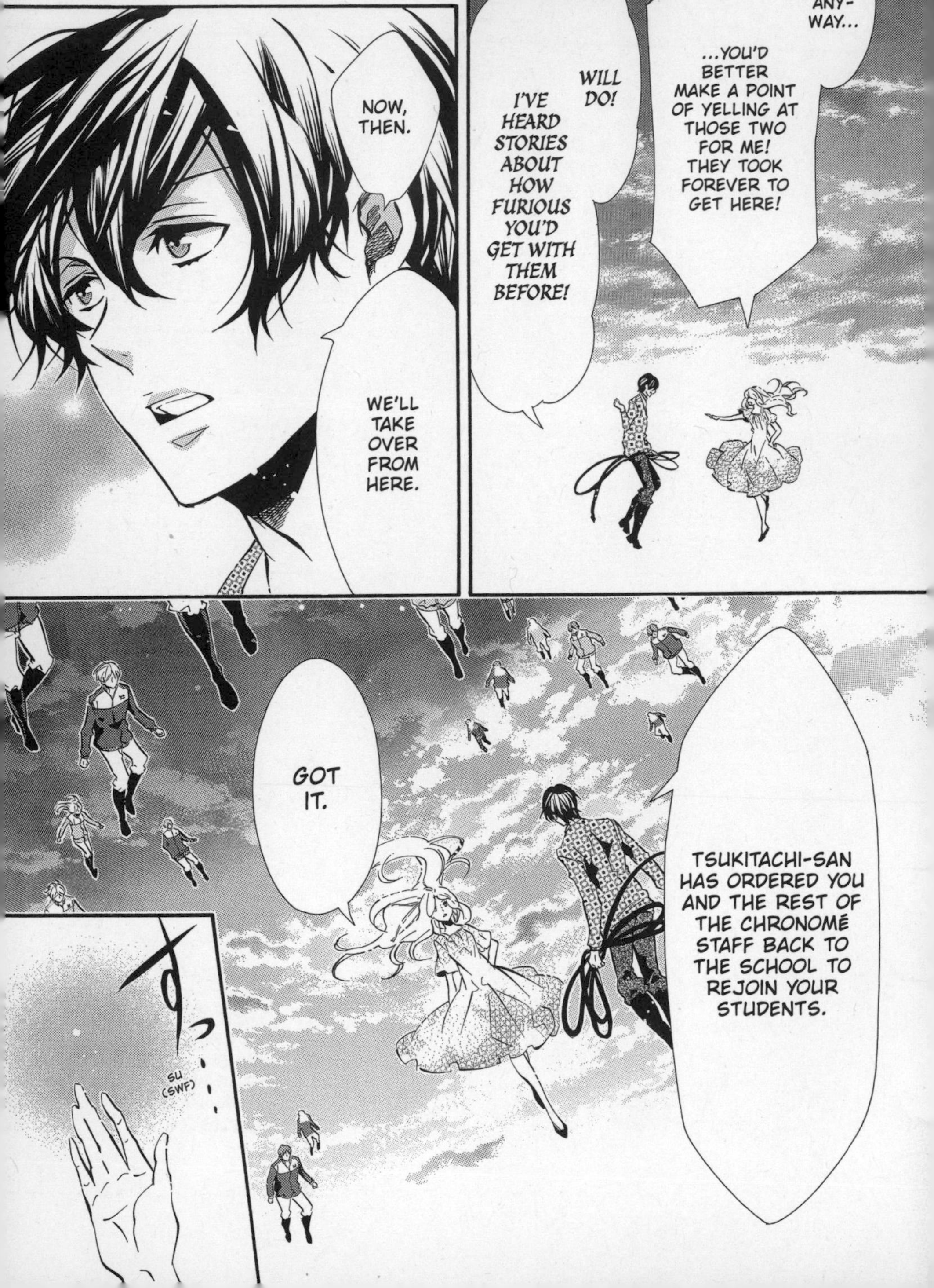
ANY-WAY...
...YOU'D BETTER MAKE A POINT OF YELLING AT THOSE TWO FOR ME! THEY TOOK FOREVER TO GET HERE!
WILL DO!
I'VE HEARD STORIES ABOUT HOW FURIOUS YOU'D GET WITH THEM BEFORE!
NOW, THEN.
WE'LL TAKE OVER FROM HERE.
TSUKITACHI-SAN HAS ORDERED YOU AND THE REST OF THE CHRONOMÉ STAFF BACK TO THE SCHOOL TO REJOIN YOUR STUDENTS.
GOT IT.
SU (SWF)

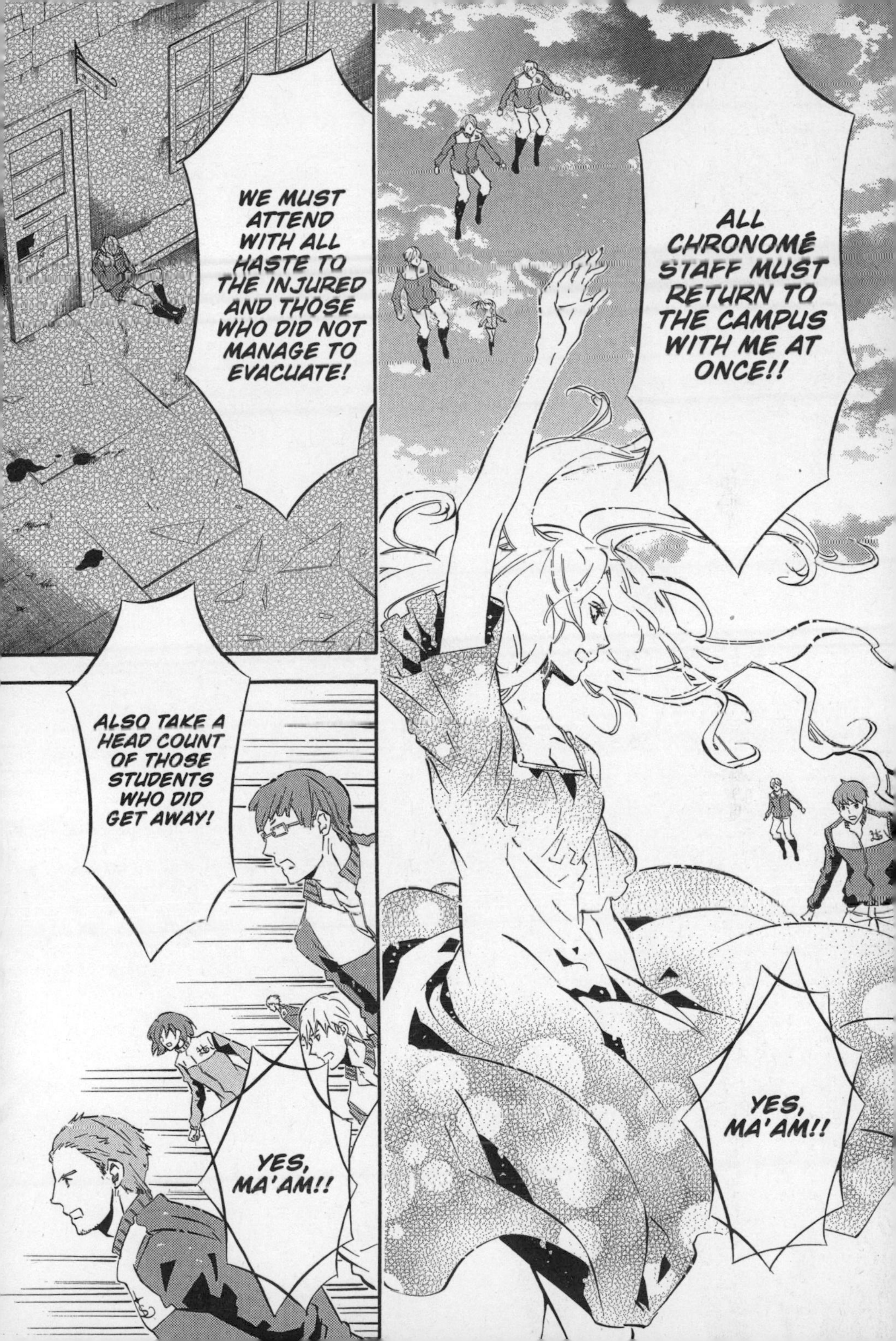
ALL CHRONOMÉ STAFF MUST RETURN TO THE CAMPUS WITH ME AT ONCE!!
YES, MA'AM!!
WE MUST ATTEND WITH ALL HASTE TO THE INJURED AND THOSE WHO DID NOT MANAGE TO EVACUATE!
ALSO TAKE A HEAD COUNT OF THOSE STUDENTS WHO DID GET AWAY!
YES, MA'AM!!

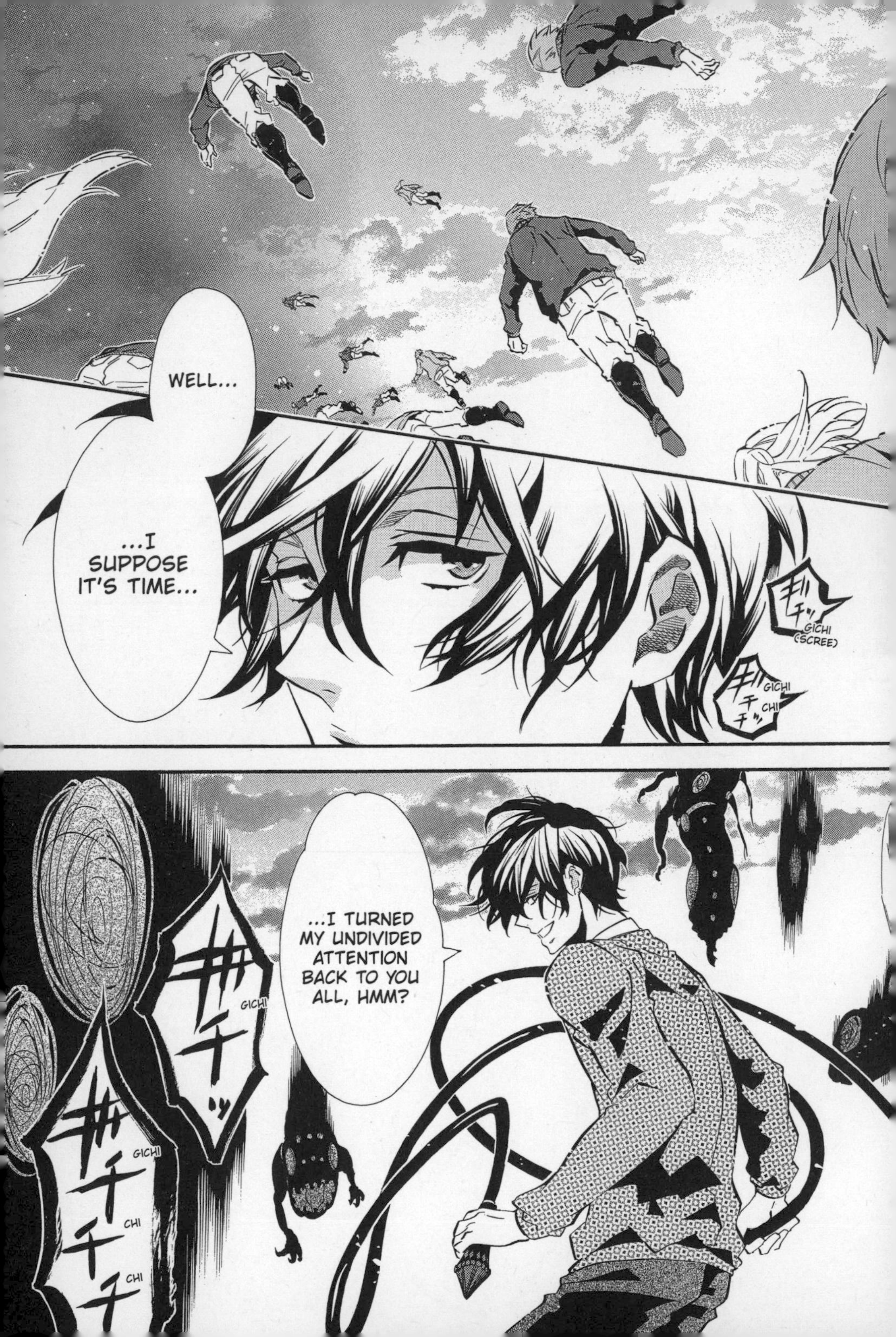
WELL...
...I SUPPOSE IT'S TIME...
GICHI (SCREE)
GICHI CHI
...I TURNED MY UNDIVIDED ATTENTION BACK TO YOU ALL, HMM?
GICHI
GICHI CHI CHI

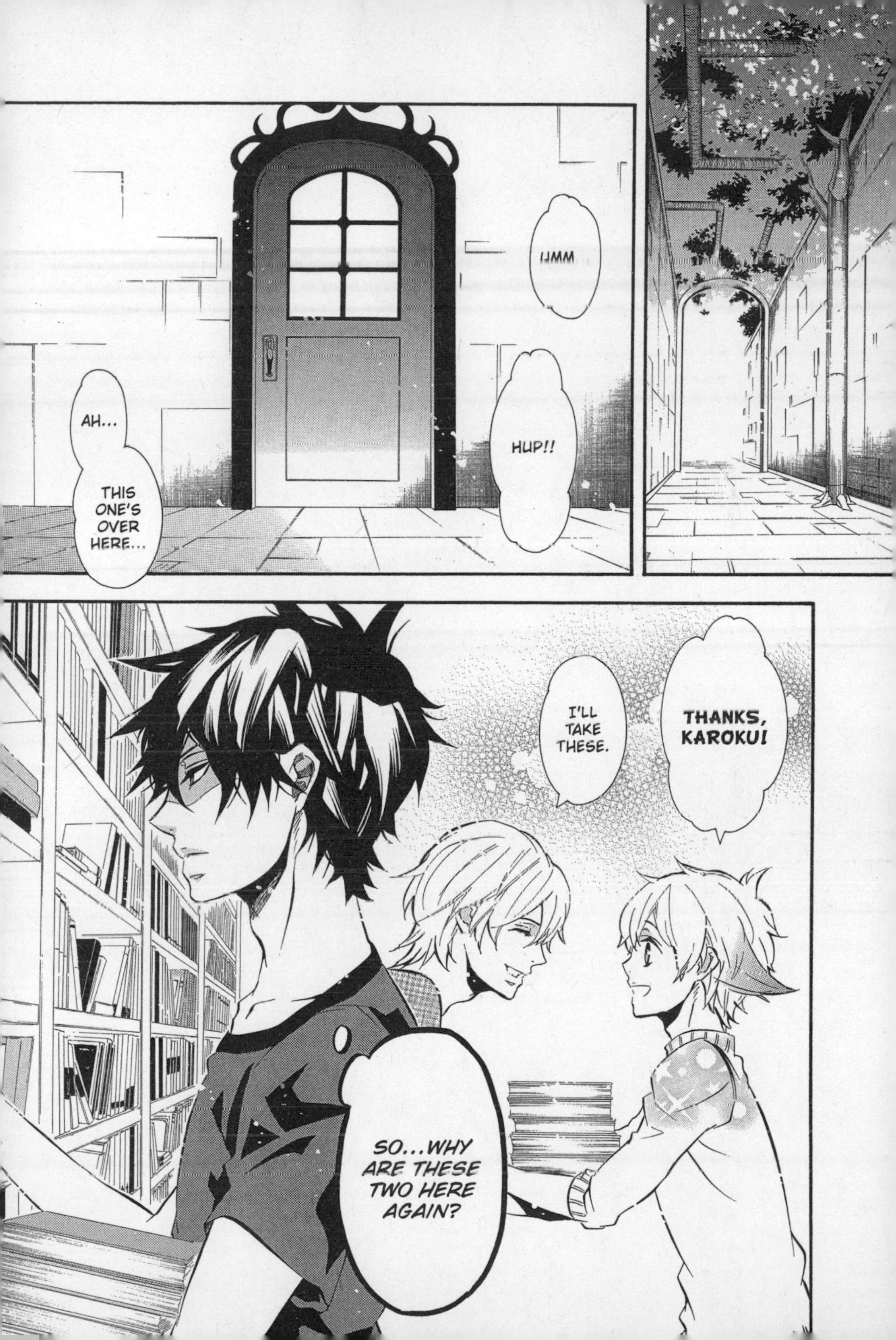
HUP!!
AH...
THIS ONE'S OVER HERE...
THANKS, KAROKU!
I'LL TAKE THESE.
SO...WHY ARE THESE TWO HERE AGAIN?

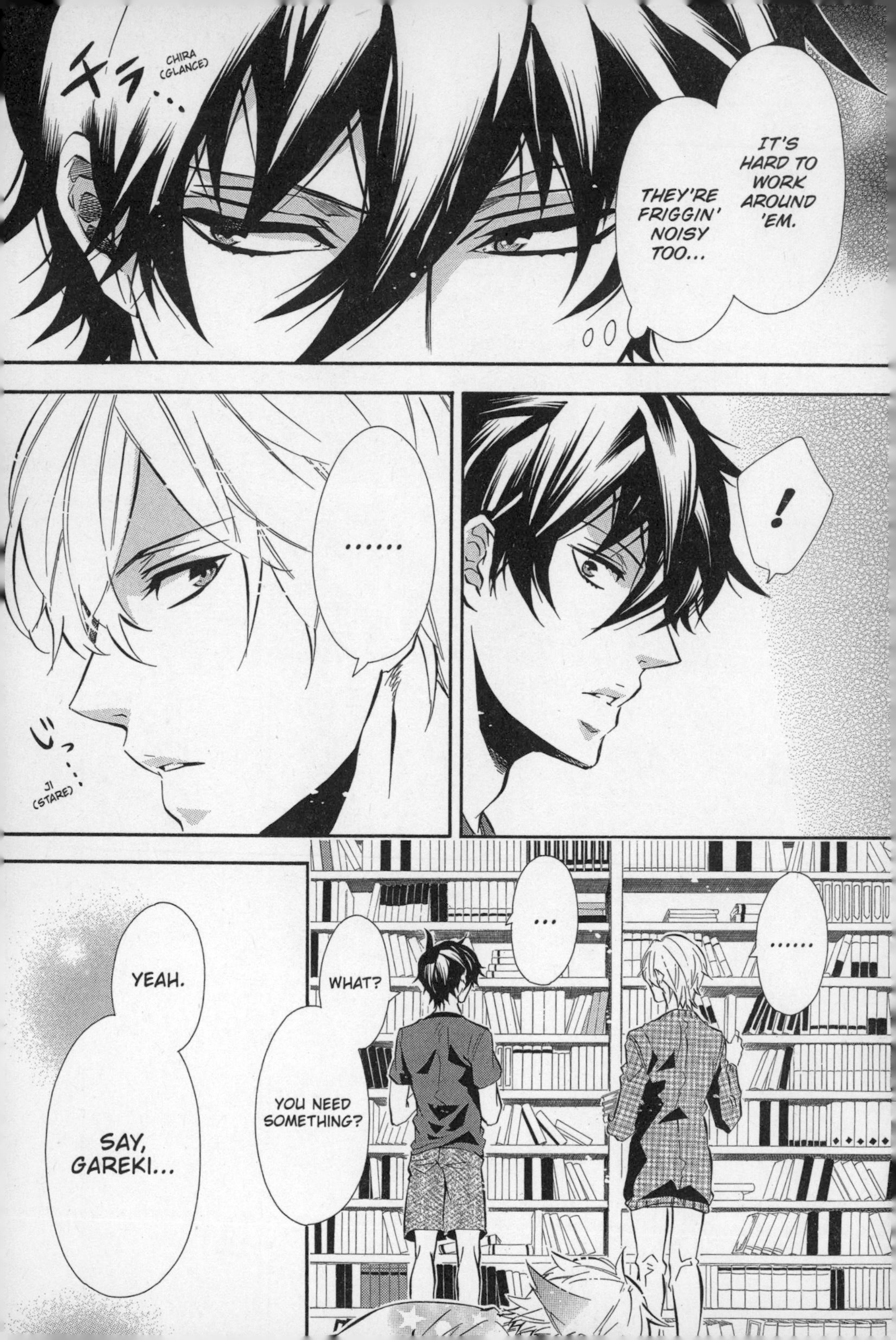
IT'S HARD TO WORK AROUND 'EM.
THEY'RE FRIGGIN' NOISY TOO...
チラ
CHIRA (GLANCE)
!
......
じっ
JI (STARE)
......
...
WHAT?
YOU NEED SOMETHING?
YEAH.
SAY, GAREKI...

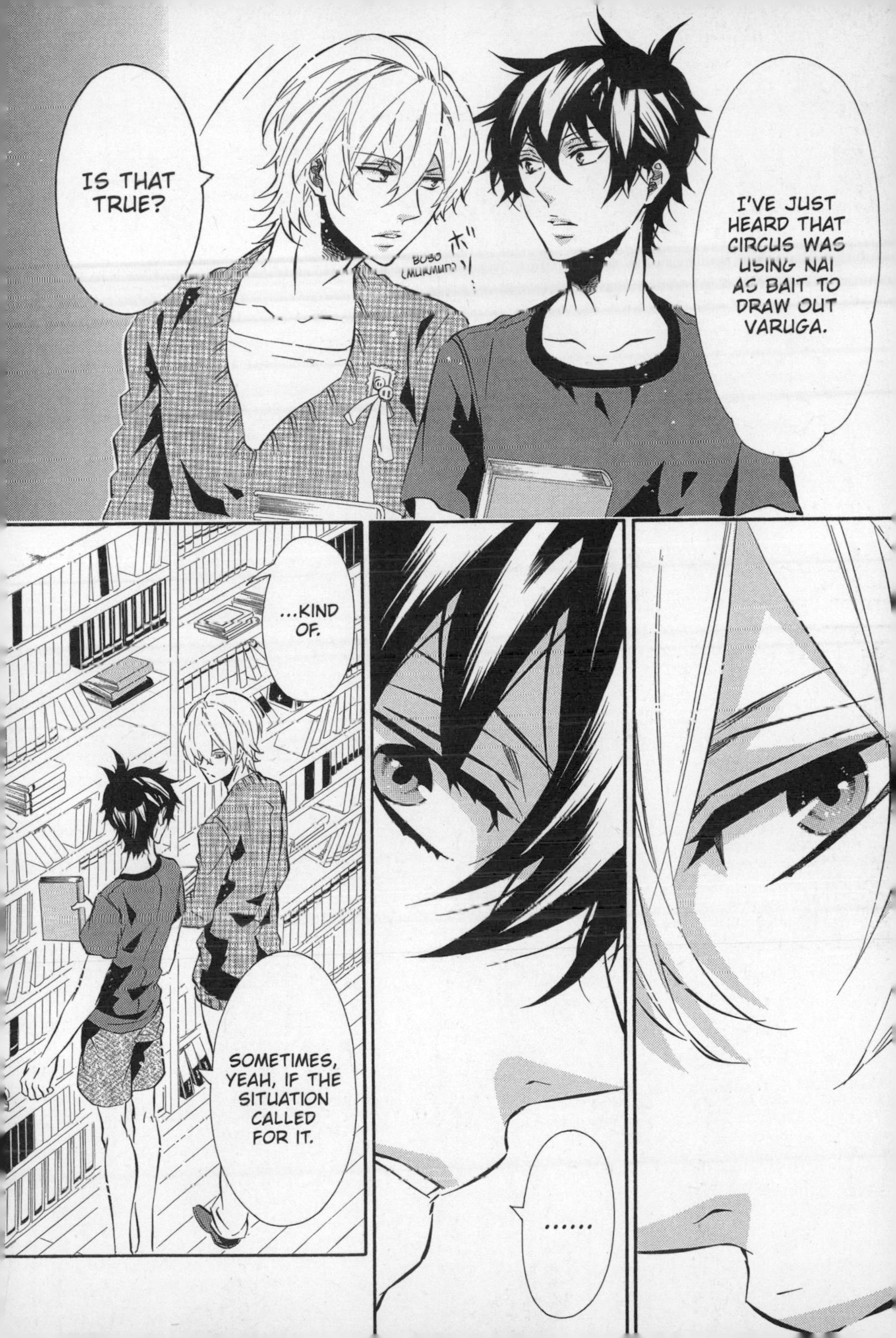
I'VE JUST HEARD THAT CIRCUS WAS USING NAI AS BAIT TO DRAW OUT VARUGA.
IS THAT TRUE?
ボソ
BOSO (MURMUR)
......
...KIND OF.
SOMETIMES, YEAH, IF THE SITUATION CALLED FOR IT.

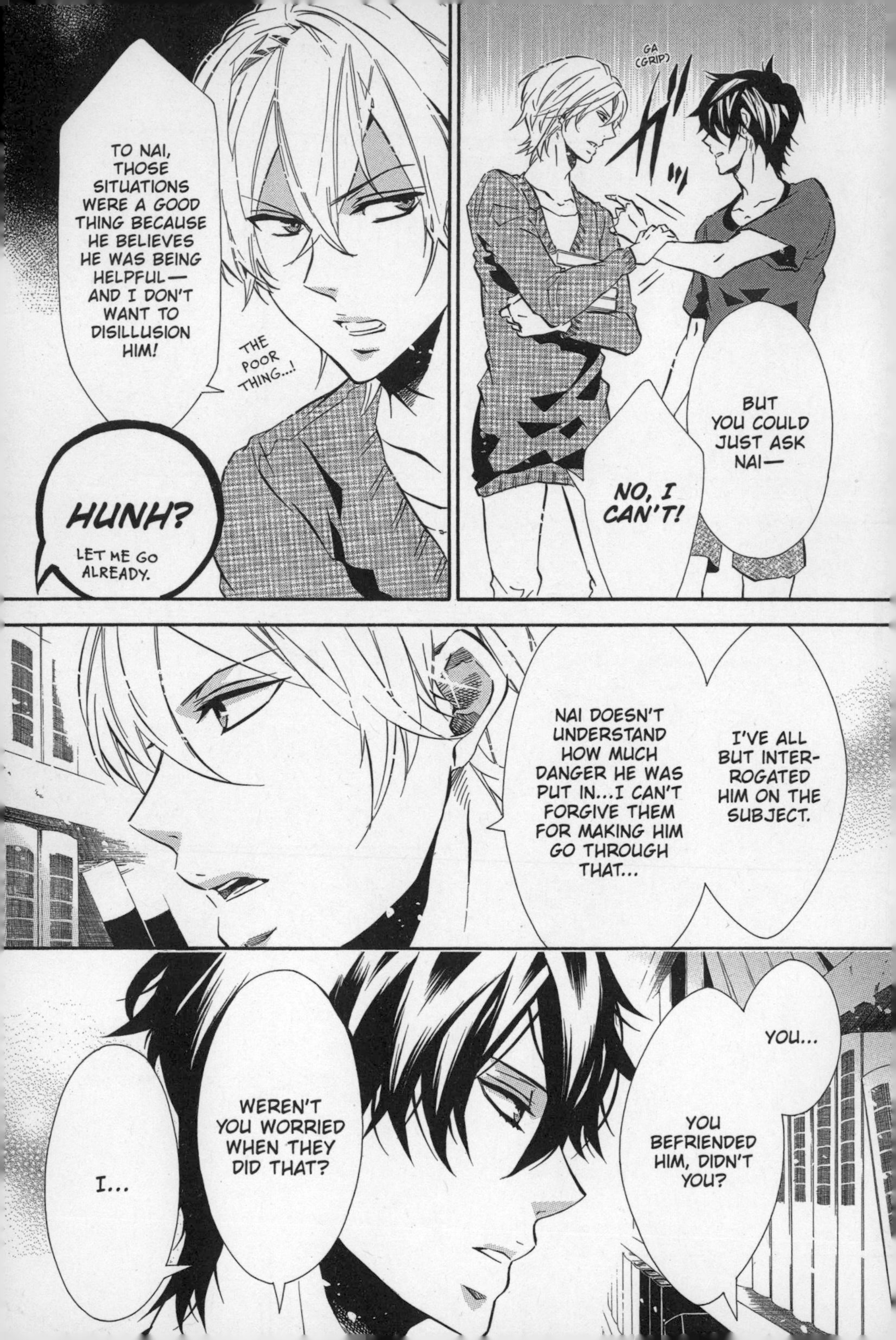
GA (GRIP)
BUT YOU COULD JUST ASK NAI—
NO, I CAN'T!
TO NAI, THOSE SITUATIONS WERE A GOOD THING BECAUSE HE BELIEVES HE WAS BEING HELPFUL—AND I DON'T WANT TO DISILLUSION HIM!
THE POOR THING...!
HUNH?
LET ME GO ALREADY.
I'VE ALL BUT INTER-ROGATED HIM ON THE SUBJECT.
NAI DOESN'T UNDERSTAND HOW MUCH DANGER HE WAS PUT IN...I CAN'T FORGIVE THEM FOR MAKING HIM GO THROUGH THAT...
YOU...
YOU BEFRIENDED HIM, DIDN'T YOU?
WEREN'T YOU WORRIED WHEN THEY DID THAT?
I...

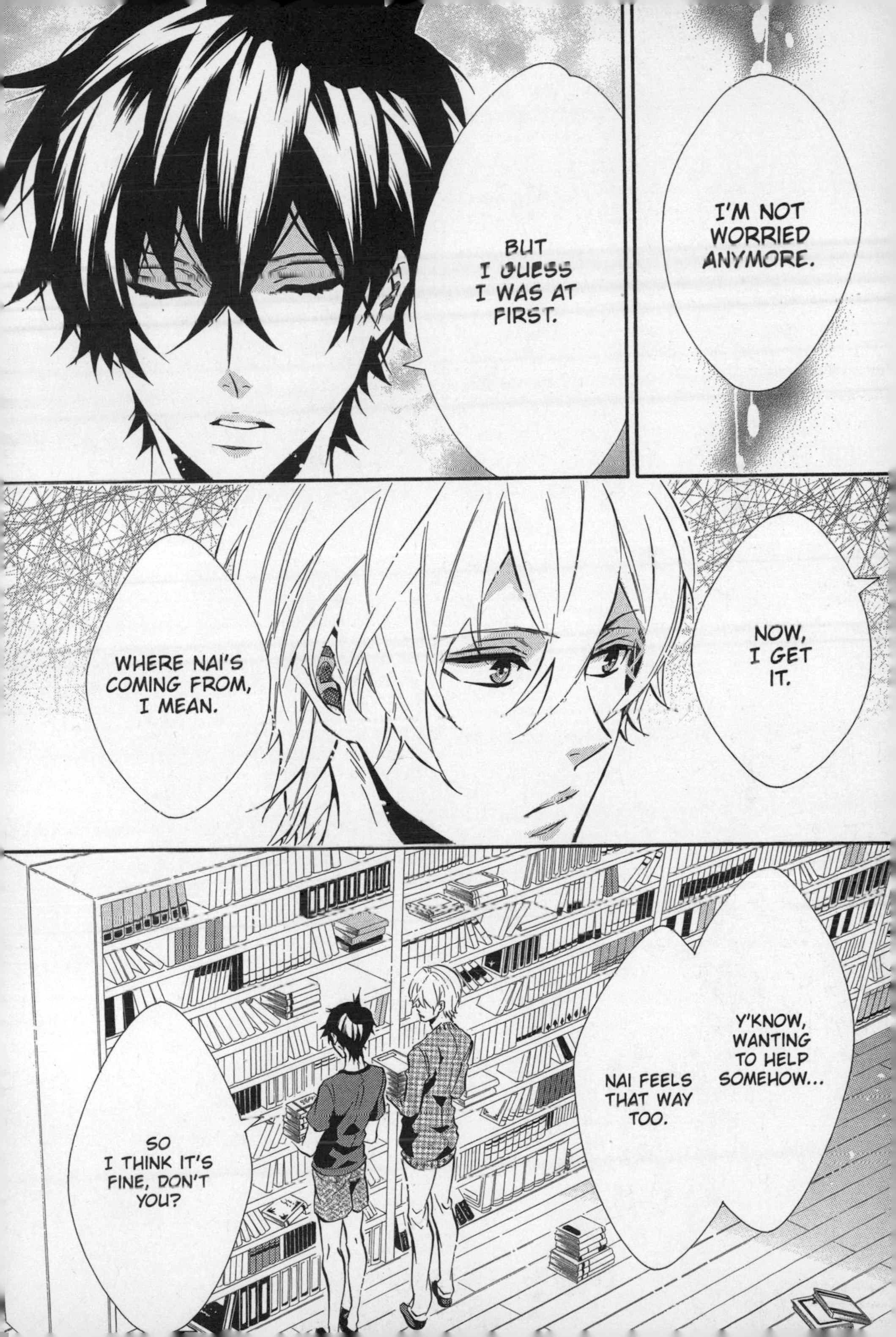
I'M NOT WORRIED ANYMORE.
BUT I GUESS I WAS AT FIRST.
NOW, I GET IT.
WHERE NAI'S COMING FROM, I MEAN.
Y'KNOW, WANTING TO HELP SOMEHOW...
NAI FEELS THAT WAY TOO.
SO I THINK IT'S FINE, DON'T YOU?

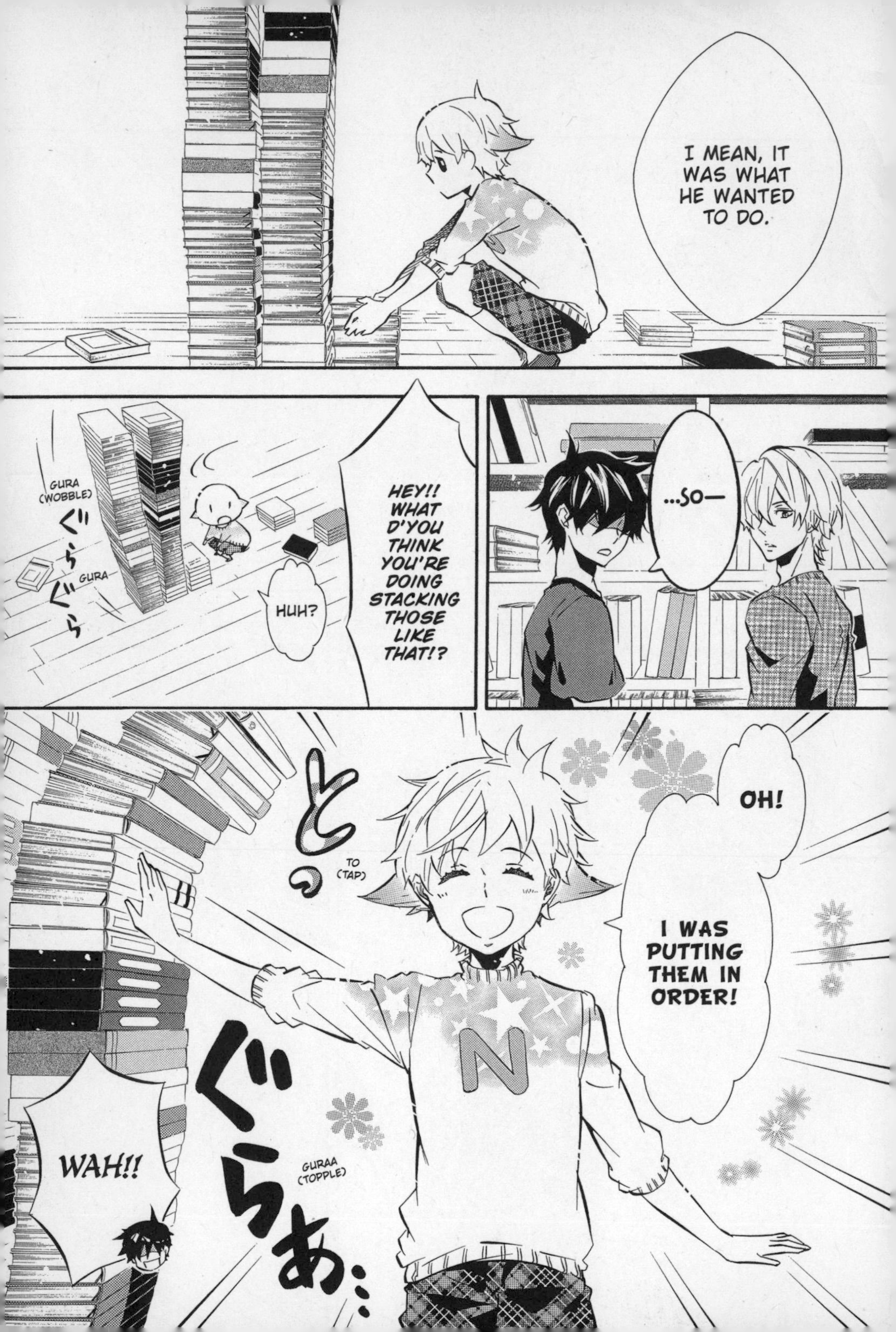
I MEAN, IT WAS WHAT HE WANTED TO DO.
...SO—
HEY!! WHAT D'YOU THINK YOU'RE DOING STACKING THOSE LIKE THAT!?
HUH?
GURA (WOBBLE)
ぐらぐら
GURA
OH!
I WAS PUTTING THEM IN ORDER!
とっ
TO (TAP)
ぐらあ
GURAA (TOPPLE)
WAH!!

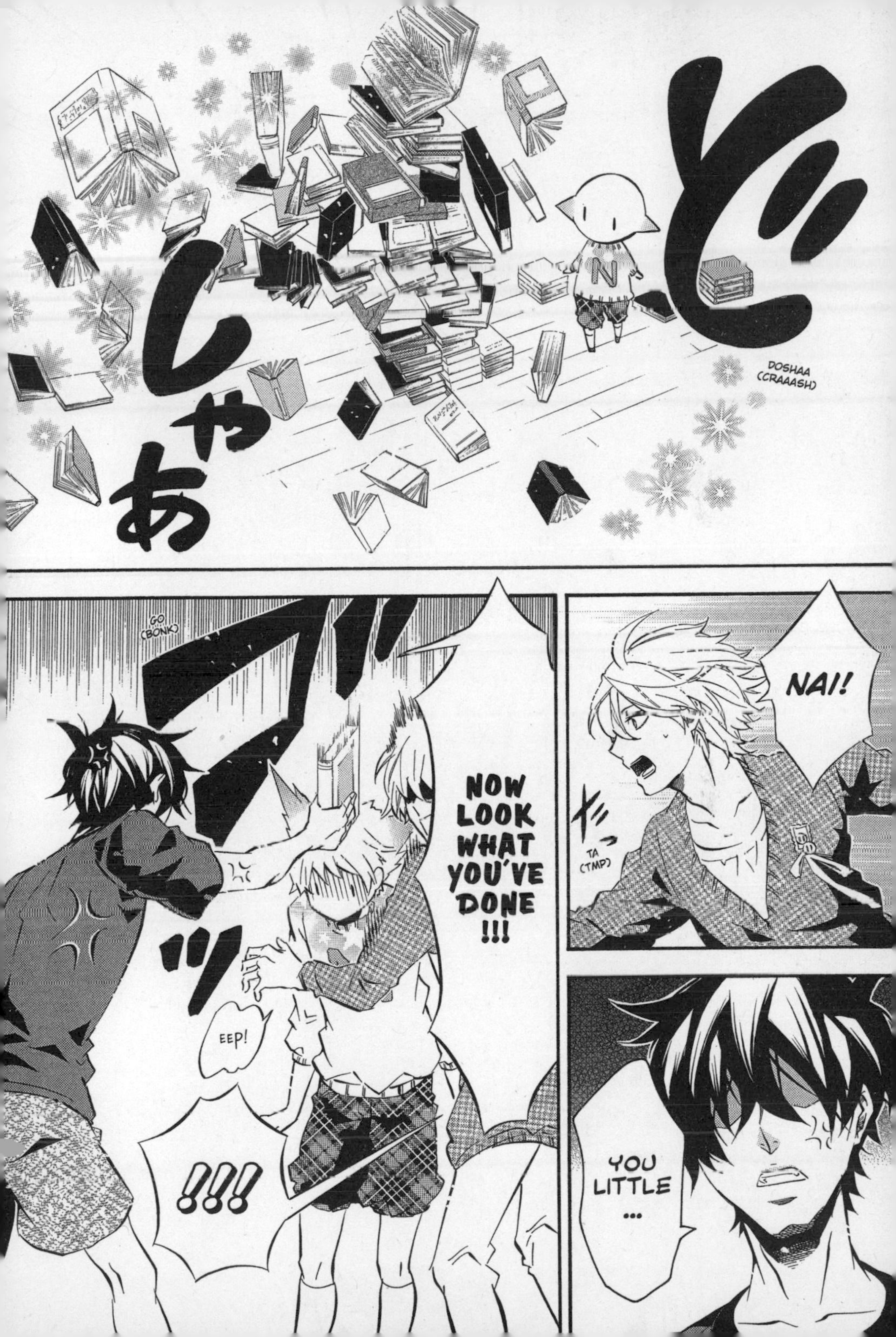

どしゃあ
DOSHAA (CRAAASH)
NAI!
TA (TMP)
YOU LITTLE ...
GO (BONK)
NOW LOOK WHAT YOU'VE DONE!!!
EEP!
!!!

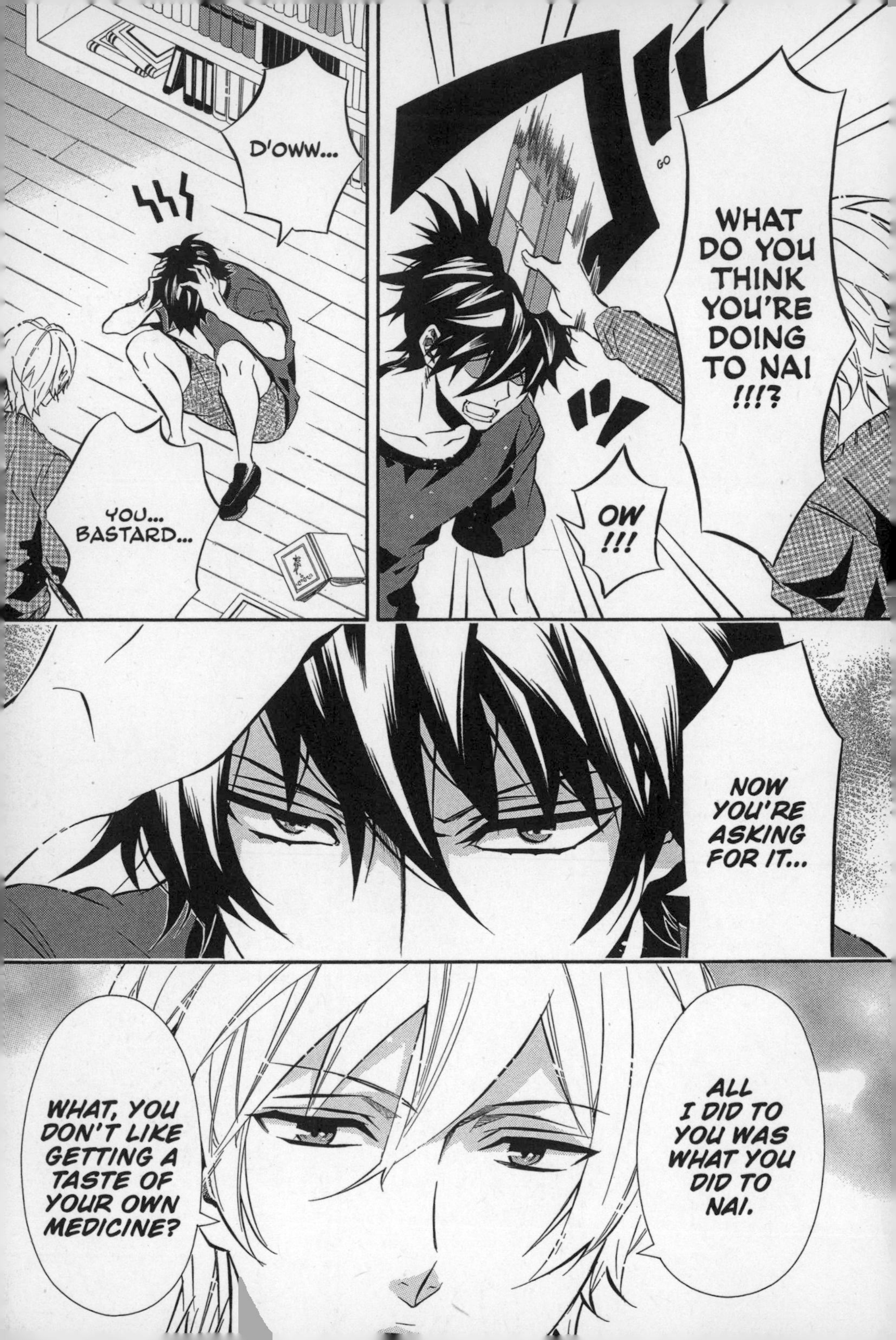
WHAT DO YOU THINK YOU'RE DOING TO NAI !!!?
GO
OW !!!
D'OWW...
YOU... BASTARD...
NOW YOU'RE ASKING FOR IT...
ALL I DID TO YOU WAS WHAT YOU DID TO NAI.
WHAT, YOU DON'T LIKE GETTING A TASTE OF YOUR OWN MEDICINE?

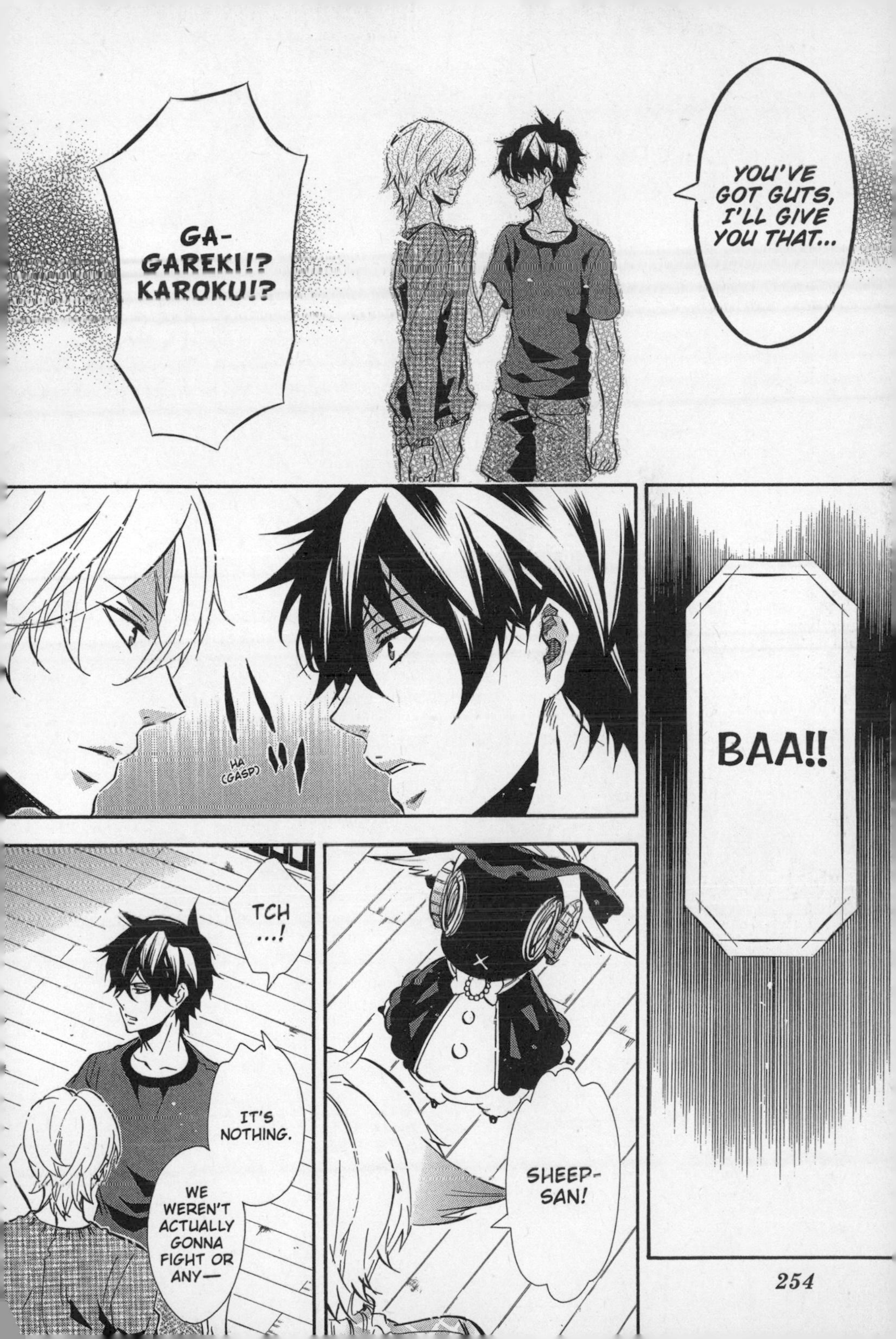
YOU'VE GOT GUTS, I'LL GIVE YOU THAT...
GA-GAREKI!? KAROKU!?
BAA!!
HA (GASP)
SHEEP-SAN!
TCH ...!
IT'S NOTHING.
WE WEREN'T ACTUALLY GONNA FIGHT OR ANY—

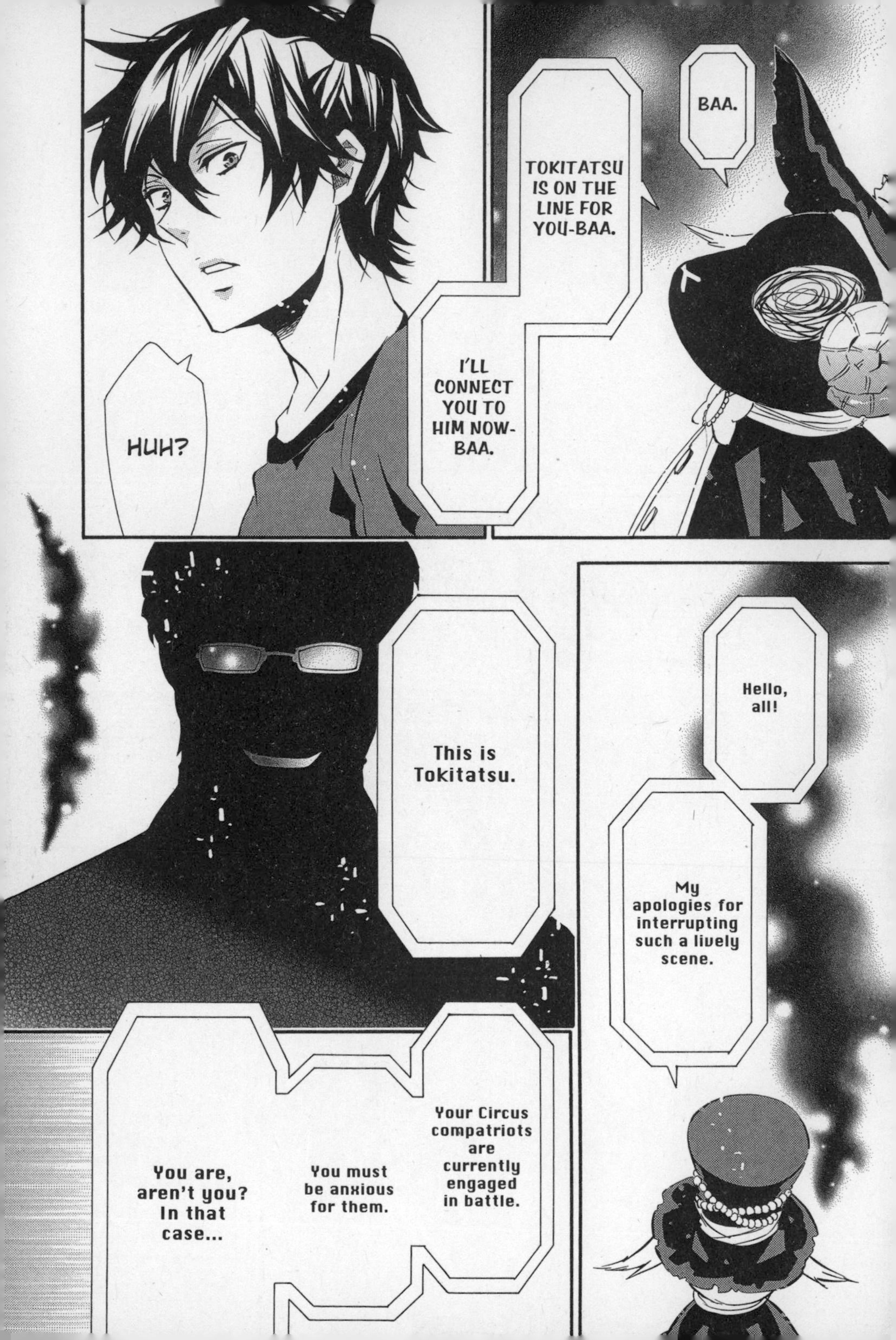
BAA.
TOKITATSU IS ON THE LINE FOR YOU-BAA.
I'LL CONNECT YOU TO HIM NOW-BAA.
HUH?
Hello, all!
My apologies for interrupting such a lively scene.
This is Tokitatsu.
Your Circus compatriots are currently engaged in battle.
You must be anxious for them.
You are, aren't you? In that case...

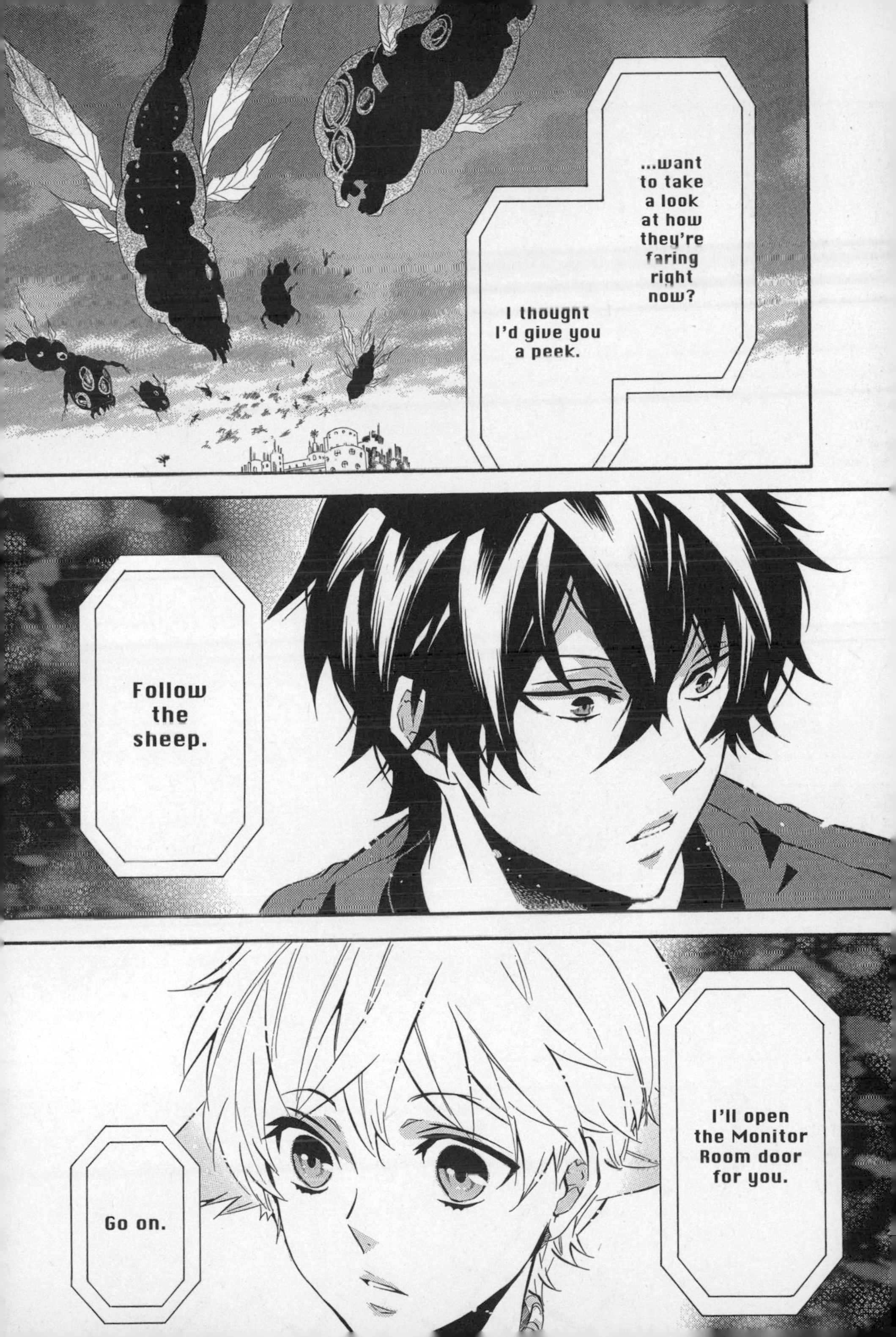
...want to take a look at how they're faring right now?
I thought I'd give you a peek.
Follow the sheep.
I'll open the Monitor Room door for you.
Go on.

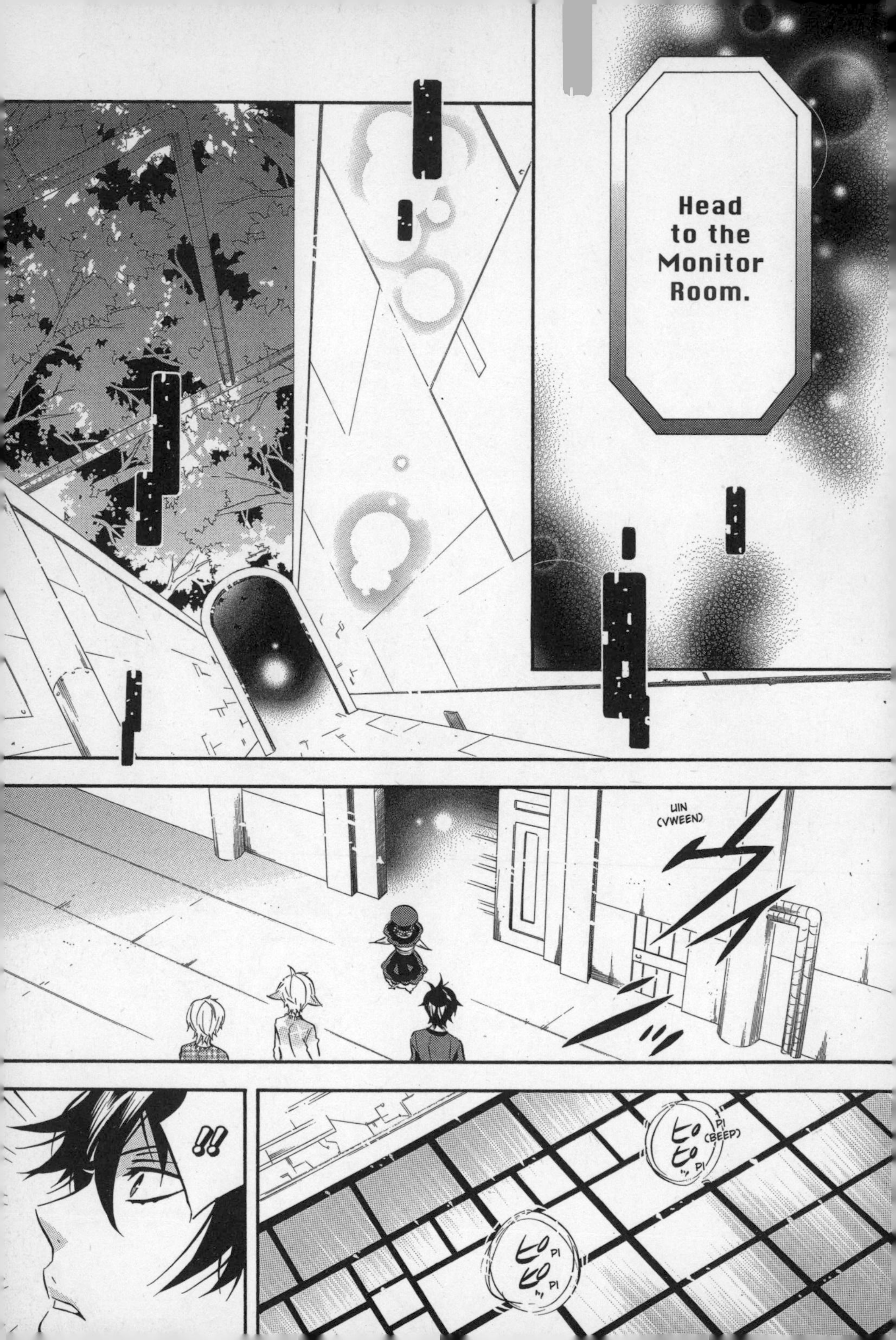
Head to the Monitor Room.
UIN (VWEEN)
PI (BEEP) PI
PI PI
!!

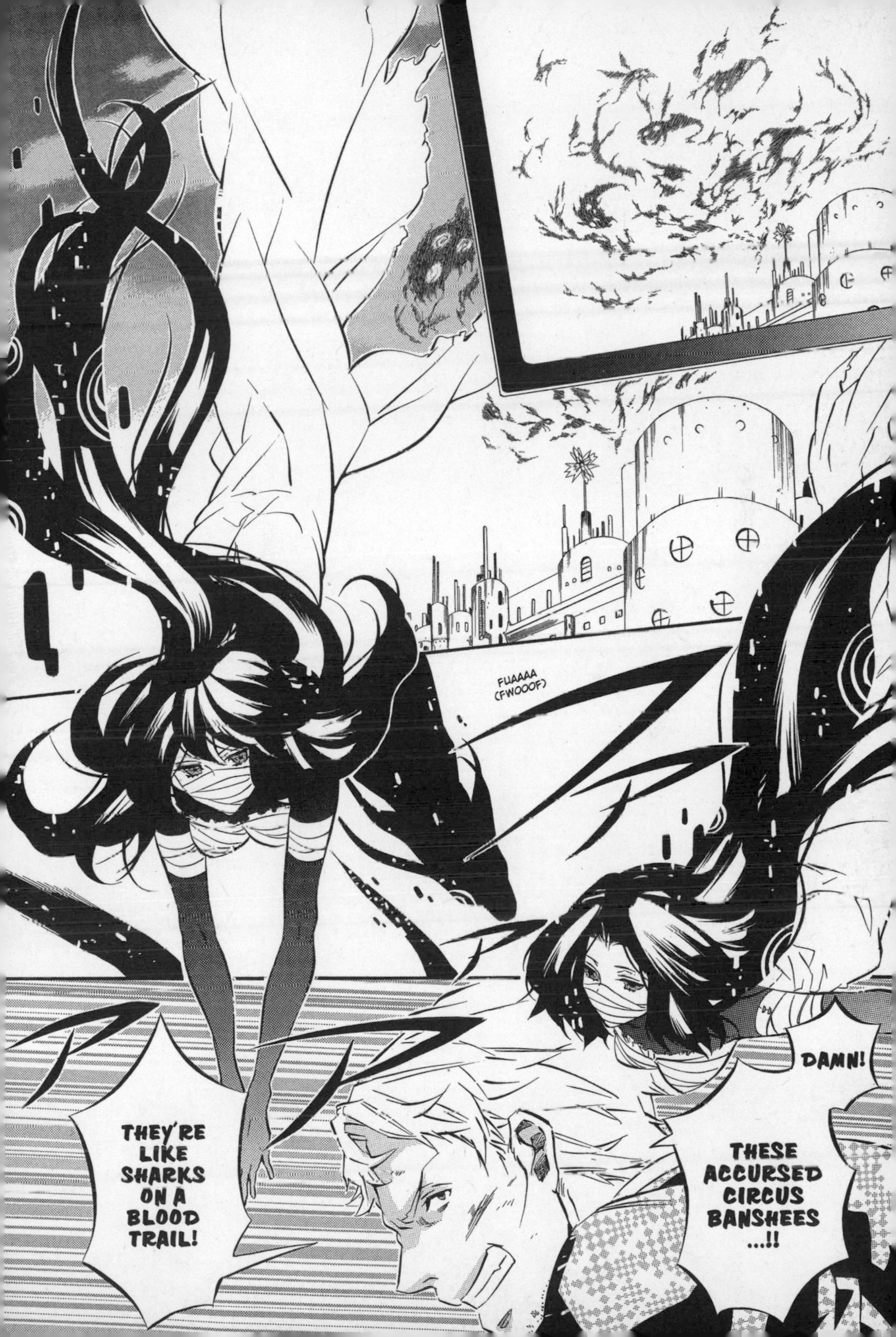
FUAAAA (FWOOOF)
DAMN!
THESE ACCURSED CIRCUS BANSHEES ...!!
THEY'RE LIKE SHARKS ON A BLOOD TRAIL!

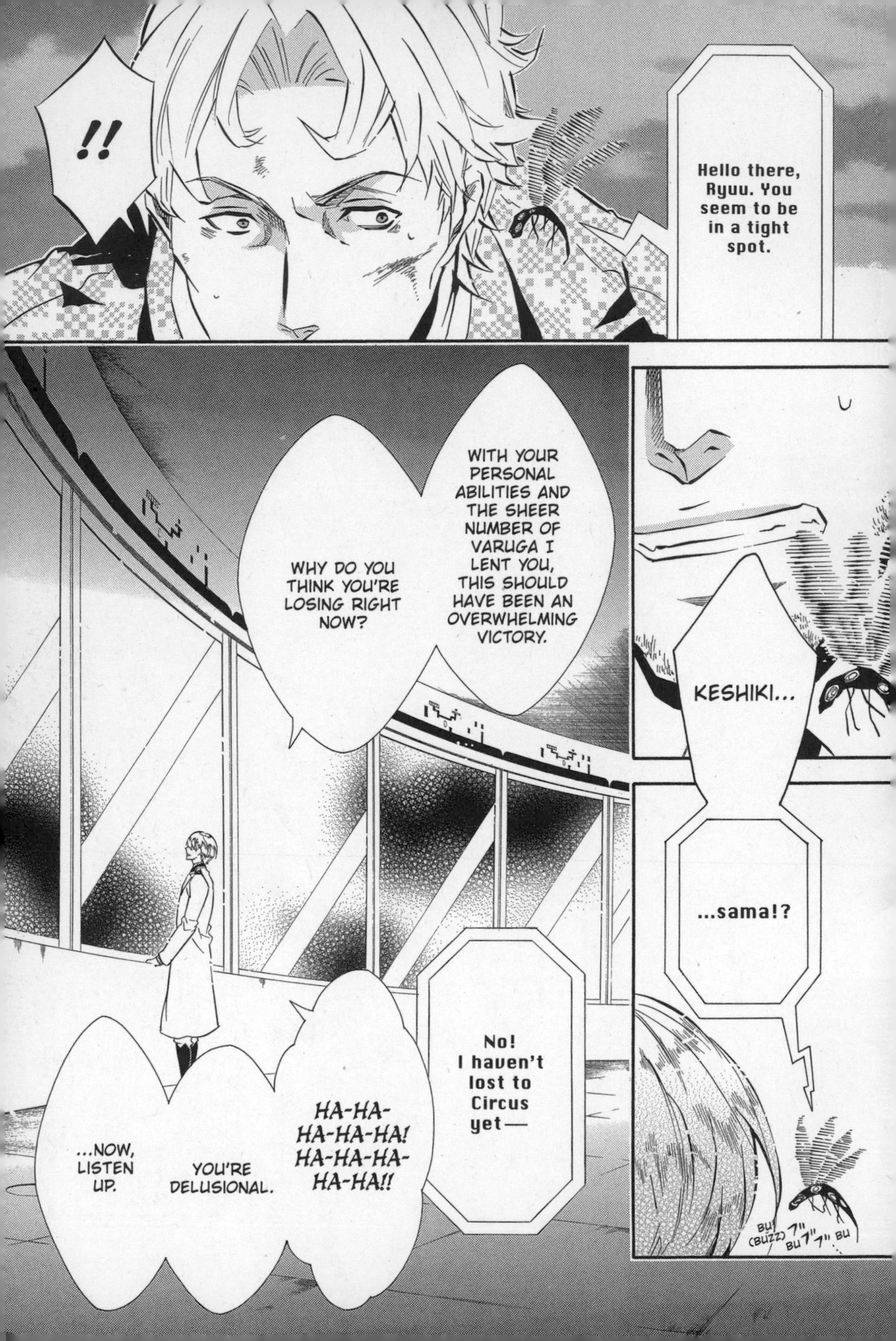
Hello there, Ryuu. You seem to be in a tight spot.
!!
KESHIKI...
...sama!?
BU (BUZZ) BU BU
WITH YOUR PERSONAL ABILITIES AND THE SHEER NUMBER OF VARUGA I LENT YOU, THIS SHOULD HAVE BEEN AN OVERWHELMING VICTORY.
WHY DO YOU THINK YOU'RE LOSING RIGHT NOW?
No! I haven't lost to Circus yet—
HA-HA-HA-HA-HA! HA-HA-HA-HA-HA!!
YOU'RE DELUSIONAL.
...NOW, LISTEN UP.

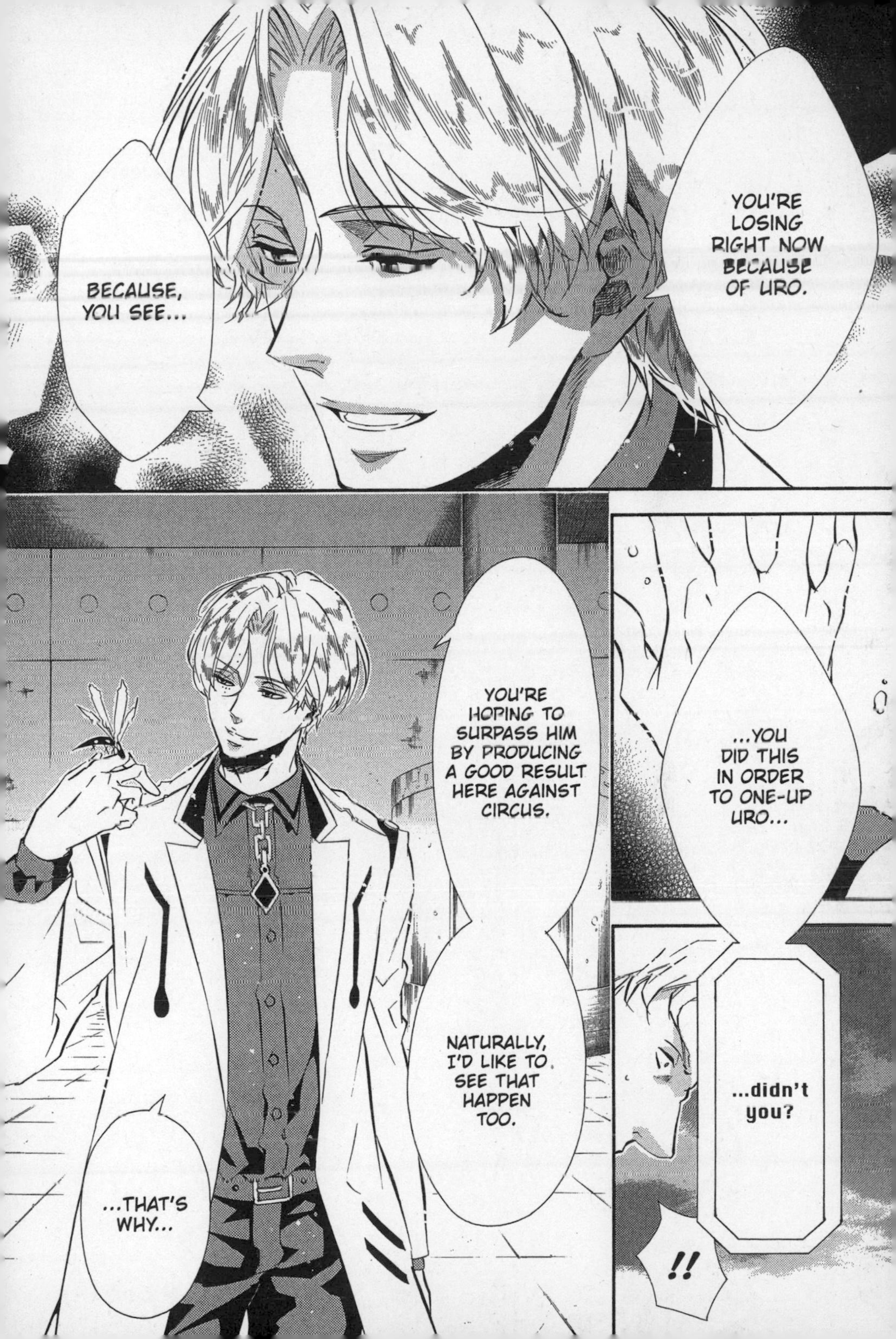
YOU'RE LOSING RIGHT NOW BECAUSE OF URO.
BECAUSE, YOU SEE...
...YOU DID THIS IN ORDER TO ONE-UP URO...
...didn't you?
!!
YOU'RE HOPING TO SURPASS HIM BY PRODUCING A GOOD RESULT HERE AGAINST CIRCUS.
NATURALLY, I'D LIKE TO SEE THAT HAPPEN TOO.
...THAT'S WHY...

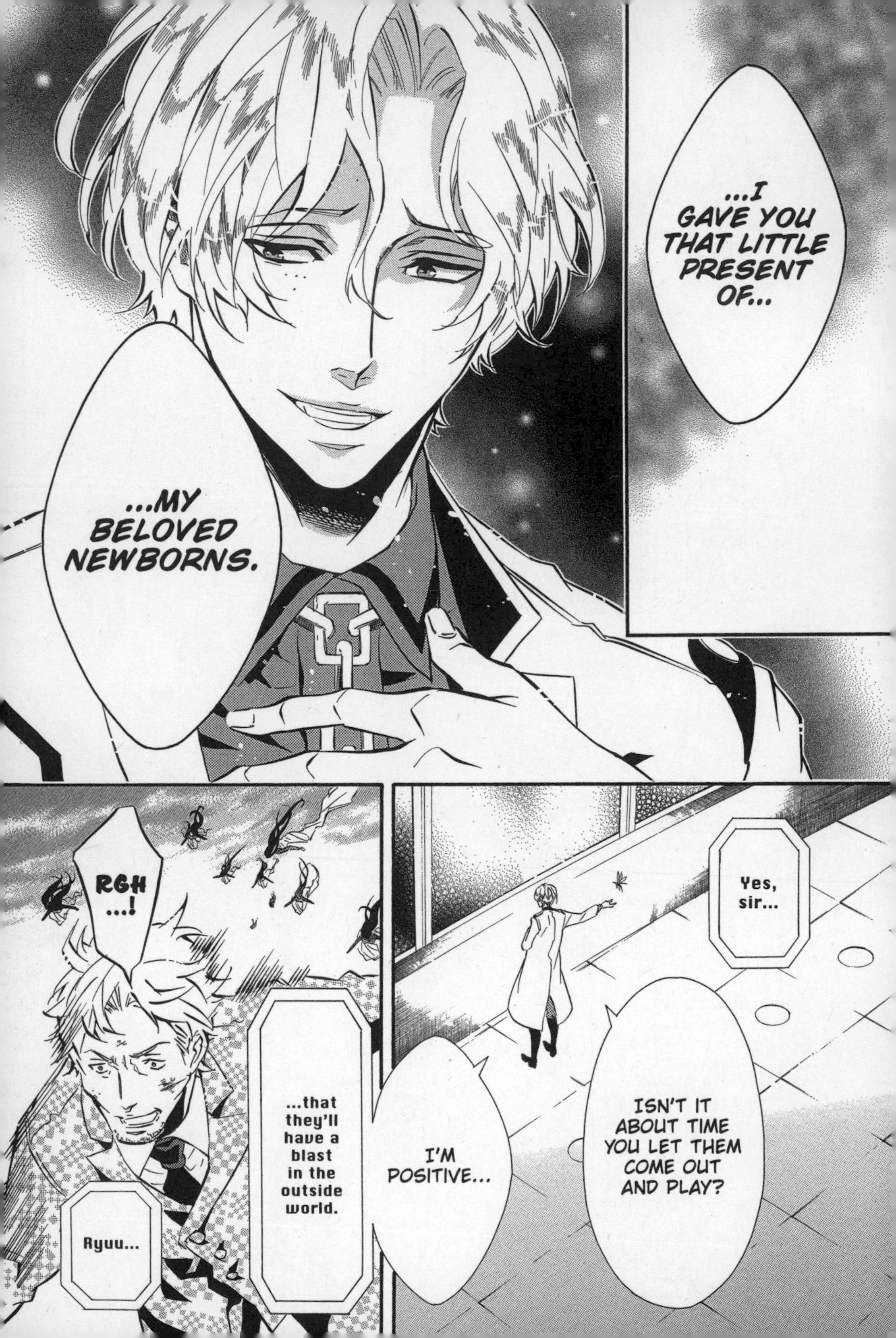
...I GAVE YOU THAT LITTLE PRESENT OF...
...MY BELOVED NEWBORNS.
Yes, sir...
ISN'T IT ABOUT TIME YOU LET THEM COME OUT AND PLAY?
I'M POSITIVE...
...that they'll have a blast in the outside world.
RGH ...!
Ryuu...

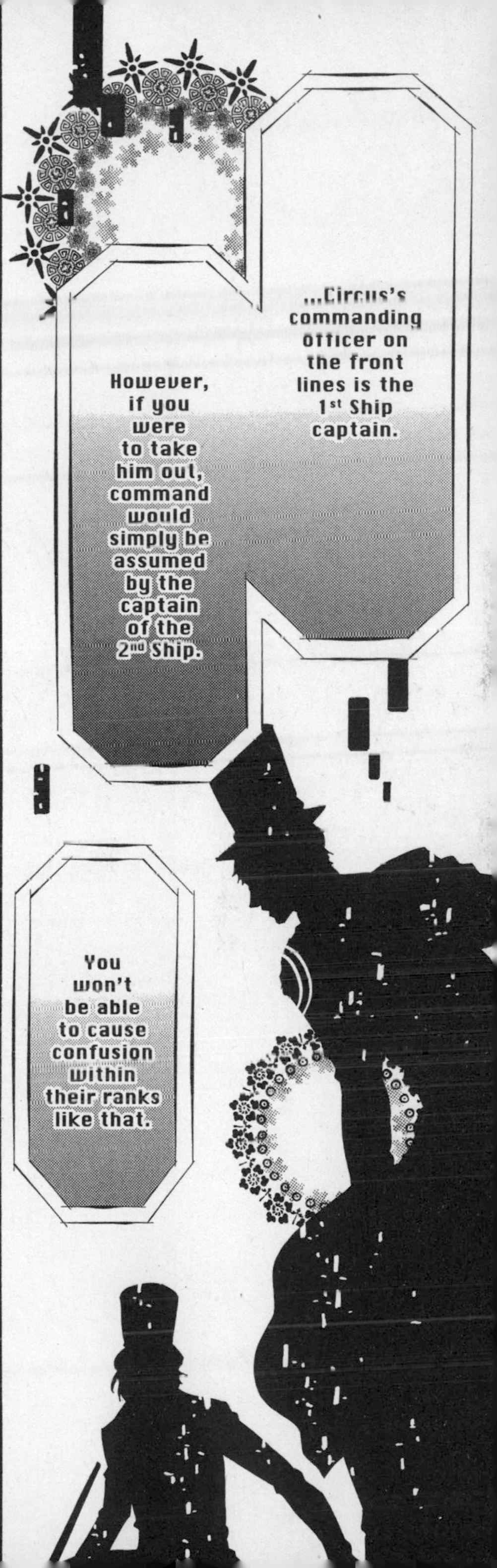
...Circus's commanding officer on the front lines is the 1st Ship captain.
However, if you were to take him out, command would simply be assumed by the captain of the 2nd Ship.
You won't be able to cause confusion within their ranks like that.
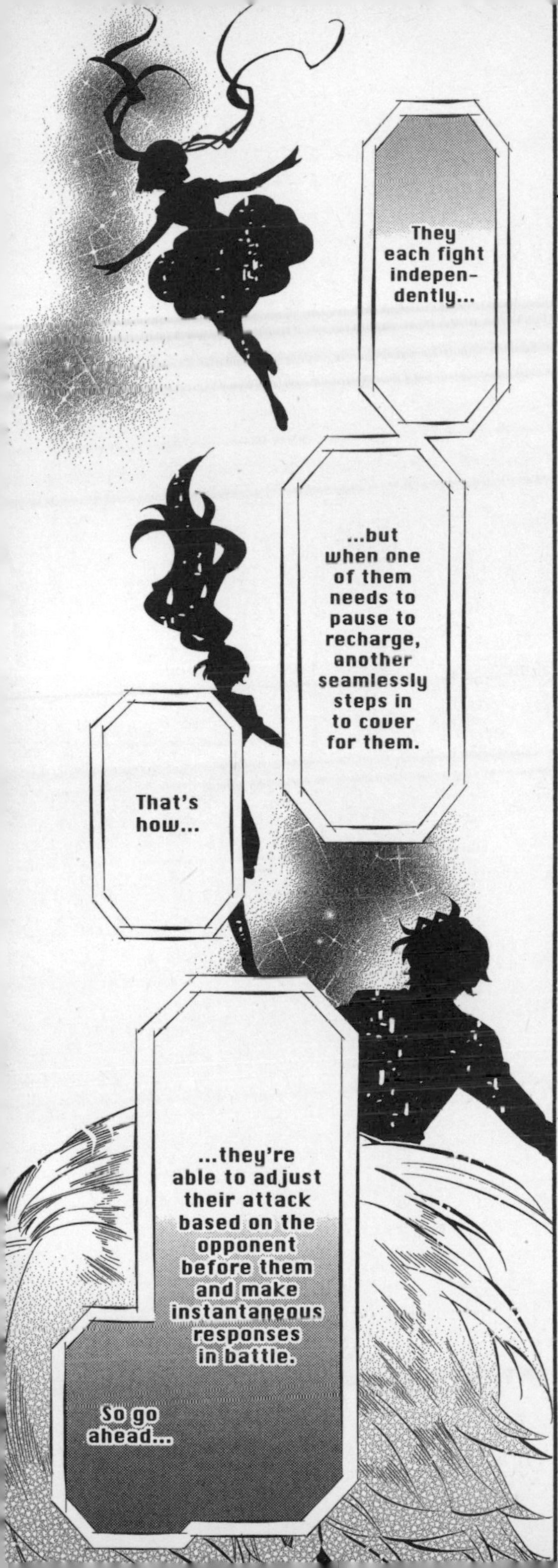
They each fight independently...
...but when one of them needs to pause to recharge, another seamlessly steps in to cover for them.
That's how...
...they're able to adjust their attack based on the opponent before them and make instantaneous responses in battle.
So go ahead...

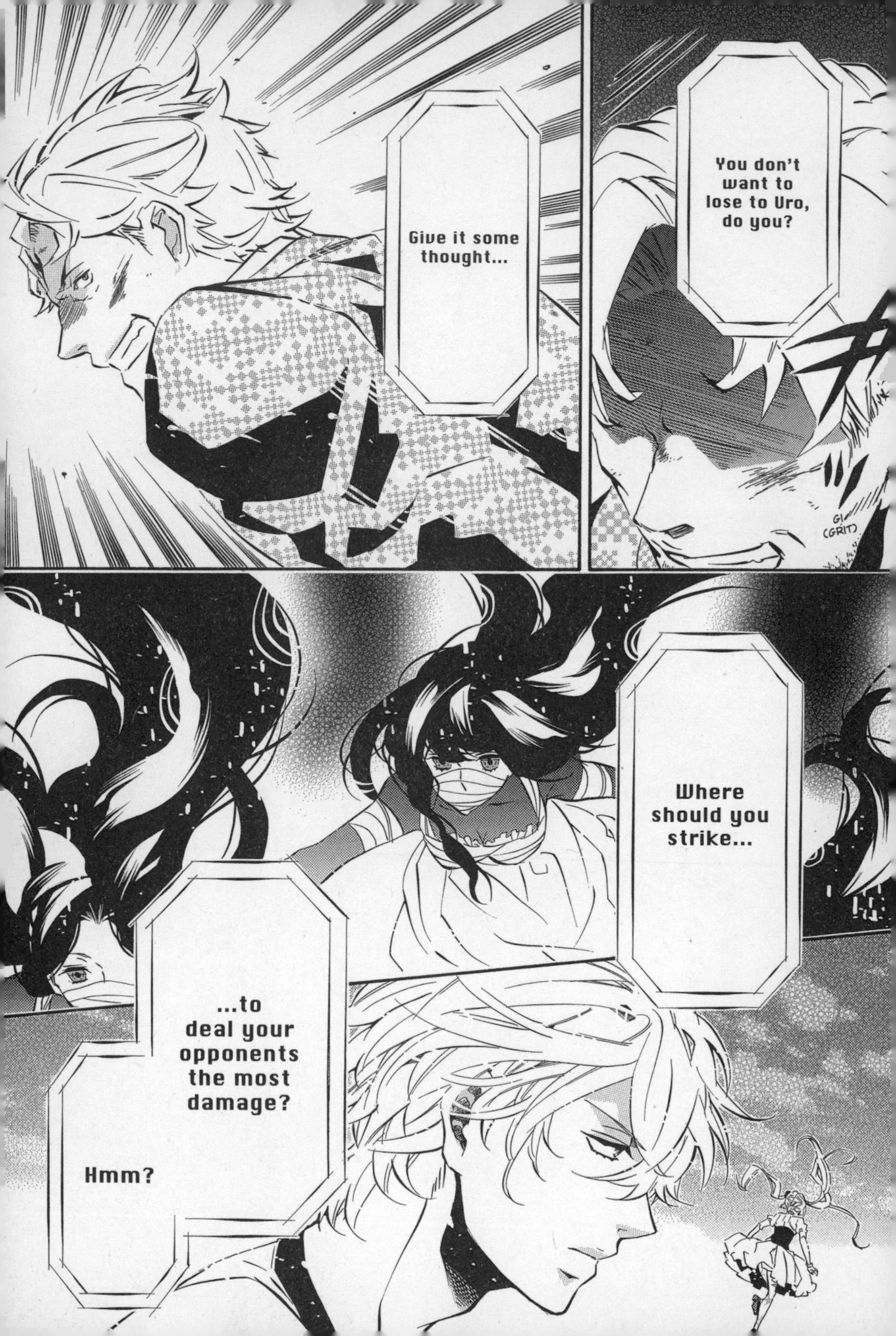
You don't want to lose to Uro, do you?
GI (GRIT)
Give it some thought...
Where should you strike...
...to deal your opponents the most damage?
Hmm?

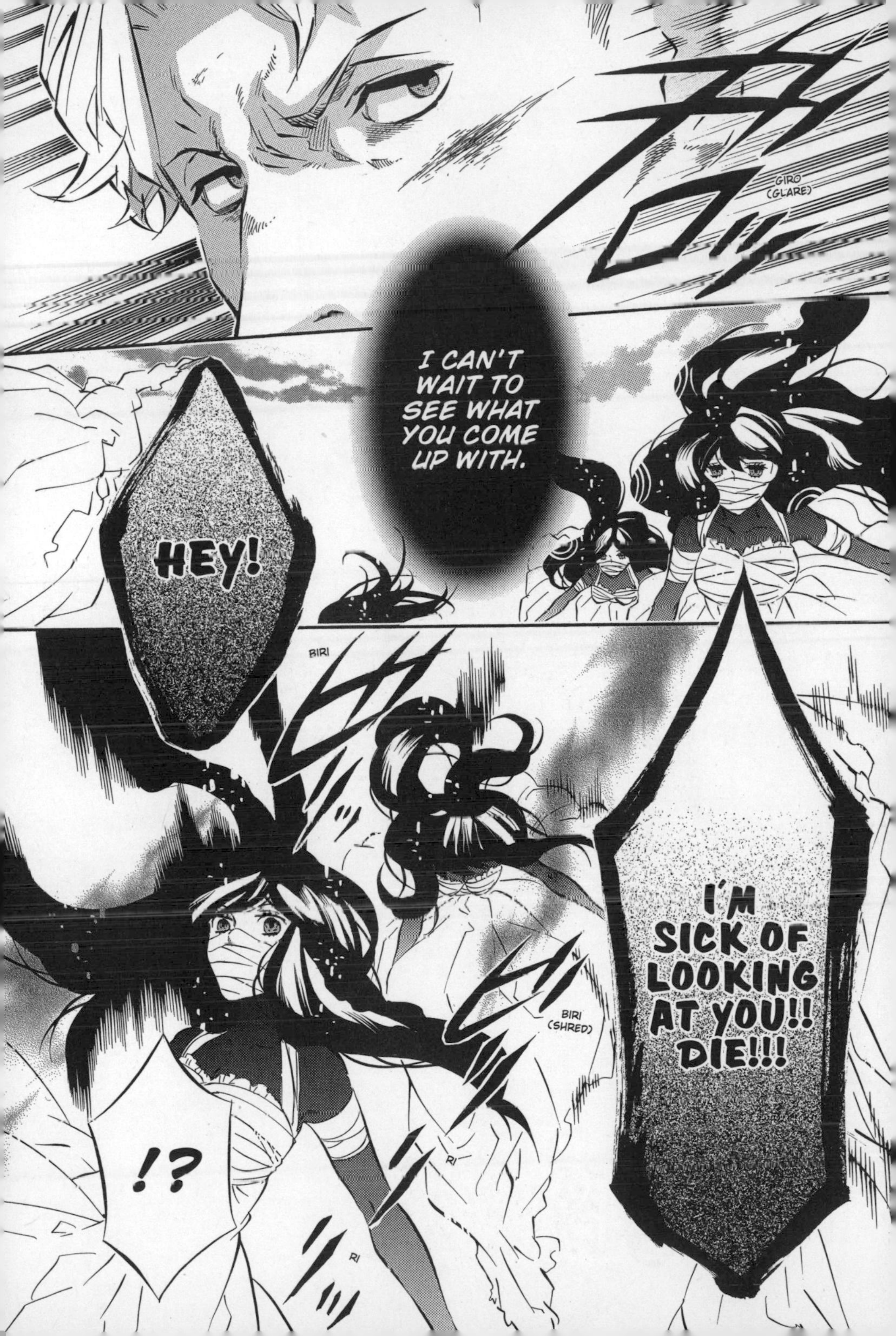
GIRO (GLARE)
I CAN'T WAIT TO SEE WHAT YOU COME UP WITH.
HEY!
I'M SICK OF LOOKING AT YOU!! DIE!!!
BIRI (SHRED)
BIRI
RI
RI
!?

KARNEVAL

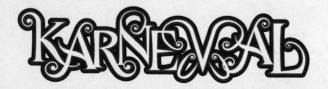

DOSHAA
(CRAAASH)

KARNEVAL

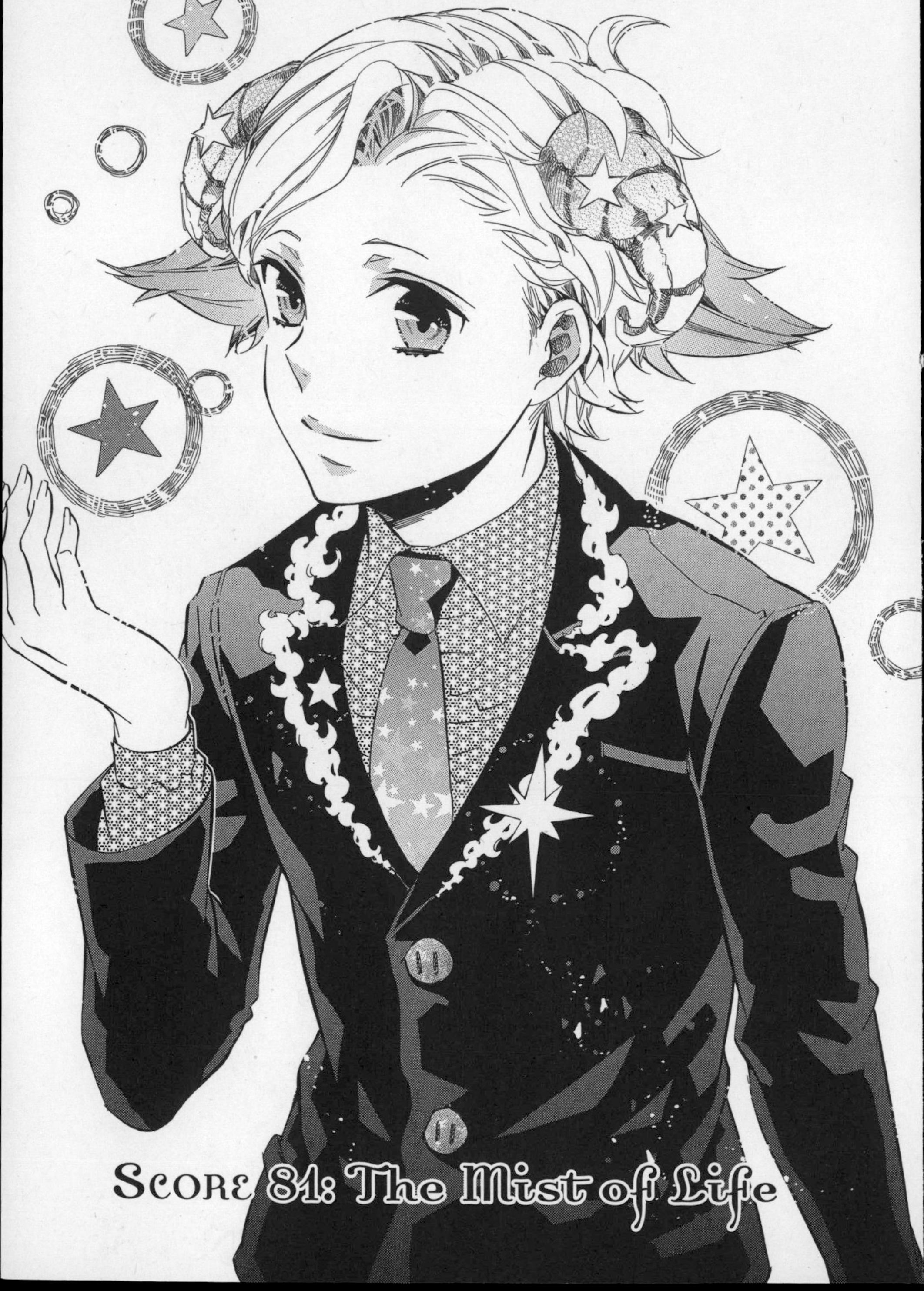

Score 81: The Mist of Life

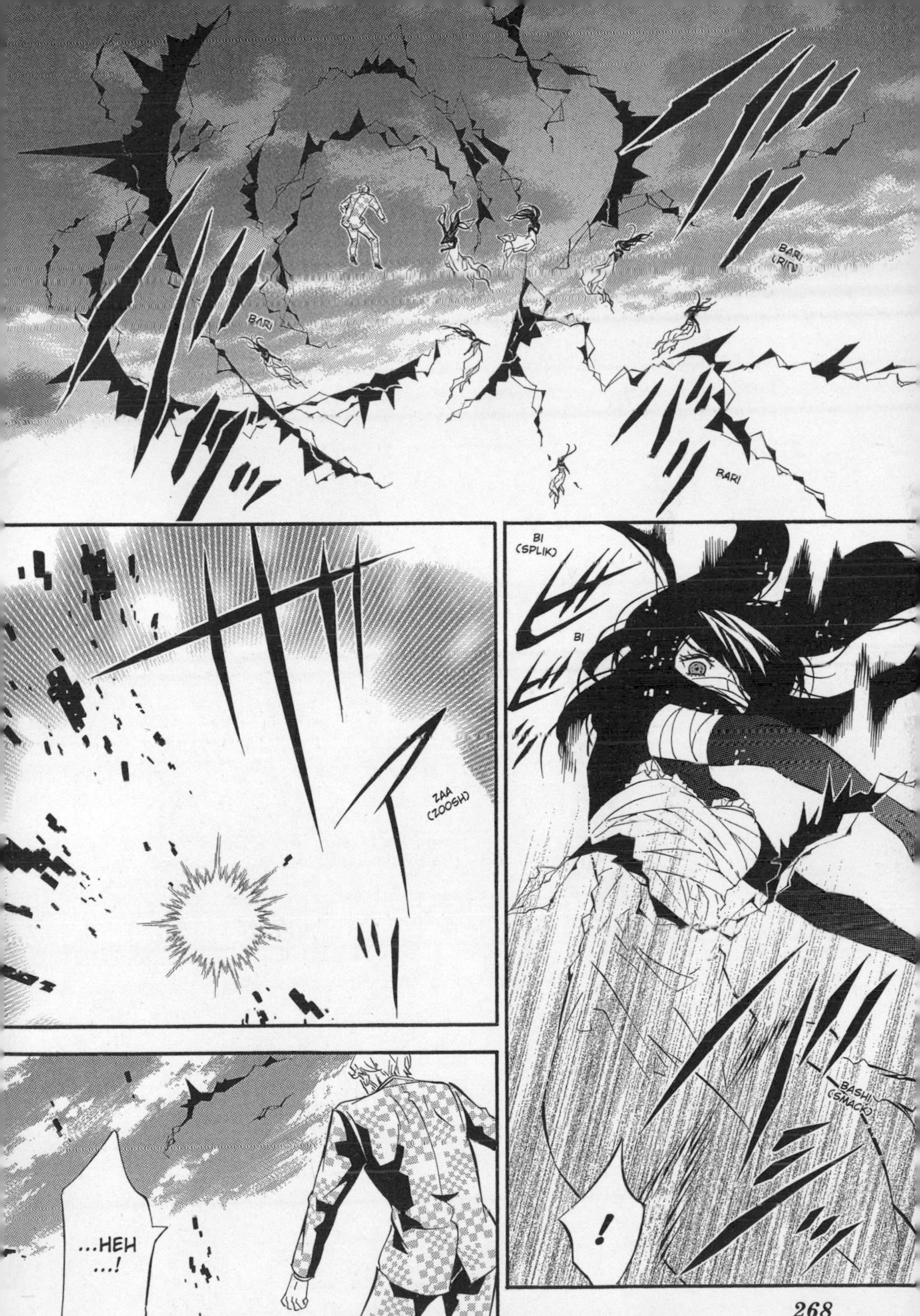
BARI (RIP)
BARI
BARI
BI (SPLIK)
BI
BASHI (SMACK)
!
ZAA (ZOOSH)
...HEH ...!

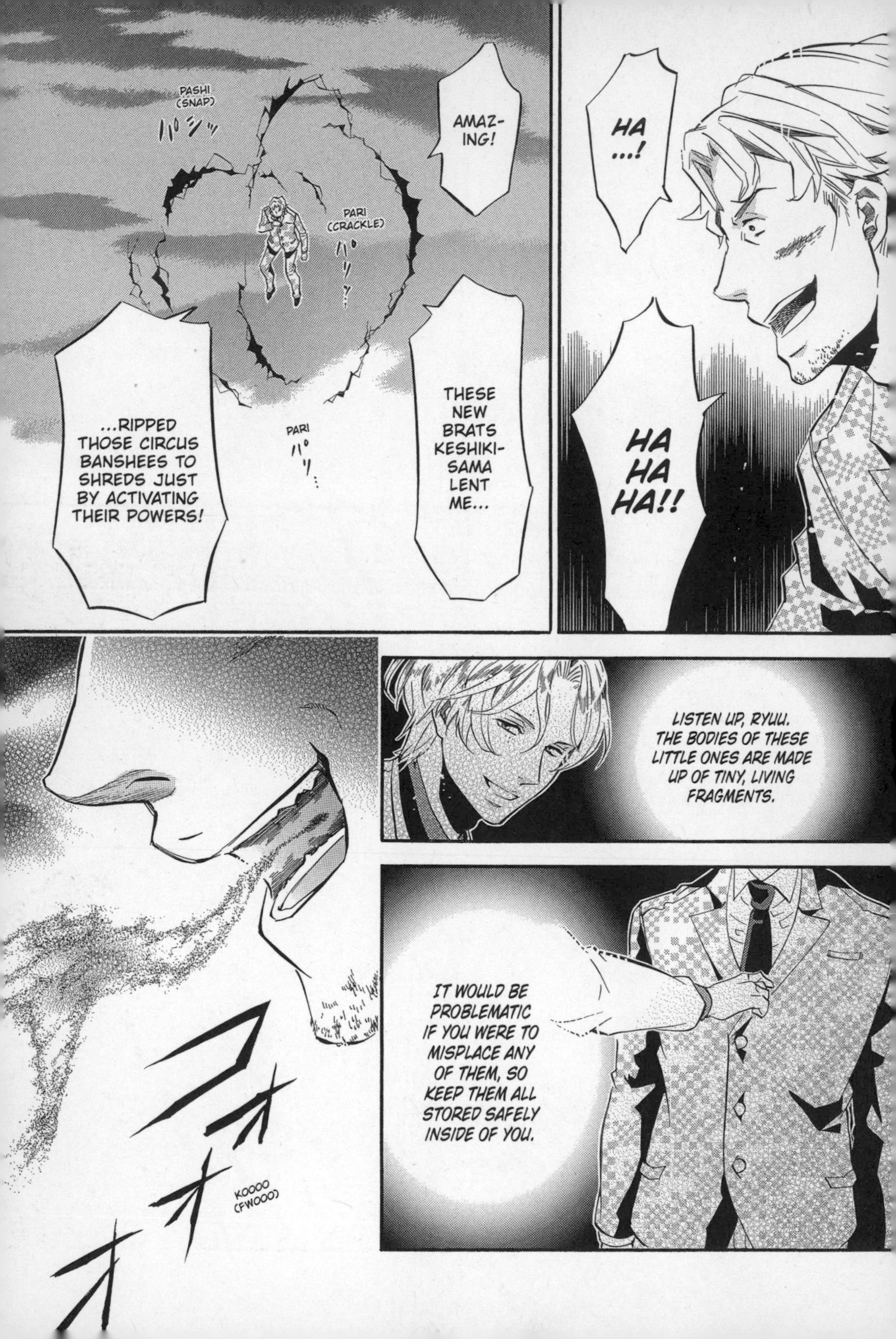
HA ...!
HA HA HA!!
AMAZ-ING!
PASHI (SNAP)
パシッ
PARI (CRACKLE)
パリッ
THESE NEW BRATS KESHIKI-SAMA LENT ME...
PARI
パリ...
...RIPPED THOSE CIRCUS BANSHEES TO SHREDS JUST BY ACTIVATING THEIR POWERS!
LISTEN UP, RYUU. THE BODIES OF THESE LITTLE ONES ARE MADE UP OF TINY, LIVING FRAGMENTS.
IT WOULD BE PROBLEMATIC IF YOU WERE TO MISPLACE ANY OF THEM, SO KEEP THEM ALL STORED SAFELY INSIDE OF YOU.
KOOOO (FWOOO)

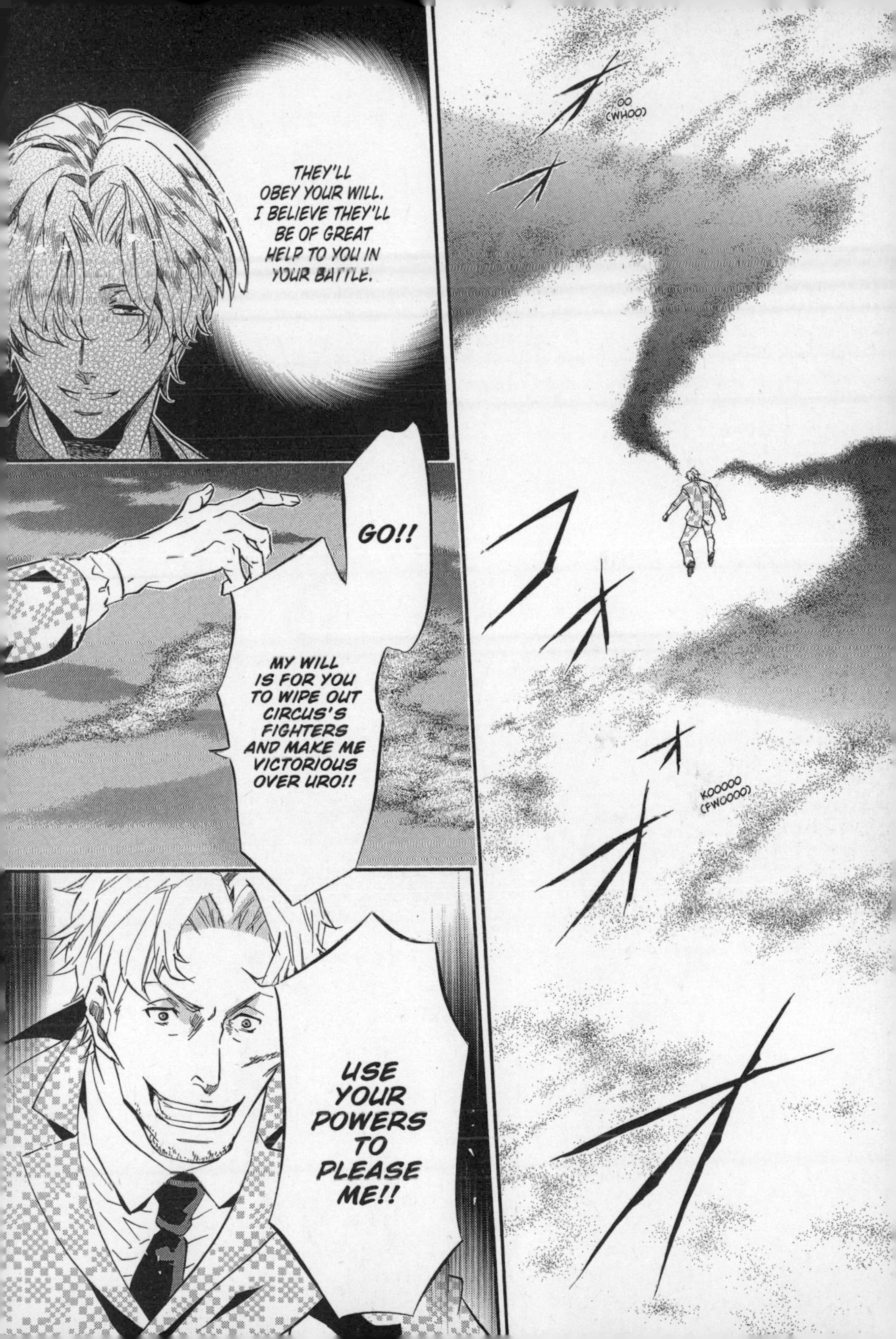
OO (WHOO)
KOOOOO (FWOOOO)
THEY'LL OBEY YOUR WILL. I BELIEVE THEY'LL BE OF GREAT HELP TO YOU IN YOUR BATTLE.
GO!!
MY WILL IS FOR YOU TO WIPE OUT CIRCUS'S FIGHTERS AND MAKE ME VICTORIOUS OVER URO!!
USE YOUR POWERS TO PLEASE ME!!

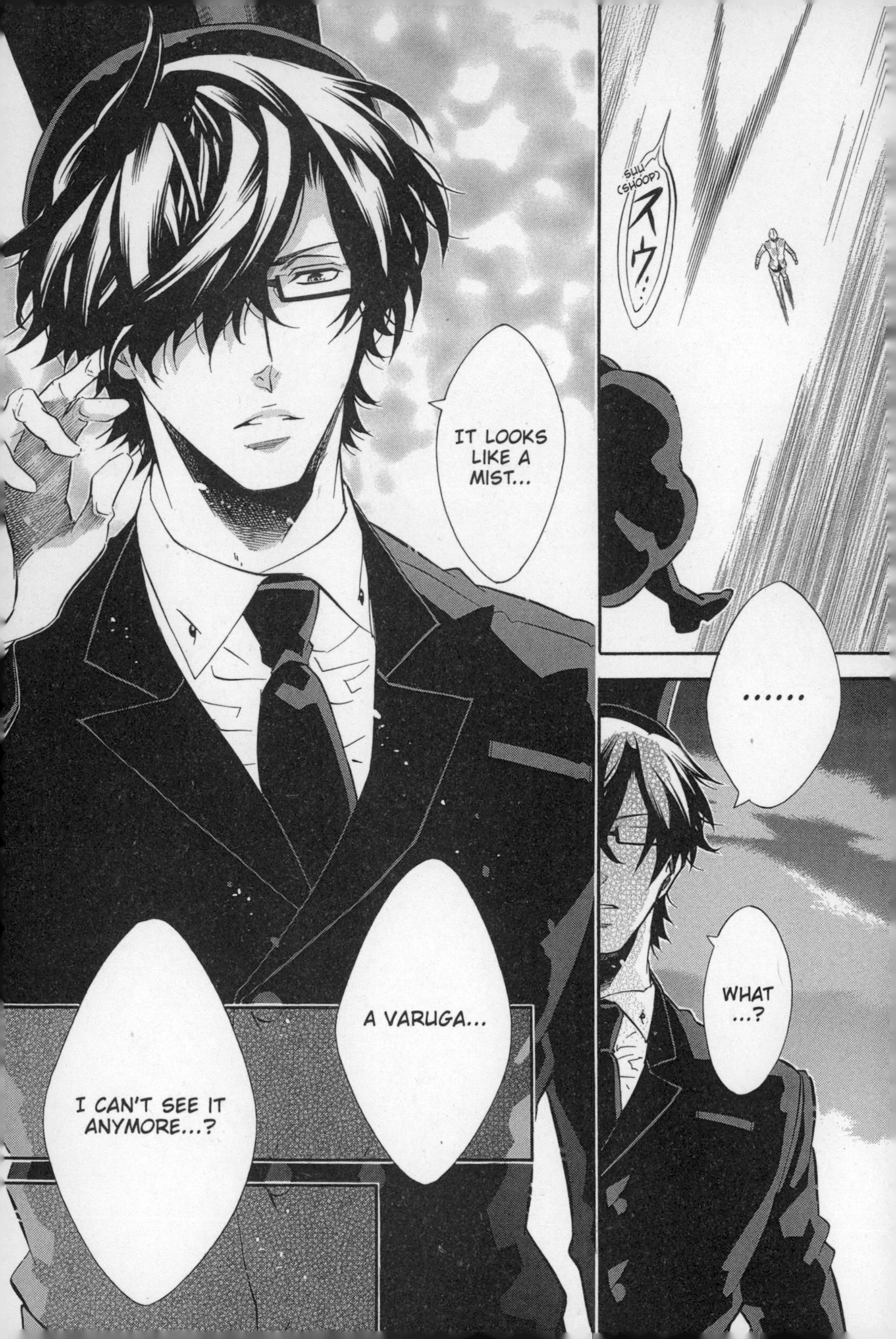
SUU (SHOOP)
スウ…
……
WHAT …?
IT LOOKS LIKE A MIST…
A VARUGA…
I CAN'T SEE IT ANYMORE…?

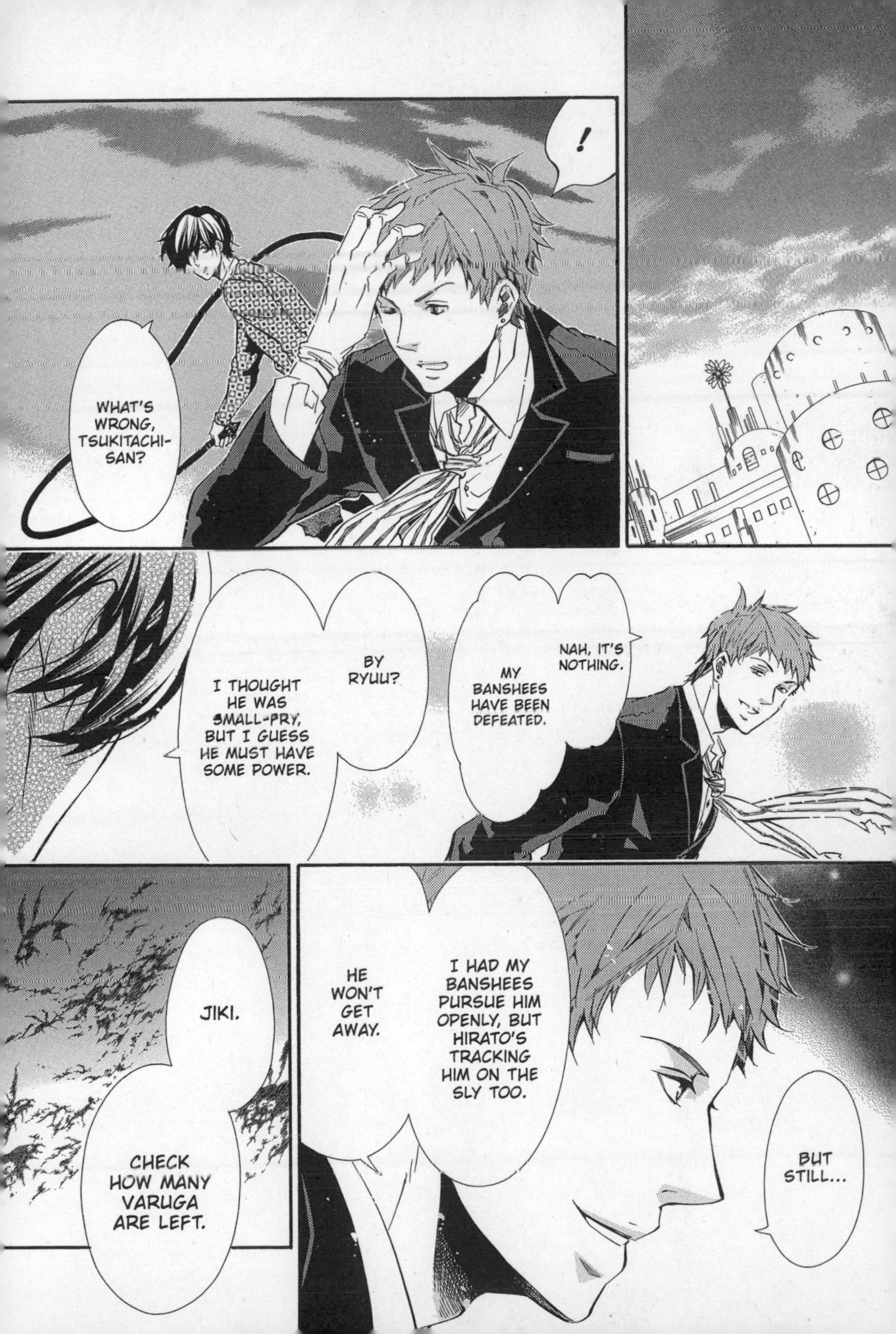
!
WHAT'S WRONG, TSUKITACHI-SAN?
NAH, IT'S NOTHING.
MY BANSHEES HAVE BEEN DEFEATED.
BY RYUU?
I THOUGHT HE WAS SMALL-PRY, BUT I GUESS HE MUST HAVE SOME POWER.
BUT STILL...
I HAD MY BANSHEES PURSUE HIM OPENLY, BUT HIRATO'S TRACKING HIM ON THE SLY TOO.
HE WON'T GET AWAY.
JIKI.
CHECK HOW MANY VARUGA ARE LEFT.

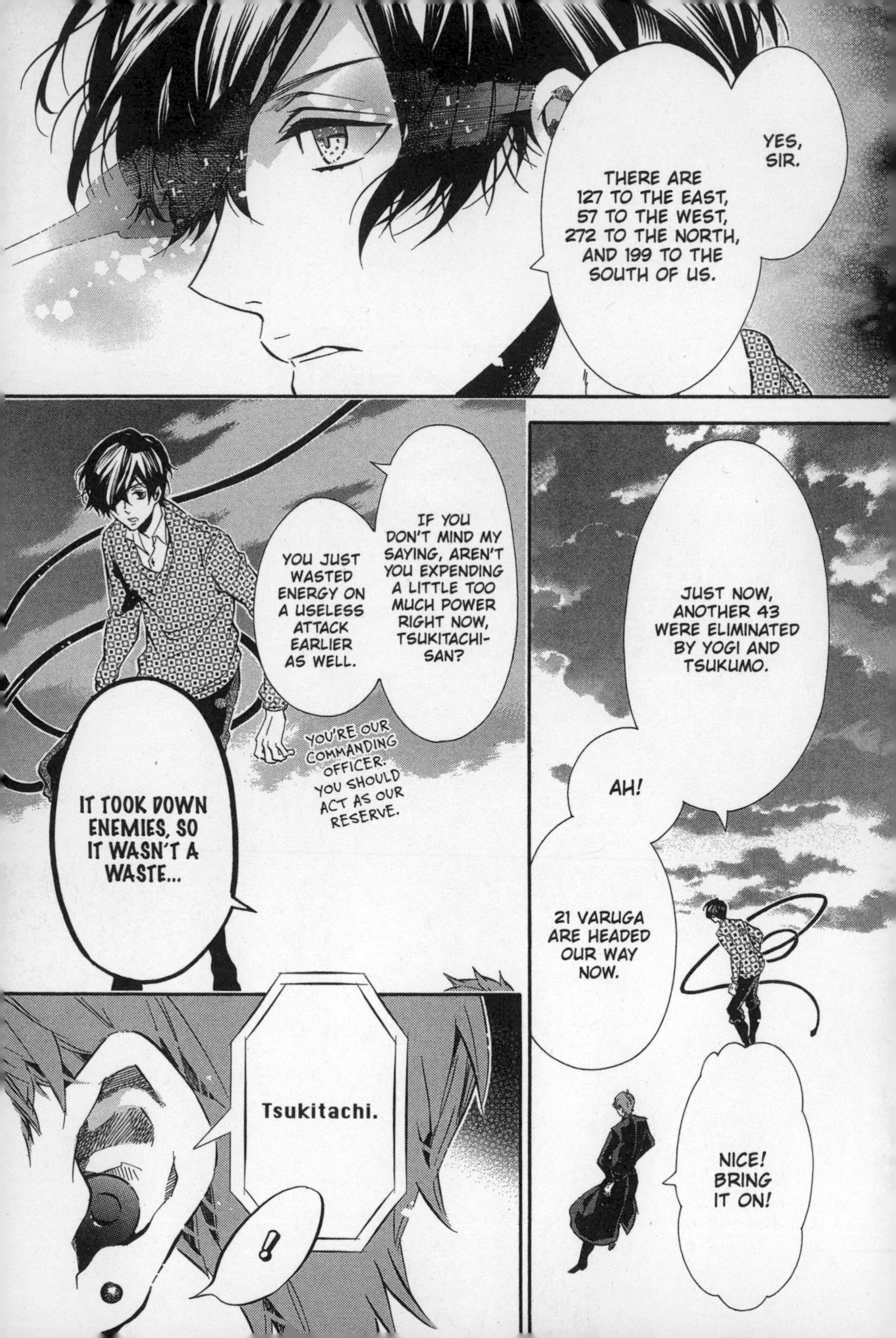
YES, SIR.
THERE ARE 127 TO THE EAST, 57 TO THE WEST, 272 TO THE NORTH, AND 199 TO THE SOUTH OF US.
JUST NOW, ANOTHER 43 WERE ELIMINATED BY YOGI AND TSUKUMO.
AH!
21 VARUGA ARE HEADED OUR WAY NOW.
NICE! BRING IT ON!
IF YOU DON'T MIND MY SAYING, AREN'T YOU EXPENDING A LITTLE TOO MUCH POWER RIGHT NOW, TSUKITACHI-SAN?
YOU JUST WASTED ENERGY ON A USELESS ATTACK EARLIER AS WELL.
YOU'RE OUR COMMANDING OFFICER. YOU SHOULD ACT AS OUR RESERVE.
IT TOOK DOWN ENEMIES, SO IT WASN'T A WASTE...
Tsukitachi.
!

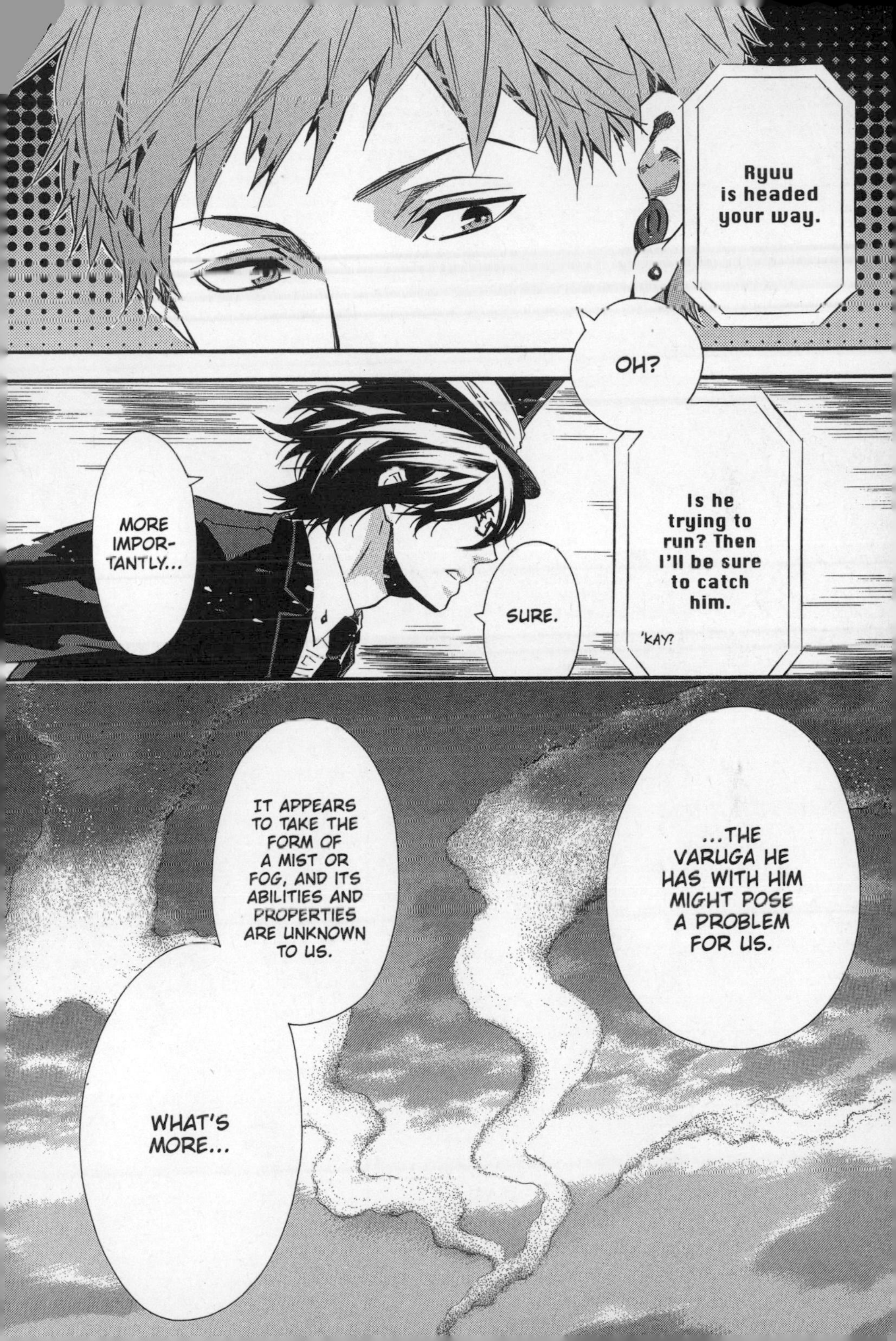
Ryuu is headed your way.
OH?
Is he trying to run? Then I'll be sure to catch him.
'KAY?
SURE.
MORE IMPORTANTLY...
...THE VARUGA HE HAS WITH HIM MIGHT POSE A PROBLEM FOR US.
IT APPEARS TO TAKE THE FORM OF A MIST OR FOG, AND ITS ABILITIES AND PROPERTIES ARE UNKNOWN TO US.
WHAT'S MORE...

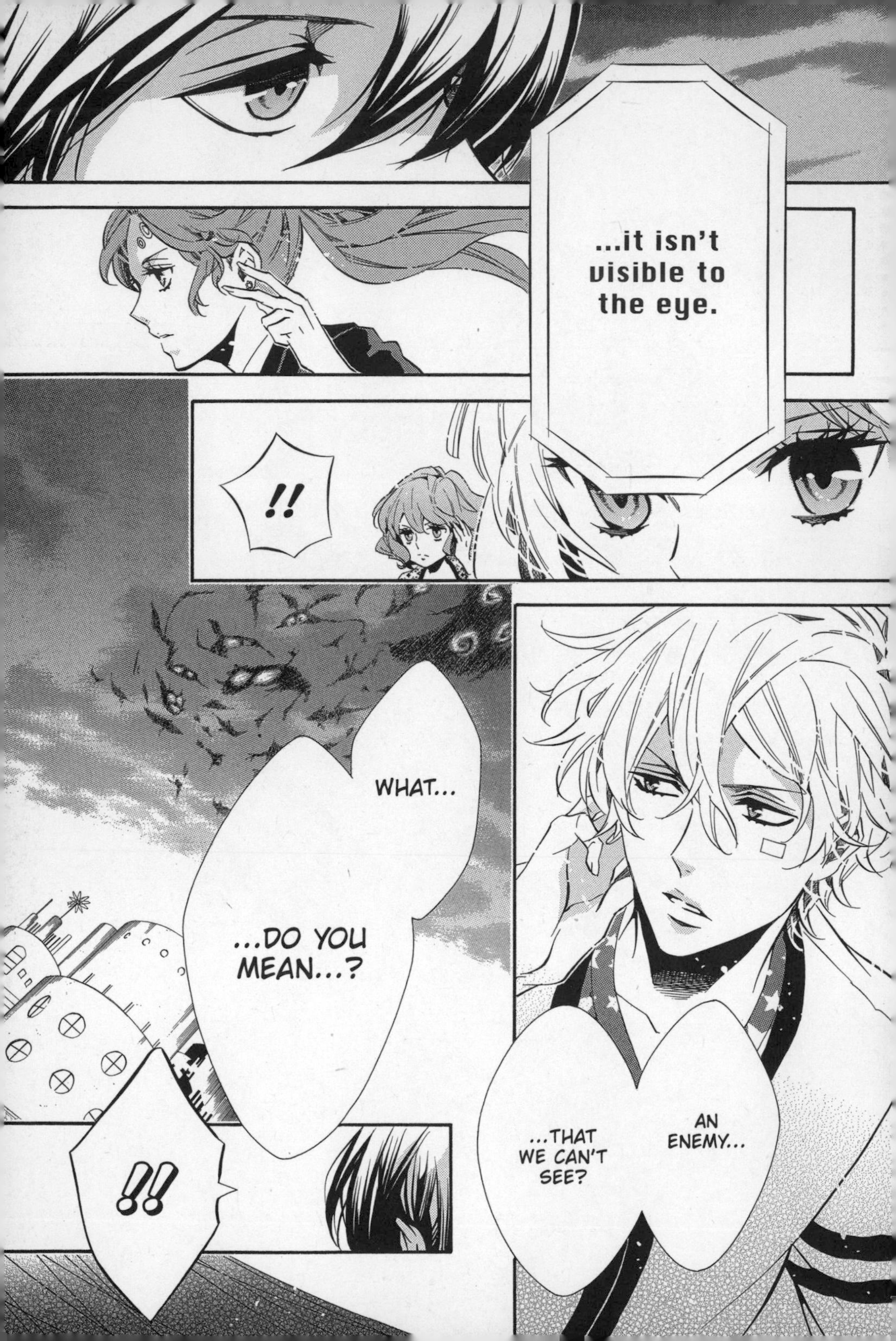
...it isn't visible to the eye.
!!
AN ENEMY... ...THAT WE CAN'T SEE?
WHAT... ...DO YOU MEAN...?
!!

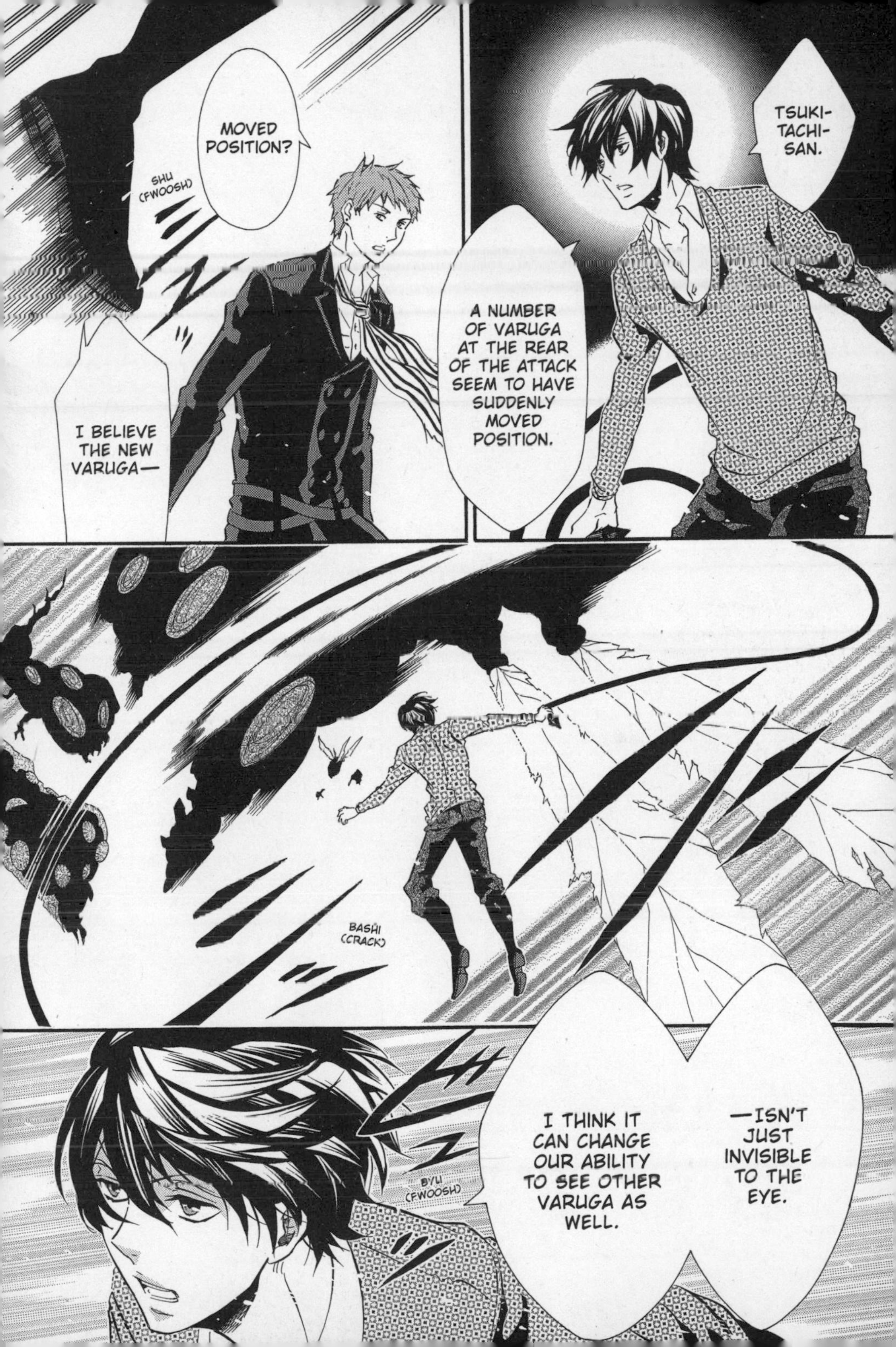
TSUKI-TACHI-SAN.
A NUMBER OF VARUGA AT THE REAR OF THE ATTACK SEEM TO HAVE SUDDENLY MOVED POSITION.
MOVED POSITION?
SHU (FWOOSH)
I BELIEVE THE NEW VARUGA—
BASHI (CRACK)
—ISN'T JUST INVISIBLE TO THE EYE.
I THINK IT CAN CHANGE OUR ABILITY TO SEE OTHER VARUGA AS WELL.
BYU (FWOOSH)

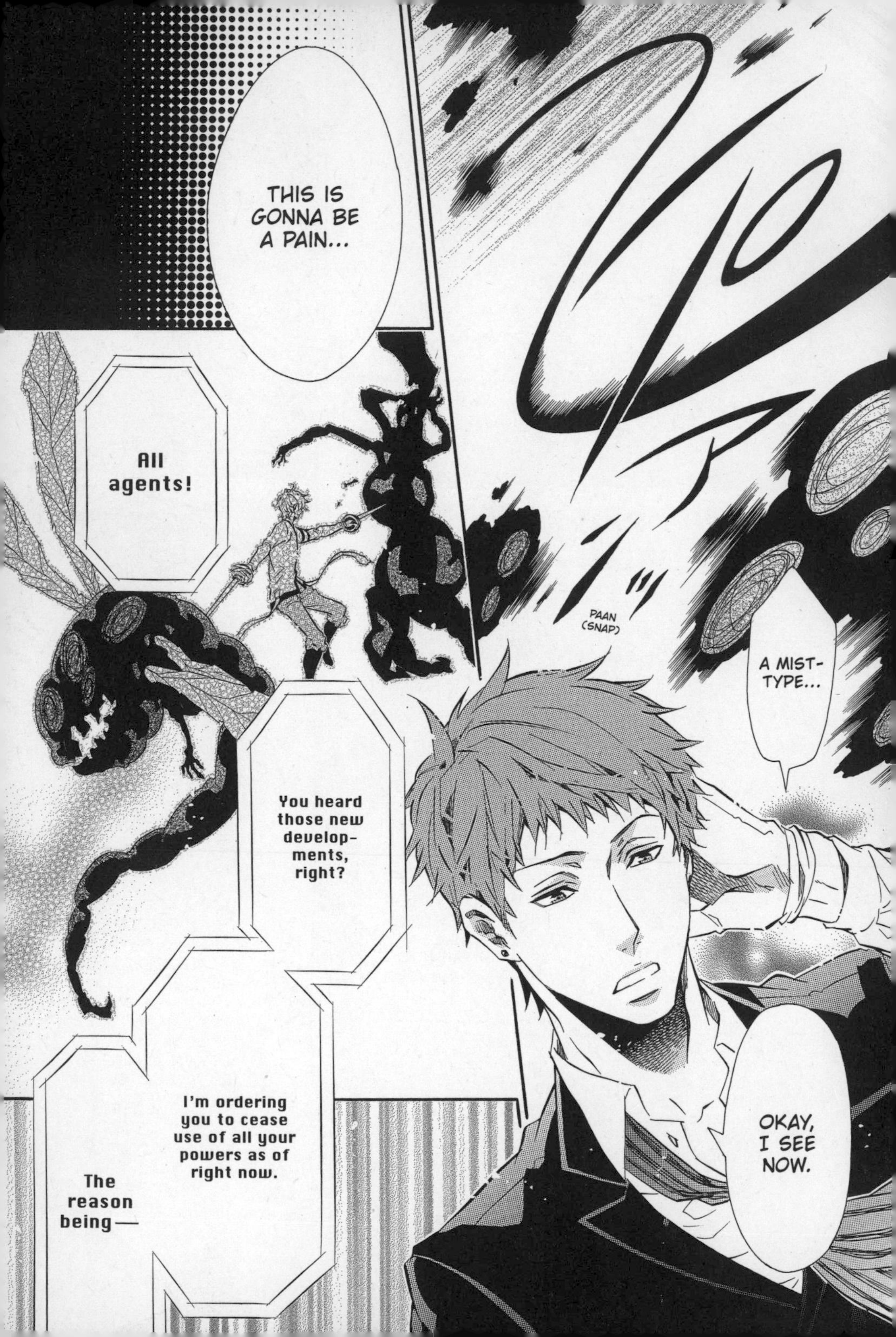
PAAN (SNAP)
A MIST-TYPE...
OKAY, I SEE NOW.
THIS IS GONNA BE A PAIN...
All agents!
You heard those new develop-ments, right?
I'm ordering you to cease use of all your powers as of right now.
The reason being—

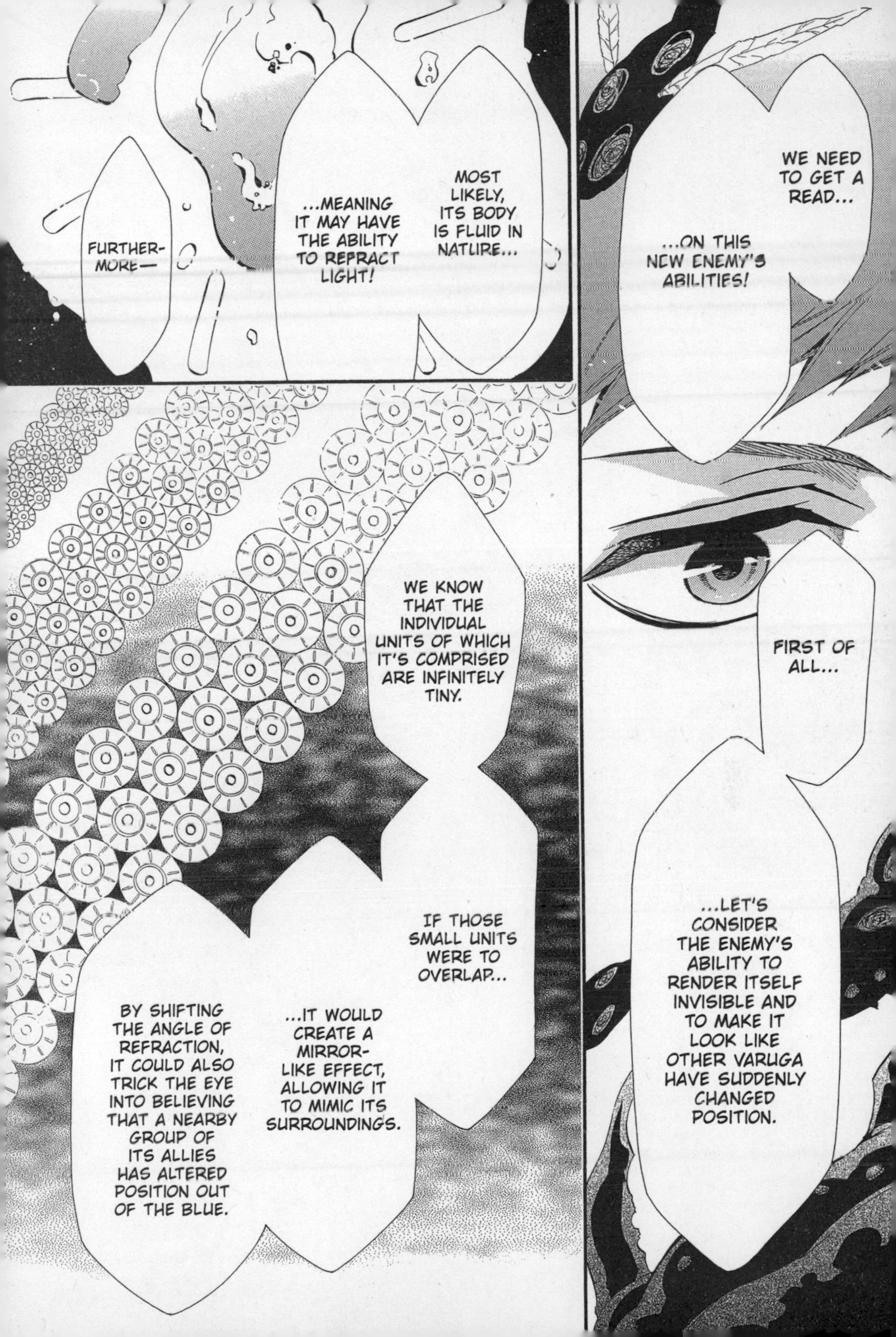
WE NEED TO GET A READ...
...ON THIS NEW ENEMY'S ABILITIES!
FIRST OF ALL...
...LET'S CONSIDER THE ENEMY'S ABILITY TO RENDER ITSELF INVISIBLE AND TO MAKE IT LOOK LIKE OTHER VARUGA HAVE SUDDENLY CHANGED POSITION.
MOST LIKELY, ITS BODY IS FLUID IN NATURE...
...MEANING IT MAY HAVE THE ABILITY TO REFRACT LIGHT!
FURTHER-MORE—
WE KNOW THAT THE INDIVIDUAL UNITS OF WHICH IT'S COMPRISED ARE INFINITELY TINY.
IF THOSE SMALL UNITS WERE TO OVERLAP...
...IT WOULD CREATE A MIRROR-LIKE EFFECT, ALLOWING IT TO MIMIC ITS SURROUNDINGS.
BY SHIFTING THE ANGLE OF REFRACTION, IT COULD ALSO TRICK THE EYE INTO BELIEVING THAT A NEARBY GROUP OF ITS ALLIES HAS ALTERED POSITION OUT OF THE BLUE.

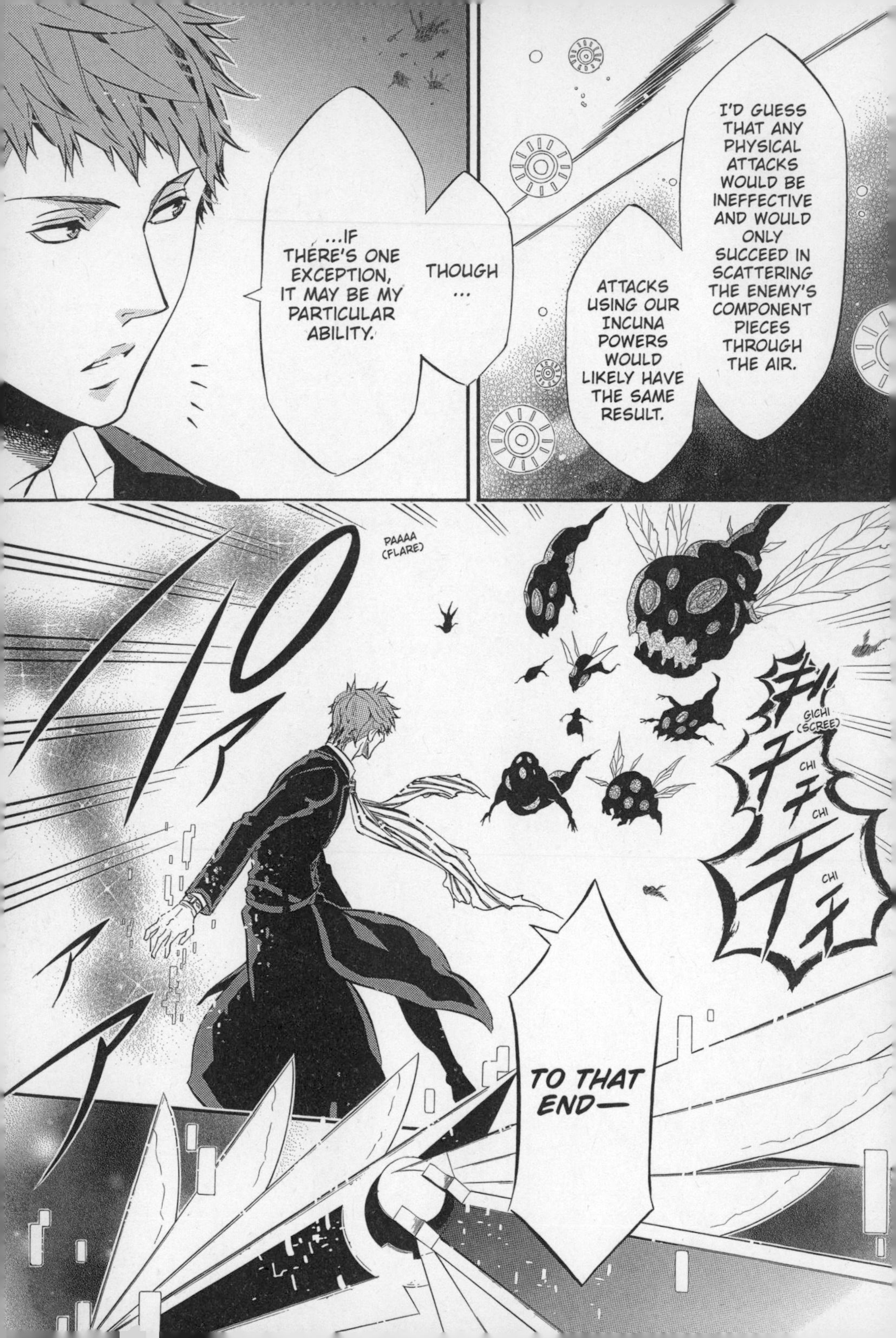
I'D GUESS THAT ANY PHYSICAL ATTACKS WOULD BE INEFFECTIVE AND WOULD ONLY SUCCEED IN SCATTERING THE ENEMY'S COMPONENT PIECES THROUGH THE AIR.
ATTACKS USING OUR INCUNA POWERS WOULD LIKELY HAVE THE SAME RESULT.
THOUGH ...
...IF THERE'S ONE EXCEPTION, IT MAY BE MY PARTICULAR ABILITY.
GICHI (SCREE)
CHI
CHI
CHI
PAAAA (FLARE)
TO THAT END—

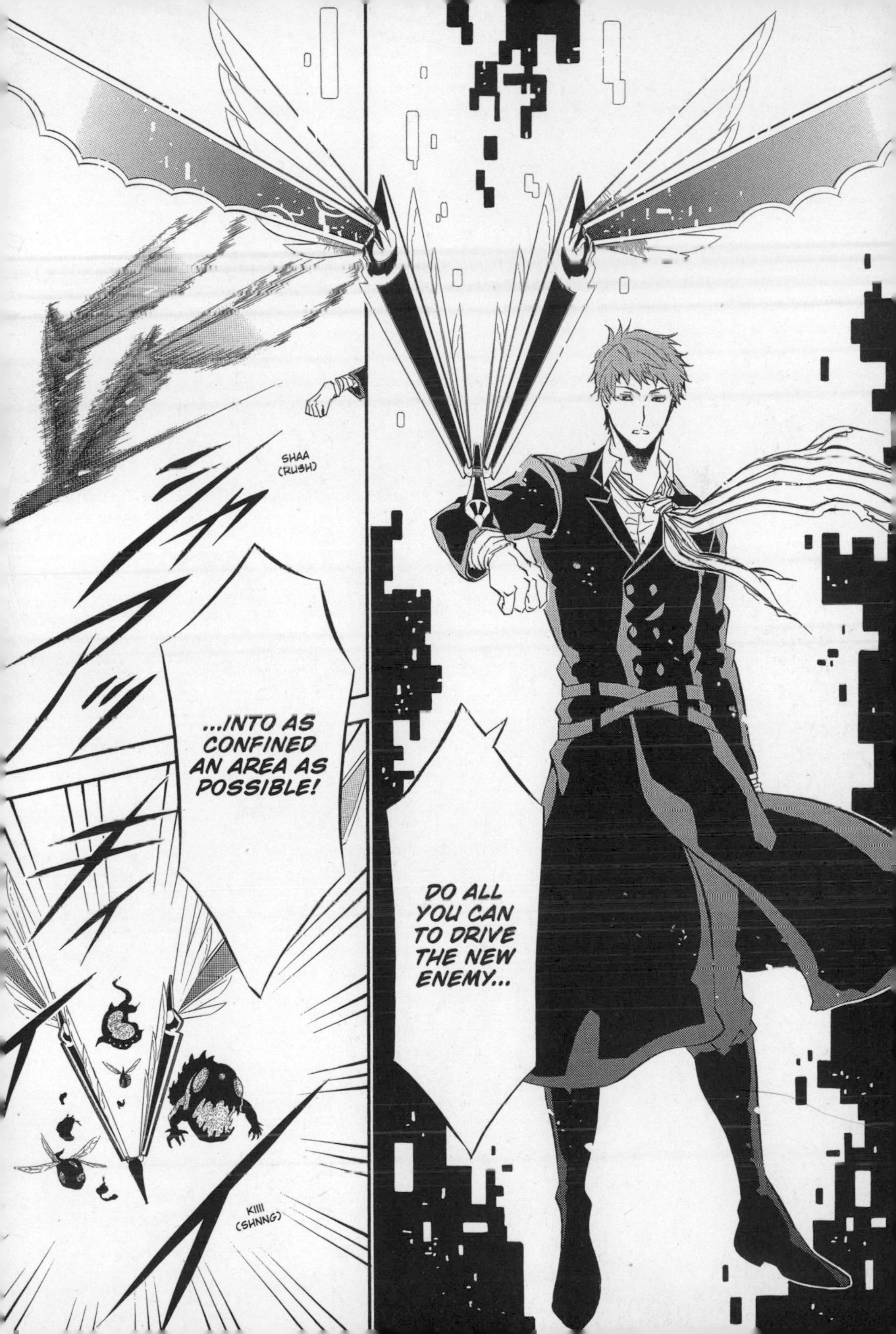
DO ALL YOU CAN TO DRIVE THE NEW ENEMY...
...INTO AS CONFINED AN AREA AS POSSIBLE!
SHAA (RUSH)
KIIII (SHNNG)

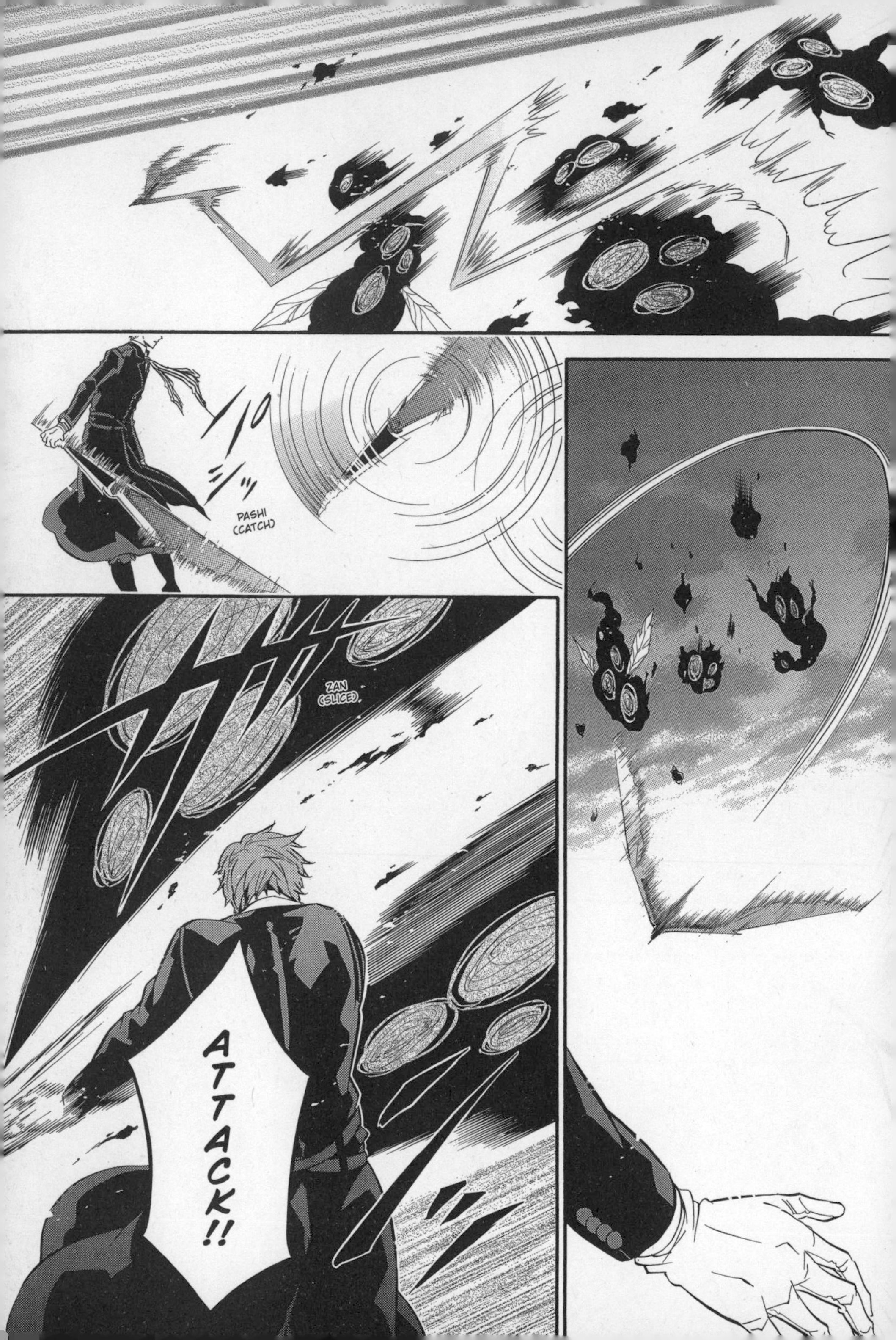
PASHI (CATCH)
ZAN (SLICE)
ATTACK!!

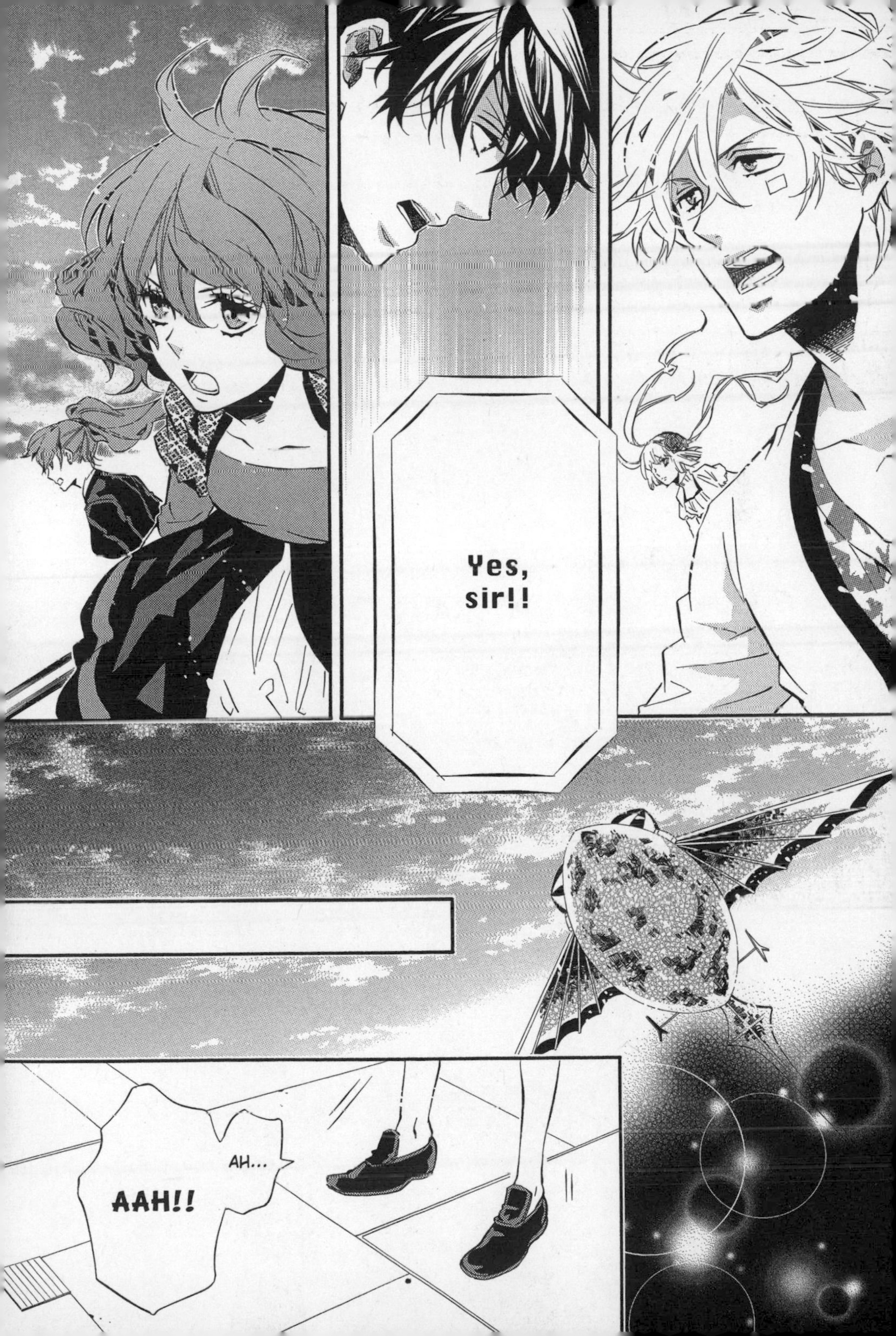
Yes, sir!!
AH...
AAH!!

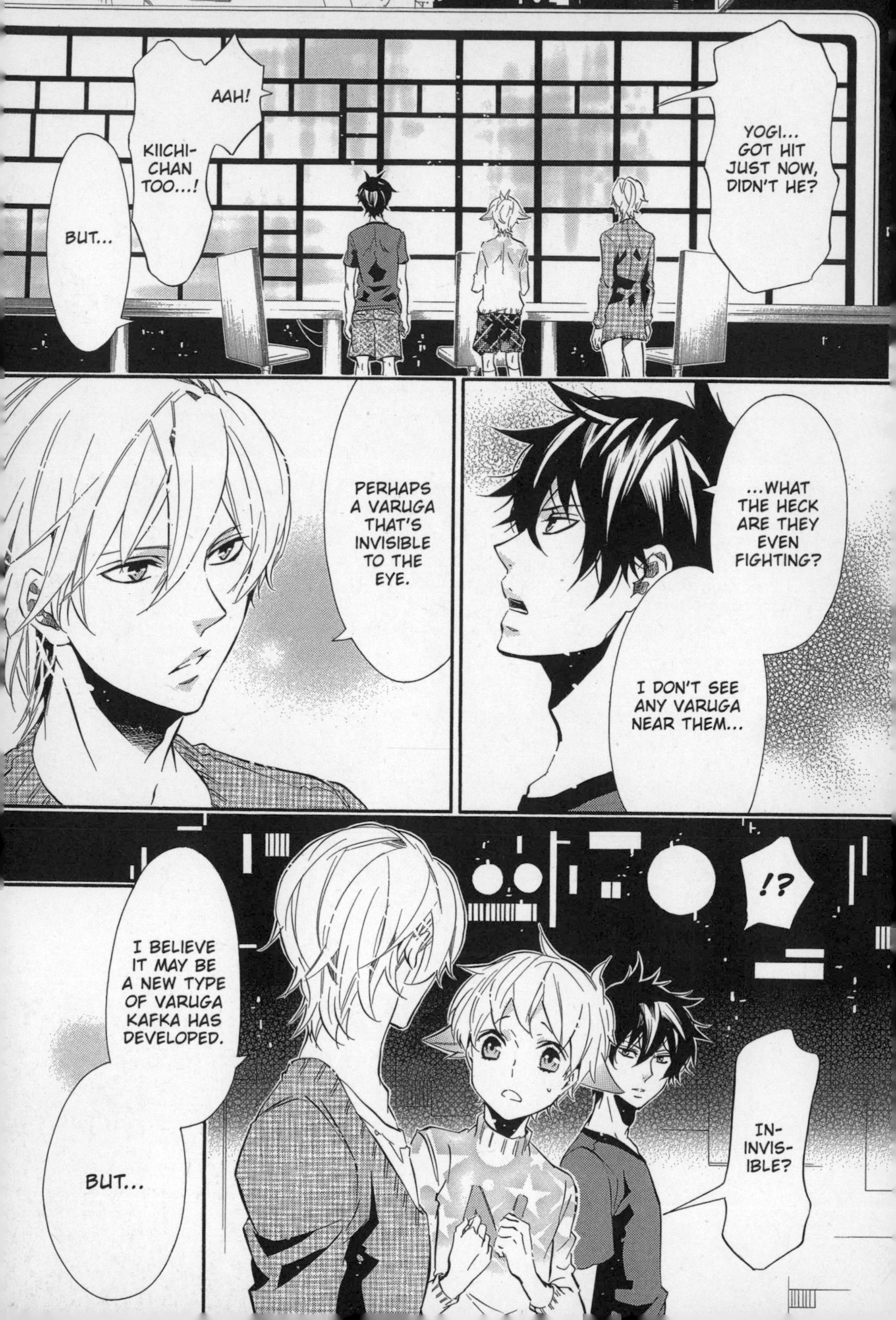
YOGI... GOT HIT JUST NOW, DIDN'T HE?
AAH!
KIICHI-CHAN TOO...!
BUT...
...WHAT THE HECK ARE THEY EVEN FIGHTING?
I DON'T SEE ANY VARUGA NEAR THEM...
PERHAPS A VARUGA THAT'S INVISIBLE TO THE EYE.
!?
IN-INVISIBLE?
I BELIEVE IT MAY BE A NEW TYPE OF VARUGA KAFKA HAS DEVELOPED.
BUT...

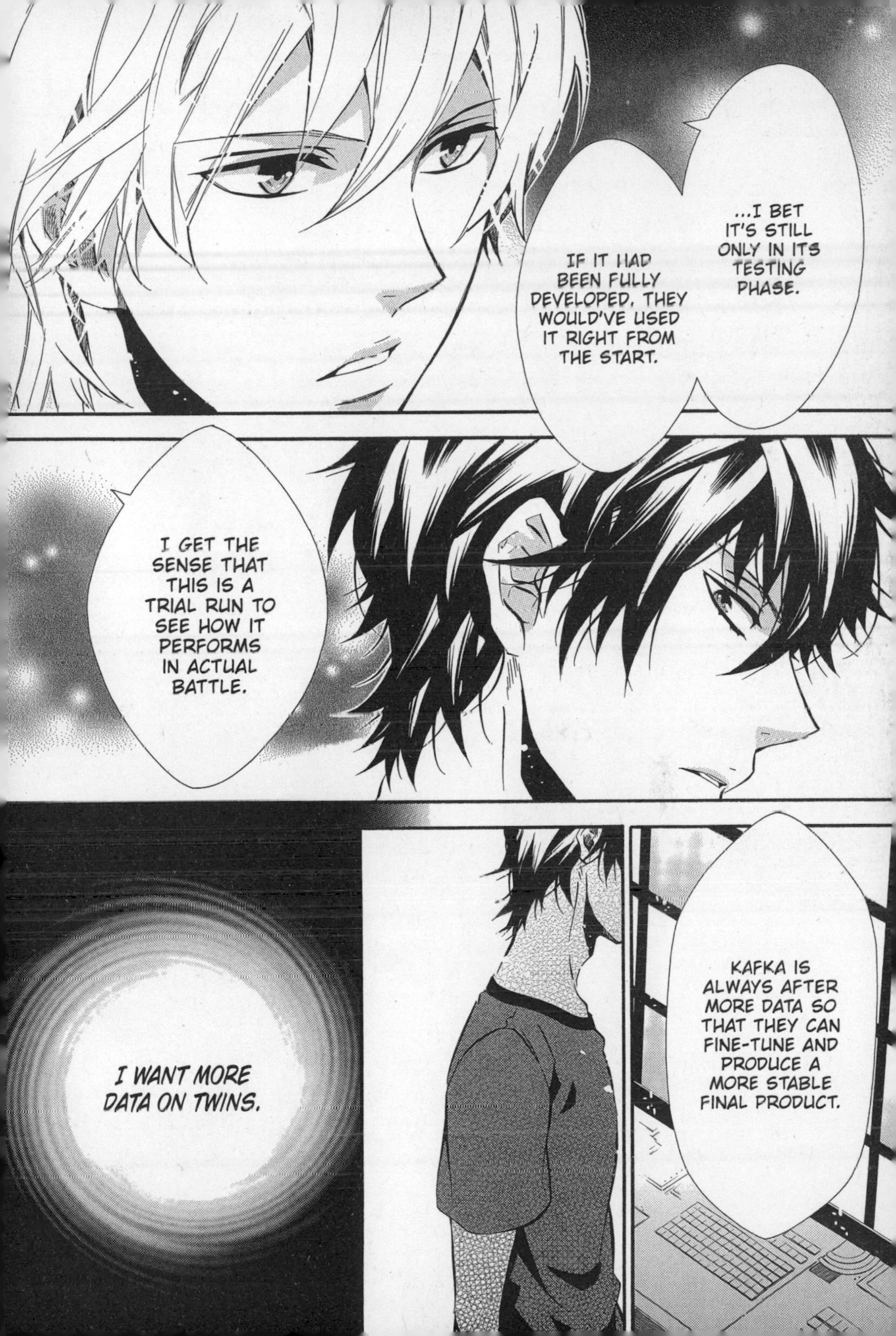
...I BET IT'S STILL ONLY IN ITS TESTING PHASE.
IF IT HAD BEEN FULLY DEVELOPED, THEY WOULD'VE USED IT RIGHT FROM THE START.
I GET THE SENSE THAT THIS IS A TRIAL RUN TO SEE HOW IT PERFORMS IN ACTUAL BATTLE.
KAFKA IS ALWAYS AFTER MORE DATA SO THAT THEY CAN FINE-TUNE AND PRODUCE A MORE STABLE FINAL PRODUCT.
I WANT MORE DATA ON TWINS.

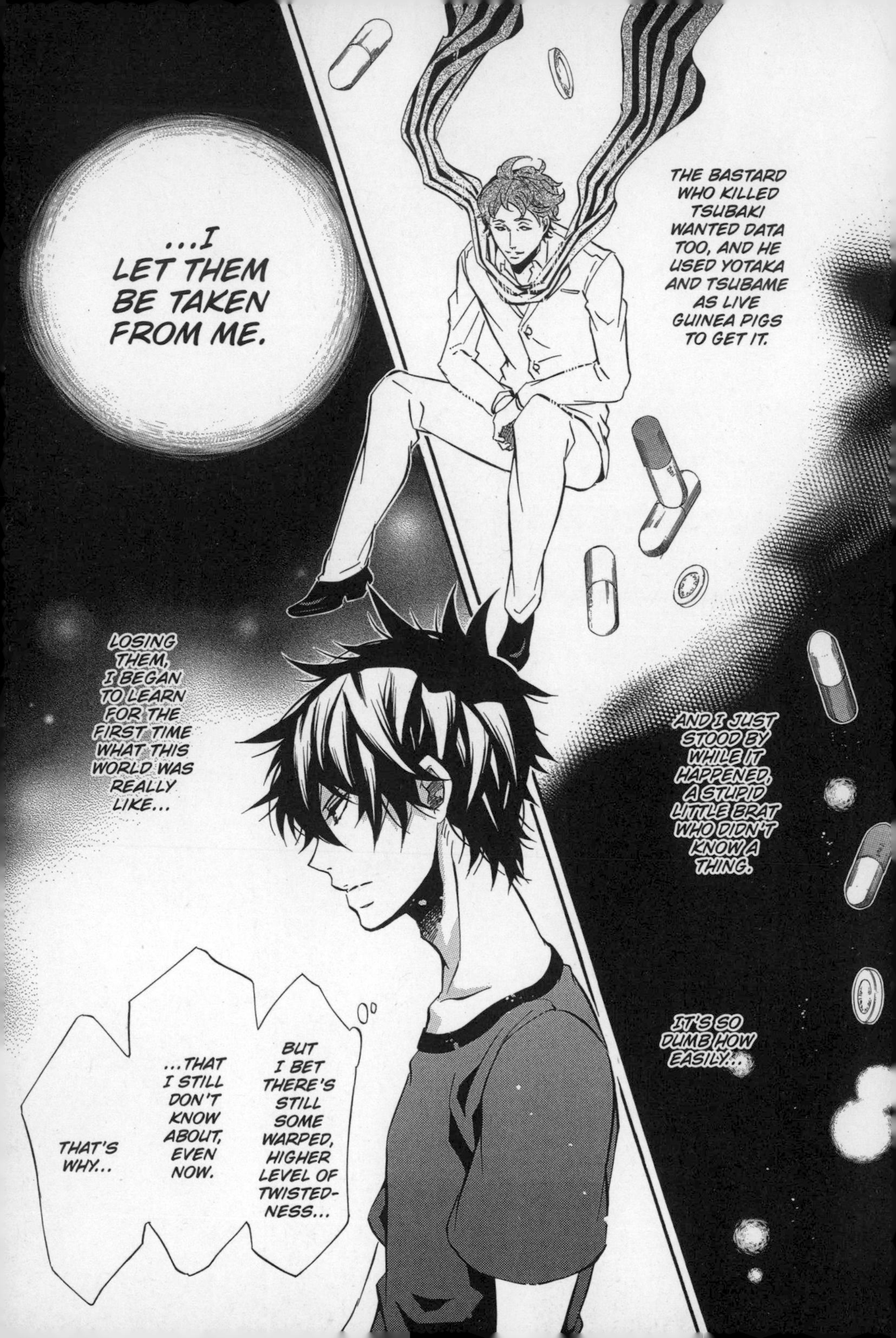
THE BASTARD WHO KILLED TSUBAKI WANTED DATA TOO, AND HE USED YOTAKA AND TSUBAME AS LIVE GUINEA PIGS TO GET IT.
AND I JUST STOOD BY WHILE IT HAPPENED, A STUPID LITTLE BRAT WHO DIDN'T KNOW A THING.
IT'S SO DUMB HOW EASILY...
...I LET THEM BE TAKEN FROM ME.
LOSING THEM, I BEGAN TO LEARN FOR THE FIRST TIME WHAT THIS WORLD WAS REALLY LIKE...
BUT I BET THERE'S STILL SOME WARPED, HIGHER LEVEL OF TWISTED-NESS...
...THAT I STILL DON'T KNOW ABOUT, EVEN NOW.
THAT'S WHY...

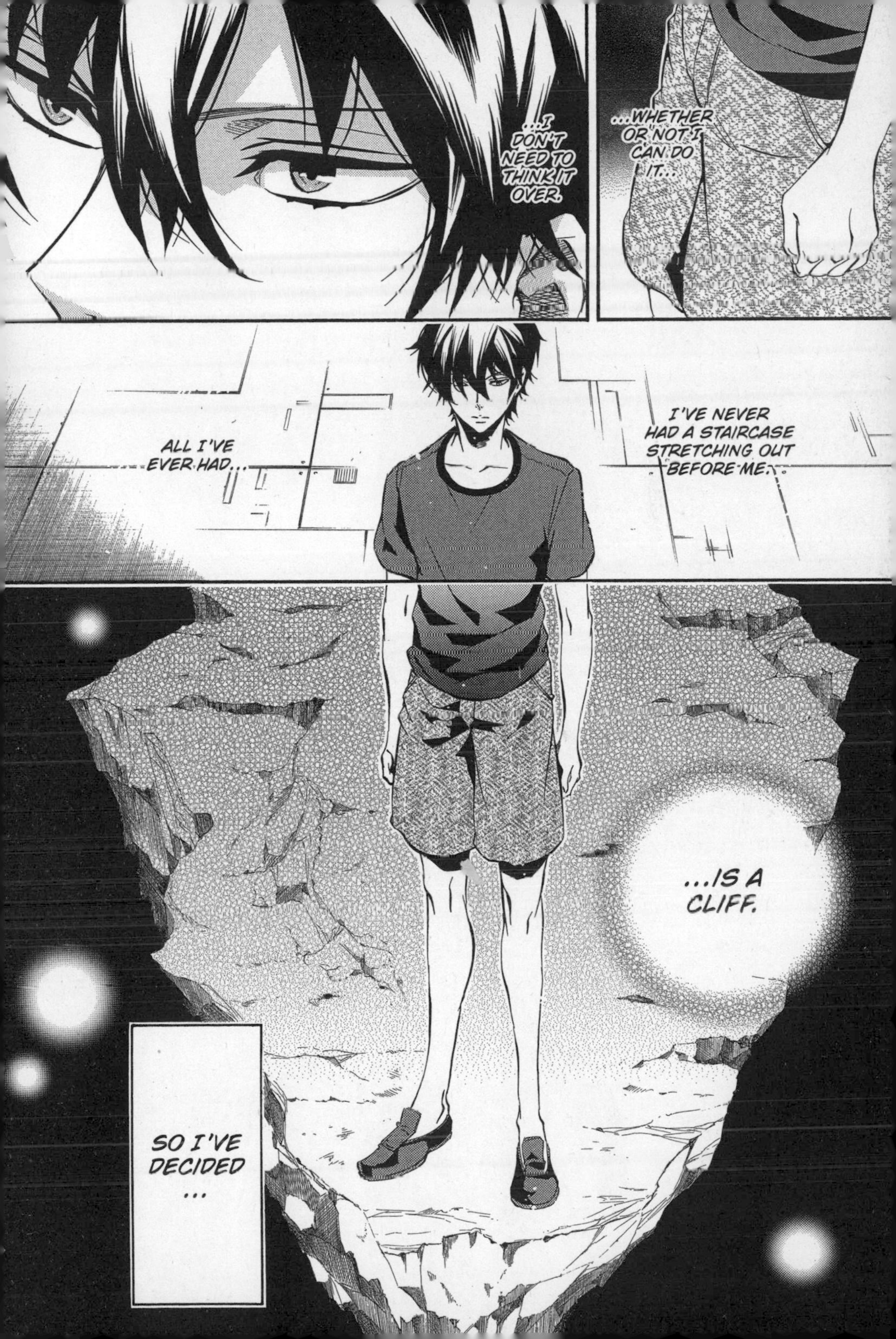
...WHETHER OR NOT I CAN DO IT...
...I DON'T NEED TO THINK IT OVER.
I'VE NEVER HAD A STAIRCASE STRETCHING OUT BEFORE ME...
ALL I'VE EVER HAD...
...IS A CLIFF.
SO I'VE DECIDED ...

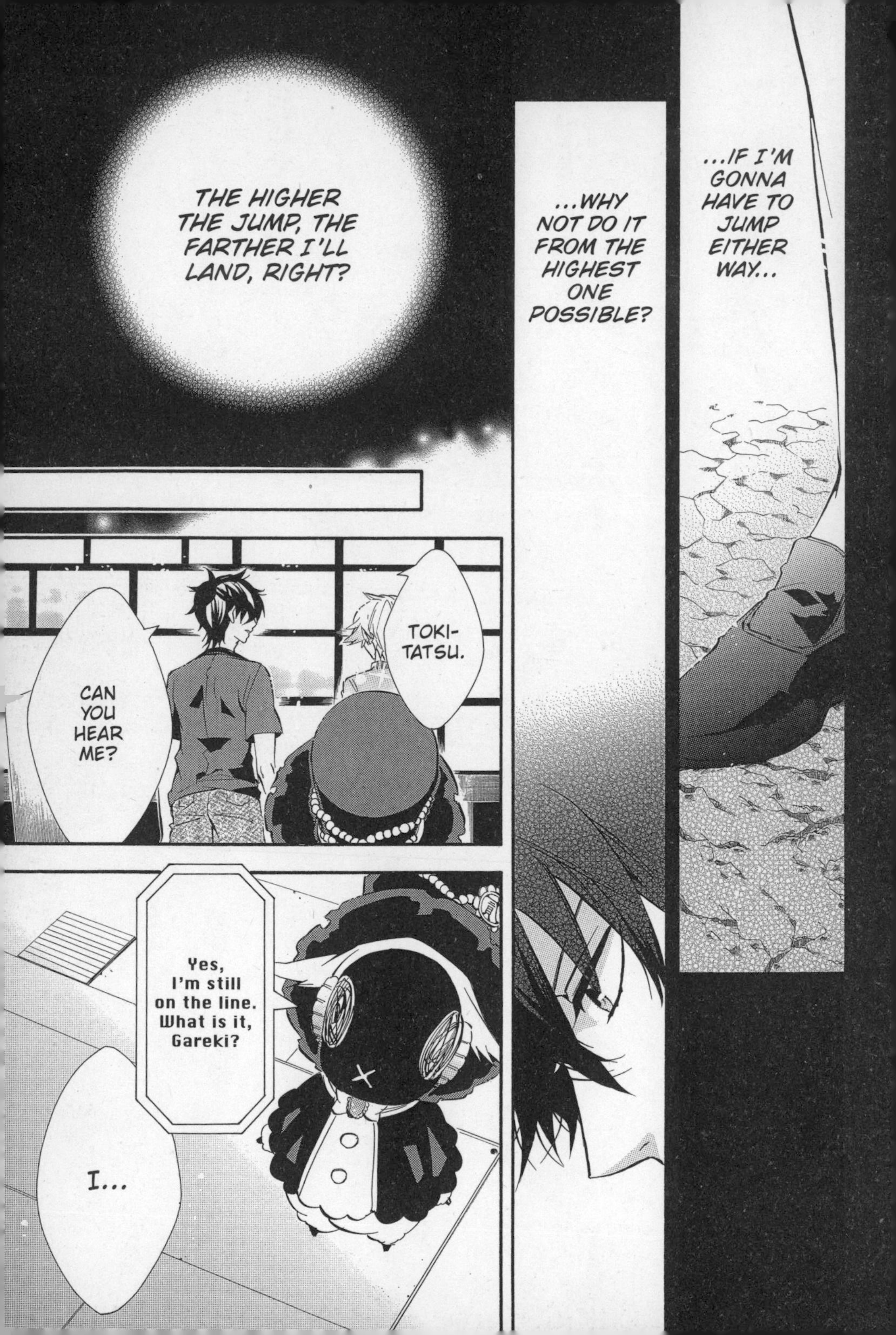
...IF I'M GONNA HAVE TO JUMP EITHER WAY...
...WHY NOT DO IT FROM THE HIGHEST ONE POSSIBLE?
THE HIGHER THE JUMP, THE FARTHER I'LL LAND, RIGHT?
TOKI-TATSU.
CAN YOU HEAR ME?
Yes, I'm still on the line. What is it, Gareki?
I...

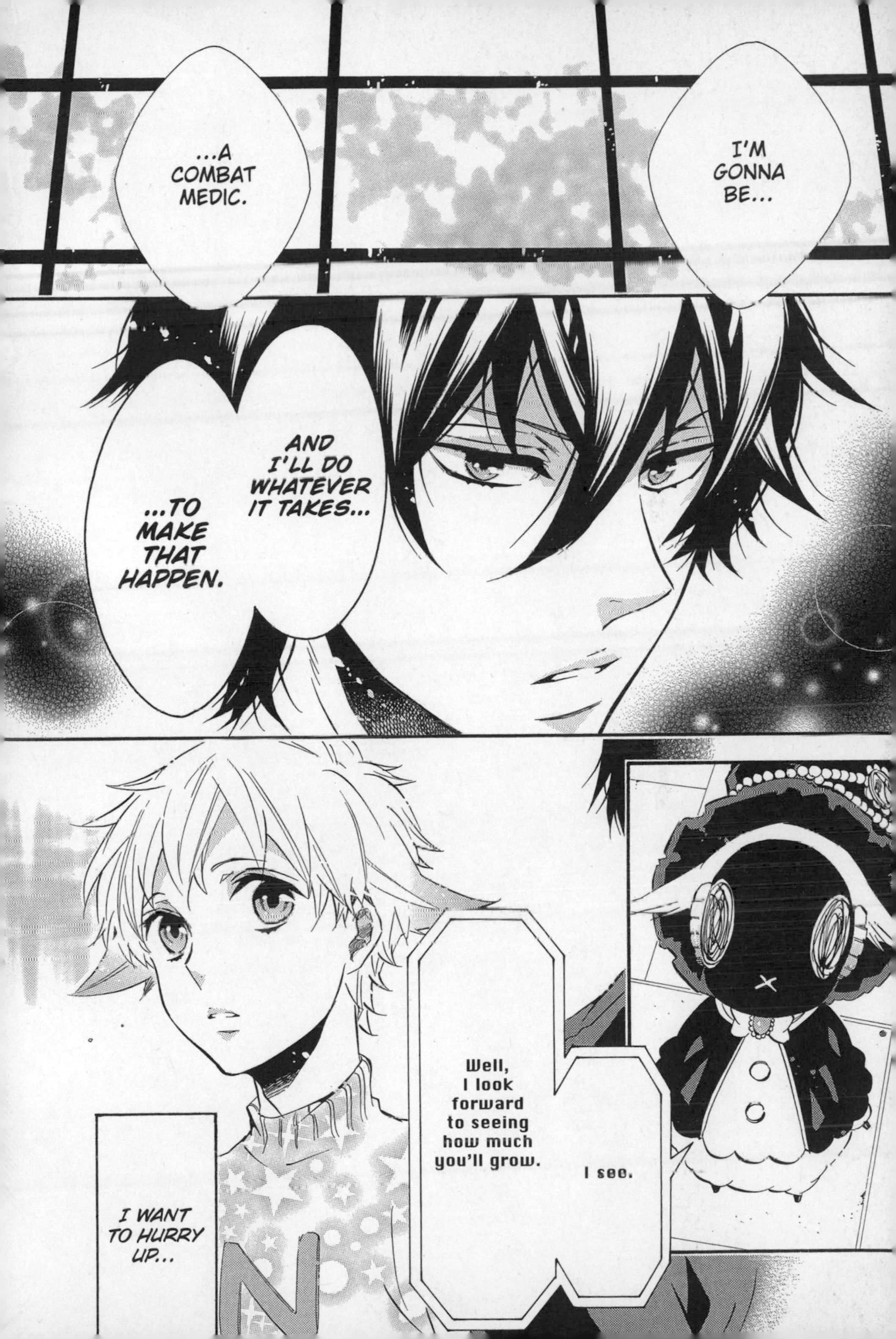
I'M GONNA BE...
...A COMBAT MEDIC.
AND I'LL DO WHATEVER IT TAKES...
...TO MAKE THAT HAPPEN.
I see.
Well, I look forward to seeing how much you'll grow.
I WANT TO HURRY UP...

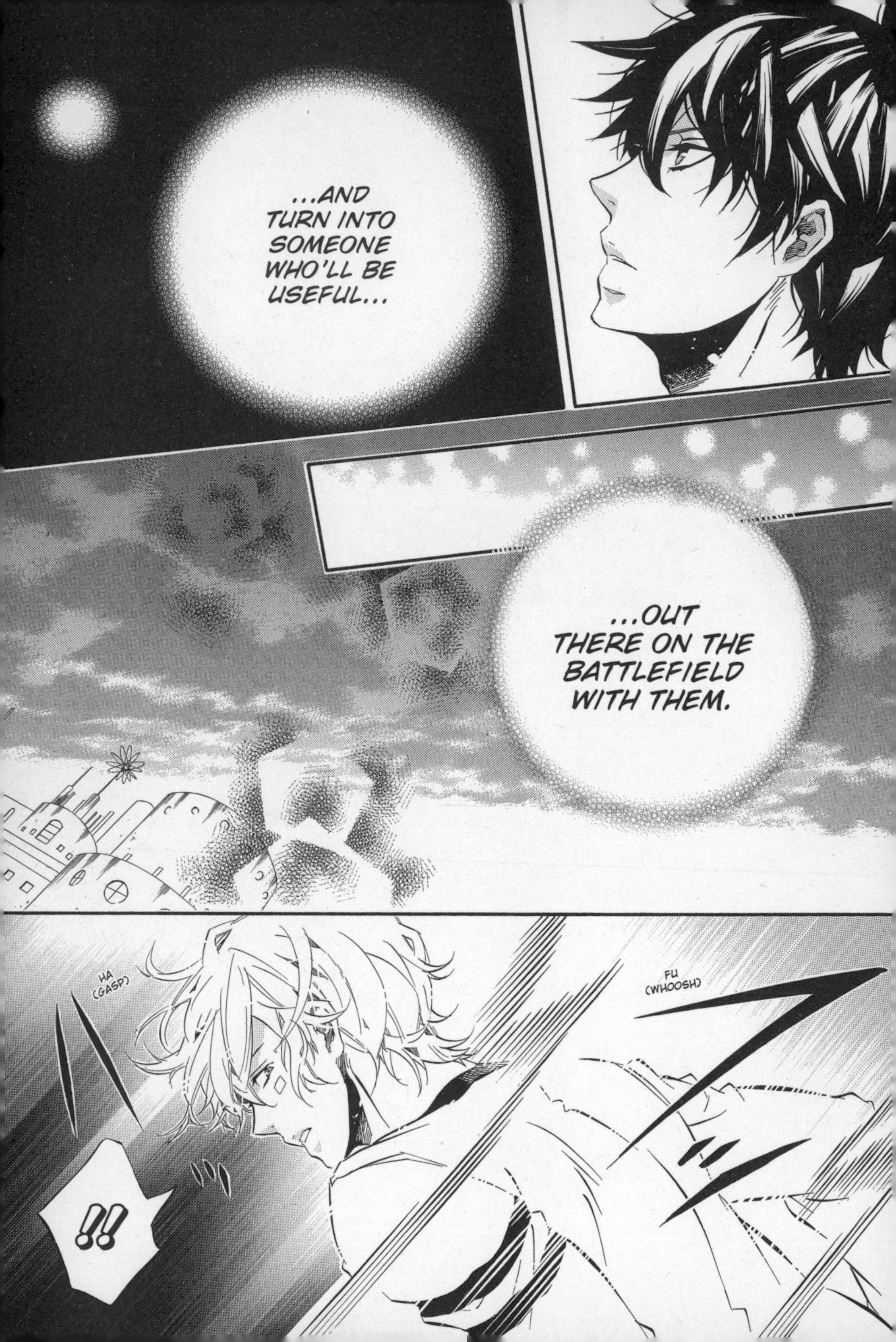
...AND TURN INTO SOMEONE WHO'LL BE USEFUL...
...OUT THERE ON THE BATTLEFIELD WITH THEM.
FU (WHOOSH)
HA (GASP)
!!

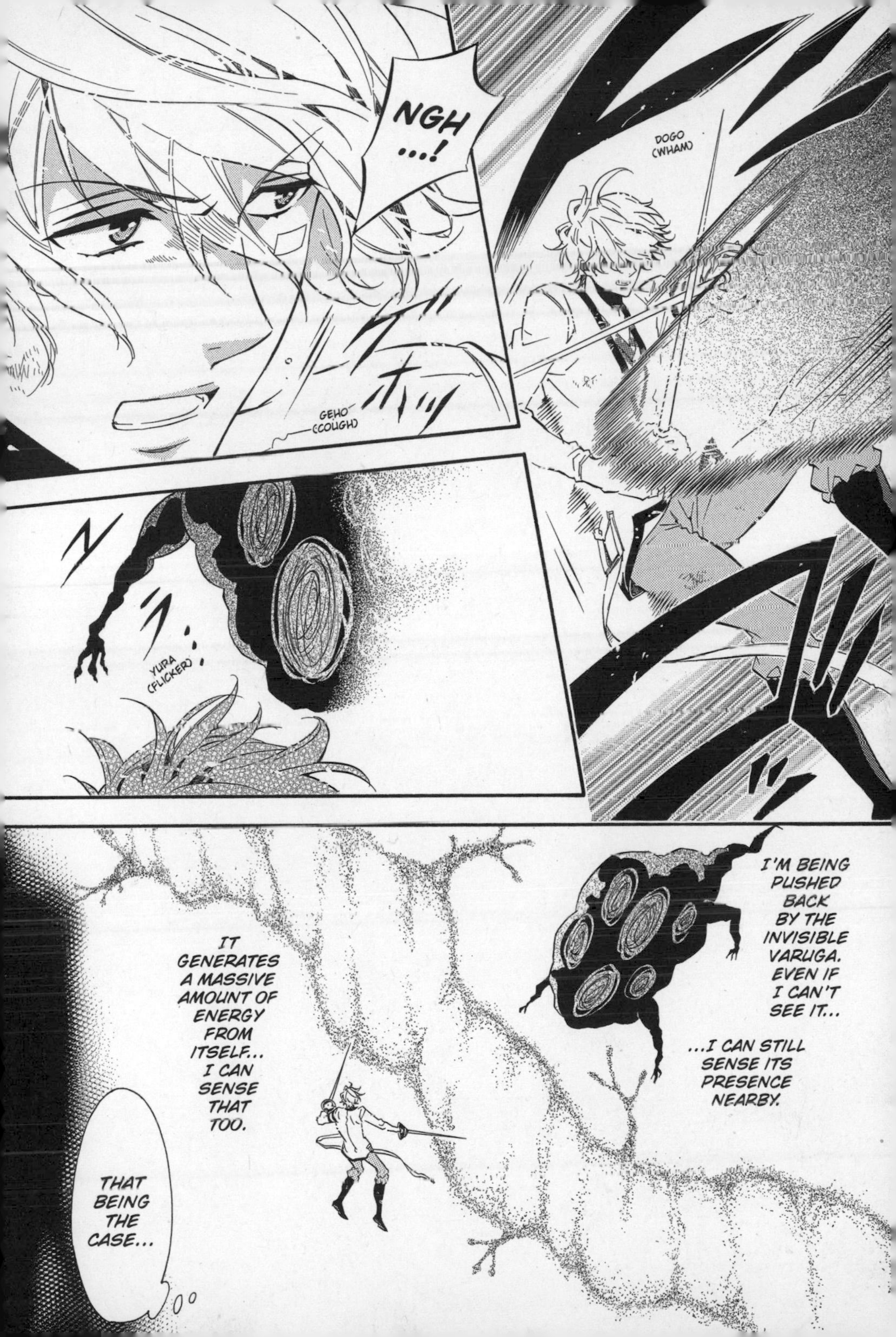
DOGO (WHAM)
NGH ...!
GEHO (COUGH)
YURA (FLICKER)
I'M BEING PUSHED BACK BY THE INVISIBLE VARUGA. EVEN IF I CAN'T SEE IT...
...I CAN STILL SENSE ITS PRESENCE NEARBY.
IT GENERATES A MASSIVE AMOUNT OF ENERGY FROM ITSELF... I CAN SENSE THAT TOO.
THAT BEING THE CASE...

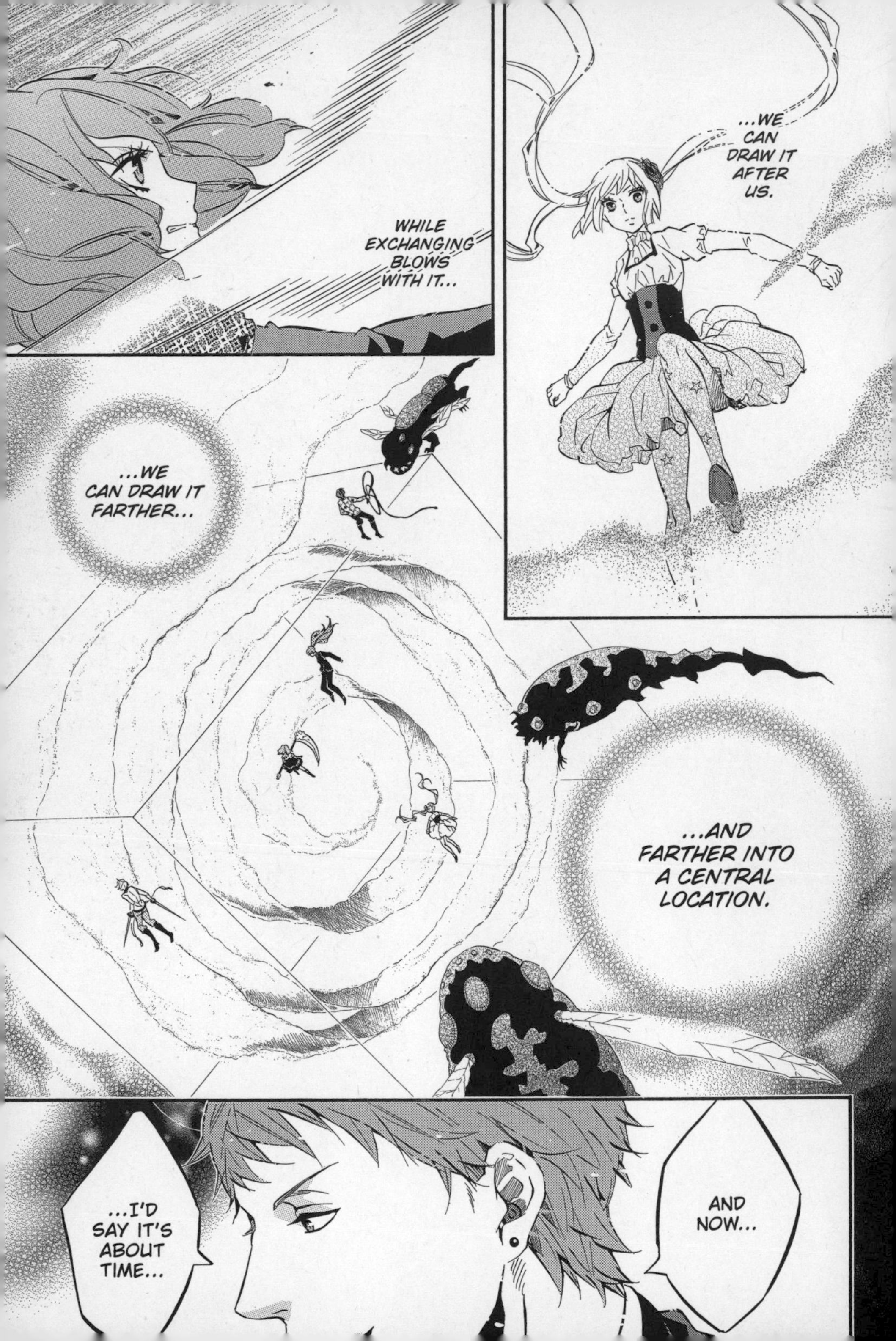
...WE CAN DRAW IT AFTER US.
WHILE EXCHANGING BLOWS WITH IT...
...WE CAN DRAW IT FARTHER...
...AND FARTHER INTO A CENTRAL LOCATION.
AND NOW...
...I'D SAY IT'S ABOUT TIME...

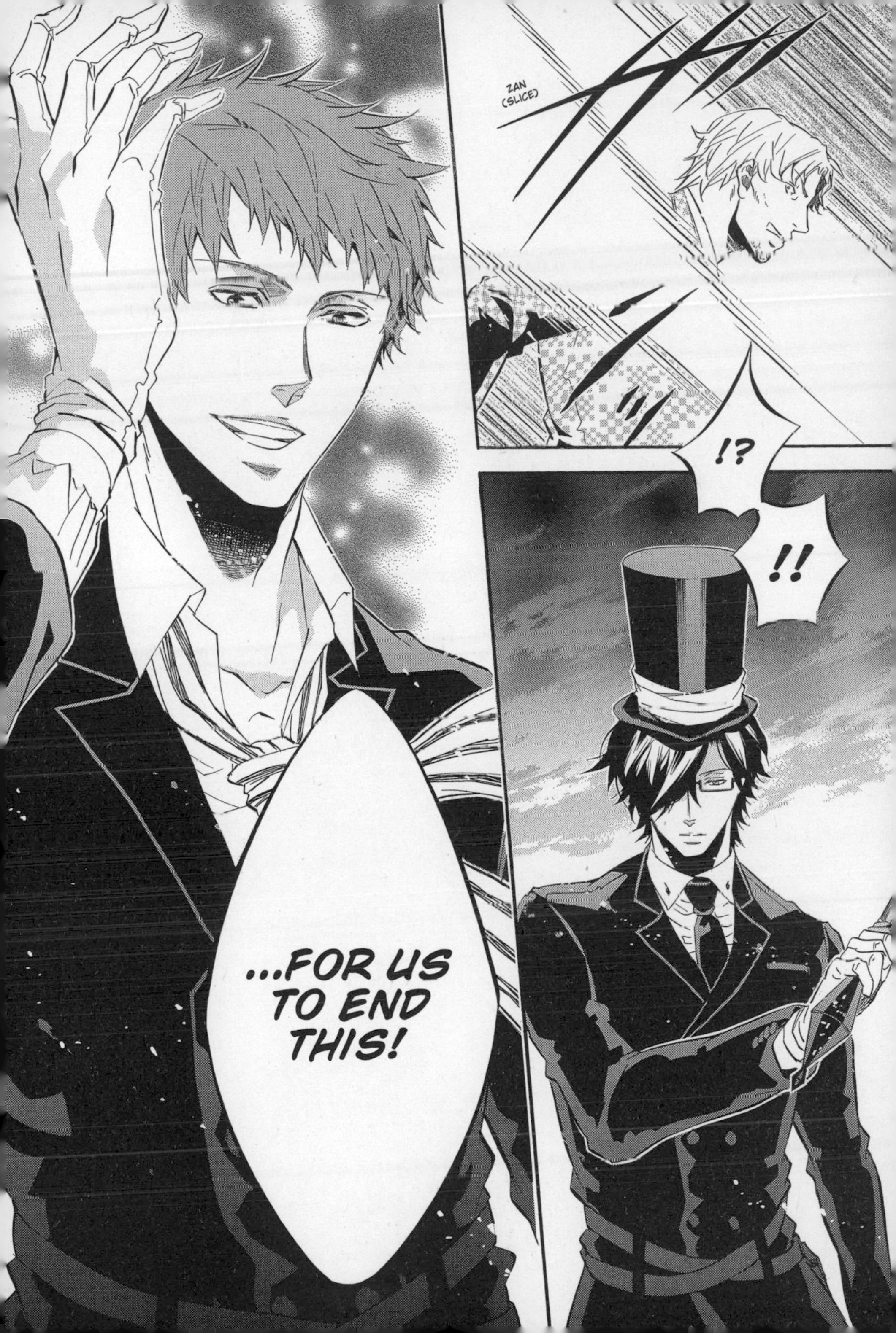
ZAN (SLICE)
!?
!!
...FOR US TO END THIS!

KARNEVAL

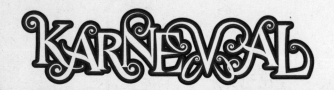

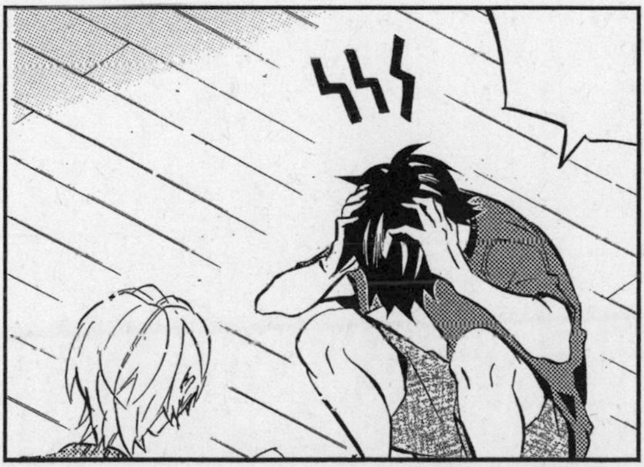

KARNEVAL

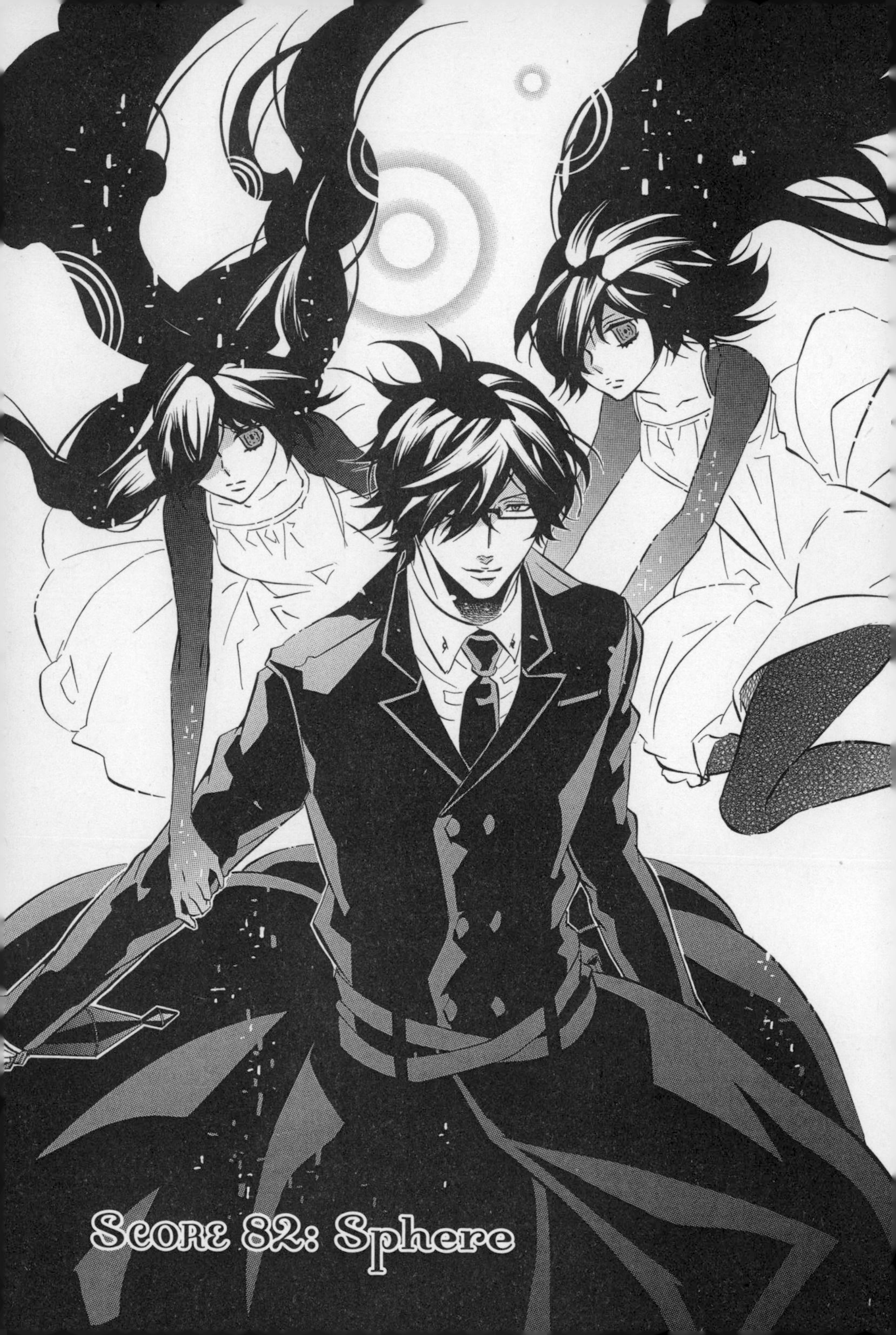
Score 82: Sphere

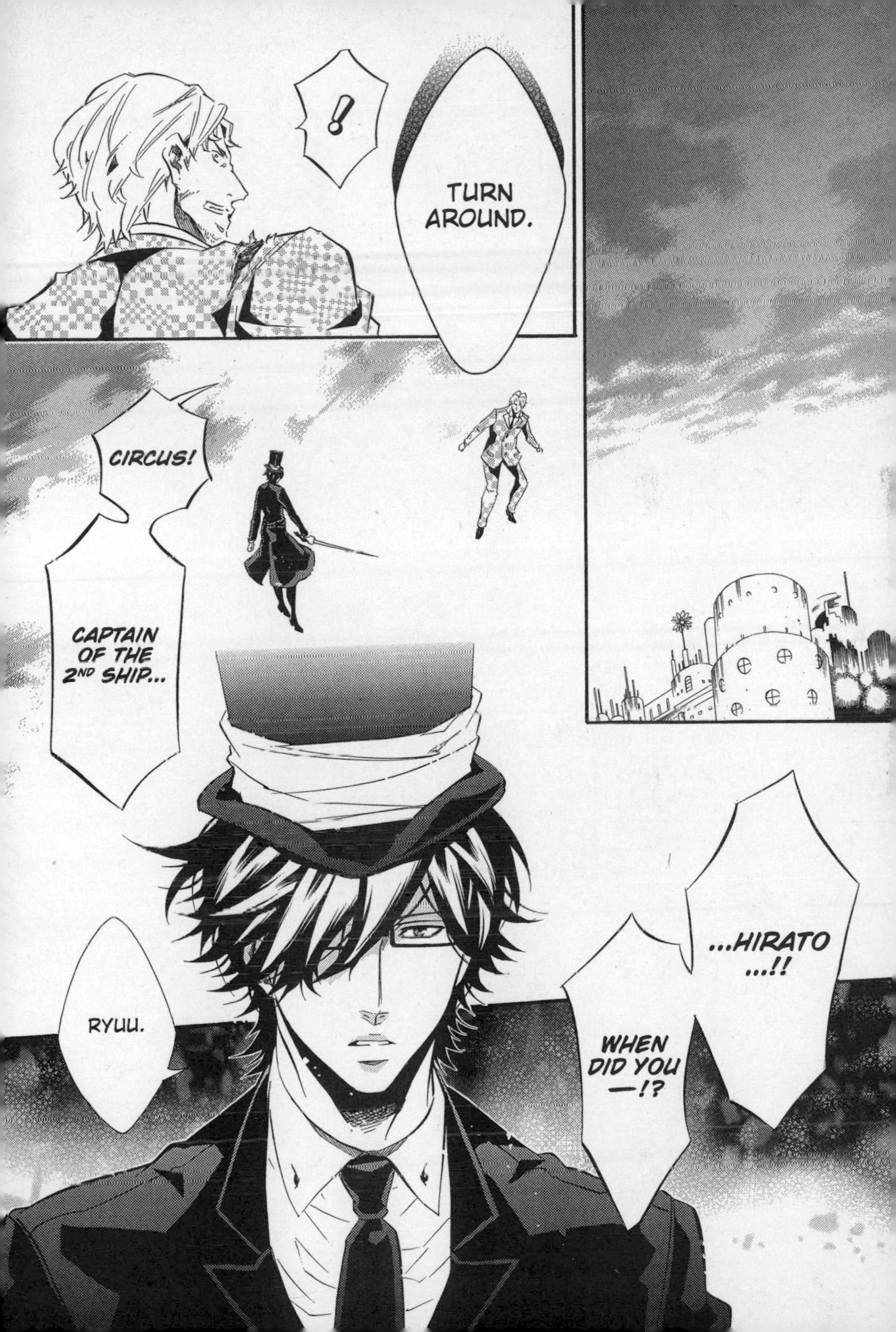
TURN AROUND.
!
CIRCUS!
CAPTAIN OF THE 2ND SHIP...
...HIRATO ...!!
WHEN DID YOU —!?
RYUU.

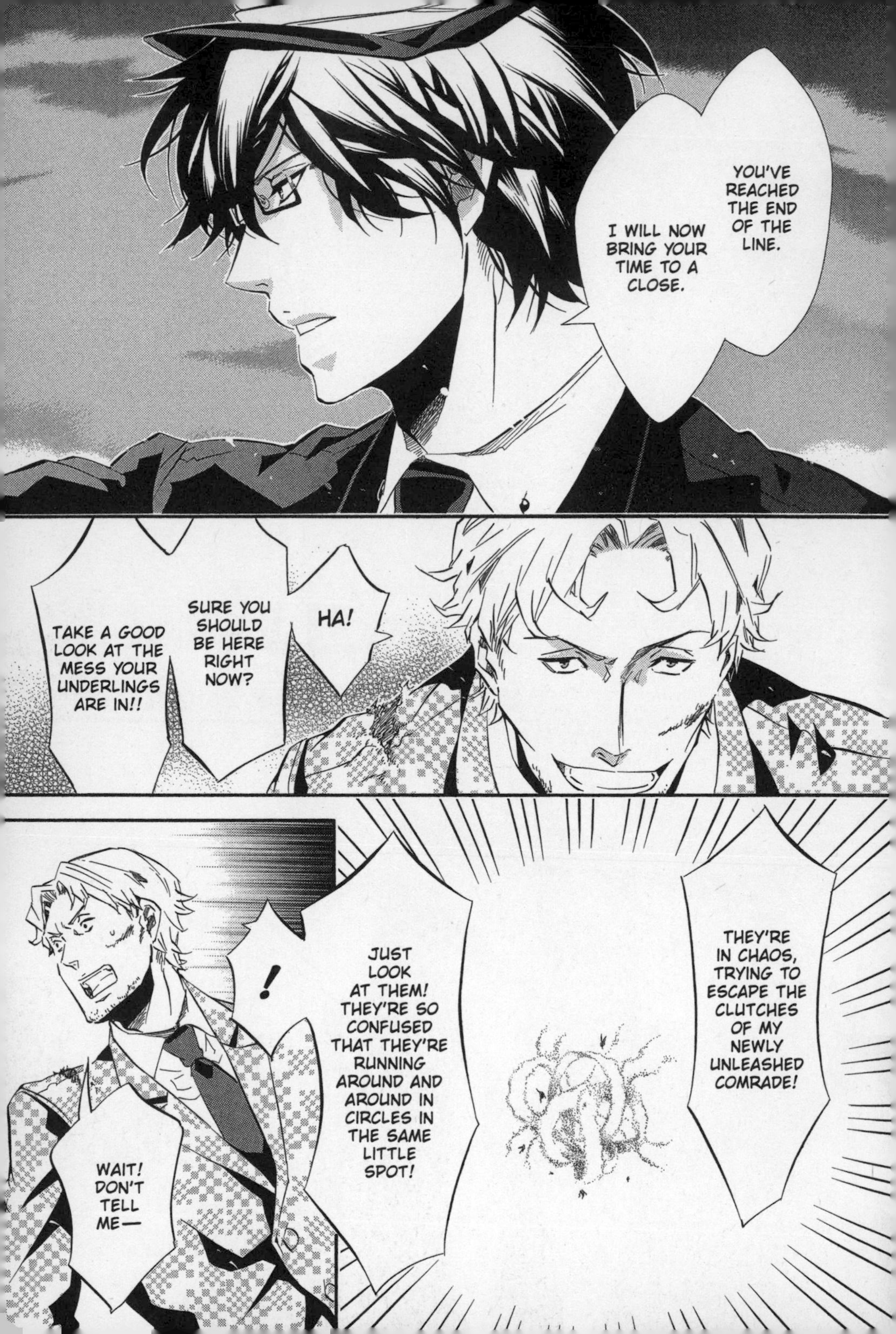
YOU'VE REACHED THE END OF THE LINE.
I WILL NOW BRING YOUR TIME TO A CLOSE.
HA!
SURE YOU SHOULD BE HERE RIGHT NOW?
TAKE A GOOD LOOK AT THE MESS YOUR UNDERLINGS ARE IN!!
THEY'RE IN CHAOS, TRYING TO ESCAPE THE CLUTCHES OF MY NEWLY UNLEASHED COMRADE!
JUST LOOK AT THEM! THEY'RE SO CONFUSED THAT THEY'RE RUNNING AROUND AND AROUND IN CIRCLES IN THE SAME LITTLE SPOT!
!
WAIT! DON'T TELL ME—

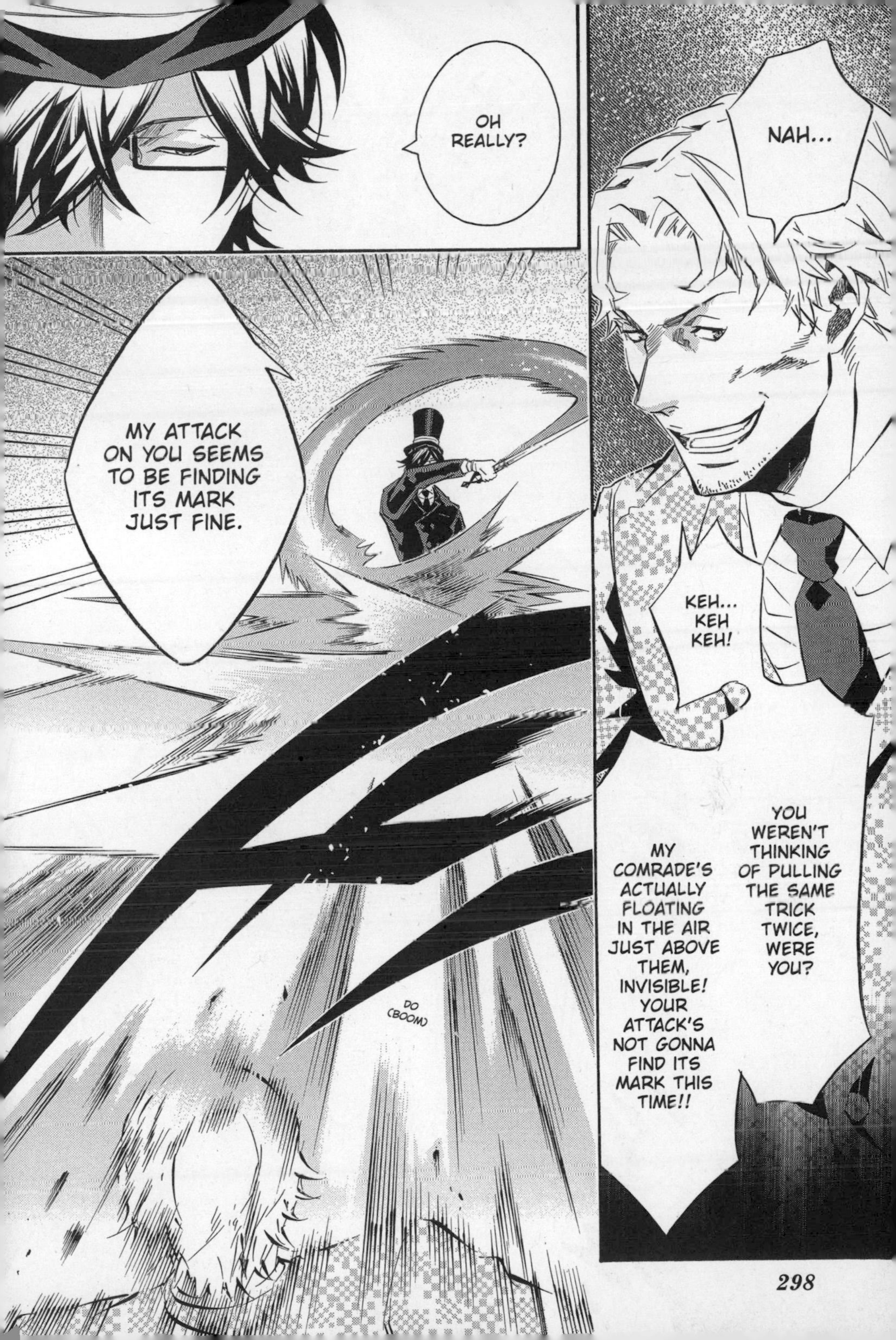
NAH...
KEH... KEH KEH!
YOU WEREN'T THINKING OF PULLING THE SAME TRICK TWICE, WERE YOU?
MY COMRADE'S ACTUALLY FLOATING IN THE AIR JUST ABOVE THEM, INVISIBLE! YOUR ATTACK'S NOT GONNA FIND ITS MARK THIS TIME!!
OH REALLY?
MY ATTACK ON YOU SEEMS TO BE FINDING ITS MARK JUST FINE.
DO (BOOM)

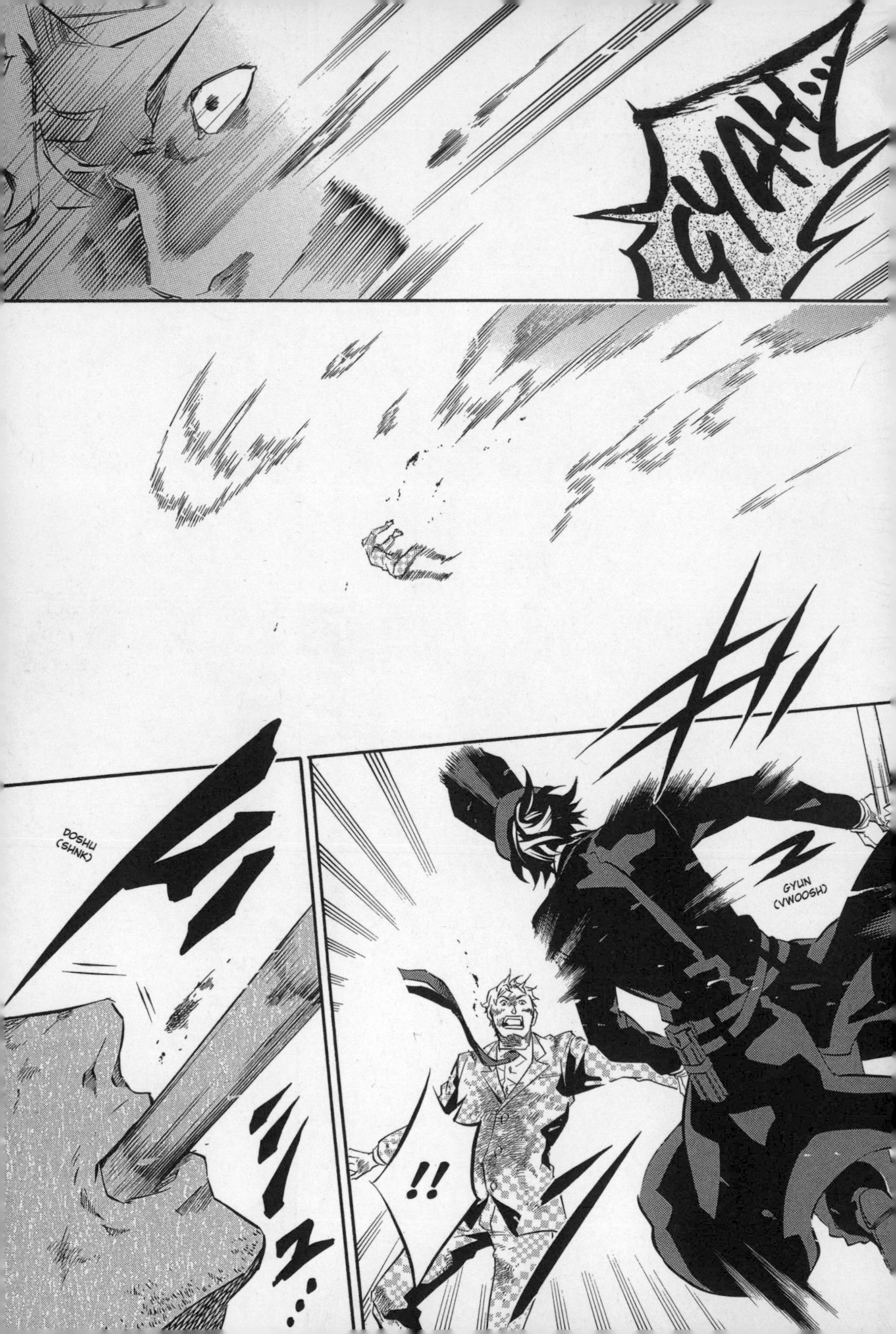
GYAH...
GYUN
(VWOOSH)
!!
DOSHU
(SHNK)

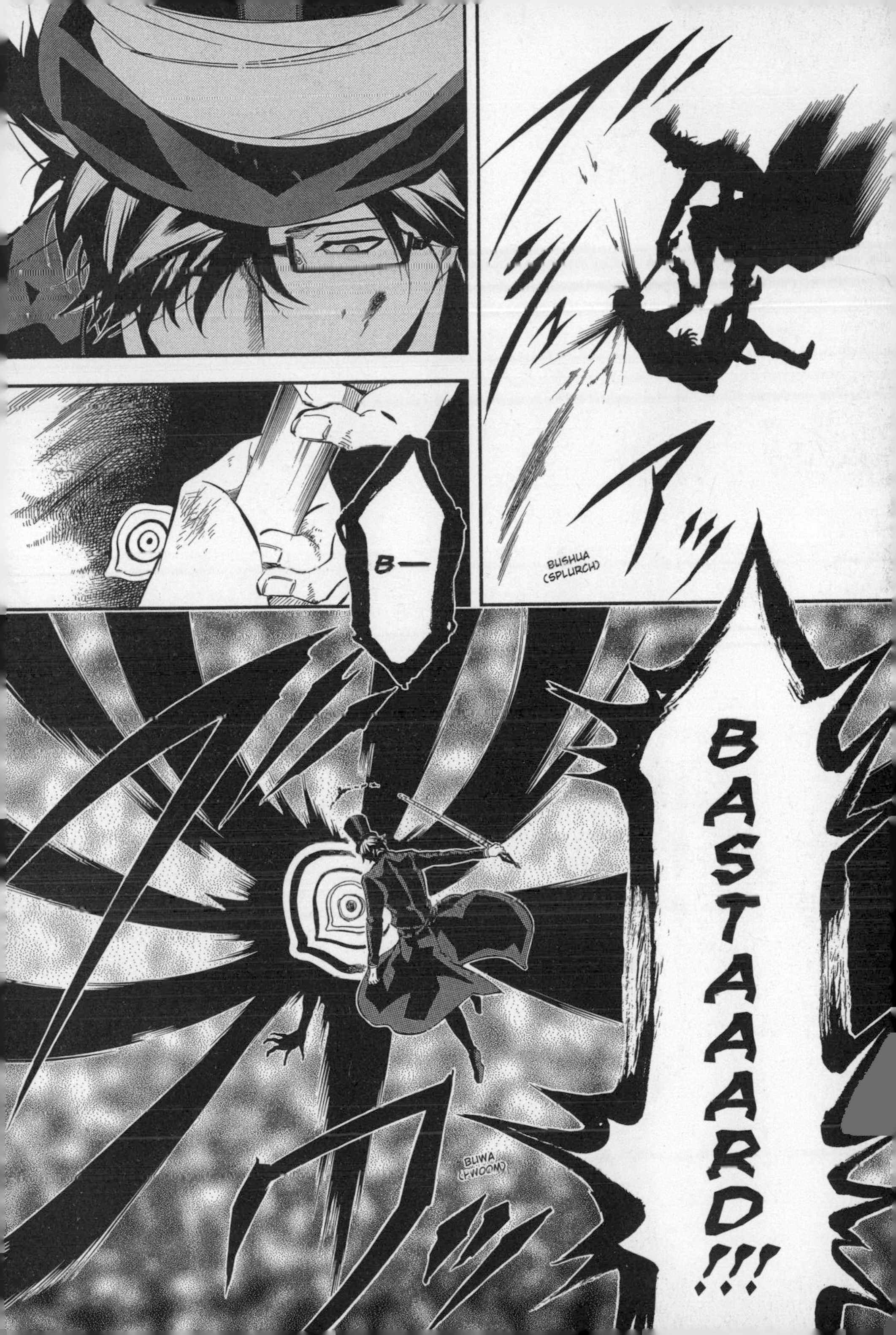
BUSHUA (SPLURCH)
B—
BASTAARD!!!
BUWA (FWOOM)

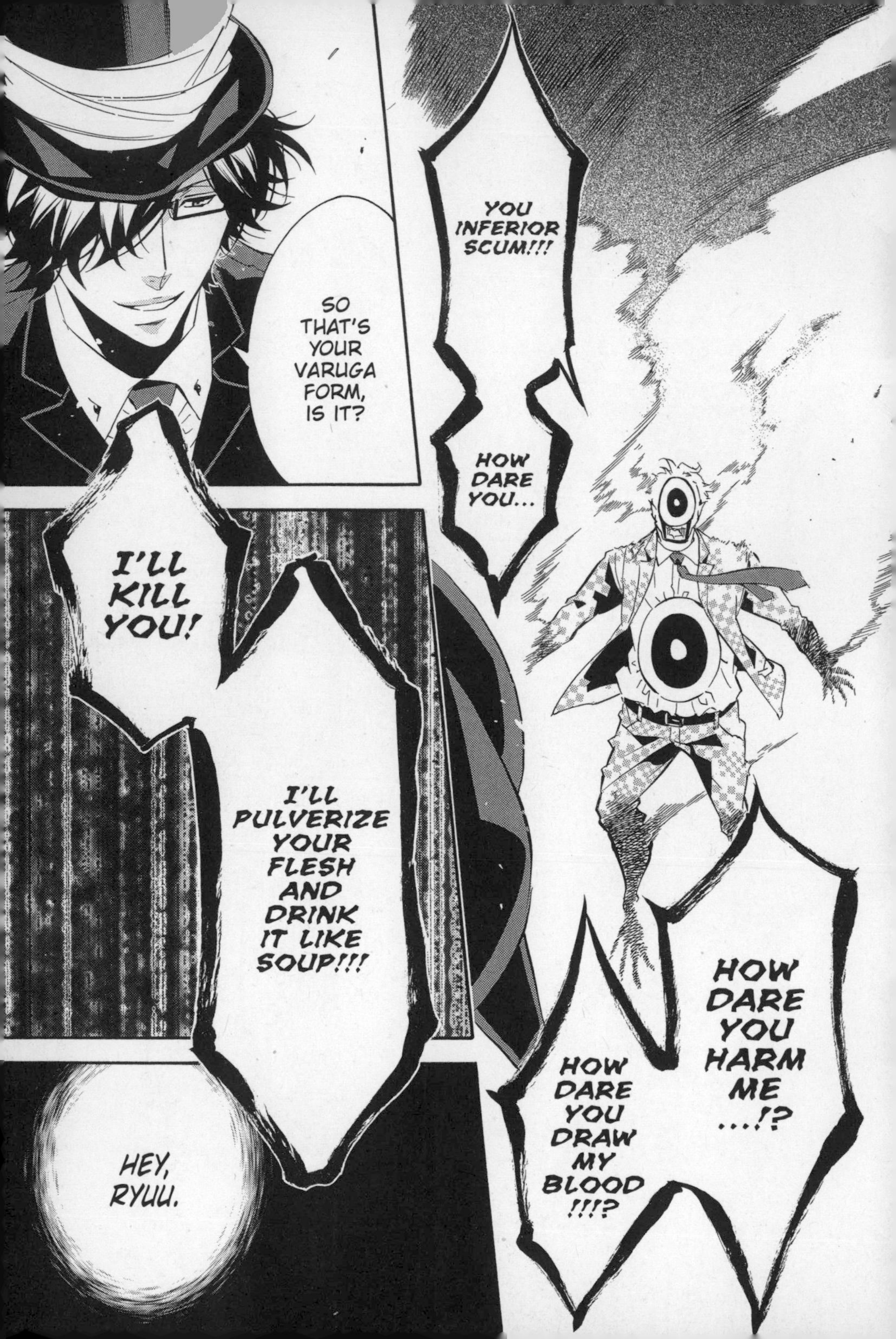
YOU INFERIOR SCUM!!!
HOW DARE YOU...
HOW DARE YOU HARM ME ...!?
HOW DARE YOU DRAW MY BLOOD !!!?
SO THAT'S YOUR VARUGA FORM, IS IT?
I'LL KILL YOU!
I'LL PULVERIZE YOUR FLESH AND DRINK IT LIKE SOUP!!!
HEY, RYUU.

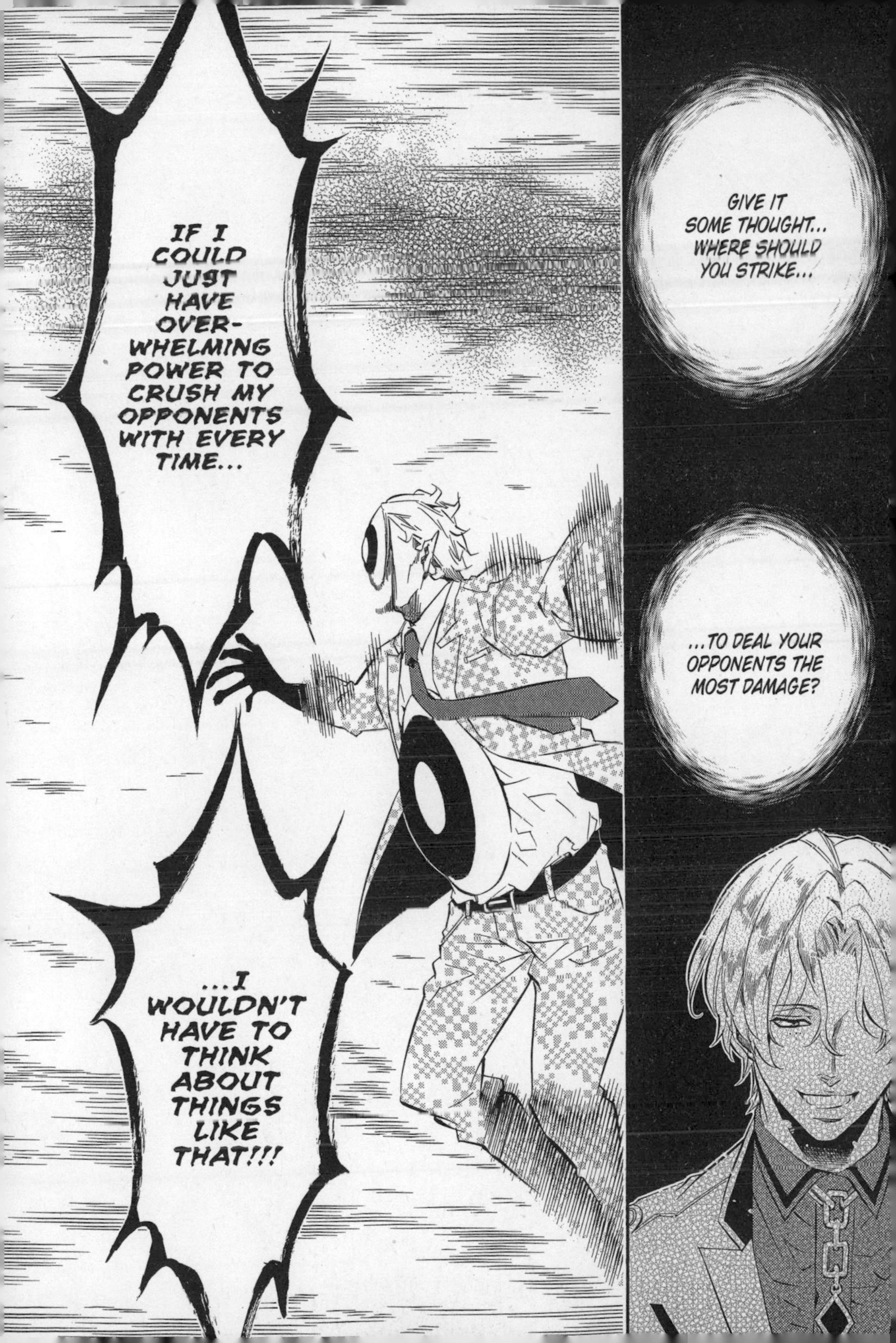
GIVE IT SOME THOUGHT... WHERE SHOULD YOU STRIKE...
...TO DEAL YOUR OPPONENTS THE MOST DAMAGE?
IF I COULD JUST HAVE OVER-WHELMING POWER TO CRUSH MY OPPONENTS WITH EVERY TIME...
...I WOULDN'T HAVE TO THINK ABOUT THINGS LIKE THAT!!!

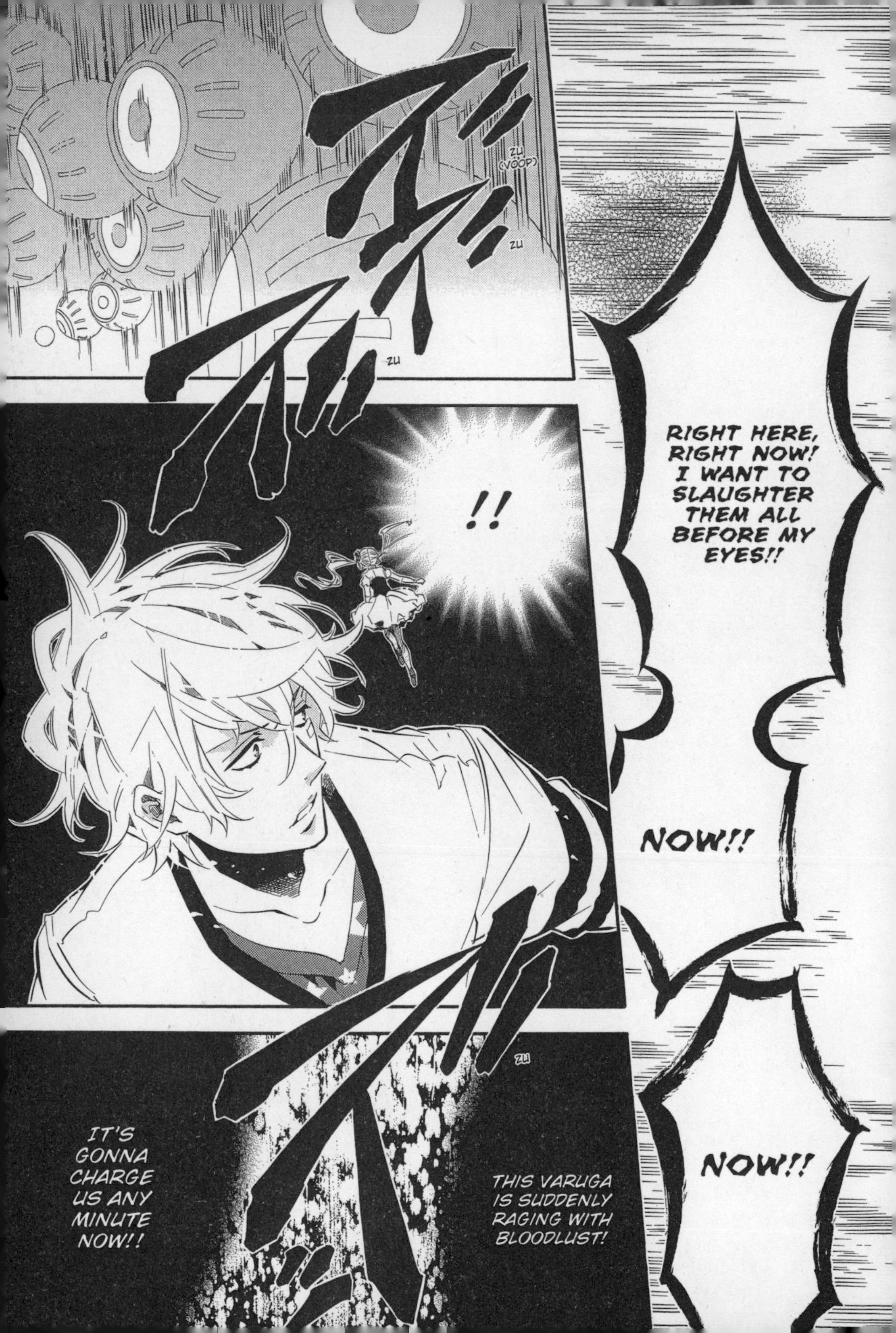
RIGHT HERE, RIGHT NOW! I WANT TO SLAUGHTER THEM ALL BEFORE MY EYES!!
NOW!!
NOW!!
ZU (VOOP)
ZU
ZU
!!
ZU
THIS VARUGA IS SUDDENLY RAGING WITH BLOODLUST!
IT'S GONNA CHARGE US ANY MINUTE NOW!!

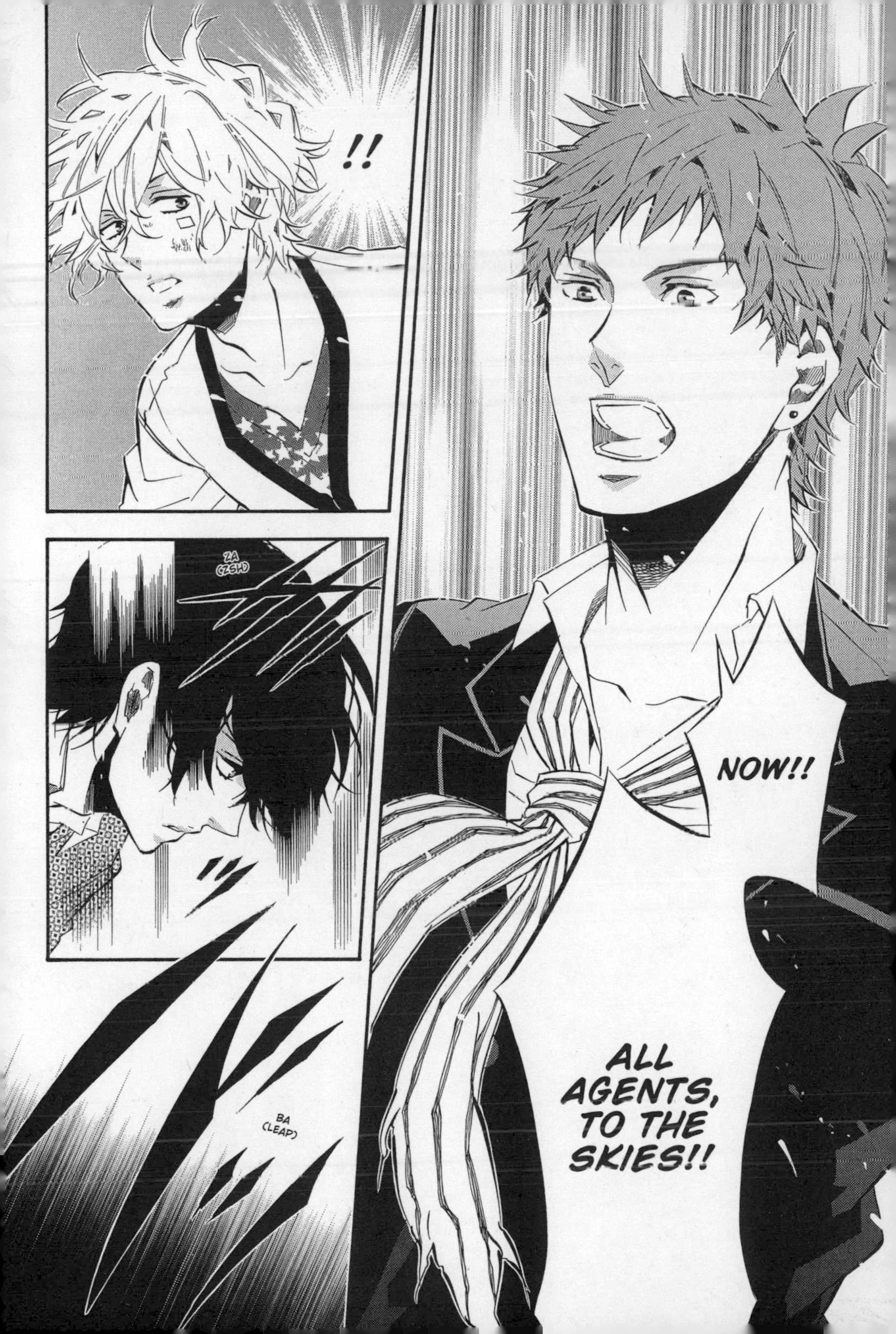
NOW!!
ALL AGENTS, TO THE SKIES!!
BA (LEAP)
!!
ZA (ZSHD)

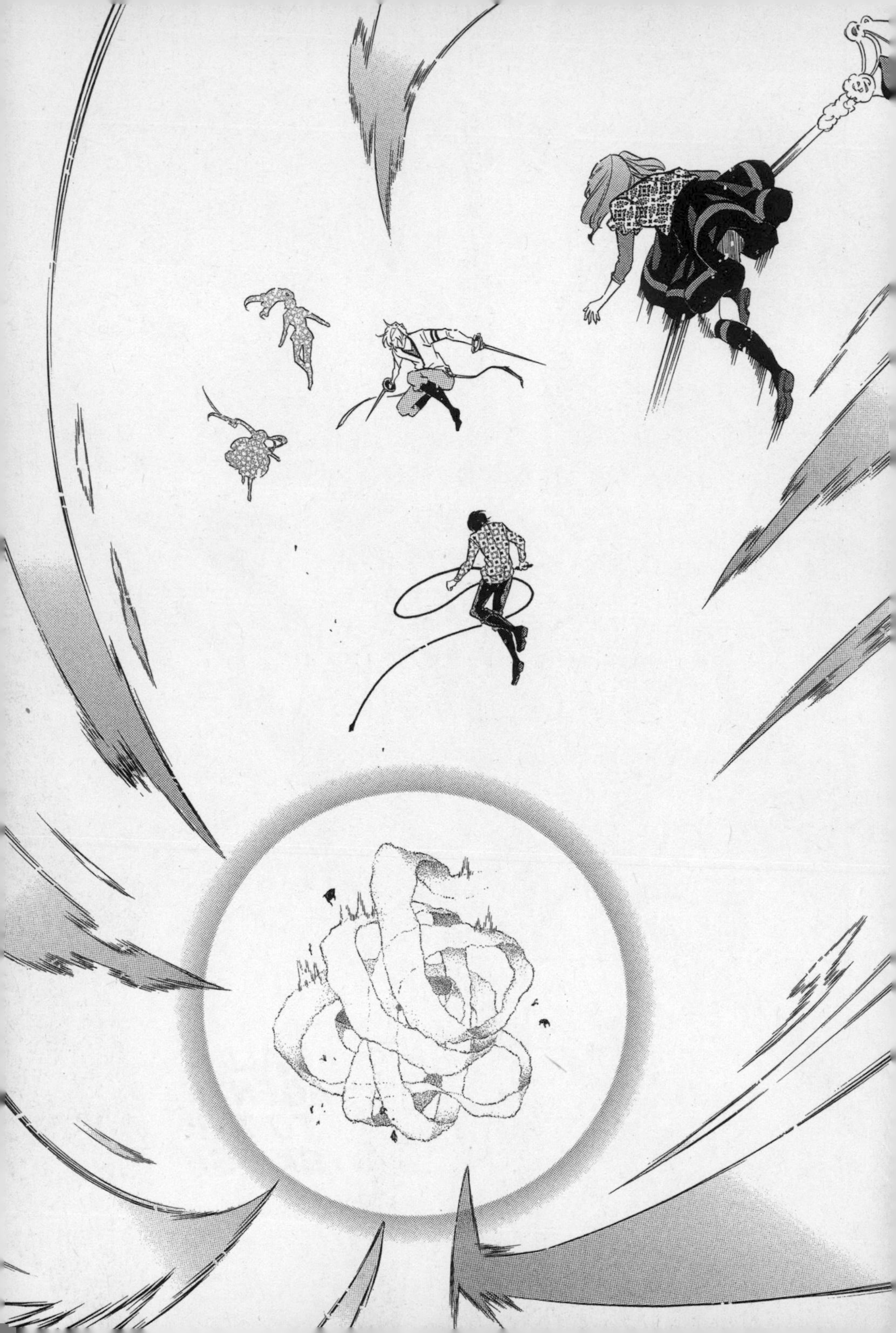

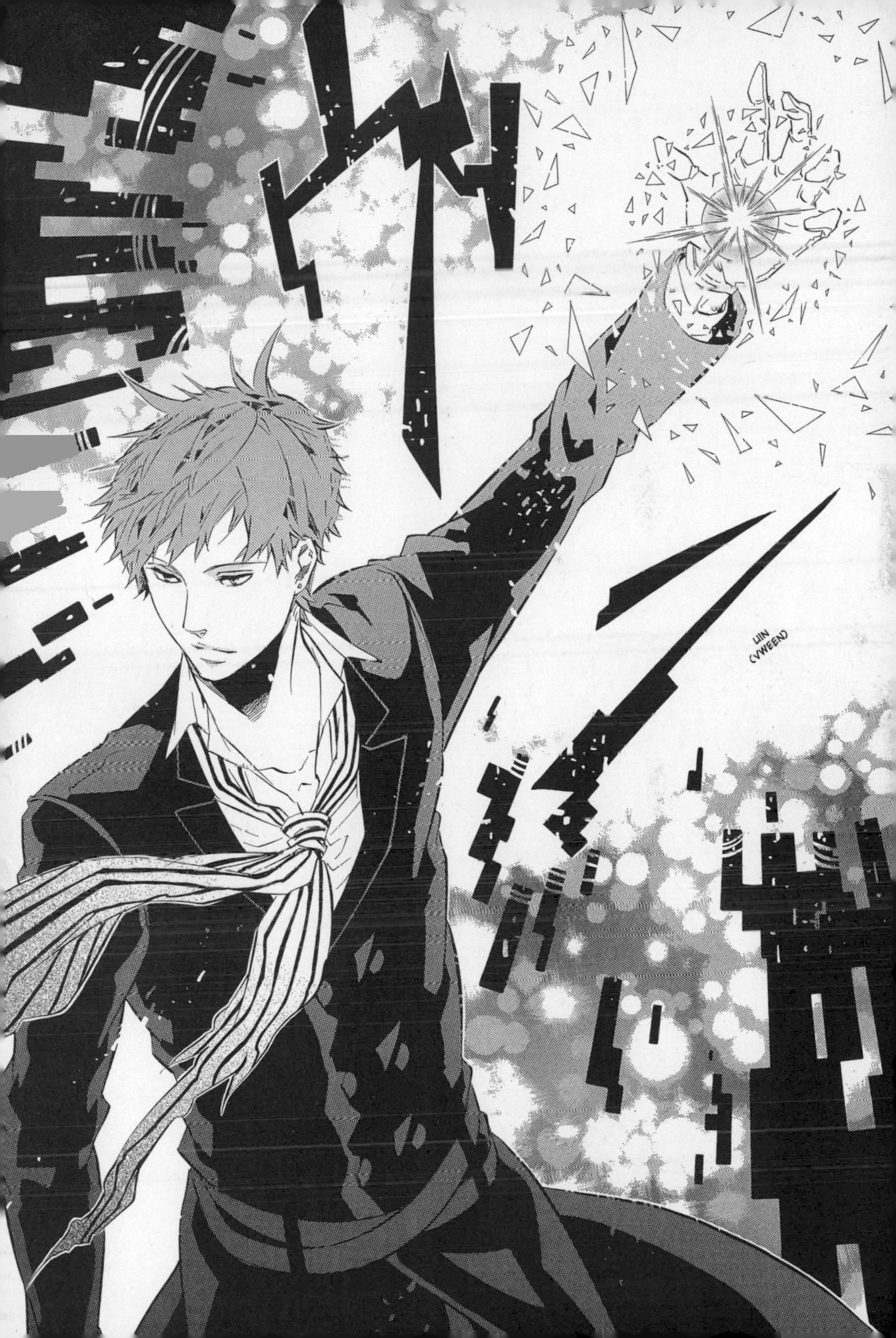
UIN (VWEEN)

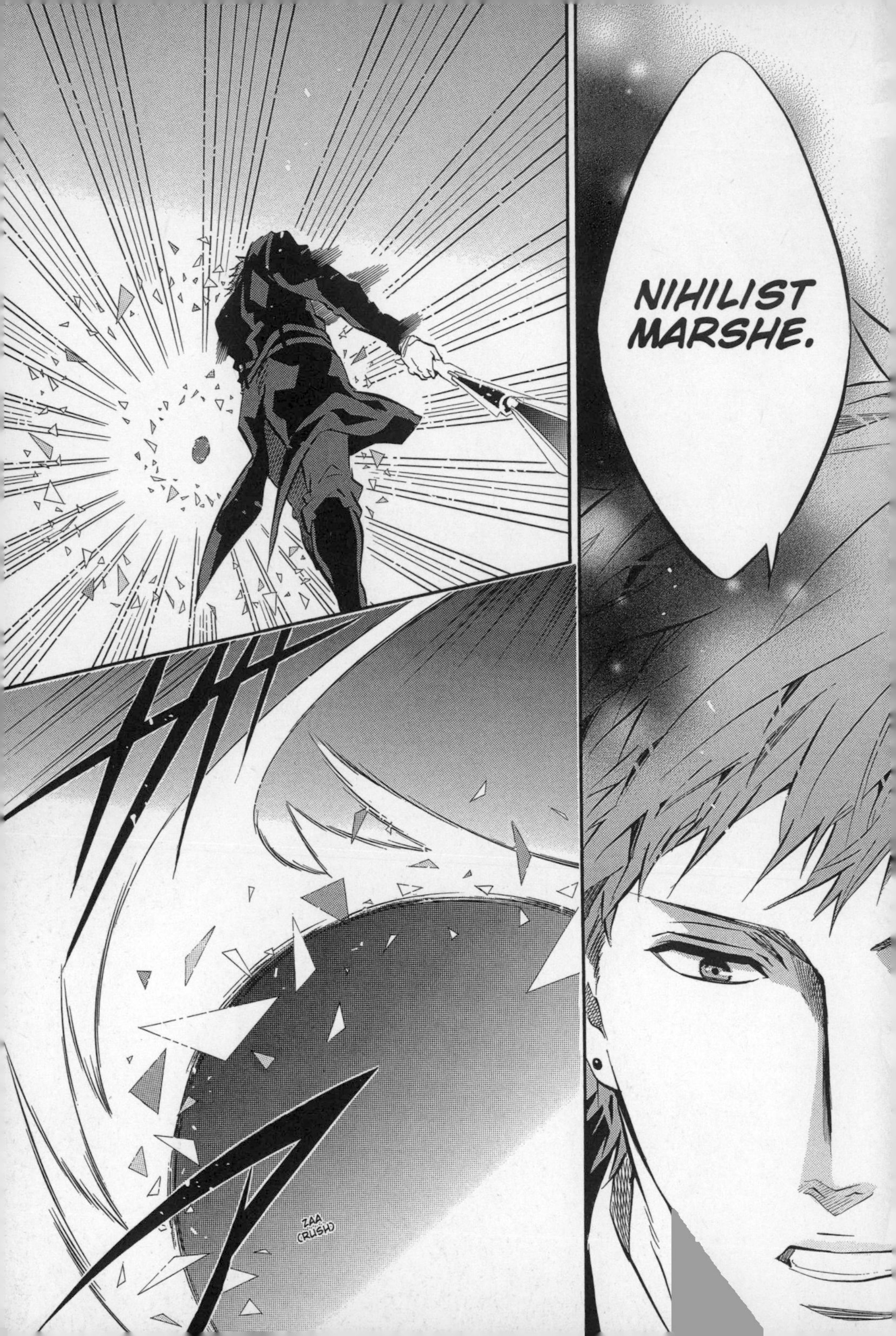
NIHILIST MARSHE.
ZAA
(RUSH)

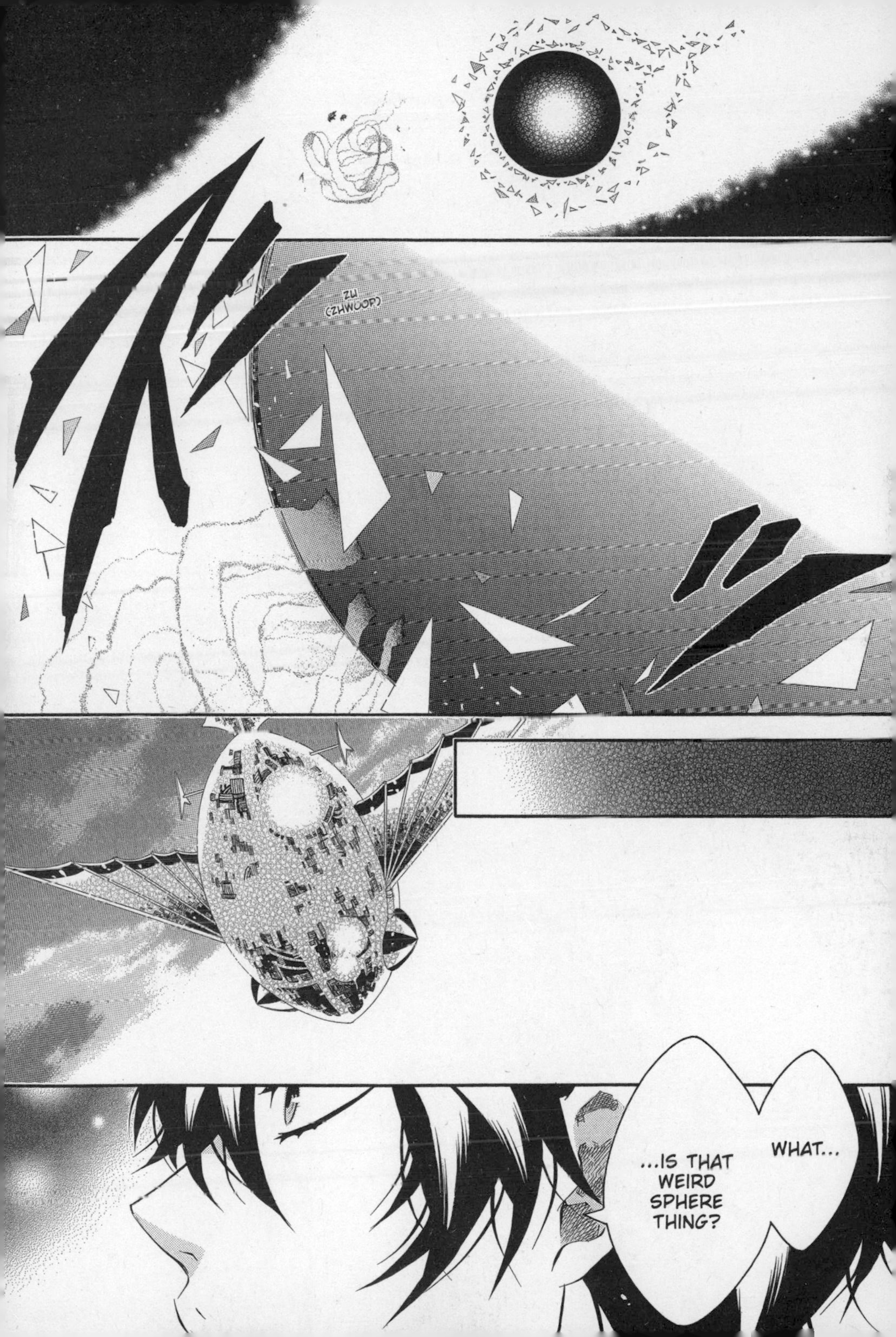
ZU (ZHWOOP)
WHAT...
...IS THAT WEIRD SPHERE THING?

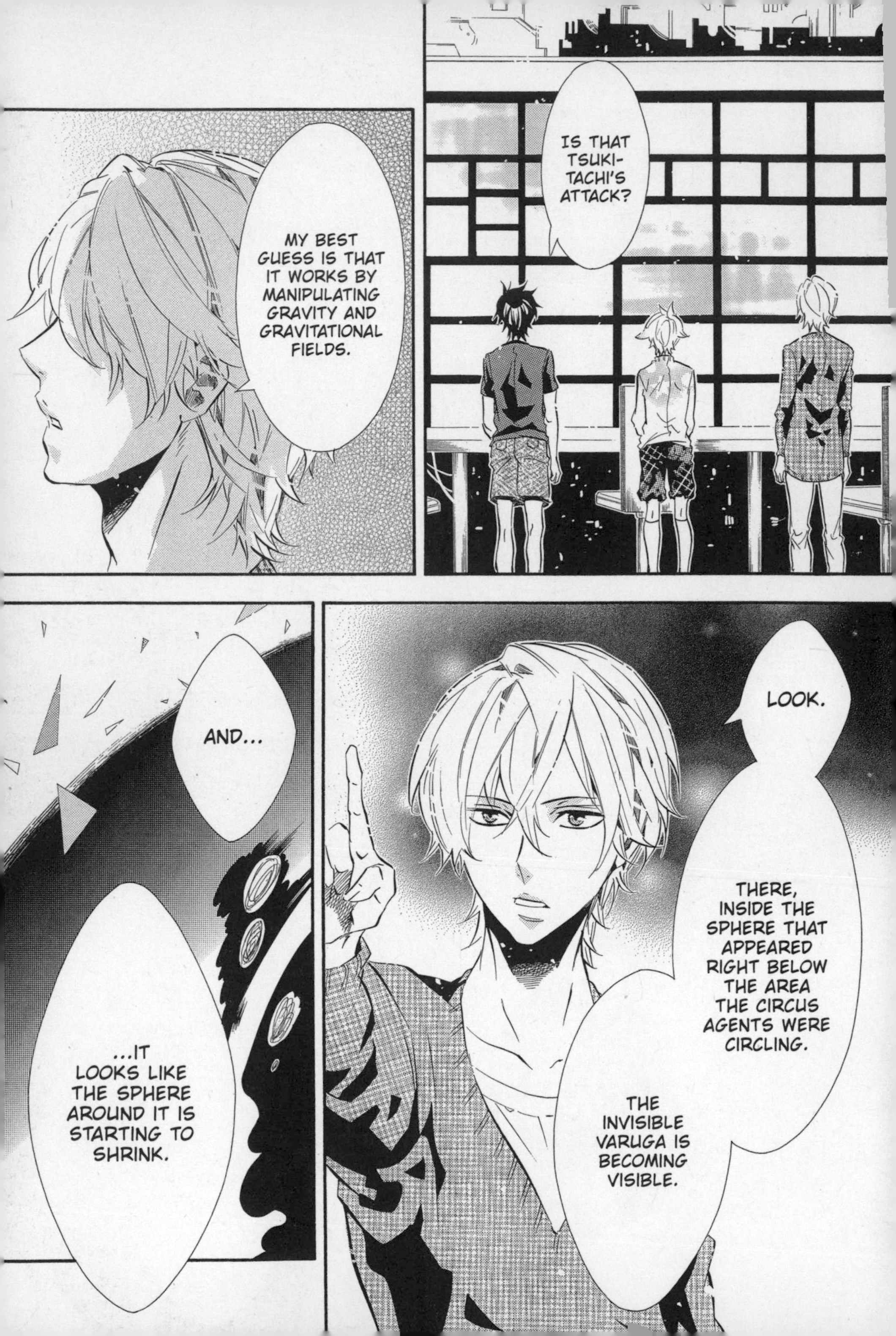
IS THAT TSUKI-TACHI'S ATTACK?
MY BEST GUESS IS THAT IT WORKS BY MANIPULATING GRAVITY AND GRAVITATIONAL FIELDS.
LOOK.
THERE, INSIDE THE SPHERE THAT APPEARED RIGHT BELOW THE AREA THE CIRCUS AGENTS WERE CIRCLING.
THE INVISIBLE VARUGA IS BECOMING VISIBLE.
AND...
...IT LOOKS LIKE THE SPHERE AROUND IT IS STARTING TO SHRINK.

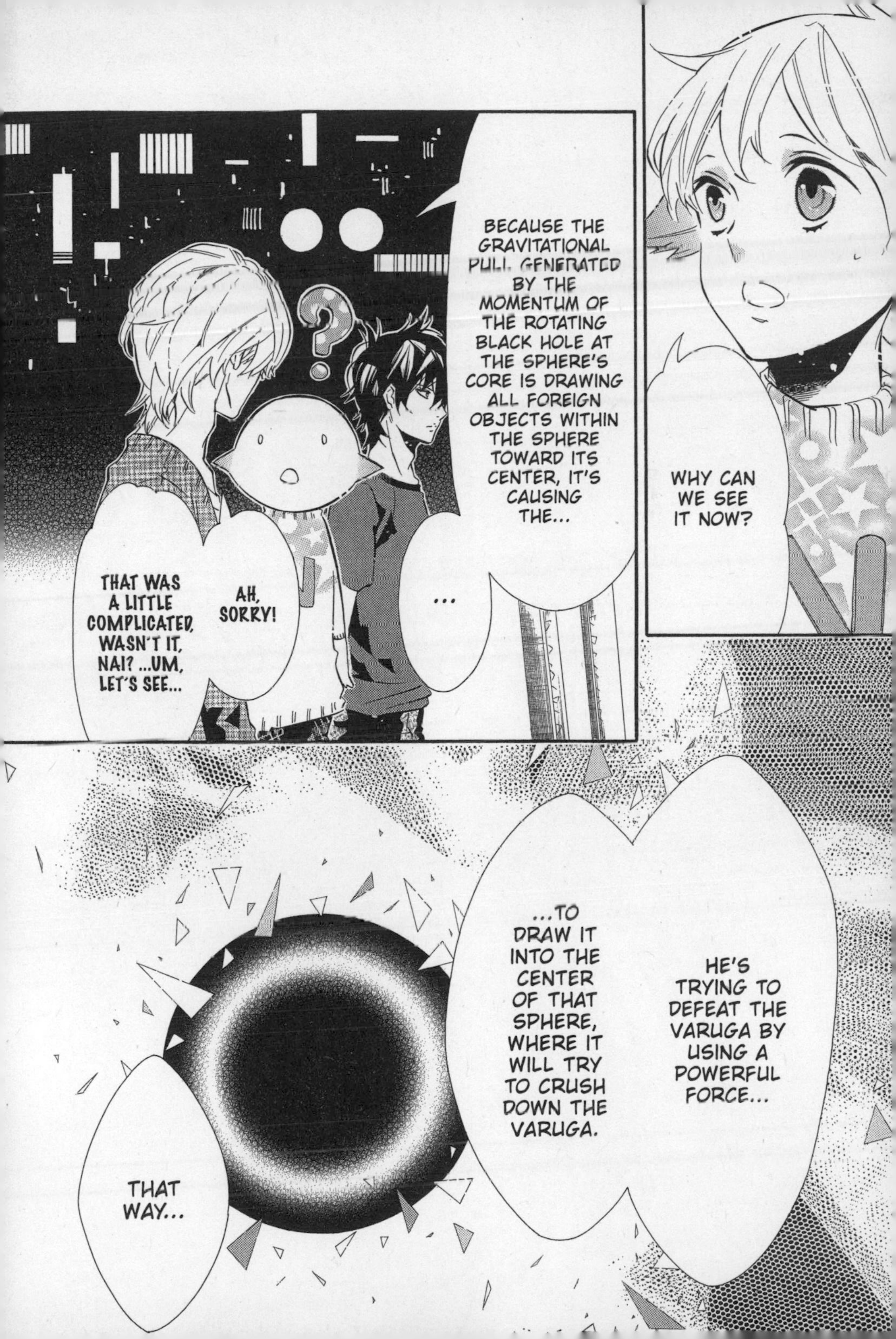
WHY CAN WE SEE IT NOW?
BECAUSE THE GRAVITATIONAL PULL GENERATED BY THE MOMENTUM OF THE ROTATING BLACK HOLE AT THE SPHERE'S CORE IS DRAWING ALL FOREIGN OBJECTS WITHIN THE SPHERE TOWARD ITS CENTER, IT'S CAUSING THE...
...
AH, SORRY!
THAT WAS A LITTLE COMPLICATED, WASN'T IT, NAI? ...UM, LET'S SEE...
HE'S TRYING TO DEFEAT THE VARUGA BY USING A POWERFUL FORCE...
...TO DRAW IT INTO THE CENTER OF THAT SPHERE, WHERE IT WILL TRY TO CRUSH DOWN THE VARUGA.
THAT WAY...

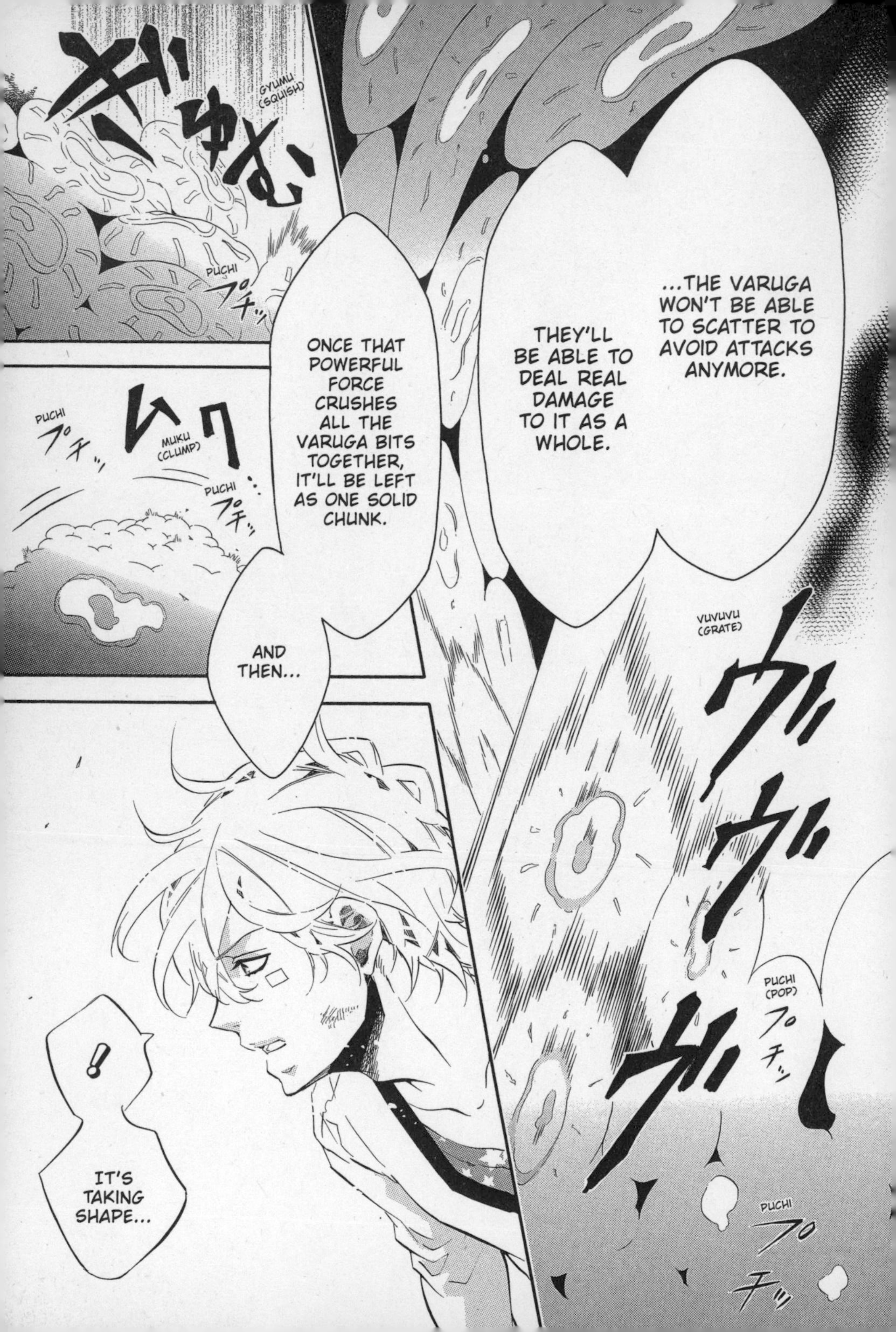
GYUMU (SQUISH)
PUCHI
PUCHI
MUKU (CLUMP)
PUCHI
ONCE THAT POWERFUL FORCE CRUSHES ALL THE VARUGA BITS TOGETHER, IT'LL BE LEFT AS ONE SOLID CHUNK.
AND THEN...
...THE VARUGA WON'T BE ABLE TO SCATTER TO AVOID ATTACKS ANYMORE.
THEY'LL BE ABLE TO DEAL REAL DAMAGE TO IT AS A WHOLE.
VUVUVU (GRATE)
PUCHI (POP)
PUCHI
!
IT'S TAKING SHAPE...

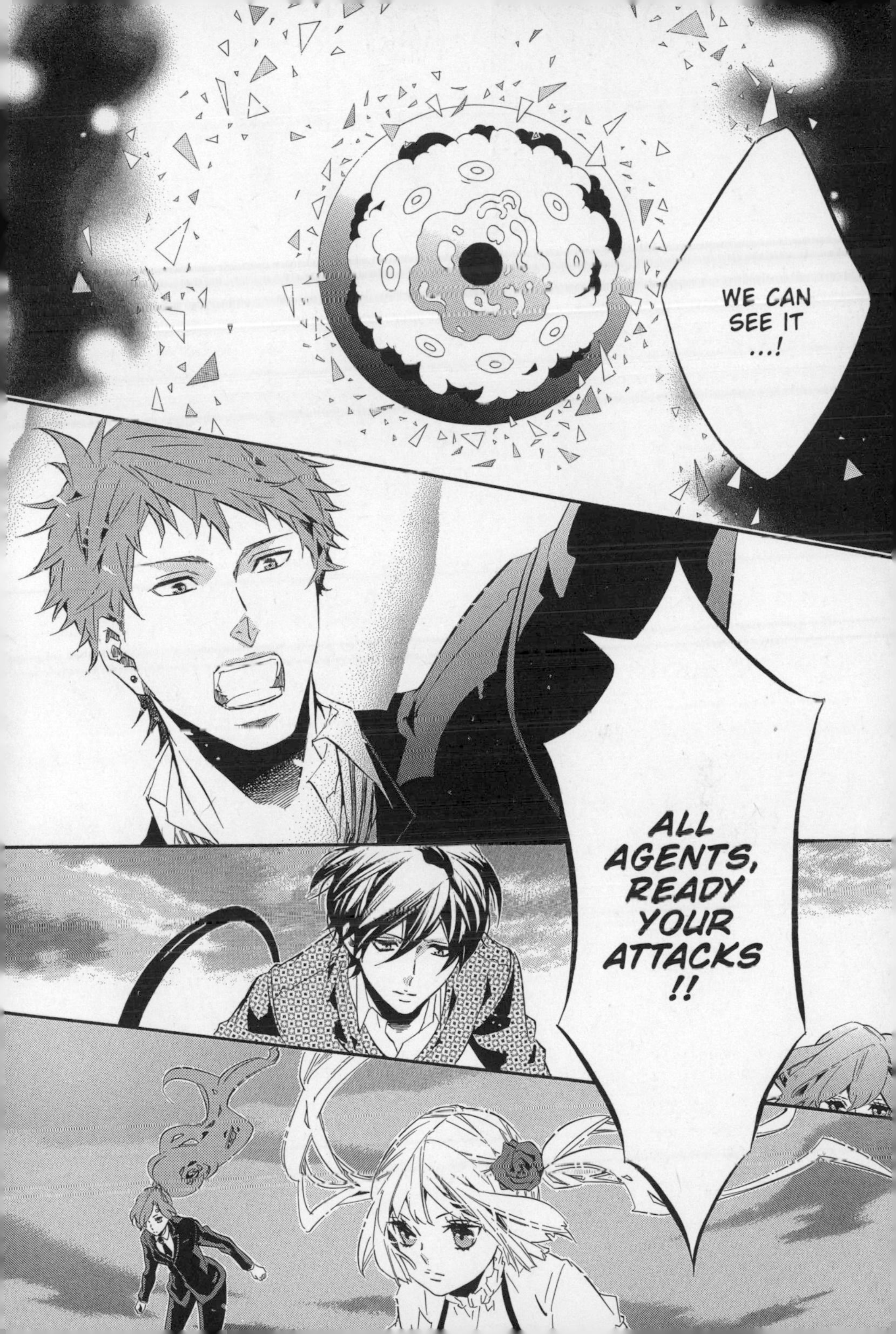
WE CAN SEE IT ...!
ALL AGENTS, READY YOUR ATTACKS !!

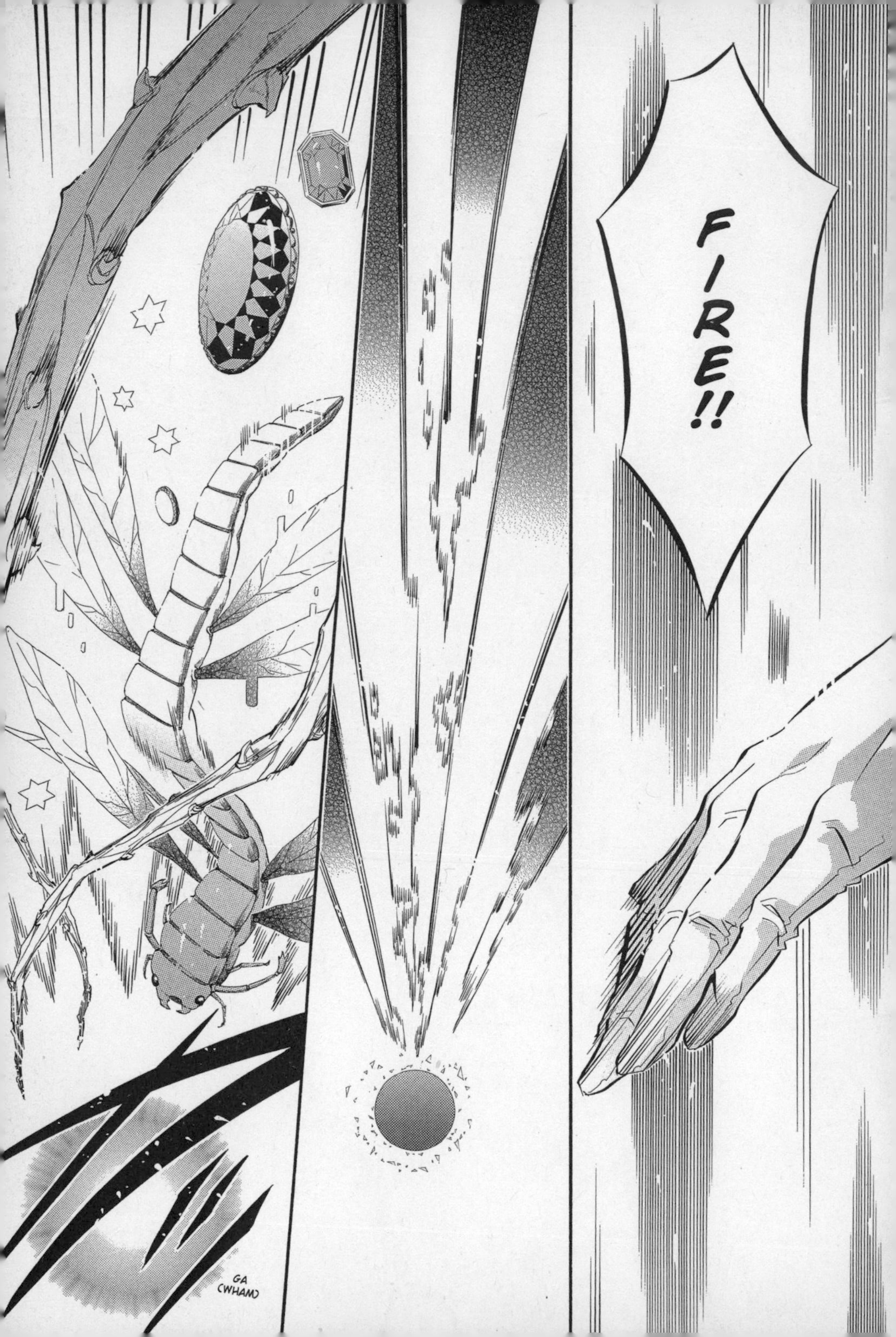
FIRE!!
GA
(WHAM)

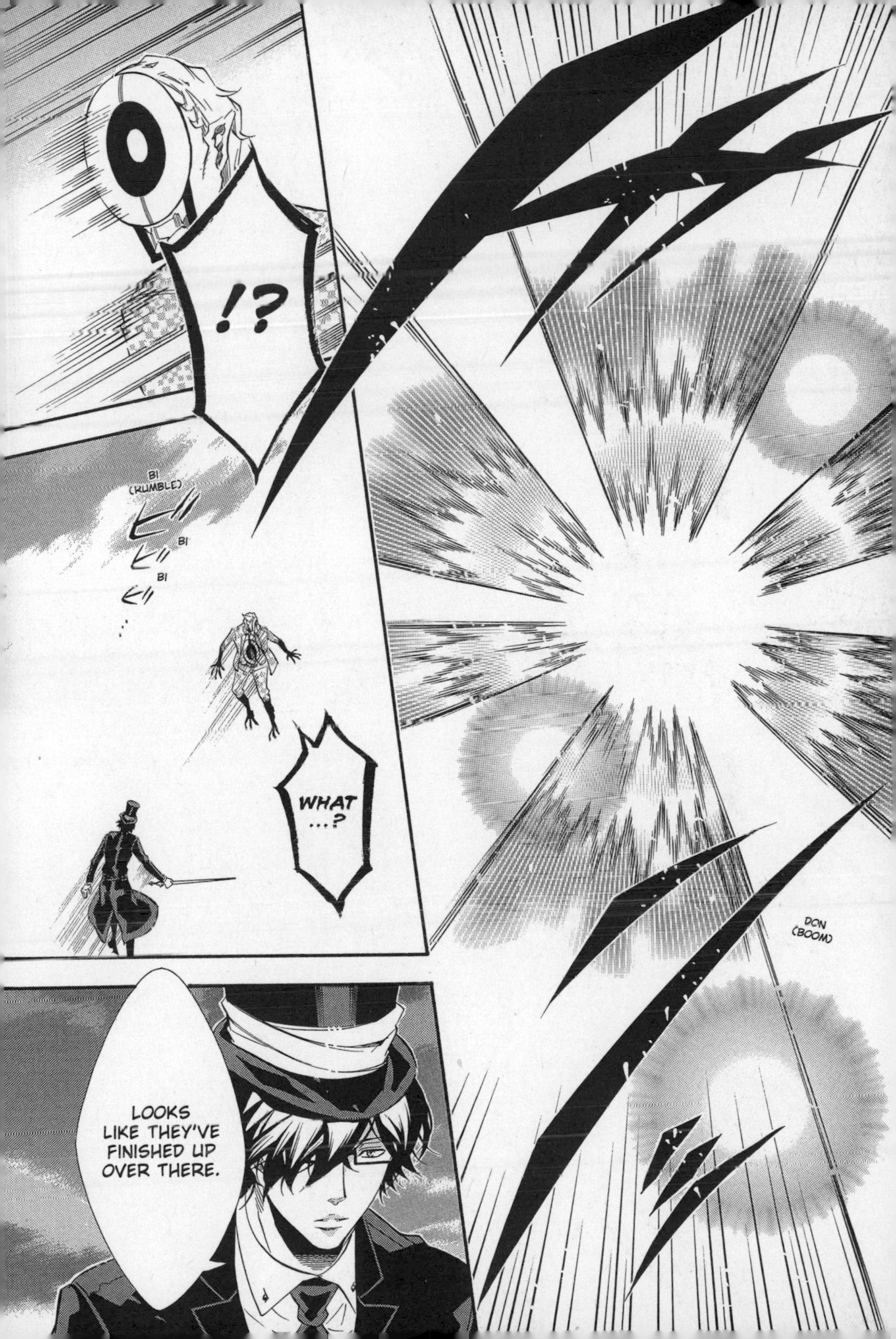
DON (BOOM)
!?
BI (RUMBLE)
BI
BI
WHAT ...?
LOOKS LIKE THEY'VE FINISHED UP OVER THERE.

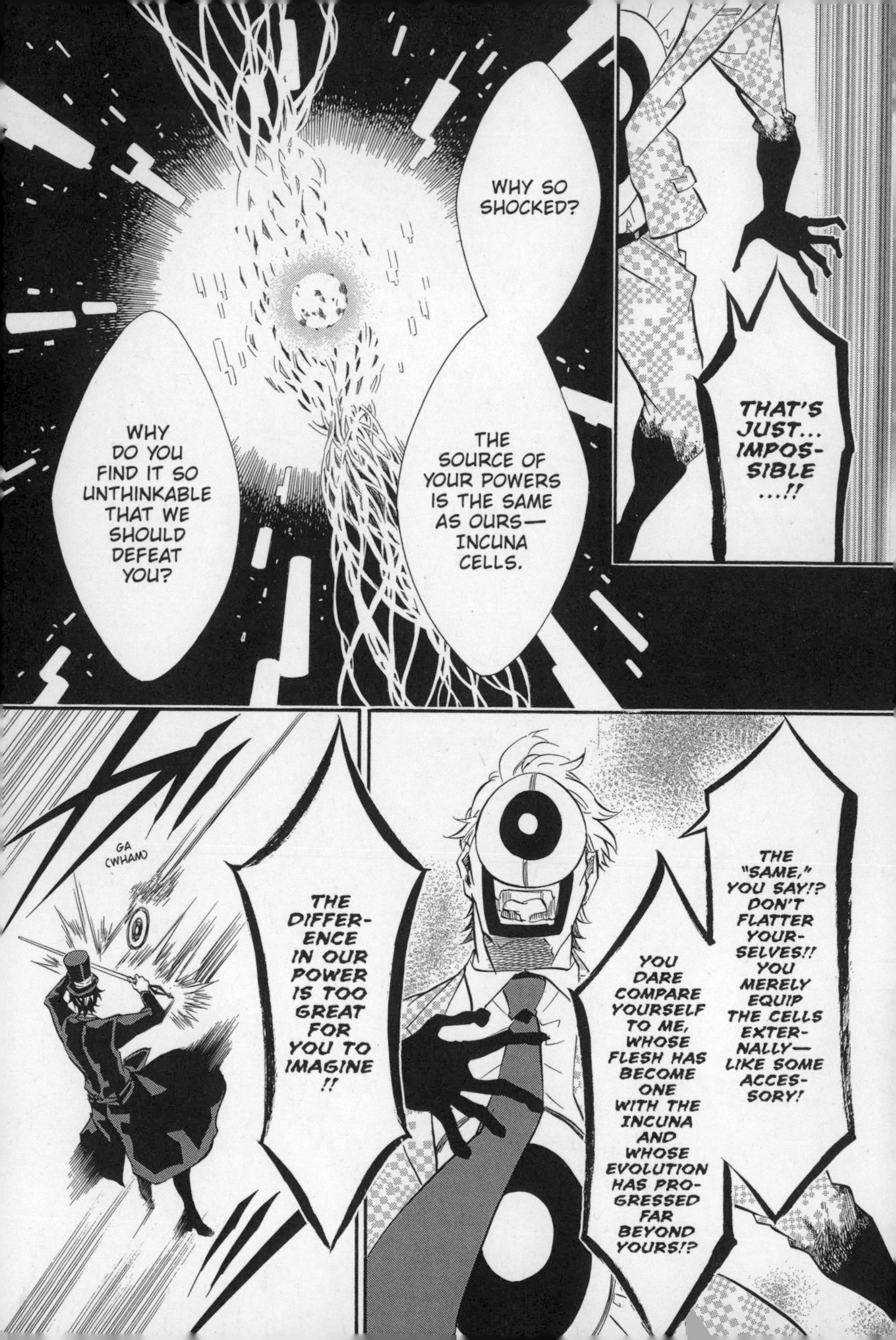
THAT'S JUST... IMPOSSIBLE ...!!
WHY SO SHOCKED?
THE SOURCE OF YOUR POWERS IS THE SAME AS OURS— INCUNA CELLS.
WHY DO YOU FIND IT SO UNTHINKABLE THAT WE SHOULD DEFEAT YOU?
THE "SAME," YOU SAY!? DON'T FLATTER YOURSELVES!! YOU MERELY EQUIP THE CELLS EXTERNALLY— LIKE SOME ACCESSORY!
YOU DARE COMPARE YOURSELF TO ME, WHOSE FLESH HAS BECOME ONE WITH THE INCUNA AND WHOSE EVOLUTION HAS PROGRESSED FAR BEYOND YOURS!?
THE DIFFERENCE IN OUR POWER IS TOO GREAT FOR YOU TO IMAGINE!!
GA (WHAM)

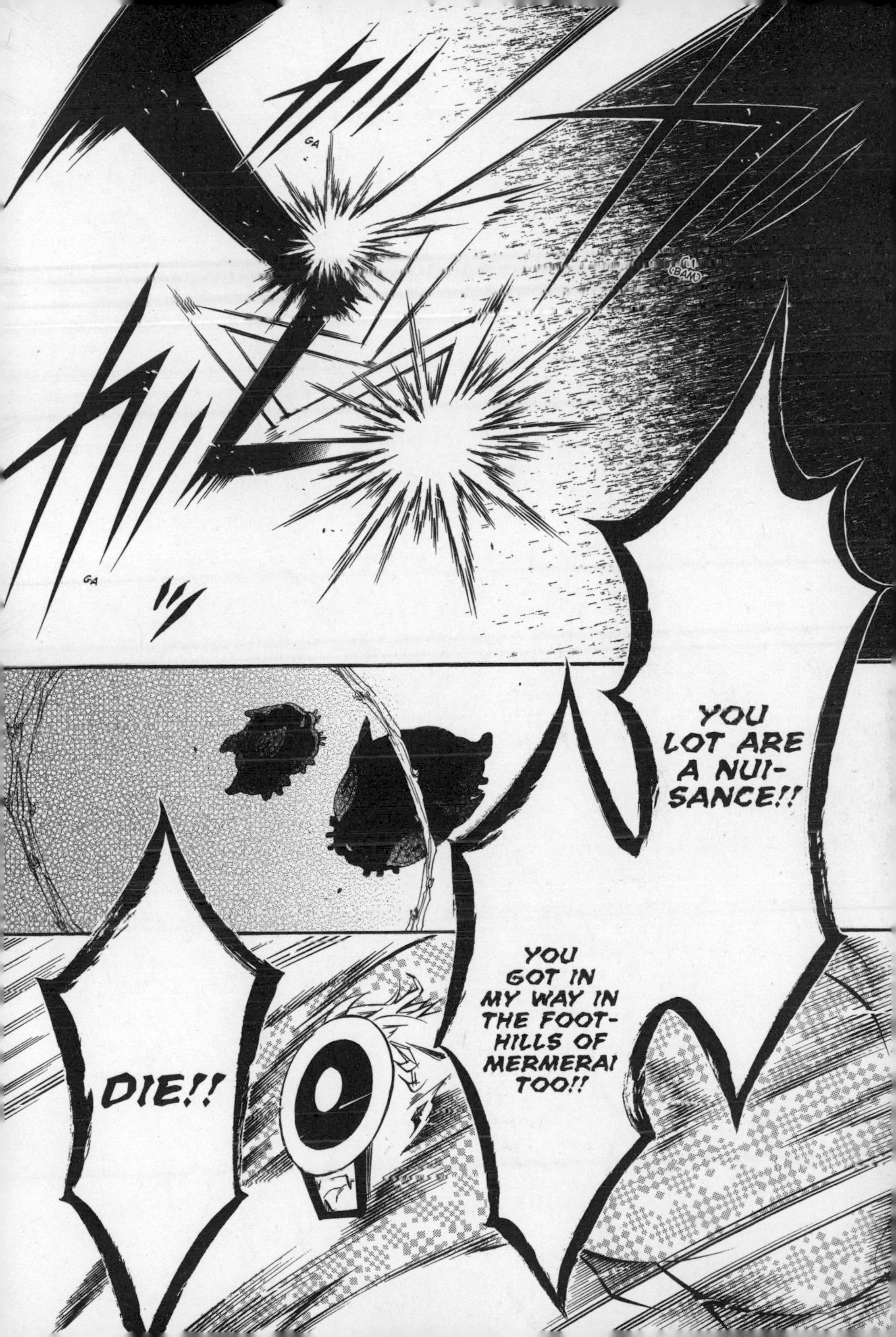
BAM
GA
GA
YOU LOT ARE A NUI-SANCE!!
YOU GOT IN MY WAY IN THE FOOT-HILLS OF MERMERAI TOO!!
DIE!!

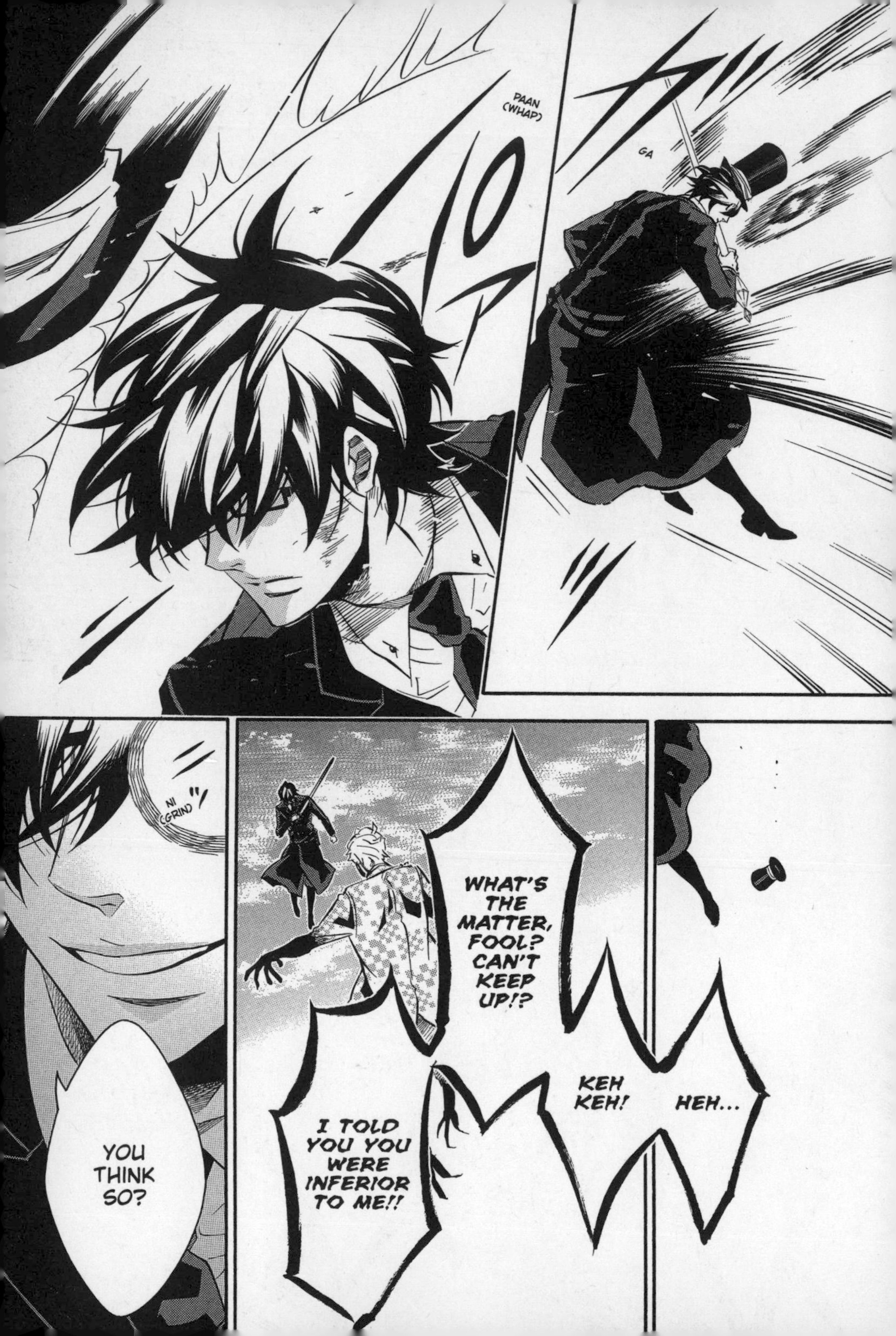
GA
PAAN (WHAP)
HEH...
KEH KEH!
WHAT'S THE MATTER, FOOL? CAN'T KEEP UP!?
I TOLD YOU YOU WERE INFERIOR TO ME!!
NI (GRIN)
YOU THINK SO?

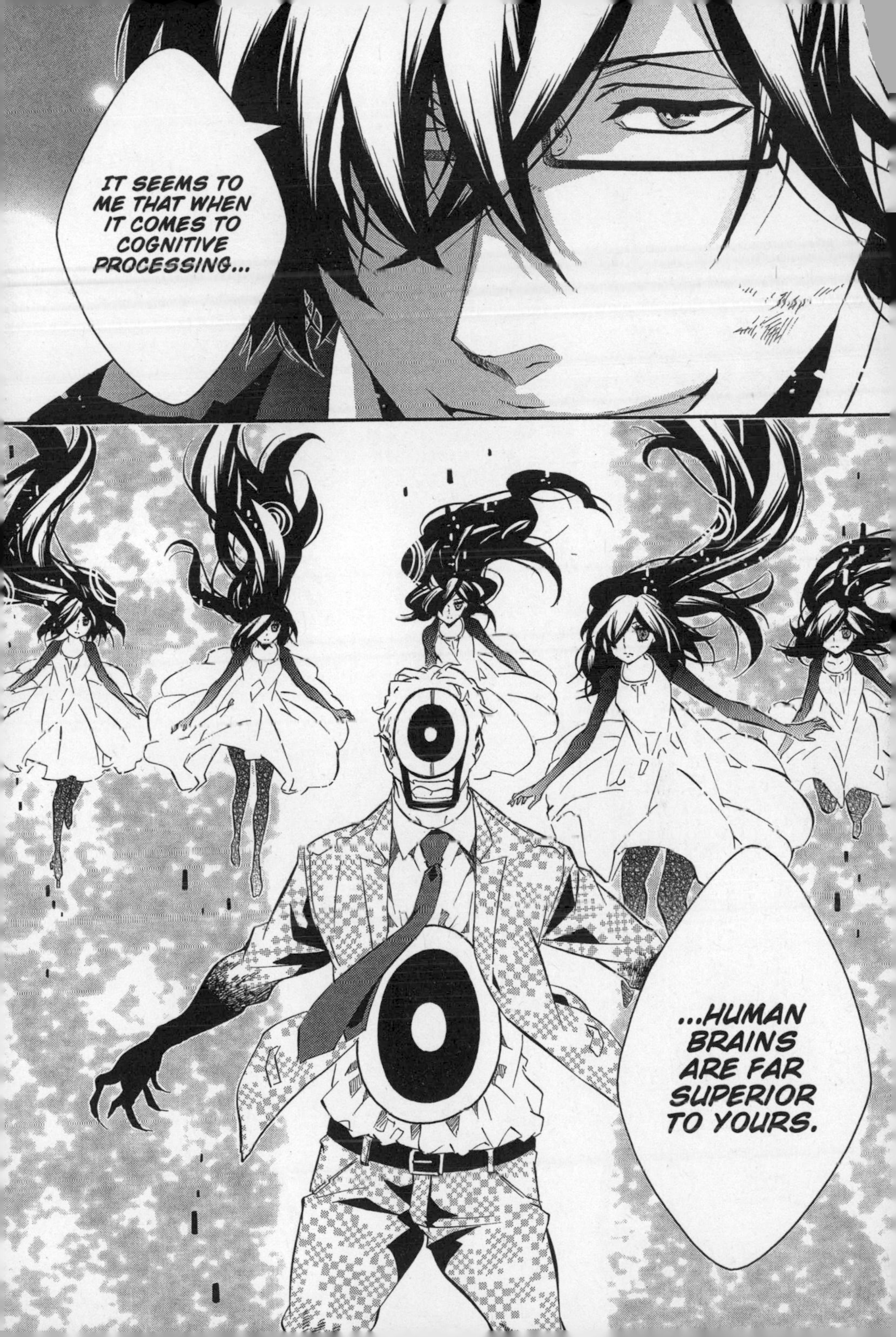
IT SEEMS TO ME THAT WHEN IT COMES TO COGNITIVE PROCESSING...
...HUMAN BRAINS ARE FAR SUPERIOR TO YOURS.

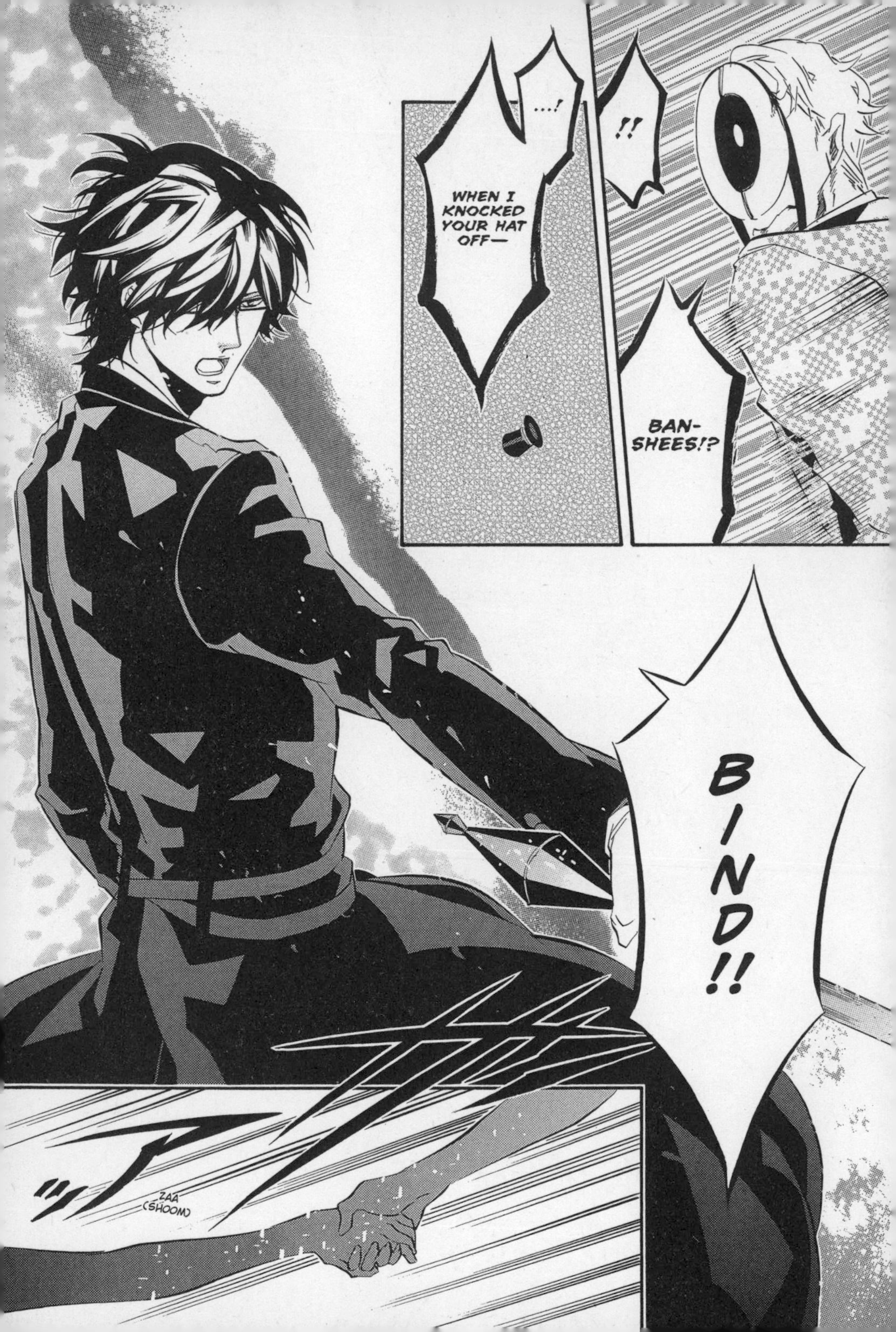
!!
BAN-SHEES!?
...!
WHEN I KNOCKED YOUR HAT OFF—
BIND!!
ZAA (SHOOM)

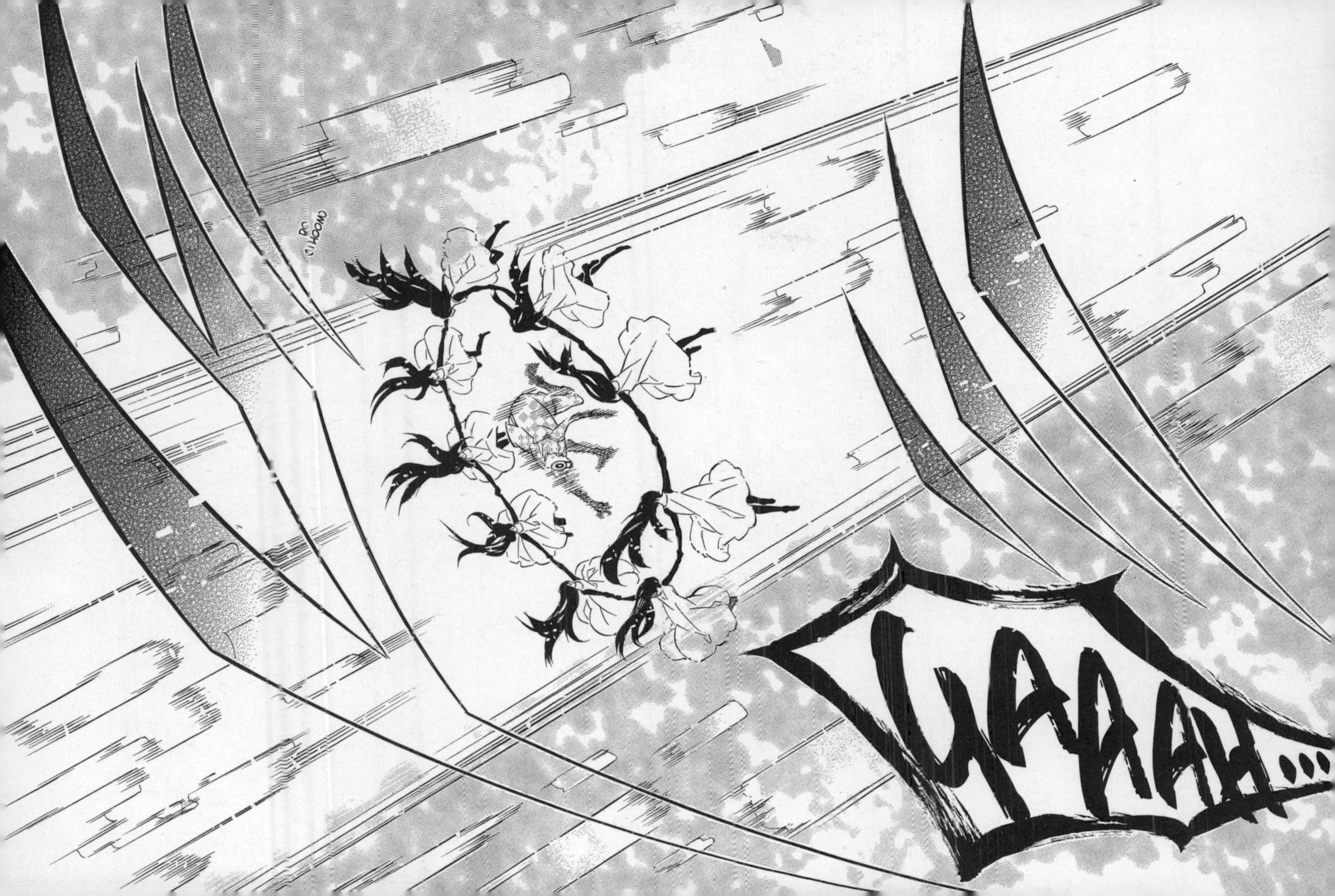
VAAAH...

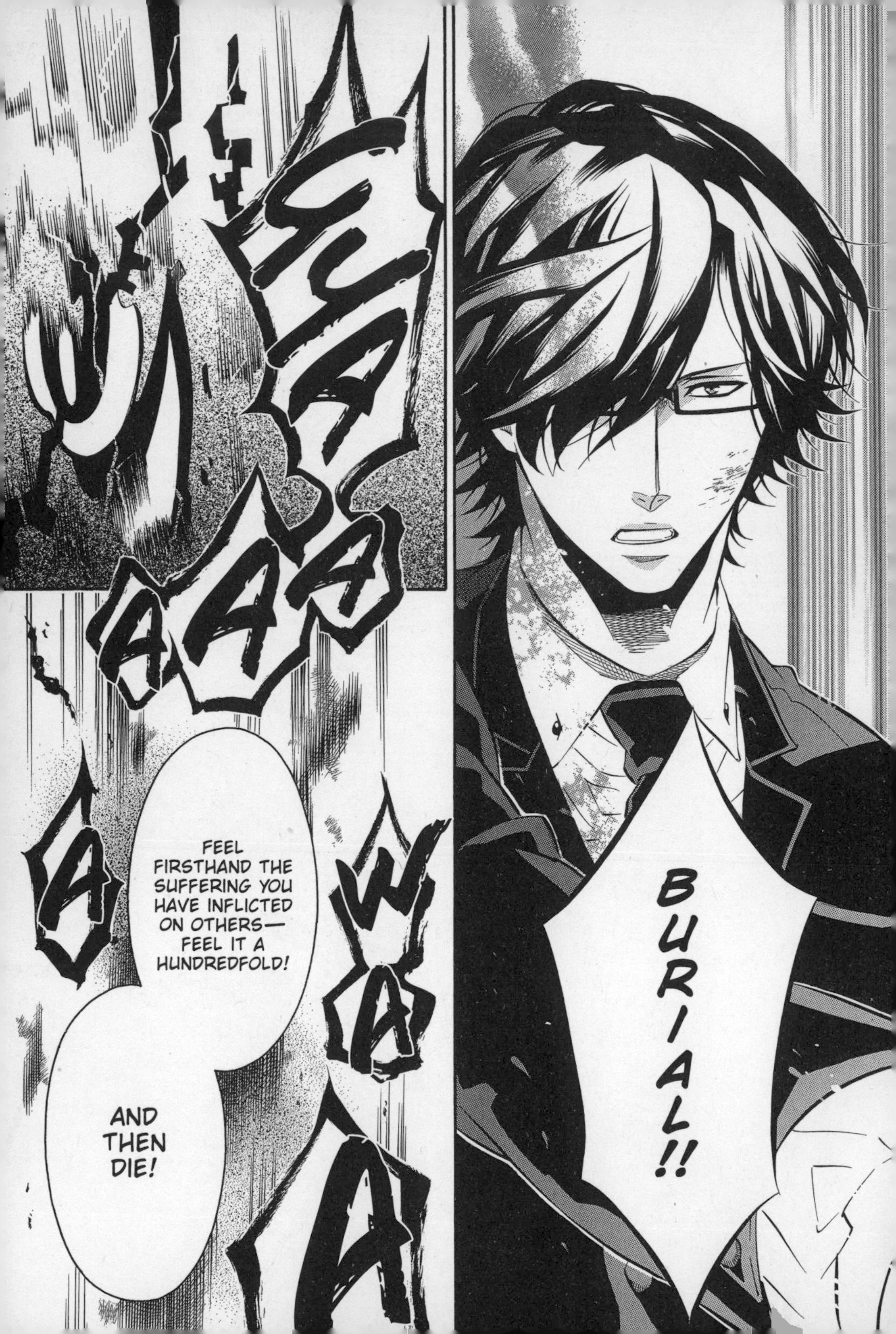
BURIAL!!
FEEL FIRSTHAND THE SUFFERING YOU HAVE INFLICTED ON OTHERS—FEEL IT A HUNDREDFOLD!
AND THEN DIE!

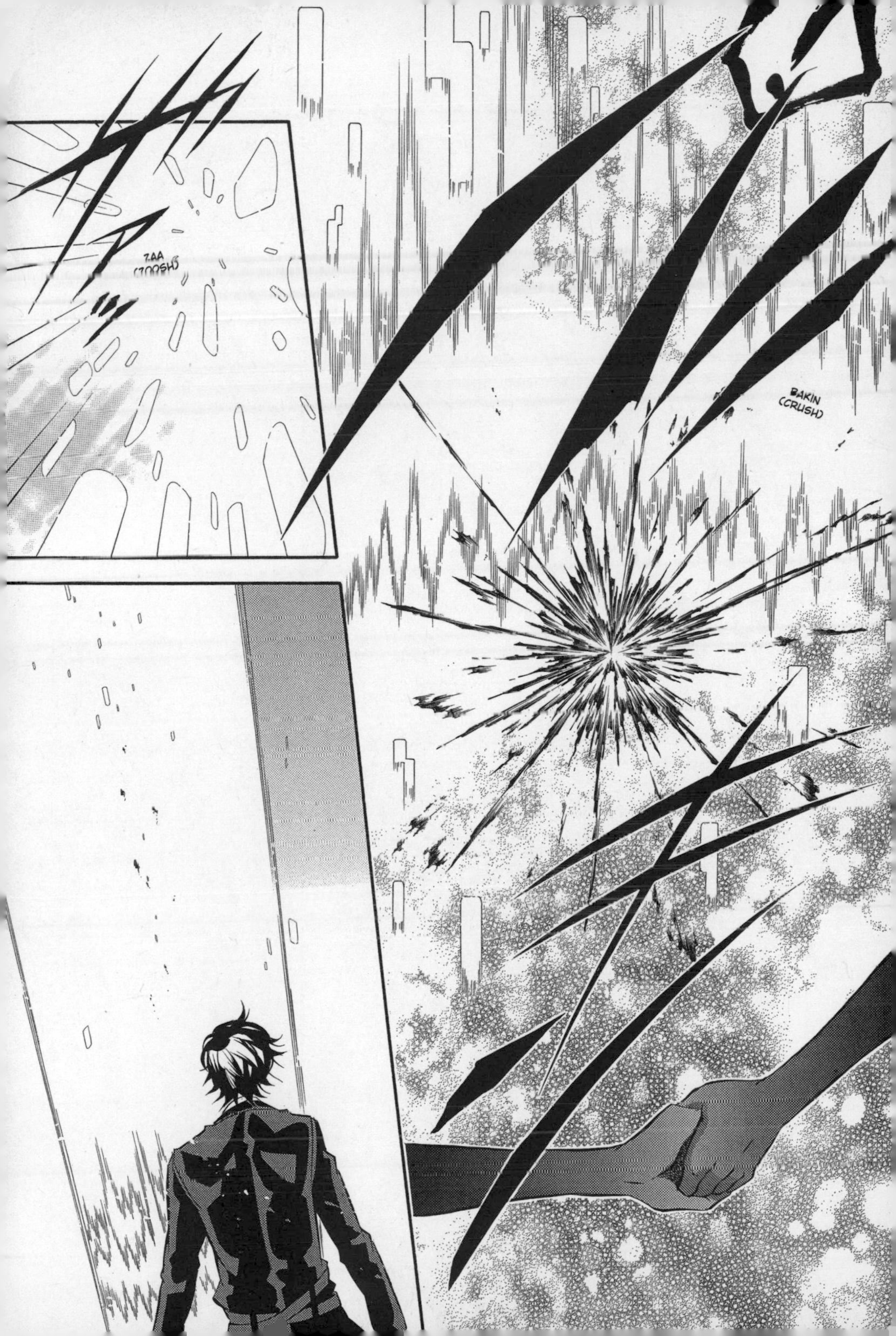
BAKIN (CRUSH)
ZAA (ZOOSH)

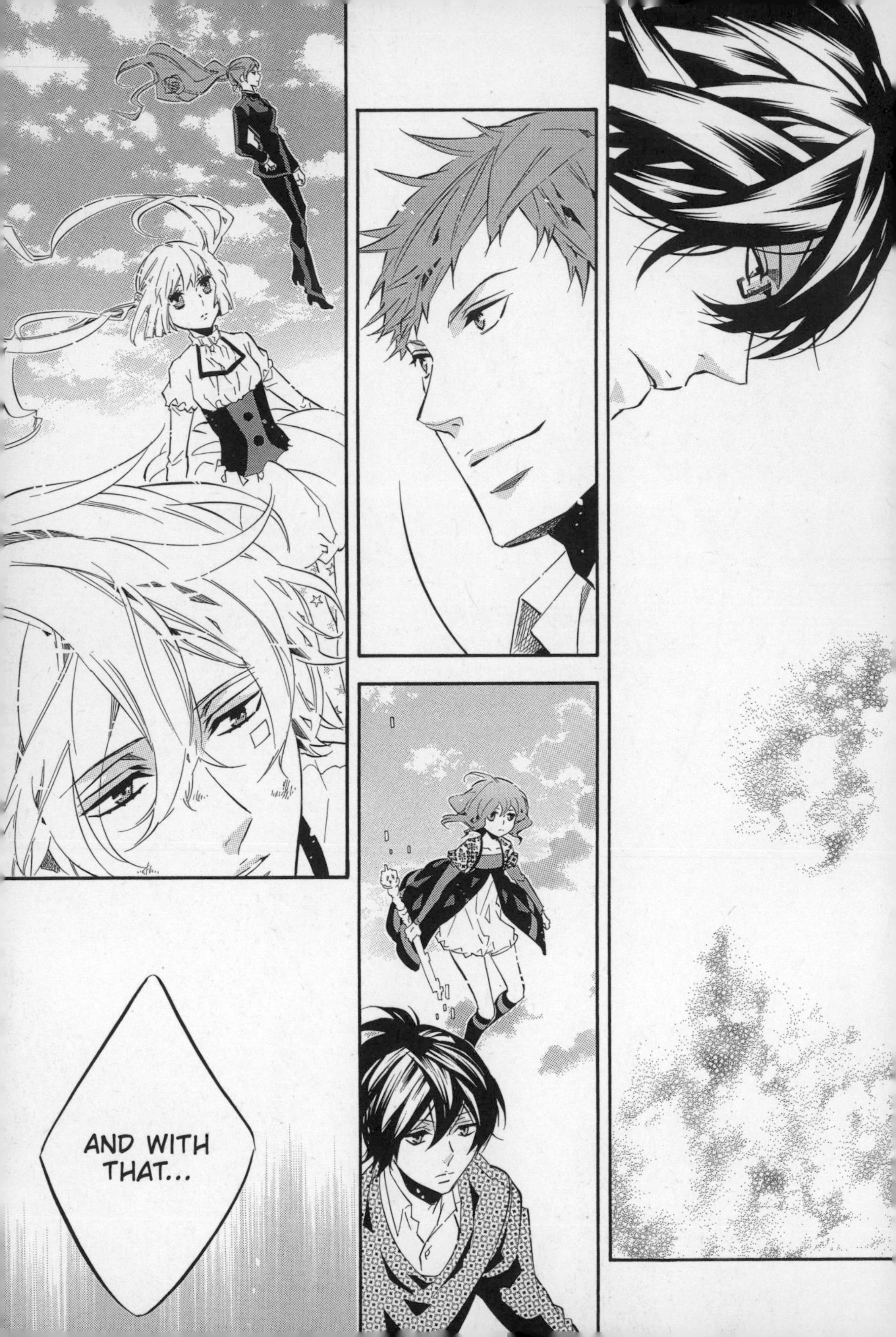
AND WITH THAT...

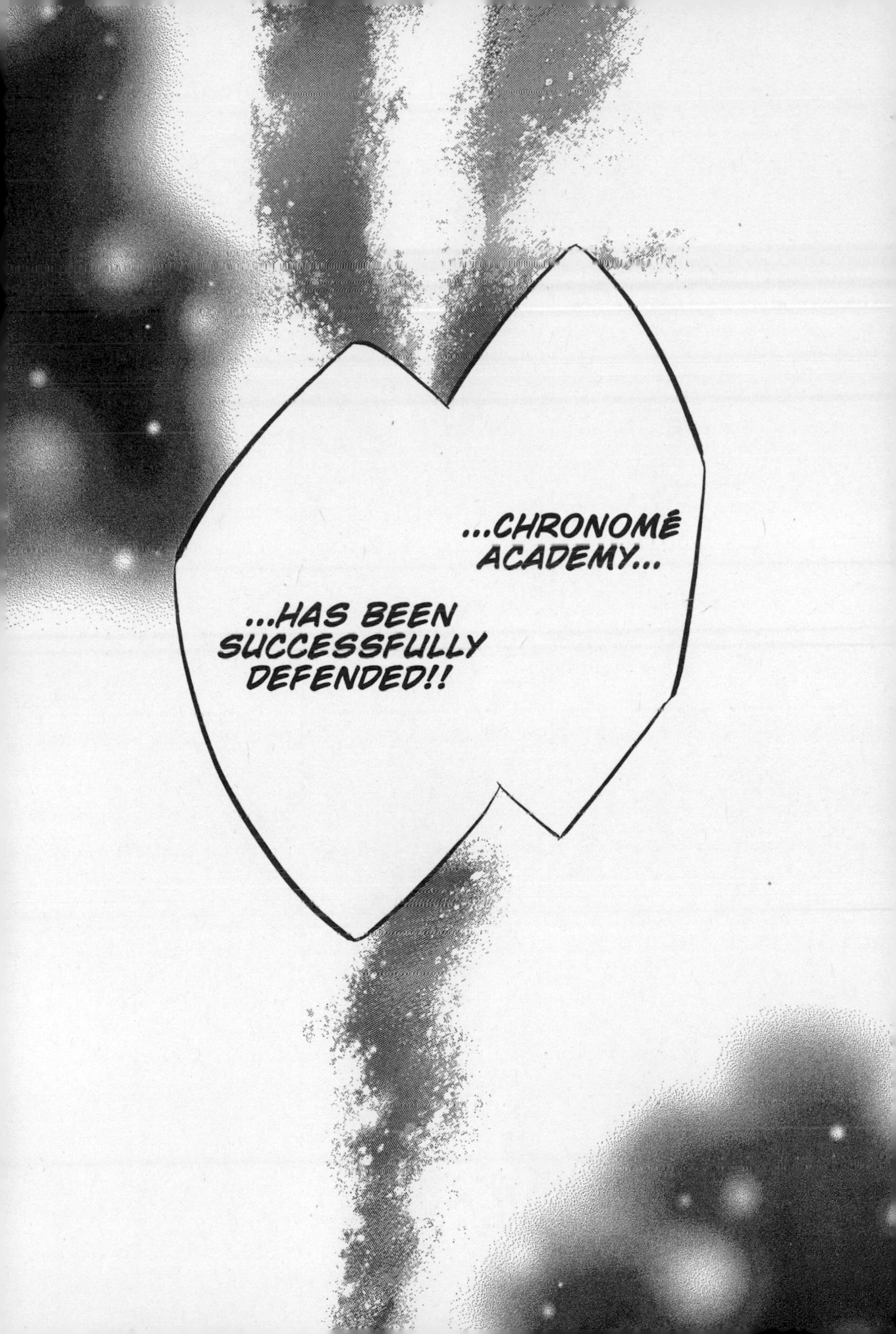
...CHRONOMÉ ACADEMY...
...HAS BEEN SUCCESSFULLY DEFENDED!!

KARNEVAL

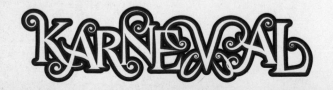

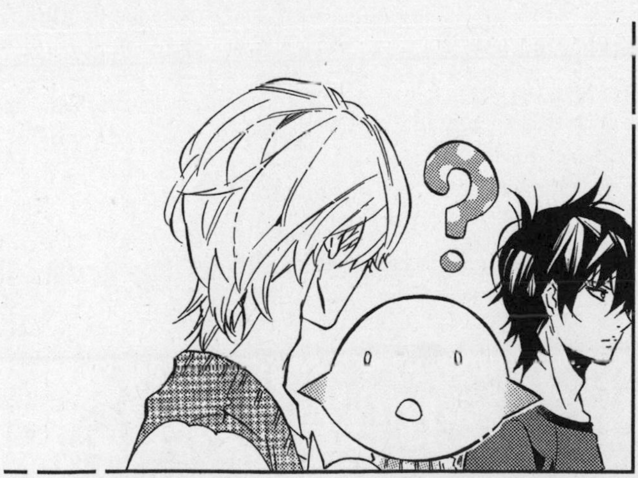

KARNEVAL

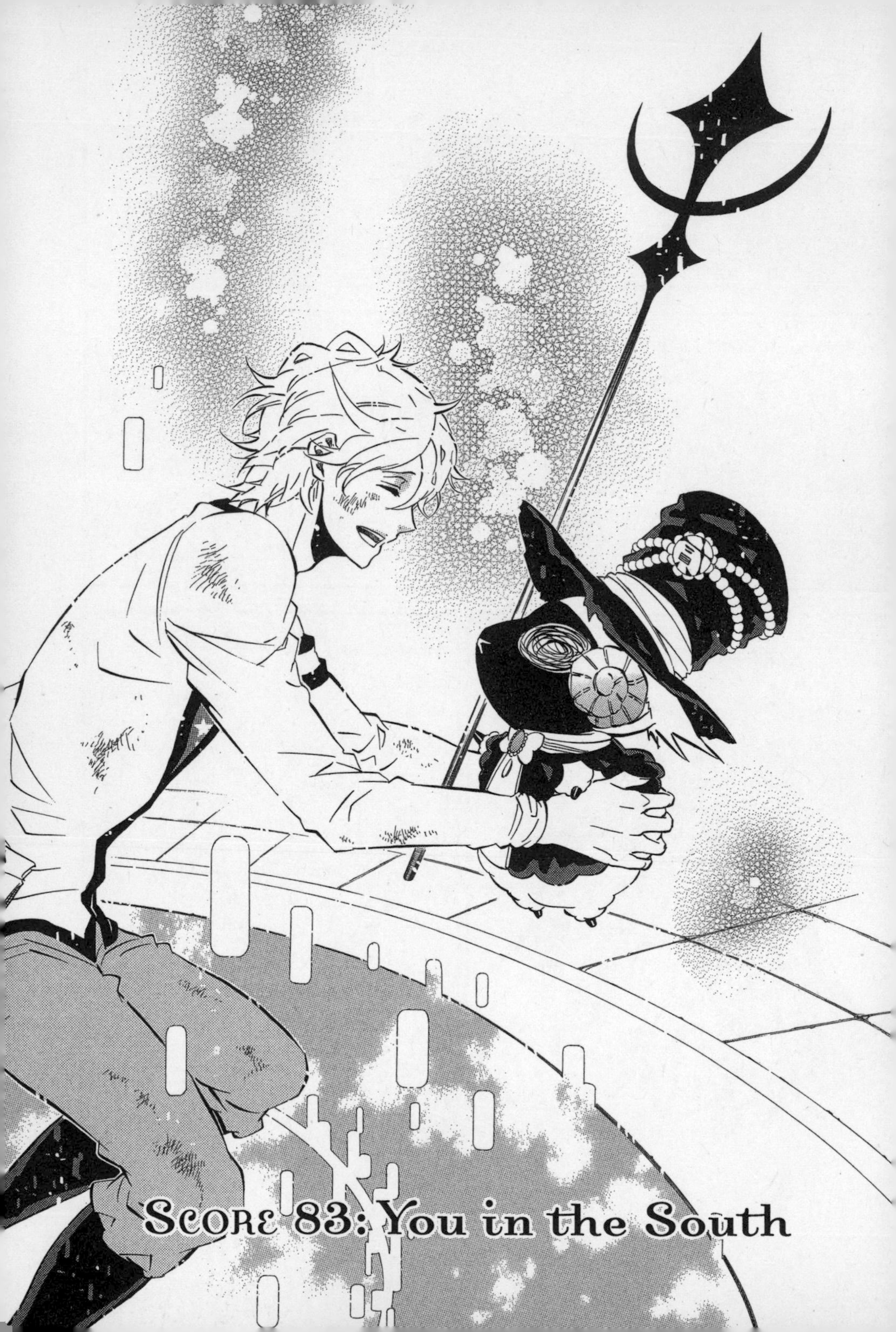
Score 83: You in the South

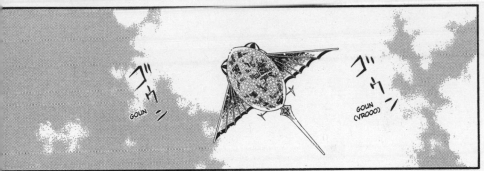

GOLIN
GOLIN
(VROOO)

SULUU
(BREATHE)

SULUU

SUPIII
(ZZZ)

SUPIII

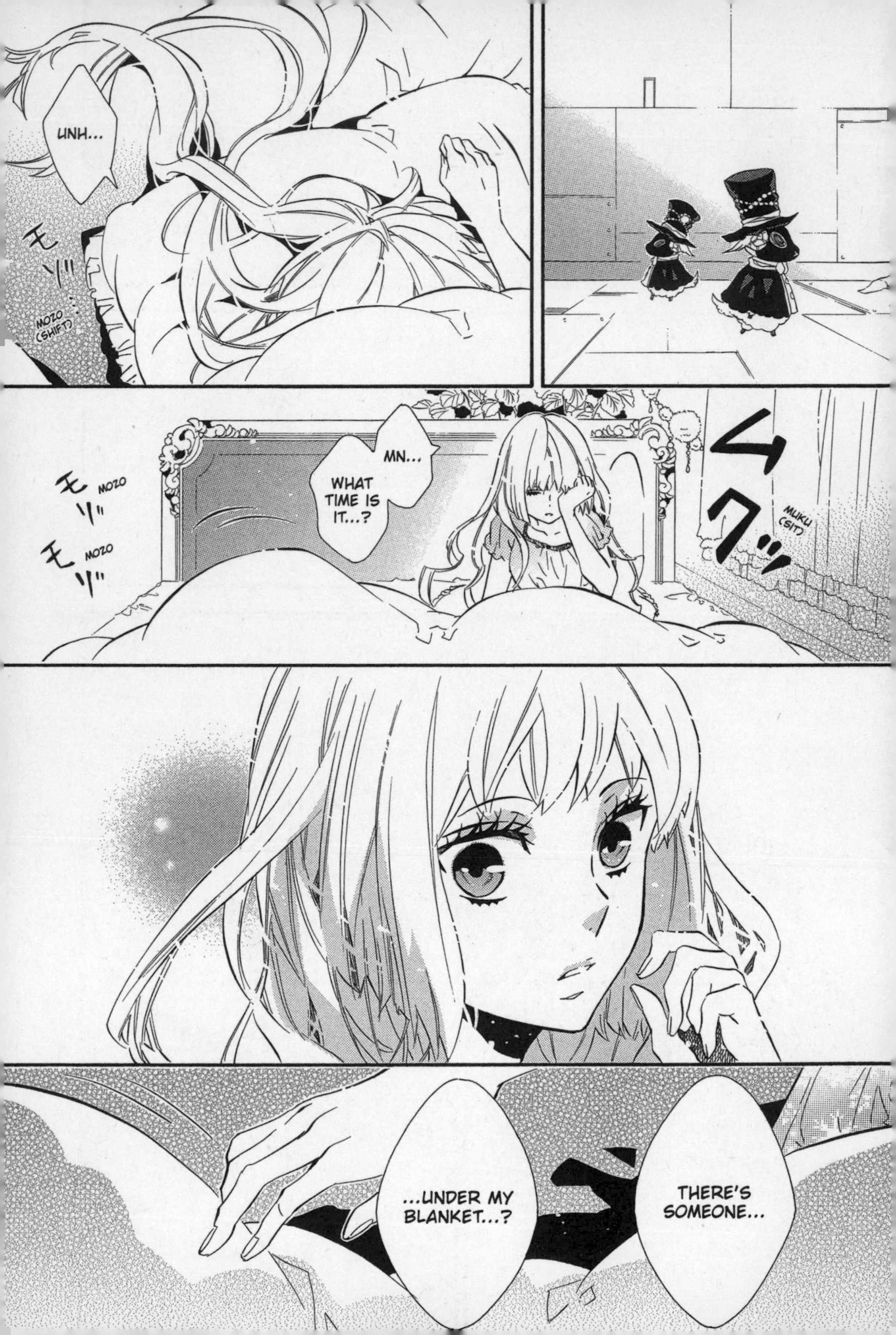
UNH...
モゾ
MOZO (SHIFT)
ムクッ
MUKU (SIT)
MN... WHAT TIME IS IT...?
モゾ MOZO
モゾ MOZO
THERE'S SOMEONE...
...UNDER MY BLANKET...?

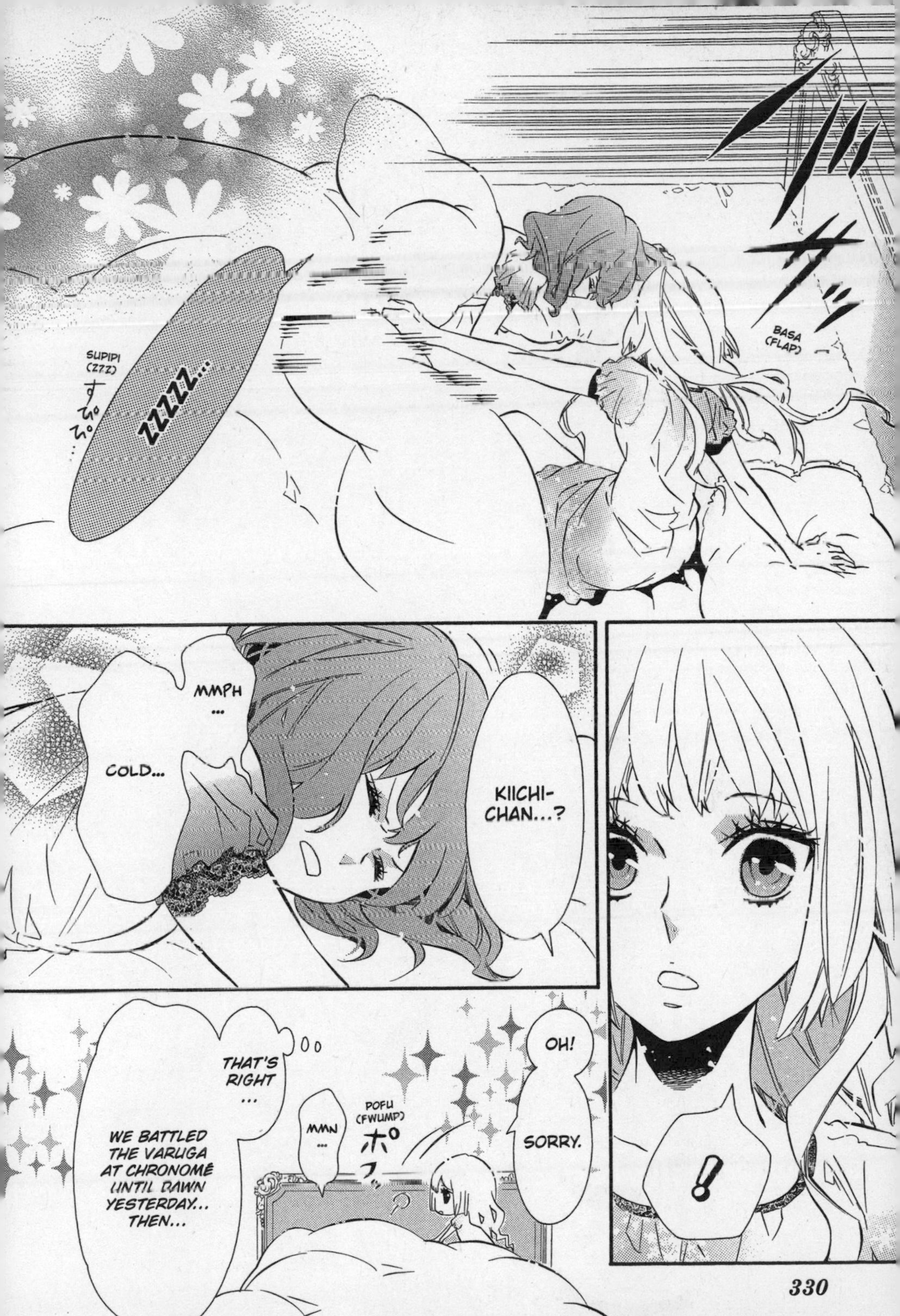
BASA (FLAP)
ZZZZZ...
SUPIPI (ZZZ)
すぴぴ…
!
KIICHI-CHAN...?
MMPH ...
COLD...
OH!
SORRY.
POFU (FWUMP)
ポフ
MMN ...
THAT'S RIGHT ...
WE BATTLED THE VARUGA AT CHRONOMÉ UNTIL DAWN YESTERDAY... THEN...

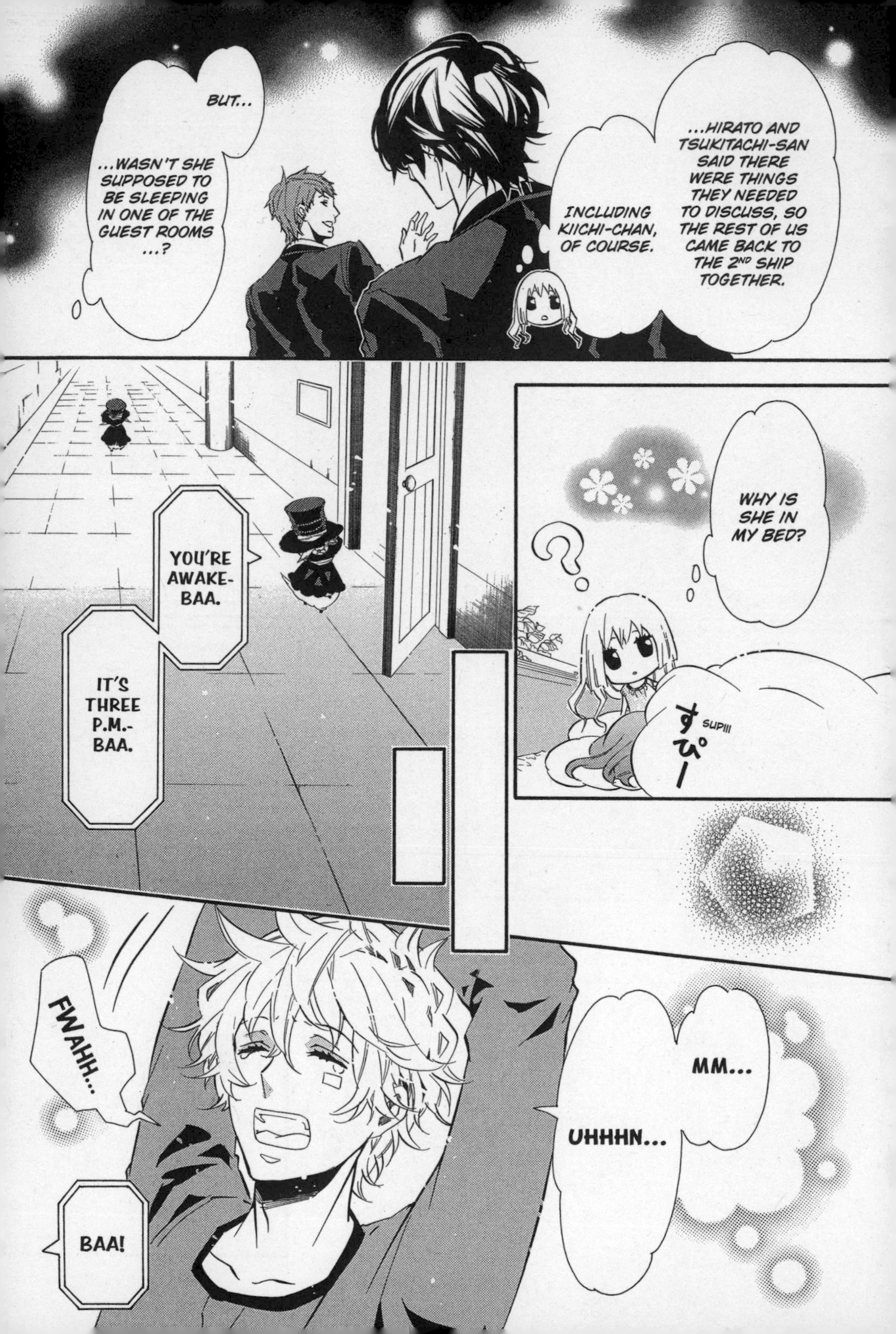
...HIRATO AND TSUKITACHI-SAN SAID THERE WERE THINGS THEY NEEDED TO DISCUSS, SO THE REST OF US CAME BACK TO THE 2ND SHIP TOGETHER.
INCLUDING KIICHI-CHAN, OF COURSE.
BUT...
...WASN'T SHE SUPPOSED TO BE SLEEPING IN ONE OF THE GUEST ROOMS ...?
WHY IS SHE IN MY BED?
すぴー
SUPIII
YOU'RE AWAKE-BAA.
IT'S THREE P.M.-BAA.
MM...
UHHHN...
FWAHH...
BAA!

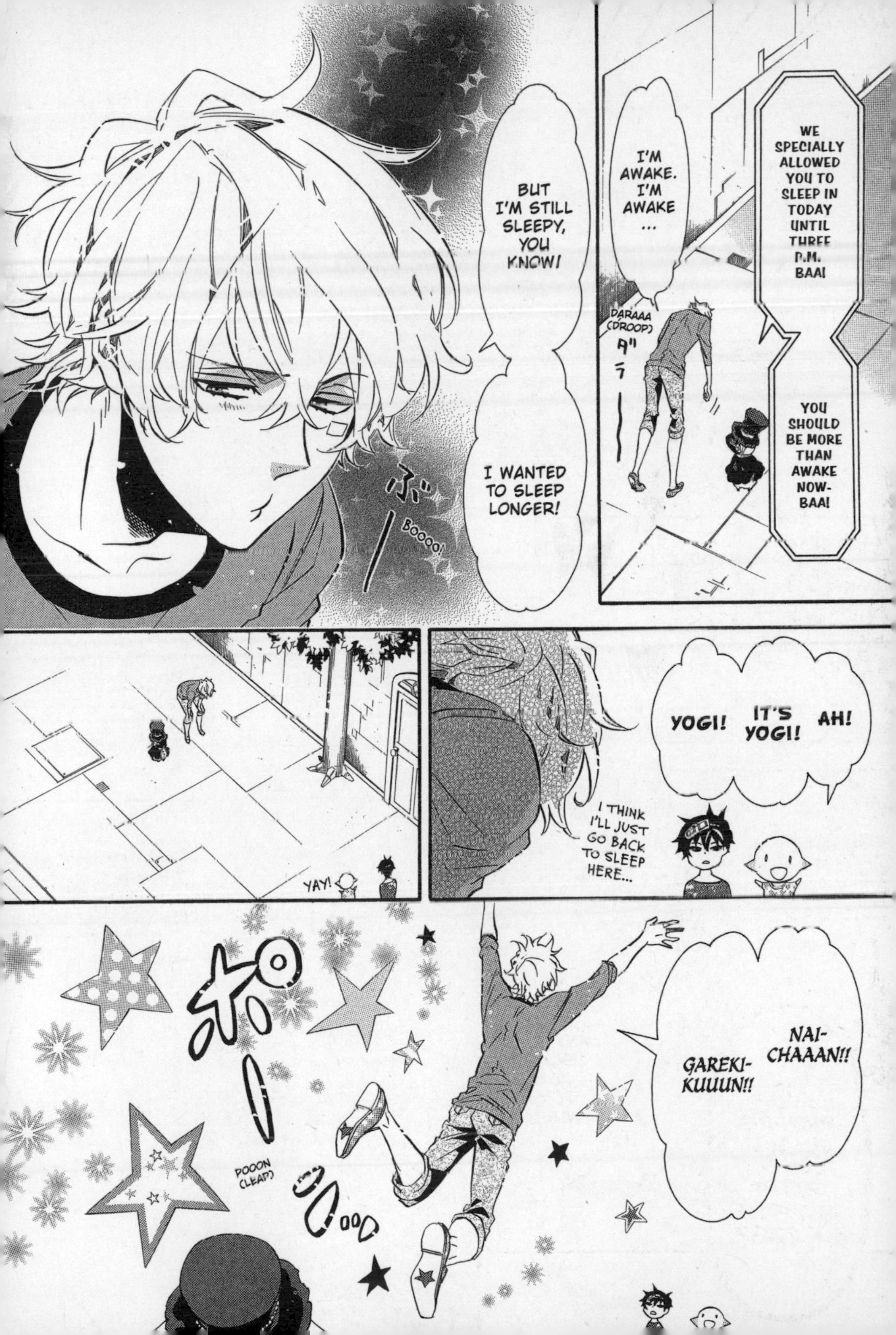
WE SPECIALLY ALLOWED YOU TO SLEEP IN TODAY UNTIL THREE P.M. BAA!
YOU SHOULD BE MORE THAN AWAKE NOW-BAA!
I'M AWAKE. I'M AWAKE...
DARAAA (DROOP)
BUT I'M STILL SLEEPY, YOU KNOW!
I WANTED TO SLEEP LONGER!
BOOOOO!
AH!
IT'S YOGI!
YOGI!
I THINK I'LL JUST GO BACK TO SLEEP HERE...
YAY!
NAI-CHAAAN!!
GAREKI-KUUUN!!
POOON (LEAP)

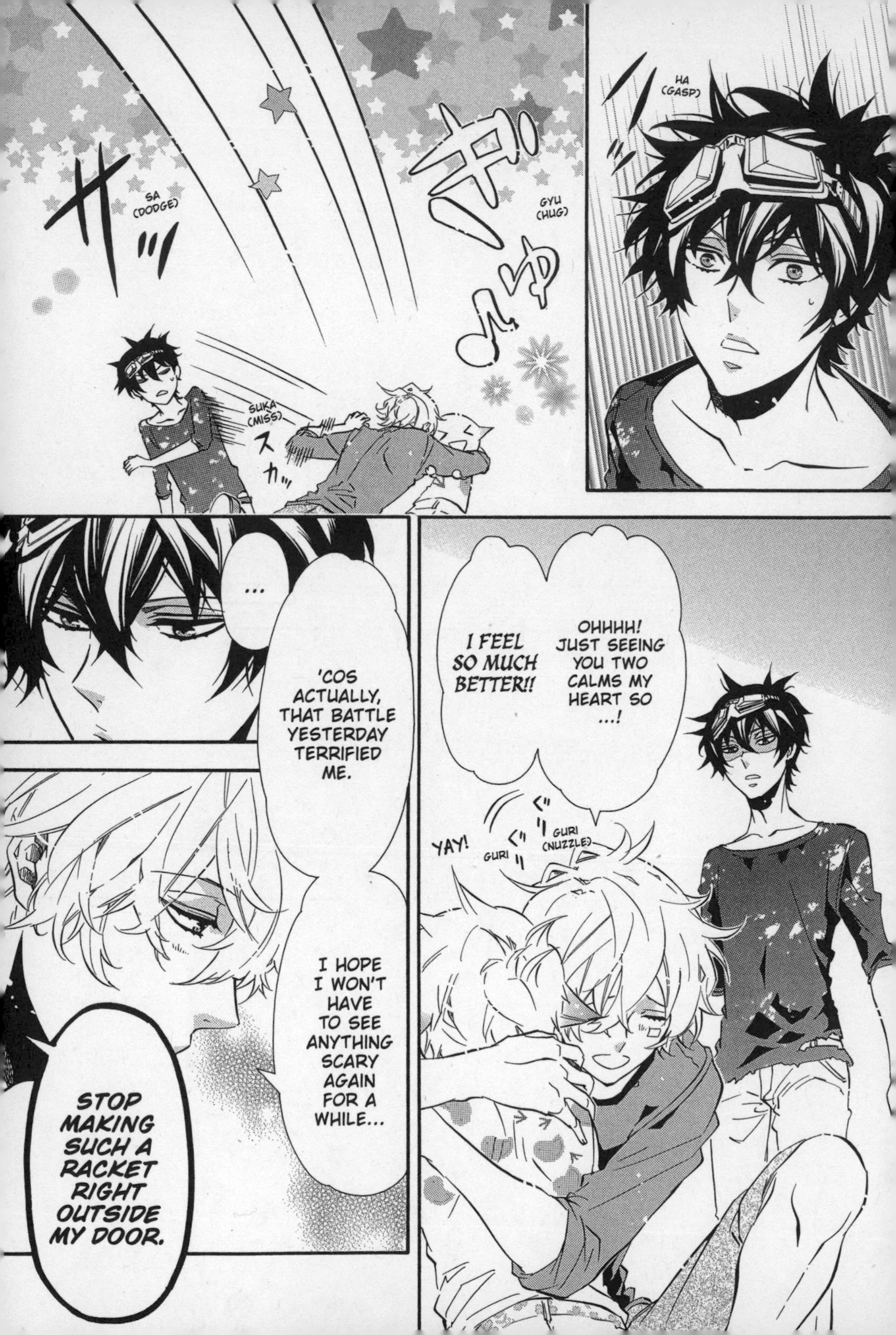
HA (GASP)
ぎゅ
GYU (HUG)
ザッ
SA (DODGE)
スカッ
SUKA (MISS)
OHHHH! JUST SEEING YOU TWO CALMS MY HEART SO ...!
I FEEL SO MUCH BETTER!!
ぐりぐり
GURI (NUZZLE)
GURI
YAY!
...
'COS ACTUALLY, THAT BATTLE YESTERDAY TERRIFIED ME.
I HOPE I WON'T HAVE TO SEE ANYTHING SCARY AGAIN FOR A WHILE...
STOP MAKING SUCH A RACKET RIGHT OUTSIDE MY DOOR.

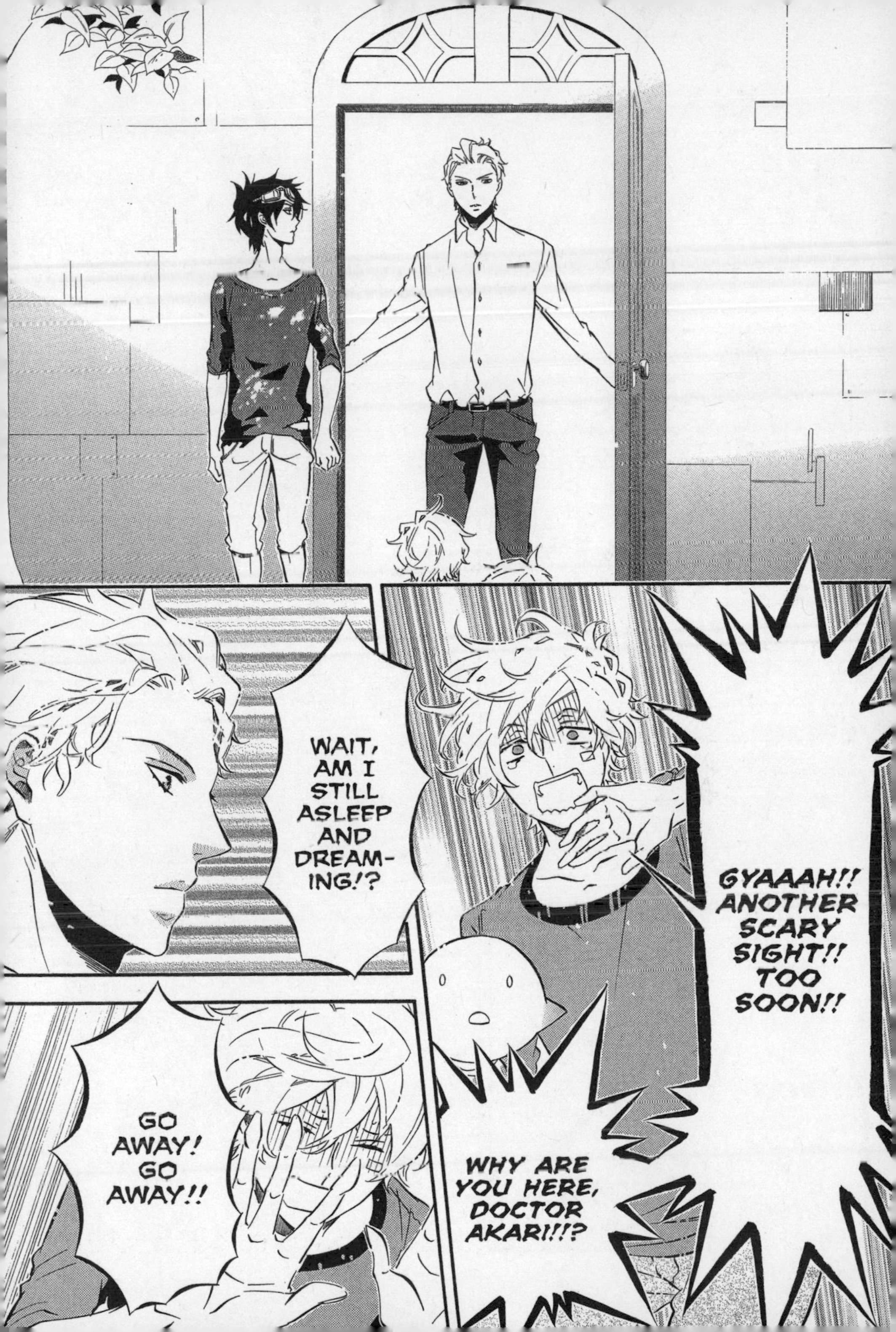
GYAAAH!! ANOTHER SCARY SIGHT!! TOO SOON!!
WHY ARE YOU HERE, DOCTOR AKARI!!?
WAIT, AM I STILL ASLEEP AND DREAMING!?
GO AWAY! GO AWAY!!

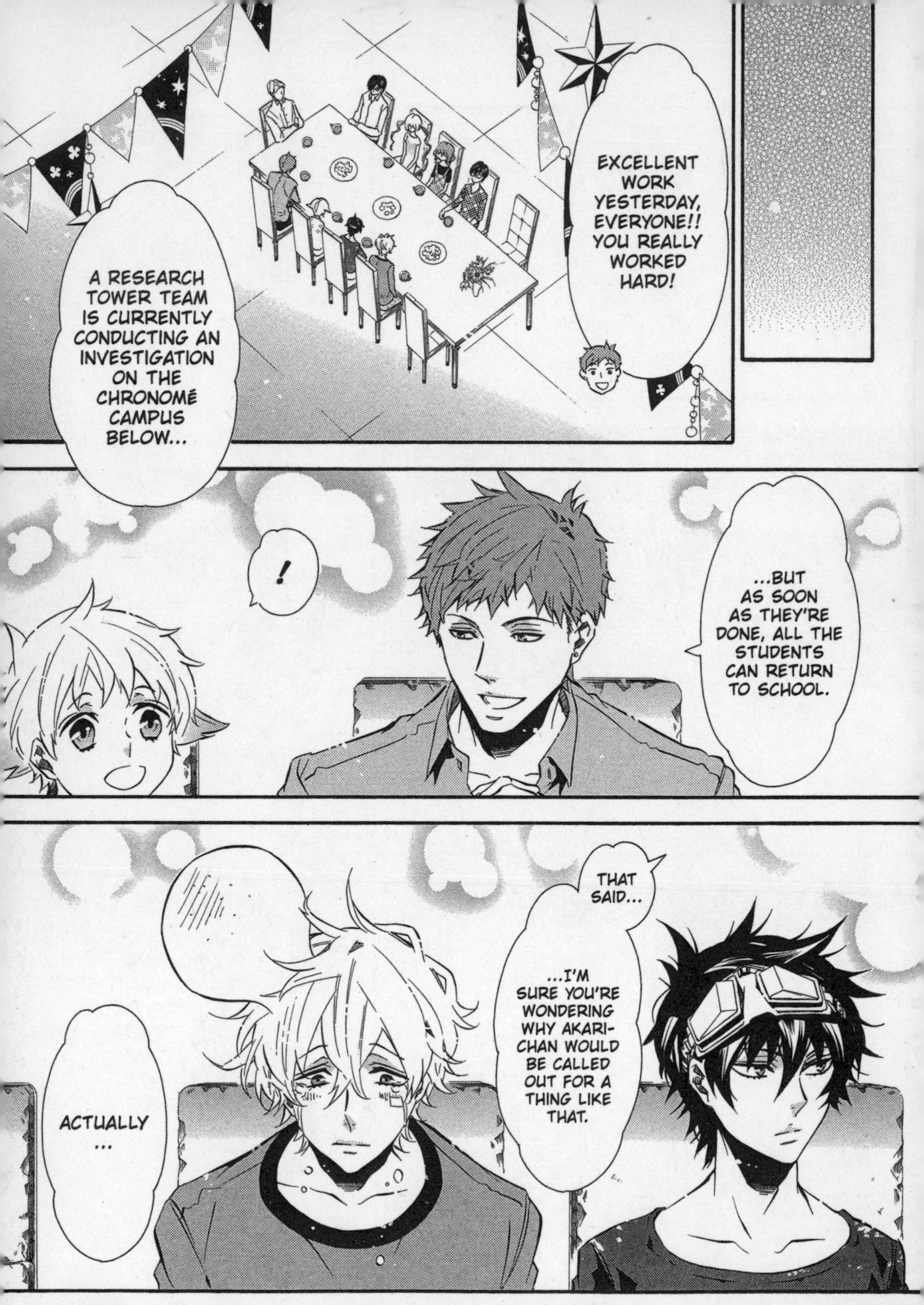
EXCELLENT WORK YESTERDAY, EVERYONE!! YOU REALLY WORKED HARD!
A RESEARCH TOWER TEAM IS CURRENTLY CONDUCTING AN INVESTIGATION ON THE CHRONOMÉ CAMPUS BELOW...
...BUT AS SOON AS THEY'RE DONE, ALL THE STUDENTS CAN RETURN TO SCHOOL.
!
THAT SAID...
...I'M SURE YOU'RE WONDERING WHY AKARI-CHAN WOULD BE CALLED OUT FOR A THING LIKE THAT.
ACTUALLY ...

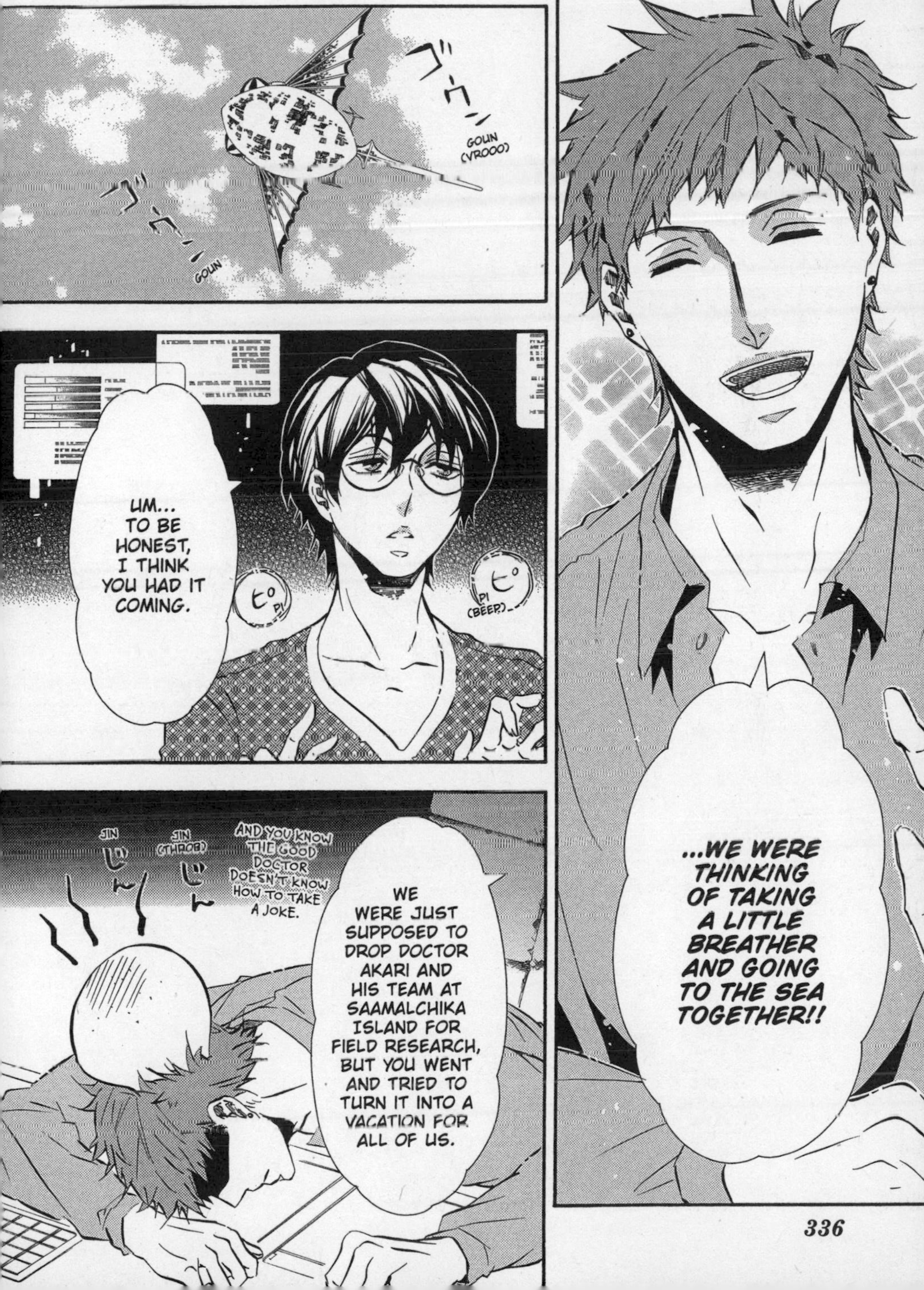
...WE WERE THINKING OF TAKING A LITTLE BREATHER AND GOING TO THE SEA TOGETHER!!
GOUN (VROOO)
GOUN
PI (BEEP)
PI
UM... TO BE HONEST, I THINK YOU HAD IT COMING.
WE WERE JUST SUPPOSED TO DROP DOCTOR AKARI AND HIS TEAM AT SAAMALCHIKA ISLAND FOR FIELD RESEARCH, BUT YOU WENT AND TRIED TO TURN IT INTO A VACATION FOR ALL OF US.
AND YOU KNOW THE GOOD DOCTOR DOESN'T KNOW HOW TO TAKE A JOKE.
JIN (THROB)
JIN

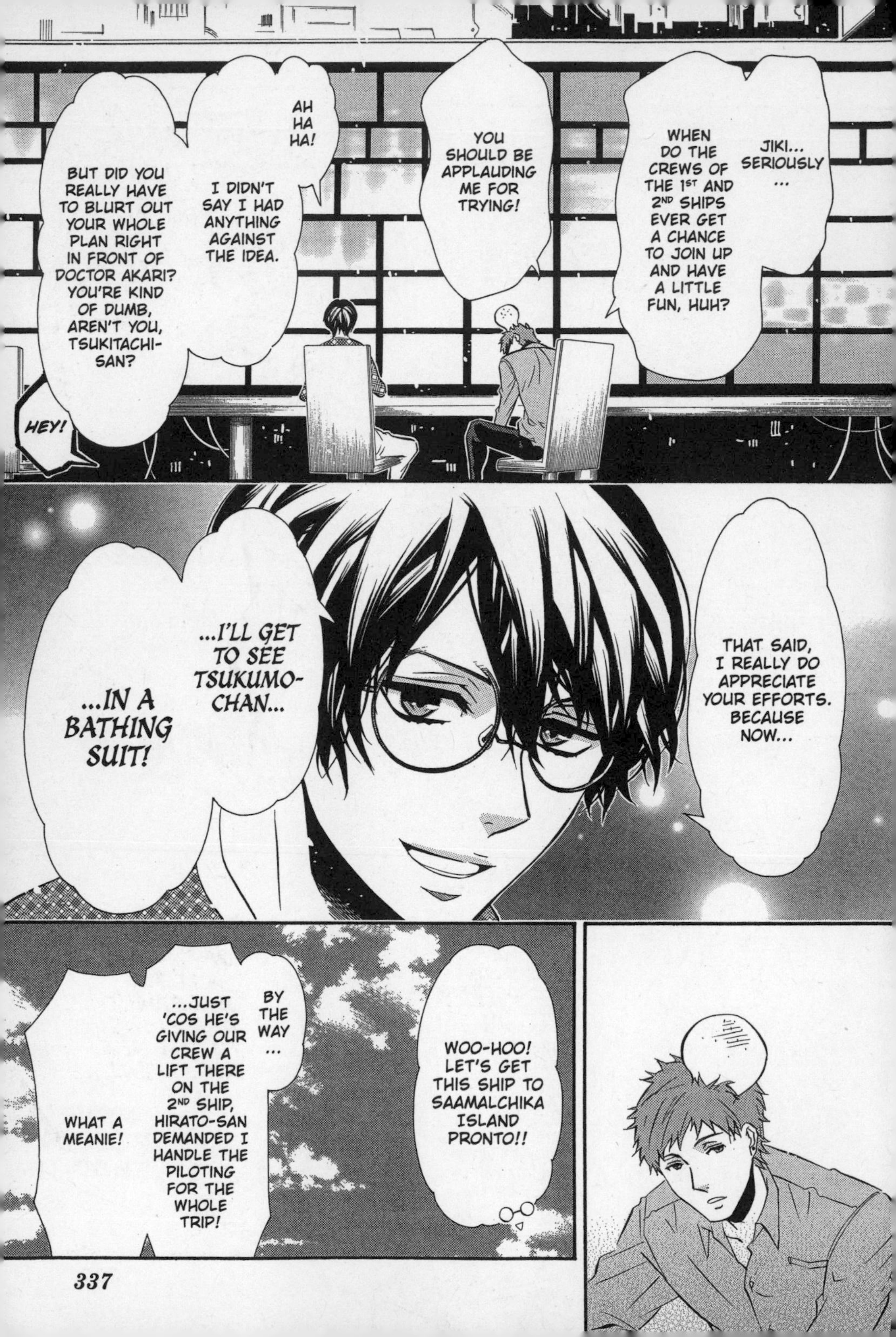

JIKI... SERIOUSLY...
WHEN DO THE CREWS OF THE 1ST AND 2ND SHIPS EVER GET A CHANCE TO JOIN UP AND HAVE A LITTLE FUN, HUH?
YOU SHOULD BE APPLAUDING ME FOR TRYING!
AH HA HA!
I DIDN'T SAY I HAD ANYTHING AGAINST THE IDEA.
BUT DID YOU REALLY HAVE TO BLURT OUT YOUR WHOLE PLAN RIGHT IN FRONT OF DOCTOR AKARI? YOU'RE KIND OF DUMB, AREN'T YOU, TSUKITACHI-SAN?
HEY!
THAT SAID, I REALLY DO APPRECIATE YOUR EFFORTS. BECAUSE NOW...
...I'LL GET TO SEE TSUKUMO-CHAN...
...IN A BATHING SUIT!
WOO-HOO! LET'S GET THIS SHIP TO SAAMALCHIKA ISLAND PRONTO!!
BY THE WAY...
...JUST 'COS HE'S GIVING OUR CREW A LIFT THERE ON THE 2ND SHIP, HIRATO-SAN DEMANDED I HANDLE THE PILOTING FOR THE WHOLE TRIP!
WHAT A MEANIE!

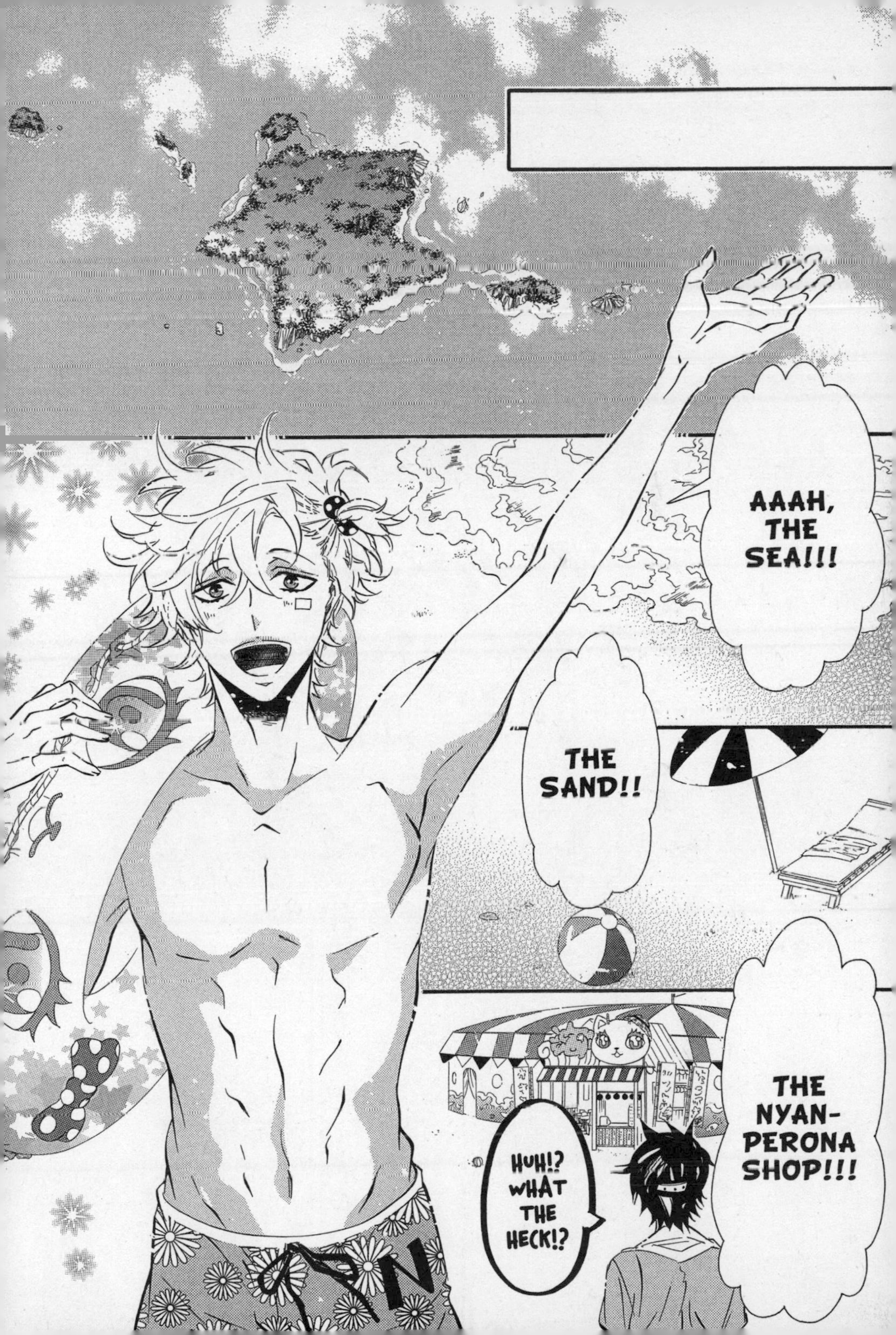
AAAH, THE SEA!!!
THE SAND!!
THE NYAN-PERONA SHOP!!!
HUH!? WHAT THE HECK!?

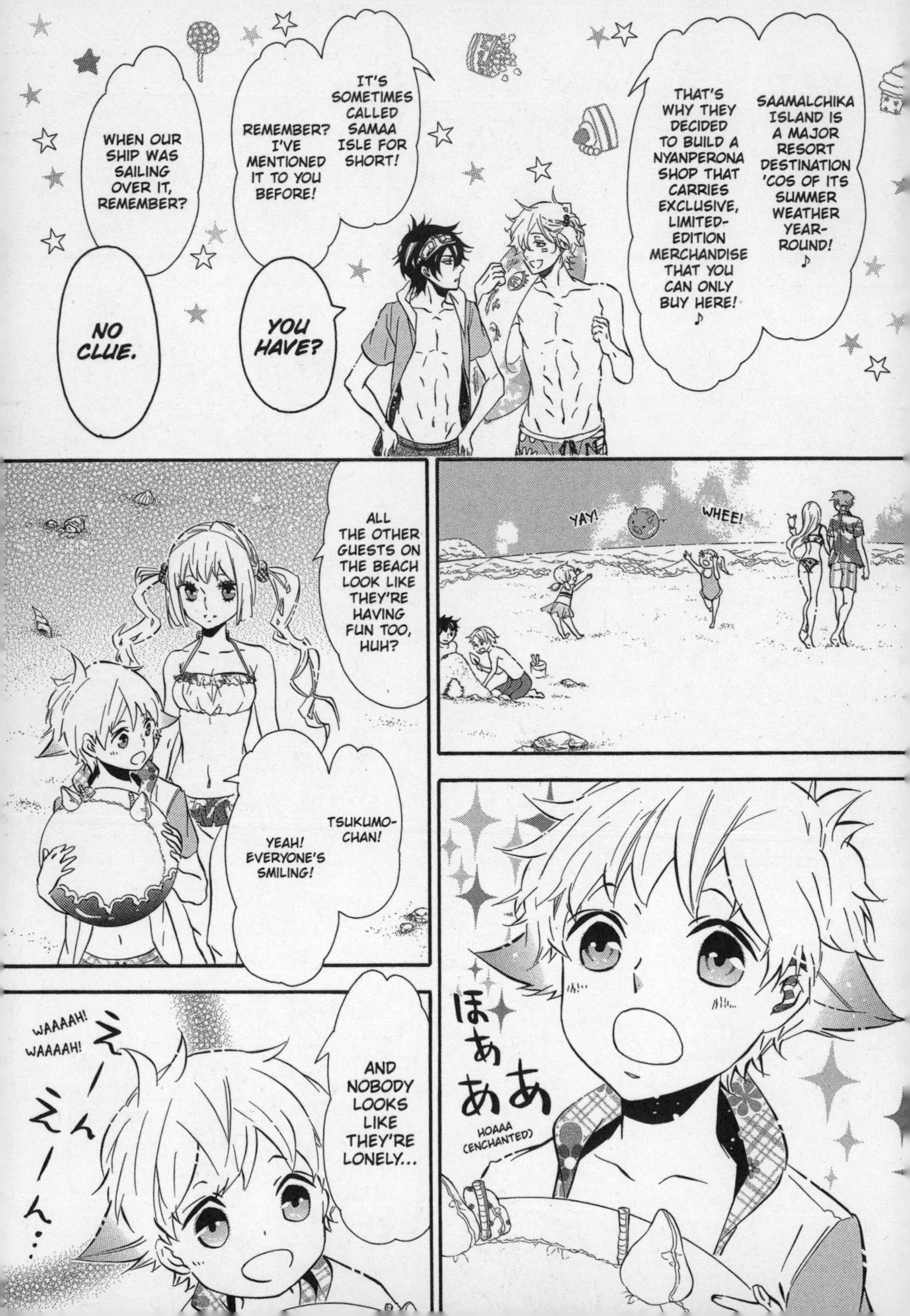
SAAMALCHIKA ISLAND IS A MAJOR RESORT DESTINATION 'COS OF ITS SUMMER WEATHER YEAR-ROUND! ♪
THAT'S WHY THEY DECIDED TO BUILD A NYANPERONA SHOP THAT CARRIES EXCLUSIVE, LIMITED-EDITION MERCHANDISE THAT YOU CAN ONLY BUY HERE! ♪
IT'S SOMETIMES CALLED SAMAA ISLE FOR SHORT!
REMEMBER? I'VE MENTIONED IT TO YOU BEFORE!
YOU HAVE?
WHEN OUR SHIP WAS SAILING OVER IT, REMEMBER?
NO CLUE.
WHEE!
YAY!
ALL THE OTHER GUESTS ON THE BEACH LOOK LIKE THEY'RE HAVING FUN TOO, HUH?
TSUKUMO-CHAN!
YEAH! EVERYONE'S SMILING!
ほあああ
HOAAA (ENCHANTED)
AND NOBODY LOOKS LIKE THEY'RE LONELY...
えーんえーん...
WAAAAH! WAAAAH!

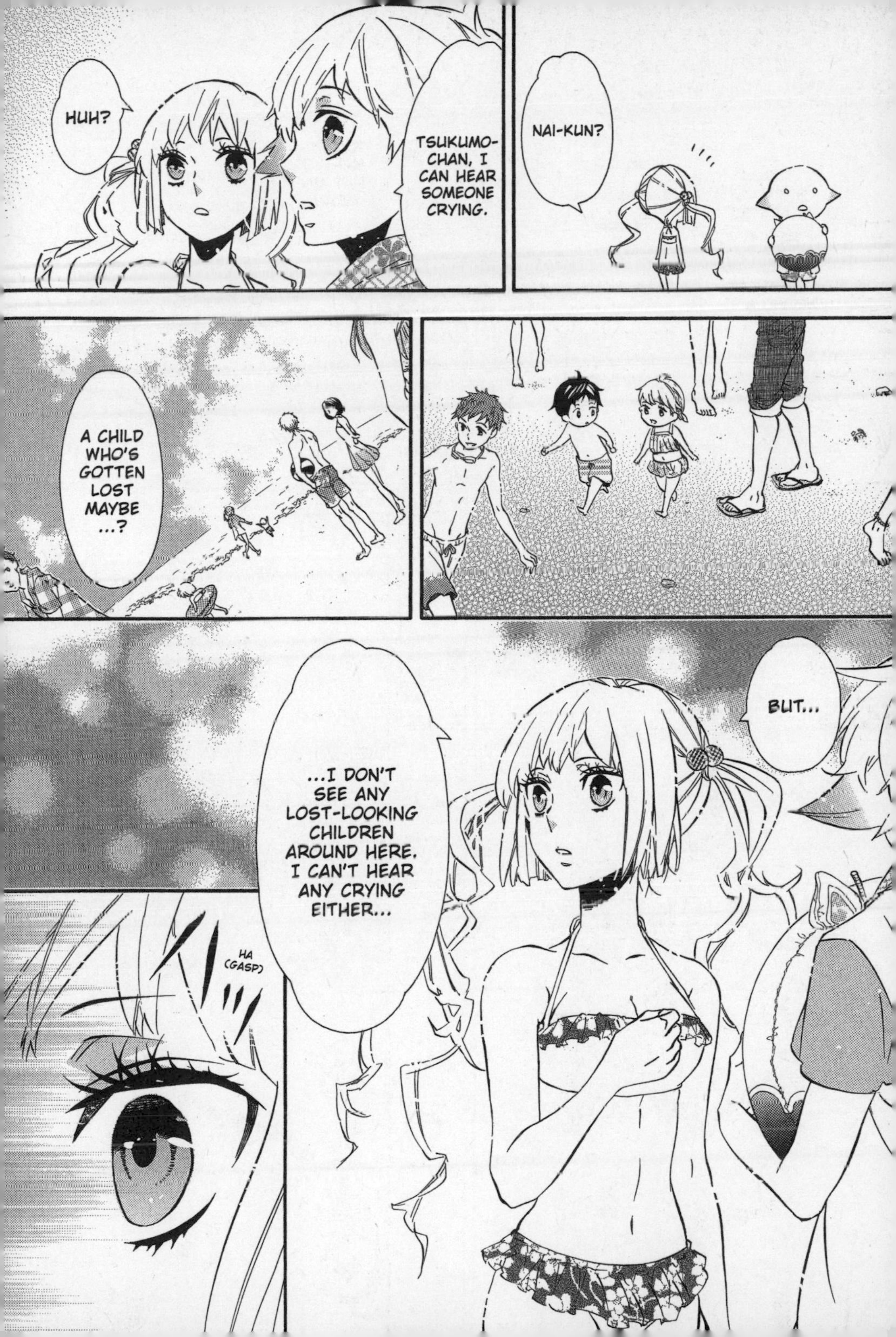
NAI-KUN?
TSUKUMO-CHAN, I CAN HEAR SOMEONE CRYING.
HUH?
A CHILD WHO'S GOTTEN LOST MAYBE ...?
BUT...
...I DON'T SEE ANY LOST-LOOKING CHILDREN AROUND HERE. I CAN'T HEAR ANY CRYING EITHER...
HA (GASP)

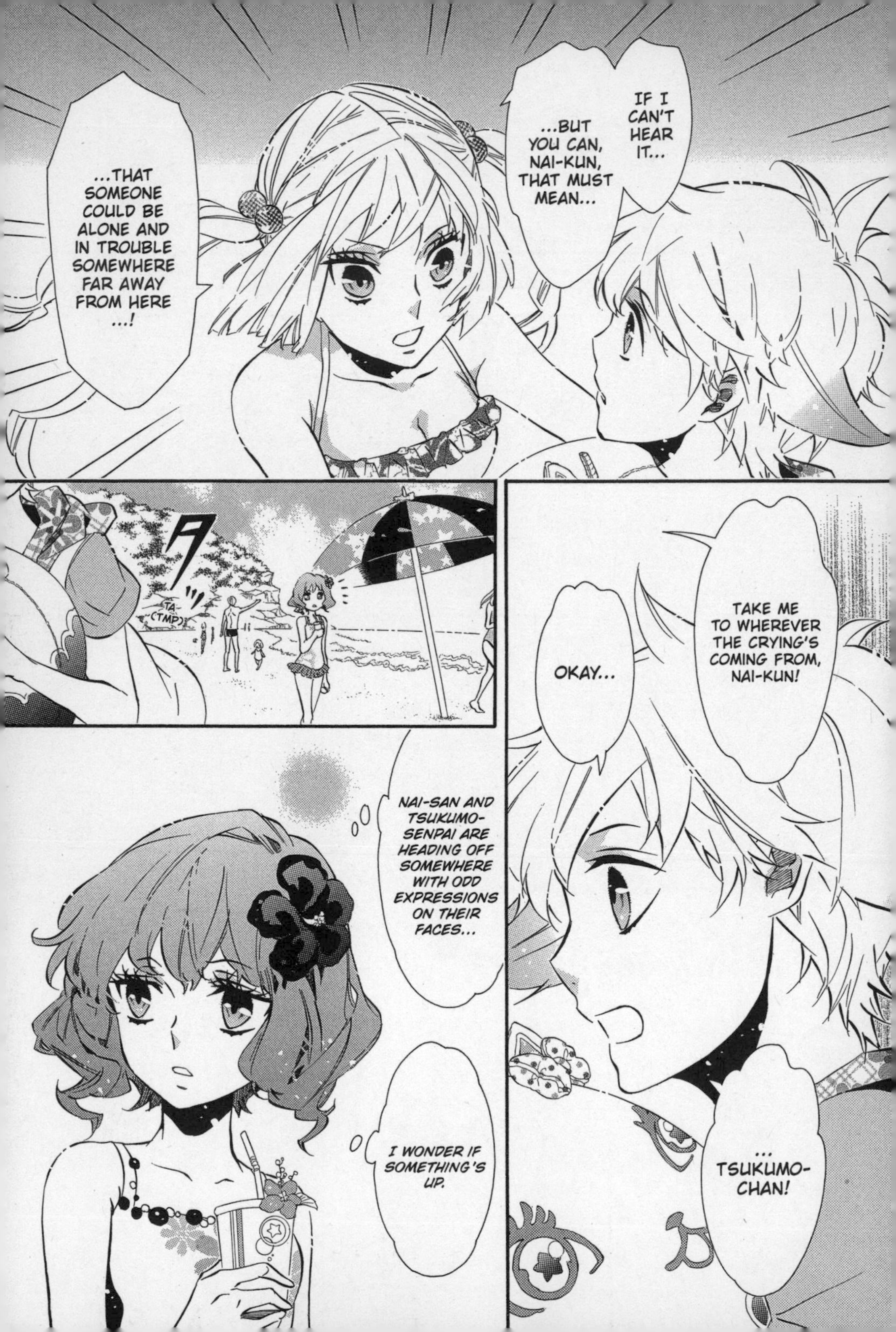
IF I CAN'T HEAR IT...
...BUT YOU CAN, NAI-KUN, THAT MUST MEAN...
...THAT SOMEONE COULD BE ALONE AND IN TROUBLE SOMEWHERE FAR AWAY FROM HERE ...!
TAKE ME TO WHEREVER THE CRYING'S COMING FROM, NAI-KUN!
OKAY...
... TSUKUMO-CHAN!
TA (TMP)
NAI-SAN AND TSUKUMO-SENPAI ARE HEADING OFF SOMEWHERE WITH ODD EXPRESSIONS ON THEIR FACES...
I WONDER IF SOMETHING'S UP.

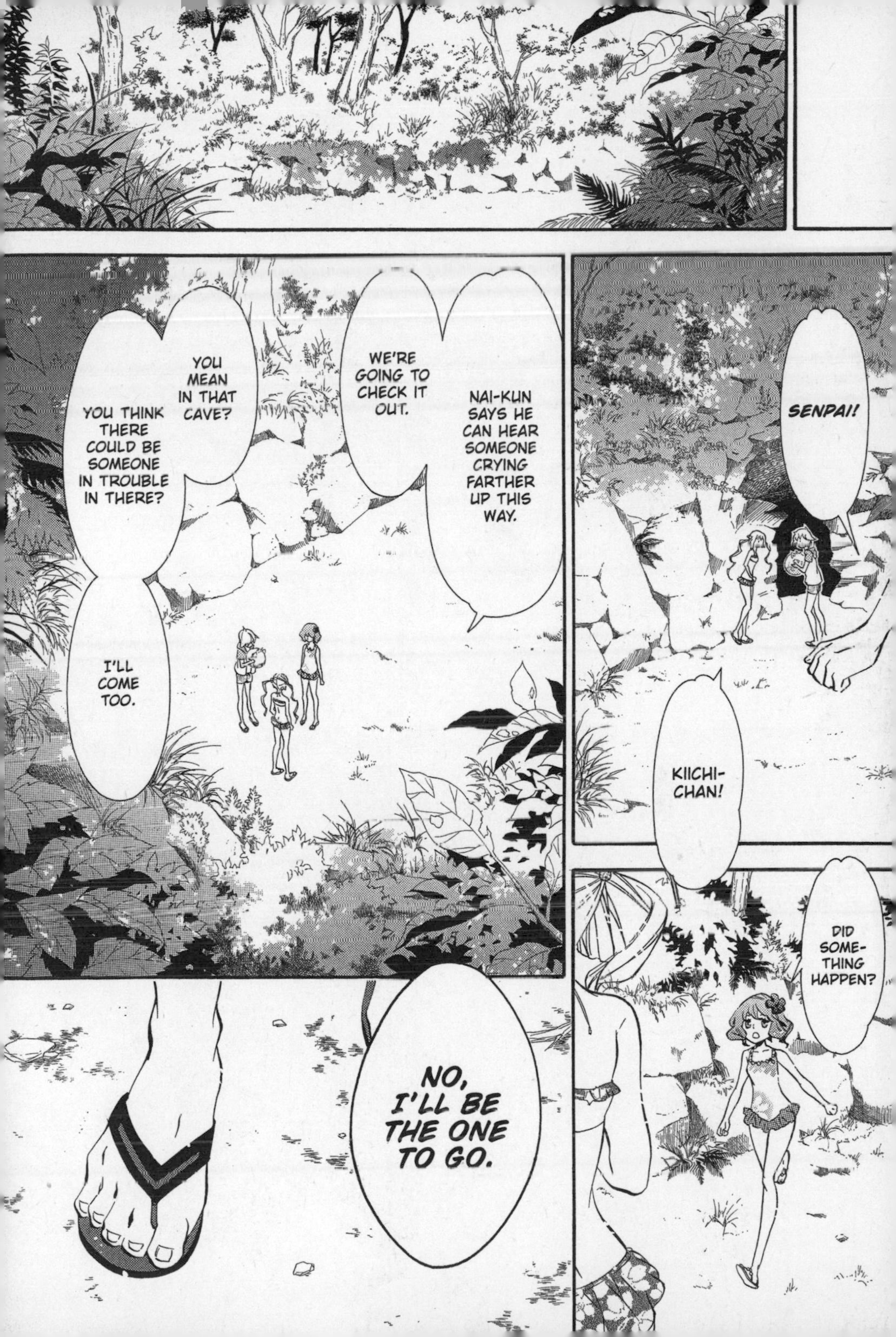
SENPAI!
KIICHI-CHAN!
DID SOMETHING HAPPEN?
NAI-KUN SAYS HE CAN HEAR SOMEONE CRYING FARTHER UP THIS WAY.
WE'RE GOING TO CHECK IT OUT.
YOU MEAN IN THAT CAVE?
YOU THINK THERE COULD BE SOMEONE IN TROUBLE IN THERE?
I'LL COME TOO.
NO, I'LL BE THE ONE TO GO.

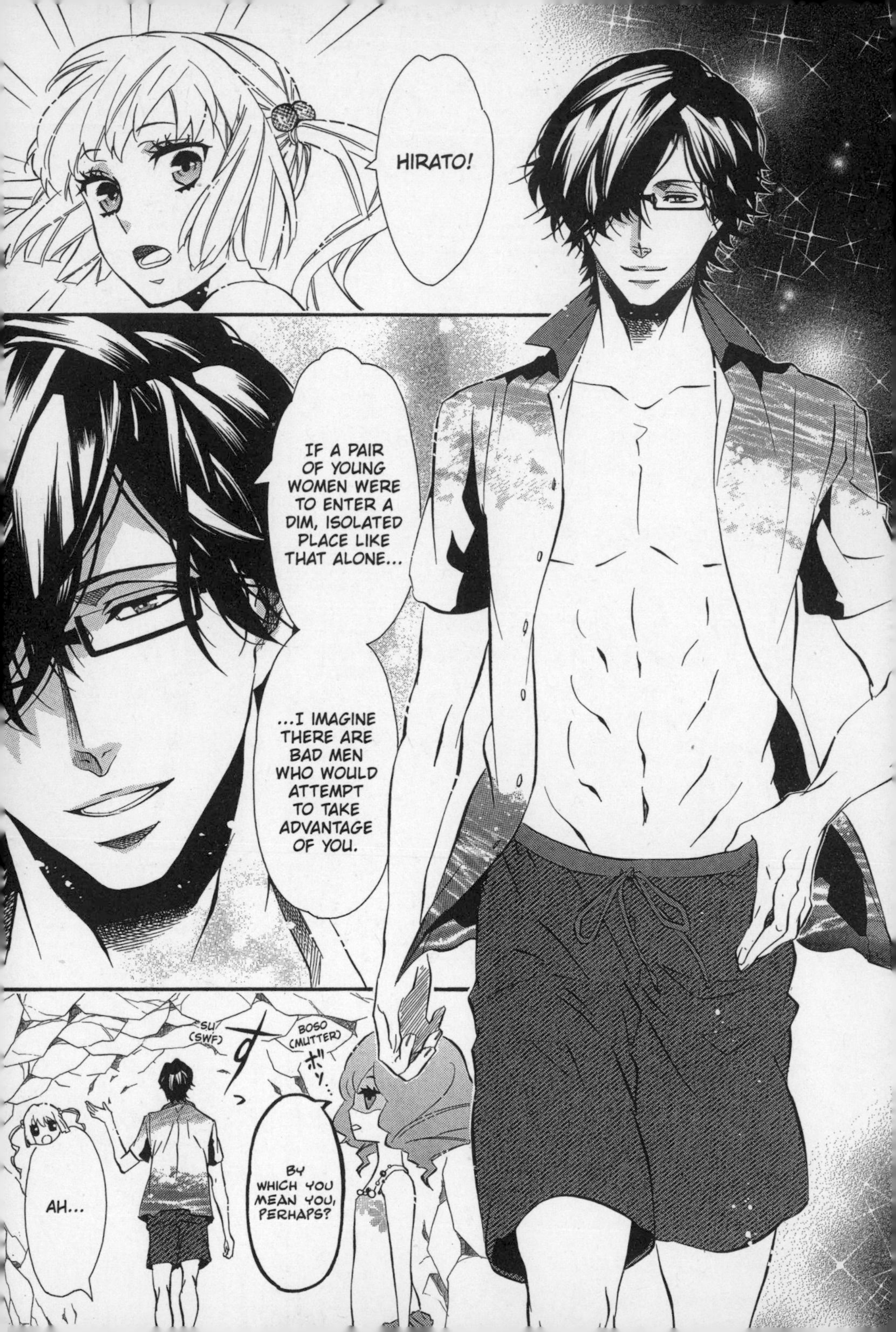

HIRATO!
IF A PAIR OF YOUNG WOMEN WERE TO ENTER A DIM, ISOLATED PLACE LIKE THAT ALONE...
...I IMAGINE THERE ARE BAD MEN WHO WOULD ATTEMPT TO TAKE ADVANTAGE OF YOU.
BOSO (MUTTER)
ボソッ…
BY WHICH YOU MEAN YOU, PERHAPS?
SU (SWF)
AH...

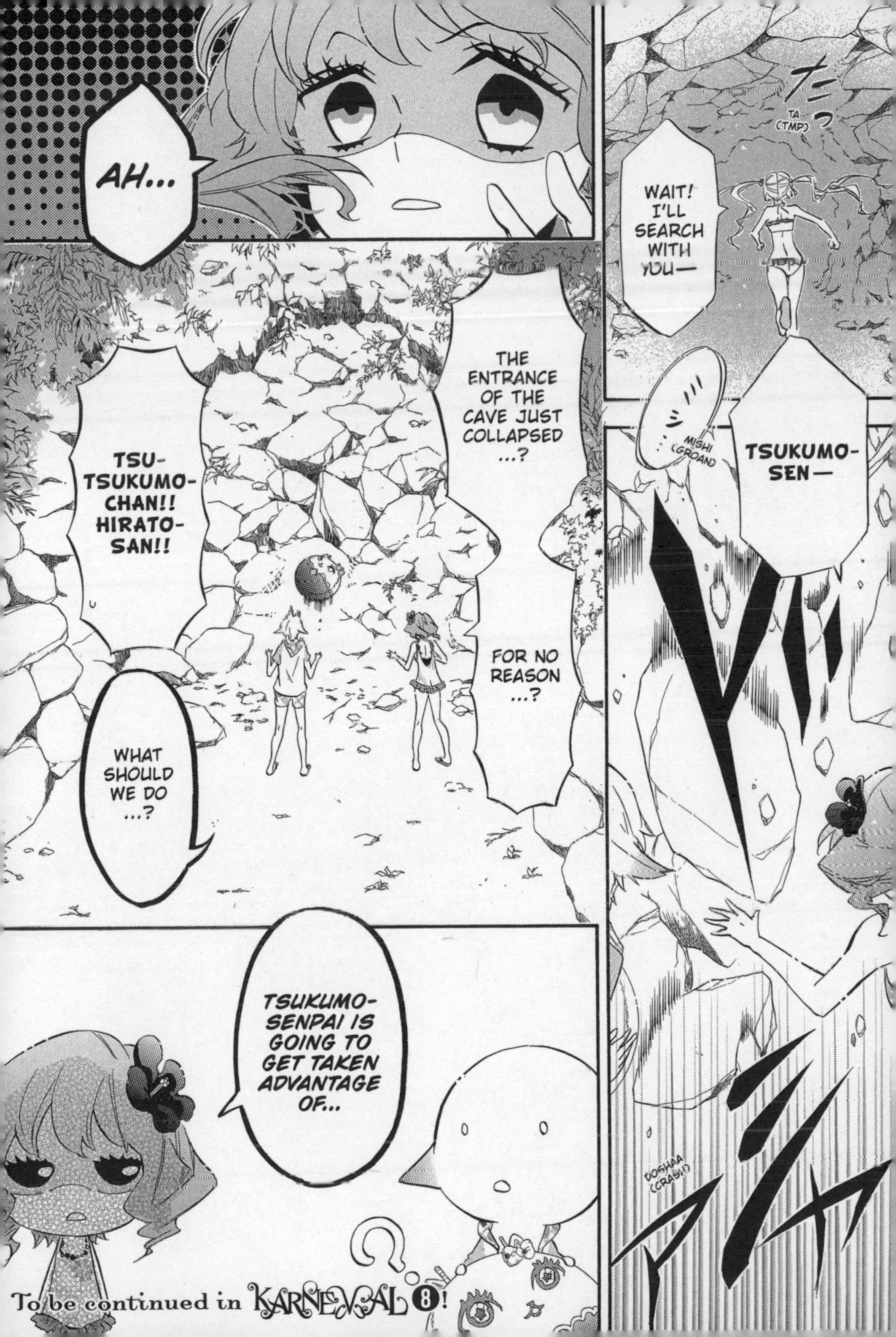
TA (TMP)
WAIT! I'LL SEARCH WITH YOU—
MISHI (GROAN)
TSUKUMO-SEN—
DOSHAA (CRASH)
AH...
THE ENTRANCE OF THE CAVE JUST COLLAPSED ...?
FOR NO REASON ...?
TSU-TSUKUMO-CHAN!! HIRATO-SAN!!
WHAT SHOULD WE DO ...?
TSUKUMO-SENPAI IS GOING TO GET TAKEN ADVANTAGE OF...
To be continued in KARNEVAL 8!

KARNEVAL

KARNEVAL

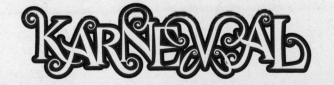

KARNEVAL

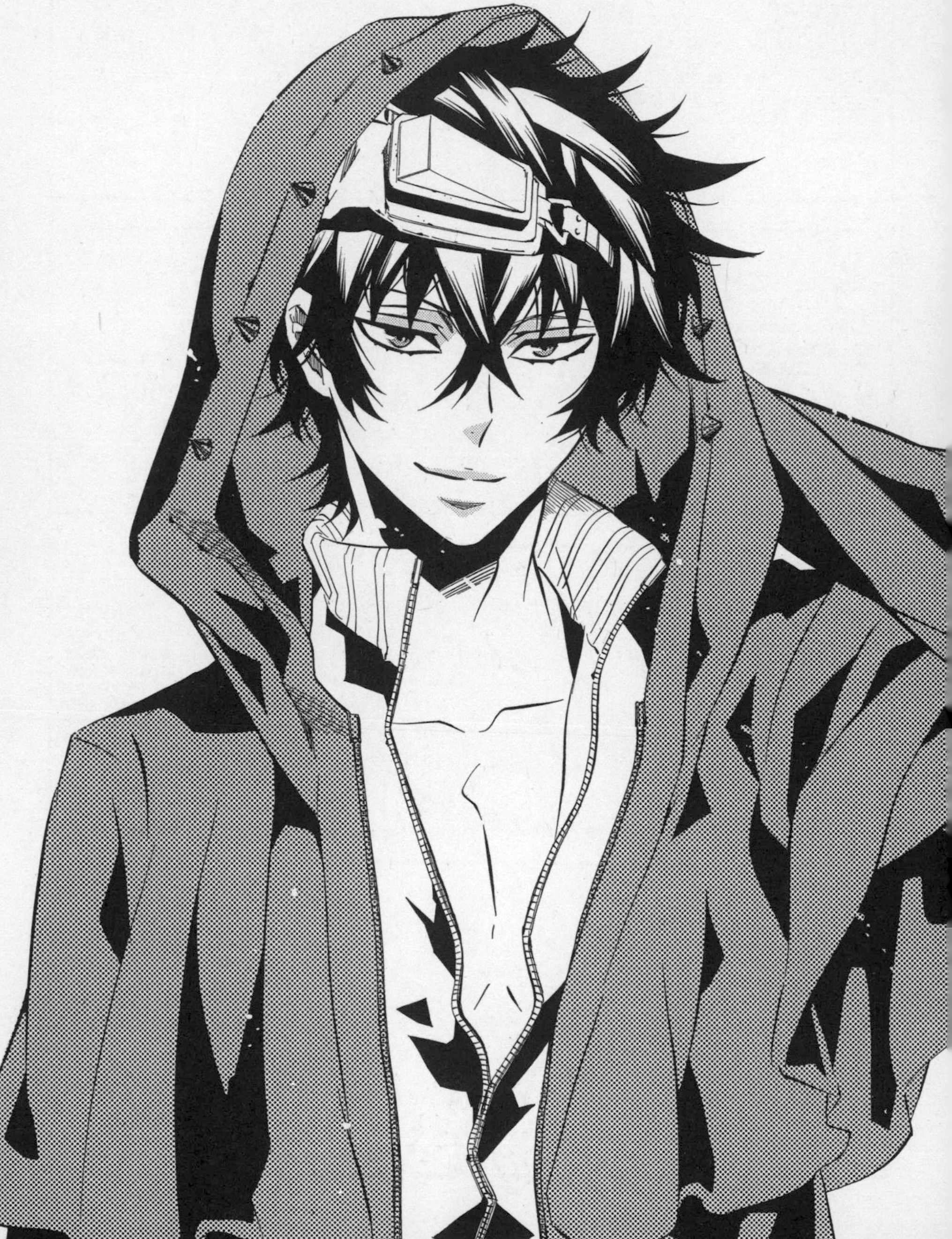

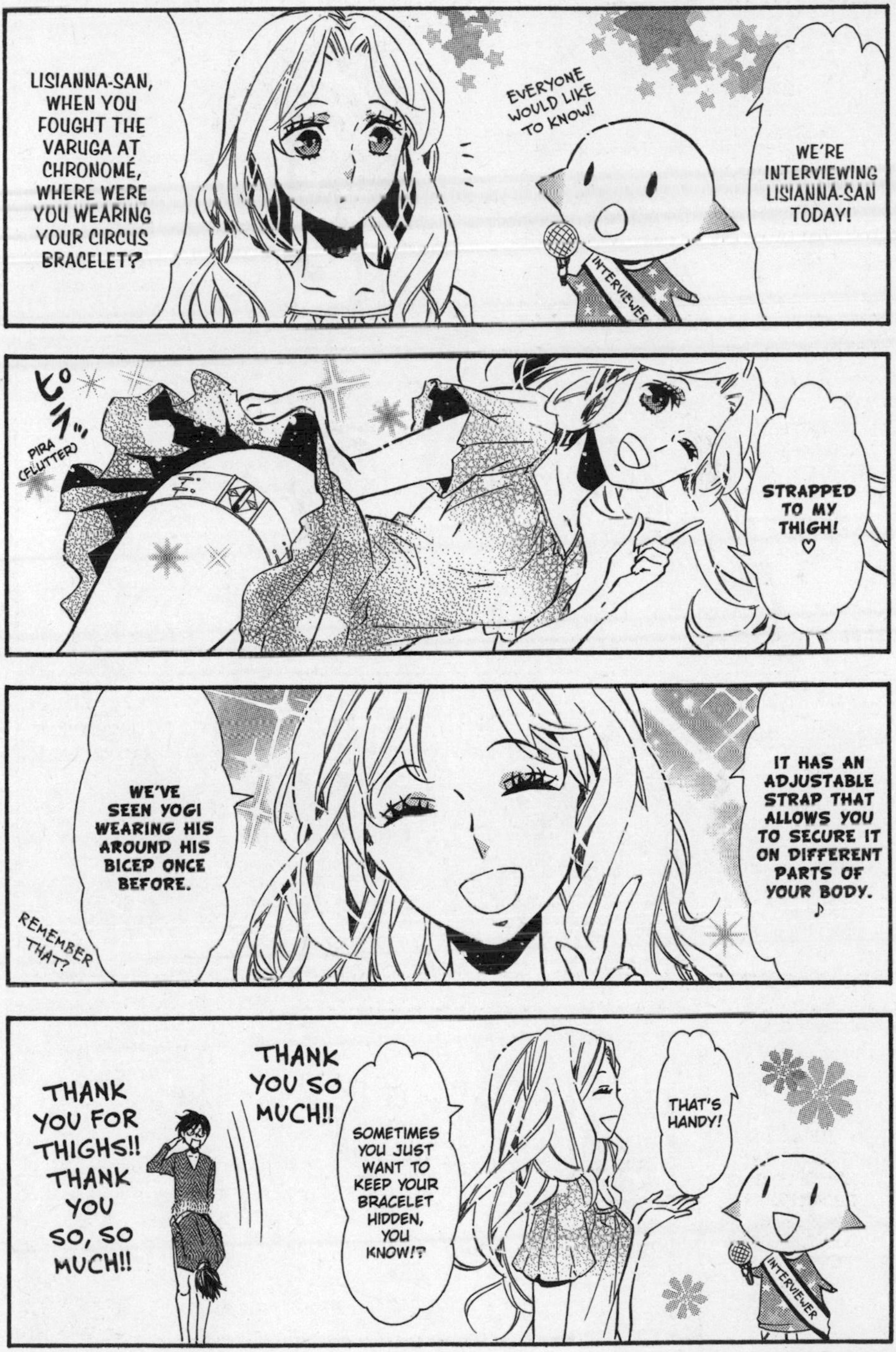
WE'RE INTERVIEWING LISIANNA-SAN TODAY!
EVERYONE WOULD LIKE TO KNOW!
INTERVIEWER
LISIANNA-SAN, WHEN YOU FOUGHT THE VARUGA AT CHRONOMÉ, WHERE WERE YOU WEARING YOUR CIRCUS BRACELET?
STRAPPED TO MY THIGH! ♡
PIRA (FLUTTER)
IT HAS AN ADJUSTABLE STRAP THAT ALLOWS YOU TO SECURE IT ON DIFFERENT PARTS OF YOUR BODY. ♪
WE'VE SEEN YOGI WEARING HIS AROUND HIS BICEP ONCE BEFORE.
REMEMBER THAT?
THAT'S HANDY!
INTERVIEWER
SOMETIMES YOU JUST WANT TO KEEP YOUR BRACELET HIDDEN, YOU KNOW!?
THANK YOU SO MUCH!!
THANK YOU FOR THIGHS!! THANK YOU SO, SO MUCH!!

Bonus Comic 2 - Small Actions

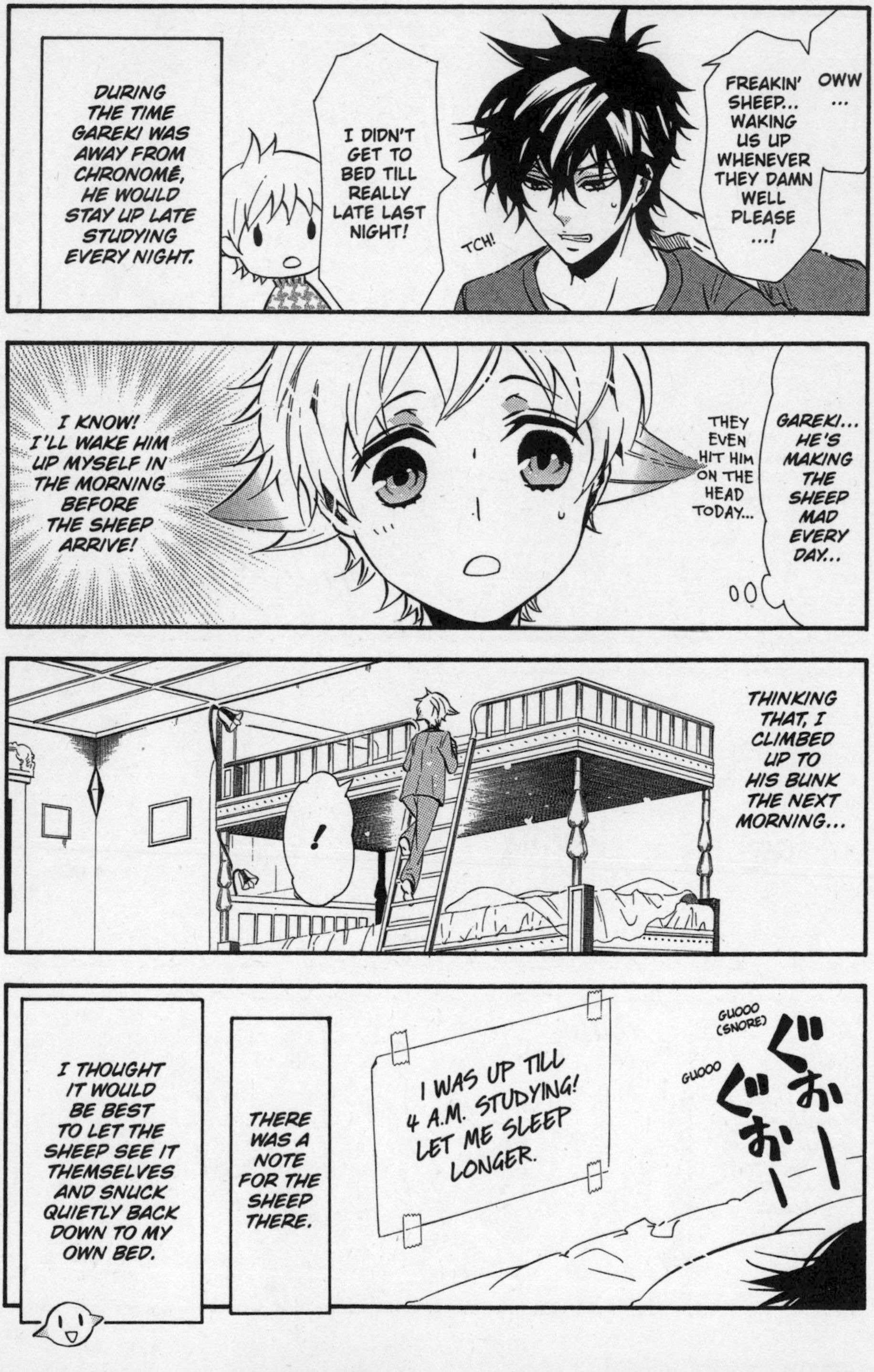
OWW ...
FREAKIN' SHEEP... WAKING US UP WHENEVER THEY DAMN WELL PLEASE ...!
TCH!
I DIDN'T GET TO BED TILL REALLY LATE LAST NIGHT!
DURING THE TIME GAREKI WAS AWAY FROM CHRONOMÉ, HE WOULD STAY UP LATE STUDYING EVERY NIGHT.
GAREKI... HE'S MAKING THE SHEEP MAD EVERY DAY...
THEY EVEN HIT HIM ON THE HEAD TODAY...
I KNOW! I'LL WAKE HIM UP MYSELF IN THE MORNING BEFORE THE SHEEP ARRIVE!
THINKING THAT, I CLIMBED UP TO HIS BUNK THE NEXT MORNING...
!
ぐおー
GUOOO (SNORE)
ぐおー
GUOOO
I WAS UP TILL 4 A.M. STUDYING! LET ME SLEEP LONGER.
THERE WAS A NOTE FOR THE SHEEP THERE.
I THOUGHT IT WOULD BE BEST TO LET THE SHEEP SEE IT THEMSELVES AND SNUCK QUIETLY BACK DOWN TO MY OWN BED.

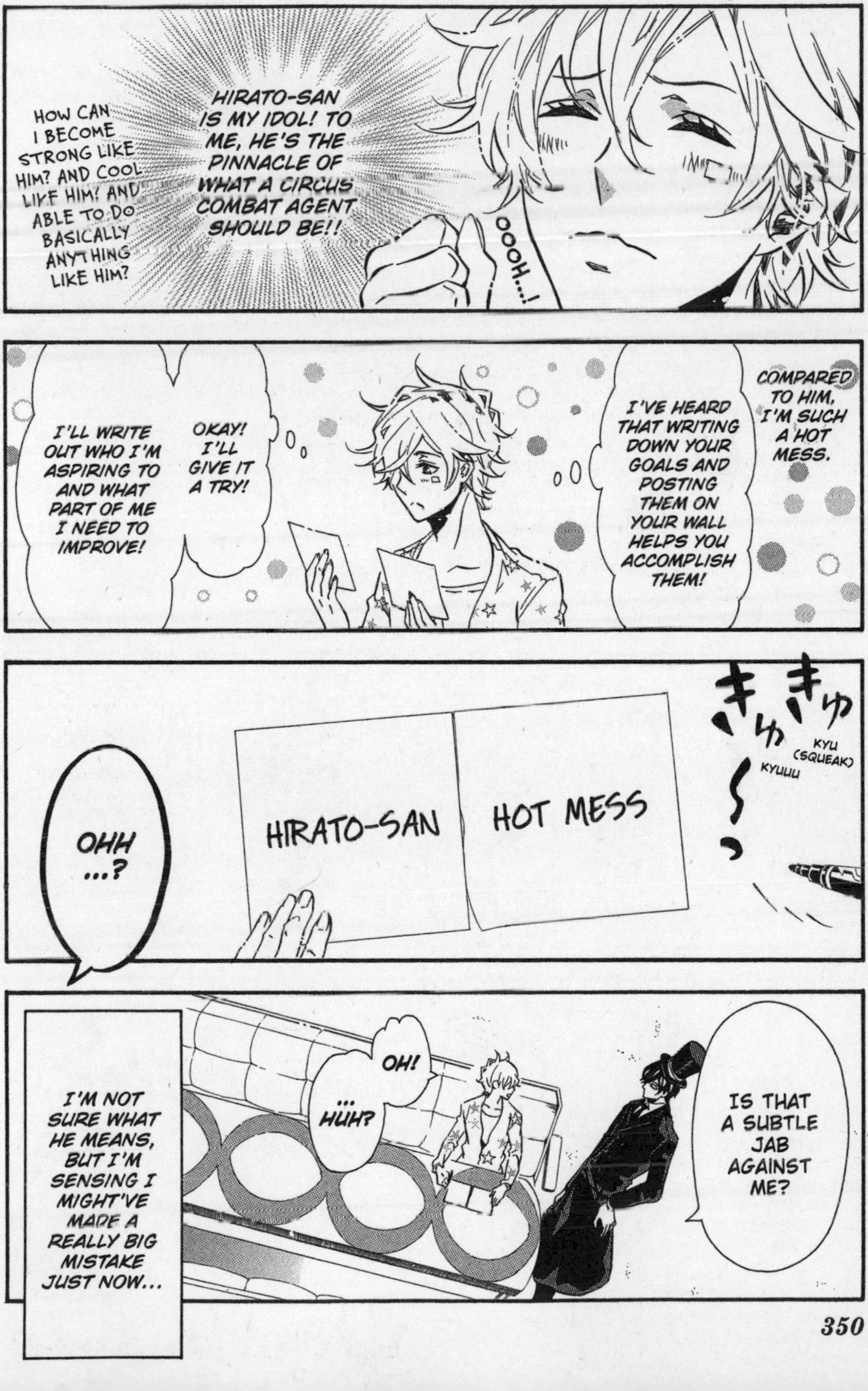
HIRATO-SAN IS MY IDOL! TO ME, HE'S THE PINNACLE OF WHAT A CIRCUS COMBAT AGENT SHOULD BE!!
HOW CAN I BECOME STRONG LIKE HIM? AND COOL LIKE HIM? AND ABLE TO DO BASICALLY ANYTHING LIKE HIM?
OOOH...!
COMPARED TO HIM, I'M SUCH A HOT MESS.
I'VE HEARD THAT WRITING DOWN YOUR GOALS AND POSTING THEM ON YOUR WALL HELPS YOU ACCOMPLISH THEM!
OKAY! I'LL GIVE IT A TRY!
I'LL WRITE OUT WHO I'M ASPIRING TO AND WHAT PART OF ME I NEED TO IMPROVE!
きゅ きゅ〜
KYU (SQUEAK)
KYUUU
HOT MESS
HIRATO-SAN
OHH ...?
IS THAT A SUBTLE JAB AGAINST ME?
OH!
... HUH?
I'M NOT SURE WHAT HE MEANS, BUT I'M SENSING I MIGHT'VE MADE A REALLY BIG MISTAKE JUST NOW...

BUT I'LL WORK REALLY HARD NOT TO MAKE ANOTHER MISTAKE, SO PLEASE CHEER ME ON IN THE NEXT VOLUME! ☆ —YOGI

THANK YOU SO MUCH FOR READING VOLUME 14! I REALLY HOPE YOU ENJOYED THIS ONE. VERY UNUSUALLY FOR ME, MUCH OF THIS VOLUME WAS DEVOTED TO PAGES OF BATTLE SCENES. WHAT DID YOU THINK OF THEM? I'M REALLY HOPING I WAS ABLE TO SHOW THE CHARACTERS AND THEIR INTERACTIONS WELL IN A VARIETY OF SITUATIONS. THIS YEAR, ASIDE FROM KARNEVAL, I ALSO GOT TO WORK AS A CHARACTER DESIGNER ON THE VIDEO GAME ROOT ∞ REX BY OTOMATE, WHICH JUST WENT ON SALE RECENTLY. WHEN I RECEIVED THE STORY FROM THEM, I WAS VERY SURPRISED AND HAPPY. I ALSO RECEIVED VARIOUS SCENES FROM THE DIFFERENT CHARACTERS' ROUTES IN THE GAME TO ILLUSTRATE. THE CHALLENGE OF FINDING A WAY TO PUT MY PERSONAL TOUCH ON THOSE ILLUSTRATIONS WAS A NEW AND DIFFICULT EXPERIENCE FOR ME, BUT ALSO LOTS OF FUN. PERSONALLY, I FOUND THE HEROINE'S SHORT, BLACK HAIR INCREDIBLY FRESH. I WAS VERY HONORED THEY WANTED ME TO DO THE MANGA ADAPTATION FOR THE GAME AS WELL, SO I HOPE YOU ALL WILL GIVE IT A READ AS YOU CONTINUE READING KARNEVAL AS WELL! AS FOR THE KARNEVAL DRAMA CDS, THE NEWEST ONE, THE TWO YOGIS, WAS RELEASED TWO MONTHS PRIOR TO THIS VOLUME'S JAPANESE RELEASE, IN DECEMBER! I DREW SOME NEW ILLUSTRATIONS FOR BOTH ITS COVER AND BOOKLET, SO I'D BE VERY HAPPY IF YOU ALL WOULD GIVE IT A LISTEN.

TOUYA MIKANAGI

Special Thanks

o KANA-CHAN, 🐱-SAN

o MOTSU-SAN, SUAMA-SAN

o MY EDITOR, ABE-SAN

o EVERYONE AT ICHIJINSHA PUBLISHING

o ALL THE COLLABORATORS AND EVERYONE AT OUR AFFILIATED COMPANIES WHO'VE TAKEN CARE OF ME

o TEN-CHAN AND JUN-SAN AND MY FAMILY

and To You !!

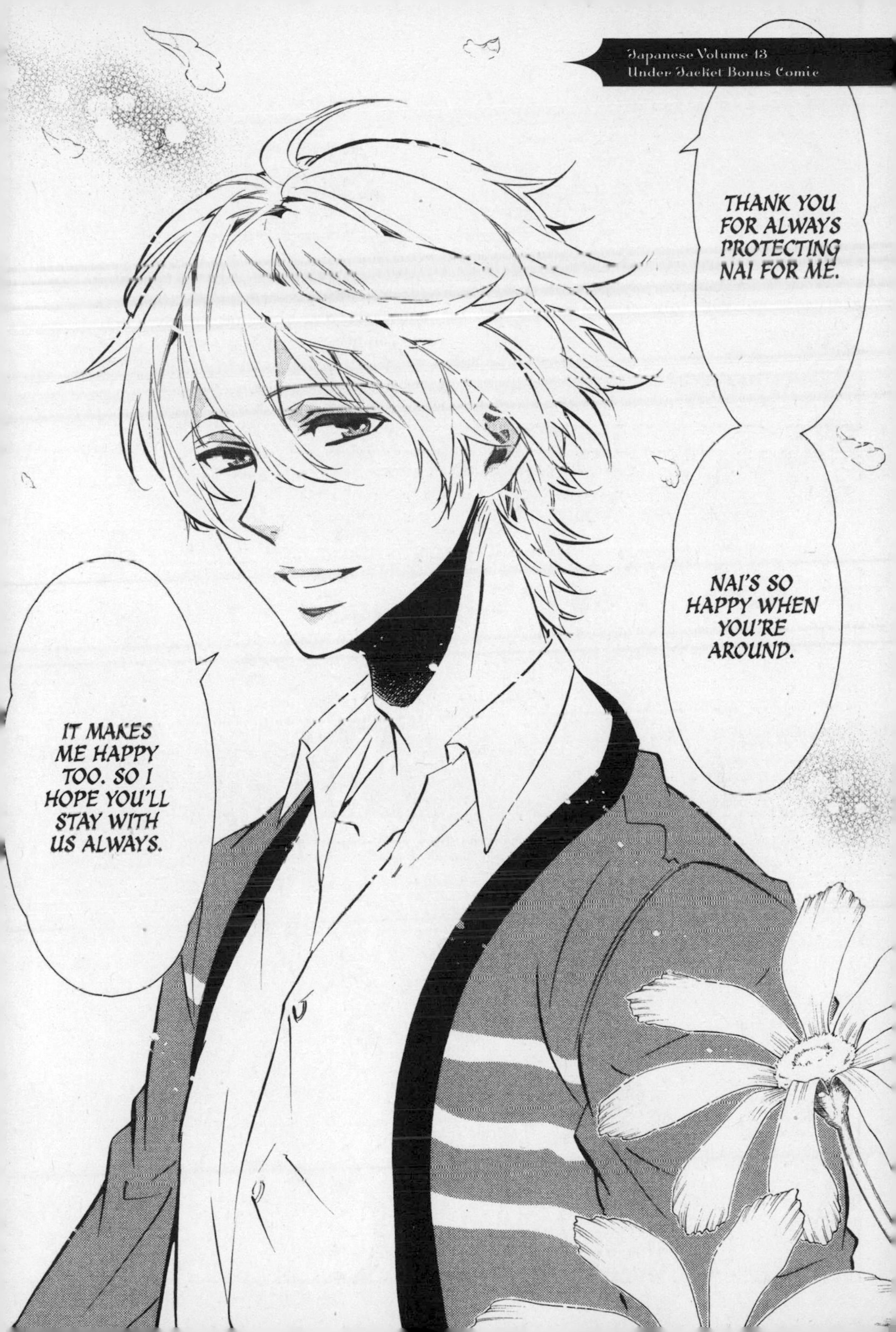
Japanese Volume 13
Under Jacket Bonus Comic
THANK YOU FOR ALWAYS PROTECTING NAI FOR ME.
NAI'S SO HAPPY WHEN YOU'RE AROUND.
IT MAKES ME HAPPY TOO. SO I HOPE YOU'LL STAY WITH US ALWAYS.

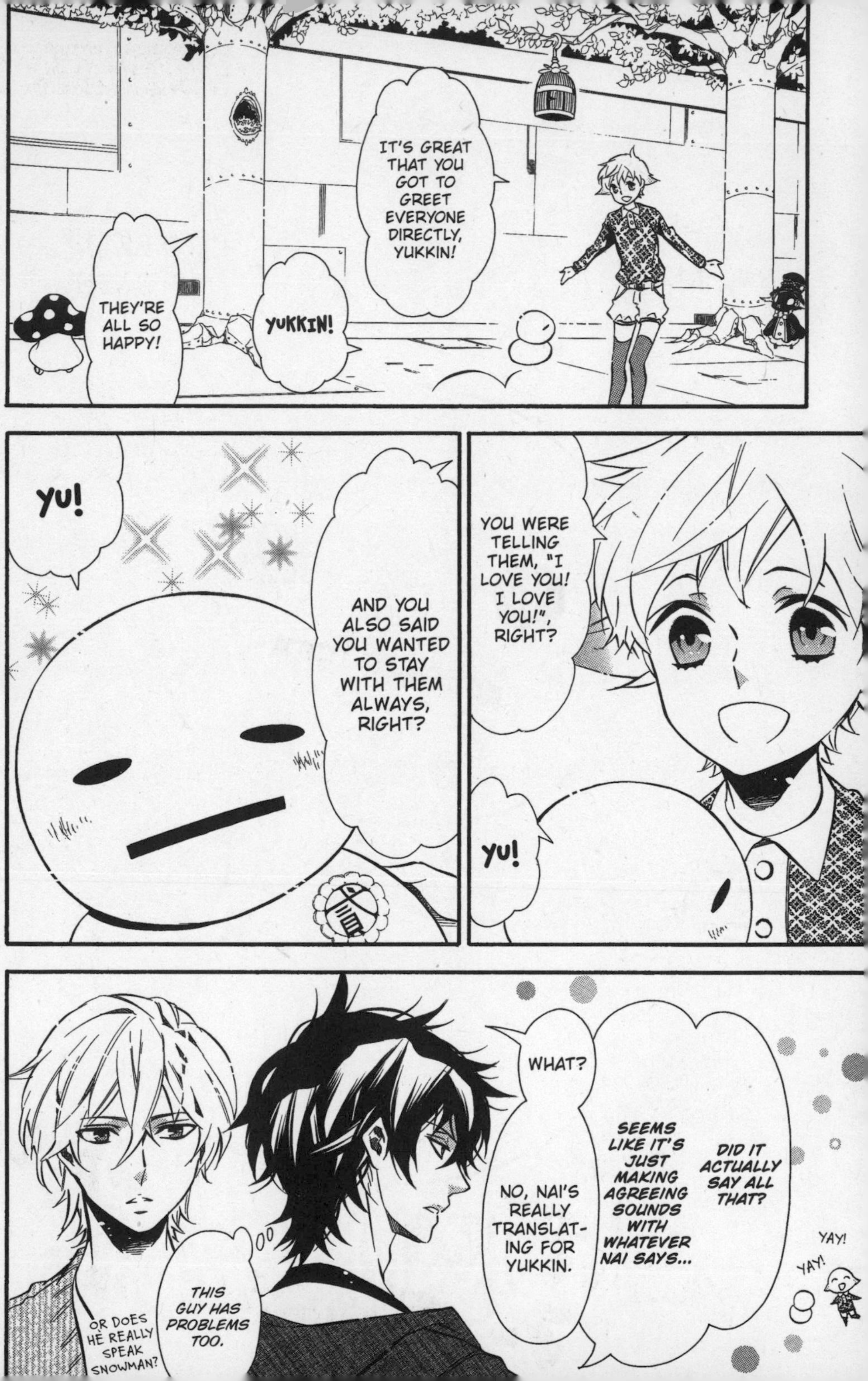
IT'S GREAT THAT YOU GOT TO GREET EVERYONE DIRECTLY, YUKKIN!
YUKKIN!
THEY'RE ALL SO HAPPY!
YOU WERE TELLING THEM, "I LOVE YOU! I LOVE YOU!", RIGHT?
YU!
AND YOU ALSO SAID YOU WANTED TO STAY WITH THEM ALWAYS, RIGHT?
YU!
YAY!
YAY!
DID IT ACTUALLY SAY ALL THAT?
SEEMS LIKE IT'S JUST MAKING AGREEING SOUNDS WITH WHATEVER NAI SAYS...
WHAT?
NO, NAI'S REALLY TRANSLAT-ING FOR YUKKIN.
THIS GUY HAS PROBLEMS TOO.
OR DOES HE REALLY SPEAK SNOWMAN?

KARNEVAL

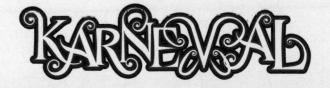

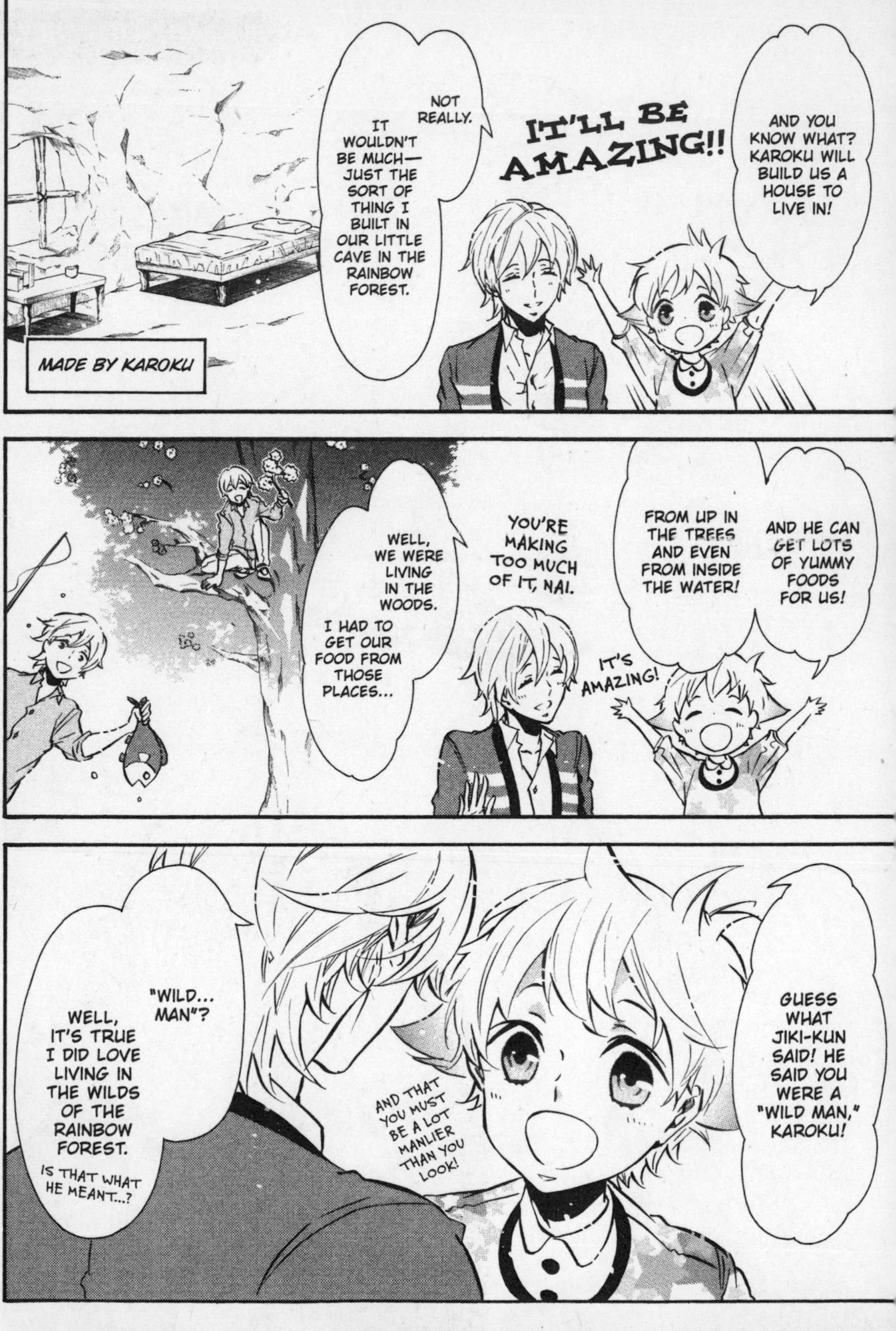
AND YOU KNOW WHAT? KAROKU WILL BUILD US A HOUSE TO LIVE IN!
IT'LL BE AMAZING!!
NOT REALLY.
IT WOULDN'T BE MUCH— JUST THE SORT OF THING I BUILT IN OUR LITTLE CAVE IN THE RAINBOW FOREST.
MADE BY KAROKU
AND HE CAN GET LOTS OF YUMMY FOODS FOR US!
FROM UP IN THE TREES AND EVEN FROM INSIDE THE WATER!
IT'S AMAZING!
YOU'RE MAKING TOO MUCH OF IT, NAI.
WELL, WE WERE LIVING IN THE WOODS.
I HAD TO GET OUR FOOD FROM THOSE PLACES...
GUESS WHAT JIKI-KUN SAID! HE SAID YOU WERE A "WILD MAN," KAROKU!
AND THAT YOU MUST BE A LOT MANLIER THAN YOU LOOK!
"WILD... MAN"?
WELL, IT'S TRUE I DID LOVE LIVING IN THE WILDS OF THE RAINBOW FOREST.
IS THAT WHAT HE MEANT...?

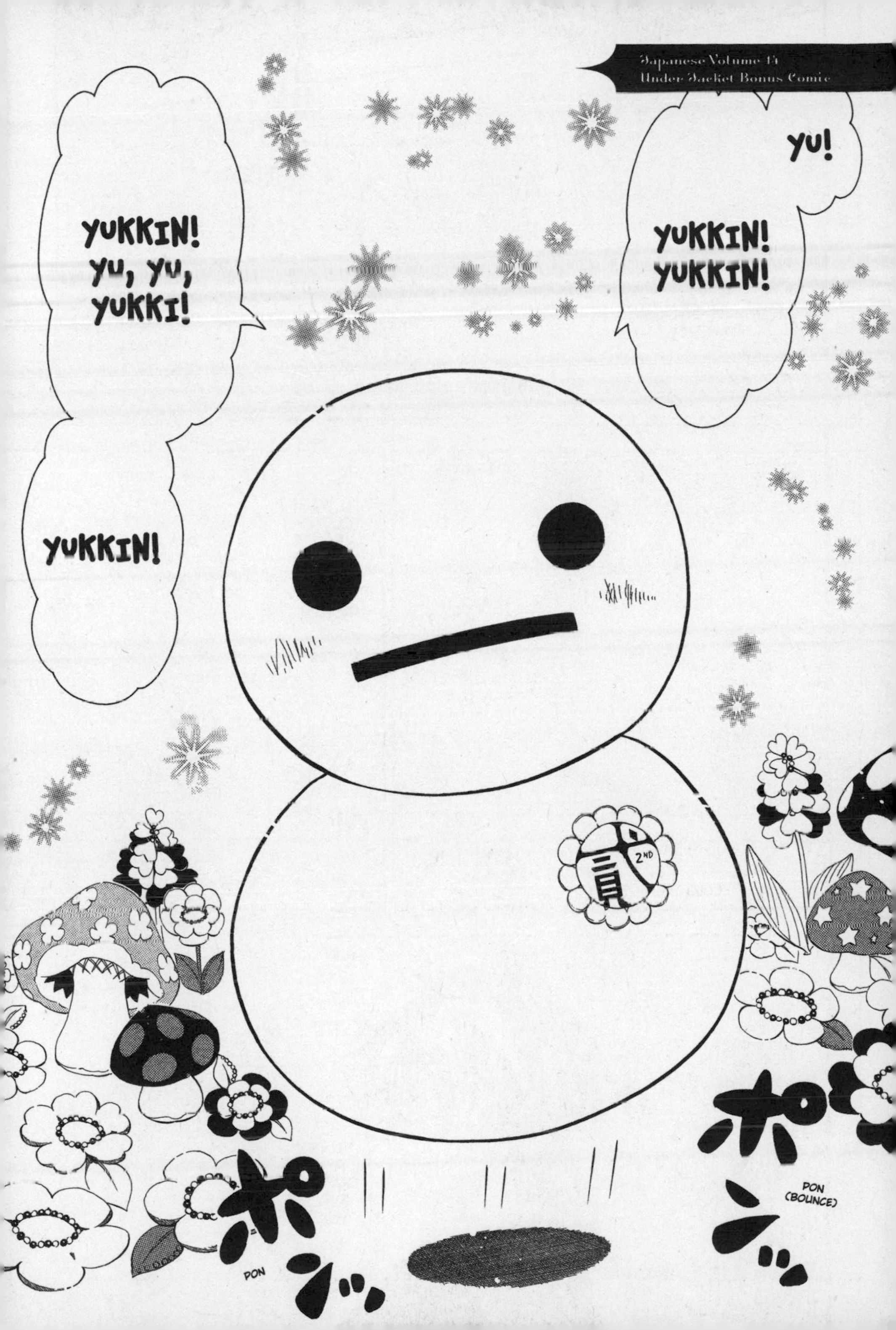
Japanese Volume 14
Under Jacket Bonus Comic
YU!
YUKKIN! YUKKIN!
YUKKIN! YU, YU, YUKKI!
YUKKIN!
PON (BOUNCE)
PON

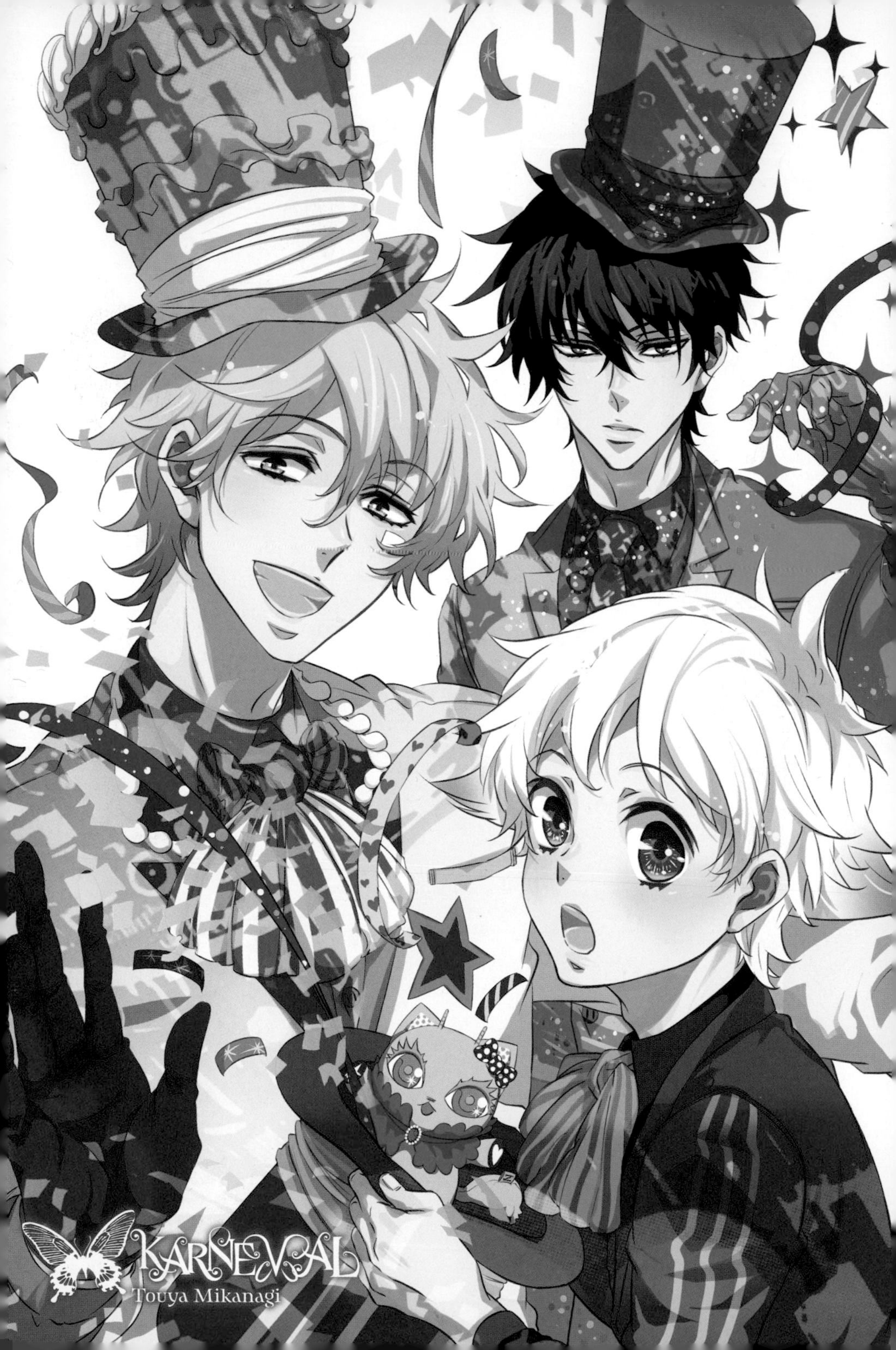
KARNEVAL
Touya Mikanagi

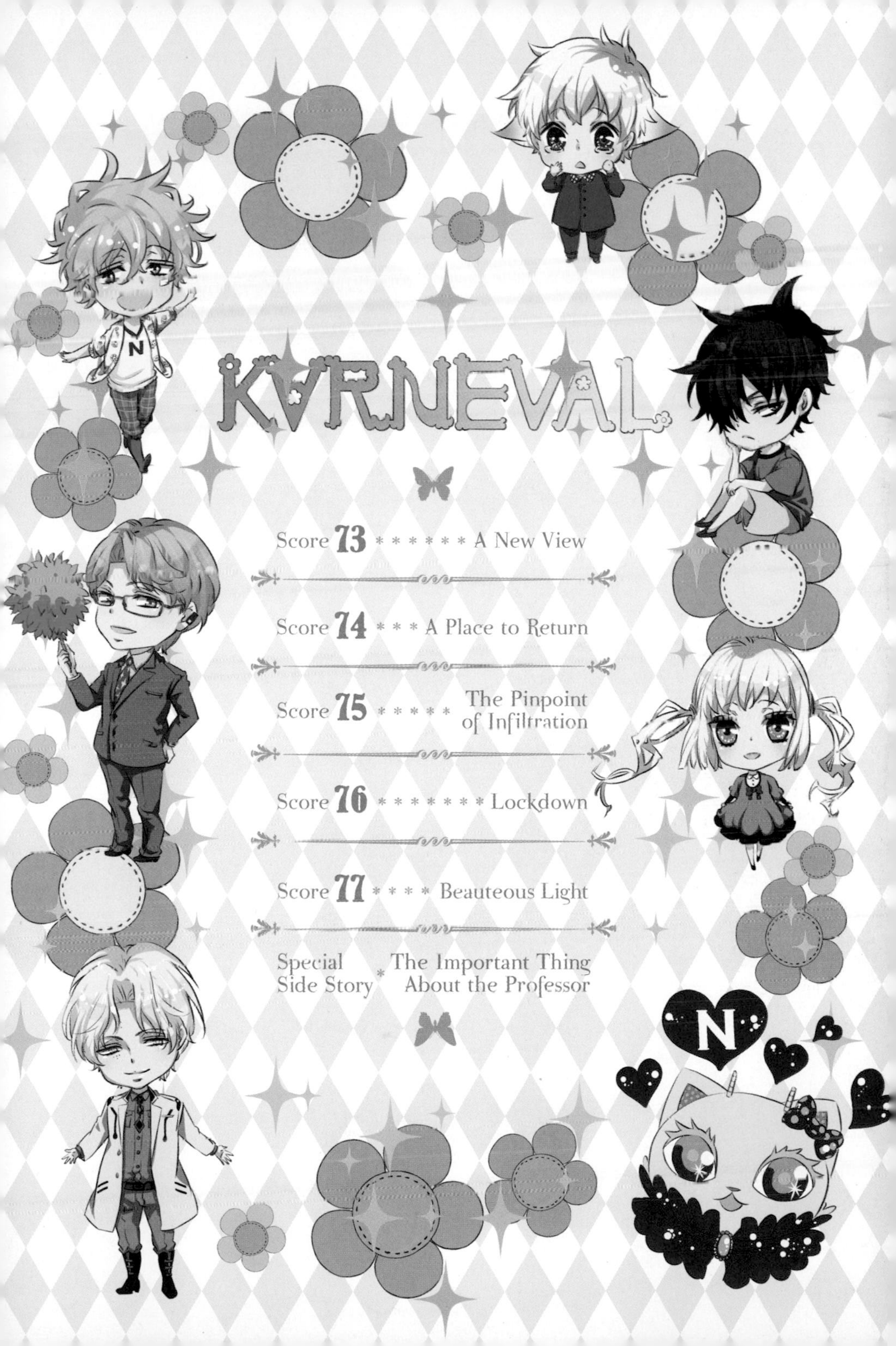

KARNEVAL

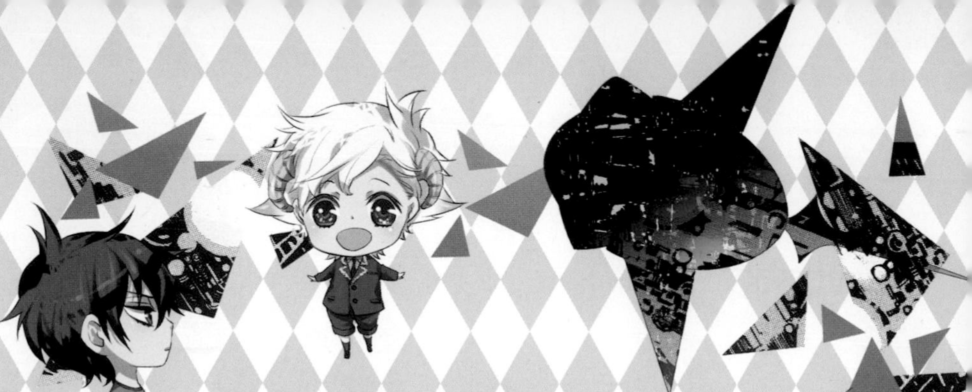

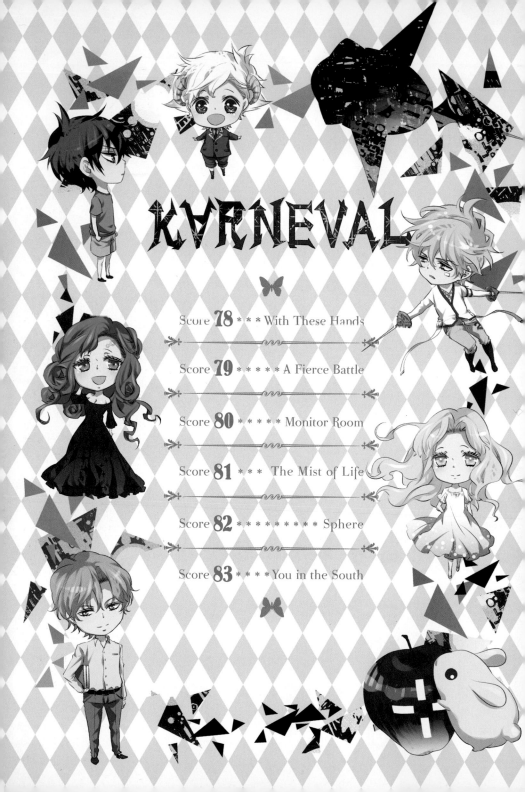

KARNEVAL

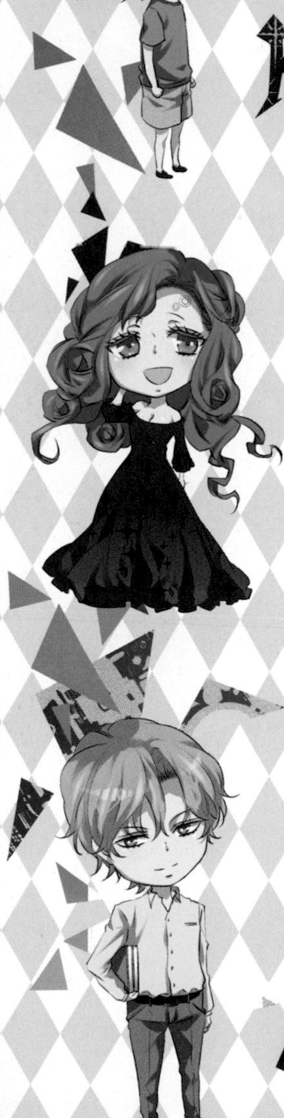

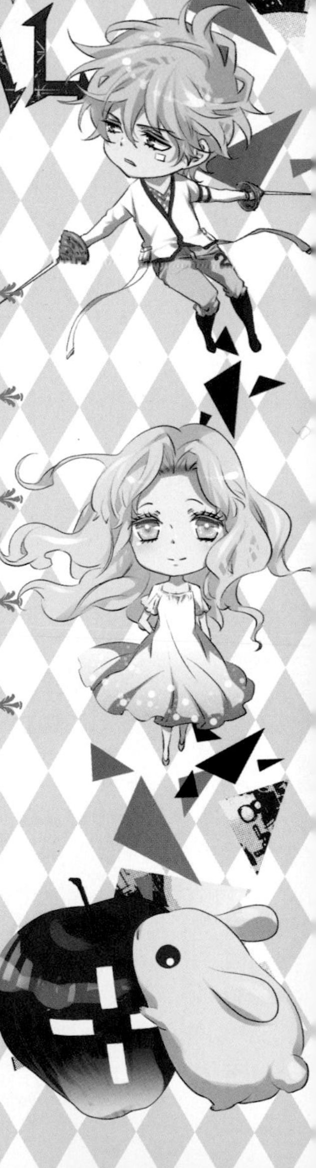

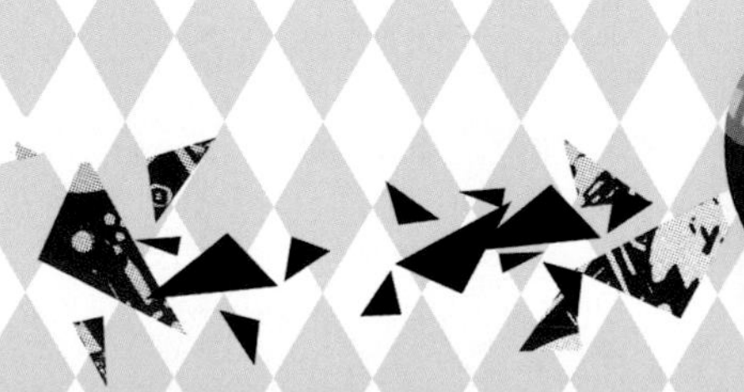

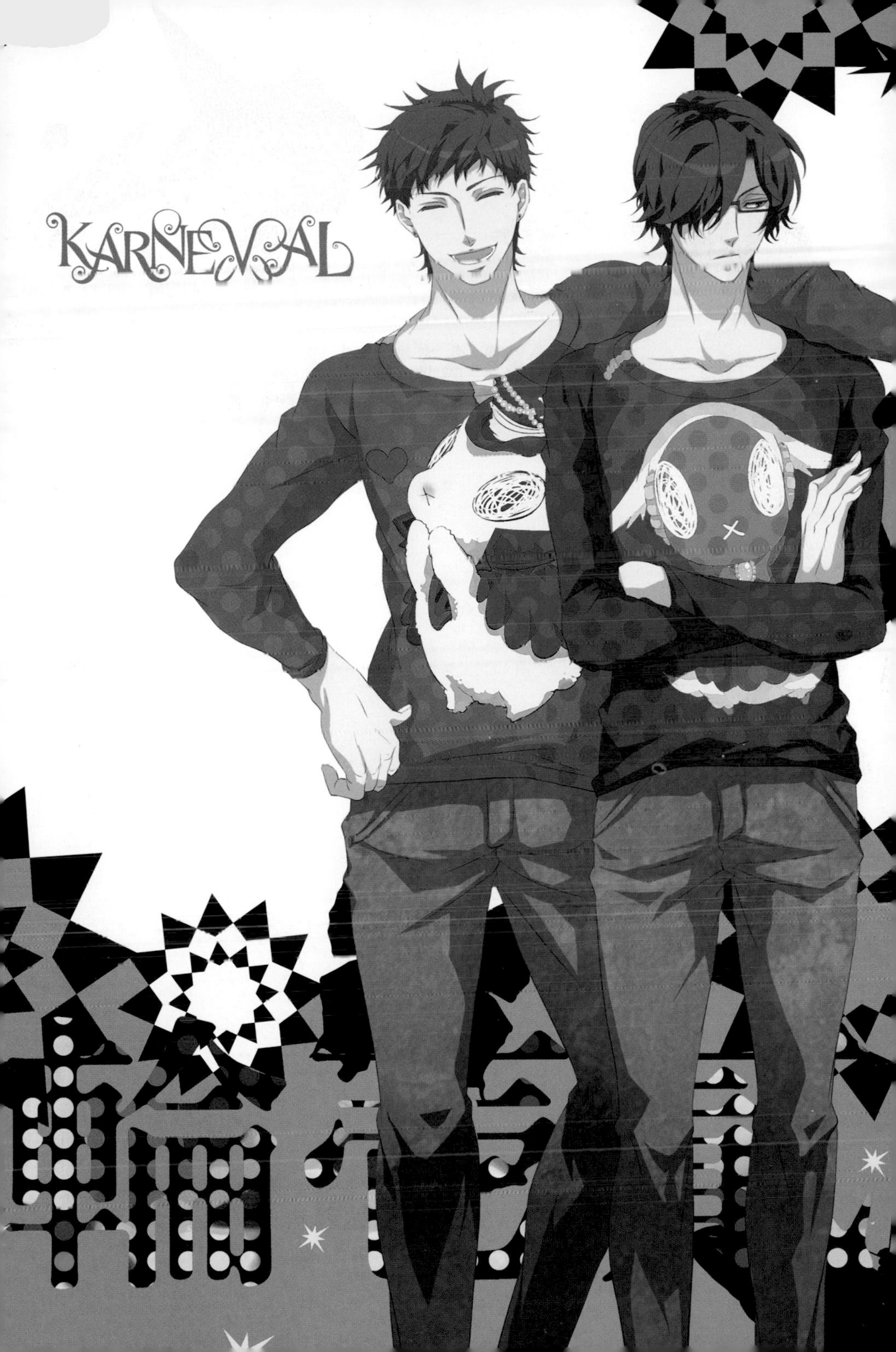
KARNEVAL

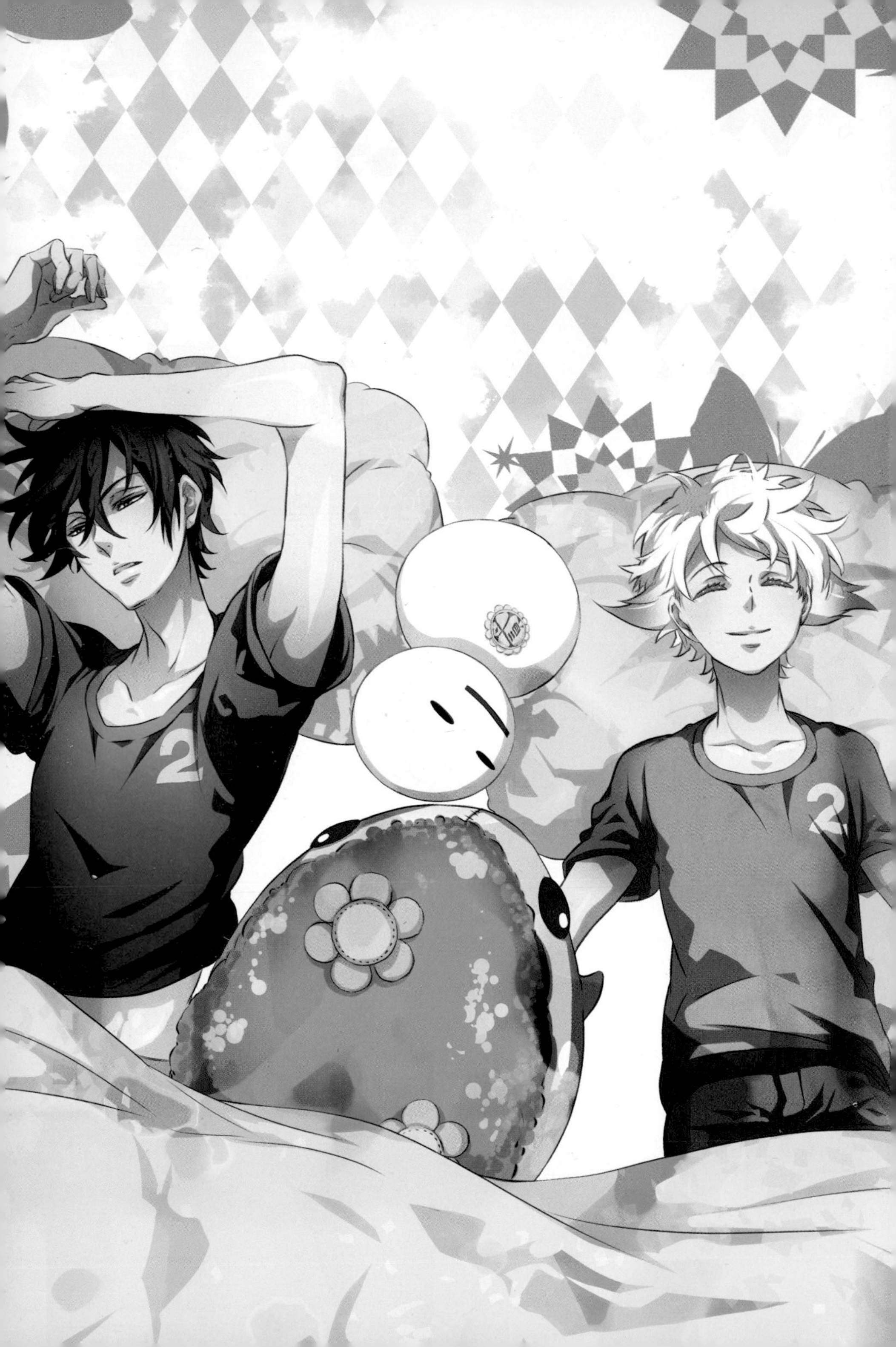

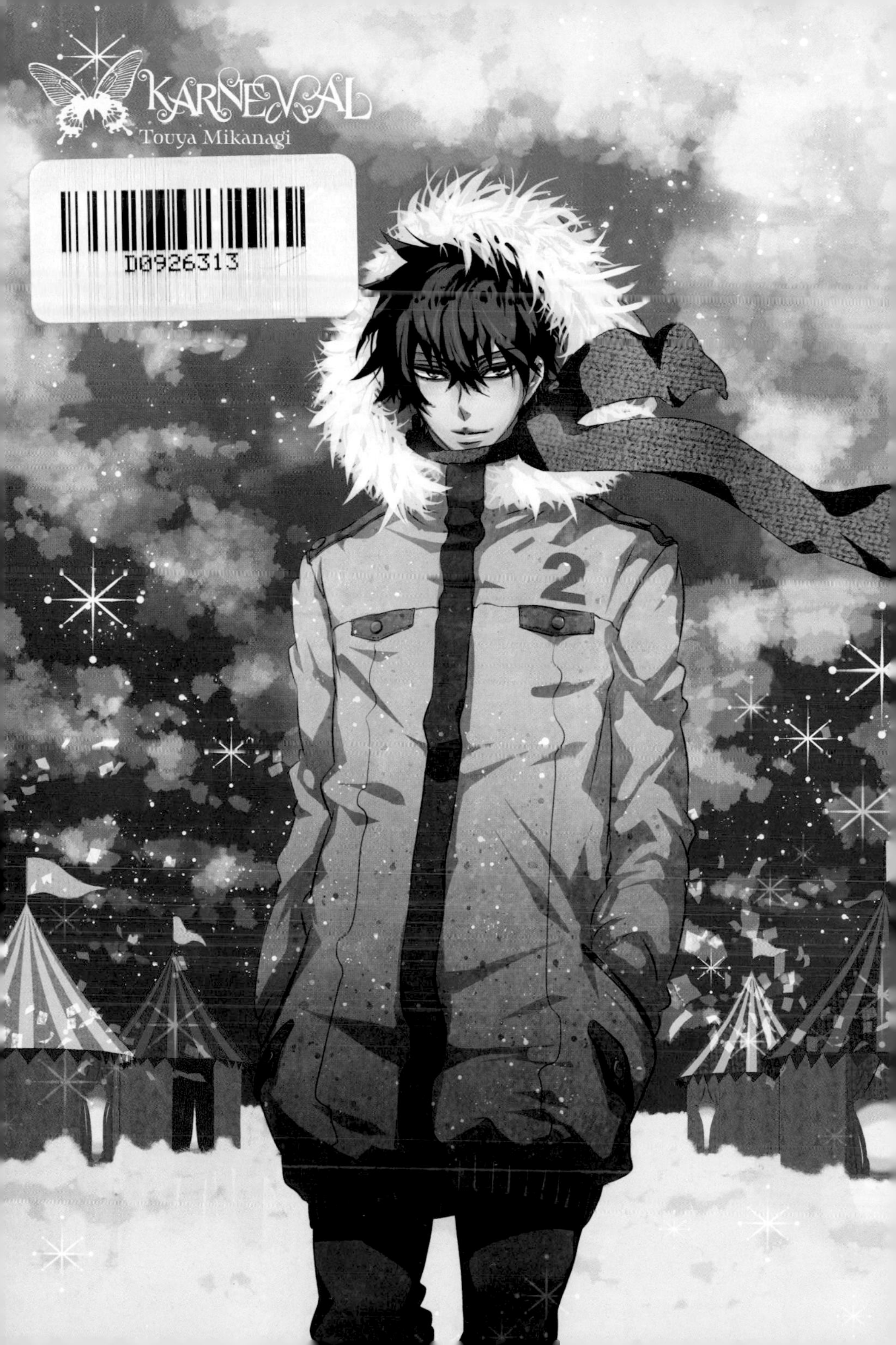
KARNEVAL
Touya Mikanagi
2